The Cinema of Hockey

The Cinema of Hockey
Four Decades of the Game on Screen

Iri Cermak

McFarland & Company, Inc., Publishers
Jefferson, North Carolina

LIBRARY OF CONGRESS CATALOGUING-IN-PUBLICATION DATA

Names: Cermak, Iri, 1957– author.
Title: The cinema of hockey : four decades of the game on screen / Iri Cermak.
Description: Jefferson, North Carolina : McFarland & Company, Inc., Publishers, 2017 | Includes bibliographical references and index.
Identifiers: LCCN 2016059029 | ISBN 9781476666259 (softcover : acid free paper) ∞
Subjects: LCSH: Hockey films—United States—History and criticism. | Hockey films—Canada—History and criticism. | Hockey on television.
Classification: LCC PN1995.9.H5225 C47 2017 | DDC 791.43/6579—dc23
LC record available at https://lccn.loc.gov/2016059029

BRITISH LIBRARY CATALOGUING DATA ARE AVAILABLE

ISBN (print) 978-1-4766-6625-9
ISBN (ebook) 978-1-4766-2696-3

© 2017 Iri Cermak. All rights reserved

No part of this book may be reproduced or transmitted in any form or by any means, electronic or mechanical, including photocopying or recording, or by any information storage and retrieval system, without permission in writing from the publisher.

Front cover: Paul Newman as Reggie Dunlop in the 1977 film *Slap Shot* (Universal Pictures/Photofest)

Printed in the United States of America

*McFarland & Company, Inc., Publishers
Box 611, Jefferson, North Carolina 28640
www.mcfarlandpub.com*

To the hockey researchers whose work built up the field
and the players who inspired it.
And to my father and grandfather
who passed on to me their love of sport.

Table of Contents

Acknowledgments ix

Preface 1

Introduction 3
  Why Study Hockey as a Repertoire? 5
  Hockey, Masculinity Archetypes and North American Scripts of Nationhood 10
  Cultural Archetypes and the Quandaries of Depicting Hockey in Film 16
  Approaching the Hockey Lineup in This Book 21

1. Critiques of Hockey as Aggressive Muscularity 25
  Bully Hockey in Canadian Film: *Paperback Hero*, *The Last Season* and *Gross Misconduct* 27
  Bully Hockey in Hollywood Film: *Ice Castles*, *Love Story*, *The Deadliest Season* and *Youngblood* 39

2. Spoofs of Aggressive Muscularity: The Pleasures of Sporting Excess 48
  The Bully-Clown in Hollywood Film: *Slap Shot*, *Happy Gilmore*, *Tooth Fairy* and *Just Friends* 49
  The Bully-Clown in Canadian Film: *Score: A Hockey Musical*, *Goon*, *Keep Your Head Up, Kid: The Don Cherry Story* and *Wrath of Grapes: The Don Cherry Story II* 62

3. Critiques of the Business of Hockey 77
  The System Against the Athlete: *Face Off (Winter Comes Early)* 77
  Hockey in Crisis: *Net Worth* and *Sudden Death* 81
  The Hockey Protagonist on the Frontier: *Mystery, Alaska* 90
  The Disillusioned Protagonist: *No Sleep 'til Madison* and *Slap Shot 2: Breaking the Ice* 97

4. Hockey and Family Entertainment 104
  Disney's Vision of Hockey: *The Mighty Ducks*, *D2: The Mighty Ducks*, *D3: The Mighty Ducks*, *H-E-Double Hockey Sticks* and *Den Brother* 106
  Hockey in Canadian Family Fare: *Ronnie and Julie*, *MVP: Most Valuable Primate*, *Slap Shot 3: The Junior League* and *Sticks and Stones* 116

5. Hockey, Masculinity and Nationhood in Quebec Cinema 130
  Quebec and the Montreal Canadians: *The Mystery of the Million Dollar Hockey Puck* and *The Sweater* 132

    Les Boys I, II, III, IV: Hockey, Identity and Commercial Success   138
    Il était une fois les Boys: *Les Boys* and the Family Genre   148
    Quebec's Hockey Icon and the Nation: *Maurice Richard/The Rocket*   153
    Mending Canada's Cultural Divide: *Bon Cop, Bad Cop*   159

6. Hockey Biopics and the Nation   167
    The Memory Work of Allegiance: ABC's *Miracle on Ice* and Disney's *Miracle*   168
    Negotiating the Nation: *Canada Russia '72*   177
    Coaching and Honing Character: *The Hounds of Notre Dame, Keep Your Head Up, Kid/Wrath of Grapes* and *Waking Up Wally: The Walter Gretzky Story*   185

7. Hockey, Race and Sexuality   199
    Ethnicity and the Hockey Protagonist: *The Love Guru* and *Breakaway/The Speedy Singhs*   199
    Sexuality and the Hockey Protagonist: *Perfectly Normal, Breakfast with Scot, Grown Up Movie Star* and *The Sheldon Kennedy Story*   207

8. The Women's Game   220
    Forging a Path for Women in the Game? *Hockey Night, Ice Angel, Go Figure, Chicks with Sticks*, National Lampoon's *Pucked* and *Les Pee Wee 3D: L'hiver qui a changé ma vie*   221

9. The Hockey Spectacle in Film   239
    The Grammar of Hockey in Film   239
    Goal-Orientation   241
    Toughness   246
    The (Lesser) Role of Goaltending   248
    The Dream and the Work Ethic   250
    The Use of Archival Footage   251
    Overview   254

Conclusion   258

Filmography   265

Chapter Notes   268

Bibliography   305

Index   323

Acknowledgments

This project would not have been possible without the help of many individuals who generously shared their research and provided source material as well as encouragement. The author extends appreciation to Amy Ransom for her insightful observations and for generously sharing her work on hockey in Quebec culture. Warm thanks also to Brian Kennedy for going through the manuscript and sending along invaluable comments. I've had the chance to work with Brian on two separate occasions and the result is always inspiring.

Embarking on a lengthy project like this also entails spending a lot of time hunting down films, and, in this case, there were movies that took many years to obtain. The help of each and every one of these individuals in locating source material was crucial in contributing to the broad range of films in this volume. My heartfelt thanks to: Jean-Patrice Martel of the Society for International Hockey Research (SIHR) who runs the Society's excellent film database and generously referred me to numerous data sources; CBC archivist Roy Harris, who kindly made available two films I would have otherwise been unable to see, and CBC producer Alex Shprintsen for his discussion of Russian hockey and culture, and for his assistance in procuring films; filmmaker and hockey researcher Brett Kashmere, for generously sharing his essay film *Valery's Ankle* and other creative work; director-writer May Chambers for making available her *Lovers in a Dangerous Time*; Darren J. Harkness for enabling a viewing of *The Hounds of Notre Dame* and Evelyn Ellerman for insights that helped me situate the film in proper historical context. Many thanks also to Robert Ligtermoet and to Marco Lienhard both of whom assisted me in locating important source material for chapter seven; and to Rebecca Frank for the heads-up about a film that extended my work on the women's game.

I also wish to thank the following individuals for generously making available a number of movie stills that bring alive the discussions in this book. My deep thanks to Mongrel Media's Hussain Amarshi who kindly made available images from *Score: A Hockey Musical*, *Breakfast with Scot*, and *Grown Up Movie Star*, and Ai Tsuzuki who considerately assisted; Entertainment One and Carrie Wolfe who generously supplied several stills from the popular *Goon*; Greg Dunning at Cinépix for kindly giving me access to however many stills I needed from the early French-Canadian film, *The Mystery of the Million Dollar Hockey Puck*; Kevin Tiernan at Park Ex Pictures for coming through on short notice with stellar images of *Bon Cop, Bad Cop*; Marie Guegan at Films Séville for key referrals; Brenda Carroll for her tireless assistance in obtaining over a dozen images from the CBC archives; Ron Mandelbaum and the Photofest staff for patiently assisting me with my queries and ensuring the best results, and Tricia Gesner for her invaluable help in obtaining Associated Press images.

Acknowledgments

The following scholars also generously gave me access to their work. My sincere appreciation to: Richard Harrison for his original take on *Slap Shot* and always stimulating discussions at hockey conferences; Glen Jones for his early essay on the sport film, which proved essential to clarifying my own ideas about the genre; Steve Hardy for his articles and discussions on New England hockey; Stacy Lorenz and Geraint Osbourne for their work on early hockey coverage in Canada; Len Kotylo of the SIHR for sharing his research on Theodore Roosevelt's view of the game; Linda Williams who made available her seminal article on the function of the melodramatic mode in Hollywood cinema; Tobias Stark for his inspiring article on Swedish, Soviet, and Canadian hockey; and Peter Dahlén for stirring discussions of the game in film early on. I also thank the following individuals and institutions who enabled me to extend the scope of my research: Patricia Hughes-Fuller and James Gifford; Merja Ellefson and Eva Kingsepp, and Nordicom editor Ulla Carlsson; Colleen Coalter, commissioning editor of the Continuum Publishing Company; Loren P.Q. Baybrook, editor-in-chief of *Film & History*; Blaine Allen, editorial board chair of the *Canadian Journal of Film Studies*; Marilyn Bittman, managing editor of the *Canadian Journal of Communication*; author Don Gillmor and the staff at *The Walrus*; and Felicia F. Campbell of the *Popular Culture Review* for use of important source material.

Inside the sports industry, I wish to thank the *SportsBusiness Journal* for allowing me access to the World Congress of Sports conferences held in New York City and Newport Beach, which brought home this research as lived experience. Many thanks also to the Hockey Hall of Fame Archives, in particular, Ron Ellis for his discussion of the 1972 series and the Soviet team, and Tyler Wolosevich for helping me locate important sources. Thank you as well to Hockey Canada and Sean Kelso for lending me a hand with source material on Canadian hockey coverage. My heartfelt appreciation also goes to Teemu Selänne for his insights on Finnish and European hockey, and to the San Jose Sharks organization for facilitating that meeting.

Preface

I first began this work in early 2004 a couple months before Disney's *Miracle* saw its theatrical release. Eager to start my research at the movie theater, I attended the very first matinee screening. Three older ladies with tickets to another screening caught a glimpse of the *Miracle* poster and one of them enthusiastically noted that it was the story of the 1980 U.S. Olympic victory over the Soviet team and a must-see. Inside the theater a couple of rows ahead, more than a dozen seven- to eight-year-old boys and girls sat accompanied by two adults. This bit of hockey history would certainly come down to the next generation. At the time, I was in the San Francisco Bay Area where hockey enclaves are not ubiquitous like they are in Canada, and I thought that my research was off to a good start.

Shortly after, and to my great chagrin, I realized that very few of the other hockey-themed films I was aware of were readily available for sale or rent. What of the ones I didn't know about? Sports film anthologies, even Canadian film anthologies, which I hoped would take into account hockey's ranking as a national sport, listed at best one or two films. In contrast, sports collections featured much greater numbers of boxing, baseball, and football entries.[1] Pearson, Curtis, Haney and Zhang's statistical study of Hollywood sports films between 1930 and 1995, published in 2003, also corroborated the lopsided ratio of hockey productions vis-à-vis those of other sports. Between 1930 and 1939, for instance, only four hockey films had received theatrical distribution as opposed to 44 boxing, 38 football, 24 horse racing, and 16 auto-racing and baseball films. The 1940s and 50s showed a similar pattern with only a couple of hockey films released as opposed to 59 boxing, 33 horse racing, 25 football, 21 baseball, and 13 auto racing films. Hockey's film profile apparently increased somewhat between 1970 and 1995 with seven pictures seeing their theatrical release as opposed to 34 baseball, 32 boxing, 20 basketball, and 10 football films.[2]

I was keen on doing this work because, as a media studies and film researcher with an interest in hockey, I found remarkably little scholarly material about it. And as far as I could tell, the public's awareness of hockey films was also inadequate. "Best of" internet sports lists at the time consisted of little more than the usual suspects—*Slap Shot, Youngblood, The Mighty Ducks* trilogy and *Mystery, Alaska* as well as the recent *Miracle*—occasionally flavored by documentary entries. Most of these pictures were also Hollywood movies since, as a general rule, few if any Canadian films made it into these lineups. The difficulty in finding films and the scarce research about them were a problem not only because they gave the impression that hockey had not been present in the cinema for long, but that the sport was a flash in the Hollywood pan with only a few entries. The game had an acceptable profile on television, especially through NHL and Olympic broadcasts, but it was rather invisible as a broad, cross-cultural, decades-long movie repertoire.

The ten years–plus worth of research this work adds up to is therefore meant to close the gap between hockey and sports whose surfeit has made possible this kind of investigation early on. The films of the 1970s and 80s in this volume are some of the most intriguing big- and small- screen hockey pictures of all time, on both sides of the border. Their totals nonetheless pale in comparison with the increasing number of hockey films packaged as part of the new entertainment genre over just the last decade, which are highly saleable in both the domestic and export markets for their youth and family focus.[3] Even as some motion pictures and telefilms remain tucked away in studio vaults or network archives, the wide availability of recent releases alongside new distribution channels means that it is now possible to examine the game in a way that was difficult even in 2004. As late as 2006 the great majority of films in "top 10" lineups were also Hollywood productions, yet recent lists include English-Canadian and Quebec pictures.[4] The sport's cultural and commercial ties increasingly lie in various parts of North America (and beyond), and the growing hockey repertoire stands as an expression of this diverse impulse.

Introduction

The hockey player in film safeguards the myth of superior physicality and vigorous masculinity. The cinema ordinarily depicts the hockey exemplar through the muscularity, grit, and offensive mindset that popular culture associates with the professional game. This character is typically a formidable sort who does not hesitate to engage in fisticuffs and shakes off any bruising with almost studied nonchalance. Whether bold and alluring or ruthless and menacing, he champions his trade as a space where physical and psychological mettle, as well as the boundaries of the permissible, are put to the test. Although decidedly stereotypical, this iconography recurs not only in motion pictures, but also in game broadcasts, fictional and nonfictional TV programs, news media content, and retail advertising.

An Electronic Arts (EA) commercial for "NHL 13" video games titled *Our Game*,[1] for example, pays homage to hockey and its principals through sequences of players tangling with opponents, blocking shots, and enduring high sticks from behind. It also emphasizes the hockey player's popular iconography via gladiatorial-like images of unflappable competitors filing into an open-air stadium ready to do battle, and poetic drill segments that highlight the proficiency and kinetic allure of the athlete's body in movement. Every detail of the piece avows that these players are the lionhearted of men, specimens at the height of their power deftly wielding their skills and hardiness for the benefit of devout followers.

The hockey acolytes in the ad come off as similarly robust sorts who express their allegiance to the sport by forcefully rapping on the plexiglass and celebrating plays with open-mouthed abandon. Women only occasionally surround their male cohorts, seemingly happy to be counted among the game's cast of supporters. Children are nowhere on this stage except perhaps symbolically in locker room color as a player bounces a puck on his stick encapsulating the child's classic playfulness and hinting, hope against hope, that what he does is not all *that* serious or difficult. References to hockey's national and regional North American footprint, by way of a sizeable Canadian flag and an energetic fan swinging a hapless octopus (a reference to Detroit Red Wings hockey traditions), are also curiously bereft of multicultural stand-ins.

The words "ritual," "beauty," "sacrifice," "justice," and "sense of right and wrong" in the voice-over narration conjure images of hockey as a creed, and convey the athlete's pursuit in terms of a moral code that transcends the limits of time and space. These words also provide a clue to the ad's primary image work: to proffer a primal, exalted vision of men venerating the game because it affords them the opportunity to be men.

Although designed to sell video games to a target demographic, the images of hockey players in *Our Game*, also sum up the primary representation of these athletes in Hollywood, English- and French-Canadian films. This portrayal by no means accounts for important variations in the film repertoire. Still, as *Our Game* suggests, the insistent use of hockey as a timeless site where men continue to perform a heroic model of masculinity is not without import given that exclusive male spaces for expressing valor and initiative are perceived as eroding in North American cultures. Hockey iconography, in other words, articulates popular desires to preserve a space for a traditional model of masculinity and its social arrangements at a time when rapidly developing media technologies, global consumption, and access to communities of compatibility worldwide have also made for increasingly hybridized identities.

Albeit not all individuals consume popular culture in the same way, the above representation remains compelling because media depictions of elite-level athletes are an important source of imagery about masculinity in the culture. Media hold up these athletes, much in the way *Our Game* epitomizes, as symbols of virile performance in its prime, consistent with a model of dominant masculinity that affirms the foremost status of men who express cultural standards of utility and desirability.[2] Michael Messner observes that media constructions of elite athletes as embodiments of male superiority typically oppose their masculinity to the social identity of lower ranking groups—cultural minorities and, in particular, women.[3] The hockey athletic ideal is not only white, male, and heterosexual, but according to this scheme, it is first and foremost "not-feminine."[4] This model, then, assumes the superiority of men in situations that require strength, physical adeptness, and self-control.[5]

The cinema corroborates the above assumption and makes similar use of hockey to heighten a character's agency and desirability. Because the ideal represents physical prowess, resilience, and stoicism, hockey is especially helpful to a character in situations that prove potentially feminizing and enfeebling, which reassure the audience that he is a vigorous sort. Stella Bruzzi observes in her discussion of Stephen Neale's 1983 essay "Masculinity as Spectacle" that dominant masculinity first appeared in genres that openly showcased men's bodies, such as gladiatorial pictures and westerns.[6] Hockey's utility as shorthand for muscular masculinity is not unlike the dashing fighting displays, hurdle-soaring, and brawn-requiring tasks in early film that set men apart from the passive spectating positions of female co-actors at a time when critics regarded the cinema as a voyeuristic medium best suited to the display of the female body.[7] The standard of manliness that hockey offers a character in film is so pervasive that even when narratives undermine the agency of protagonists to articulate the need to temper aggression and recalibrate masculinity vis-à-vis social norms, they do not tamper with popular assumptions of hockey as a game of power.

Much as *Our Game* illustrates, the dominant masculinity of the hockey player also draws on romantic metaphors of the warrior that conflate the sport's high contact aspects with combat. Warrior culture prioritizes physical competence, goal-orientation, high tolerance for pain and injury, as well as self-sacrifice for the good of the group.[8] When translated to the sports arena, these values enshrine the hockey contest as a stage for performing male heroism. Hockey characters in the cinema dramatize warrior masculinity by exemplifying grit and resilience, showing determination in the face of risk, and harmonizing individual goals with those of the team. They profess allegiance to the martial code by respecting the hierarchical setup of organized sport and abiding by the directives of coaches, team managers, owners, and officials. Hierarchical setups are not always beneficial to all stakeholders, however, for as Don Sabo and Sue Curry Janssen note, these arrangements can entangle the worker-athlete in complex power relations that lead to exploitation and loss.[9] The cinema amply acknowledges this reality and readily deploys the hockey player's warrior masculinity to push back against the interests of power blocs and express allegiance to coworkers in high populist form.

Aside from expressing agency as breadwinners, hockey films also represent characters "being men" outside the locker room in (heteronormative) sexual relationships and fathering roles. To express social adjustment, male behavior and practices must take into account gender relations and athletic models that grant characters flexibility in male-female associations in the service of masculine success. Sport also serves as an arena for modeling masculinity and passing on "the facts of life" to the next generation,[10] and in film the father-son link in sport exemplifies this tradition. Like other sports films, hockey narratives express the desirability of close-knit parent-offspring, and even sibling bonds, and for this reason signal when a breakdown in these relationships occur.

Because hockey allows viewers to witness both the ideal and transgressive aspects of dominant masculinity in action, dramatizations of the hockey player in the movies also guide cultural expectations about national character. The relationship between masculinity, sport, and the nation is not unexpected given that sport has historically conveyed male values and practices and the exercise and rituals of nationhood are also expressions of male identity, as Joseph Maguire observes.[11] Hockey's leading men in film, therefore, stand out as best expressions of the nation or amplify a cultural problem by depicting masculinity in opposition to social norms. Since hockey speaks to the social fabric of particular cultures, protagonists also dramatize regional identities and rivalries, which films may depict much in the way *Our Game* suggests, by formulating the sport as akin to a creed, its practitioners as combatants, and its followers as acolytes whose fierce support and attire recall ancestral tribal loyalties. The cinema in any case reiterates the vision of the hockey protagonist as a physically resilient and resolute type, steadfast in the yearning for masculine heroism and ritualistic rivalries that mattered greatly when nations were smaller and less complicated social ventures.

Why Study Hockey as a Repertoire?

Although hockey is played in many cultures and in the least expected of places, the mythic blueprint "Canada is hockey and hockey is Canada" echoes in popular discourse as a natural encapsulation of identity and nationhood. In his study of Canadian hockey novels, Michael Buma argues that the commonplace cultural assumption in the country is that "Canadians think about hockey simply because that is what Canadians think about," and that these literary works do their part to "hold this 'truth' as self-evident."[12] Hockey is also integral to French-Canadian or Québécois self-conceptions of identity, mirrored in French-language media productions and a distinct and sturdy film industry that reflects a concern with modern-day nationalism. Amy Ransom notes in her study of the game in Quebec's popular culture, that hockey is paramount to how French-Canadians perform their cultural identity, though they may only appear at the margins in representations of the Canadian game.[13] Hockey likewise has its own history of development and iconography in the United States, and because of Hollywood's historical supremacy in meeting global demand for film and TV content,[14] in film the sport features a decidedly American imprint.

Treatises of hockey in the cinema are not lacking and a number of authors such as Bart Beaty, Janice Kaye, André Loiselle, have made noteworthy contributions to the field by tackling a sample of films or zeroing in on a single film's subject matter. Amy Ransom's in-depth work on hockey in Quebec's popular culture also includes exhaustive analysis of feature films and TV series.[15] No work, however, has taken on an extensive overview of the North American repertoire as a whole, perhaps because the full repository of films has neither seen wide release nor been available on VHS, DVD, video-on-demand or streaming formats. Yet it is only when considering hockey in film as a broad body of work that it affords a more nuanced view of film practitioners' use of hockey, whether to evince shifts in social norms, or negotiate the relationship between sport and the nation.

Examining hockey as a film repertoire entails tackling the game as part of the sports film genre. Rick Altman provides a functional definition of genre formats as clearly identifiable and recognizable categories that share a common topic and approach to structuring film narratives.[16] Genre as a cogent concept nonetheless is not set in stone as a multiplicity of actors on the production side (studios, individual filmmakers, editors, and other talent), as well as in the circulation (distributors and marketers) and reception (critics and audiences) sectors have contributed to the formulation of genres and remain central to their decoding. There is also great variance among film practitioners, critics, and scholars about recognizing and giving the sports film its due.

Hollywood producers, writers, and directors, for example, shun the idea of marketing a film by way of its sports aspects since members of the Academy of Motion Picture Arts and Sciences favor middle-of-the-road movies that appeal to mass audiences and the above labeling dashes the prospects of an Oscar.[17] Producers also take a cautionary approach not only in marketing these films but also in making them in the first place. At the 2004 Octagon/Street and Smith *SportsBusiness* World Congress of Sports conference on sport in film and entertainment, Mandalay Entertainment Group Chairman and CEO Peter Guber noted that sports movies are "worrisome," risky fare that, unlike action-adventure movies, "don't translate internationally, " and can only be justified when made for "the right price," and aimed as "local repertoire, like French making French films and Italians making Italian films." Producers Mike Tollin and Kathleen Kennedy, for their part, insisted that sports be tucked safely into the narrative edifice by bringing the drama and characters to the foreground." And although producers discussed the commercially successful *Miracle*, released a month prior, the hockey aspect was not brought up. Disney also marketed the film as a drama.[18]

On the film criticism front, the sports genre—much like the western, science fiction, horror film, and other genres—remains in contention because of the distinct ways in which researchers tackle these motion pictures.[19] Emma Poulton and Martin Roderick in their introduction to their special edition of *Sport in Society* (2008), for example, note that the varying perspectives on sport in film make it difficult to substantiate the idea of a genre as anything but tentative.[20] Garry Whannel cautions that because sport in film has its own particular relationship to identity narratives and sports themes can be affixed to other genre structures, this category cannot be articulated as distinct.[21] Glen Jones, for his part, traces the history of sports film production and the shared assumptions, visual motifs, and conventions that critics define as part of a genre, but argues that these films nonetheless remain "invisible" as a bona fide category because they are viewed as too formulaic to deal with serious subject matter and are lacking the cultural cachet of classics.[22]

Bruce Babington, whose work falls on the other side of the debate, proposes that whether film theorists affirm the existence of a sports genre or not has much to do with whether they relegate sports to the background or take active interest in it as a cultural form.[23] He rejects arguments about sport in film as lacking in the most basic elements of genre by defining this category through plot lines that are substantially constituted around sport, a *mise-en-scène* comprised by the stadium or playing field of the sport in question, sports iconographies whose specificity depends on the athletic activity portrayed, and essential themes (i.e., respect and its loss, the public hero as role model, locker room bonding, the parent-child relationship, the character's conflicting loyalties to his/her sport vis-à-vis other responsibilities, the tension between the individual and the group, the dystopian aspects of fame and corruption, and sport in the context of gender, ethnic, and sexual identity, and regional and national affiliations.)[24] Seán Crosson also makes a detailed case for the sports film genre and defines this category as comprising narratives that depend on sport to motivate and resolve the plot and feature a dualistic hero-villain character set as well as a dualistic structure through which the sport and social worlds connect either in utopian or problematic ways.[25]

Ken Dancyger and Jeff Rush in their screenwriting volume draw up a more succinct definition of the sports genre as follows: (a) the main protagonist is a talented athlete who must prove himself within the game's parameters; (b) he faces superior opponents, who are nonetheless not as important to the story as the principal's struggle or pursuit; (c) his quest drives the plot forward and motivates relationships with a mentor (coach), teammates, a love interest or partner, and likely a family member; (d) his ultimate testing occurs in a final game that culminates the narrative and serves as his wish-fulfillment.[26] Sifting out narratives with appended sports motifs from ones that occur in sports films proper may also be accomplished by looking at differences in plot and characterization; that is, by examining what the principal character wants and how the plot structures the sojourn toward his/her goals. Case in point, *13 Going on 30* (Winick, 2004) and *Slap Shot* (Hiller, 1977) both feature a hockey player doing a strip tease that plays out to very different effects. In the first film, New York Rangers player Alex Carlson (Samuel Ball), boyfriend of principal protagonist Jenna Rink (Jennifer Garner), attempts a stripping act as part of a sexual role-playing routine, without realizing she has been regressed to the age of thirteen as part of a journey to retrieve her authentic self. Jenna sheepishly puts a halt to the proceedings and avoids the entanglement to Carlson's

Alex Carlson's (Samuel Ball) striptease in *13 Going on 30* (Columbia Pictures/Photofest).

befuddlement. The sequence exploits for laughs the stereotype of the elite hockey player as an object of desire, as Alex engages in a buffoonish dance that is the very antipode of alluring male performance on the playing field. It is also relevant that the stripping hockey player in this romantic story is not the leading man but a character in a tangential role that serves to call attention to Jenna's change of heart and help her realize that her true love is a childhood friend (Matty, played by Mark Ruffalo).

In the second film, which is also the hockey repertoire's most popular, Charlestown Chiefs star player Ned Braden (Michael Ontkean) sheds his gear during the final game, and much to the horror of his thuggish opponents and the enjoyment of the crowd, upstages the devolution of the matchup into an all-out brawl. While his act also plays on the allure of the elite athlete, Ned's disrobing packs a punch because it underscores the athlete's and the game's commodification through violence. Because this film boasts a plot structure and other aspects of characterization that align with the sports film proper, Ned's act also disrupts the ending's archetypal goal-scoring sequence through which the Hollywood sports film project delivers its promise.

The message of the Hollywood sports film is intrinsically connected to traditional conceptions of manhood that draw on American mythic archetypes. In this context, the sports film's ending operates as the clincher, so to speak, the act that conveys the assurance of social and material ascendance inherent in American myth. As Babington notes in regard to baseball biopics, these films express "American sports as a symbol of Americanness, with success in them a means of moving from society's margins to its centre…."[27] Ned's disruption, then, not only fractures the ideological underpinnings of dominant masculinity, but also skewers the Hollywood sports film project itself. The clichéd ending, which is part and parcel of the genre's repetitive and saccharine aspects,[28] is not as unimportant as seen at first blush because it is full of ideological innuendo and its rupture impales the promise inherent in American cultural myth. Elfriede Fürsich advocates looking at mythic imagery not only in film but also in televisual and other media in order to understand how producers—as participants in the culture and shapers of public memory and collective identity—influence audience expectations, whether

Ned Braden's (Michael Ontkean) striptease in *Slap Shot* (Universal Pictures/Photofest).

consciously or not.[29] The repetitive aspects of genres and myth are also relevant in that they work to construe narrative setups and resolve problems in ways that accord with normative beliefs, ultimately helping make the case for particular configurations of reality.[30] Even though hockey motifs and themes can be affixed to narratives that bear the imprint of other genres, films like *Slap Shot* demonstrate that identifying sport as a bona fide genre is nothing short of pivotal since breaks in genre conventions can signal a crisis or turning point in the culture's values.[31]

There is no denying that sport narratives and motifs appear in conjunction with other genres and/or blended with aspects of these film formats.[32] In the hockey repertoire, the sports film is most commonly found in combination with family fare, specifically the new genre of family entertainment that emerged in the early 1990s (discussed in chapter four), since production companies rely on this format to sell content globally. Therefore the idea that sport in film primarily appeals to national audiences is true only in cases when narratives memorialize national icons. In any case, rather than weaken the case for the sports film, genre hybridity acts to reinforce the impact of particular messages and ideologies. Hockey themes in conjunction with family fare, for example, feature an augmented didacticism. The hockey hero's toughness, for its part, draws on combat genre referents because sport speaks to a very traditional, militaristic model of masculinity. Protagonists in hockey stories additionally tap frontier or western genre archetypes that activate national myths and perpetuate particular sets of cultural values. The sports narrative, which is frequently cast off for its sentimental tenor, also borrows from the melodramatic as part and parcel of how Hollywood film rewards protagonists for their tribulations. These blended motifs, above all, amplify screenwriters' flexibility in telling stories. Dancyger and Rush speak to this point in outlining elements of the sports film genre but also in urging treatment of film narratives through a multi-genre approach, as this strategy mirrors the way in which intellect and intuition customarily combine in the creative process.[33]

In tackling hockey as part of Hollywood sport repertoire, this project seeks to dispense with the idea that the sports film is for the most part an American genre populated by American sports like baseball, football, basketball, and its principals, which undergird the bulk of academic writing. Identifying hockey as part of the sports genre is also relevant in gauging how Canadian canonical film—which is drawn up "out of difference" with Hollywood classical storytelling and is buttressed by a complex mythology and a different set of conventions—breaks with game archetypes even though hockey is said to be intrinsic to Canadian identity. Identifying the sports film as a bona fide genre will also assist in gauging how Quebec film practitioners, who are proficient in numerous genres and who typically blend classical and canonical film motifs in their stories, negotiate representations of the French-Canadian hockey player. In addressing the game's cultural complexity by way of a multicultural cinematic approach, this volume then aims to extend the investigation of sport in film and to contribute to the burgeoning and multidisciplinary study of hockey.[34]

As noted at the outset, hockey in film filters particular mythical imagery that perpetuates specific standards of masculinity and validates cultural norms in speaking to regional and national audiences. Examining national myths and the game's historical role in contributing to these models of manhood provides a basis for gauging how these archetypes operate as antecedents in contemporary film. After a historical tour of this topic, the discussion will follow up with the quandaries of portraying hockey in film.

Hockey, Masculinity Archetypes and North American Scripts of Nationhood

The three North American cinemas in this study share key commonalities in portraying the game and its protagonists, but they also outline distinct starting points for articulating the connection between masculinity, sport, and the nation. To understand the assumptions underlying the construction of the game and the hockey player, it is necessary to refer to older cultural archetypes that have come down in history encoded in literature and theatre, and now circulate in film and media.[35] Albeit lyrical repositories of the nation's history, these symbols are far from neutral since their very selection privileges particular social groups and their cultural practices. André Légaré sheds light on the process of identity production in noting that social actors who seek to influence how a group defines itself commonly use archetypes and other symbols in public forums and mass media to amplify "the truth" of who they are. Because cultural identity is not etched in stone but depends on the continual chronicling of the past, social actors who have an investment in these accounts for reasons of political gain also strive to impact how a group remembers its history.[36] Therefore, although national archetypes may appear to take on a life of their own by binding a nation together and creating a sense of difference vis-à-vis neighbors, they also implicitly preserve the worldview and interests of influential groups who leveraged these symbols to safeguard their power.

The North American cultural archetypes that inform the hockey player's masculinity in film have sturdy links to larger scripts of nationhood,[37] scripts that nineteenth-century nationalists consolidated for political interest by way of older cultural elements. Canadian and American national scripts share a point of convergence that is based on the originary New World character of North America as uncharted land, a frontier territory available for conquest to youthful males who embodied the best qualities of the nation. But they also diverge in line with identity blueprints that presuppose group differentiation from geographical and political others. The Canadian script prioritizes cultural traits by way of the country's location in the climate and environment of the North. Hockey intimately features in this script by dramatizing Canadians' successful adaptation to the immensity, algidity, and harshness of the Northern wilderness. South of the 49th parallel, hockey developed and flourished in the Northern tier of the U.S.—the Eastern Seaboard, the Midwest and other Northern states—and also primarily alludes to the geography of snow and ice. But because the United States lacks a distinct tradition of writing and reading the North,[38] the hockey player in the American imaginary exemplifies frontier ruggedness through the script of the West, a concept that denotes the frontier's (westerly) advance[39] to allegorize Americans' unlimited prospects.

National scripts of the North and West—i.e., Nordicity and Westering—have their roots in environmental determinism, a variant of modern geography that emphasized the link between character and the natural landscape as scientific representation.[40] Although these constructs dramatize frontier national character, they also have an economic component that along with the exaltation of the nation's landscape entails the exploitation of its resources. Donald Worster regards these origin scripts as development myths that serve to explicate a nation's inception, make-up, and promise. Development myths assumed prominence at a time when the narrative of progress from primitive origins came to the fore, and Canada and the U.S. emerged as nation-states, helping nationalist interests hone unique national identities as their countries jostled to secure a footing in the international economy.[41]

In Canada, a rising professional and business elite approached the question of national character by differentiating the Dominion from its neighbor, the U.S., and the Mother country, Britain. The Canada First Movement, which emerged after Confederation (1867), zeroed in on the role of the North, its climate and rugged, unpopulated wilderness, in instilling endurance and fortitude in the nation's citizens in a way that its neighbor's more southern climate and environment could not do for its nationals. Canada's Northern robustness also facilitated the moral regeneration of the Old World, allowing the country to honor its British roots by way of its political and cultural colonial traditions. This mythic blueprint further reaffirmed Canada as peaceable kingdom, boosting the cultural life of communities by fomenting a respect for civil liberties.[42] Canada's Northern pedigree also superseded the Anglophone-Francophone divide by submersing early French-Canadian iconography into the greater myth of the North through the symbolism of the *coureurs de bois* and *voyageurs*—trappers, wood-rangers and other frontiersmen—who arrived in Canada during the late seventeenth and eighteenth centuries to advance the fur trade.[43] Because ease in navigating the harsh climate of the North informed the script of Northern robustness, nationalists underscored how these early icons prospered in the harsh conditions of the rugged Canadian wilderness. Michael Robidoux explains that the *coureurs de bois* chose to adopt First Nations' emblematic lifestyle emulating native skills when hunting, trapping, snowshoeing, and canoeing, and assessing their skills by indigenous standards. In allying with native tribes, these figures existed outside the control of the Catholic Church and skirted oppressive French government laws, driving the new economy that supplied beaver pelts to Europe while exerting an aura of "renegade heroics" in the manner of frontier outpost inhabitants.[44]

Robidoux notes that the elite expanded on Canada's Northern character by borrowing concepts from First Nations' sporting traditions and ethos because the genteel European masculinity did not suit the Canadian colonial setting, whose harsh conditions, particularly in rural communities, necessitated a more self-reliant and hardy attitude toward everyday life. To articulate a more contemporary vision of Canadian sport and national character, the nineteenth- and early-twentieth-century colonial elite drew on First Nations' games as well as indigenous attitudes toward sporting contests, which framed the expression of distress or anger in the face of physical punishment as a sign of vulnerability to the intemperate North. Early Canadian Nationalists regarded lacrosse and hockey as infused by a vigorous bush masculinity that exemplified the audacious feats of the First Nations' mythological male figure. Robidoux makes clear that hockey was nothing short of pivotal in transforming the Northern wilderness from an "unbearable reality" into "the essence of Canadian virtue and identity."[45]

Along with its important anthropological functions, the North articulated Canada's potential for development by focusing attention on the abundant resources its vast frontier spaces. Not all scholars saw the country's framework for development as benefiting its future prospects, however. Economic historian Harold E. Innis understood resource extraction as a dilemma for the nation because it primarily served powerful outside concerns. In *The Fur Trade* (1930), he outlined the Canadian material economic state as defined by the extraction of "staples"—beaver, fish, and lumber—designed for export to European metropolitan centers. Because Innis considered Canada's colonial conditions to be detrimental to the economy and culture, he advocated for the instatement of a strong nexus of communications to offset the American influence in Canadian life.[46] William Katerberg explains that Innis strove to define the country on its own terms, reaffirming "the 'wildness' of the North" as the source of the Dominion's distinctive and vital character. He argues that this romantic vision of the North notwithstanding, Innis also stressed Canada's dependence on Old World economic and cultural structures, leading Canadians to take for granted the permeability of their borders and to conceptualize national life as greatly influenced by outside forces.[47]

Although a number of American commentators theorized that the Old World perforce influenced the mores and cultures of the colonies and its expanding territories, the American mindset ultimately came to prioritize the radical separation between the Old and New Worlds. The script of the West objectified the Old World as corrupt and decadent and heroized the residents of the New World for honing a brand new identity by way of the revitalizing forces of the landscape.[48] Among those who specified the break with the old heritage was Wisconsin-born historian Frederick Jackson Turner, who put forth his argument in his "frontier thesis," first presented in an 1893 lecture to the American Historical Association at Chicago's World Columbian Exposition.[49] Turner regarded the frontier as the boundary line of Americanization, and fashioned it as a westerly process. The structuring premise of Turner's thesis was the rhetoric of progress and equal opportunity, which specified that "the game be played according to the rules … no artificial stifling of equality of opportunity, no closed doors to the able, no stopping the free game before it was played to the end."[50] Turner characterized the free space garnered by the westward-moving frontier as bustling with incessant productivity and driven by the prospect of material and intellectual wealth. His essay "The Problem of the West" (1896) alludes to the western frontier's arbitration of the nation's destiny where Americans negotiated the concrete and allegorical ramifications of progress with implications for the continent as a whole.[51] Richard Slotkin argues that for Turner frontier development inherently fostered democratic values, as the historical agents at its center were not the captains of industry or the bold men of adventure, but the everyman: the yeoman farmer, the artisan, and small entrepreneur. Turner was at heart a populist who subordinated the directives of the state and the corporation to the prerogatives and desires of communities. He saw the frontier as an environment in which all classes had the opportunity to attain wealth and power.[52]

Turner's thesis consolidated many of the elements of the Westering myth that had circulated in the culture since colonial times, such as the notion of pioneering as national calling, the idea of "Manifest Destiny," and the concept of the West as an enormous repository of natural resources which offered endless opportunity to the enterprising individual.[53] By the turn of the century, "the West" had ceased to refer to an actual geographical region and had transformed into a mythological script through which to reify American history and national character, much as "the North" had transformed into a liminal icescape that symbolized the rightful heritage of Canadians. And just as historians, scientists, writers, artists as well as business and political elites in Canada had a role in disseminating the script of Northern sturdiness, so did their American counterparts promote the idea of the West as a threshold for immensity and limitlessness.[54] Turner regarded the prospect of improved living standards through labor and wealth accumulation as a level playing field, and his influential ideas and rhetoric perpetuated U.S. citizens' expectations of an unending array of political, economic, and intellectual prospects to explore and exploit, as Catherine Gouge notes. Turner's theories effectively buttressed the growth of American capitalism by proposing the validity of "a utopian narrative of unlimited sociopolitical resources" that in time became the foundation of American nationalism, as Gouge confirms.[55]

As the real geographic West disappeared by the turn of the century and became an object of nostalgia, the region persisted as a fulcrum for American masculinity.[56] Alongside Turner, President Theodore Roosevelt contributed to the consolidation of the Westering myth by playing up the role of the New World's revitalizing geographies in fomenting the sturdy masculinity necessary for good citizenship. Roosevelt linked athleticism with frontier imagery by way of the metaphor of the heroic male who tested his mettle in wild frontier spaces.[57] He advocated the necessity of living a "strenuous life" to cultivate "resolution, courage, endurance, and capacity to hold one's own and to stand up under punishment," manly virtues which were best "instilled by out-of-door sports" with an "element of risk."[58] In his February 23, 1907, Harvard Union address, Roosevelt forcefully extended support for manly sports, noting, "I emphatically disbelieve in seeing Harvard or any other college turn out mollycoddles instead of vigorous men," singling out "[r]owing, baseball, lacrosse, track and field games, hockey, football" as "all of them good" for fostering a dependable masculinity.[59]

The "strenuous life" was effectively an aggregate of discursive bundles combining outdoor adventure with the concept of self-made manhood through which Roosevelt addressed the ruling elite class. Outdoor adventure, which drew from the regenerative quality of the American landscape, promoted the production of fit, virile (Anglo-Saxon elite) males for nation- and empire-building. The concept of self-made manhood—a construct that had heavily influenced American middle-class men's conception of manhood through the early postbellum years starting in 1865[60]—brokered the idea of personal attainment and economic success. Strenuous manhood honored the masculine achievement of the family man through capital accumulation and promoted physical courage, a chivalrous spirit, and patriotic duty as ideals.[61] The concept of strenuous manhood served to energize the nation by politically resonating with Progressive Era reforms and a budding overseas American empire.[62]

Roosevelt's rhetoric articulated a triumphant model of manhood at a time when social commentators deemed masculinity to be in crisis. Large-scale transformations in the economy which bound men to less than virile white-collar jobs, and changes in the social order which amplified women's demands for active participation in the industrializing workplace and disputed men's exclusive hold over social and political power, magnified fears of over-civilization and feminization. These trepidations extended to cultural life, as ministers and lady novelists favored pious displays of virtue and emotional excess, in the process displacing a more stoic masculine ethos.[63] To offset the threat of emasculation, North American social models highlighted the more aggressive, violent aspects of masculinity by incorporating strong physicality and Social Darwinist elements. A host of movements concerned with honing physique and behavior in line with the ideals of sturdy manhood also emerged during the late nineteenth and early twentieth centuries, including the modern Olympic Games, fraternal lodges and youth movements like the Boy Scouts.[64]

With the crisis and renewal of masculinity as backdrop, conceptions of hockey drew on the socially acceptable middle-class ideal of self-made manhood, the amateur ideal, and working-class preference for rough play.[65] The amateur leagues privileged the concept of sportsmanship as the defining norm of athletic competition. Sportsmanship originated in the nineteenth century values of the English public schools and articulated upper-class conceptions of athletic activity. Michael Oriard explains that because "[t]he gentleman ... had already 'won' in life by the very fact of his class," and sports primarily instilled the skills to perform the duties that his rank had bestowed on him, deportment in athletics mattered more than winning. Respect for the rules of the game and losing with grace were therefore paramount to the sportsman.[66]

John Fiske amplifies that elites justified the superiority of particular sports and competing styles based on moral legibility. Nineteenth century processes of industrialization and urbanization had revealed stark class differences about work and leisure among social groups, and elites, worried that these disparities in social values threatened their hold on power, reacted by reining in the recreational activities of the subordinate ranks. In short order, they put in place legislative measures buttressed by an ideological discursive overlay of "morality, law and order, and the Protestant work ethic" to imbue so-called vulgar sporting pastimes with respectability. They also discredited certain leisure activities and preserved the integrity of gentlemanly sporting pursuits.[67] Fiske notes, however, that the upper echelons also saw sport as a means of creating strong national bonds, and for political reasons did not always discourage these coarse pursuits.[68]

Developments in hockey attested to similar class contestations while allowing for the broad appeal of rough play across social strata. In Canada, hockey had originated in the upper-middle class urban centers of Montreal, Toronto, and Ottawa, where it remained under the aegis of the Canada Amateur Hockey Association (CAHA)[69] supported by an ascendant class of professionals, businessmen, bureaucrats, and clerks. Stacey Lorenz and Geraint Osborne note that the rising bourgeoisie adhered to the ideal of self-made manhood, which reinforced respectability and breadwinning responsibilities in the context of Christian morality. This social group also embraced amateur values and codes of sportsmanship. At the opposite end of the masculinity spectrum, an emergent working-class culture in the industrializing urban centers engaged in leisure activities that involved fighting, drinking, and bloodsports in pool halls and saloons. This group espoused toughness, physical proficiency, and the imperative of good repute, and not surprisingly, had a preference for rough hockey.[70]

In the U.S., a similar dynamic took hold as hockey developed parallel to the amateur movement of the 1870s and 1880s. Historian Steve Hardy notes that elites and bourgeois interests, who sought to control hockey by carving out a separate sporting space from the working-class, alleged that "butchers, blacksmiths, and saloon owners" had ruined sports like baseball, rowing, and boxing by encouraging match-fixing and gambling. Early hockey also took root in the elite high schools and colleges of the Northeast, as institutions like Harvard, Boston College, Princeton, and Yale took to the game and other top-notch sports to buttress their athletic powerhouse status alongside their intellectual cachet.[71] Amateurs also espoused sportsmanship in hockey, with the colleges adhering to scientific play after the introduction of the Montreal game with its more controllable puck.[72]

Rink promoters in the amateur leagues on both sides of the border, however, had no qualms about exploiting violence to sell the game through the media, while disavowing displays of violence as part of the corrupt professional's toolbox.[73] Lorenz and Osborne indicate that newspaper coverage of the 1907 game between the Montreal Wanderers and Ottawa Silver Seven of the Eastern Canada Amateur Hockey Association, professed outrage at the spectacle of "brutal butchery" while conveying the potential appeal that violence brought to the sport.[74] Hardy also alludes to Harvard athlete Ralph Winsor's account of early hockey in the U.S. as "controlled brawling" with few rules and plentiful hitting, even as athletes played for the love of the game. He notes that the amateur leagues flaunted "mayhem and bloodshed" to set themselves apart from the college game, which increasingly featured scientific play and skill. As happened North of the border, pre-game media accounts titillated audiences with the promise of the violent spectacle and denounced rough play post-game.[75] The absorption of amateur leagues by high profile professional leagues through expansion and mergers during the first two decades of the twentieth century only solidified hockey's repute as a violent sport.[76] This signature remained in place because the game developed at a time when primitive and aggressive elements were readily enlisted in the construction of manly character.[77] Revitalized masculinity models combined with mythological scripts of nationhood to produce sport as an exclusive space through which to hone the skills of citizenship.

National scripts of the North and West, which reify engagement with the landscape in the performance of masculinity, have proven to be remarkably durable in the way they prescribe and interpret experience and identity in North America. This mythological masculinity deploys the power of the will and formidable physical attributes in the work of citizenship and nationhood, a prototype that also recurs in North American sports literature. Robert Hollands notes that writers of North American sports novels typically emphasize the hockey protagonist's manly virtues through superior physical and mental attributes that allude to biological and/or ethnic inheritance.[78] This protagonist, who is almost always male, is on the whole individually rather than socially-constituted. Like the "positive hero" who is a "producer, man of 'action' or statesman," he engages in mundane hard work if necessary, but retains for himself the ability to lead.[79]

About the Canadian sports hero, Hollands stresses that this protagonist is a powerful character who is able to surmount obstacles through sheer personal will. He molds the external world to suit his needs albeit not at the expense of moral imperatives or his estrangement from society. Importantly, the protagonist's decisive agency necessitates little input from secondary characters, as he resolves all conflicts by the end of the story. Hollands also highlights sports writers' notorious tendencies to describe a character's social relations as stemming from a "predisposed personality structure" which originates in the individual's national temperament and heritage. Sports novelists thus may go as far as to attribute the protagonist's hockey talents and skills to his ethnic or cultural status.[80]

Jason Blake in like manner corroborates that English language Canadian hockey fiction runs into essentialist discourse by articulating the ability to play the game as a matter of nature rather than nurture. He notes of hockey protagonists that they must be able to handle various modalities of aggression on the ice, but the moral sorts also stand out for their ability to grasp and adhere to limits.[81] Michael Buma in his treatise of hockey in Canadian novels also traces how hockey in these works is ontologically equated with Canadianicity and is seen as equipping youth with physical and mental fortitude, self-control, focus, dedication, honor, and the ability to sacrifice for the collective, all considered necessary for the effective work of citizenship. Buma makes the case that, despite the recent proliferation of anti-heroes as part of high culture's reaction to postmodernity, the heroic hockey archetype retains currency in popular genres for embodying a model of masculinity that harks back to a state more interconnected with primal Nature, reliant on muscularity for survival, and infused with moral conviction.[82] In other words, in Canadian novels, the hockey player's heroic masculinity remains conversant with the New World character of North American myths.

The above outlines of the hockey player amplify that North American sports literature encodes national character in the performance of masculinity by delineating the sports hero's decisive agency in the context of national specificities. Although most of the characters in the above works are Canadian-born and bred, Canadian and American sports literature share similarities in the way they structure plots, resolve conflicts, and adhere to the myth of sports success.[83] This means that they borrow heavily from the conventions and story structures of nineteenth-century literary forms and draw on ideological discourses about masculinity and nationhood to develop their protagonists.

Cultural Archetypes and the Quandaries of Depicting Hockey in Film

National scripts of the North and West bestow male protagonists with a formidable toughness that stems from their interface with the North American wilderness landscape. This baseline trait lends characters dramatic appeal, and for mainstream cinema, which heavily trades in white male leading figures, it also means ready marketability. The athlete-hero of American popular lore is a composite of the bold, adventurous exemplar of frontier narrative and the archetype of the self-made man, the restless, ambitious operative of the industrial age that came to the fore at a time of market revolution.[84] American sports discourses call on the populist Turnerian element that stipulates attainable wealth and social ascendance through individual and/or local initiative and weds it to conceptions of sport as a heroic project popularized by Theodore Roosevelt in his advocacy of the "strenuous life."[85] The Hollywood sports film genre in like manner configures the hockey archetype through the superior physicality and self-reliance necessary for navigating the frontier landscape, combining it with the self-willed, hard-working, meritocratic- and competition-respecting attributes of the self-made man. The story structure of the Hollywood sports genre, in addition, encodes the Westering myth's emphasis on a limitless and open future through "destiny" or "triumph-over-obstacles" plot lines.[86] These story lines, which dramatize social mobility, showcase protagonists winning the final game to convey the idea of underdogs steadily advancing toward brighter prospects.

In Canadian film hockey also metaphorically alludes to the durability necessary for thriving in the Northern landscape in line with the Canadian origin script.[87] The Canadian hockey protagonist recreates the distinct, self-affirming masculinity of myth and combines it with the concept of the self-made man by denoting social mobility in the context of breadwinning responsibilities and respectable morality. Canadian film also attaches to this archetype a courteous, self-effacing aspect that articulates the idea of Canada as a Victorian British colony and peaceable kingdom.[88] The hockey player and his (or occasionally, her) game must express with integrity and straightforwardness and without any grandstanding, embellishment, or unsportsmanlike behavior that vexes the opponent. Richard Gruneau and David Whitson note hockey's dual mandate in their concept of the exemplar as a principled individual of scant words, who also has a keen gauge of his own capacity for physical toughness and confidence in his ability to manage demanding conditions. The ideal is someone whom others hold in esteem and also think twice about challenging. While taking note of social norms and the customary way of doing things, the exemplar can also operate outside those rules when required.[89] This means that the Canadian culture of hockey also assumes that hockey is a self-contained universe that allows players the discretion of acting beyond the stated rules. Hockey codes also apply to French-Canadians since they are exposed to similar acculturation and marketplace pressures. Quebec film likewise portrays ruggedness and durability as part of the allure of the French-Canadian player for his ability to withstand physical punishment and show resilience in the performance of his duties.

Just like hockey comes with built-in dramatic and commercial benefits by amplifying characters' masculine appeal, the sport also exacts a price from Hollywood and Canadian film. The standard Hollywood hockey story features a protagonist who experiences some sort of setback and sets out to prove—to a coach, a family member, or the community—that he, and occasionally she, has the goods to win the big prize. The hero prepares as best as possible and either wins in good order or manages to eke out the coveted victory. Above all, the protagonist is an honorable sort who, if haunted by past failure, secures redemption by the end of the story. The above formula, which structures the typical hockey narrative, stretches the believability of story lines and too often rehearses familiar themes and character stocks. These films often come across as derivative and trite because they trade in the emotional trappings of the melodramatic mode. Linda Williams makes a substantial case for viewing melodrama as the fundamental operative approach of Hollywood popular film. She notes that melodrama's aim is to showcase the protagonist's innocence and the villain's culpability, as it capitalizes on the hero's suffering and victimization with the ultimate purpose of staging his/her "moral legibility," and pronouncing right and wrong in a post-sacred world beset by ethical uncertainty.[90] In the sports genre, melodrama's incentive is to moralize that our guys or gals are better than the players on the other bench, and that our approach to sport is superior to theirs. The nefarious and often overwhelming quality of the opposing forces creates indignation in the audience, and the protagonist's humble origins coupled with his long-suffering mien all the more amplify his labors.[91]

Therein, however, lies the catch-22 of popular film's fielding of hockey themes. The melodramatic approach distorts the pragmatic, skill-driven underpinnings of sport by equating success with exemplary morality.[92] The genre's primary function is not to accord the athlete-hero success because of superior aptitude or fair competitive edge, but to do so on the basis of his dark horse markers and virtuous agonizing, which create the foundation for his moral authority. Films that operate in the melodramatic mode may give the impression of update and overhaul, festooning themselves in the realist accouterments of acting, setting, narrative motivation and physical encounter to speak to audiences. But as Williams advises, the realism of the sequences and the virile quality of the engagement in masculine action-oriented genres serve the melodramatic impetus of these films, not the other way around.[93]

Sports film producers typically fret over depicting hockey and other athletic pastimes with accuracy. But this focus often distracts from deploying characters' psychological motives for action and from delivering setups that mirror adequate historical complexities. Even when narratives individualize social conflict as metaphor for power relations, they often aim for denouements within plausible boundaries of the conventional social order. Williams makes the case that the fundamental problem of the melodramatic mode is that it attempts to resolve social issues without confronting traditional moral ideologies, because those are the very cultural spaces to which the melodramatic mode seeks to return.[94] The same can be said of the conservative ideologies of the sports film, whose prescriptions guide hockey's representation in Hollywood film. Marjorie Kibby maintains that the genre's preoccupation with reaffirming the link between masculinity and athleticism via an old form of nationalistic sport that emphasizes character-building through physical pain is not unexpected given that this model of manhood appears ever more difficult to achieve.[95] The conservative arrangement that this masculinity encapsulates is also symbolic of traditional social compacts, as the archetype does not seek to test and transform the social order but to return to nostalgic origins. The orderly resolution of problems that this arrangement represents may consequently appear too facile and simplistic, a utopia that deflects social tensions and inequalities in the culture.

For Canadian film, hockey presents another quandary. Canadian-produced films, from high art to popcorn movies, come in a variety of guises, and popular films more often than not resonate with Hollywood genre conventions and mobilize the premises of the melodramatic mode. Canadian canonical film as defined by critics and historians, on the other hand, is a highbrow cultural form that expresses "out of difference" with Hollywood genres in characterization and plot structure, trading in loser, silent, or weak heroes and their truncated quests.[96] The social-realism of canonical films addresses the weaknesses of Hollywood genres by acknowledging that life is complicated and social-economic conditions may not produce winners in large numbers. Film theorist Jim Leach amplifies this notion in arguing that Canadian film traditionally refuses to generate exultant heroes, and for this reason, Canadian filmmakers' work continues to echo the ambiguities and discrepancies that have historically supported canon conventions.[97] There is a literary precedent for loser hero motifs, which have spilled into film by way of critic Northrop Frye's and novelist Margaret Atwood's readings of the North as an overwhelmingly hostile terrain that must be survived.[98] Atwood's stories, for example, specify the Canadian experience through its interface with "the North, snowstorm, the sinking ship—that killed everyone else," but the individual who lived to tell the story. Her work also connects to the Innisian critique that denounces outside control of Canadian resources by postulating that Canadian literature's concern with survivalist motifs stems from the country's colonial origins, which positions Canada as "a place where profit is made and not by the people who live there."[99] As highbrow or art cinema, Canadian canonical films additionally express a bias against the popular motivated by critics' view of genres as American, which in the Innisian tradition connote the Americanization of Canada.[100]

Highbrow sensibilities prioritize hockey by way of its skilled, artistic merits and agonize over reconciling the sport's aggressive elements with the Canadian character.[101] The hyperbolic template of masculinity endorsed by the Canadian culture of hockey is a popular blueprint of athletic performance that has been in ascendance for over fifty years and shows no signs of losing leverage.[102] Highbrow tastes regard violence as a by-product of the NHL's pandering to audiences in the U.S. who indiscriminately consume the league's product and crave the rough spectacle. In expressing a bias against the popular, highbrow culture does not value the physical game of the Canadian culture of hockey as a legitimate indigenous expression internationally recognized as such, even though film theorists insist that the subjects and protagonists of Canadian film should be homegrown to contribute to the cultural life of the nation.[103] This conflict persists despite that highbrow culture also expresses apprehension over surrendering, indeed "losing," hockey to other nations because it means forfeiting part of Canadian identity.

Canadian canonical films consequently seek to rein in any indications of hockey excess, castigating violence as misbegotten particularly when it spills out of the confines of the ice. Films may chastise the athlete for his inability to restrain himself as the hockey player in film narrative is typically endowed with prodigious strength and fighting skills that can quickly lead to mayhem. Gruneau and Whitson note that decline-into-tragedy or decline-and-fall narratives that center around hockey are often about former players who, once back in their small Canadian communities, "run afoul of the law or become prominent town drunks trading on their past successes for free beer and conversation with strangers."[104] These narratives may depict the protagonist's difficulties in adjusting to a life after hockey, but they also critique the excesses of masculinity in and outside the rink as fundamentally contravening the well-regulated, peaceable nature of the Canadian social order. These characters are moreover consistent with the antiheroic figures of postmodern "high culture" texts, which Buma describes as "marginalized, ineffectual ... and more concerned with escaping their surroundings than improving them."[105]

Despite their social-realist proclivities, films that replicate canon conventions do not always elude the melodramatic mode as they take on violence as a social problem, only to shrug off the role of institutional forces and assign blame to a character from the lofty perches of high culture. The iconic loser, weak, or silent protagonist also clashes with the mythical ideal of the hockey hero, as the latter is anything but weak since mental and physical feebleness contradict the very essence of the hockey archetype. A film like *Gross Misconduct* thus may negotiate this dissonance by denying a character masculine success and truncating his quest. Films may also pair up a protagonist who does not attain his objectives with an Innisian critique by dramatizing the NHL as a business cartel that furthers the American domination of the Canadian resource of hockey, just as *Face Off* and *Net Worth* do. These films express the impossibility of escaping setups inimical to a protagonist's wellbeing because of larger economic or cultural constraints that cannot be magically waved away. Other times, much as in *The Last Season* and *Paperback Hero*, films may be caught in dead ends because of the characters' own shortcomings which stand in the way of his objectives.

In any case, iconic loser heroes who never reach their goals can scarcely accommodate the refrain that second place is fine in a sport other than hockey, widely echoed by the Canadian media and fans in prestige international competition.[106] English-Canadian filmmakers who work with canon conventions typically endorse less committed displays of masculine dominance[107] and routinely refrain from pronouncing triumphalist endings. Yet, the culture cannot consistently promote hockey as premier amplifier of Canadian identity and see itself mirrored in the cinema by way of systematically defeated hockey protagonists, even if it means representing them out of difference with Hollywood cinema. Such films are likely to result in lukewarm reception at the box office.[108] Even when a picture's cultural value supersedes its lack of commercial viability, the public still wants to relate to characters that express parts of itself and its place in the world.

The above discrepancies allow for a range of characters and stories that make for intriguing variations of the hockey player in the three national cinemas. However, even formulaic films with simplistic Manichean characters and plot lines are deserving of serious consideration. Tim Edensor makes a case for carefully considering popular culture texts for the way they unwittingly filter and recreate national identity.[109] Williams, for her part, argues that the melodramatic inflection of genres, including that of the masculine action-oriented formats, amplifies their cultural resonance by propelling debates about weighty social issues of the day. She also interprets the hero's redemption and the restoration of his innocence as a powerful and very American form of democratic justice-procurement.[110] A number of films in the U.S.-made repertoire, however, also feature endings that although consistent with genre codes, fail to provide a convincing narrative of the hero's future prospects. As noted, breaks in genre conventions can signal a crisis or turning point in the culture's values, and these films question the solidity of the scheme of heroic masculinity, sport, and nationhood. Because hockey in film preserves a space to enact the ideological project of traditional white masculinity, these symbolic cracks point to a puncturing of cultural myths that may result from shifts in social norms, intense cross-cultural contact, and the hybridization of nations.[111]

Like Williams who acknowledges the melodramatic mode of Hollywood genres for their inspirational American attributes, Ryan Diduck argues that the Canadian loser archetype is meaningful for its power to express vigorous opposition to the "culture machine" and commercial standards of American film and TV. Although characters who consistently succeed at failing may frustrate the viewer, Diduck underlines that producers' motivation is "to take possession of something rightfully belonging to the Canadian experience, negative or not."[112] Hockey in Canadian movies, however, also hardly expresses singularly "out of difference" with the generic by way of marginal characters and outcomes, since the sport reifies masculine success and this motif, at least in popular film, can only withstand so much quashing and invalidation. Peter Urquhart indeed questions why Canadian film must always defy genre conventions to play an important part in cultural life. He also puzzles over the national historiography's apprehensive view of Canadians' consumption pleasures and popular tastes as evidence of colonization.[113]

Pierre Véronneau and André Loiselle, for their part, echo a similar concern in underlining that the English Canadian "imaginary Québécois" in cinema studies bears little resemblance to Francophone protagonists in commercial genres because critics and scholars alike privilege auteur films and narrow critical approaches. They counsel widening the study of Quebec film to popular movies in order to get a handle not only on the actual range of this cinema but on the authentic Québécois movie-goer.[114] As chiefly popular fare, Quebec's hockey movies also evince their own blend of genre and anti-genre conventions. Even in burlesque turns of the hockey player that dramatize the iconic dysfunction of the loser hero as a comical send-up of hockey masculinity—seen for example in the *Les Boys* films—film practitioners do not sacrifice the propitious ending denoted by the final game because it resonates as a potent national myth and embodies the dreams of North American Francophones, as Loiselle notes.[115] Moreover, these films play up the courageous hues of protagonists who struggle against a superior enemy, downplaying violence but also extoling physicality as a site for expressing honorable resistance. The hockey-themed popular movies of Quebec indeed are some of the most interesting in the entire repertoire because filmmakers not only entertain genre conventions but also lampoon their protagonists and repurpose larger myths and themes in the culture.

The values and perspectives that hockey protagonists dramatize in the three cinemas effectively represent not only distinct allegiances to the game, but also differences in hockey's relationship to masculinity/femininity, race/ethnicity, and sexuality, as well as to the nation and its myths as they mirror the interests of the game's diverse stakeholders on both sides of the 49th parallel.[116] Crosson speaks to this argument in noting that because of the sports film's excessively formulaic features this genre is most productively examined for its functional aspects rather than for its aesthetic or artistic value.[117] The diverse cultural codes and motifs that mold the game's representation in the cinema, in any case, amply suggest that as a category of film sport is hardly a minor format and deserves more in-depth study.

Approaching the Hockey Lineup in This Book

The films selected for analysis in this book loosely follow Dancyger and Rush's definition of the sports genre and feature a main protagonist who draws his/her identity partly or entirely from the game, whose quest drives the plot forward and motivates relationship with significant others, and who must test himself in a final game to attain his goals. This project, however, does not solely feature films that depend on hockey to move along the story or drive the character's development. That is, this volume includes not just sports films, but sports films in combination with other genres, as well as central protagonists who play hockey in non-sports narratives. These generous outlines are necessary to procure a large enough sample that assesses filmmakers' use of the game in film.

Hockey-themed films like *The Tooth Fairy*, *The Mighty Ducks* trilogy, and *Miracle*, which adopt classical storytelling conventions, adhere to the sports genre and follow Dancyger and Rush's format prescriptions. Canadian popular fare like *Goon* also displays sports genre conventions like a final game and a main protagonist with a clear opponent. Canadian productions that follow canonical parameters and trade in "loser" heroes, on the other hand, introduce game sequences at any point of the plot to precipitate the principal's demise, effectively shunning the use of a final game with dramatic goal-scoring to disrupt the heroic trajectory. *Paperback Hero*, for example, features a truncated game that serves as metaphor for the protagonist's own truncated dreams of glory. Other times hockey sequences may express through a scant few plays that allow the viewer to situate the protagonist's social identity, as is the case of the Don Cherry biopics, *Keep Your Head Up, Kid* and *Wrath of Grapes*, which conflate aspects of both popular and Canadian canonical film. Even Hollywood movies may veer away from genre conventions depending on narrative needs. TV movie *The Deadliest Season* in like fashion deploys a game sequence mid-story to precipitate the principal's demise and follow up with a courtroom trial to dramatize hockey as a lethal game. In *Ice Angel* the coach is missing, and in *The Love Guru* teammates mostly appear as NHL stand-ins because these figures are not central to the story. Despite the utility of genre conventions, then, the above variations illustrate that film practitioners do not utilize them in prescribed form but blend motifs to entertain audiences with unexpected twists and augment a story's salability.[118]

To gauge the images and themes of the films under study, this project adopts a textual analysis approach that serves to decode the visual, sound, dialogue and other elements of the cinematic text and elucidate how the film's creative team—producers, writers, directors, and others—puts forth particular meanings. This approach takes into account comments from writers, directors and other individuals from the creative team who may make themselves accessible in media junkets to elucidate on particular aspects of moviemaking as this information is helpful in pinpointing the target audience that film practitioners aim to reach. The interpretation of the cinematic text, however, must perforce go beyond film practitioners' explicit intentions, since motion pictures are rife with contradictions. Indeed, the nature of film is such that it can accommodate discordant meanings, enabling filmmakers to speak to disparate constituencies by averring particular values in one segment and disowning those same values in another. Those moments of ambiguity are significant because they amplify the text's understandings.

The topics that the film industry chooses to depict, the approaches to the subject matter, and the timing of a movie's release also depend on a complex set of contingencies. While a proponent of textual analysis, Elfriede Fürsich nonetheless also advises against remaining too close to the text and failing to examine other aspects of media content, including production, distribution, and reception or consumption, as well as the text's historical positioning.[119] Pierre Véronneau echoes this sentiment in admonishing film scholarship's almost exclusive use of textual analysis in the study of Quebec national cinema because it lends itself to distortions and precludes social science practices that can more aptly assess these texts.[120]

This study takes note of this guidance by tackling the wide array of films in the three national cinemas, outlining separate cultural histories, referencing sport and media industry developments, and incorporating clips from television programs, journalistic reports, and other content to supplement a text's interpretation. This multipronged, more systemic "media studies" approach is critical because hockey in the cinema uses to advantage television's own economic and cultural relationship with sport by harnessing topical matter as well as game broadcasts' viewing angles, reportage styles, and archival footage. Although any film can encode developments in the North American game, this exchange is very much in evidence in the Canadian Broadcasting Corporation's telefilms, which draw on issues aired in the pubcaster's news and public affairs programming as well as *Hockey Night in Canada* broadcasts. Leakage between the TV/cinema and sport industries also shows up in film texts through frequent NHLer cameo appearances that amplify a film's realist aesthetic, augment its promotional cachet, and signal to audiences the existence of corporate synergies.

The Cinema of Hockey comprises nine chapters that mirror the study's thematic emphasis. The first two chapters explore hockey masculinity as aggressive muscularity. Chapter One grapples with critiques of muscular excess as depicted by the bully or goon aspect of the hockey player in the Canadian-produced *Paperback Hero, The Last Season,* and *Gross Misconduct*. It also looks at the muscularity of the hockey player in Hollywood films *Ice Castles, Love Story, The Deadliest Season,* and *Youngblood*. Chapter Two scrutinizes spoofs of the hockey player's hyper-physicality through the archetype of the bully-clown in Hollywood's *Slap Shot, Happy Gilmore, The Tooth Fairy* and *Just Friends*, and in its Canadian counterparts *Score: A Hockey Musical, Goon,* and the Don Cherry biopics, *Keep Your Head Up, Kid* and *Wrath of Grapes*. Chapter Three examines films that critique aspects of the business of hockey prior to and after the game's transformation into upmarket sport—*Face Off, Net Worth, Sudden Death, Mystery, Alaska, No Sleep 'til Madison* and *Slap Shot 2: Breaking the Ice*. Chapter Four takes up Disney's entry into the NHL and hockey's production as part of the family entertainment genre. This section appraises *The Mighty Ducks* trilogy and Disney TV movies *H.E. Double Hockey Sticks* and *Den Brother* as well as Canadian popular family fare *MVP: Most Valuable Primate, Ronnie and Julie, Slap Shot 3: The Junior League* and *Sticks and Stones*.

The remaining chapters assess the hockey protagonist and his/her relationship to the nation. Chapter Five considers films produced in Quebec, including the English-language *Mystery of the Million Dollar Hockey Puck*, the French-language *Les Boys* tetralogy and the prequel *Il était une fois les Boys, Maurice Richard,* and *Bon Cop, Bad Cop* to gauge how hockey validates French-Canadian masculinity and identity. Chapter Six probes renditions of the "Miracle on Ice" in the TV movie *Miracle on Ice* and the Disney feature *Miracle*, as well as the depiction of the Summit Series in *Canada Russia '72*. This section also explores portrayals of seminal coaches in *The Hounds of Notre Dame*, the aforementioned Cherry biopics, and *Waking Up Wally: The Walter Gretzky Story* for the way they prioritize aspects of the national character. Chapters Seven and Eight weigh in on ethnic and gay minorities as well as women in the game to gauge how these characters, whose identity opposes that of the archetype, fare in leading hockey roles. Black American and the Indian Canadian hockey players take center stage in *The Love Guru* and *Breakaway*, respectively, while *Perfectly Normal, Breakfast with Scot, Grown Up Movie Star*, and *The Sheldon Kennedy Story* take up mild and gay expressions of masculinity and deal with the subject of sexual abuse in the game, respectively. With respect to the women's game, *Hockey Night, Ice Angel, Go Figure, Chicks with Sticks*, National Lampoon's *Pucked*, and *Les Pee Wee 3D: l'hiver qui a changé ma vie* trace the trajectory of girls and women in hockey and examine the reasons for its limited scope. Chapter Nine focuses on the spectacle of hockey in the movies and explores how the thematic and technical aspects (cinematography, soundtrack, editing, etc.) of game action, player roles, and other facets of storytelling convey their ideological messages. A brief Conclusion sums up the findings.

The selection and placement of films in this volume is also not fixed because texts are polysemous and open to multiple readings. Many of the above pictures incorporate at least a partial critique of the hockey business because this commentary enhances both the realism and the entertainment value of the subject matter. As noted, a number of these films qualify as family fare, a genre that the film and broadcast industries have increasingly relied on to appeal to a mass audience. These narratives do not all appear in chapters three and four because they highlight more forceful themes. The placement of the women's game toward the end of the book also does not mean the subject is unimportant. Quite the contrary, it is designed to call attention to glaring absences and misconstructions as an entreaty to enlarge and actualize this representation.

While the films chosen for analysis straddle four decades—from the 1970s through the 2000s—this volume by no means secures the full gamut of hockey movies in existence. Films from early cinema are not examined at length because they have not seen wide release and are difficult to see, particularly the Hollywood pictures. Nonetheless, it is important to underscore that hockey's presence in the cinema dates back to the silent era with the 1898 Edison Company's black and white *Hockey Match on the Ice*,[121] which depicts players jostling for the puck on a patch of natural ice in line with sports representation of the time as part of newsreels and actualités. Later pictures feature the narrative structure, quick dialogue, and compelling characters that came out of the studio system. By this time sport in film also evinces now familiar sports values, like the importance of the level playing field, recurrent motifs about underdogs beating the odds, and the idea of sport as a masculine realm.[122] Numerous hockey films see their theatrical release at this time, such as *King of Hockey* (Smith, 1936),[123] *The Game That Kills* (Lederman, 1937), *Idol of the Crowds* (Lubin, 1937), *The Duke of West Point*[124] (Green, 1938), *Gay Blades* (Blair, 1946) and *White Lightning* (Bernds, 1953).

The early Canadian hockey repertoire, which depended on state subsidies and institutional production and borrows heavily from the documentary tradition, for its part, assigns the game a nation-building role. *Hot Ice: The Anatomy of Hockey, Canada's National Game* (Jacoby, 1940), a Canadian Government Motion Picture Bureau release, portrays hockey as integral to the nation-building effort, where it is presented as transcending all socio-economic differences consonant with the way the game developed in the country early on.[125] The National Film Board of Canada (NFB)[126] also released *Here's Hockey*[127] (Mcfarlane, 1953), a tour of hockey from peewee to the professional ranks featuring Montreal Canadiens star Jean Béliveau, which shows why the sport had the makings of an exciting national spectator game. *Is Commercialism Changing Canadian Sport?* (1955), for its part, incorporates a discussion of

Here's Hockey and focuses on the role of commercialism in the game. Later on, the agency released *Blades and Brass*[128] (Canning, 1967), a 10-minute short that showcases footage taken during the NHL season joined with a musical soundtrack that blends sixties Latin-flavored, light swing, and other motifs and amplifies the game's multiple cadences. A western theme highlights fighting and other skirmishes.

It is worth underlining that the cinematography of matches in the early films is quite sophisticated even by today's standards. *King of Hockey*, for example, features long overhead shots of the play that cover both ends of the ice, medium (upper body) close-ups of the puck carrier, low camera shots that give close views of skilled maneuvering, and medium shots of tallies from varying angles. The hockey of the period, as noted, was quite rough and the movie depicts players tripping and interfering with opponents as well as involved in all-out brawls. What's more, this film includes an over-the-head hit by the goalie (Bill "Jumbo" Mullins, played by Wayne Morris) on the star player of his *own* team (Gabby Dugan, played by Dick Purcell), which has an inadvertent comical effect but also alludes to hockey as a no-holds barred sport. Quite telling also is how the plot quickly resolves the tension brought on by the vicious interlude, and brings the two players back together as friends by film's end.

Here's Hockey, a 10-minute black and white documentary, plays like a short feature driven by game sequences in which the narration takes a backseat. Medium shots follow players en route to the goal from a variety of angles and mostly from a camera above the ice. The hockey is also quite physical and skilled which the quick edits make sure to convey as exciting spectacle.

Many of the above films also use real players from both college and professional leagues. *Gay Blades*, for example, deploys athletes from the high profile but now defunct Pacific Coast pro league to supply most of the game action.[129] A notable exception is *Idol of the Crowds* starring John Wayne as erstwhile minor league hockey star-turned-chicken farmer Johnny Hanson. Laurel Zeisel observes of the film that although it was one of the 147 of Wayne's prosperous career, it was also one of his worst, in part because it showcases the "Hollywood star legend skat[ing] around on the inside of his ankles … try[ing] to shoot the puck."[130] A University of Southern California (USC) football player who had grown up around horses, Wayne had always wanted to star in motion pictures and got his chance when Universal Studios signed him up to an eight-picture deal. The hockey film was part of the package, and judging from the actor's remarks, he did not enjoy the role: "I'm from Southern California. I've never been on goddamn skates in my life. I was in the hospital for two fucking days after that."[131]

Many of the early films, as noted, are unavailable and, as a result, are difficult to study as a repertoire. The pictures examined at length in this volume, on the other hand, although not all easy to secure, are deemed to be the most representative in articulating the concerns of the game's contemporary stakeholders. They also supply guidelines about the kinds of realities and blueprints of masculinity that hockey in film furthers across four decades. These critical readings, in any case, are offered in an effort to advance the study of sport in film and augment the game's understandings in popular culture in the expectation that they will kindle future work.

• 1 •

Critiques of Hockey as Aggressive Muscularity

The dominant masculinity that hockey mythologizes is a proxy for the robust resourcefulness that made possible North America's frontier opening. The frontier masculinity that inspires the hockey exemplar, however, is more complex than the myth intimates, since the process of exploration (and conquest) made for tenuous institutional and cultural sway over the individual, and suffused male occupational culture with individualism, resistance to authority, and violence.[1] Hockey's frontier referents, as a result, also dramatize the tension between institutional control and forceful opposition to this order. This tension is evident in the highbrow and lowbrow readings of the game. Popular culture identifies hockey by way of the aggressive muscularity that is necessary in procuring the satisfying spectacle of the professional game. Aggressive muscularity's variants—forceful checking, grinding, hard hitting, fighting and other bold displays—designate the hockey player as a committed athlete. The game's high contact aspect makes it amply clear that most players must be able to defend themselves to forestall prospective attacks, or at least have someone to protect them from assault. Players who make a living by way of their fighting skills tend to be underdogs "who otherwise might have no business in the game," as *New York Times* writer John Branch notes.[2] These athletes model a working-class ethos by offsetting gaps in talent with hard work, and heartily engaging in fisticuffs bouts that fans enthusiastically applaud. Valerie Walkerdine underscores the importance of physical skills and fighting for individuals whose position in life expresses masculine success by way of manual rather than intellectual labor, noting that they are a sure way of confirming heroism and advancing personal empowerment.[3] Evidence of aggressive muscularity, whether through brawling or other tests of durability, is also expedient in confirming that pieces of old school hockey retain currency in the culture regardless of rule changes across the decades.

Although popular culture privileges hockey as a suitably rugged performance of manhood, power blocs that seek to contain an excess of masculinity are liable to brand this muscularity as incongruous with social mores. Norbert Elias and Eric Dunning shed light on the dynamics behind the struggle for control over leisure activities, noting that while competitive games are the one area that allows for affective expressions of exuberance, elites consent to these displays within boundaries by way of civilizing directives that advocate propriety, respectability, and self-restraint. Elias and Dunning argue that the complex process of balancing out the effervescence of the sports contest with the social checks of the civilizing process can never be fully settled as the popular can easily blot out societal controls.[4] John Fiske similarly argues that the body and physical displays remain critical sites of social contestation between the elites and the people, as the outstripping of civilizing checks can readily expose the fragility of the social enterprise and threaten the power blocs who oversee it.[5] Elias and Dunning's and Fiske's ideas of the body, physicality, and affective expressions as sites of containment and resistance are useful in assessing readings of hockey as highbrow or lowbrow cultural form. Highbrow sensibilities express a preference for the aesthetic and didactic features of the game in line with the Victorian amateur's reading of sport as civilizing social agent.[6] Popular or lowbrow tastes, on the other hand, favor the use of physicality as legitimate performance of masculinity. Historically this contestation has articulated a social divide between upper- and middle-class predilection for respectable (sportsmanlike) competition and working-class preference for rough play, although the institutional development of hockey confirms that brawling and other forms of violence have been a staple of the game from its inception.

Because hockey is a fast, reactive sport, and players retain for themselves the discretion to overstep the boundaries of the game's codes, the dividing line between restraint and the unbridled expression of emotion can be unusually thin. Canadian canonical films express a bias against the popular and agonize over the game's rough edges because they lack the uplifting quality that contributes to cultural life, and motion pictures in this section follow suit by

Felix Batterinski (Booth Savage, with moustache) with the Philadelphia Flyers in *The Last Season* (CBC Still Photo Collection).

critiquing violence as maladaptive. These motion pictures articulate the tension in hockey's dramatization of frontier virility by chastising hyperphysicality and bloodletting as proof of masculine courage. Hollywood movies also articulate physical excess as counterproductive to masculine success, although they make an exception with upper-class and educated protagonists by framing their relish for the robust game as a necessary statement of virility. These films, then, voice a range of critiques about violence in hockey. Some denounce its use as a vulgar cultural form that is transgressive of the moral order and incompatible with the project of citizenry and nation. Others condemn the heavyweight ideal of masculinity as set for displacement for having overstayed its welcome in the sport.

Bully Hockey in Canadian Film: *Paperback Hero,* *The Last Season* and *Gross Misconduct*

The model of dominant masculinity that the hockey player embodies in popular culture as a forceful and tough character diverges from preferred masculinity models in English-Canadian canonical films, which favor more muted expressions of male social identity and nationhood. Lee Parpart proposes that Canadian realities—resulting from the country's colonial past, its premium on cultural heterogeneity, and the social and political implications of having the U.S. as neighbor—have made for variants of masculinity that are milder, gentler, peaceable, and more tolerant of peripherality.[7] In the sports film, the contrast between this mild Canadian masculinity and the triumphal, proactive masculinity of classical Hollywood is so pointed that protagonists who attempt "to assume classical heroic proportions in the American mould ... [are] generally rendered ridiculous, if not completely insane," as Katherine Monk proposes.[8]

English-Canadian films typically chastise dispositions that exceed the parameters of mild masculinity, and needless to say, take issue with the frontier virility of the hockey player who wields violence to attain his objectives. This position is consistent with the civilizing directive and cultural elites' desire to manage the popular and its penchant for physical excess. Canadian film's aversion toward shows of force and expressions of triumphalism also aligns with highbrow culture's conventions that balk at pronouncing winners. As a result, these pictures turn hockey characters into bona fide loser heroes by framing their masculinity through the game's contentious aspects, and severely punishing them for an outlaw disposition that is incongruent with social norms.

Many of the films that critique hockey's aggressive muscularity dramatize the seventies game for a reason. Violence saturated the amateur and professional games at this time and commentators pinned the responsibility on elite-level players, who deployed violence as legitimate strategy to garner a winning record. The endemic violence in the seventies game had originated with a 1960s rule change that broadened the use of body checks to the entire ice surface, enabling new playing strategies for winning match-ups to take root.[9] Critics, however, blamed the violence on the 1967–1968 NHL expansion, which despite shrinking attendance doubled the number of teams from six to twelve, and paved the way for role players or goons. Deploying an Innisian critique of Canada's status as U.S. branch plant, commentators accused the league for actively marketing violence to enlarge the U.S. fan base, who were largely ignorant of the game's finer points. In this scheme, the violent spectacle not only ruined the game for connoisseurs but substantiated Canada's takeover by American commercial interests and the lowbrow tastes of U.S. pop culture.[10]

Whether for structural or strictly commercial reasons, systemic use of violence in the seventies game promptly became a means to field competitive playoff teams. Brawling and brutality were part of the game of the 1969–1970 Stanley Cup winner "Big, Bad" Boston Bruins, whose legendary center Derek Sanderson confirmed that violence helped players score goals. Brutal plays intimidated the opponent who coughed up the puck for the greater part of the game.[11] Violence was also in plain evidence during the eight-game Canada–U.S.S.R. 1972 series, and extended into the two-time Stanley Cup winning game of the Philadelphia Flyers, best known for their Broad Street Bullies moniker.[12] The 1974–1975 expansion enlarged the league again to eighteen teams, further diluting talent and reinforcing the use of bruiser tactics. But with the emergence of speedier players in the mid–1970s and especially in the 1980s, violence stood out like a sore thumb, warranting even louder calls to curb brutality. A 1987 *Washington Post* report denounced that "[t]he NHL, which has a long history of tolerating excessive violence, is supposedly trying to cut down on it…. The next time there's a mugging on the ice, forget about the NHL: somebody go out and call the cops."[13] Critics in Canada similarly argued for drawing a line on unacceptable levels of physicality, debating its ethics, and calling for the institution of checks on the rough play of seventies hockey.

Felix Batterinski (Booth Savage, facing camera) with Tapiola Hauki in *The Last Season* (CBC Still Photo Collection).

If hockey was the theater of the national psyche, the high incidence of violence and the cultural doubling of hockey into highbrow and lowbrow variants were problematic because they mirrored the fractured character of the nation. The tough-man ideal existed at odds with the aesthetic and didactic features of hockey favored by the Victorian amateur view of sport as civilizing agent,[14] and hockey typically bridged this duality by containing violence as a highly regulated ritual of manhood. But the violence of the seventies game also left cultural commentators shaken, engendering concerns about its discharge into other social arenas. Canadian identity was synonymous with peaceful and well-mannered citizenry, yet on the ice, this identity played out as a dark alter ego.

Hockey's cultural doubling also resonated with the duality expressed in the period's cinema. Cultural nationalists argued that Canadian media's permeation by American production values and genres had resulted in the country's invisibility on the nation's screens. To counter this lack of visibility, the government stepped up subsidies to spur an indigenous film industry and culture in the form of a tax-shelter scheme termed the "Capital Cost Allowance" (CCA).[15] Films slated for material assistance explicitly broke with the conventions of Hollywood genres by stressing unpleasant loser protagonists, aimless plots, and truncated outcomes, among various disruptions of generic storytelling.[16] Janice Kaye notes that the protagonists of CCA films were conspicuous for their inability to bridge two worlds—Canadian-American, Anglophone-Francophone, center-periphery, metropolis-hinterland, local-global—and were therefore obsessed with performing a form of psychological border-crossing that masked a deep sense of insecurity and manifested in a desire to escape reality.[17]

Influential Canadian film theorist Robert Fothergill in his memorable essay in 1973 titled "Coward, Bully or Clown: The Dream-Life of a Younger Brother," critiqued the psychological dysfunction of the unpleasant characters of CCA cinema, which he categorized as Cowards, Bullies, or Clowns. Fothergill pondered that if the cinema mirrored the nation, why would English-Canadian films insist on producing an inordinate number of problematic types, hardly the sort with whom the nation's citizens could identify. Offering a social-psychological theory for this dysfunctionality, he noted that it stemmed from Canada's colonial past, and the country's sense of inferiority vis-à-vis the U.S., the more powerful older brother who thwarted little brother's self-realization.[18] Of the three character categories, Fothergill chose the bully to typecast the hockey player in two semifinal films of the period, *Face Off* (1971) and *Paperback Hero* (1973), defining it as the "ugliest" of the archetypes because of his "insubstantial male ego," fits of rage, and inconsiderate treatment of women.[19] Fothergill's use of the bullying frame to describe the cinematic anti-heroes of the national game was not far off from the kind of hockey played across North American rinks during the 1970s and into the next decade. His essay, however, also conflated nation and gender to reiterate disquietude over Canada's branch plant status, which as cultural nationalists argued, dramatized the country's economic dependence on the U.S.

One of the acclaimed films of the CCA, *Paperback Hero* (Pearson, 1973) epitomizes many of this cinema's preoccupations in its depiction of a bully protagonist who is caught between two identities and reaches an impassable juncture in antiheroic form. Rick Dillon (Keir Dullea) is the film's hockey player, a reckless top-liner with the local team of Delisle, Saskatchewan, who has a dual identity as a fantasy officer of the law. When not in hockey gear, Dillon goes about town in costume, toting a gun and wearing a 10-gallon hat, and speaking of himself as the Marshal of the Prairie hamlet, after the Marshal Matt Dillon of Dodge City in the 1950s-1970s western TV series *Gunsmoke*. Dillon's coach does not buy his pretentious, reckless ways on the ice warning that, "this stuff you're doing is going to make this team a liability...." But like his Marshal persona, Dillon makes the laws and lives life on his terms, a lifestyle that includes plenty of womanizing and brawling. Despite the town's slumping economy and an offer for a building janitor position, he refuses to relocate to the city: "Go some place where I'm just a little guy that nobody knows? ... I'm the Marshal in this town.... I've got respect." Big Ed (Franz Russell), father of collegiate girlfriend Joanna (Dayle

Haddon) and an entrepreneur with interests in cattle and the local hardware store MacLeod's where Rick plays at working, is also the owner of the town's hockey team. Players complain that the ice in the rink is "soup," but Big Ed waves them off as alcoholics and refuses to put down the $75,000 needed to replace it. Instead, he decides to sell the team after the last game of the season. He informs players that although he is unable to a make firm commitment, he will make every effort to relocate them and help them secure jobs. But the players know this likely means the end of their hockey careers. To prove to Joanna that he remains a "somebody," and the odds against him, Dillon enters into a senseless shootout with the town's police, and much to the chagrin of barmaid girlfriend Loretta (Elizabeth Ashley), ends up dead in front of a barn that sports a "Pioneer" sign.

Dillon embodies the extreme psychological border-crossing and sense of invisibility of characters in CCA films, an invisibility he attempts to relieve by appending an American Old West persona that emulates the Hollywood version of the North American prairies through the clash between lawmen and reprobate sorts. His virility-boosting American masquerade notwithstanding, Dillon also doubtlessly longs to embody national North American identity myths, wearing NHL sweaters, and dreaming of a life in the big leagues. Along with teammate Pov (John Beck), who is married but restless, he fantasizes about playing NHL hockey out in the American West, and as Pov pictures himself in one of the newly-minted expansion teams of the sixties, Rick joins in the reverie, "Twenty grand a year.... Cadillacs.... California, instead of that I'm sitting here." The men's musings call forth images associated with the Westering myth and its immense prospects, which all the more show up their small potatoes, dead-end lives. In equating their current bearings with dashed prospects, the film expresses disquietude over hockey's shift away from its roots in small Canadian towns to large American sunny enclaves where fans are not familiar with the game,[20] reiterating the Innisian critique of Canada as branch plant of the U.S.

Dillon's chronic fantasizing, which spills into a dysfunctional use of violence, also exacerbates his disconnection from the organic life of the region, as his relationship with the townsfolk is defined by a series of perks that he sums up as respect. In short order, Rick proceeds to abuse the community's goodwill, taking every opportunity to brawl at the local drinking establishment, goad Constable Burdock (George R. Robertson), and provoke the hockey referees. Although his elevated status as a hockey player in a small town is appealing to the opposite sex, his macho posture quickly leads to transgressive violence against female partners. He labels his sexual associations as woman-handling and deploys various gradations of physical force on Loretta and Joanna. In contrast to the long-suffering Loretta who waits patiently for Dillon to commit, Joanna yields but also spurns his outsized male ego sardonically offering to role-play and cry when he slaps her so he can feel like a man. Instead of grasping the motives for her ridicule, Rick retrenches further into his Marshal bravado, a hollow veneer of self-importance that stems from his inconsequential life, to which director Peter Pearson alludes in his assessment of Dillon as a tin god.[21]

The film's opening shot speaks to this image as Rick in his Marshal get-up engages in target shooting with the beautiful Prairie landscape as backdrop. The setup recalls the romantic masculinity of the cowboy, but the target shooting of beer bottles simultaneously downsizes this iconography. Gordon Lightfoot's "If You Could Read My Mind" accompanies the sequence and alludes to a hero that cannot be set free as long as he remains a ghost that cannot be seen. Visuals and lyrics illustrate the conundrum at the center of Dillon's life: a hopeless sense of invisibility that has ties to the regional realities of Prairie life and the economic downturn of the period. Unlike the West's immensity in the American imaginary, which functions as symbol of unending prospects, the Canadian Prairies in literature and film dramatize "a sense of confinement by limited space," as Gerald Horne observes.[22] In *Paperback Hero*, this sense of confinement translates into an oppressive invisibility, one that Pov also expresses when he complains to his wife, "You know what the trouble is, honey? There's too much goddamned sky, not enough of me." Like Rick, Pov feels inadequate, and he attempts to assuage his sense of diminishment by building himself a new house. According to Ronald Tranquilla in his discussion of Dick Harrison's work, the house in Canadian Prairie literature represents not only man's buffer against the elements, but operates as a Western heroic response to the overpowering New World landscape.[23] Pov's unfinished house, a result of the team's disintegration and his forced relocation, dramatizes the failure of heroic masculinity, mirroring the experience of settlement as one of alienation. *Paperback Hero* also associates the failure of heroic masculinity with the economic deprivation of the Prairies, which it amplifies by way of Delisle's marginal status and its lack of an NHL team to enable hockey's myth of success and procure Rick and Pov's profitable move out of the area. The dilapidated arenas in the film contribute to the image of a mid-seventies rural Canada in decline and depict the erosion of hockey in local communities.[24]

Beset by an agonizing sense of diminishment, the characters face further cultural erasure. The film's only and final hockey matchup parodies the seventies game of unbridled violence and ends in an absurd fight that immerses referees and fans. It stands out, however, because it never gets started in the first place, dramatizing Rick and Pov's truncated quests of social mobility and dreams of masculine glory. The film sets up the unraveling by framing Pov's eager expectation to measure himself one last time against the Prince Albert Chiefs. When the referees cancel the game because of the unfit state of the rink's ice, Pov refuses to be denied and breaks out the mayhem, punching an official. Pov's actions cue in Rick, who proceeds to take on an opponent just as his buddy moves on to the fans. Not to be outdone, Dillon assails Constable Burdock, but having literally transgressed the law, and with his prospects imploding, he flees in his convertible set to kidnap Joanna who is on a bus bound out of town. The fight continues and takes on a buffoonish aura as players do battle with their sticks to the relish of those in attendance.

The wielding of physicality in a pivotal game that is not allowed to run its course acts as a proxy for redressing the characters' social downsizing, but as Joanna mocks after Rick has forcibly taken her from the bus, it is all to no avail since "five years from now nobody will even remember you." The anxiety of the characters who strive to write themselves on the landscape and on the ice can also be felt throughout the car chase segments by way of kinetic camera pans over the flat immensity of the Prairie landscape, and in the spectacle of excess that arises from the truncated hockey game. Dillon's reckless hockey moves and his joy rides across the Prairie fields are reminiscent of literary critic Eli Mandel's description of the archetypal Prairie character as "a man not so much in place, as out of place and so endlessly trying to ... write himself into existence."[25]

Having failed at the myth of sports success, Rick strives to reassert himself through his Marshal persona. But on this front too his efforts are overlaid with absurdity. Like the gunslingers of the American West, the Marshal makes the laws, but in the Canadian context this formula is delusional as Canadian Western expansion presupposed the embedding of a police force, the Royal Canadian Mounted Police (RCMP), who were, in turn, superseded by the larger power of the British Empire.[26] As a result, the Marshal is caught between the historical American "indulgence in violence" and the Canadian "necessity of self-restraint," to use Ronald Tranquilla's view of the antipodal forces that animate Canadian and U.S. national identity myths.[27] He ends up the loser because he cannot succeed at a game that is stacked against him from the outset. Because Canadian "Mild West" narratives framed movement into the West as a peaceful enterprise, the Marshal's American "Wild West" façade appears painfully misguided.[28] The local police, whom Dillon engages in the final shootout, are in reality a source of institutional constraint and order in the small town, and in the context of the community's isolation in the Canadian North, very much a part of the Canadian identity.[29] The tone of the film captures the insane connotations of the Marshal's dual bully personas that lead to his futile end. Bordering on black comedy, the character's outrageous behavior makes light of the audience's values, but by farcically precipitating his own death, he underlines his own insignificance.[30] Rather than heroic, the Marshal's demise comes off as pointless and absurd, an unsound exercise in psychological border-crossing by a protagonist who carries the seeds of self-undoing.

Peter Harcourt suggests that in a number of CCA films, the viewer seldom encounters larger-than-life characters and the landscape often works to arrest the protagonists' movements. Canadian films like *Paperback Hero*, Harcourt proposes, don't move relentlessly or inevitably in the direction of a resolution, nor are their protagonists able to make sense of their quandaries.[31] Dillon's masculinity of excess and his disruption of social checks express an underlying need to extract greater agency. But the animating energies of Prairie life, which seek to contain the primitive, anarchic elements of masculinity,[32] only recapitulate his sense of confinement and reaffirm that neither facet of his border-crossing can make up for his very real lack of hockey prospects. The film subverts the prescriptions of the heroic protagonist in the western and avers the impossibility of escape, suiting up the hockey anti-hero and setting him on a downhill slippery slope toward his demise.

The CBC telefilm *The Last Season* (King, 1986), based on the novel by Roy MacGregor, explores the foibles of another bully hockey protagonist whose scheme to exploit heavyweight tactics backfires and leads to his downfall. The film frames violence as strategy for garnering wins akin to a thorn on the side of the Canadian psyche. It weighs in on professional hockey's use of violence through the physical game of Felix Batterinski (Booth Savage), a twelve-year veteran of the NHL and winner of two Stanley Cups with the Philadelphia Flyers. Of a Polish family from the rural town of Pomerania, Ontario where he grew up playing hockey, the thirty-two-year old Batterinski figures he's not done with the game and accepts an offer as player-coach of the Tapiola Hauki team in Finland. He promptly instates the Bully tactics he mastered with the Flyers, and to habituate his charges to the rough game, he gets the Board overseeing the team's management to reward them with bonuses for winning, moving up in the standings, and dropping a man "on his rear," as he puts it. Despite vocal resistance by a number of players, Felix informs his Finnish squad that if it is fancy skating they're entertaining they should head for the Ice Capades. The coach is unwavering in his conviction that a more physical form of hockey will hone a winning team. The proprietary attitude he feels toward the Finnish game and toward architect girlfriend Kristina (Johanna Raunio) is one and the same as Felix is intent on transforming both to suit his tastes.

Unlike his girlfriend's values, however, the team's game gradually begins to change turning more physical as they move up in the standings. On the ice, Felix puts his own lessons to good use and when he is sent to the penalty box after a clean check, a fan taunts him and he retaliates. Outrage follows and newspaper headlines scream: "Kanadalainen Skandal!" Even as he apologizes for his affront and explains that the passion of the moment often gives way to deplorable actions, journalists get wind of his other machinations and accusations mount. Felix claims ignorance stressing that he is only the coach but he is forced to return to Pomerania and soon after, out of options, he ends his life.[33] *Helsingin Sanomat* sports journalist Arto Kurri (Seppo Wallin) considers Felix's end, observing that although Finnish hockey could certainly do with a little more assertiveness, no real fan could condone violence. Still, matters should not have come to pass quite in the manner in which they did.

The Last Season aligns Felix Batterinski's obsession with the violent game with his desperation to climb out of his rural Ontario town. The film opens with scenes of the Northern landscape and zeroes in on a group of boys, among them an eight-year-old Felix, playing the game on the pond. While he is away, his grandfather dies, and his Polish grandmother blames his death on the youngster for forgetting to collect the morning eggs from the chicken coop. Dad Walter (John Colicos), who is invested in Felix's success in the hope that it will bring glory to the family and match the Batterinski's social status in the old world, sticks up for his son. The scene, however, is visually dark, pointing to his grandmother's superstitions as a clue to Felix's own primitive makeup, which will color his quest and lead to his demise. The host of *Canada Magazine*, the news outlet investigating the player's story, reiterates the motif of underdevelopment by describing him as a "simple, uncomplicated" individual whose rise to the NHL was fuelled by a sense of desperation to leave his rural backwater, and whose failure to put his career with the Flyers into perspective contributed to framing his sojourn as a "pathetic story." In *The Last Season*, the North, typically a source of self-affirming Canadian vitality that is consistent with the entrepreneurial spirit of the positive hero, inscribes Felix with unsophisticated characteristics that turn his efforts to extend the athletic lifespan into misfortune.

Since the NHL dramatizes hockey's myth of success, and Batterinski's rise from junior hockey in Pomerania to the Flyer ranks makes him a paragon of achievement, to articulate his decline and fall, the film must formulate his migration to a European team and his insistence on a form of hockey that is inimical to highbrow tastes as misguided. *The Last Season* consequently downplays Felix's transatlantic export of the seventies game by designating it as the colonizing undertaking of a fanatic. In Joseph Maguire's typology of sports migrants, the pioneer or colonizer is a zealot who seeks to "convert the natives to … [his] body habitus and sports culture."[34] Batterinski's proselytizing of rough hockey in short order wreaks havoc with his close relationships, with the team he coaches, and the game he loves. His insistence on physical play to win games recalls the bully tactics of the Philadelphia Flyers, who were the first club to win the Stanley Cup while leading the league in penalties. Batterinski dramatizes this disfigurement as he capitalizes on the advice of his childhood Lake Vernon–Huntsville coach—"talent makes you dress; heart makes you win"—by merchandising it to his Finnish players as "work produces blood, which makes up for talent." Ironically, Fred Schero's poetic words to his Flyers—"we know that hockey is where we live … and life is just a place where we spend time between games"—words which Felix Batterinski takes to heart, make no sense in a culture in which professional hockey was a part-time amateur endeavor until 1975,[35] and winning at all costs was an unreasonable and perplexing expectation. Given that Felix's game is dislocated from its regional and historical roots, his attempts at the successful transatlantic export of seventies hockey can only amount to a miscalculation that truncates his potentially invigorating sojourn.

The Last Season also articulates Felix's repertory of breaches as bypassing the unspoken guidelines of the physical game. His former coach warns about transgressing into bully territory noting, "You fight, you fight hockey players. You fight a jerk, you become a jerk." He advises Felix to pick his fights to no avail. Dad Walter similarly objects to Felix's cheap-shotting of an opponent. But the son responds by waving off the father's consternation and noting that his bully tactics are part of hockey. Even though as a coach Batterinski is responsible for firming up the game of his Finnish players and making the team more competitive, his Broad Street Bullies tactics evoke mixed feelings on the bench. Some players take to Felix's brand of play, but others categorically reject it. When the team loses the game, Felix commends that "it was a brave try," hardly the picture of an uninspiring bully ill-suited to steer a transatlantic team. However, the film undercuts his statement by seguing to visuals of players who do not take to the bullying game to reassert Felix's Flyer-Bully disposition as a foregone conclusion.

The player's relationship with girlfriend Kristina in like fashion dramatizes the player's intemperate ways. Kristina's professional background and the Scandinavian culture that informs her feminist views make her solid internal moorings difficult to upset. Kristina is also patently attracted to the Canadian tough, however, as a shot of her in the stands cheering for Felix and her statement that he is unlike the men she has dated confirm. She also expresses utter shock at Felix's death, noting that she did not see any signs that he would take his life. But the film leaves no doubt that the relationship is on perilous footing because of the player's penchant for over-reaction. A sequence in which he trashes a phone booth after a dissatisfying long-distance conversation with her illustrates the point. The sequence recalls Fothergill's argument about the inadequacy of bully protagonists in their relationships with women, and Felix's inability to parlay his connection to Kristina into a rewarding future and successfully improve his professional circumstances configure him as backward on several fronts.

Mary Jane Miller notes in her analysis of four decades of CBC series and dramas that telefilms like *The Last Season* grew out of the network's need to explore perennial issues in sport such as the ethics of professional hockey.[36] *The Last Season*'s particular critique of violence came at a time when speedy and offensively minded players diminished employment opportunities for the league's enforcers.[37] Influential commentators like the CBC's Peter Gzowski contextualized the play of the period primarily through the multiple successes of the high-scoring NHL's Edmonton Oilers as reestablishing Canadian ownership of the game, which articulated the use of violence to garner wins as obsolete.[38]

The Last Season technically sets out to examine the systemic use of violence by zeroing in on the export of hockey brutality to another nation's game: "how much was caused by the man and how much by the system that shaped the man," as *Canada Magazine*'s host announces at the onset of the film. Although the statement hints at criticism of the NHL's role in fostering violence, the film fails to reliably examine the systemic pressures behind Felix's game. Instead, it lays the blame squarely on Batterinski's shoulders as the player acknowledges that he created a particular brand of hockey that he now has to live with. Joseph Maguire, however, argues that the process of athlete migration cannot be disassociated from the global commodification of sport, which, in turn, cannot be explained by any one factor as it involves interactions

Felix Batterinski (Booth Savage, left) and teammate restrained by Finnish refs in *The Last Season* (CBC Still Photo Collection).

among transnational organizations, corporations, government officials, entrepreneurial classes, and the beliefs and cultural practices of individuals.[39] *The Last Season* reduces these processes to a matter of character and circumstance by arguing that the bully game is the preserve of primitive men and by framing the player's sojourn as a last ditch effort to extend the athletic lifespan.[40] Felix's childhood friend Danny Shannon (David Ferry) speaks to this perspective when he notes that the former Flyer, cut off by the league and swindled by his agent, was running out of options. It is no surprise, then, that *The Last Season* should repurpose the motif of player migration to Europe to articulate Felix's misguided game and failed quest. As Maguire notes, aging Canadian players have frequently sought the lure of more comfortable European arenas to recapture the feeling of glory days gone by, even as the decision has resulted in an "inevitable downward spiral."[41] By rendering Felix's story in terms of an emblematic unraveling—an argument voiced by *Canada Magazine*'s host when he explains Batterinski's demise as an inability to recognize the situation for what it was: "a dead end"—*The Last Season* categorically sounds the death knell for the systemic use of violence in the game.

A third film, the hockey biopic *Gross Misconduct* (Egoyan, 1993), reiterates the critique of seventies hockey violence through the familiar loser hero motif and his decline and fall narrative arc. Based on a screenplay adapted by Paul Gross from journalist Martin O'Malley's 1989 novel, *Gross Misconduct* tells the story of NHLer Brian "Spinner" Spencer's (Brian Kash) climb out of the British Columbia outpost of Fort St. James, his stints with Toronto, Buffalo, and Pittsburgh, as well as a post–NHL life as a drifter in West Palm Beach, Florida where he ends up murdered during a hold-up. From the very outset the telefilm makes clear that the viewer cannot make sense of Brian's outback masculinity without understanding the father's input in his upbringing and for this reason, it insistently links them throughout the story line. Although Martin O'Malley reduces the father-son relationship to one page of his 1989 account,[42] director Atom Egoyan amplifies the relationship by way of inter-titles that textually link Brian and dad Roy (Peter MacNeill) and portray them as unhinged characters. The film's establishing sequence focuses attention on Brian by way of black and white archival footage that depicts the player taking to the ice with the rest of his Leafs teammates. The accompanying musical score, which evokes Wild West gunslinger motifs merged with the sound of the wind in desolate places, clue the viewer in to Brian's character. The film then segues to Fort St. James by cutting to a jagged peak that towers over a rugged landscape and moving on to an extreme close-up of Roy Spencer looking into the distance and smoking a cigarette. As he spots a raptor overhead, he aims his gun and takes it down needlessly. The overhead shot amplifies Roy's "Wild West" referents by way of his thick dark coat and shotgun, as well as ominous marks on the snow that give the impression of outsized bullet holes. The introductory setup deftly connects father and son and studiously hints at their analogous demise.

Roy's input also extends to Brian's formative hockey experiences. In a poignant exercise of masculinity training, Roy instructs the youngster (Shawn Ashmore) to purposely collide with his twin brother Byron (Aaron Ashmore). Brian refuses, and as punishment, he is forced to skate figure eights until the next morning. When dad queries his boy whether he is angry and Brian quietly acknowledges his vexation, the elder Spencer instructs him to harness his emotions. The father teaches his young sons the function of pain in honing character in line with the old form of nationalistic sport and its role in training for manhood. He also underscores sport's link to warfare by using military imagery to teach strategy. Amplifying that "hockey is God's game," and for this reason, its make-up is quite intricate, Roy stresses that, "the only guy that's got more angles to worry about is a fighter pilot." The father moreover counsels that the physical game can serve as an escape valve from economic desolation as he points to the dreary surroundings and makes clear that there isn't much to life at the Fort. "You can live here and be buried here," he cautions, "or you can play hockey." Roy sums up for his sons the role of the game in promoting the myth of sport success by facilitating a way out of the hinterland, leaving no doubt about the outback status of the small B.C. outpost from which the Spencers hail. The stark landscape, bracketed by immense mountains and augmented by the presence of hefty logs stacked up and ready for transport, alludes to Brian's upbringing in the backcountry and his honing of an outback masculinity conducive to raw violence. Like the logs waiting to be shipped out to large metropolitan centers, Brian's bush masculinity is set for export to sell the game in hockey meccas. Both are natural resources, but Brian turns out to be a dubious commodity, as he puts to questionable use the formidable strength he accrues working in the log camps and lumber mills and the lessons he learns by way of the elder Spencer's austere training methods.

To dramatize Brian's active courting of violence, *Gross Misconduct* integrates documentary footage of the player's on-ice exploits with dramatic reenactments. When he is queried in *Hockey Night in Canada* archival footage whether the Leafs acquired him to "thump" opponents, the real Spencer quietly dismisses the allegations but explains that his style invariably features hard-hitting. Since in the context of violent seventies hockey Brian's behavior does not appear misplaced, over-the-top acting must convey the player's volatile character. The resulting dramatic sequences depict Spencer trespassing the boundaries of legitimate play by tricking opponents and hitting them unexpectedly, picking up individuals who happen to cross him and dropping them on their heads, and viciously reacting at the slightest provocation. Brian, the boy, explains this volatility as grounding the very essence of the hockey player, noting that hockey presupposes the existence of clear boundaries that delineate whom to protect and whom to assail.

Much like *The Last Season*, *Gross Misconduct* avoids examining the systemic pressures faced by NHL players who make a career of the game, articulating Spinner's own raging personality as the cause for the player's downfall. The film alludes to these pressures in passing when the Leafs coach informs recruits to put their game faces on and have their mean game ready since "nobody's job is secure." However, the telefilm suggests that the platform of organized elite-level hockey merely provides Spencer with an outlet to express normative behaviors learned in the bleak and violent landscape of his youth since the player appears to be incapable of self-restraint.[43] Following yet another loss by his then Pittsburgh Penguins team, Brian vents his frustration during an interview by castigating that the main problem with the team is its name—one that denotes "incompetent little birds"—after which he proceeds to violently lash out in the studio. The Penguins subsequently demote the player to the minors, and now deserted by his second wife who refuses to follow in his journeyman's steps, he abruptly walks off the team, abandoning his hockey commitments for a seedy life in Florida.

The film lays out Brian's masculinity of excess in the context of an underachieving career and a life of failure, as the boy Brian reads from Robert A. Stebbins' scholarly study *The*

Brian Spencer (Daniel Kash, left) engages in fisticuffs in *Gross Misconduct* (CBC Still Photo Collection).

Retirement of Professional Hockey Players: Process of Change and Career Identity (1987), and notes that over-identification with the game is eminently hazardous to the health of the individual when his career has the markings of failure. By labeling Spencer's life a flop, the tale ultimately attenuates the lessons of the father—lessons vividly illustrated in Bobby Orr's compliment: "Hey, Spinner, you hurt!" which equate making a living through physical skills with competence. By negating the directives of the father, *Gross Misconduct* renders inconclusively the escape from the hinterland and ultimately associates the wilderness-wasteland with Brian's own untamed character and wasted life. The film's dramatic finale not unexpectedly connects Roy and Brian's deaths, even though they originally occurred in separate time frames. Their demise is set up by a scene in which Brian, the boy, speaks of a nightmare in which he and his dad resemble trains on the same track headed for a collision. The Spencers' end subsequently unfolds through six sets of back-and-forth edits of Roy's holdup of local CBC headquarters for failing to broadcast his son's inaugural Leafs game, and Brian's armed robbery by a thug who demands his wallet just as he is recounting the particulars of an encounter with dazzling Bobby Orr. The edits prolong the tension and confirm the men's characters as reckless, and Brian's especially as driven by a misguided bravado that warrants his untimely end.

The film grounds Spencer's vulgar character and consequent demise in his working-class, interior B.C. roots, suggesting that a Toronto-centric cultural-nationalist perspective is at work in Spencer's portrayal. Bart Beaty argues that *Gross Misconduct*'s condemnation of violence in the Canadian culture of hockey should be considered in the context of director Atom Egoyan's art cinema credentials, which recapitulate both the cultural nationalist bias against hyperphysicality in hockey and a center-margins view that takes for granted that the values and symbols of the Canadian center regions animate those of the rest of the country.[44] He adds that by undermining Spencer's status as fan favorite and linking his game to his vulgar lifestyle and subsequent demise in Florida, the telefilm reprises the player's journey as a moral tale about "repressed Canadians and libidinous Americans."[45]

The above formula through which Canadian identity is expressed "out of difference" from its southern neighbor harks back to the myth of Northern robustness.[46] The 1994 CBC documentary *Going South*, which examines the relocation of NHL teams to areas like tropical Florida, similarly portrays Miami as a "city built for pleasure" and the game's merchandising in the context of commercialized American popular culture to reactivate the notion that hockey is ill-suited to its transplantation to southern shores because of its organic link to the icescape of the North. The reprise of Brian Spencer's seventies career in a nineties film through a similar cultural lens recapitulates the advisory of unhinging the game from its Canadian poles.[47] Back in the 1970s critics blamed the league's merchandising of hockey to American audiences for the flare-up of violence, a development that nonetheless allowed players like Spinner Spencer to become popular with fans. In the 1990s, pressure on the game came from globalization processes and the opening of Sun Belt markets, which the Canadian media again interpreted as the Americanization of hockey[48] and whose effects *Going South* encapsulates through a Florida Panthers fan's comical assertion that she has "complete understanding and complete knowledge of the game," but she hopes to see more fighting. *Gross Misconduct* comments on the consequences of employing unsavory bully types to market the game to audiences unacquainted with its finer points because doing so inevitably degrades the cultural heritage. Brian Spencer's Florida death from a gunshot wound during a botched robbery relays the message that the player's use of physical excess to carve out a career in hockey fittingly spilled out of the arena to become his foil.

Bully Hockey in Hollywood Film: *Ice Castles, Love Story, The Deadliest Season* and *Youngblood*

Sports literature and genre film rehearse the relationship between masculinity, sport, and the nation by enlarging on the athlete's formidable physical aptitude, courage, and staunch will. Hollywood movies that emphasize the dual nature of hockey, like Canadian films that critique violence in the game, express the concern with physical excess mirrored in the period's influential reports and commentaries.[49] These films feature protagonists who either relish the game's high-contact edges, or upon entering the high-pressure professional arena, must deal with the systemic uses and deleterious effects of hyperphysical tactics in the game. Collegians Nick Peterson (Robby Benson) in *Ice Castles* (Wrye, 1978) and Oliver Barrett IV (Ryan O'Neal) in *Love Story* (Hiller, 1970) are prime examples. Pre-med student Nick plays the game with reckless abandon, which he shows off at the Minnesota North Stars tryout camp by fighting the first player who checks him into the boards. When the head coach (Leonard Lilyholm) counters that he should be concerned that there is always someone more dangerous, Nick takes it as an affront: "There ain't nobody, nobody more suicidal than me." Instead of encouragement, however, he gets a surprise scolding: "I don't know why you wanna beat yourself to death playing hockey…. You can speak English, for Christ's sake…. What would a smart kid, not too ugly, wanna be playing hockey for? If I had any brains, gone to college…." When Nick queries whether he made the cut, the troubled coach, realizing he will not dissuade the prospect, relays that he is headed to the North Stars farm club in Lincoln: "You go down and play with some of those killers for a while." Nick joins the minors but before long quits the game after he grows disillusioned with the professional ranks.

As *Ice Castles* illustrates, this period's films convey hockey as an extreme sport, in a different league than major-league baseball or basketball, by bandying about about the term "suicidal" or communicating much the same message through the protagonists' actions. *Love Story*'s own main character, wealthy Harvard student Oliver Barrett also shows his zest for hockey by garnering multiple penalties and game misconducts against other Ivy Leagues teams, though he "always make[s] the other guy look worse," as he brags. As a quintessential All-American, Oliver plays squash and touch football, but it's his feisty hockey markers that set him apart as a seventies protagonist of unmatched allure.

Hollywood films typically make clear that characters from wealthy and/or educated backgrounds are well served by hockey's muscular markers because elitism in U.S. popular culture often smacks of effeteness. The Beadle & Adams dime novel series of the late nineteenth and early twentieth centuries, based on western and frontier narratives reprinted from paper serials, for example, reaffirm the ideal of a robust masculinity exemplified by the heroized masculinity of frontier protagonists as it contrasts with the effeteness of the bookish, appearance-fixated, and self-preoccupied Easterner.[50] The protagonists' hockey markers, however, also run counter to class expectations because fighting and physical skills, as Valerie Walkerdine aptly notes, primarily embody "the fantasy of working-class male omnipotence over the forces of humiliating oppression…."[51] Contravening class expectations is also a source

Oliver Barrett IV (Ryan O'Neal) playing for Harvard in *Love Story* (Paramount Pictures/Photofest).

of tension for its implicit threat to the social order, and in these films these pressures show up by way of familial rifts. When Oliver's father (Ray Milland) presses him to relinquish his attachment to the game and focus on his future by attending prestigious Harvard Law School, the tough man refuses because "they haven't got a hockey team," straining the already distant relationship between them. The satire of all hockey films, *Slap Shot* (Hill, 1977), for its part, opts to poke fun at the rift between father and son by pointing to the game as an inappropriate career choice for upwardly-mobile middle-class males. When radio announcer Jim Carr (Andrew Duncan) queries Ned Braden (Michael Ontkean), the Chiefs star player and best forward of the Federal League, "Why would someone with your background and education still be playing hockey?" Ned comically retorts, "because I hate my father!" Since sport is central to the archetypal bond between father and son, in taking up organized hockey, these upper- and middle-class characters articulate shifts in the value repertoire of the culture that accord with the period's political critique of traditional masculinity and institutional authority.[52]

Although the sports genre stages the athlete's commitment to the job by way of his laboring body, the bully game short-circuits the myth of success in sport by amplifying the transgressive and socially dysfunctional elements of dominant masculinity. This focus is prominent in movies that deal with violence in the game and the player's collusion in the shady side of sport. *The Deadliest Season* (Markowitz, 1977) depicts its central protagonist through an analogous bully motif, and debates the parameters of legitimate hockey as well as the responsibility for its breach. The CBS telefilm pronounces its acerbic commentary through the figure of American defenseman Gerry Miller (Michael Moriarty) who after three seasons on a professional Wisconsin team is sent down to the minors because he refuses to play a retaliatory game. Noting that he's been competing since turning eight, Gerry protests, "That is *not* hockey!" But the manager argues that he cannot carry a man who doesn't see any ice time, warning that he can do without figure skaters on his team. Gerry confides in teammate and best friend Dave Eskenazi (Paul D'Amato), who encourages him to give in to management and the coaching staff's demands. Miller works his way back to the majors by ratcheting up his game into sheer aggression, rationalizing: "It's hockey. It's a violent game.... How many years have I got left to play? ... It's a job." In time he becomes "the Penalty Killer" on the team with a record 22-minute penalty points and soon receives his first "ball-and-chain" award. The crowd clamors: "We want Gerry!" spurring him on until, in a retaliatory move that turns fatal, Miller spears his own friend Dave, now with a Seattle team, rupturing his spleen. District Attorney Horace Mead (Walter McGinn), who is at the game with his son, decides to bring charges of aggravated assault with a deadly weapon. After a lengthy trial, and with the help of personal attorney George Graff (Kevin Conway), Gerry is exonerated from jail time, but he is banished by the league from the game he loves.

A pivotal film in its critique of hockey violence, *The Deadliest Season* sports courtroom scenes that fiercely argue the issue of violence as spectacle and place owner greed at the center of the debate. Team attorney Bertram Fowler (Patrick O'Neal) queries Meade over lunch why he intends to turn Gerry into a sacrificial scapegoat when he poses no social risk. But the D.A. questions he should let the player walk simply because he's a professional athlete in a highly lucrative business. Team owner Bill Cairns (Mason Adams) secretly longs to drop Miller as the team's main sponsor balks at having his beer brand associated with violence. Attorney Fowler, whose job is to look after the interests of important client Cairns, for his part, proposes to get Gerry to plead guilty to save the team's reputation. It falls to George Graff to make the case that the league and the team must share the guilt for the mishap for courting society's basest instincts by selling violence. The Defense argues that Gerry was only required to play hockey, not be a goon. Although sorry for the death of his best friend, Miller explains the dynamics of the game as akin to instinct, noting that when a player gets hit, he instantaneously hits back, and that his friend had doled out "a real shot." The film conveys professional hockey as both a game of reaction and implicit compliance by the opponent to some mode of assault. Deploying Graff's voice, *The Deadliest Season* places responsibility for Gerry Miller's actions on the ice squarely on the lap of the league, team, and spectators. Graff admonishes that Miller strove to hold down a job that supported his family, making the case that ownership, driven by rising profits, and fans who "like their hamburger raw," equally depended on the player performing his role. In framing Gerry's actions as driven by the crowd's "darkest fantasies," Graff portrays the player as an expendable commodity controlled by a professional hockey cartel and a white canvas on which to project a social thirst for violence.

The Deadliest Season contextualizes violence in hockey in terms of the wider societal upheaval of the sixties and seventies and public appetite for fighting, bloodshed, and lawlessness. Indeed, the period saw the release of several notable reports on violence, which the film conflates in its commentary on hockey brutality. The first, the June 1969 *Report of the National Commission on the Causes and Prevention of Violence*, came about in response to the Robert Kennedy and Martin Luther King assassinations and the social and political anarchy of the sixties, citing violence as principal cause for the escalation of social problems. Richard Slotkin observes that the Commission had faulted the U.S. "frontier heritage" for the negative features of the American character and the frayed national experience, in the process formulating an "inverted Turnerism" as the root cause of the widespread violence.[53] The second, a 1974 report by Ontario attorney William R. McMurtry, came about in response to the Canadian government's concerns over violence in amateur hockey. McMurtry blamed hockey brutality on parental expectations of victory and the influence of elite professionals, who deployed violence to win at all costs.[54] *The Deadliest Season* integrates McMurtry Report references to comment on hockey violence in the context of commercial imperatives to sell the game and combines them with a crime motif that amplifies public appetite for bloodshed. Slotkin notes that the inversion of the frontier myth in urban crime dramas of the period depicted violence as an offshoot of corporate collusion, ominous power wielding, and obscene wealth accumulation and exploitation.[55] *The Deadliest Season* foregrounds, in similar fashion, violence as a by-product of corporate interests that short-circuit sport's agency in promoting social mobility.

Joan Mellen elaborates that the cinema of the seventies mirrored the anarchy that typified the movements of the sixties through a thematic "jungle brutality" that merged oppression and victimization in the figure of the central protagonist. In these films, male characters are explicitly initiated into violence to enable their effectual agency in the swell of chaos and disorder.[56] *The Deadliest Season* similarly contextualizes Gerry Miller's violent tactics as a scheme to retain his hockey job during a period of intense economic dislocation, and in the context of the increasing social demands made on men by the women's movement. A bedroom scene between Gerry and wife Sharon (Meryl Streep) after a six-week separation on account of his duties depicts masculinity under pressure-cooker conditions. Turning to her nightly ablutions, Sharon lets her husband know she's aware of his newly refurbished play, a bully game that she cannot condone. When Gerry dismisses her concerns by underscoring that "it's hockey" and it has nothing to do with her, she retorts that she cannot compartmentalize her emotions and let him put his hand on her, a hand that earlier ran a young player into the boards and busted up his mouth. Uneasy with the direction of the conversation, Gerry gets up from the bed and approaches a window with open blinds that resemble prison bars. The setup is a poignant metaphor for the checks on his masculinity represented by the social demands for full partnership that Sharon expresses. As Gerry continues to argue that "it's a job" and she need not watch if she's vexed, with arms crossed Sharon counters that his explanations amount to "a lot of crap" and that he cannot pull the veil over her eyes for she understands the game full well. At the window, Gerry takes a look at the cigar he's been holding and lowers it in complete disbelief at his wife's turn-about, noting that because of eight penalty minutes he's about to be kicked out of bed. The scene succinctly encapsulates the protagonist's quandary as he is caught between the demands of the job and his mate's expectations for equal partnering, a role that exceeds the typical displays of emotional support and self-sacrifice ascribed physically inactive female leads in sports films.[57]

The window setup also foreshadows the death of friend Dave and the prospective jail time Gerry faces. Although in seventies films violence enables the effectual agency of the protagonist in the face of corporate agendas, in *The Deadliest Season* violence magnifies the character's dual oppressor-victim position. The film depicts Gerry's downward spiral into brutality when the referee calls a penalty on both Gerry and Dave with the crowd hollering for the player to beat up the opponent. Inside the penalty box the two players yell at each other despite their close friendship, and as the tension mounts and the clock ticks down, the spectators stamp their feet and ever more loudly chant Gerry's name. With the penalty over, and out of the box, Dave high-sticks Gerry in the head, and Gerry responds by spearing Dave in the stomach, rupturing his spleen and eventually costing his friend his life. Post-game, President Macloud (George Petrie) relays that the team's management and ownership intend to back Gerry fully because he's a true American, although "Dave was a real Canadian, but it's the same thing." As it turns out, Gerry and Dave end up as mere casualties of the commercial imperatives of the seventies game, sacrificed to the whims and interests of ownership and management.

But the film hardly exonerates Gerry over his actions. Despite the D.A.'s own career ambitions and his harsh description of the player as "a hired bully," his accusations about the "license in professional hockey for violence for blood" ring true. Even as Graff argues that the upper echelons were fully invested in the "Philadelphia style of play," Gerry admits that while he dislikes beating people up, he promptly became "a member of the goon squad." He defines the line between legitimate hockey and brutality noting that, "playing tough, hard hockey is one thing. Fighting all that, that's something else." He confesses to wife Sharon at film's end that he conned himself and fooled everyone but her, and that she was justified in expressing her displeasure. The film affirms the place of physicality in hockey as legitimate in the context of very specific strategies, which Sharon underlines as necessary defensive actions to prevent an opponent from scoring, and which she specifies as skills that contributed to her husband's allure: "When I watched you … hitting, checking, it would turn me on." She also makes clear, however, that she recognizes the difference between legitimate tactics and unwarranted attack. The film, then, critiques the hockey athlete's ability to transcend the rules and engage in physical excess as transgressions of the sportsman's codes, a critique that draws on the systemic use of violence by seventies' teams to garner wins. *The Deadliest Season* showcases a protagonist who has fallen into the role of bully but at enormous social costs that he fully and plainly recognizes. When attorney Graff offers to appeal his case, Gerry declines noting that a new trial would be unlikely to settle matters differently, since "[w]hen you come right down to it I killed him." The ending sequences, which portray the player taking shots on net and reminiscing about the time he went through a whole team to score the perfect goal, underline his profound love for the game and all the more highlight violence as a project of corporate exploitation. In banishing Gerry from the league and truncating his opportunities for social mobility, *The Deadliest Season* renders its verdict of the professional game of the seventies as decidedly dystopic.

Despite the emergence of skilled and speedy players in the 1980s and calls by critics on both sides of the border to check violence in professional hockey, the use of physical tactics continued unabated. However, as Timothy Scheurer notes, the eighties sports film was "no longer a difficult and unpopular genre,"[58] but recapitulated the power of sports in forging real heroes and regenerating communities.[59] The coming-of-age narrative *Youngblood* (Markle, 1986) combines both motifs in showcasing a heroic protagonist who must push back on the Canadian culture of hockey's heavyweight ideal of masculinity. The film casts its lens on the sojourn of Dean Youngblood (Rob Lowe), a 17-year-old talent from upstate New York who decides to try out for the Hamilton Mustangs across the border from his father's farm. Dean makes clear at the dinner table that he doesn't want to be a "goddamned farmer" for the remainder of his life, and he must play junior if he ever wants to make it into the pro leagues. Despite his 5'10" and a 160-pound frame, Dean is confident he can make an effective playmaker: "They'll never catch me!" His first tryout ensures a run-in with hyperphysical Karl Racki (George Finn) who repeatedly lands the young gun sideways on the ice. Despite the confrontation, Dean draws on his scoring skills and handily makes the team. As a Mustang, the rookie befriends hotshot forward Derek Sutton (Patrick Swayze) but the Hamilton topliner ends up seriously injured by the infamous Racki, now team goon of the arch-opponent Thunder Bay Bombers. Despondent about the bad break that ends his teammate's career, Dean returns to the farm to the disgust of older brother Kelly (Jim Youngs), a onetime minor hockey player forced to retire after suffering the loss of an eye. While initially upbraiding Dean for quitting the team, Kelly and dad Blane (Eric Nesterenko) ultimately rally to teach him the intricacies of self-defense, and upon his return the player helps the Mustangs win the championship game against the Bombers. His work done, he proceeds to avenge teammate Sutton by confronting Racki and ultimately leaving him knocked out cold on the ice.

Youngblood vividly contests the masculinity codes of the Canadian culture of hockey built into the junior game[60] by pitting scorer Dean against the physically more imposing Racki and insisting on a game that expunges gratuitous violence. The industrial town of Thunder Bay where Racki and his Bombers are based operates as a signifier of the hard-man tradition that celebrates hockey's tough-man ideal.[61] With 378 penalty minutes under his belt, Racki is the film's bully villain. The team's plentiful skill notwithstanding, the Bombers, including the goalie who wears a mask painted with an ominous-looking human skull, are stand-ins for the violent game of the seventies and eighties. The Mustangs, in contrast, feature

Left to right: Dean Youngblood (Rob Lowe), Coach Murray Chadwick (Ed Lauter) and Derek Sutton (Patrick Swayze) in *Youngblood* (MGM/UA Entertainment Co./Photofest).

the services of players who chiefly deploy skill and speed to score goals. The Mustangs-Bombers opposition dramatizes the scorer's hampering and enfeebling by the masculinity codes of the physical culture of hockey, which the unabashed Derek Sutton protests when he notes, "They've got us by the balls.... It's more than just a game. You gotta play it according to their rules." Boasting physical durability, a decided size advantage, and 92 points in the season, Sutton nonetheless expresses his dissatisfaction with professional hockey's institutionalization of physical excess.

Derek also shows relief that there is still a way for him and his teammates to realize their dreams of social mobility. Watching a televised basketball game, the otherwise confident Sutton notes, "Thank God there is still a sport for the middle-sized white boy." *Youngblood* fashions hockey as an athletic harbor for the Caucasian male in the context of the increased visibility of black athletes and perceived dwindling opportunity for working-class white males in professional sport. The film reiterates that hockey in the eighties remains a pathway through which working-class white men can achieve social mobility as Coach Murray Chadwick (Ed Lauter) admonishes his charges when his team is staring a losing record in the face: "Do you want to go back to the mills and mines?" Racki's unmotivated from-behind attack of Sutton during a stoppage of play, which goes unpunished and the film renders viscerally by way of slow motion, poignantly critiques the pervasive use of violence in junior hockey as an attempt against the very social and economic viability of the scorer.

The film's commentary on physical excess also plays out as a critique of the Canadian culture of hockey's controlling influence over the game. This perspective is not unexpected in view of the hockey background of Peter Markle, who both wrote and directed the film. As a member of the 1972 U.S. Olympic team who trained under the innovative eye of celebrated coach Murray Williamson, Markle was exposed to play that stressed aspects of the game other than physicality as a winning tactic. Coach Wiliamson, who was invited by premier Soviet hockey coach Anatoli Tarasov to learn Russian hockey techniques, incorporated new strategies into the American game early on, enabling an unexpected and now celebrated silver-medal victory for his 1972 U.S. Olympic squad at the Winter Games in Sapporo, Japan. Williamson also coached Herb Brooks, passing on the Russian influence into the American game, as Brooks incorporated similar techniques to further innovate play, resulting in another unexpected gold medal at the Winter Games in Lake Placid. In a 1990 *New York Times* interview, Coach Brooks explicitly aligned his team's victory with the U.S. history of the game, noting that "we didn't exactly come out of nowhere: people forget that the US team won the silver medal in 1972."[62] Privately, too, he acknowledged Coach Williamson's legacy in a note written after the 1980 triumph: "Murray, your influence as a teammate and coach helped produce this victory."[63] Given the above history, it is no coincidence that Markle sketches his American protagonist as someone who, while required to build up physical resilience by virtue of his participation in a Canadian-dominated arena, relies primarily on skills to win games.

To dethrone Racki and his Bombers, the film makes clear that Dean must traverse territory that he hesitates crossing because he lacks the physical aptitude that hockey demands. As he throws in the towel and returns to the farm after Sutton's injury, he gets a talking-to from Kelly who berates him for relinquishing his dream so readily: "You never quit, ever!" Kelly's input in acculturating Dean to the norms of the hockey arena is significant given that good sibling relationships in the cinema of the game occur infrequently and typically showcase strains when one brother successfully remains part of professional hockey. *The Rhino Brothers*

(Beaver, 2001) and *Lovers in a Dangerous Time* (Charters and Hug, 2009), for example, dramatize sibling jealousies that end in physical disputes to amplify the dysfunctional family motifs of Canadian canonical film. Since the culture defines males who make a living in the sport as powerful and physically superior specimens, the childhood rink acts as theater where characters vie for validation by putting muscles on display. In *Youngblood*, Dean is the American ingénue facing the intricacies of reality,[64] and Kelly must help his younger brother assert a bolder, physically durable, and self-reliant masculinity that accords with the muscular aptitude of the ideal.

Dean's dad, played by hockey tough Eric Nesterenko, also resolves to coach the young gun in the finer points of the two-man hockey fight. Blane Youngblood tells his son that if he's headed back, he wants to see that he is ready. When Dean wonders aloud why earlier he had offered no help, the father replies that he did not wish to see his younger son hurt like his first-born. Blane reiterates Hollywood dads' pervasive emotional inarticulacy, but since Dean has an absent mother—"she got tired of the farm too," as he remarks—the father must transcend any inadequacies and fully reclaim his paternal role. The son has pointed need for the father because he must undertake a rite of passage to separate from home and make it on his own as a man, and the film encapsulates the father's allegorical return by way of a lyrical sequence in which Blane trains Dean in the open air backlit by the setting sun. The farm transforms into the preparatory site for the son's rite of passage into self-sufficiency, much like the pond on which young Dean celebrates his first goal serves as the initiatory site of his hockey talent.

Primed for the confrontation, Dean makes a return to the team and informs the injured Sutton he intends to put Racki in his place, even as his teammate advises otherwise. Dean also faces the prospect of losing the coach's daughter, Jesse (Cynthia Gibb), who detests the violent aspects of hockey. But the player's mind is made up. Before he can measure himself against his nemesis, he must first score the game-winning goal with a final ten seconds left. After a long setup, he finally makes his move by making a wide turn and kicking the puck with his skate onto to his stick, ending up in the back of the net and cleanly beating the goaltender with a pretty goal. With three seconds left and the game won, Dean signals Racki by hitting him with his stick unprovoked. Almost in disbelief, the enforcer accedes with a sneer and both players engage in lengthy circling and stick fighting. Racki lands the first punch, and Dean stumbles but remains on his feet, responding with a dramatic hit that makes his opponent's head swing backward. After another round, Dean has managed to pull off his opponent's jersey and placed four brutal punches that land his nemesis on the ice. The final punch puts a bloodied Racki out of commission, and with the heavyweight ideal of hockey masculinity vanquished, the arena erupts in cheers. The completely unnecessary fight in the context of the championship game conveys that the protagonist has assimilated the lessons of the father, sealing his rite of passage and propelling him toward masculine success. The hero bounds into questionable territory, but the film frames his crossing into violence necessary to avenge the ills suffered by the community. In the manner of the western, the movie enmeshes Dean in the violence, but leaves him unsullied by the aggression. In clearly spelling out his triumph over Racki, *Youngblood* also forcefully conveys the demise of hypermasculinized seventies hockey.

The Last Season and *Youngblood* voice a stark critique of the bully element at a time when the professional game found itself at a crossroads. Even though *Youngblood* amplifies hockey's rough edges through bench-clearing brawls and suitably hostile working-class fans that harass visiting teams and coaches, the film's symbolic vanquishing of the goon decisively stages the closing of an era of controversial hockey. In similar manner, the above motion pictures articulate the limits of aggression in accomplishing sports masculinity. Although these films authenticate hockey as a working-class sport, they refrain from honoring physical excess as the hard labor of the worker-athlete or from conducting an in-depth debate of systemic forces behind the use of brutal tactics in the game. Instead, these movies look upon physical excess as eminently transgressive, a cultural problem that necessitates surmounting for its subversion of the civilizing process. It is also clear, however, that there is a fine line in Hollywood films especially, between the use of physicality as evidence of adaptive masculinity and outright dysfunctional behavior. Nick Peterson's enjoyment of "suicidal" hockey, Oliver Barrett IV's routine fisticuffs display and heavy penalty minutes, and Dean Youngblood's unnecessary use of physical force to put away Thunder Bay punisher Racki, all marked as part of the protagonist's allure, only differ from Gerry Miller's physical spectacle as the "Penalty Killer" in that the latter accidentally ends in the death of the opponent. Indeed, these Hollywood films appear to frame as transgressive—and here they concur with their English-Canadian counterparts—physical punishment that is concentrated in the labor of the enforcer, as if the structure of the game itself had nothing to do with this role division.

Moreover, while English-Canadian films with canonical hues dress up maladaptive behavior as lowbrow American frontierism and un–Canadian by nature, Hollywood films do much the same by casting Canadians as needlessly violent enforcer types. Hence, Oliver complains to girlfriend Jennifer that "I was nearly massacred by the wild Canadian hordes," even as he boasts that he always has the final say. The bully archetype in these Hollywood films hints that the real threat to the moral order are protagonists of upper- and middle-class backgrounds who defy hockey's working-class values by integrating them into their masculine identity. Indicative of the melodrama's function to return to traditional ideologies, *Love Story* and *Ice Castles* resolve these social tensions by having their protagonists give up hopes of establishing themselves in the sport. *Slap Shot*, for its part, culminates the definitive matchup of the film as Ned parodies the working-class aspects of hockey through the memorable striptease discussed earlier. English-Canadian films also veil class issues by placing the blame on "bad apples" who have an unfortunate penchant for violence, all the while diverting attention from the existence of a Canadian demographic that fiercely defends toughness in hockey as integral to the national character because it shatters claims of "a classless and nationalized Canadian identity," as Bart Beaty notes.[65] These films, then, deploy the hockey bully to both air and suppress issues of importance in the culture in accordance with melodrama's tendency to put back in the box or project onto an Other the very fears its raises, a strategy that the sports film, as a genre which inherently ratifies traditional compacts, easily manages.

2

Spoofs of Aggressive Muscularity: The Pleasures of Sporting Excess

Hockey's aggressive muscularity in comedic situations is deployed to satirize the game and its characters as a mockery of the ideal. Outbursts of physical excess are easy pickings in the cinema because these expressions straddle a fine line between legitimacy and deviance. Although hockey's frontier referents ideally hone character in the service of the national project, frontier symbolism is a double-edged sword as it invokes the implicit tension between elites' claim on power and the active subversion of their authority by popular forces. Spoofs of hockey capitalize on this tension, snickering at the (sometimes futile) effort of keeping rambunctious males in check. Because some movies frame physical excess as part of the game but also as detracting from hockey's potential to bring the protagonist authentic masculine success, films that celebrate hockey's popular froth insert only token guidance about heeding the directives of the civilizing process. These pictures unabashedly celebrate the inversion of rules that govern mundane life as a form of the carnivalesque.

John Fiske explains that the carnivalesque provides evidence that the vitality of popular forces is alive and well. Although these creative moments are frightening to power blocs who oversee the moral and aesthetic order as they bring to light popular resentment toward social checks, they are freeing to those whom such controls are meant to restrain. Fiske notes, however, that not all unruly impulses are populist. Only when the carnivalesque deploys the people's notions of pleasure and gratification to challenge the power of elites by contravening its strictures, does it operate in full populist mode. Whether the carnivalesque takes on populist overtones or not, the threat to the higher orders nevertheless lies in its potential to do so. And although this popular form of resistance is not necessarily a progressive force since it can seek to rein in the effects of immoderate liberalism, in saluting the disruptive joys of popular excess it has the power to show up upper-/middle-class ideas of honor, morality, and the belief in sport as expelling insalubrious, unruly impulses.[1]

In hockey comedies, the farcical archetype of the bully-clown is a sure way of spotting the presence of the carnivalesque.[2] The archetype sanctions expressions of tough-guy physicality while satirizing the sport's rowdy elements. This function allows for the interplay between the sports genre's didacticism and the proverbial cynicism of the spoof, which questions the ability of the civilizing process to contain irrepressible popular forces. Wes Gehring notes that in comedy genres the Clown is an anti-heroic, wise guy who is either unsophisticated and inept or cool and self-centered.[3] Robert Fothergill, for his part, describes the clown archetype in Canadian canonical film as an individual who shirks adult responsibilities and acts up with decided ebullience, often under the indulging eye of a supportive partner, who in time also comes to tire of his infantile expressions.[4] Whether of the Gehring or Fothergill variety, when the clown combines with the bully archetype, the protagonist's actions communicate rashness and lack of restraint. For this reason the character often comes across as a man-child in various stages of growing up or as someone who epitomizes the wild, anarchic masculinity that upper-class conceptions of sport seek to suppress. When the protagonist is only passing through a bully-clown phase, the situations that entangle him are often a cause of mirth as the audience laughs at his folly while he tries in vain to make sense of his dilemma. The bully-clown's entertaining quandaries are meant to re-size his ego, humorously communicating that he is likely a redeemable project if he will only change his ways and move on to the next stage of maturation.

Whether the bully-clown realizes his mistakes and adjusts his responses, or whether he embodies the chaotic forces that the civilizing process cannot ultimately subdue, films are likely to leave in the viewer the indelible impression of hockey protagonists as zany sorts and of the game as a mad undertaking. Because these movies fall on different sides of the propriety-excess divide, they also engage the bully-clown and his game in disparate ways. A film may celebrate the pleasures of excess by extolling the manly vigor of the fight and laugh at other aspects of the character, such as his thickhead, clod-like or artless ways. Another may take the time to delineate the codes that govern brawling, with the ultimate intent of labeling the aggressive buffoon-like muscularity of the bully-clown as a senseless macho scheme. The inversion of rules that the bully-clown game dramatizes may also enable the athlete-worker to reclaim some measure of power, commenting on his masculinity as sports commodity, and calling attention to the clashes at the heart of the social order. Even though the satirical aspect of these films emphasize the joys of hockey excess, the bully-clown archetype also dispels the idea of dominant masculinity as a secure project.

The Bully-Clown in Hollywood Film: *Slap Shot, Happy Gilmore, Tooth Fairy* and *Just Friends*

No film in the repertoire satirizes the rugged game and the bully-clown archetype better than *Slap Shot* (Hill, 1977). Inspired by the experiences of screenwriter Nancy Dowd's brother Ned with the professional minor league Johnston Jets, the film depicts corrupt owners and managers and the predicament of small market teams at a time of deep economic malaise.[5] At the center of the story is aging player-coach Reg "Reggie" Dunlop (Paul Newman), who after coming off a lackluster career for the money-losing minor league Charleston Chiefs, gets a wind that his team will be shutting down at the end of the season. The steel mill that serves as the town's economic engine is about to lay off 10,000 workers and the small Pennsylvania enclave will no longer support professional hockey. In the middle of the season three new arrivals called the Hansons (Jeff Carlson, Steve Carlson, and David Hanson) make their grand entrance. Disturbed by their appearance, Reggie scolds the team manager: "Those guys are retards.... Every piece of garbage that comes on the market you gotta buy it." But as he notices the excitement that the Hansons generate with their hyper-aggressive style of play, Reggie decides to sell the team on the idea to increase attendance numbers and improve his players' future job prospects.

A handful of Reggie's charges balk at his maneuvering, in particular, American college grad Ned Braden (Michael Ontkean), the Federal League's most skilled player, who resists the new bullying style of play as unsportsmanlike. Reggie threatens to bench Braden but he remains undaunted, and refers to the Chiefs' first victory as a junk win. For his part, Chiefs radio announcer Jim Carr calls the new style of play an "upsetting display," but entreats fans to "bring the kids; we have entertainment for the whole family." Buoyed by a newfound confidence, the team soon garners a strong following and begins to rise in the rankings. To keep players motivated, Dunlop plants the story that the team's owner has plans to sell the club to a wealthy retirement community in Florida if they manage to win the league title. When Reggie finally locates the secretive owner, Anita McCambridge (Kathryn Walker), the wealthy widow is unwilling to negotiate and matter-of-factly lets him know she stands to bank a larger profit from a tax write-off if the team folds. Exasperated, Reggie keeps the conversation to himself as the Chiefs make it to the championship final with NHL scouts in attendance. As a predictable bench-clearing brawl ensues, Ned upstages the fighting baring everything except for a jock strap. And when one of the opponent goons assails the referee in protest, the Chiefs are given the title on a technicality.

Slap Shot's lasting appeal is rooted in the Hansons' attendant personalities. The trio, who profess the joys of the "old-time hockey" of Gordie Howe and Bobby Orr[6] and make the sign of the cross as they take to the ice and pound the opposition, personify the mayhem with which hockey is associated in popular culture. Along with the other goons in the league,[7] the Hansons serve as caricaturesque expressions of the chaotic, hard-edged masculinity that the sport recalls in the comedic genre. In line with enforcer attributes, their mas-

Reggie Dunlop (Paul Newman) questioned by police in the locker room in *Slap Shot* (Universal Pictures/Photofest).

culinity has working-class overtones, which Nancy Dowd, a native of Boston, underscores when noting that growing up "hockey was the sport of the working-class and had a rough-and-tumble edge to it."[8] The film portrays a game punctuated by regular brawls between opponent teams and even with spectators, and police visits to the locker room to investigate potentially criminal behavior. Players' provoked-at-a-glance postures and idiosyncratic pre-game rituals reveal seventies minor league hockey as a culture of pain overlaid with sheer folly.

As in *The Deadliest Season*, hockey violence in *Slap Shot* expresses the wider context of social turbulence of the period, but the film reroutes the element of victimization by depicting the league's goons, and the Hansons in particular, as powerful, ungovernable forces. In one of the many humorous scenes, the brothers take the ice during the Peterborough Patriots pre-game warm-up and immediately instigate a fight by casually thumping one of their opponents. With no referee in sight, a bench-clearing brawl ensues thoroughly bloodying opponents and instigators. Order resumes in time for the game's start, and as the players dutifully line up, a slow pan reveals the Hansons' comedically grotesque, beat-up façades respectfully listening to the National Anthem. A medium shot next shows the referee fuming over the pre-game mayhem. Unable to contain himself, he skates over to one of the brothers and tells him he's out of the game. The official continues his diatribe warning that he runs a clean game and he'll be watching closely for further disturbances. But the player abruptly interrupts him with a shrill "I'm listening to the fucking song!" turning the tables on the official and leaving him contrite and bewildered over his faux pas. The two-shot sequence contrasts the small stature of the referee with the player's towering physique and unruffled expression, conveying that the game's arbiter, a stand-in for institutional authority, is clearly out of his league and up against a force of nature.

Aaron Baker in *Contesting Identities* posits that these characters, who literally play with children's toys off the ice but engage in the most aggressive hockey in the lineup, effectively embody "an adolescent outlaw masculinity."[9] The Hansons express the unbridled virility of young working-class males who act in defiance of social rules, and whose insubordination organized team sport is meant to stamp out or, at the very least, curb.[10] *Slap Shot* satirizes sport as a civilizing agent by showcasing a burlesque version of the professional game steeped in seventies violence. Although bully-clown characters in film are portrayed in various stages of development, the Hansons are not en route to any stage of maturation. They do not rise above thuggery at any point in the story, but are its very blissful and oblivious embodiment, satirizing not only hockey's masculinity of excess but parodying the sports film genre's clichéd heroism.

The overtly sexual expressions of female fans and the hordes of groupies that follow the team bus around attest to the Hansons' masculine allure. These players perform the gritty role of the enforcer with relish yet also matter-of-factly encode an enticing ability to get the job done. The support for this masculinity is no small matter in the context of seventies economic decline and lack of jobs, and the displacement of men from the workforce.[11] The cinematography's use of gritty realism renders the era's economic downturn palpable through drab depictions of small towns, unassuming accommodations, and dark watering holes. In contrast, arenas and all aspects of the game are brightly lit, highlighting the excitement and newfound sense of regeneration procured by the hockey spectacle offered by the Chiefs. By transgressing the game's stated rules and allowing the carnivalesque pleasures of excess to come to the fore, the Hansons provide much-needed distraction for the disenfranchised residents, acting as proxy for their deep-seated yearning to bust up the rules.[12]

Reggie's use of violence also effectively plays out as a de facto response to management and owner subterfuge at a time when sport was growing increasingly impersonalized, a reality that Dowd underscored decades after the film's release: "It was incredible to me that my brother did not know who owned his team…. If you didn't know who owned you, what did you know?"[13] Hoping to buy some time, and resonating with the betting culture associated with the game's working-class roots, Reggie adopts the Hansons' tactics as a prospective game-changer to offset the machinations of both ownership and management. In attempting to turn the tables on higher-ups, Reggie affects a gamesman ethos that historian John Dizikes defines as "acknowledg[ing] the rules but refus[ing] to recognize the existence of any code."[14] In his discussion of Dizikes' work, Michael Oriard notes that gamesmanship was as integral as sportsmanship to the early sporting ethos that developed in the U.S. at the end of the nineteenth century. Gamesmanship valued intrinsic fairness between contestants while embracing the athlete who engaged in skillful displays against both the opponent and the rules.[15] Sportsmanship, which upheld fair and meritocratic play under strict rules, was the operating principle of athletic masculinity, but many lauded clever coaches and players who devised winning stratagems that thwarted stated guidelines and regulations.[16] Gamesmen, in other words,

The Hanson Brothers climb the glass in *Slap Shot* to take on fans (Universal Pictures/Photofest).

implemented a type of tricksterism that exploited loopholes in the rules and operated to level the playing field. In *Slap Shot*, Reggie's gamesman instincts in short order enable him to gauge the loophole—the Hansons' adolescent outlaw tendencies—necessary to win matchups and recover the team's marketability. The brothers' enjoyment of the robust game denotes a kind of innocent abandon that transforms these characters into accidental champions who save old-time hockey from the clutches of corporate ownership. Juxtaposed against the Machiavellian maneuvering of ownership and management, the Hansons come off as populist figures who fight back against unscrupulous big money, even as they do so eminently without a plan or agenda.

Slap Shot's take on labor politics, as it feeds into the realities of the seventies economic slump, is therefore at the base of the film's critique of violence. Commenting on the boom-and-bust economic cycles of the 1950s–1970s, Clay Motley notes that during the post-war years, the American economy fuelled expectations for high-paying, stable jobs as steel factories prospered in places like Cleveland and Pittsburgh.[17] These jobs sustained the post-war economic boom, supporting the expansion of suburbia and its consumerist directive as represented by large malls and the increasing disposable incomes of white workers and their families. During the late 1970s, however, those very same steel mills were on the verge of closing as America's economic prosperity began to bottom out and rampant unemployment and social and economic ills became the order of the day.

Because Reggie's use of violence is fundamentally a marketing ploy to further his players' employment prospects, it has indelible populist connotations that seek to protect the worker-athlete from vested interests. Populism originally made its mark during the Depression by upholding the individual rights of the rural middle-class in the face of an industrializing economy and increasing corporate economic control. According to Aaron Baker, Populist rhetoric profoundly resonated during economic crises, for while it sided with the worker, the farmer, the common man, and professed a return to agrarian values based on the idea of collective brotherhood, it preserved the tenets of capitalism by upholding free enterprise and the work ethic.[18] Populism also ascribed integrity to those charged with performing physical labor, and moral wrongdoing to mercenary bosses profiting from the work of underlings.

Populism also converged on the Turnerian vision by prioritizing the material gain and political power of individuals and communities rather than that of the corporation and the state.[19] Brian Baker argues, however, that the opening of the West, which Turner saw as key to disseminating the democratic ideal and constructing the nation-state, cannot be considered without acknowledging the violent, martial masculinity that made the process possible. Frontier narrative, then, implicitly bound violence with notions of American maleness, and this idea has survived in the western's Code of Honor, a form of morality that distinguishes "the 'good' man of violence from the bad" in male affiliative networks,[20] and ensures that the protagonist who resorts to violence for the good of his community remains unsullied by it. In looking after his team's welfare by appropriating violence to counter manager and owner subterfuge, Reggie embodies the "good" man of violence much in the way the outlaw or social bandit utilized his managerial expertise to extract fair wages for the producing classes.[21] *Slap Shot* connects the dots between Turnerism, Populism, and martial masculinity in the service of the athlete-worker's social mobility, putting forth a potent critique with deep American roots. By installing the populist impulse of gamesmanship behind the bench, the coach deploys the violent spectacle to improve the Chiefs' chances in reclaiming a form of fair play[22] that celebrates the underdog's triumph and rescues masculinity at a time of dwindling economic opportunities. Since gamesmanship arose as a reaction to power and wealth inequalities, and economic crises are consistently cyclical,[23] it is no surprise that *Slap Shot*'s evocative force should have endured.

The film's popularity also rests in its rescue and simultaneous satire of dominant masculinity and physical excess. Indeed, although Reggie's fatherly leadership preserves his players' economic prospects, it comes at the expense of the sports values he cherishes. The coach readily accepts his squad's responsibility in popularizing the bully game, and seeking to redress these improprieties, he informs his charges prior to the championship matchup: "We've been clowns ... we've been goons ... a side show. We oughta be in jail.... Violence is killing us." The spectators, however, are already on their feet screaming: "Kill! Kill! Kill! This is hockey!" The violence-habituated crowd, who craves the same spectacle of excess night after night as a cathartic exercise for their frustrations, summarily derails Reggie's attempt to do away with the team's ruffian image and restore the sportsmanlike play that star forward Ned Braden had insisted on all along. Ned, for his part, sees where the championship game is going, and after it predictably devolves into a buffoonish fight, he seizes the opportunity to mock the bully game one last time in carnivalesque form. Stripping down to his jock strap, he spoofs audience appetite for spectacle and simultaneously protests the cheap shenanigans of the coach and his infantile recruits. The burlesque interlude shows up the crowd's thirst for sexual fantasy veiled in conventional interpretations of athletic masculinity to highlight players' increasing objectification as commodities (by way of violence) at a time when sports businesses were transforming from small-scale outfits into larger more profitable franchises.

The ending also has an up-in-the-air feel as team members are farmed out to minor professional squads across the country. Although the players' individual careers don't dead-end, the wholesale disbanding of the Chiefs leaves a veil of uncertainty about the myth of sports success, articulating the limits of dominant masculinity in line with the antiheroic project of the seventies sports film.[24] While embracing Turner's view of capitalism, then, the film also acknowledges that the American Dream is hardly a guarantee.[25] Because the carnivalesque offers the prospect of rescuing the insecure project of dominant masculinity, and protagonists' exploits can expedite the venting of the audience's vexation,[26] the Hansons come off as mythic embodiments of the game's propensity to devolve into mayhem.[27] Ned's stripping, which the film overlays on the final game, however, also registers as a burlesque response to the ruinous use of violence in hockey, which traditional social arrangements regard as evidence of real manhood. As Richard Harrison aptly notes, Ned's striptease is Dowd's satirical commentary on the tragedy of men's wounded bodies, which the premise of violence performed in a team's name and the slapstick language with which it is described in game commentary commonly cover up.[28] By downgrading the sports film's nostalgia for character-building through pain, Ned's parody pronounces the rehearsal of traditional masculinity as an outworn scheme. The mythic status of the Hansons as proponents of "old time hockey" nonetheless also attests to the endurance of conventional standards of masculinity, in turn, corroborating the satirical complexity with which *Slap Shot* delivers its message about violence in the game.

Protagonists who combine the physicality of the tough man with the irrepressible tendencies that the civilizing process seeks to contain are good candidates for the comical role of the bully-clown. The Adam Sandler film, *Happy Gilmore* (Dugan, 1996), features another working-class goon-buffoon who grows up with hockey and has dreams of making it to the big leagues. From a young age, Happy (Adam Sandler) boasts a powerful shot, which he demonstrates by breaking his dad's camera. Because his hockey game is also untamed, he makes up for it in raw emotion. The brash rascal is so bent on his hockey ambitions that he dutifully shows up at the annual tryouts, even though the coach repeatedly leaves him on the sidelines laughing at his futile persistence. The day that his hopes of making the team are dashed for the umpteenth time, his girlfriend walks out on him, and a government bureaucrat repossesses the house his grandfather built with his own hands, consigning his beloved grandma (Frances Bay) to an old people's home overseen by a miscreant attendant (Ben Stiller). Happy must find a way to pay the hundreds of thousands in taxes she owes to recover the house, and he discovers that he can repurpose his powerful hockey shot into a 400-foot golf drive.

Chubbs Peterson (Carl Weathers), a former player-turned-coach who lost his hand to an alligator, spies out Happy's powerful shot and attempts to persuade him to take up golf professionally. But the rascal dismisses the advice stating nonchalantly that golf is about "goofy pants and a fat ass," as opposed to a "normal" sport like hockey or football. Upon entering his first golf tournament, Happy predictably wins the $275,000 title prize, but as he presses on with his quest and nears the upper echelons of the PGA tour, he comes face to face with contender Shooter McGavin (Christopher McDonald), an unsportsmanlike sort who is not about to lose his top standing to an uncouth parvenu. Even though Happy's unpolished manner presents a problem for the tour, like the prizes he consistently racks up, he also pulls in a sizeable and economically diverse group of supporters, and soon the big sponsors take note. The pretty publicist who works for the tour, Virginia Venit (Julie Bowen), coaches Happy to temper his style and focus on pleasing the sponsors. But Shooter, who complains fruitlessly that Happy is a disgrace to the sport, will not be fazed and secretly calls in a heckler to exploit the upstart's short fuse and throw him off his game. He gets up to the same tricks in the championship final, calling in the heckler who arrives in a VW, mows down Happy, and promptly slams onto a TV tower at the 18th hole. The tower crumbles and blocks the path to the target,

Happy (Adam Sandler) on the golf circuit in a Boston Bruins jersey in *Happy Gilmore* (Universal Pictures/Photofest).

but Happy recovers and deploys an expert shot he practiced with Chubbs to clinch the victory. Wearing the tour's champion jacket, with his arm around his grandmother and accompanied by now girlfriend Virginia and his caddy, Happy reclaims ownership of the house.

Happy is the proverbial bully-clown, a man-child with a brash and untempered character that purportedly makes him suitable for hockey. His strategy in dealing with life's vicissitudes is to verbally or physically attack anyone or anything that frustrates him. When at the film's outset his girlfriend leaves, he intersperses verbal aggression with sweet coaxing to prevent her from walking out. He also pummels the hockey coach who denies him a spot on the team, attacks the IRS agent who turns up to repossess his grandmother's house, humorously strangles the young caddy supplied by the tour, and vociferously berates his golf ball for not dropping into the final hole. Despite his blustery approach, Happy also boasts resilience and grit in keeping with the standards of the hockey tough. His idea of training for the next hockey season is to stand inside a batting cage and take hits on various parts of his body. Happy objects to golf because he perceives it to have an enfeebling effect. He plays with his grandfather's golf clubs, afraid that having his own will strip him of his virility. When Chubbs attempts to teach his student to relax into the swing instructing that "it's all in the hips," Happy retorts with a firm "get off of me!" scolding that he just wants to get the ball into the hole. Happy's technique is instinctive and uncomplicated, one that he believes is closer to the true approach to sport.

Because his male identity is entirely wrapped up in hockey and he perceives golf as emasculating, Happy superimposes many of the game's conventions onto his golf performance. He wears Original Six NHL sweaters and caps on the grass, particularly the Boston Bruins logo that recalls the rough and tough hockey of 1971 Stanley Cup-winning Big Bad Bruins. He holds his golf club like a hockey stick, and when he gets a hole-in-one he celebrates by cheering, "He shoots, he scores!" He also guzzles beer from a hose, and refuses to have a caddy carry his golf clubs, relenting only because of tour rules and choosing a homeless man for the role. When he racks up prize after prize in the form of the large cardboard checks, he unceremoniously stacks them in the back of his beat-up car, counting down the amount needed to get back his grandmother's house, all the while repeating that he's a hockey player. In the eyes of the tour Happy is a bad boy, because he refuses to conform to the genteel, upper-class behavioral codes of golf. He epitomizes a character in "the comedy of infracted rules," which Bruce Babington describes as principals who, through inexperience or purposeful intent, defy a sport's rules and norms.[29] Happy nonetheless regards these values as gimmicks, mere externalities that get in the way of authentic manhood and its feistiness, displayed through the use of imprecations. Happy's manly pluck and cursing resonate with the socially diverse crowd who boisterously roots for him at every hole, confirming Fiske's view of "excessive speech" and gestures as a sign of the carnivalesque and its transformation of sporting conflict into social conflict.

Happy's approach, however, is also oafish and not wholly productive. His signature hard "hockey" shot confirms that he understands the performance of masculinity in sport through large, aggressive moves rather than skill, control, and composure, which are key to success on the playing field. Happy is so anxious about overhauling his masculinity that Coach Chubbs guesses that he cannot forcefully remove his pupil's hockey identity for he is bound to compensate with more aggression. Although the coach advises against raw emotional outbursts that are more appropriate to hockey than golf, he also gives Happy a modified putter with the markings of a hockey stick to calm him down and get him to work on his short game. Honing his short game entails taming his inner bully-clown, and in short order Happy must find a way around the sinister Laughing Clown hole at the Happy Land miniature golf course where Chubbs takes him to practice finesse shots. The Laughing Clown appears to taunt Happy about his inadequacies, deriding him every time he misses a shot and throwing him into a rage. Only when he overcomes the clown in the third attempt is there a hint that he might yet conquer his irrepressible nature and learn that competence in sport is not merely about sheer force, but also about control and skillful adaptation to extract desired outcomes. The clown metaphor is all too pertinent in signaling that Happy must overcome his unsuccessful, buffoon-like ways by modulating his penchant for physical excess. Even though the Clown spits his ball back and Happy takes revenge on him, by the time he arrives at the final and most challenging stretch of the mini-golf course, he is able to go to his "happy place," as Chubbs instructs, and manage a difficult, calibrated shot that will serve him in the final hole of the championship game. The shot also marks a turning point that shows he is ready to claim the champion's jacket.

Wes Gehring notes that the childlike antiheroic protagonist of comic genres represents the thoroughly frustrated contemporary man.[30] Happy is the classic thwarted sports protagonist who must accomplish masculine success by embracing the athletic exemplar's self-restraint. The genteel sport of golf appears to offer Happy the chance to hone the self-discipline he needs, but unlike professional hockey players who take happily to golf during the off-season, the tough man cannot get past its devitalizing image. Happy's adversary, Shooter McGavin, albeit well-versed in the niceties of the golf world, represents the sport's racist, upper crust echelons who resent Happy's diverse following and whom he admonishes to "go back to your shanties!" Even though the champ's place in the circuit is hard-earned, he also resorts to preposterous forms of sabotage to bring down his rival, and the film rightly appends to his character a western musical motif with decided farcical overtones that denote his outlaw proclivities. When the unsportsmanlike Shooter takes off with the champion's jacket, the restless crowd, led by Happy's gargantuan erstwhile boss, Mr. Larson (Richard Kiel), enthusiastically gives chase in hot pursuit intent on thrashing the miscreant. The scene, which ends with comically inflected off-camera sound effects that capture the beating, conveys the people as an unstoppable, justice-seeking force and sporting conflict as social conflict.

Happy Gilmore deploys its populist commentary by foregrounding the working-class attributes of the athlete-protagonist. The power of Happy's long golf—a.k.a. hockey—shot depicts the raw force that elites associate with the people, which the film relays through medium shots that closely follow behind the aloft ball as it travels above the landscape and offers a panoramic and cathartic view of the green. These shots, which occur at the start of each tournament and when Happy must garner an advantage, expeditiously capture the ability of sport to procure economic empowerment to the everyman and rehearse his vital manhood. The character's "hockey" proclivities and unswerving integrity also leave him unsullied while selling sponsors' brands, much like the hero in the western is untarnished by the necessary violence he must perform. Indeed, this salesmanship is justified as part of the much-needed income stream Happy needs to recover his grandma's house and conveyed in line with the business savvy of the professional golfer.[31] Even after he becomes a golfer, Happy does not dispense with his "hockey" identity, winning the tournament with his "hockey putter" and fine-tuning his ways to achieve masculine success. The final scene, which features Happy arriving in his old, beat-up car at his grandparents' house, and taking back possession of it with his arm around his grandma alongside his homeless caddy and girlfriend Virginia, confirms that he does not stray from his principles but merely conquers his inner bully-clown to attain social mobility. Happy's vision of Abraham Lincoln, the spirit of Chubbs—who checks out earlier in the film because of a mishap—and the alligator that ate his hand, all waving at him in the sky as he toasts victory with a glass of champagne, reiterates this premise.

Sandler's predilection for lowbrow characters convey the rituals of uncomplicated masculinity that old-time hockey represents with characteristic entertaining hijinks.[32] These rituals are in keeping with the comic *shtick*-driven routines in which the actor specializes, which hinge on the over-reaction and zaniness he popularized in his *Saturday Night Live* clownish, intemperate man-child act. The sketch-like performance combines the rascal aspects of the clown with incompetent, underdog elements to express physical humor, and in film these traits assure the audience that despite the character's evolution, he will stick to his unorthodox populist antics through to the end. The clown in the comedic genre lacks both a moral and a motive as these plot lines are typically connected by just a clever idea.[33] With more than a dash of *Slap Shot*, however, *Happy Gilmore*'s depiction of physical excess celebrates sport as carnivalesque resistance against the influence of the moneyed classes, and rolls out potent social commentary about masculinity and class.

Tooth Fairy (Lembeck, 2010) offers another version of the bully-clown by way of wrestling personality Dwayne "The Rock" Johnson. Johnson plays Derek Thompson, an erstwhile first draft pick of the New Jersey Devils sidelined with a shoulder injury. Demoted to the minor-league Ice Wolves in Lansing, Michigan, Thompson repurposes his formidable size and strength into a bruiser job. His knack for thunderous hits and for knocking out opponents' teeth promptly earns him the nickname of Tooth Fairy, and transforms him into a fan favorite. Soon he garners the league record for penalties and has his own recliner installed in the penalty box for good measure. After a game, the coach (Barclay Hope) introduces Derek to Mick "the Stick" Donnelly (Ryan Sheckler), a new recruit whom he calls "the future of our franchise," and asks Derek to look after the young gun. But shirtless and with muscles bulging, the hockey tough summarily instructs the newcomer to lower his expectations and get used to being in the minors. Unimpressed by either Derek's size or his advice, the rookie wonders aloud whether there is "an old-timer's game" later on that day.

Mick is merely the beginning of Derek's problems. He also fumbles his way around girlfriend Carly (Ashley Judd) and her children, five-year old Tess (Destiny Whitlock) and teen Randy (Chase Ellison). One night, playing poker with his buddies and babysitting Tess, Derek finds himself short on cash and decides to borrow the dollar bill that Carly left for the tooth the little girl just lost. When Carly returns home, Tess wakes up and sees the tooth gone but no sign of the money. Derek has not had a chance to replace the dollar bill and he attempts to smooth over the situation by explaining to the youngster that there is no Tooth Fairy, only to be hushed by mom who happens to discover the money on the floor. Privately, Carly chides Derek for his carelessness and lectures that children need their fantasies. But the goon goes home unrepentant.

Tossing and turning during the night, Derek wakes up to find a summons for Violation 70136: "Dissemination of Disbelief" under his pillow, punctuated by a solemn voice that booms: "Mr. Thompson, you, sir, are guilty of killing dreams." He dismisses it as a joke, but still smiling, he suddenly sprouts large wings, is decked in a pink tutu with matching tights and slippers, and sucked into a vortex on the way to Fairyland. There, Derek is met by caseworker Tracy (Stephen Merchant) who brands him a "dream crusher" and sends the goon into a mayhem-causing panic as he hollers to be rescued from the nightmare. When Head Fairy Lily (Julie Andrews) arrives on the scene, she shows Derek little clemency and promptly sentences him to two weeks of performing Tooth Fairy duties for busting up children's dreams. To aid in the successful completion of his assignment, gadget procurer Jerry (Billy Crystal) provides the big lug with the necessary tools of the trade: Invisibility Spray, Shrinking Paste, Dog Bark Mints, Cat-Away, and Amnesia Dust, along with a small bag to collect teeth. As expected, Derek fights the assignment from the outset and bumbles task after task. In shrunken form he is smashed by an opening door, scared to death by the frightening screams of a child who has caught sight of him, hunted by an enormous cat, and flushed down the toilet to avoid being caught by teammates in his froo-froo outfit. To buck up his resolve, he imports his enforcer persona into the job complete with hockey paraphernalia, only to bumble the exercise some more. In the process, he also incurs the displeasure of the Head Fairy who despairs that Derek "might just be the worst Tooth Fairy ever!"

As he struggles to fulfill his Fairy tasks, Derek's hockey career also takes a turn for the worse. His fans have shifted their support to rookie Mick and the young hotshot appears to have taken to the role with relish. Derek's family life is also suffering as Randy keeps his distance sensing that the player only wants a rapprochement to court his mom's favor. Derek finally succeeds by encouraging Randy's knack for the guitar and helping him practice for the high school's talent show. As he gets close to the teen, he also wistfully relays that he was once an up-and-coming NHLer but a shoulder injury put an end to that trajectory. The two of them make a pact to conquer their fears and go for their dreams. After a few bumps on the road, Derek manages to score his first goal in nine years, and complete his Tooth Fairy assignment. He proposes to Carly, and when the L.A. Kings call him up, he scores another goal with Tooth Fairies Lily and Jerry in attendance.

Like *Happy Gilmore*, which encourages the protagonist to temper his bully-clown disposition, *Tooth Fairy* exploits Johnson's hypermasculine physique to contain the shadow side of the enforcer as it spills out of the confines of the arena. In this film, the moderating force is not a genteel sport, but a feminizing fairy getup meant to teach the character important lessons about accomplishing masculine success. Derek is a selfish man-child who has taken on the task of downsizing children's dreams. Because as a consummate model of fandom, the child takes to sport and its stars without reservation and bestows on the game and its principals an unqualified heroic status, s/he is the most valuable asset of sports franchises.[34] Albeit as a franchise asset Derek is expected to help popularize hockey among young audiences, he routinely fazes boys by advising them to lower their hopes of playing the game in the big leagues. True to his bully clown aspect, he is oblivious to the folly of his ways, and the Tooth Fairy role into which he plunges is meant to expand his notion of what is possible and set him on a path of maturation. The film's fantasy theme is merely a symbol of what the plot is meant to teach the bully-clown. Derek is in need of an attitude adjustment that will temper his unreasonable outbursts, and in line with the carnivalesque's disruption of social hierarchies, his chastening entails deflating his formidable bruiser position. The film plays with The Rock's iconic wrestling musculature[35] by decking the character in a fairy costume that downsizes his tough-man charisma, and proves doubly entertaining because it downgrades the masculine competence of the hockey player. Strapping The Rock's physique into a tight feminizing outfit acts as a training suit of sorts and the satiny baby-blue pajama-like outfit that he subsequently dons communicates that the situation offers him the prospect of rebirth. But like the prototypical bully-clown, Derek is also clueless about his bearings and attempts to make up for his diminishment by superimposing his hockey gear over his fairy getup, placing his glove on the face of the evening's target and dressing himself up in an ominous voice as he mumbles "Just here for the tooth, sir, just the tooth."

Because Derek was an erstwhile scorer who took on the mantle of bully-clown to remain in the game, his enforcer ways amount to a stage of development from which he must move on, quite unlike the Hansons who are an uncomplicated embodiment of the archetype. In superimposing his bruiser persona on his sprite ensemble, Derek merely confuses the issue for none of his subterfuges help him fix his hampered game, as his hindered Tooth Fairy flying faculties rightly denote. Only when Derek stares his fear in the face and helps others with their dreams, does he begin to gain full use of his game. To illustrate that he is ready to dispense with his inner bully-clown, he takes a brutal hit by the opposing team's goon that leaves him flat on the ice as the crowd gasps in astonishment. The opponent, who sports Philadelphia Flyer colors, a moustache and longish hair that liken him to a seventies goon, sets Derek apart from the real bullies of the league, particularly since he is a bully-clown in disguise only. The brutal hit conveys that Derek has changed his ways because instead of retaliating, he seizes the opportunity to score his first goal in nine years. With the crowd hollering loudly, the rink fades into silence and an angelic chorus takes over, highlighting the parallel universe in which Derek lives. Looking in the direction of the net, the player sees caseworker Tracy sitting atop egging him on. Smiling and with renewed conviction, Derek takes off, and the camera elongates his advance through various gradations of slow motion that amplify the tension. A subsequent lower body shot that highlights Derek's skill level and shows him deftly stealing the puck corroborates that he has the heart and talents of a scorer. A stick in the face follows but he catapults into the air scoring the long-awaited goal. The yeoman-like effort communicates that Derek's transformation is real and that his efforts in rerouting his bully-clown life are nothing short of heroic. The team's celebration framed by the Ice Wolves stained glass logo gives the feel of a church and authenticates the numinous nature of Derek's restored scorer identity in line with the fairy motif.

Although most sports films end with a goal that expresses the protagonist's yearning for better circumstances and wish fulfillment, Derek's masculine success must

Derek Thompson (Dwayne Johnson) in his hybrid hockey-fairy outfit in *Tooth Fairy* (20th Century Fox/Photofest).

extend to the familial front. In the manner of the bully-clown's partner, Carly has put up with Derek's antics with patience to the point where she is no longer able to rationalize away his folly. Consistent with the depiction of the single mother in the cinema, she appears in need of a mate and a surrogate father for her children, and the film makes clear that Derek must get the surrogate father role right. To atone for his juvenile behavior, with 00:20 to go in the game, Derek decides to take his final Tooth Fairy assignment at Carly's home where Tess has lost another tooth. With the coach yelling at him to get back in the game, Derek sprouts wings and in full Tooth Fairy costume prepares to go airborne much to the astonishment of teammates and spectators. Taking a turn to pick up speed, an extremely long shot mimics the ice as a runway and tracks Derek's move overhead like a plane taking flight. He disappears in golden light above the crowd, communicating that he has risen above his psychological blocks, leaving Tracy to clean up by happily taking over the zamboni and shooting Amnesia Dust over the crowd with a large canon. Derek heads to Carly's house to attend to Tess' childhood fantasies and nurture Randy's aspirations by getting him to the school concert on time so he too can prove himself. Proposing to Carly, getting called up by the Kings, and scoring in his first L.A. game are merely the icing on the cake and ratify that Derek has recovered what he once lost. Head Fairy Lily and Gadget Master Jerry's attendance at the game merely confirms that the Derek Thompson case has ended successfully and the future of children's fantasies and adults' belief in possibilities is safe. Like Happy, Derek has traveled the narrative arc and succeeded in recalibrating his bully-clown ways for the sake of a more authentic life.

Although in *Happy Gilmore* the protagonist's carnivalesque antics take after Reggie's populist harnessing of the Hansonian game in *Slap Shot*, in *Tooth Fairy* the quest is less ambitious, merely seeking to re-size the bully-clown's ego to augment his chances for success. The convoluted situations that the character experiences because of his flaws and faltering as well as his amusing appearance augment the film's entertainment value. *Tooth Fairy*, in addition, portrays hockey in line with the norms of family fare, expedited by the game's transformation into family entertainment during the 1990s. The film makes heavy use of special effects that amplify gags aimed at children and the child within the adult, even if the violent aspect of the hockey spectacle conflicts with this focus. The bully-clown signature is consistent with this theme for it comically communicates that the hero must reform his ways in line with the sports film's principled moralizing but without the extremes of villainy that characterize opponents in the genre.

Because Hollywood films deploy hockey to buttress the virile allure of male characters, narratives with central protagonists who draw their identity from the game can more easily downsize their manly vigorousness if they are required to modify their behavior. *Just Friends* (Kumble, 2005) presents a variation on the theme by upending the hockey skills of protagonist Chris Brander (Ryan Reynolds) to convey his symbolic regression to his chubby loser high school persona and enable his maturation. Brander, who since his teen years has turned into a skilled forward, also has a successful career in L.A. as a record producer with the accompanying perks of the bachelor lifestyle. When he comes across high school love interest and popular girl Jamie Palamino (Amy Smart) on an unplanned trip home, he eagerly attempts to convey his refurbished persona to his former crush, but through sheer circumstance he finds himself back in his effete best-friend high school role.

One morning as Brander is set to meet up with Jamie for a free skate on the pond, he is unable to find his hockey skates, and is forced to don figure skates instead. He predictably ends up stumbling his way around, confirming to Jamie he has not retired his former awkwardness. To make matters worse, when the two of them are hastily recruited to join a children's pickup game, Brander can do little to help the team, struggling mightily to find the puck and falling repeatedly on his rump. The children brand him "Suckster" and one of the players on the opposing team who turns out to be a girl, labels him a wuss for not dropping the gloves and fighting her. Exasperated, Brander morphs into a bully-clown, and intent on proving he has the skills of a scorer, he makes his way to the net through sheer effort. But as he takes a vigorous slap shot, which the film humorously displays in slow motion, the puck hits the crossbar and ricochets backward hitting him in the mouth and putting him out of commission. He is bloodied and disabled, strapped into an EMT cart as a metaphor of his bound masculinity, and told he will need several stitches. To make matters worse, the incident brings into the picture emergency technician Dusty Dinkleman (Chris Klein), a high school peer who quickly transforms into a rival for Jamie's affections, infinitely complicating matters for Brander.

In *Just Friends* the pond turns into a stage for the character's masculine enfeeblement since, as the initiatory site of talent, it is an environment he has already mastered. The more Brander aims to show off his metropolitan sophistication, the more circumstances conspire to show up his virility, so that children easily outstrip him of his prized hockey expertise and of his corresponding masculine allure. However, just as with Derek Thompson's infantile pajama-like outfit, the pond is full of allegorical significance, denoting the prospect of rebirth and the need to revert to a state of innocence. As clueless as his *Tooth Fairy* counterpart, Brander perceives the setup as a step back, since situations repeatedly backfire on him when he resorts to his smart aleck ways. Although actor Ryan Reynolds' fit but slim physique, apposite with the vulnerable romantic-comedy protagonist in *Just Friends*, hardly approximates The Rock's in *Tooth Fairy*, the effect is the same: an infantilization of his masculine competence. Brander's hockey markers corroborate that he has shed his teenage portliness and acquired a dashing cockiness that masquerades as masculine success. But off the ice he has transformed into a smooth operator, going from one short-lived affair to another to avoid putting himself through the heart-wrenching prospect of falling in love again and remaining just friends with his love interest, as transpired in his high school relationship with Jamie. Like Derek, who is sitting on an outsized wound, Brander is stifling a deep-seated vulnerability that has stunted his maturation process. He has become too slick for his own good, and he must be set on a slippery slope to mend his ways, which *Just Friends* accomplishes by deploying Reynold's rascal film persona and conveying the character's circumstances as humorously self-defeating. Like Derek, Chris must confront his fears and revamp his life, a turning point he reaches at the end of the film by unveiling his true feelings to Jamie.

The Bully-Clown in Canadian Film: Score: *A Hockey Musical*, *Goon*, *Keep Your Head Up, Kid: The Don Cherry Story* and *Wrath of Grapes: The Don Cherry Story II*

Spoofing the masculinity norms of the Canadian culture of hockey in Canadian film must take into account the emotionally loaded debate on physical excess. This debate, which echoes throughout Canada's funding outlets and in the media, as illustrated by the CBC telefilms in the previous chapter, traditionally frames the bloody workmanship of the hockey tough man as deviance, dismissing it as misguided in catering to popular tastes. The guidelines for depicting hockey in film, however, have also expanded through the years, in response to political changes that have affected Canadian funding agencies and distribution outlets, allowing for the production of films that appeal to popular tastes.[36] The next few films revealingly depict bully-clown characters as expressing gradations of legitimate hockey masculinity. In these films, the enforcer knows his role,[37] jumping into action at the behest of the coach, who makes use of the player's services not only to protect the more talented players on the team, but as part of game tactics. Films consequently make clear that the tough guy's workmanship is fundamental to the team ethos of hockey and not merely the curiously random feature of an exotic sport. Canadian films naturally also depict hockey's potential for mayhem, acknowledging that the line between bedlam and self-restraint can be excessively thin. Films that reprise the bully-clown's hijinks all the same focus on comical aspects of the character, poking fun at the physical excess dictated by the role, laughing at the character's obtuseness, or simply reveling in the carnivalesque elements of hockey as a people's game.

Score: A Hockey Musical (McGowan, 2010) plunges its young protagonist into the pressure-cooker of organized hockey, challenging his deeply-held beliefs and demanding that he honor its premium on physical excess. Farley Gordon (Noah Reid) is the film's 17-year-old talent in question, a phenom who hones his skills in the neighborhood shinny game. He is home-schooled by progressive-utopian, pacifist-anarchist parents Ed (Marc Jordan) and Hope (Olivia Newton-John), who go to great lengths to tutor him in the social issues of the day. When owner of the minor-league semi-pro Brampton Blades Walt Acorn (Stephen McHattie) spots Farley during a pick-up game, he is confident he just found "the next Sidney Crosby." Ed and Hope, who don't believe in competition and for whom hockey is "Neanderthal and ne'er-do-well," make clear they have no intention of signing up their son for such a preposterous scheme. Torn between wanting to try his hand at the organized game and respecting his parents' wishes, Farley confides in childhood friend and next-door neighbor Eve (Allie MacDonald), who tells him to follow his heart. The teen decides to give organized hockey a try and promises his parents he will do nothing that will embarrass them.

When Farley shows up at the rink, a suitably rough-shod Coach Donker (John Pyper-Ferguson), who has not been kept in the loop about the new prospect, wastes no time in driving home the point that he should either join the figure skating circuit or the team's booster club. But Farley insists he is there at the behest of the owner, and unable to get rid of him, the coach decides his best option is to humiliate the upstart. He sends in two of his best forwards but Farley easily weaves around them, proving that he's got the goods for the job. Donker steps up the pressure and Farley soon runs into a "brick wall" named Moose (Dru Viergever), the team's enforcer, who lands the over-confident young gun on the ice unconscious. The coach catches up with Acorn and insists that taking on this insensate into the toughest league in the nation is liable to get him killed. But the owner remains certain that the teen will avoid a Moose-like encounter a second time. Farley's first introduction to a bona fide organized game promptly turns into an utter farce. Led by Moose, the warm-up quickly transforms into an all-out brawl to the delight of the rowdy crowd, confirming Hope and Ed's expectations about the hare-brained project. Farley tries to make sense of the explosive ongoings but Acorn, who is close by, tells him not to concern himself too much, explaining that the players are just letting off steam and that "hockey without fighting is like gratin without cheese," a saucy ingredient without which the proceedings cannot sparkle. Once the game gets started, Farley easily breaks the record for fastest goal and promptly turns from a complete unknown into an unremitting sensation. TV commentators rave that he is the kind of prospect that will live up to the likes of "Howe, Orr and Gretzky," and slowly but surely the teen begins to feel that he's in his element.

During one of the de rigueur melees, the first roadblock appears in Farley's path when the opposing team's goalie heads straight for him, and instead of gearing up for a fight, the young gun ducks and remains in a crouching position for the duration of the pummeling. The team and the fans are nothing short of stunned at the spineless display, and turn against Farley no matter how passionately he defends his pacifist views. Soon magazine covers blare that Farley Gordon is "ruining hockey." The pressures mount as his parents insist that his hockey venture has carried on long enough. Farley's friendship with Eve also takes a turn for the worse when he walks in on her and music partner, pianist Marco (Gianpaolo Venuta), misconstruing the scene as a romantic encounter. Angry and confused at the intense feelings for his best friend, he takes it out on Eve who attempts to explain her circumstances to no avail. In his next game, predictably, Farley buckles under public pressure and pummels the opposition. Ceding his own values only compounds his misery, and out of solutions, he quits hockey. Away from the game and unable to reconcile the many emotions pulling at his heart, he soon loses the will to do anything. But the calling to be a champion will not subside, and alone in a half-lit arena pondering his bearings, he is greeted by a vision of hockey icons who sing that he can play the game the way he wants as he's "got the goods to be ... [his] own man." Soon Farley makes up with Eve and declares his love, and rejoining the team, he finds

Farley Gordon (Noah Reid, left) with Brampton Blades owner (Stephen McHattie) in *Score: A Hockey Musical* (Mongrel Media/Michael McGowan).

a surprising way of reconciling his pacifism with the rugged directives of the organized game so that it rings true to his nature.

Score airs both sides of the hockey debate on fighting and advocates for a tempered masculinity that neither dips into the artistic "effeminacy" of the male figure skater nor rushes headlong into the rough-and-tumble world of the goon, both of which the film handles through cartoonish stereotypes. *Score* satirizes the male figure skater by way of dad Ed's humorous flashback, as he recalls the reason for his dislike of hockey. Nostalgically noting that, "figure skating was my world," Ed appears as a boy dressed in a long, buttoned-up woolen coat gliding carefree on one leg when he is bulldozed nonchalantly by a much bigger teen in hockey gear. The boy's getup and the musical score make clear that the child is a ninny and on the wrong track as far as the normative masculine ideal. Marco's unconvincing masculinity, structured through extremes—when he forces a kiss on Eve and dons a figure skating outfit and toe-picked skates at the rink with her—also signals to the viewer the character's inability to hit the right note. As pop culture insists, artistry and bookishness denote questionable manhood, and in this equation the male figure skater can only play second fiddle to the hockey player.

The film also makes clear that Ed and Hope's views of hockey, albeit not completely unfounded, are quite harsh. When Farley argues that hockey features fighting but pummeling others is not why he plays the game, dad interjects that his argument amounts to "saying that the KKK are a bunch of swell guys." Mom, for her part, will not be dissuaded from the view that professional hockey players' lineage can be traced to baboons. Although Ed and Hope indulge their son's proclivities for shinny, they choose to remain blissfully ignorant that he is a true sport talent, which frames their helicopter parent tendencies as counterproductive to the development of Farley's potential. At the opposite end of Ed and Hope's views of hockey are the standards of masculinity on which Coach Donker insists, norms his players embody through bully hockey moves because "the code" expects it of them. In one of the more buoyant sequences of the film, which recalls the militaristic imprint of the real-life Brampton Battalion junior team on which the Blades are modeled, Moose clearly spells out the significance of the enforcer role: "I don't make fancy passes. I right wrongs by kicking asses. Without me, most would agree, the game would devolve into anarchy." The big defenseman's refrain amplifies the enforcer's work as policing a moral code without which the game would escalate into unmitigated violence. Moose, however, remains just as intractable as Farley's parents in his views about hockey, warning his young teammate that he cannot refuse to conform and remain part of hockey's "band of brothers."

Although *Score* authenticates the ice as a masculine domain with its own sets of rules and prerogatives, and a proxy for enacting human primal instincts that are restricted in the course of ordinary social interaction, it also disavows this argument by painting players with the broad caricaturesque brush of the bully-clown. Writer-director Michael McGowan approaches the first brawl as a circus act prompted by the seemingly innocent remark of an opponent who points to food on Moose's shirt. The Blades enforcer responds by decking the player and provoking a melee that is cheered by the disheveled fans, and applauded by the coach who goads, "Mess him up!" If there are rules that govern brawling, none are in evidence, as players indiscriminately punch one another in the stomach, head, and face to the dismay of Ed, Hope, and Eve in the stands. A farcical musical score led by trombones accompanies the long sequence and an ensuing right pan shows the bloodied players on the bench nodding to the music as if anesthetized. At first blush the brawl might appear to have the Hansons' vigorous imprint, but the scene communicates that this kind of play neither reinvigorates the team nor serves the community by dramatizing sport conflict as social conflict. Although the hockey player's feistiness has the power to spur the carnivalesque by injecting the pleasures of excess with a populist spirit, the scruffy, indiscriminating fans who celebrate the display come across as the unlikable "moronic ... clientele" to whom Farley's parents earlier allude. The bully-clown players also exhibit a hollow bravado that rears its head when a mouse enters the locker room and Moose and his teammates scramble onto a bench and clamor to have it removed. Without a second thought Farley does the honors, picking up the little rodent by the tail and looking on with amusement as these purported macho men in the nation's most feared league file out to take on their hated opponents. Coach Donker and his right-hand man Ace (John Robinson), for their part, appear to be thoroughly regimented by professional hockey's hierarchical system and see Farley as a freeloader who has catapulted to stardom without having paid his dues. The coach, in other words, absurdly inverts Felix Batterinski's directive that work produces blood which makes up for talent, by insisting that talent is not enough, for blood and sweat are necessary.

The final game offers Farley a chance to solve the quandary of articulating a stout masculinity that speaks to the hockey code but allows him to remain true to his values. When he finds himself on the receiving end of another attack, this time the teen faces his opponent squarely. In the manner of the two-man hockey brawl, a high shot frames the circling players to create tension, shifting to side-by-side reaction shots and bringing in the expectant audience. But after avoiding a few punches, Farley takes advantage of an opening and lunges at his opponent with a bear hug that both immobilizes and humiliates him. Predictably, the coach is dismayed at the unmanly display, but the opponent is in noticeable physical and psychological discomfort as the maneuver has a clever emasculating effect. He pleads for a truce and Farley, in true gamesman form, wholeheartedly acknowledges the player's outburst of love and asks whether others will take a run at him because he will embrace them "'till eternity." The exchange sequence starts out like *Youngblood*'s final fighting scene, but drastically abridges the confrontation to bring home the message that short-circuiting, rather than emulating, the bully-clown's behavior is the way to vanquish his misguided bravado. Farley has crossed over into bully territory only to find an astute solution that shows up the absurd machismo of perpetual aggression and helps his teammates onto a further stage of maturation.

Score advances legitimate issues on both sides of the fighting debate, spelling out the enforcer's code but also commenting on the undue emphasis on fighting as proxy for virility. The movie also strives to delineate the hockey ideal as a middle-of-the-ground yet courageous standard that differs from both the effeteness of the effeminate artist-skater and the faux masculinity of the goon-buffoon. The musical format that structures the story, however, undermines the film's message because it is antithetical to the masculinity hockey embodies in the cinema. Although *Score* astutely deploys the choreographed style of *West Side Story* (Robbins and Wise, 1961) to emphasize players' forceful gestures and depict hockey in musical format as the "anthropologically correct outpouring of a ... culture,"[38] these song and dance numbers also convey the body as the object of the male gaze, and in so doing, contravene the athlete's performative feats.[39] In addition, although a sports match is informed by tactics, it is not perceived by the audience as choreographed but as unscripted, straightforward, and instinctive.

This intrinsic spontaneity grounds fans' views of sport as a charged, thrilling undertaking, the very reason why producers insist on depicting hockey in the movies by realistically deploying elements of the sports contest.

Even though the hockey player in film can potentially move into feminizing situations without danger of emasculation because his virile signature supersedes any so-called suspect attributes, players engaging in song and dance call attention to the very objectification that the sports contest strives to disguise. *Slap Shot 2: Breaking* the Ice (Boyum, 2002) illustrates a similar point in deploying the figure of a gay Broadway director hired to transform the game into a series of choreographed acts as a metaphor for large media conglomerates' enfeeblement of the athlete by turning hockey into family entertainment. Although *Score* features a number of simple but well-constructed hockey game sequences, the song and dance numbers disrupt the focus on the sports performance, distracting from the debate by feminizing and objectifying the hockey players in the film. Despite the innovative premise offered by the musical format, the image of singing and dancing hockey players may have startled viewers, explaining, in turn, *Score*'s low box office numbers.[40]

The film, however, also explicitly bridges the idea of the athlete's objectification in a gigantic ad of Farley in briefs plastered on a Times Square high rise under the headline "the New Macho." The ad is designed to sell metrosexual beauty products and Farley's acquiescence to the scheme shows he does not grasp the implications of his stripping. The salesmanship foisted on him reduces his masculinity to the realm of ornamentality, contravening the idea of maleness as predicated on men's performance and utility to society. Although Farley is hardly effeminate and certainly not incapable of large muscular acts, he is an innocent who doesn't see through agent Don Mohan's (Brandon Firla) marketing ploys. The satire cleverly conveys that the teen is ill prepared to gauge the pitfalls of participating in organized hockey as a star player, an inexperience that leads to complications when he naively breaches hockey's codes for philosophical reasons.

The film's opening montage, which features poetic black and white archival footage of players engaged in a game of shinny and on professional ice accompanied by a beautiful John McDermott rendition of "O Canada," as well as the catchy musical finale by the entire cast who ratify hockey as "the greatest game in the land," serve as paeans to the sport as communal ritual and people's game. *Score*, however, circumvents the notion that populism is also about sweat and blood, and that the people applaud the hard-man ideal embodied by the enforcer's game. In waving off the legitimate masculinity that the tough man represents by depicting it through the guise of the bully-clown, *Score* settles little about the debate on fighting, merely shoving the issue under the rug.

Goon (Dowse, 2011) serves up the enforcer as a legitimate force in hockey, and conjures a character that, while embodying features of the bully-clown, remains curiously untainted by its unflattering aspects. Inspired by the experiences of Boston Bruins enforcer Doug Smith who came to the game at the age of 19, Canadian-born writers Jay Baruchel and Evan Goldberg draw up Massachusetts native Doug Glatt (Seann William Scott) as the starring goon. Doug works as a bouncer, by his own admission too stupid to do anything else, much to the chagrin of his father (Eugene Levy), a prominent Jewish doctor. Doug, however, is neither callous nor cold-hearted, but rather a courteous, self-effacing sort who apologizes before taking on a nonpaying or unruly customer at his employer's behest. He bumps into the enforcer role unwittingly when he attends an Orangetown Assassins game with best friend, hockey vlogger

Pat Hoolihan (Jay Baruchel). As the visiting team's enraged defenseman climbs the stands fed up with the home crowd's taunting and food-pelting, Doug steps up to the plate and puts on a fisticuffs display that transfixes fans and players alike. Impressed with Doug's prowess, Coach Rollie Hortense (Nicholas Campbell) calls in to Pat's *Hot Ice* low-rent cable show the following day and offers him a tryout. Doug "The Thug" Glatt can barely skate, but it is a small detail in the scheme of his gift for the fist. Soon Rollie's brother Ronnie (Kim Coates) comes calling, seeking Doug's services at his minor-pro Halifax Highlanders team in return for protecting the team's young hotshot, Francophone Xavier Laflamme (Marc-André Grondin). Laflamme, an erstwhile top Montreal draft demoted to the minors after suffering a potentially life-threatening hit from veteran enforcer Ross "The Boss" Rhea (Liev Schreiber), is smarting and turning to drugs and a suspect lifestyle. Making matters worse is Rhea's demotion to the St. John's Shamrocks in the same league for injuring yet another player, a move that also prompts the 40-year-old hardened hitter to cap his career at season's end.

Doug's arrival in Halifax is an eye-opener, a far cry from hockey's NHL glamour. The inebriated team captain, Gord Ogilvey (Richard Clarkin), who is going through a tough divorce, offers a bird's eye view of hockey in the minor leagues as "pretty much the shitter." The Highlanders are also only a squad on paper, a disparate bunch for whom the concept of team loyalty is an oxymoron. During Doug's first chat with Laflamme in their low-rent lodgings, the young hotshot laughs out loud at the ingénue's sincerely stated commitment to protect his teammates. In Xavier's view, these are people Doug barely knows, and he jeers with relish: "Wait one month and tell me if you feel the same." But Doug's rugged performances do the job and quickly turn into decided crowd-pleasers. His star rises meteorically and newspapers soon crown him as the next Rhea, stoking the fires of a prospective confrontation between the two. Laflamme, for his part, watches Doug's growing popularity with anguish, and soon his bewilderment turns into unsuppressed anger as Coach Rollie divests him of his assistant captain rank and taps a hatchet man for the position.

In the meantime, Doug falls in love with Eva (Alison Pill), a local with a taste for "hockey players ... the violence, the beer," as she matter-of-factly observes. But Eva also holds on to her attachment to her straight-laced boyfriend, doing her best to fight her powerful draw to the player. Like the others on the team whom Doug touches with his sincerity, Eva soon succumbs, but their long-awaited get-together only comes after he sacrifices the body in a teeth-grinder finisher that Halifax wins to keep its playoff chances alive. The Highlanders'

Enforcer Doug Glatt (Seann William Scott) in *Goon* (No Trace Camping/Entertainment One).

final encounter for the eighth playoff spot is against their nemesis Shamrocks, where Rhea and Doug go at each other for the heavyweight title and Doug manages to put the veteran out of commission, even as he himself ends up badly battered. Laflamme takes up where Doug leaves off and scores two goals to lift the Highlanders into the playoffs.

As an American hockey protagonist envisioned by its two Canadian writers to appeal to both U.S. and Canadian audiences, *Goon*'s disarmingly charming character is both the personification and the very opposite of the assorted bully-clowns of Canadian and Hollywood film. With a patent lack of facility with words and a tentative nature rooted in others' underestimation of his qualities, Doug comes across as an amusing dunce who cannot properly express what his big heart contains, but whose upstanding moral character rescues his goon-buffoon status. He goes quietly about his task with a sense of purpose that speaks to the hockey ideal of the honorable man of few words who has the aptitude to handle whatever comes his way.[41] And although he misses the mark more than once, he also comes to grasp the consequences of his actions. After Laflamme accuses him of not being a real hockey player, leading the rookie enforcer to flail in his duties and costing Laflamme a concussion that takes him out of the game in a stretcher, Doug compensates for his mistake by pummeling Xavier's assailer to a pulp. The move lands him a suspension and has a ricochet effect on the whole squad as the team captain, a graybeard who has only fought three times in his career, must take on tough man Rhea in the next game to get him off the ice. Seeing the obvious mismatch and the captain's sacrifice, Doug grasps the fallout from his actions and vows to never again let his ego and insecurities stand in the way of his duties. In a subsequent scene, he touchingly appeals to Xavier's own better self by pledging unstinting support: "I'm an idiot. From now on, no matter what happens … I'll always be watching your back." Using a childlike metaphor that invokes *E.T.* (Spielberg, 1982), he notes that the two of them have a special light burning in their stomachs and that the team needs both to light the way: "My stomach light needs your stomach light. We can all phone home together."

Doug's humility and the way he embraces the testing ground rescues him from being indelibly stamped as a full-fledged bully-clown. His childlike quality harks back to the Hansons, who despite their archetypal force-of-nature aspect operate primarily in the service of the coach and take nothing personally. Although more self-aware, Doug has some of the same childlike qualities, but his make-up and manner more closely resemble that of the heroic holy fool. Peter C. Phan describes the holy fool as an "untutored and simple-minded" character who has the ability to "penetrate … profounder truths than the lettered and the learned." Albeit others deride him as a "dull-witted … buffoon," the holy fool has faculties that are close to supernatural.[42] Coach Rollie invokes this supernatural quality when he apprises Doug that he has been "blessed by the fist of God." Indeed, proponents habitually find him almost impossible to fell, whereas he is able to handily dispatch them into oblivion with his signature boxing style. Doug's childlike authenticity and heart also support his commitment to the enforcer's messy job through the nonjudgmental outlook and unfaltering courtesy that illustrate the holy fool's trademark "contradictory elements without pretension."[43] This winning temperament allows him to imagine superlative outcomes in a way that jaded teammates, coach, and counterpart Rhea cannot.

Although *Goon* does not take itself very seriously, it succeeds in addressing the issue of fighting in hockey by focusing on the enforcer's role within it, doing so through a series of encounters between Doug and Rhea that begins when the innocent runs into the hardened

Hockey whiz Xavier Laflamme (Marc-André Grondin, center) in the Highlanders locker room in *Goon* (No Trace Camping/Entertainment One).

pro at a diner as he is taking a late-night stroll. Sitting across from each other, the crafty veteran imparts wisdom to the neophyte. The advice reveals Rhea's unsentimental view of his function on the team. He has done one thing well for twenty-three years and he is proud of his career as a foot soldier. But he also knows the contours of his role extremely well. He informs Doug that while he, much like himself, has the goods that make him a superlative fit for the role, like himself, that's all he's got and that's all he's good for. "What I'm saying," he admonishes, "is don't go trying to be hockey player. You'll get your fucking heart ripped out." When Doug insists that he plays hockey, the veteran counters by forcefully stating he is nothing more than a goon. As a mentor, Rhea attempts to make clear that enforcers are expendable and that the job does not fall within the parameters of real hockey. But Doug remains unwavering in his conviction and argues that his role entails doing whatever the coach and team need him to do, including bleeding. The film casts Doug's heartfelt statement in a close-up shot that captures the player's absolute commitment to the role. Rhea's reaction close-up shows him quietly acknowledging the statement, for the first time coming around to the poetic character of the enforcer's calling. With the advice bit over, Rhea issues a warning. He makes clear that he will not go out like a "nancy boy," and apprises the rookie, in an extreme close-up that conveys the dramatic character of the ultimatum, that if an encounter between them is in the cards, he will not hesitate to lay him out. The Boss then unceremoniously gets up and leaves, and as the apprentice watches him go out the door, just as unceremoniously he grabs a cracker from the veteran's plate and eats it with a noticeable crunching sound. The intimation is that the "kid" will finish what the veteran started and without much ado polish off his plate.[44]

In this debate about the legitimate parameters of hockey, neither character argues that the enforcer creates the space necessary for the scoring chance. No matter, because *Goon* makes the case amply by way of Rhea's wily tactics. Although the veteran characterizes the enforcer's role as that of the quintessential bully, nothing more and nothing less, his actions on the ice paint a different picture of his playmaking abilities. Visually the film underscores Rhea's role as vital in counteracting the talent of stars like Laflamme. In the Halifax-Newfoundland game, Xavier opens up the ice by balletically creating space using speed, agility, and puck-handling skills, augmented by way of twelve edits that follow him all the way to net. Despite the difference in size between Laflamme and Rhea, the star forward's talents are clearly of a superior order, and *Goon* makes the case that Rhea's enforcer contributions are necessary to enable his team to open up a lead with less gifted athletes. By taking several Halifax players out of the play, Rhea enables teammate Norris to score, after which the excited forward celebrates with a cheer: "Real hockey, let's go!"

Rhea's borderline actions, like checking a Highlanders player into the bench and taunting the entire Halifax team with his stick, register as a form of astute intimidation. TV footage of Rhea in penalty trouble, which features him with an Ace of Spades on the front of his jersey instead of a Shamrock, alludes to the iconography of the enforcer in like manner. As the highest card in the deck, the Ace of Spades, has associations with physical and psychological warfare as *carte de revenge*, connections which allude to the enforcer as a trump card that coaches deploy to physically and psychologically intimidate the opposition. The Ace of Spades also has "all-seeing eye" connotations, which point to the enforcer as someone with more self-awareness than any other player on the bench.[45] Through this heady symbolism, *Goon* redresses Rhea's limited view of the role as mere fodder, and calls attention to the many talents the enforcer must have to properly discharge his function in hockey.

The musical score "Scotland, the Brave," which plays as the Shamrocks disembark from the bus in slow motion coupled with a medium close-up of Rhea staring straight at the camera, pays homage to his formidable stature. In the number-retiring ceremony, the camera frames the veteran giving a speech about bleeding for his team with the portrait of a young Queen Elizabeth II in the background, suggesting that he is not unlike the honorable soldier who performs his duties for country and Queen. The film also calls attention to Rhea's warrior masculinity as no-frills and working-class in a scene in which he watches the televised Highlanders-Concord Minutemen game wearing a black toque and gray

Ross "the Boss" Rhea (Liev Schreiber) in *Goon* (No Trace Camping/Entertainment One).

flannel shirt, smoking a cigarette, and flanked by a beer bottle, a donut on a side plate, and a donut ash-tray, all of which identify him as a man of the people in the Canadian game.

Goon is a paean to the heart and commitment of the enforcer, to which Baruchel points in his remark that "violence is part of what makes the sport beautiful."[46] Although this tribute does not touch on the psychological toll that fighting extracts from athletes,[47] it does direct the viewer's gaze to the grimy but courageous work of the enforcer by portraying violence with brutal detail that vividly illustrates the physical price that these players must pay in the dispensation of their duties. Up-close over-the-shoulder shots bring the viewer into bouts that are highlighted by loud punching sound effects even through cutaways to audience reaction shots. The bloody mess that results from these fights harks back to the raw edges associated with brawling in seventies hockey. Doug's orange and black Assassins colors and lettering, and Ross Rhea's long hair and tricolor moustache, also call to mind the bully play of the Philadelphia Flyers during the seventies. Clearing bench brawls and players tangling with fans in the stands suggest similar imagery, as do police sirens that echo in the background as Doug enters Pat's home at the outset of the film, harking back to police visits to the locker room to investigate incidents of brutality.

The final game that brackets the highly expected fight between Doug and Rhea makes the final confrontation in *Youngblood* look like kid's play. Rhea lands no less than fifteen shots on Doug, the last of which takes the rookie down to the horror of the crowd. The veteran signals the referee not to intervene, and when Doug recovers, he gets in a shot of impressive proportions bloodying Rhea's nose. Before he is able to finish the veteran off, Doug tumbles felled by weak ankles. A total mess, and with a loud crunching sound, the rookie manages to stand up again and in a series of rapid shots, knocks out his opponent to the accompanying triumphant musical score of Turandot's "Nessun Dorma." After teammates carry Doug to the locker room, a close-up of Rhea shows him lying sideways on the ice with his eyes closed. As the veteran turns to lie flat on the ice, he spits up a tooth and cracks a smile. The tooth lands on the ice alongside drops of blood, replicating the sequence that opened the film. The sequence is a take on the sanitized tooth effects featured in the opening scene of *Tooth Fairy*, which highlight not the enforcer's work ethic, but his play as family-friendly spectacle.

Goon reiterates its critique of family entertainment through farcical allusions to Disney films *Miracle* and *The Mighty Ducks*, which expunge the sweat and blood aspects of hockey. When in a surprise move Coach Ronnie Hortense deploys Doug on a power play, the announcer remarks, "Do you believe in miracles?" alluding to the 1980 U.S. Olympic win over the Soviet team to underscore Doug's American markers and sardonically comment on his narrow role on the team and the limited range of hockey in Disney's rendition of the event. When Pat comforts Doug by reiterating praise for his inordinate abilities after the rookie's parents have disparaged the enforcer role, he satirizes *The Mighty Ducks* noting that watching him is like "watching a bunch of fucking birds flying in a V ... like it was instinct, purpose." In taking on the family genre's sanitization of hockey, the spoofing communicates that without the enforcer the game is less authentic, and by implication, less Canadian, as happens in movies that either critique the working-class masculinity of the enforcer as maladaptive or displace this aspect of hockey by projecting it onto their bully villains.[48] *Goon* speaks to the populist roots of hockey as Canadian game through the enforcer's sweat and blood markers, which Baruchel underlines in his statement that the film was made with "Canadian kids" in mind.[49]

The film clearly resonated with audiences, garnering CAD 1.2 million at the box office, an amount that for an independent Canadian film was described as an "unheard of" success.[50] Without a doubt, a large reason for the film's popularity lies in the way it portrays the doubled nature of the game and its main protagonist. Although opponents give each other notice before a fight and adhere to a code that avoids belittling the other player, bench-clearing brawls that celebrate the carnivalesque pleasures of excess also portray hockey as a game of mayhem. In like fashion, the protagonist's butcher game unfolds with brutal honesty, but the player also comes across as an endearing, self-effacing sort that never loses track of his commitment to the team. Part of Doug's magic is that he refuses to dispose of his sense of awe for the job, countering his father's arguments that his hockey post is no different from his bouncer job by adamantly noting, "for once in my life, I'm part of something.... I can protect people."[51] Through sheer example, without a trace of self-righteousness, and all the while taking his lumps in learning the business of the trade, Doug redirects his teammates' cynicism into optimism and transmutes bully-clown notions of the enforcer into wide-eyed belief in the task.

The next film discussed here and its sequel, while not overlooking the protagonist's bully-clown flaws, also pay homage to the enforcer's trade. *Keep Your Head Up, Kid* (Woolnaugh, 2010) and *Wrath of Grapes* (Woolnaugh, 2012) showcase the life of Canadian hockey icon Don Cherry.[52] The first film opens with a classroom scene that portrays Cherry's stoutness of heart from a young age, which makes him suitable for hockey but also gets him in trouble with the bureaucratic power structure. When a young Don details his father's view on properly saddling a horse by kneeing the animal in the midriff to tighten the harness, the teacher deems the comment crass and asks him to rephrase his account. The youngster refuses and he is summarily taken to the Principal's office, where he is whipped harshly on his tender young hands. The boy has done nothing wrong, having only expressed a view that grates the public sensibilities of higher-ups, but he takes the punishment stalwartly. Visuals of the youngster's whipping give way to snapshots of a grown-up Cherry (Jared Keeso) taking shots on net in a half-lit rink. The sequences are linked by sound effects that magnify both the visuals of the belt hitting the boy's hands and the hockey blade hitting the puck. The scene, although grim, also features a lighthearted musical score that amplifies Cherry's half-laughing voiceover as he relays that his father taught him to never retreat from a fight. The only problem with not keeping his big mouth shut, Cherry notes, is that later on it would invariably get him in hot water with the "front office." The introductory scene sets up Don Cherry's life journey in a nutshell. It also showcases his self-deprecating style and larger-than-life personality, which integrate a buffoon-like impishness with a solid moral compass that serve him well throughout his life.

The two-part mini-series makes clear that as an enforcer, Cherry has an unsentimental view of his job, one that resembles Ross Rhea's foot soldier outlook. In the first telefilm, Cherry explains the ethos that fuels the enforcer's work and notes that, "It's not how many you win, it's how many you show up for." He outlines the hard-man's code as "never pick[ing] your spots" and never engaging a smaller guy, and elaborates that the tough guy must protect the star player. However, neither film sets up his jousts in such a manner. Rather, the visuals always focus on a suitably rugged and bloodied Don engaged in the courageous fight. Because of the player's commitment to the job, the film also plays up the enforcer's role as hardly a walk in the park. The toughest job in hockey entails a give-and-take element that lands Cherry in the stitching room remarkably often, so much so that he turns down the use of numbing agents because it cuts into his drinking time. At the same time, Cherry's workmanship is never garish or flashy, a detail that Keeso confirms in an interview: "Don wasn't too animated when he was on the ice. He was never yelling. Even on the bench, he would stay pretty still." The sheer frequency of fights establishes brawling as part of the job, and Cherry's vigorous fighting masculinity is always suitably committed, supported by his belief that once in, a player must never hesitate.

The normative codes of the enforcer are also on display throughout the second installment, which covers less of Cherry's journeyman life in the minors but features bloodier, more brutal fight segments. The brawling starts out the second part of the biopic with a medium close-up of the opponent as he is tackled by a disheveled Cherry, who subsequently places enormous punches in the midsection from below and on the face, accompanied by sound effects of loud thumping. The opponent counters with a spectacular blow that doesn't seem to affect Cherry's resolve or destabilize his footing in any way, although he experiences profuse bleeding in the upper-eye area. Jerseys off, and with others engaged in two-man brawls, the fighters continue with their synched routine, as Don's voiceover explains that after seven of the last nine seasons with the Rochester Americans, the NHL dream had faded: "I was fighting for ice time with younger, faster players. After a while, I was mostly just fighting." Cherry had fallen into the role player part and brawling had become his mainstay. But the films define it as a cornerstone of his breadwinner function and in the context of a full day's worth of honest labor.

Although the fights are brutal and unsanitized, the narratives deploy Cherry's game in line with the norms and occupational duties of the cultural ideal of heavyweight masculinity. As sports biopics often do, the narrative also underscores the social costs of the journey, and albeit Cherry crosses into nasty bully territory merely once in an incident in which he knocks out five teeth from an opponent who barely runs into him against the boards, he recalls the episode with deep regret and as a life-changing event. Nonetheless, the films must mitigate Cherry's unsentimental approach to the job by deploying two figures whose excessive behavior frame his game within the normative boundaries of hockey. Teammate Larry "The Rock" Zeidel (Sean Bell), whom Don dubs a "wild card," gives a glimpse of the furthest reaches of bully territory, busting up opponents' mouths and engaging in skirmishes at every turn. Cherry describes Canadian minor professional hockey of the period as "every man for himself" and one of the sequences portrays an injured player, another of Larry's casualties, out of commission on the ice while his teammates merely look on at their fallen comrade.

Zeidel's work comes off as merely high-spirited when compared to Eddie Shore's (Stephen McHattie) short work of players. As owner, manager, and coach of the Springfield Indians based out of Massachusetts, Shore terrorizes his charges, skimps on their equipment, and recruits them for concession stand work and arena upkeep and restoration. He forms a repair corps, the Black Aces, consisting of players with permanent doghouse status whose services he enlists without pay in a number of tasks that range from changing light bulbs to handyman work. He also threatens to fine his charges for wrongheaded plays, takes offense at imaginary insults, and delves out so-called medical assistance by practicing extracurricular therapies that purportedly undo misaligned spines and heal broken toes overnight. Shore also meddles in his players' personal lives, demanding that wives maintain their distance because intimacy presumably affects the quality of play. For some reason, he delights in torturing Cherry, humiliating him at every opportunity and nicknaming him Madagascar for the part of the world he would have shipped him to had he managed.

A skilled athlete mentioned among the likes of Hobey Baker and George Owen, Shore played at a time when coaches viewed developing strategies and team play as a science and an important component of the game's brand.[53] The films hark back to these roots as Shore loudly admonishes Cherry that "in most hockey players' hands a hockey stick is a scientific tool. In yours it's a blunt instrument." Little of Shore's brilliance, however, is on display in his coaching sessions. Although Don repeatedly refers to Shore's hardiness during his hockey-playing years, citing his fractured neck and back and over a dozen instances of a broken nose, for his players, his tenure of the Springfield Indians proves to be a testing ground bordering on torture. The CBC telefilms portray Shore's short temper and peculiar ways as doing more harm than good and alienating players around the league. Cherry explains that the owner-coach was so hated he precipitated the formation of the Players Association which banished him from hockey. Shore inhabits the outer limits of bully territory, extending beyond the parameters of normalcy and bordering on the sociopathic. In comparison, Cherry's game, even though not that of a schoolboy, is well in line with the normative codes of the Canadian culture of hockey.

The films' bloody fight scenes dramatize Cherry's tough man exertion in line with the laboring body of the working-class exemplar who struggles to feed his family. Although popular culture romanticizes hockey as a dream occupation that opens many doors, Cherry's story flips this perspective and shows his struggle post-hockey to find construction-related jobs, indeed any job, with which to support his family. "I had no education, no trade, now no job. I was at the lowest point in my life," as he notes in a voiceover in *Keep Your Head Up, Kid*.[54] The retired player is so desperate he tries his hand at selling soaps and fragrances for men, a role ill-suited to a man who built up his physique doing back-breaking construction work, and who made his living working the corners and taking on the more grubby, unglamorous aspects of the game. Cherry finally opts for a Cadillac salesman position uncomfortably repurposing his hockey image to pitch the brawny upscale vehicles in commercials. Despite his snappy attire and the masculine image he projects, he proves too outspoken and not nearly crafty enough for the business. At this time, he also accedes to try his hand at coaching youngsters with stellar results, and the opportunity prompts his return to the game with the Rochester Americans, who begin to make use of his talents as a coach mid-season.

If there is one refrain throughout the Cherry biopics, it is that the protagonist will remain true to himself despite the pressure to conform. Cherry explains that his dad made sure to prepare him for his hockey role by instilling the values that served him throughout his life. Don's father nurtures the tough-man ideal by pulling his young son (Tyler Johnston) from a painting job because he is given the day off, and sends him off to toil on the railroad, a grueling line of work where older men resent him for doing a man's job. But the kid learns to stand his ground, finishes up his stint, and in the process hones a tough physique that prepares him for his job on the ice. Unlike Roy Spencer's outback disposition which echoes in son Brian's maladaptive bush masculinity and leads to both men's untimely demise in *Gross Misconduct*, Cherry's father is a man of integrity who teaches his son to conduct himself with probity, to protect those weaker than himself, and never shirk his duties or recoil from sacrifice. Because the player lives according to an unshakable moral code and his work amounts to honorable labor, the films do not debate whether fighting is a legitimate part of the game or inimical to it. Fighting and hockey go together just as Cherry's construction, painting, and railroad jobs sharpen his healthy habits, values, and work ethic. As a player Don neither has the size or the talent to distinguish himself as an athlete. But he clearly makes up with heart and commitment—with sweat and blood—what he lacks in skill and speed. At the same time, the biopics cannot forgo laughing at Cherry's idiosyncrasies because they contravene the spectrum of mild masculinity that Canadian culture and English-Canadian film prioritize.[55] The bully-clown's entertaining quandaries are meant to teach the character to mend his ways, but he typically finds himself at a loss about his predicament. Don humorously bellyaches about why he must find himself in hot water so often as Eddie Shore punishes him for yet another imaginary slight: "I'd try to work hard, tell the truth like my parents had taught … why's everyone always picking on me!" Cherry's wife, Rose (Sarah Manninen), also provides running commentary about her husband's irrepressible character as she assumes the forbearance of the bully-clown's partner. Don loves the brawl and their repartee calls attention to his zany proclivities as she holds down the fort as standard-bearer of sanity in the marriage. Despite his polarizing, over-the-top opinions, the films show that Cherry's patriotic, proactive martial views are well received by viewers in part because he prioritizes hockey as a rugged people's game. Hockey in Canada remains one of the last nostalgic refuges of white sturdy masculinity[56] where such a contestation for dominance can occur, and it is no coincidence that the biopics show that despite opposition, Cherry's popularity also remains high.[57]

The above pictures make clear that all out spoofs of the bully-clown's approach to the game are not palatable to either Hollywood or Canadian film because this signature also celebrates the vitality of popular forces as rightful resistance to power blocs, even as fighting and other aspects of the enforcer's toolkit lie at the center of the Canadian cultural debate about hockey. The sports film's didacticism nonetheless is also on display in the humorously tortuous situations that the bully-clown experiences on account of his excesses. Because these characters are redeemable projects, they remain at heart sympathetic figures, as they articulate the people's notions of pleasure and gratification by contravening elite preference for the sportsman's propriety and restraint.

3

Critiques of the Business of Hockey

Canadian popular culture dramatizes the practice of hockey as the genuine expression of a people. While in the U.S., the game's regional markers prevail,[1] the idea of hockey as a popular practice that engages localized identities also links sporting loyalties to the idea of communal ritual. In these schemes, the play aspects of sport at first glance appear distant from the nitty-gritty of work and commerce. But the hard facts of the athletic job as defined by training routines, physical injury and burnout, strained compensation negotiations, and the sports enterprise's risk and competition corollaries also figure prominently in cinematic discourses of hockey. Films in the previous chapters, such as *The Deadliest Season*, *Slap Shot*, *The Last Season*, and *Youngblood* comment on physical excess as part of the culture of hockey and in the context of job pressures.

The films that follow embark on a more developed critique of the systemic aspects of the business of sport, leaving little doubt that romanticizing hockey as a cultural dream is inadequately fragmentary. These films crush myths about the game, featuring protagonists who grapple against structural constraints and power blocs that are difficult to counter or remove. They critique the dark side of institutional sport for disfiguring the original expression of hockey as liminal practice and for ripping athletes from communities, leaving fans bereft by the loss of sports traditions. Films also denounce the role of unscrupulous corporate interests that fail to remunerate athletes appropriately or act to sanitize hockey to grow their media empires. The forces of commercial terrorism also take center stage and threaten all of the game's stakeholders to allegorize mounting tensions in the business of sport that resonate with developments on the ground. These movies enrich the repertoire at large with their commentary, illustrating that aspects of the game besides the skill-physicality problem remain contentious in the cinema of the sport.

The System Against the Athlete: *Face Off* (*Winter Comes Early*)

Canadian movies with hockey at their center are characterized by a persistent focus on identity myths that amplify hockey as performance of masculinity and nationhood. The following film inflects this commentary with the critiques of the social projects of the seventies—the counterculture, anti-war, civil rights and women's liberation movements—and opposes their progressive values to the masculinist norms of elite level hockey. *Face Off*

(McCowan, 1971), a telefilm based on the 1971 novel by Scott Young and George Robertson, articulates its critique of capitalism and the league's practices by way of the relationship between fictionalized Maple Leafs forward Billy Duke (Art Hindle), and acclaimed flower-child pop singer Sherrilee Nelson (Trudy Young). A top draft that commands $120,000 for a two-year contract, Billy makes a dazzling debut in his first NHL game, scoring a goal and chalking up the third star. Although he initially garners the approval of Leafs' head coach Fred Wares (John Vernon)—"He's got guts!"—before long he compromises his team's ability to win with untimely penalties. His reputation as a no-holds-barred rugged type soon begins to precede him, and when the player takes the ice a reporter wagers that he will botch his first play. By the end of the film and with six games left in the season, Billy is suspended for roughing up the referee just as the team needs two more wins to make the playoffs. When he complains about the suspension, the same coach that once lauded him for his aggressive disposition informs him that whatever his gripe, he most assuredly cannot assault the official. He chastises the player for never needing anyone in his life and mutters that the team will do better without him in the lineup.

Robert Hollands describes Billy Duke, as he appears in the novel, as one of the most extreme individualists in sports literature.[2] With a questioning, rebellious bent and a pointed distaste of rules apposite of the time, Billy accepts institutional control only to the degree required to retain his hockey job. Even as he enjoys the financial rewards of his labor, for a hockey star, Billy behaves problematically, as he relentlessly pushes against the hierarchical structure of the league in a way unfitting of the North American sports exemplar. For all his aversion to regimentation, Billy's relationship with Sherry exposes the great ideological rift that exists between the conservative, regimented masculinist order of the professional sports world and the values of the progressive movement that she represents. Sherry literally stands for the sixties countercultural ethos as an acclaimed peacenik pop culture icon whose pacifist sensibilities clash with the hierarchical masculine codes of elite-level sport. When Billy describes his setup as professional athlete as "like the army," the best remunerated army in the world, Sherry rejects the role of institutionally-derived wealth in carving out a meaningful life: "Yeah, but how much can you pay for someone's life?" Her position is consonant with the identity politics of the period's social movements, which indicted commodity culture and constructed a space for cultural nationalism outside the dictates of the market, institutional politics, and the military-industrial complex.[3] The neglected wife of Leafs owner Graydon Hunter (Susan Douglas Rubes) also augments the political critique of the league in a restroom chat with Sherry, delineating the realities behind institutional sports and calling attention to all the players who preferred not to be traded, and the plethora of fired coaches and wives suddenly uprooted without input. Mrs. Hunter ends with the poignant observation, "you have to wonder which gains most, people or the system." Her commentary conveys players as a natural resource extracted for profit, mere commodities to be traded like sports cards in a scheme that pulls apart social networks in the interest of big capital.

Face Off also exposes cracks in the ethos of dominant sporting masculinity that requires athletes maintain careerist, disciplined lives. When coach Wares announces a 9 o'clock curfew, a player registers a minor but not unimportant complaint scoffing whether team members' mothers will also be there to tuck them in. Billy also pushes against the controls placed on him, and intent on defying the curfew set by the coach, he grumbles that he's not a mere working stiff following orders. Teammate Chief, played by (real-life) Leafs captain George

Armstrong, promptly throws light on the futility of Billy's aversion to institutional checks, summarizing in a less than a flattering manner the constraints that players must live with as NHL property. "You're a slave by choice. We all are.... Great white Hunter says 'Jump!' We jump. Great white Hunter no like Billy Duke, sell Billy Duke to new master." The captain adds for full effect that, if the rookie intends to remain part of the game, he'd better get with the program. Armstrong's First Nations status, which inflects his speech with the history of colonial oppression, serves to reify Billy's status as commodity. Chief's comments, like Mrs. Hunter's, lay out players' lives as nothing short of contracted out to the prerogatives of management and ownership. But Billy will not be denied. He ignores the curfew and leaves to rendezvous with Sherry.

Robert Hollands proposes that by outlining a rebellious protagonist in Billy Duke, *Face Off* puts forth a cultural ideal of autonomy that pushes against "American influence and cartel control of the professional game."[4] The character's non-conformism on the one hand heralds increased player profile and athletes' assertion of rights during the seventies as sports clubs transformed from small franchises into corporatized and highly profitable entities. On the other, he represents a national archetype of independence at a time of great cultural angst about Canada's branch plant status vis-à-vis the U.S. As noted, cultural-nationalist backlash against American political and economic influence over Canada's culture[5] reached a crescendo with the 1967 NHL expansion and with the progressive incursion of U.S. capital into elite-level hockey that presided over the downturn of senior amateur development programs. Critics blamed the expansion's fallout on NHL owners who, intent on marketing hockey to American audiences, prompted the dilution of talent and promoted hooliganism in the seventies game and beyond.

Billy's representation through iconography of hunting—he appears as both hunter and hunted in the film—also defines him as an archetype of national difference. Hunting speaks to conceptions of Canada through an organic, revitalizing rurality and scenes of Billy in his hometown show him in an idyllic setting hunting small game accompanied by his dog. The sequence alludes to the circumscribed role of guns in Canadian life, dating back to the settlement of the Canadian West when small arms were primarily used in "hunting, varmint control or reserved for the use of RCMP officers,"[6] as Lorry Felske and Beverly Rasporich observe. As conjured by the image of the small-town hunter, Billy communicates an unadulterated pastoralism that evokes the manufacture of Canada as "small, rural, innocent, and old-fashioned," a concept that Patricia Hughes-Fuller notes explicitly distinguishes the country from its southern neighbor.[7] Leafs owner Graydon Hunter (Austin Willis), to whom Chief also refers in a hunting context, conveys precisely the opposite, and recalls the slave-trader who disrupts the organic life of the community.

Billy's association with hunting also highlights the tough masculinity favored by the Canadian culture of hockey. As Billy lands in the hospital with a concussion, newspaper reports warn that this "cocky kid ... better keep looking over his shoulders for bounty hunters" and play up the abandonment and recklessness with which the rookie plays the game as highly dangerous and liable to hurt the team in the standings. Yet, even as coach Wares chastises Billy for not prioritizing his squad by carefully picking his fights, he is also fully aware that the young, feisty player was brought in because of his ability to dish out and take punishment, and he relies on Billy to mix things up, prodding: "Let's get something started!" Billy certainly plays the game like many a protagonist of seventies film, for even when he crosses the line he never apologizes for his toughness. Indeed, when Sherry accuses him of being like the rest of the lot, he lets her know in no uncertain terms, "I'm younger and stronger and tougher. That's why you dig me." Billy's grit and his rural roots evoke the durability of the mythic exemplar in the Nordicity myth, and Sherry clearly responds to his masculine allure. But she also has mixed feelings about her attraction because the ideologies that elite-level hockey represents oppose her own progressive principles. Her attitude toward violence in the NHL game is captured during her first attendance of a live matchup. A dark close-up shot, consistent with the neo-realist hues of the film, isolates her from the crowd as she winces with visible discomfort at her boyfriend's rugged play. Unlike Gerry Miller's wife Sharon, who in *The Deadliest Season* understands the intricacies of the professional game and regards her husband's use of legitimate physicality as an aphrodisiac, Sherry is repulsed by such expressions. She rejects the league's patriarchal values which prioritize the masculine order matter-of-factly and in a way that contravenes her pacifist ideals and the women's struggle to achieve equality at home and in the workplace. Her concerns are not unfounded as the film highlights this masculinist ideology at the team party where coach Wares prods Billy to make a commitment to the Leafs, arguing that "everything in life" must assume its proper place, including "the wife."

The rookie's non-conformism notwithstanding, *Face Off* frames the rift between Sherry's worldview and the professional choices that her boyfriend must make as a matter of irreconcilable differences. Billy, for his part, must also decide between his dreams of stardom and duties to team and fans, and his commitment to his love interest. But like a many a movie of the seventies in which the project of masculinity is defined by compromise and loss, the film solves Billy's conundrum inexorably as Sherry dies in a car accident before he is able to reach her. Her death, although presented as part of the fallout of the sixties' drug culture, also registers as a sacrifice of the relationship to the NHL's altar. Her immolation is foreshadowed in a party conversation with owner Graydon Hunter as he refers to players and their wives as a "brave group" who must have outright devotion to the game. Her loss helps to fracture the myth of sports success by communicating that "the system" works to effectively annihilate the individual as obligations to the team and the league take precedence over personal commitments.

Billy's return to the Leafs bench, however, highlights the ultimate futility of his rebellion and deflects his defiant stance toward management and coaching staff. The ending performs this symbolism by freezing his figure as he takes the ice and subsequently appending an aerial shot of a boy skating on a strip of ice in the vast, desolate backcountry as he is cheered on by his father. Book-ending the story through imagery of the father-son link in sport suggests that despite the protagonist's defiance of institutional strictures, he cannot deny the organic link that exists between the game and his Canadian identity. The final scene reminds the viewer of hockey's mythic origins in the vast, unpopulated wilderness of the North as source of Canadian vitality. Linking the Canadian icescape to NHL ice, and reaffirming the connection between the Nordicity myth and the game as both organic pastime and professional sport, also frames Billy's rebellious stance against the league as problematic. Despite his frontier-like defiance of NHL rules, then, the rookie remains circumscribed by his professional role as a primary source of identity, pointedly conveyed by his return to the bench after his suspension is over.

Face Off presents the viewer with a protagonist who attempts to buck the systemic forces of capital and the hierarchical structures of sport, even as he desires to remain part of a game profoundly informed by national identity myths. The film expresses a distinct tension between popular imaginings of hockey as cultural dream and a view of the league as a sport cartel governed by unsentimental business practices that demand conformity to patriarchal norms at the expense of personal prerogatives. In fielding the need for autonomy from the economic regime that the NHL represents, *Face Off* expresses difficulty and ambivalence in escaping the order it critiques. Indeed, the movie's extensive NHL game sequences, which feature the real Leafs, amply convey the professional hockey player as Canada's foremost cultural status symbol and the highest expression of the Nordicity myth.[8] In its indelibly stark view of the hockey business, however, *Face Off* stands by itself in the repertoire.

Hockey in Crisis: *Net Worth* and *Sudden Death*

On April 14, 1994, the CBC aired in its Primetime news slot the documentary the *Going South*, which investigated the fallout from the impending relocation of small-market Canadian NHL teams to U.S. Sun Belt arenas.[9] The report compared Winnipeg, poised to lose its beloved Jets, with Miami, a megalopolis and home to the newly minted Florida Panthers. *Going South* made clear that in forfeiting its team Winnipeg stood to relinquish both credibility and identity, swapping the distinction conferred by its NHL signature for backwater status. Conversely, Miami, "capital of the Americas ... beachfront and bronze ... dazzling, daring, dangerous ... a city built for pleasure..." where hockey players were "aliens," boosted its cachet and moved to empower Latino and African American youngsters' newfound hockey dreams. Through a tale of two cities, the CBC news feature fittingly encapsulated nineties Canadian media discourse about the threat posed by the league's expansion into regions where hockey was non-indigenous. The expansion came about because of owners' inability to meet mounting player payrolls, and a Canadian citizenry who, weighing priorities like education and health, refused to subsidize an NHL team in their backyard. Alongside the commodification of sport and the unstable relationship between capital and labor, *Going South* fielded the familiar motif of Canadian resources extracted for profit by foreign interests. Juxtaposing Canadian warmhearted concern to American wealth and technological know-how, the narrator pointed out cheerlessly that "far, far from Canada, Canada's national passion [had] ... become a cash crop in Florida."[10]

The issues aired in the CBC piece were relevant in that Winnipeg's descent-into-tragedy story line mirrored larger concerns about the economic status of Canadian cities in the era of new globalized markets. Corporations' search for economies of scale prompted by U.S. legislation that removed cross-ownership barriers early in the decade led to a series of mergers between entertainment conglomerates and large sports outfits.[11] Moving to parlay media conglomerates' increased interest in sport, the NHL had set out to court the giants of the new communications industry: Michael Eisner's Disney, Wayne Huizenga's Blockbuster Video, and Ted Leonsis' AOL. Of the three corporations, Disney's partnership with the league proved most fruitful.[12] Disney's icing of a sparkling new team christened the Mighty Ducks of Anaheim at the start of the 1992–1993 season, and the Company's long association with American cultural codes, spurred fears about Canada's marginalization in regard to the national game. Expansion had not only led to the relocation of the Winnipeg Jets to Phoenix but the transplantation of the Quebec Nordiques to Colorado, where the franchises re-emerged as the Coyotes and Avalanche, respectively. Rumors about the prospective sale of other small Canadian teams like the Edmonton Oilers and Calgary Flames only exacerbated fears that hockey, the Canadian resource, was being picked off as mere staples for the benefit of vested interests outside the country.[13]

The CBC's inability to consistently secure match-ups for its trademark *Hockey Night in Canada* Saturday night broadcasts, due to league scheduling that favored U.S. networks, also caused furor about the NHL's failure to protect Canadian interests in the game. The 1993 sale of hockey equipment manufacturer CANSTAR to U.S.–based Nike, an NHL stoppage in the latter part of the 1994–1995 season, as well as Rupert Murdoch's Fox Networks' introduction of a red glowing puck during the 1996 NHL All-Star game in Boston also dominated headlines and were viewed as tantamount to "the Americanization of Canada,"[14] according to Dan Mason. Mason notes that Fox, which had become the fourth-ranked TV network in the U.S., introduced the glowing puck to grow the American audience for the sport.[15] Although Fox's survey had demonstrated that seven out of ten American viewers liked the new technology, negative reaction to the Fox-Trax Puck from American viewers who were longtime hockey fans and U.S.–based reporters who covered the game added to the discontent. Commentators in Canada, for their part, lamented the NHL's lack of leverage in enforcing the traditional way of broadcasting hockey,[16] fueling accusations of American interference in Canadian culture and framing developments in the context of a larger Canadian crisis of identity.[17] The introductory paragraph of an April 1994 report in the *International Herald Tribune*, for its part, succinctly summarized hockey's decade-and-a-half metamorphosis by pronouncing that hockey had at no time seemed "less Canadian" and "more American,"[18] while Commissioner Bettman assessed the game's prospects in the U.S. as "limitless."[19]

Ted Lindsay (Aidan Devine, right) with Red Wings Manager Jack Adams (Al Waxman) in *Net Worth* (CBC Still Photo Collection).

Much as *Going South* had done, the CBC's film division aired concerns over control of hockey as it coincided with an NHL player-owner impasse over salary cap negotiations that threatened the partial shutdown of the 1994–1995 season. The telefilm

Net Worth (Ciccoritti, 1995), based on the 1991 nonfiction book *Net Worth: Exploding the Myths of Pro Hockey* by David Cruise and Alison Griffiths, offers a fictionalized examination of the role of owners and managers in depriving players of pensions during the Original Six NHL era. The docudrama's storyline centers on the Herculean efforts of Red Wings star Ted Lindsay (Aidan Devine) who attempts to organize a Players Association in 1956–1957 against owners' wishes. Lindsay takes on the league's powerbrokers: Leafs owner Conn Smythe (Robin Gammell), league president Clarence Campbell (Michael J. Reynolds), and owner-at-large James Norris (Richard Donat), who through interests in four out of six teams (the New York Rangers, Chicago Blackhawks, Detroit Red Wings, and Boston Bruins), effectively controlled the league since the early 1940s.[20] A popular player on the Production Line with Gordie Howe (Kevin Conway) and Sid Abel, Ted Lindsay's[21] struggle begins as he and his teammates are refused a small raise by Red Wings general manager Jack Adams (Al Waxman). Adams epitomizes the league's clout, bellowing that players are obligated to play for whatever he decides to pay them because, as he notes, "I made you guys into heroes…." He promptly and unceremoniously orders the squad: "You must eat, sleep, walk, talk … hockey." Adams takes on Lindsay, in particular, mocking his "Terrible Ted" moniker for his failure to contain Montreal's Maurice Richard during the playoffs. Lindsay endures Adams' humiliating remarks but decisively moves to organize as he comes across indigent former players and begins to suspect NHL team owners are cooking the books. Despite great initial resistance from other teams, he manages to gain enough signatures for a first NHLPA. Ultimately, however, as Jack Adams points out, players lack the staying power to carry on with their demands, and owners break the organization by trading those involved to other NHL teams and to the minors.[22]

In the introduction to *Artificial Ice*, Gruneau and Whitson write that Griffiths and Cruise's pioneering work on which the TV film is based questions many of the game's foundational myths and challenges the standing of its legendary figures.[23] *Net Worth* similarly depicts how, in the move to have players look after their interests, Lindsay punctures the widespread belief that "there is no money in hockey; the owners are barely scraping by … [and] are in it only for the love of the game," as Adams notes. Those very owners, of course, are nothing short of veritable moguls whose interests range from hockey to horseracing and boxing.[24] Although the film depicts NHLers routinely playing past their prime in order to avoid sinking into poverty, Lindsay's battle is an uphill one on account of the anti-union outlook fostered by the small Canadian towns from which most NHLers hail.[25] Even as Lindsay scales down his efforts and opts for a Players Association, the press frames his actions as Leftist strategizing, accusing him of betraying team owners by employing "commie tactics." League rules also prevent NHLers from talking to teammates and to players on other teams, as well as interviewing with the press on income-related issues. Part of Ted Lindsay's battle entails breaking down the wall of distrust that team owners promote and reconfiguring entrenched habits in the culture of hockey. The telefilm also exposes management's underhanded methods to pressure and intimidate players. Teammates are played against one another, yet also warned not to let "rabble rouser" Ted Lindsay imperil team unity and irreparably damage the game they love. Higher-ups also equate team with family and community, reaffirming the NHL game as the "stuff of your dreams." Clarence Campbell (Michael J. Reynolds), for his part, perpetuates the myth that "Hockey is not about money…. Hockey is about the dreams of boys on frozen ponds and backyard rinks all … across Canada," deflecting attention from the role of capital in the game by way of its ties to the Northern landscape.

Unlike *Gross Misconduct*, which two years earlier put forward a staunch condemnation of Spinner Spencer's tough-man attributes, *Net Worth* focuses on players' laboring bodies, visually depicting the hard edges of the era's game to dramatize the physical price players must pay to belong to the NHL's exclusive club. Doug Beardsley notes in *Country on Ice* that despite his small size, "Terrible Ted" Lindsay was one of the toughest players of the league in a game that was by all accounts much rougher, but he, along with players who doled out regular amounts of clog also enjoyed highly calibrated skills.[26] Rather than Lindsay's skills, *Net Worth* captures the player's courage and durability in the professional arena. In the lone game of the film between the Red Wings and the Leafs, Lindsay takes brutal punches in the face from an opponent as a referee ties his arms from behind. Close-up slow motion pummeling sequences from the perspective of the player on the receiving end highlight the NHL's premium on physicality, as Jack Adams yells cheers from the stands, "That's my Teddy Lindsay ... who I want to see out on the ice!" Lindsay goes to the penalty box bloodied but smiling, only to be taunted and spat upon by Leafs fans. Out of the box and undaunted, he takes the ice positioning his stick to simulate shooting at the crowd, where Leafs owner Conn Smyth sits mumbling that no matter what, he will hit upon the man who will destroy Ted Lindsay.

That man, of course, is Chicago Blackhawks owner Jim Norris, who threatens to shut down the league and leave the players out in the cold if they do not put an end to their plans. As Lindsay remains steadfast in his quest, the conflict escalates. Black and white shots of players doing practice drills downgrade the romance of hockey in favor of the stark realities

Ted Lindsay (Aidan Devine) in the penalty box harassed by Leafs fans in *Net Worth* (CBC Still Photo Collection).

they must face in their dealings with management. As Lindsay presses on with his efforts, players repeatedly rebuff him, refusing to see through the enactment of a Players Association lulled by empty promises from higher-ups. In taking a behind-the-scenes view of the NHL's Golden Era, the telefilm repurposes hockey's myth of success by framing athletes as a natural resource extracted from small towns for the benefit of power blocs. By depicting the business of elite-level hockey of the 1940s and 1950s through catchphrases like the "good of the game," *Net Worth* warns about using myths about hockey to veil the vested interests of institutional authority.[27] Even as the film's ending frames Ted Lindsay's trajectory as another decline-and-fall story, an adjunct interview makes clear that his efforts ultimately paved the way for a Players Association.[28] Despite *Net Worth*'s narrative arc, then, Lindsay's journey is one of decisive agency and vision. Through this textual addendum, the telefilm rescues Lindsay's antihero status, and transforms the story into a cautionary tale about conflating the romance of hockey with the business of sport, reaffirming the need for a cultural exemplar that has the best interests of the community at heart to set things right.

Net Worth's critique of the appropriation of Canadian national symbols was timely given that in 1995 the NHL had endured a lockout and seen its season shortened by 468 games. Robert Berry and William Gould provide context for this escalation in their explanation of the evolution of the North American sports enterprise. They note that early sports franchises resembled overgrown small-scale outfits that were operated in that capacity and had lower revenues than the insurance, automobile, and oil industries.[29] Although the NHL operated as a de facto cartel with interests in diverse sectors of the North American economy, franchising practices by professional leagues, especially in the U.S., evolved to stress the need for television contracts profoundly transforming the business of professional sports. Steady access to male demographics on a national scale and increasing profits from advertisers spurred bidding wars by the networks for sole rights to broadcast games. In an attempt to secure a share of the revenue pie, athletes moved to confront inflexible labor practices in court, appointing agents and player reps and reinforcing their elevated profile through membership in player associations and collective bargaining agreements.[30] The emergence in 1972 of a new professional hockey league, the World Hockey Association (WHA), also enhanced athletes' leverage in negotiations by escalating player salaries to multi-million dollar levels, particularly for franchise players. But the relative advantage offered by the WHA remained short-lived as the budding league folded in 1979 and the NHL reabsorbed the best players. Berry and Gould indicate that even as sports profits grew at this time, "[e]xistent industrial models ... [remained] unclear and [p]eople ... in the industries ... [were still] feeling their way,"[31] with player-management infighting likely beyond the 1980s.

In its look at team relocation, *Going South* addresses the tensions between labor and ownership on account of mounting player salaries. Critiquing the owners, Wayne Gretzky, then with the L.A. Kings, stated in the CBC piece that players and owners were morally obliged to look after the needs of small-market teams. Citing that the New York Rangers had a duty to help the Winnipeg Jets just as the Montreal Canadiens had lent financial assistance to the Quebec Nordiques to allow the team to remain viable, Gretzky nevertheless concluded that the likelihood of such a development was slim. Then Panthers Manager Bobby Clarke also asserted that even as the situation concerned all Canadians, he did not see how small Canadian markets could effectively support NHL teams. Owner Wayne Huizenga, for his part, elaborated that skyrocketing player salaries were untenable and inherently unfair to fans,

Ted Lindsay (Aidan Devine, right) takes on an opponent in *Net Worth* (CBC Still Photo Collection).

who would be forced to subsidize the rising cost of player salaries in addition to the construction of new arenas. The rift between NHL and the NHLPA over the implementation of a player salary cap and the plight of small-market franchises ultimately resulted in the partial lockout of the 1994–1995 season. Owners sought in vain to tie player salaries to revenues, while the Players Association got behind a revenue-sharing scheme to help subsidize smaller teams. In the final analysis, the lockout only instated a rookie salary cap, leaving other key issues unaddressed.

The Universal Studios blockbuster *Sudden Death* (Hyams, 1995), produced by Pittsburgh Penguins part-owner Howard Baldwin and written by wife Karen Elise Baldwin, procures an allegorical view of ownership's side in the NHL dispute, dramatizing in timely fashion concerns over the forces of commercial greed that hold hostage all of the game's stakeholders: VIPs, players, and fans alike. In a plot that features hockey as backdrop, Jean-Claude Van Damme's Canadian-born Darren McCord, assigned to fire security duties at Pittsburgh's Civic Arena, walks into a terrorist trap set up by rogue Secret Service agent Joshua Foss (Powers Boothe) that endangers his children, the Vice President of the United States, and the 17,000 in attendance at the seventh game of the Stanley Cup playoffs between the Penguins and the Chicago Blackhawks. Foss wires the building with explosives and takes everyone in the owner's box hostage. He then demands a transfer of over $1 billion from the U.S. Treasury into his bank accounts after each of the three periods of the hockey game. Among the hostages is McCord's young daughter, Emily (Whittni Wright), forcing the former fireman to single-handedly take on Foss' thugs, disarm every bomb in the building, and for the grand finale, deliver the derelict into oblivion.

Sudden Death establishes McCord as a gentle and secure sort from the very outset, the kind of resolute working-class hero that will fight off the forces of commercial terror and their assailment of the hockey community. In the introductory locker room scene, the erstwhile fireman-goalie and his son Tyler (Ross Malinger) spot boyish NHLer Luc Robitaille (appearing in cameo) working on his gear. McCord greets the player in French and casually inquires about the team's prospects for the evening. An otherwise innocent-looking Luc responds with a vulgar colloquialism, noting that his team will obliterate the opponent. Taken aback by the language, McCord turns his boy away and relays to him that Robitaille is counting on a win. Next McCord and Tyler move to greet fictional goalie Brent Tolliver (Jay Caufield), who resembles a goon more than a goaltender. Tyler makes the mistake of disclosing dad's opinion of Tolliver as someone who belongs in a rocking chair. When McCord relates he used to play pro hockey in Canada, Tolliver menacingly suggests, "Come by some afternoon. I'll show you the difference between the game you played and the one I play." Seeing the goalie's part-toothless smile, McCord calmly replies that he can indeed notice the difference. The locker room scene establishes that the protagonist is not a bloodthirsty character, not even a violent type like the average NHL player, but someone who in the mode of the western hero will be forced to take matters into his hands for the good of his community. As a caring, divorced father who is helping to bring up children, McCord's character is automatically granted lenience for the violence and brutality in which he is about to engage.

Tellingly, before McCord gets on with the task of saving the world, the would-be hero must first set his relationships aright specifically by redressing his bond with Tyler. In the aforementioned Penguins locker room scene, the film makes clear that McCord is a fallen icon in his son's eyes. Answering Robitaille's question as to whether he plays hockey, Tyler replies in a muted tone, "My dad played. He was a goalie." Because McCord is no longer a heroic figure—he is neither a fireman risking his life for others, nor a hockey goalie defending the net against opponents—he must act to reinstate himself in the eyes of his son. Pursued by terrorists, unbeknownst to Tyler who is watching the game in the stands, McCord enters the locker room and dons Tolliver's gear as the goalie lies prostrate on a table with an oxygen mask on. As the acting goaltender, McCord must now worry about the game at hand rather than the crooks. At a crucial juncture, he makes "the save of the year!" per the TV announcer's remark, and immediately signals the youngster that he loves him. McCord acts to regain Tyler's respect before he can move on to save daughter Emily's life, reaffirming the father-son link in sports.

In so doing, he embodies the new man of nineties cinema, a self-effacing character who as a father must address any chasms in his relationship with his children. Stella Bruzzi notes that in nineties Hollywood film the muscular virility of the preceding decade was no longer in vogue since traditional masculinity and fatherhood were both constructed as in crisis and new paradigms of manhood were being probed.[32] Although *Sudden Death* upholds Van Damme's "muscles-from-Brussels" image, his character must first and foremost heal familial rifts before the monumental task ahead. McCord's actions thus claim hockey as a quintessential arena for negotiating heroic masculine agency and redressing the social relevance of the father's role in sport as a legitimate way of strengthening familial bonds.[33]

Having rehabilitated himself in the eyes of his son and saved the Penguins' hide, McCord must now get on with his mission to save daughter Emily and the world. He punches a Blackhawks player to leave the ice on a game misconduct, and resumes his hunt for the assailants, expeditiously slamming Penguins mascot Icey against a ceiling fan to reveal one of Foss' henchwomen. McCord's actions in short order link the violence of the hockey world with the savagery of the terrorists. Although stressing that the terrorists are evil incarnate, the film amply makes the point that hockey is synonymous with unremitting brutality. At the same time, deploying the hockey game as backdrop for the hero's thuggish actions serves to attenuate the harshness of the off-ice proceedings, providing a degree of distraction without having to cede the violence altogether. By presenting a contest of hard edges, the film openly formulates hockey as Canadian, reminiscent of the game Disney set out to sanitize, but with a twist. When the U.S. Vice President (Raymond J. Barry) asks the players in the locker room, "Are you Democrats or Republicans?" the forthcoming reply is, "Neither, Sir, Canadians." By locating Canadians squarely within the cultural parameters of the game but outside the North American political power structure, *Sudden Death* attenuates Canada's international political and economic agencies and activates the idea of Canadians as labor implied in *Net Worth*.[34] Montreal-based Seagram's acquisition of Universal Studios, which occurred prior to the film's release, did not change this representation, charging a Canadian transnational at the head of a major Hollywood studio with promoting U.S. cultural codes that marginalized Canadians to the role of sports labor.

As a blockbuster film, *Sudden Death* must also capitalize on Jean-Claude Van Damme's action hero persona. John Lyden in his work on film and myth argues that action films take their thematic cues from westerns where "good and evil ... fight to the death without the

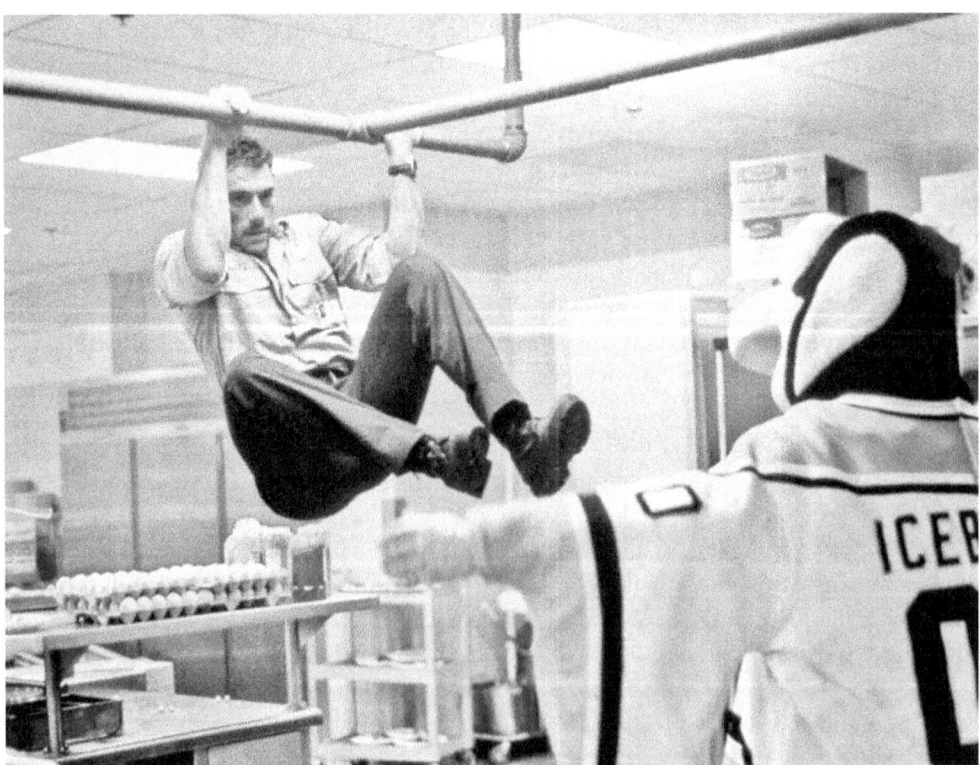

Darren McCord (Jean-Claude Van Damme) intercepts Pittsburgh Penguins mascot Icey in *Sudden Death* (Universal Pictures/Photofest).

impediments of social convention."[35] In the manner of the classic western hero, McCord's fighting skills and potential for violence are on par with those of villainous forces. Although the classic western protagonist's character is such that it allows him to operate on both sides of the divide,[36] McCord's civil servant background, which expresses the values of the social order and the stability of the community and its institutions,[37] amplified by his nurturing-father profile, grant him moral authority to engage in acts of restorative violence in the face of colossal threat.

Through the metaphor of hostage-taking of the game's constituents, *Sudden Death* foregrounds greed as the primary menace facing elite-level hockey in the 1990s. *Going South* and *Sudden Death* appear to concur over the fallout caused by the negotiating parties' intransigence, particularly as it is visited on the game's youngest demographic. *Going South* scripts the hockey dreams of young boys as beholden to owners' and players' whims, by noting that as Ivy League lawyers on both sides of the owner-player divide were going at each other, a team of Winnipeg youngsters suited up to skate during a Jets-Kings game intermission, the very group that stood to be disenfranchised when the team relocated to Phoenix. *Sudden Death*, for its part, foregrounds commercial terror as primarily harming the game's youngest fans by inserting McCord's daughter in the line of fire along with the VIPs held hostage in the owner's box. The film's final sequences interrupt the climactic overtime of the Stanley Cup playoffs' seventh game as the conflict between Foss and McCord escalates, and players and fans are sent scrambling toward the gates. This disruption registers as a dramatic analogy of the game's takeover by the forces of commercial greed.

The final sequence culminates the white-knuckled game of chess between good and evil as McCord dangerously dangles from a ladder of the helicopter holding Foss, and shoots into the belly of the craft bringing it down and risking his life in the process. Supported by shots from outside and inside the arena, the sequence draws out the helicopter's thunderous crash, first into the jumbotron sporting the score of the interrupted game, and then onto the ice in spectacular blockbuster fashion. This elongated and extremely tense finale allegorizes the fallout from the potential destruction of small-market teams in Canada and historic U.S. franchises like the Pittsburgh Penguins, which at the time were in danger of folding because of inadequate, aging rinks. Penguins co-owner Mario Lemieux had hoped to obtain public funding for the construction of a modern arena with amenities for the upmarket consumer, much in the way that the city had financed its NFL and NBA stadiums. Struggling to secure the monies, Lemieux considered selling the team, warning time and time again that the Penguins could not remain solvent at their present location, an assertion that NHL Commissioner Gary Bettman corroborated.[38]

The destruction of the Penguins arena that *Sudden Death* enacts in the final sequences speaks specifically to Pittsburgh's case, but also warns of a wide unraveling of the hockey business that stands to affect all of the game's constituents. The film argues for unstoppable progress by depicting the hero as acting and succeeding on behalf of all of hockey's stakeholders. Its reliance on an underdog exemplar to represent not only the game's followers but the owner's side of the debate is not unusual given that Hollywood typically depicts the businessman as a greedy, evil character who inflicts the ruinous effects of corporate monopoly on the community.[39] Through imagery of VIP hostage-taking, *Sudden Death* reiterates the untenable position of owners expressed by Wayne Huizenga in *Going South*, as he relayed that skyrocketing player salaries were interfering with owners' ability to secure the necessary funds for building new arenas. By aligning the interests of owners with those of the average fan, *Sudden Death* makes the case for rescuing corporate hockey as necessary social capital, underscoring the cachet of sports practice under corporate intervention.

Sudden Death's cautionary tale about the game's disruption resonated with the 1994–1995 lockout that preceded the film's release. Owners and players had attempted to address the fate of small-market franchises, but ultimately proved ineffective in ending the transfer of Winnipeg- and Quebec-based teams to the U.S. Ownership's commitment to tie salaries to revenue also lingered unresolved and remained relevant well into the next decade, culminating in the 2004–2005 lockout of players and the cancellation of an entire season for the first time in NHL history. Pittsburgh Penguins owners, for their part, only reached an agreement for construction of a new arena in early 2007.[40]

The Hockey Protagonist on the Frontier: *Mystery, Alaska*

The transformation of the hockey landscape in the 1990s by American/global entertainment combines, in particular Disney's re-fashioning of the sport to coincide with its corporate brand, was much maligned by traditional North American hockey constituencies who resented corporate tampering of the game. As a testament of the contradictions that the cinematic text can withstand, Disney's NHL foray did not hamper a critique of professional hockey practices in its films, much like Seagram's acquisition of Universal Studios did not change Canadian players' representation in *Sudden Death*. Case in point, *Mystery, Alaska* (Roach, 1999), an R-rated feature originally dubbed *Disney's Hockey Project*, deploys the myth of the West to mark the game as American and castigate the excesses of professional sport. This critique nonetheless ultimately amounts to a surface rebuke, because in basing the plot out of Alaska and calling forth the open spaces of the West, the story foregrounds the frontier as primary engine in supporting the growth of American capitalism and its utopian account of boundless sociopolitical resources.[41] Frontier imagery in short order allows for a concomitant disavowal of this critique by endorsing the expansion of sport under the aegis of corporations in synergy with the Company's NHL interests.

The film opens with the forces of disruption making their way into the Northern backcountry outpost of Mystery, as Charlie Danner (Hank Azaria), an erstwhile town resident and writer for *Sports Illustrated*, arrives bearing news involving the New York Rangers. Danner proposes an exhibition game between the town's amateur whiz players and the NHL professionals. The prospective match is founded on the premise that on sheer skating ability, Mystery's team can hold its own against any National Hockey League team, and the townspeople must decide whether the game is a smart idea for the small enclave whose identity is tightly wrapped around a form of pond hockey labeled the "Saturday Game." Mayor Scott Pitcher (Colm Meaney) calls a meeting for the purpose, noting that hosting the game could give a boost to the local economy. Judge Walter Burns (Burt Reynolds), Mystery's voice of reason, quickly counters the Mayor's suggestion as he cautions that the Rangers are elite professionals who will undoubtedly shatter any illusions Mystery has about its game. The judge's son, Birdie (Scott Grimes), who is a Saturday Game regular, however, adamantly states that he's ready to play those Rangers. The Rangers, it turns out, have better things to do than to spend their scarce vacation time playing "a bunch of Eskimos." But the community fiercely wants the game and sues to enforce the agreement. After they win the fight, preparations for the match ensue with the big media in tow. The pond game promptly turns into a highly structured affair with boards and sponsors. "We agreed to a game of pond hockey on open ice; no one in a rink playing on a box, boards, blue lines, referees," town sheriff and team captain John Beebe (Russell Crowe) tells Danner to no avail. And as game day arrives, the NHLers outnumber the Mysterians eleven skaters to eighteen, albeit the Alaskan cold, a bitter -10° F, temporarily stops the professionals in their tracks. Mystery ultimately loses the match 4–3, but the Rangers draft two of the town's most skilled players, Connor Banks (Michael Buie) and Stevie Weeks (Ryan Northcott), into their farm team, handing the community a belated and relished victory.

Mystery, Alaska's opening sequence depicts a young male, Saturday Game talent Stevie Weeks, in his hockey skates and with stick in hand traversing a frozen river. The introductory overhead shots of the immense and pristine snowy landscape, surrounded by rugged mountains and vast glaciers, establish the player as one with the terrain. As he skates the length of the river to a heroic soundtrack inflected by indigenous flutes and drums, he gives the viewer an intimate view of the sublime landscape. The poetic opener exceeds the training montage of the sports film, and succinctly conveys hockey as a successful adaptation to the frontier West's wild open spaces.[42] The idea of hockey as native to the landscape of snow and ice and as natural and instinctive to its inhabitants is consistent with the Nordicity myth, not with the culture of Alaska, where the practice of hockey is not common among indigenous peoples and the game is mostly played among university students and/or Lower 48 transplants from hockey states. The Alaskan setting in the film, however, activates the Westering myth and links the pond game[43] to the romance of open spaces that is emblematic of the American frontier's vastness and promise. Susan Kollin speaks to Alaska's role in the American imaginary in noting that it re-opens the frontier line that Frederick Jackson Turner had deemed closed in his 1890s lecture,[44] and in that role, guarantees the nation ongoing self-regeneration.[45] The introduction suggests, then, that as products of the West, Mystery's players appear to be a version of the leatherstocking archetype and their masculinity draws on Alaska's frontier symbolism by way of Native American imagery. Team captain John Beebe, one of the film's principals, exhorts his players to "hunt in corners!" and not to grant the Rangers too much respect because they "didn't pull a dogsled" or "skate the river." The handful of indigenous players on the team and the musical score that augments the hockey scenes equally authenticate the Alaskan character of the squad and validate players' tough disposition.

In good sports genre form, however, the narrative centers on white male dramas and relegates indigenous team members to merely picturesque status.[46] Indigenous players chiefly dramatize Hollywood's romanticization of Native Americans as embodying Nature's benign disposition and the ideal of humans blissfully inhabiting the wilderness.[47] The film imbues these characters with a pacifism characteristic of their representation in Hollywood film, which erases the grueling and oftentimes brutal quality of indigenous games prior to colonization. In a humorous scene, captain Beebe attempts only half-successfully to teach Tree Lane (Kevin Durand) to use his size in the upcoming contest with the Rangers. The project of indigenous peoples who play for play's sake also precludes their association with the business of sport, lending them an air of innocence that configures these characters as children with little or no voice. In retort to the Rangers' characterization of Tree Lane as a lumberjack, Attorney Bailey Pruitt (Maury Chaykin) provides an argument to the New York Court that is consonant with the romantic image of the native who is unencumbered by the accouterments of civilization, noting that he doesn't skate for the sake of a million-dollar salary but for sheer love of the game. In this scheme, Native Americans take on a sentimental, antimodern role that turns them into unchanging nostalgic symbols of the primordial landscape. Given their representation as primeval symbol of Nature, *Mystery, Alaska* also renders Native team members in a way that erases their specific cultures. Charlie Danner's *Sports Illustrated* article "The Roots of Hockey" describes the two Winetka brothers on the team as "forecheck[ing] like gophers," and indigenous protagonists on the whole function as minor characters assimilated into white settler culture. Although *Mystery, Alaska* puts forward a populist all-inclusive multicultural version of hockey, the pond game primarily serves to mediate the white males' relationships and dramas revealing Hollywood's discomfort with indigenous agency.

Of all the white male dramas in *Mystery, Alaska*, the most compelling is the conflict between Judge Burns and son Birdie for its congruity with the archetypal father-son feuding in 1950s westerns, which dramatizes the son's rebellion against the father's strict code. A former accomplished AA college player whose nickname "Little Bear" is symbolic of a tough defender approach to the game, Judge Burns represents an old traditional masculinity on and off the ice. His son, Birdie, a Saturday Game player who is content with his lot in life and does not harbor his father's professional aspirations, relishes the freeing quality of pond hockey, and excels at the scoring game. Judge Burns repeatedly reprimands Birdie for being a puck hog and not playing both sides of the ice, likening him to a figure skater. The Judge, brilliant and levelheaded, nevertheless emerges as an overly harsh and inflexible figure who employs stock feminization tactics to belittle his son's manhood. He embodies the precise opposite of the mythical father who roots for the son in the standard hockey movie. Birdie, for his part, astutely senses that despite multiple accomplishments, his father is trying to compensate for not making the lineup of the town's quintessential signifier of prestige, the Saturday Game. In the Judge's chambers, Birdie acknowledges to his father he is the source of his embarrassment and apologizes for not measuring up to his high benchmark of success, but he also makes clear that he sees through his insecurities.

As a nineties film, *Mystery, Alaska* clearly sides with the son in line with press and popular culture discourses about masculinity and fatherhood, which continually urged the aloof, career-driven father to go back home and revisit his parenting role. Stella Bruzzi notes that emerging representations of fatherhood at the time, shaped by demands for a gentler masculinity from the part of the women's movement of earlier decades, vigorously signaled the traditional father's discomfiture and maladjustment.[48] Despite his standing in the town, Judge Burns' maladjustment is evident as he frequently reprises opposite views from that of the townsfolk and adamantly refuses to have anything to do with the ill-advised Rangers-Mystery game. John Beebe repeatedly prods the judge to drop the harsh stance and coach the team: "You're in this town, Little Bear. You have to coach." The judge finally accedes, and although Mystery does not come out on top, the team wins the hearts of all those who witness their courageous attempt, preserving their dignity, as the judge had counseled at the outset. "Great game, son," Judge Burns says as he hugs Birdie post-game, and with this statement the film ratifies that the father has come home to the son. Unlike the protagonist of seventies films who cannot solve the gap between himself and the authoritarian father, in the nineties the father re-joins the son on the pond, ditching the self-destructive stance that had fashioned men as competent performers in the workplace to the detriment of their familial relationships.

Lending legitimacy to the new paradigm of masculinity, *Mystery, Alaska* also repudiates male chauvinism and characters' callous treatment of women. John Beebe admonishes Matt "Skank" Marden (Ron Eldard) for his offensive comments about resident Sarah Heinz's (Megyn Price) resemblance to a "wet walrus," noting that, "women don't like being referred to as fat mammals." In the context of a nineties masculinity in crisis, in which facing psychological blocks emerges as the arena for male heroism, *Mystery, Alaska* signals the need for active engagement with women in a more pliant, flexible way. Beebe, who reprises the role of the aging player who cannot transition to a life outside the game, neglects his relationship with wife Donna (Mary MacCormack), and in short order, must make amends and honor his partner's needs before the big game with the Rangers can ensue. The motif recurs in Mayor Pitcher's relationship with wife Mary Jane (Lolita Davidovich), who because of her husband's duties in overseeing the Saturday Game has been conducting an affair with Marden, a skilled player and womanizer who appropriately defines himself through two main agencies: playing hockey and fornicating. The main female characters in the movie, however, also play a limited discursive role as sexual partners and mothers, particularly as the town's identity is wrapped up in the Saturday Game and women are primarily spectators in this arrangement. The film also unsympathetically lampoons the lone female character with occupational status, SBC's female star anchor Janice Pettiboe (Beth Littleford), for her overbearing attitude as part of the New York-based media, and for succumbing to the wiles of Skank Marden post-game.

Male protagonists, on the other hand, express multiple agencies, the foremost being to secure a respectable rung in the town's male hierarchical ladder by landing a spot on the Saturday Game lineup. As occurs in the sports genre, characters' sense of allegiance depends on respect for male bonds as outlined by the sanctity of the locker room. The baseline prescription for male cohorts' punishment rests on the violation of these codes, as Beebe makes clear that, "What happens in this room, what's said in this room, stays in this room." A team member who divulges Marden's derisive comments about Ms. Heinz to his own girlfriend is punished by being forced to slide naked on open ice. Marden, for his part, also makes up for his transgression against the Mayor by taking a hit in the midsection at a crucial point in the Rangers game, articulating the role of pain and toughness in building character and making up for past misconduct. The primacy of male-male relationships alongside the men's complete investment in their hockey identity, which subsumes that of the entire town, is emblematic of the idealized role that nationalistic sport plays in encapsulating a traditional model of manhood in film and literature. In his work on Canadian hockey novels, Michael Buma discusses the hockey dressing room as a discrete space for enacting an "idealized male fraternity" both as reward for personal effort and resilience, and as respite from social duties to family, job and community demanded by the competitive pressures of life in a capitalist society.[49] Of all the films in this book, *Mystery, Alaska* dramatizes most vigorously this ideal masculinity enacted through symbolism of the mythic brotherhood. It does so both by sidelining women and other assumed weaklings, and by critiquing professional athletes for the excesses of the job in the competitive marketplace through the practice of physicality to win games and pervasive steroid use to achieve career success.

Because the film also validates the players' frontier authenticity, the East Coast media, who represent the institutional aspects of the opponent, appear far removed from this unsullied state as attested by their misuse of Native iconography. The NHL and SBC rush in to exploit the buzz created by Danner's *Sports Illustrated* article and look to the game as a publicity stunt and an opportunity for sky-high ratings. The big media machine that blows into town for the Rangers game does their utmost to turn the story about Mystery into a fairy tale and paint the team as a romantic source of hockey, but only manages to misrepresent Native life through disfiguring TV formulas. Pettiboe carelessly dubs the Mystery team "the Eskimos," describing them as mysterious snowmen with substandard dental health who skate "like the wind" on a nearby lake. Although Charlie Danner is a born and bred Mysterian, the film also contextualizes him as part of the media machine overrunning the town. With a knack for doing the awkward thing despite his local roots, Danner repeatedly attempts to woo high school crush Donna, now John Beebe's wife. He lures her with dreams of a normal life in the big city with standard amenities like a museum and urban-dwellers without incestuous tendencies. Judge Burn's teenage daughter Marla (Rachel Wilson) also alludes to Danner's outsider status when she remarks that his "homosexual" skating style prompted his exit from Mystery. The film configures Danner primarily through his intellectual and writing abilities and as sorely lacking in the frontier masculine traits required to survive the stark Alaskan environment, calling to mind the image of the effete Easterner in Beadle novels. His arrival by helicopter, a recurring motif in films about Alaska that speak to its despoilment,[50] nonetheless also stands for the impending advance of developmental forces. This advance is consistent with Turner's frontier thesis and his acknowledgment that the settlement of the West was inevitable, a theme that the film enacts by way of the Rangers' subsequent extraction of local talent.

Buttressing Kollin's observation that Alaska's symbolic importance as source of the nation's "regeneration and renewal is not merely psychological but also involves an economic dimension,"[51] large corporations also arrive in town prospecting for new business. Big box outlet Price World sends an envoy to lay the groundwork for another store.[52] Hockey ace and small grocer Connor Banks meets the challenge with suitable frontier hostility by wielding a gun against the corporate rep who threatens local jobs and small-town values. The gesture summarily calls up the American West story through the familiar motif of the small frontier settlement whose permanence is imperiled by the Eastern establishment. The big guy-little guy metaphor also plays out on the ice, and the film dualizes hockey into its professional and pond variants by dramatizing them as industrial output and liminal play, respectively. Writer Charles McGrath eloquently explains that in the pond game what matters is "the journey, not the end," as this form of hockey is "about whole stretches of time, sometimes speeded up," and recalled in a snowflake flurry against the backdrop of a crimson sky.[53] *Mystery, Alaska* suggests as much by way of the introductory sequence in which Stevie Weeks traverses the landscape in his hockey skates with stick in hand. Because the Disney film makes the case that pond hockey is the edifying source of the game rather than an inferior counterpart or extension of the NHL brand, the New York Rangers are suitable subjects of contempt as corrupt professionals, with Banks first to express disdain when watching a taped game with his teammates by suggesting fast-forwarding to the hockey portion. Weeks in like manner balks at the Rangers' physical brand of hockey and queries his teammates in dismay, "We're playing these guys?"

As expected, the Rangers game proves extremely punishing to Mystery's players, leaving in its wake injuries that necessitate stitching, a broken hand, and downcast, battered players whom the film depicts in dark hues practically disappearing into the cabin-like setting of the locker-room. The joy of liminal play is gone, and the team members must dig down for their last ounce of grit to avoid embarrassment. With the score 5–2 in favor of the Rangers, Judge Burns suggests a lineup that will help the squad sidestep further humiliation. But incensed, captain Beebe counters that they're not beaten and riles up his players bellowing that the surface out there is "still black ice and this is our pond." Revitalized, the team scores two consecutive goals. The remainder of the matchup procures another perspective of the doubled game, as Mystery's naturals engage the New York professionals. The film captures the contest from Mystery's perspective through overhead shots that amplify the game through its small-town, outdoors setting. The non-diegetic musical score, which consists of a flute motif accompanied by drums, also speaks to the organic, indigenous hues of the game in its natural western frontier environment. The structured, bruising, and highly competitive game, and the announcer broadcast style, on the other hand, are more in line with the action of NHL arenas.

The game's denouement is suitably tension-filled as the outnumbered Mysterians have a chance to tie the game. The long sequence, consisting of no less than thirty-one edits and marked by intensifying indigenous drums, begins with Beebe holding the puck behind his own net and passing it to Stevie Weeks who takes it up the ice. The tick-tack-toe plays that follow find Connor Banks in position, and as the announcer voiceover fades and the indigenous music, now blended with a conspicuous western motif, takes over accompanied by slow motion effects. As Connor takes the loud echoing shot accentuated by the sharp note of a flute and the puck travels the length of the ice, it hits the post with a clang. The final visual shows that the Rangers goalie would have not stopped the puck had he wanted to, and that the play fell short by a mere inch. But the Mysterians are deflated, and Banks and Beebe appear stunned as the pain begins to show on the faces of their teammates and the crowd. As the players hug one another and take a modest glide toward the bench, a mournful score washes over the scene. The above sequence is significant because both players and townsfolk readily interpret the loss as a failure to substantiate the superiority of the pond game, the "pure" version of hockey unsullied by commodification, over the professional game. Because the idea of hockey as masculine preserve links to American identity discourse through the Westering myth, which is, in turn, encoded in Hollywood triumph-over-obstacles plotlines, the scene comes off as dissonant and less than satisfying. Indeed, Mystery's loss emerges more in line with Anglo-Canadian cinematic conventions that put forth the notion of truncated dreams as de facto realism.

The ending edits attenuate the loss by inserting a homage sequence to the brave team with its shortened, bruised bench. Judge Burns breaks the mournful interlude and heartily applauds his squad's efforts, and the Rangers join the community in celebrating the courageous players by slapping their sticks on the ice. As both lineups shake hands, an extreme wide shot, which resembles that of a TV broadcast and disrupts the idea of a small-town frontier game, comes into view. The shot reframes the game as akin to the one played in large metropolitan arenas, positioning the two lineups as equals. The community's roar in salute of its team, which resembles that of the crowds in NHL arenas, procures a similar effect. In between, shots offer a close-up of frayed relationships that are healed by the team's lion-hearted try. With the Rangers off the ice, the Mystery players salute the town residents perched on the rustic stands as they file out, revisiting the original framing of hockey in a small town. Through this interpellation of shots, the final sequence attempts to convey that Mystery has played a game that is larger than life, and that frontier ice has held up its part of the bargain vis-à-vis artificial ice as legitimate source of the game.

This homage notwithstanding, the Disney film must also negotiate the dilemma of circumventing the genre's archetypal ending, which melodramatically stages the underdog beating the odds and activates the Westering myth's unlimited prospects through the symbolism of Alaska. Since the final moments of the game do not yield Mystery the expected windfall, the film must produce success in different form. The bonanza arrives by way of recruitment, as the Rangers draft Mystery's best players. The contest thus ultimately facilitates the extraction of local talent, as players readily accede to contracts with New York's AHL Binghamton farm team and the town revels in the recruitment effort as validation of their game. The film contextualizes local player extraction in line with the ideology of sports success: as an opportunity for small-town, skilled players to go pro in the big leagues. Because the story activates Alaska's role as an agent of national revitalization, by extension, Mysterians' creative, freeing, open-space play, is also meant to reinvigorate the NHL game. This exchange then justifies the Rangers' act of plucking a community's top talent as an auspicious and revitalizing infusion of new blood, much like the function Alaska performs in the U.S. imaginary as agent of psychological and economic regeneration.

But as Mystery receives validation for producing players the league wants, reprising the pride of the small town after a local player is posted to the majors, the film makes short shrift of the community's independent frontier spirit faithful to its own brand of hockey, contravening the very reason why Mysterians play the game, one whose rhythms and bearings fundamentally hew to the cadences of Nature. Allusions to professional hockey's distortions, such as steroid use and the excessive use of physicality, and visual and aural references to the contest through the archetypal story of the frontier settlement that must withstand the pressures of metropolitan (institutional) forces, therefore also ultimately give way to the boon of having Mystery's top liners absorbed into the big leagues. The denouement effectively downplays the idea of the naturals staking a claim on hockey as an independent, autochthonous cultural practice by asserting that community-based hockey ultimately necessitates the involvement of large corporations for its legitimization.

The finale resonates with the corporate-led restructuring of sport and leisure begun in the 1990s, which led to the devastation of regional cultures throughout North America as brands from wealthier urban and suburban areas siphoned off interest from smaller regional and independent outlets by playing up their status as national or major-league outlets.[54] The Disney Company was a central player in this transformation through its acquisition of a new NHL franchise, the Mighty Ducks of Anaheim, which further leveraged the media giant's status as global entertainment conglomerate. Whatever the intent of the writers in fielding the narrative, by advancing the commodification of small-town hockey, the film synergizes Disney's NHL interests with the Company's long-time links to the Westering myth and American nationalism,[55] anchoring American hockey to frontier symbolism through the narrative of unlimited social and economic prospects. In enabling the players' dreams of social mobility through the aegis of large corporations and naturalizing the renewal of the professional game in the frontier, *Mystery, Alaska* also segues from its romance of the pond game into a virtual endorsement of hockey's transformation into upmarket spectacle.

The Disillusioned Protagonist: *No Sleep 'til Madison* and *Slap Shot 2: Breaking the Ice*

The onset of globalization in the 1990s enabled the adoption of the American standard for corporate sports entertainment around the world: a glitzy spectacle, populated by superstar athletes whose larger-than-life performances made good television and attracted hefty sponsorship monies.[56] Media companies' search for a larger consumer base by transforming hockey into an upmarket consumer spectacle, however, also alienated traditional constituencies who held on to the game's association with robust masculinity and community. The U.S. release *No Sleep 'til Madison*[57] (Fleer, Moe, and Rudy, 2002) critiques hockey's extraction from its regional roots in the Upper Midwest and speaks to fans' disillusionment with professional athletes and the commodified sports product. Inspired by the filmmakers' Wisconsin high school hockey experiences, the indie feature centers on the annual pilgrimage that thirty-year-old Owen Fenby (Jim Gaffigan) and his former hockey teammates take to the Wisconsin State High School Hockey "Big Ice" Tournament in their "quest into the true essence of sport." Against the wishes of his girlfriend, Owen arranges the trip for the twelfth year in a row, refurbishing an old laundry truck and setting off on a journey that takes the group through the Wisconsin high school hockey landscape with a few side stops. After a series of mishaps, the travelers begin to drop out one by one because of job or family commitments. Those who are left question the reason for the trip and pin it on Owen's refusal to move on. "At some point we all have to grow up," as one of them notes. But Owen remains unconvinced. He continues the trip on his own and ends up stranded in the middle of nowhere. A large black truck tailing the group throughout the journey arrives on the scene and the figure of a man in an old-timer hockey uniform emerges from it. It is Dave Dellenbach Dinger (Alex Swiggum) who, still in his hockey gear, menacingly walks toward Owen and screams that he stole his truck. This vision is a mirage, as the figure confronting him is really the owner of the laundry truck that Owen had taken over and refurbished for the trip. Delusional, he is taken to the hospital where his former teammates reunite around him. They vote on continuing on and heading for the championship at the Big Ice in Madison. Owen, however, has a change of heart and ends the trip by going back to his girlfriend.

No Sleep 'til Madison makes the case for a return to the communal roots of hockey. Behind the obvious nostalgia for the long-gone, carefree days of youth—"[it's] what we experienced," as Owen feelingly remarks—is a longing for the classic interaction of fans with players that lies at the root of communal team sports. The glitzy corporatized spectacle and the commodification of athletes as transnational superstars exacerbate the fan's alienation from leisure activities that lack the true spirit of community sport, and not unexpectedly, *No Sleep 'til Madison* extends a scathing critique of professional sport. Greg Palawski (T.J. Jagodowski), Owen's high school teammate, performs the honors as he explains the reasons for the journey: "I'm sick to hell of professional sport, a whole bunch of overpaid prima donnas, don't care where they play, what jersey they wear, because they're all in it for themselves." Palawski expresses fan disenchantment with the claims of corporate sports entities that tout the glamour of global market citizenship and promote the fielding of world-class teams for the purported benefit of regional economies. Giving voice to growing fan cynicism in the face of corporate sponsorship of professional sport, Palawski and his teammates advocate for a return to sport's local referents because of young players' authentic ties to the communities where they play.

Embedded in the landscape of ice and snow, Wisconsin high school hockey registers as small-town yet high caliber, conveyed in the filmmakers' creation of the Wisconsin High School Hall of Fame, which enshrines the status of high school hockey in the state and the characters must visit on their sojourn. Owen's mirage of Dave Dellenbach Dinger also encapsulates his longing for old-time hockey in alluding to the game's traditional ties to small towns. The producers dress one of the Wisconsin high school teams in Team USA colors to suggest that, despite the popularity of the corporatized sports spectacle, the idea of sport as organic expression of the community lies at the root of the country's sporting values. Popular perceptions of Wisconsin as America's bucolic Dairyland also reinforce the authenticity of hockey's small-town roots. As he ends his statement about the state of the game, Greg Palawski exclaims, "Here's what I want: something pure and untainted. Get me to the Wisconsin State high school hockey tournament!"

Despite the group's search for the unsullied hockey experience, Owen's fit with the culture of high school hockey comes across as uneasy. In a scene where he sets out to videotape the ongoing contest from the stands, the parents in attendance suspect him of less than virtuous motives and force him to leave the building. Owen's subsequent humorous stranding in a Wisconsin field where he suffers extreme cold and hunger plays out as a metaphor for the sense of abandonment and loss experienced by the fan who, having tasted the genuine feeling of rootedness in community through youth involvement in athletics, has nowhere to turn in the face of the growing transnationalization of sport. The road movie structure of the story also points to this motif by way of its preoccupation with masculinity. Stuart Aitken and Christopher Lukinbeal note that the road movie dramatizes the unhinging of masculinity from its traditional role by giving expression to men's desire to break free from mainstream societal and sexual roles represented by marriage, family, and breadwinning.[58] Wendy Everett discusses the road movie in similar terms arguing that the genre represents "the concept of America as locus of escape and new beginnings" as well as its relationship to masculinity by way of four elements: the road, which mirrors the failure of the family unit; the protagonist, who is typically a male engaging in an escapist fantasy from the responsibilities of domesticity; the vehicle, an object of close identification by the male protagonist; and the events encountered in the journey.[59]

In *No Sleep 'til Madison*, these elements illustrate that a deep nostalgia for youth hockey cannot make up for the estrangement suffered by the fan who is unable to find in corporate entertainment the genuine connection experienced in communal sports. The sense of freedom from domesticity and social responsibilities that the annual hockey pilgrimage affords Owen and his friends concludes ironically as one by one the participants drop out to attend to those very responsibilities they sought to elude. The truck that Owen refurbishes is also significant in that, far from the freeing transport usually depicted in the road film as key symbol of male identity, it turns out to be a laundry truck, a vehicle ill-suited to a road trip because of its alignment with routine responsibilities and female domesticity. The van is also stolen, implying that the protagonist has misappropriated a feminizing identity incompatible with the quasi-religious masculine ritual of the sports pilgrimage. It is no surprise, then, that Owen's vision of Dave Dellenbach Dinger, which dramatizes his longing for traditional hockey, is also a fleeting mirage. The repossession of the truck by its rightful owner seals Owen's disassembling of his high school sporting masculinity and his re-absorption into the social order of mundane domesticity, as he gives up his quest and goes back to his girlfriend.

As the truncated outcome shows, *No Sleep 'til Madison* provides no solution to the loss of communal sport and its integrative role in the lives of adults short of that offered by their offspring's involvement in athletics. Indeed, the film asserts that for adult males without children, nostalgia for days gone by is insufficient in assuaging the sense of isolation felt by fans who cannot recapture the experience of sport honed in small, close-knit communities. Although devoid of solutions to heal the sport fan's alienation, Palawski's indictment of corporations' oversight of organized sport serves as a vigorous form of protest against the restructuring of athletics and leisure that decimated regional sports cultures throughout North America in the 1990s. Disney's *Mystery, Alaska* dramatizes a similar motif but also hedges its potential critique by rationalizing the absorption of small-town players into the NHL farm system as much-coveted social mobility and a matter of pride for the town. *No Sleep 'til Madison*, however, does no such thing, leading the charge to indict corporate sport for annihilating regional sports and leaving fans with nowhere to turn.

Slap Shot 2: Breaking the Ice (Boyum, 2001) reiterates the critique of entertainment combines' takeover of hockey and the marginalization of traditional constituencies. Produced twenty-five years after the original *Slap Shot*, the B.C.-filmed sequel dramatizes screenwriter Broderick Miller's retort to media corporations' absorption of important sports properties. Miller wrote the script in response to Fox's introduction of its controversial FoxTrax glowing puck during its mid-to-late 1990s NHL broadcasts to expand hockey's appeal in the U.S.[60] His cautionary tale about losing the soul of the game takes up where *Slap Shot*'s critique of the role of vested interests in the sport leaves off. In *Slap Shot 2*, former NHL star prospect Sean Linden (Stephen Baldwin) reprises the role of Chiefs player-coach. English owner Matt Fox (David Hemmings) dumps the team on media mogul Richmond Claremont (Gary Busey) who is intent on fashioning a new league to garner higher ratings for his family-oriented media empire, with wealthy conservative Better America Coalition as sponsor. As part of the transfer deal, Linden, who is besieged by charges of public sex, drunken-driving infractions, and gambling allegations, is told that league owners consider his past problematic, and he is demoted in favor of a new female coach, Jesse Dage (Jessica Steen), who is also the granddaughter of a hockey legend. But the Chiefs, now the Super-Chiefs, soon find they will be playing to lose as villains in a scripted contest branded "Paradise on Ice" against the all-American New Omaha Ice-Breakers.

The bait for the players is the exposure: hockey on real TV with real money. The catch is that in this tightly choreographed league there will be no fighting, no cursing, and no bloodletting, as the show's gay director imported from Broadway tells the team. Players will rehearse, not practice; perform, not play. Claremont's right hand man expeditiously moves to dismiss the Hanson Brothers because they are not suitably telegenic, and before long, the Chiefs are incessantly upended and manhandled by the Ice Breakers in a circus-like performance. When Linden breaks into Claremont's office accusing that he is making a travesty of the game, Claremont offers to double players' salaries. Discontent among the ranks continues unabated, however, led by star player Gordie Miller (David Paetkau), who is bent on sabotaging Claremont's grand design. Linden, who continues to be hounded by credit companies for defaulting on his bills, is offered a clean slate in return for ditching the hostile stance. Claremont cajoles him into making effective use of his role as captain and re-direct his teammates' restlessness.

Sean Linden (Stephen Baldwin, right) faces off in *Slap Shot 2: Breaking the Ice* (Universal Studios Home Entertainment/Photofest).

His back against the wall, Linden accedes and prevails on his players to comply with ownership's desires and go along with the media "hype, publicity, advertisement, [and] big-time endorsements," as he notes. Following Claremont's plan, Linden furtively walks off the team only to return shortly after with the Hanson Brothers as new owners. In the locker room he gives teammates the signal to reclaim their old identity stressing that, "Claremont is trying to take away ... who we are: hockey players." As the squad takes the ice in their Chiefs jerseys, they proceed to hit their opponents to the chagrin of sponsors, and Linden scores to redeem himself and end the sell-out of "old-time hockey."

Claremont's transformation of hockey in *Slap Shot 2* conveys the corporate takeover of the professional game as tantamount to hockey's very corruption. Former L.A. Kings coach-turned-commentator Barry Melrose, playing himself, supports players' perspectives by denouncing the new league as "a bunch of crap" and protesting that professional hockey has worked for over two decades to attain legitimacy and overturn popular perception of hockey players as buffoons. NHL defenseman Chris Chelios, a familiar presence on the Team USA roster, backs Melrose's claim. When Linden accuses Claremont of debasing the game, the mogul calmly replies: "I don't respect your little game. I respect money and television ratings and this league brings a lot more of both." In the lopsided world of Better America and Claremont Media, the tightly scripted spectacle sanitizes the game by rigging the contest in favor of the squeaky-clean Ice Breakers who continually upend and batter the Super-Chiefs in a closely choreographed performance of dirty tricks.

The gritty game with which the film unfolds serves as contrast to the gimmicky travesty that Claremont Media sells as hockey. By way of half a dozen low camera shots that emphasize the opponents' skillful puck-handling, the opening scene makes clear that the Chiefs are outmatched. The opponents, who are dressed in Philadelphia Flyer colors, are not merely skilled but proceed to go at the Chiefs, smashing them against the glass, banging them against the boards, and upending them at every turn, while Linden hollers to his players from the bench to counter with hard hits. The sequence makes clear the Chiefs are not only out-classed, but unprepared for the spectacle that awaits them, as they mistake Claremont's man in the stands for a bona fide scout. As opposed to the opening set-up, the "Paradise on Ice" show unfolds with the Ice Breakers taking the ice in orderly single file. A top-down shot reveals their choreographed progress as resembling an Ice Capades number. The so-called contest is little more than an exhibition of the Ice Breakers' superiority as the Super-Chiefs slide under the opponents' legs, and find themselves on the receiving end of digs and thumps for their effort. Players also cue one another before trips and dives as the undiscerning fans cheer. The canned, nonsensical performance is meant to dodge the game's unpalatable aspects, but by placing the Super-Chiefs in an emasculating position the spectacle dramatizes the very debasement of the game. Shots of Claremont and his corporate partners socializing in high form in one of the arena suites and commenting approvingly on the proceedings make clear that the disfiguration of hockey by sanitized family-friendly entertainment is proceeding apace.

The Super-Chiefs' chagrin at their participation in an act that ensures the Ice Breakers remain "fresh, healthy and unmarked," as the Paradise on Ice Broadway director notes, is obvious and their humiliation is complete as Ice Breakers captain Skipper Day (Jonathan Scarfe) derisively apprises star player Miller that the Chiefs' loser status in the league made them ripe for the taking and expedited their transformation into a laughingstock. But the former Eastern bloc players who are part of the roster and whom the film conceptualizes as having trouble understanding the modern (i.e., Western) world—"What does mean by transvestite?" as one of them asks—quickly grasp Claremont's idea behind the new league and remark, "Hey, look, we are going to look like communist clowns again." They reassure Linden, "Don't worry coach, it's show biz!" The premise that players from socialist countries can best grasp the Super-Chiefs quandary because they are used to the dictates of an autocratic entity reiterates the notion that the game has been stolen and transformed from true sport into a circus act.

To convey Linden's need to get back to hockey's roots, memories of his boyhood spent on the pond flash before him as he watches a televised game at a bar. The memory helps him reassess his earlier stance: "You still get to play hockey every day and you still get paid to do it." Disgusted at his team's status as stooges, Linden returns to the locker room with Chiefs jerseys in tow and forcefully tells his charges that this is who they are. Old-time hockey officially retakes center stage as the Hansons make their entry in a cloud of smoke and under a golden spotlight that communicates that they are the real stars of the game. One of the brothers assumes his position for the face-off against the Ice Breakers captain and the players stare at each other as a prelude to the showdown. But as the whistle blows, instead of making off with the puck, the helmet-less, feral Hanson punches his opponent without much ado, catching him completely off-guard, and humorously showing off his trademark signature as "heart and soul" of the game.

Slap Shot 2 rehearses numerous motifs of the original installment: the player-coach with a shady past and willing to resort to gamesmanship to keep his team in business, the talented sportsman who balks at game's disfigurement, greedy managers and owners who see hockey as a tool for attaining wealth and status, the long-suffering team who has no real grasp of the behind-the-scenes manipulation, and the colorful announcer who strives to keep abreast of the on-ice shenanigans. Although the Hansons are the one constant, in *Slap Shot* their chaotic play registers as a satirical statement about seventies hockey violence, a Daemon-like expression that Reggie Dunlop harnesses to counteract the Machiavellian strategizing of management and ownership. Because the second installment disparages the valorization of hockey as family entertainment, the film elevates the Hansons' role to the status of exemplars who embody the hard-man's approach to the game. Their collective untamed signature remains, but they are now held up as symbols of hockey's roots and virile archetypes untainted by transnational corporate agendas.

Slap Shot 2's call to enact a reinvigorated masculinity illustrates Michael Kimmel's argument that globalization has engendered forceful male opposition to outside forms of control.[61] Resistance to these kinds of dynamics through cultural expressions such as rugged hockey is not unexpected as sport conflict can be a proxy for social conflict, and populism can block the schemes of power blocs by way of carnivalesque formats, as the Hansons aptly convey. In the nineties, hockey's upmarketization alienated traditional demographics by downgrading the sport's sweat and blood markers and served notice that strategic power now lay firmly ensconced in the hands of managers and executives.[62] Corporations also boosted the cachet of their brands by appropriating the physique of elite athletes, appending them to the purchase of corporate boxes to market these setups as the ideal environment for conducting business, networking and entertaining, quite distant from the brawls and unruly crowd behavior of the seventies and eighties game. The Chiefs' transformation into Super-Chiefs thus dramatizes the enfeeblement of athletes as expendable workers of the entertainment economy likely to be benched on short notice as victims of corporate downsizing or simply as a result of the corporation's need to reinvent its products and image. *Slap Shot 2*'s mechanical use of its predecessor's misogynist and homophobic imagery, which the film passes off as male camaraderie, also registers as a by-product of the enfeeblement of traditional sports masculinity. Kimmel notes that disenfranchised males respond to emasculation by "problematizing the masculinity of ... various 'others'" through homophobia and sexism to redeem their virility.[63] Although unpalatable, crass misogynist and homophobic remarks convey players' projection of their own disenfranchisement onto vulnerable referent out-groups, particularly in the face of eroding traditional male spaces in the workplace.[64]

Slap Shot 2's *deus ex machina* ending, which reprises the theme of the Hansons rescuing old-time hockey by winning the lottery, also offers no solutions to corporate control of sport short of individual ownership of teams by former athletes, resembling media coverage of Mario Lemieux (Pittsburgh Penguins) and Wayne Gretzky (Phoenix Coyotes) during 2004–2005 NHL lockout negotiations as intercessory in saving the season.[65] Whatever their actual roles, this simplistic response reiterates social actors' inability to redress the problems resulting from corporate inroads into sport. As Gruneau and Whitson observe, despite the range of reactions, they do not constitute "sustained resistance to current tendencies in the political economy of major league sports."[66] Despite vigorous protest about the game's forced unhinging from working-class male identities, then, *Slap Shot 2*, like *No Sleep 'til Madison*, ultimately unfurls as a tale of disillusionment about the game's disfigurement by entertainment combines.

The above films show that many of the issues in the business of hockey that reared their collective head decades earlier are still in contention and have turned more complex with globalization. Corporations' courting of the upmarket consumer and family entertainment's focus on bland subjects have downgraded hockey's pleasures of physical excess, tampering with sport's connection to robust masculinity and isolating traditional demographics.[67] The solutions offered by these films with good reason appear tenuous, pointing to the melodramatic mode's airing of cultural debates and anxieties only to put them back in the box, and indicating that concerns may have to be continually fought and negotiated as economic conditions change and leverage accrues differentially to one side of the stakeholder divide. Nonetheless, these motion pictures play out as valuable registers for the evolving business of hockey and as reactions to the game's transformation into upmarket transnational consumer product from various sides of the stakeholder divide.

4

Hockey and Family Entertainment

In the sixties and seventies hockey did not figure much in family films, since the game was synonymous with violence and its ferocious edges were everywhere, spilling into amateur development programs and spurring concern for its impact on children and youth. The cinema of the period focused on derisive portrayals of athletes in setups featuring nudity, sexual situations, and coarse language,[1] all of which were unsuitable for children. The antiheroic treatment of characters, which disrupted the myth of success in sport, also mirrored the profound questioning of core cultural myths at this time. The period's social tumult deeply impacted the family structure, with half of the children born in the seventies witnessing the breakup of their parents by the time they graduated from high school.[2] The cynicism of the era and the disruption of public myths were inimical to the values of the family film, a genre, which from its inception operated as a pedagogical instrument that reaffirmed conservative ideals and bolstered the integrity of the familial unit.[3]

Consistent with the social upheaval of the era, seventies hockey-themed films feature a plethora of fractured families as well as protagonists who express defiance of social expectations that are in line with the values of Middle America. Nick Peterson in *Ice Castles* epitomizes youth's resistance to marriage and children when he tells girlfriend Lexie (Lynn-Holly Johnson) that while he is aware that he is meant to attend college, get married, and have kids, "I see where it's going and I don't like it, but that doesn't mean I don't love you." These films also disrupt the father-son bond in sport by fashioning fathers as autocratic figures who enforce traditional social norms. As noted, in *Love Story*, Oliver is pressured by his father to cast aside his interest in hockey and focus on Law School only to create distance between them. *Slap Shot*, for its part, satirizes hockey's fraying of the father-son bond when Ned notes that he's still playing hockey because he hates his father. These films downgrade the father-son connection by formulating hockey as site of rebellion against patriarchal authority because of its working-class innuendos. In bucking the demands of the 1950s authoritarian father, hockey reaffirms the anti-establishment stance of seventies film, as adults, no longer invested in middle-class values prioritize self-interest.[4]

In the 1980s, with moral anxieties about the values of the youth culture mounting, media entreated Hollywood to produce more acceptable G-rated movies that embrace the values behind family fare.[5] Eighties films thus retrieve sport to heal cultural rifts[6] and reaffirm the importance of the father who raises children as a form of social capital to bolster the project of citizenry and nationhood. If seventies hockey protagonists are reluctant to become fathers, and films recurrently establish traditional fathers as unrelentingly autocratic, distant, or absent, in the eighties the father returns to reprise his role as glue for familial relationships. In *Youngblood*, Dean's dad Blane overcomes the father's emotional inarticulacy and helps the rookie through his rite of passage to enable his vanquishing of villain-enforcer Racki. In *Touch and Go* (Mandel, 1986), Chicago hockey star Bobby Barbato (Michael Keaton) conquers his restlessness and settles down with single Latina mom Denise DeLeon (María Conchita Alonso) to serve as surrogate father for 11-year-old Louis (Ajay Naidu). Although these films feature the father-son bond and dramatize the American man coming home after the turmoil of the sixties and seventies, they are not family films proper but sports films accented by family motifs as they accentuate the adult male athletic body.[7]

The TV movie *The Boy Who Drank Too Much* (Freedman, 1980) comes closer to the conservative family genre in showcasing the family unit as a safe haven in which children are honed into social capital for the community. The film features two father-son pairings: middle class Gus Campbell (Ed Lauter) and son Billy (Lance Kerwin), and working-class hockey talents Ken Saunders (Don Murray) and son Buff (Scot Baio). Billy is the star of the film, a Boston Bruins fan whose idol is multiple Byng Trophy winner Jean Ratelle and a member of his Spartans high school hockey team. Since he has yet to see any ice time, he performs his model teammate role by standing by the team's hockey whiz, Buff, as the teen struggles with alcoholism and memories of his absent mother. While Buzz's dad, Ken, a former professional player who tends bar at night, senselessly complains that raising a good kid is backbreaking

Billy Campbell (Lance Kerwin, right) with Eagles teammate Buff Sanders (Scot Baio) in *The Boy Who Drank Too Much* (CBS/Photofest).

and he can do without his son's alcoholic tendencies, Gus is a hands-on father who establishes solid parameters for his son's future success by entreating him to prioritize his studies over his hockey interests. As a movie steeped in gritty seventies realism, *The Boy Who Drank Too Much* promotes the intact (and morally superior) middle-class family as a salve for the social disintegration of urban culture, a formula that also entails taking hockey out of the equation because of its working-class hues. Despite its moral tale signature, the TV movie has visually and thematically more in common with its seventies counterparts. The opening—a wide pan of a rink unmarred by advertising with Billy practicing shots on net—also marks this film as quite unlike the spectacle-driven mass entertainment vehicle popularized in the subsequent decade.

Disney's Vision of Hockey: *The Mighty Ducks*; *D2: The Mighty Ducks*; *D3: The Mighty Ducks*; *H-E-Double Hockey Sticks* and *Den Brother*

The popular new family entertainment genre of the 1990s, which features numerous children and teens in the role of hockey protagonists, arrived on the scene thanks in part to the restructuring of Hollywood movie studios into global entertainment combines. Disney's entry into the NHL, which inaugurated the era of family-friendly corporate entertainment in professional hockey, also helped re-brand the sport as an upscale consumer product and acceptable film fare for the whole family. In no small measure the surprise trade of Edmonton Oilers' star Wayne Gretzky in 1988 by owner Peter Pocklington to Bruce McNall's Los Angeles Kings contributed to Disney's NHL foray by creating an immense amount of promotional cachet for elite-level hockey. Gretzky gave hockey greater credibility and exposure, mitigating the game's reputation as scheduled mayhem and heightening the interest of Madison Avenue.[8] His presence in California popularized the game across southern tier states, creating a window for further NHL expansion and facilitating Disney's entry into the league to transform the game into an upmarket consumer sport. Talks between Disney and the NHL began early in 1992 culminating in a joint announcement in December of the same year that the Company would ice an expansion team in Southern California bearing the name of The Mighty Ducks of Anaheim at the start of the 1993–1994 season, two months after the *Mighty Ducks* feature premiere. Commissioner Gary Bettman noted that Disney had passed over other sports and determined that "hockey is where they want to be," underlining the high standing of the sport among key players in the entertainment industry.[9] As the Ducks took the ice on October 8, 1993, Eisner remarked tongue-in-cheek that the film had served as market research for the hockey franchise.[10]

For the league, Disney's entry provided a much-needed shot in the arm. U.S. national TV hockey ratings averaged 440,000 homes for the season, approximately fifty percent of the cable audience of professional wrestling.[11] A number of teams like the Washington Capitals, Edmonton Oilers and New York Islanders had also turned into money-losing schemes. Disney offered the ultimate potential for marketing and cross-promotion and the cachet of a quintessential American company with a global reach. NHL senior vice president and chief operating officer Steve Solomon noted as much, detailing that Disney's presence over multiple

Left to right: Disney CEO Michael Eisner along with NHL commissioner Gary Bettman, NHL chairman Bruce McNall, and Mighty Ducks chairman Jack Lindquist blow duck calls during a press conference announcing the name of Disney's newly-minted team, The Mighty Ducks of Anaheim. March 1, 1993 (AP/Douglas Pizac).

media platforms comprised "an integral element in creating broader awareness for the sport and growing our television fan base."[12]

For Disney, the $50 million admission ticket into elite professional hockey also made sense since the new concept of family entertainment incorporated sports events and theme parks into the consumer experience. Noel Brown notes that Disney's early positioning as children's brand and extensive experience in producing family fare enabled it to exploit the resurgent global family entertainment market.[13] The Company was also cognizant that seventy-five percent of visitors to its Disneyland venue were adults,[14] which allowed it to tap this demographic to promote live hockey events.

Although the L.A. area at the time boasted the premier name in hockey in Wayne Gretzky, in Anaheim Disney had the opportunity to introduce the sport to a new market of would-be fans and, in the process, emboss it with its own brand. The pre-game display, for example, featured the team's Donald Duck–like mascot, Wild Wing, descending from the rafters and a video clip of the team's marquee players in larger-than-life dimensions skating through the Disneyland Park to arrive at the arena, the Anaheim Pond. Goals, stoppages of play, and miscellaneous game interludes were punctuated on the jumbotron with brief clips of Disney cartoons and movies featuring beloved Disney characters. Innumerable sideshows in the aisles also ensured that fans were being duly entertained at all times. The effect, as Jeremy Michael Ward aptly remarks, was "of sensory overload similar to the experience one would receive at Disney World or Disneyland."[15] The strategy was doubtlessly geared to make families comfortable with professional hockey by furnishing a familiar setup that reminded spectators of the "Disney experience," one in which objectionable incidents were properly effaced or obscured. In the process, the Company also tapped the large, ready-made fan base that routinely patronized its parks and bought is products.[16]

The film that opened the door, *The Mighty Ducks*, for its part, became a resounding box office success, grossing a robust $51 million in domestic receipts with millions more in video and overseas sales as well as merchandise tie-ins.[17] The first sequel, *D2: The Mighty Ducks*, also debuted in first place in its weekend March release, posting over $45 million in domestic gate receipts as it coincided with the start of the 1994 NHL season, while *D3: The Mighty Ducks* garnered almost $23 million domestically.[18]

Disney focused on delivering hockey as a consummate upmarket spectacle by merging not only its NHL team with its movies, but by subsuming the game itself into its brand in a distinct blend of the virtual and the real.[19] In short order, the company reshaped hockey on screen and off, revisioning most Americans' ideas of the sport as depicted in *Slap Shot*—"a game played by brawling apes with missing front teeth for the appreciation of blue-collar beer drinkers," as *Seattle Post-Intelligencer* national sports correspondent Bill Knight noted at the time.[20] As it set out to commodify and enhance its appeal, Disney transformed the media image of hockey in the United States from a regional or "niche" blue-collar game to trendy consumer sport. With its partnership with Disney consummated, the league proclaimed that "hockey had finally arrived" as one of America's "Big Four" national sports.[21]

In Canada, reaction to Disney's entry into the NHL engendered wide discontent fueled by CEO Michael Eisner's Hollywood background and his lack of credibility as a "hockey man." Eisner had also lobbied the league to implement changes in the game—from the shape

NHL commissioner Gary Bettman sneaks a look at an oversized puck held by Goofy, and embossed with the name of The Mighty Ducks of Anaheim, as Disney chairman Michael Eisner (left) speaks to the press. March 1, 1993 (AP Photo/Douglas Pizac).

of the helmets to the inclusion of a soccer-style shootout to decide tied games.[22] The moniker "Ducks," which corroborated the Company's association with docile animality and childhood innocence, also offended hockey connoisseurs and turned it into a target of derision, not only because it branded an NHL squad as an adjunct of a Hollywood film, but because the name ran counter to the robust image that sports teams seek to project.

Hockey in Disney's cartoon classics, after all, had been consistent with fans' vision of the game as a rough sport singularly patronized by males. In *The Hockey Champ*[23] (King, 1939), for example, speedster Donald Duck loses himself in the open spaces of the pond like a girlish figure skater, when he is casually interrupted by toque-wearing nephews Huey, Louie, and Dewey, who are bent on carving out ice time for a little pond hockey. As the young ducklings take their first faceoff, they feverishly hack at each other vying for the puck to the amusement of uncle Donald who mocks their haphazard technique. To show the youngsters the genuine article, he puts on dazzling scoring demonstration that deploys his profuse artistic talents, validating his moniker as Champ of the Swamp. However, once the brood gets a hold of the puck through a sleight of hand, the game devolves into a free-for-all that takes the players all over the ice and through the snow. The ducklings have the last say when one of them lands Donald inside the net thoroughly tangled. The piece parodies the skilled player's show of wizardry, serving notice that in short order he too will take to the rough-and-tumble tactics that he snobbishly derides. *Hockey Homicide*[24] (Kinney, 1945), for its part, features a game between the Pelicans and the Aardvarks populated by innumerable replicas of Disney staple Goofy, and takes the rough-and-tumble edges of hockey up a notch by putting forward starring players who see no ice time because they spend the game in the penalty box, spectators who contribute to the mayhem by tackling each other in the stands, and fans who cap off the proceedings by spilling onto the ice and enthusiastically taking on players in a game-ending melee. The piece features brawls from start to finish lampooning hockey through its unruly, robust edges. Both animation pieces also satirize the fierce competitiveness of the participants in a way that radically diverges from the upmarket family entertainment fare that the Company would prop up in the 1990s.

Brawling in hockey grew ill-suited to Disney's family fare because these films' address mode prioritize the child and the child within the adult, the so-called kidult. Although cartoons could easily disguise hockey violence with humor, the realism that informs depictions of athletic contests and culture in feature films was less likely to do so. Moreover, studios had renewed interest in the family film because of new genre parameters that sanitized violence. Brown explains that, in order to extract the compounded earnings from economies of scale, the new family film had to appeal to the largest audience possible by keeping to a minimum potentially offensive subject matter like violence, nudity, and objectionable language. Producers also pumped up the emotional aspect of film by way of the visual and aural spectacle, and expanded the social makeup of its cast of characters in a way that mirrored the tastes of the increasingly multicultural publics these films sought to reach.[25] Sparkling spectacle, easy-to-grasp subject matter, highly emotional content, and an enlarged multicultural context enabled the premier marketability of family entertainment. Disney deployed these conventions to amplify its child-centered stories and turn hockey into acceptable fare for its greatly expanded domestic and international markets.

The Mighty Ducks trilogy encapsulates Disney's vision of hockey by synergizing the Company's trademark motifs of childhood, animality, and the centrality of family with the conventions of the newly emerging family entertainment genre. The first installment (Herek, 1992) opens with 10-year-old Gordon Bombay (Brock Pierce), star of Hawks pewee contender team, taking the shot of his young life. He misses and is irrevocably marked by the experience. Years later, at work for the law firm of Ross, Savor and Ducksworth, Gordon (Emilio Estevez) is gamesman *extraordinaire*, excelling at covert maneuvers and finding loopholes to win every case. Concerned about the firm's reputation, Boss Gerald Ducksworth (Josef Sommer) cautions, "Score, don't spike," and warns that the practice of law requires self-restraint. Unrelenting, Gordon carries on with his tactics, until one day he is caught driving with an open container and charged with 500 hours of community service. He is assigned as peewee hockey coach to District 5, a bunch of prankster prepubescent minors whom he tells upon first blush, "I hate hockey. I don't like kids," adding for full effect that their time together is certain to be a "bonding experience" which one of them might some day write about in jail. District 5's first game is against the Hawks, headed by its long-standing coach Jack Reilly (Lane Smith), who rekindles in Gordon memories of the missed shot during the 1973 championship by reminding him of his team's second-place standing. Cut to the quick, Bombay vents on his peewees blaming them for the team's losing streak, but his young charges remain heedless. Disheartened and without a trace of credibility as a coach, Bombay heads for the local hockey outfit where owner Hans (Joss Ackland) entreats him: "Show them how to have fun. Teach them to fly," so that the youngsters remember the experience. Bombay reconsiders, and after obtaining much-needed equipment for his charges from boss Ducksworth, he re-names them "the Ducks" and instructs them in the intricacies of hockey. The Ducks end up in the championship final against the archenemy Hawks, and the game comes down to a penalty shot, which Charlie Conway (Joshua Jackson) pulls off with his signature Triple Deke. At film's end, Bombay heads off to try out for the minors but promises to return as the Ducks have a title to defend.

D2: The Mighty Ducks (Weisman, 1994) resumes where the first installment leaves off. Sidelined by a knee injury, coach Bombay is offered a sponsorship to coach the national team at the Junior Goodwill Games by senior VP for marketing corporation Hendrix in Los Angeles. Bombay reconvenes the Ducks with a few additions and pits his squad—now Team U.S.A. but ultimately in Ducks gear—against arrogant top dog Iceland. In second sequel *D3: The Mighty Ducks* (Lieberman, 1996), the team garners a scholarship at Eden Hall Academy in their home state of Minnesota after their Team U.S.A. victory. The Ducks are automatically anointed to the junior varsity berth and under coach Ted Orion (Jeffrey Nordling), a harsh taskmaster intent on teaching his charges defense, they must beat the cocky varsity Warriors, state champions two years in a row.

The Mighty Ducks reenacts the standard underdog–top dog fare favored by the sports film, pitting an ethnically and gender-diverse Twin Cities, Minnesota ragtag team against a vastly superior team in organization and performance. When first introduced, District 5 is a grouping of unruly youngsters who are scrimmaging on a frozen pond in a haphazard, unproductive way. For all intents and purposes, District 5 is not a team and only acquires legitimacy when the youngsters are procured proper attire and equipment, and are assigned a proper (upwardly mobile) coach to enable their climb to contender status. This metamorphosis articulates sports participation that is free and open to the public as somehow lacking the cachet of its sponsored counterpart, legitimizing sports practice for all classes and ethnic groups under corporate intervention. District 5's transformation into the Mighty Ducks in short order allegorizes Disney's re-branding of hockey as upmarket consumer sport by way of its NHL franchise and corporate properties.

Although Gordon teaches his charges bonafide hockey strategies and rules, what is most striking in the Ducks' game is the pivotal role of gimmickry and tricksterism, which take after the comic *shticks* of the early Disney hockey cartoons to validate children's sport as play. The first two Ducks films formulate trickster moves as tailor-made for the squad's fun-first orientation. Tricksterism suits the Ducks in a number of ways. First, as a form of gamesmanship, tricksterism allows players to seek out loopholes and attain much-coveted goals. The Ducks win tournament games through trickster moves, which result in a last-minute tally and confer great emotional charge to the destiny ending. Second, tricksterism and gimmickry anchor goal-scoring among team members, allowing characters other than the star player in on the final moment of attainment, soothing audience anxieties about the Social Darwinist implications of sport.[26] Third, because the Ducks are a socially diverse squad, trickster moves serve to flesh out the background of team members by acting as individual signatures through which each player contributes to the team. These signatures also broadcast that hockey is no longer an exclusively white male game, consonant with the design of family entertainment to appeal to multicultural audiences. Fourth, and no less importantly, tricksterist schemes displace the rogue hyperphysicality that American audiences associate with the Hanson Brothers. They entertain by obscuring the objectionable aspects of hockey, much like Disney video imagery and sideshows at the Ducks games, allowing the Company to sanitize and serve up hockey to a wider (more affluent) consumer demographic.

Because Ducks hockey amounts to quintessential play and the team rejects success at all costs as a testament of their good guy status, true to the melodramatic mode of Hollywood film, the Ducks must also come out on top. In other words, the Ducks' attitude toward hockey serves as proxy for their superior moral character, which supersedes the professionalism and commercial directives of the play-to-win drive. The catch, of course, is that even though the moral of these narratives espouses anti-commercial values, the product placement deals that Disney made in pre-production, and the validation of sport primarily through corporate sponsorship, interconnect these cherished sporting ideals with the very commercial entities whose products the Company markets in film.

Albeit marketed to the widest possible audience, popular film texts like Disney movies are also rife with contradictions as they pay lip service to multiculturalism but preserve the sanctity of dominant white masculinity's link to athleticism and fulfill the imperative of nationalistic sport's aim to return to its nostalgic roots. In spite of their multicultural veneer, *The Mighty Ducks* franchise remains consistent with the way that hockey in film expresses nostalgia for a heroic white masculinity, by reiterating the premier status of the Gordon-Charlie relationship and likening it to the father-son link in sport. Although Charlie is not as skilled as former Hawks Adam Banks (Vincent Larusso), Gordon spies out the youngster's potential early on, perhaps because his talent reminds him of his own prospects as a player. He entrusts the teen with the game-ending penalty shot, and as Charlie does the honors, revealingly he does not resort to standard Duck gimmickry like lassoing an opponent or figure skating jumps and spins that the trilogy inserts in the hockey proceedings. His Triple Deke is effectively a take on the talented athlete's repertoire, which reiterates the premium on skill and speed that phased out the physical game of the seventies and eighties. *D2: The Mighty Duck*'s lyrical introductory sequence in similar manner amplifies that Gordon always banked on his playmaker talents, but his prospects were cut short by a brutal hit that sidelined him from the game. Consonant with this primary signature, prior to the championship matchup in the first sequel, Gordon reaffirms the team's brand of hockey as dodging the bully element. In typical Disney form, Gordon exhorts: "We're not goons, we're not bullies. No matter what people say or do, we have to be ourselves." He makes this statement despite that the Ducks now feature not one but two players, the Bash Brothers (Elden Ryan Henson, Aaron Lohr), who perform the enforcer role in tandem, albeit modulated by the Company's gimmicky imprint. Gordon aims to teach his charges playful, non-violent codes that accord with the coach's own character less informed by the hard-bodied edges of traditional masculinity and more predicated on family and caring exemplified by the new model of manhood that emerged in the male-centered films of the nineties.[27] In the first *Ducks* film, Gordon embodies this new pliant masculinity in his relationship with Charlie's mom, Casey (Heidi Kling), in turn reaffirming his connection to Charlie as a surrogate father, a figure who in the cinema proves more adept than the biological father at navigating the intricacies of parenting.[28]

Gordon's gentle masculinity and Charlie's playmaking abilities showcase Disney's vision of hockey, which aligned with the courteous disposition and marquee game that Gretzky had brought to L.A., even as the upmarket spectacle that the Company favored entailed unhinging the game from its Canadian ideological moorings. Michael Jeremy Ward ratifies this argument noting that by inserting content extraneous to the game at its arena, the Company performed a "veiling" of hockey to distance itself from the sport's historical "cultural meanings … [as] a brutal blue-collar sport" played by Canadian goons.[29] The family genre in like manner sanitizes the sweat and blood of the enforcer's game, morphing brute force into clean setups that elicit grunts and deliver spills, but leave no distasteful evidence of gashes, lacerations, or blood-spilling. At the same time, because of hockey's robust markers, Disney does not do away with the sport's rugged signature but upholds the game's usefulness as masculinity training. The Ducks' Wild Wing logo, a take on Disney favorite Donald Duck augmented by a menacing façade, appears on the fictive team's jerseys to convey the Company's brand through the symbolic ferocity of the hockey competitor.[30] As innocent tricksters, however, the Ducks strategize to neutralize the opponent while seeking to cause no physical harm.

To subvert the rough game as mandated by the Disney brand, the films also enlist NHLers to support the Ducks' cause. In *D2*, Wayne Gretzky puts in an appearance in the locker room to give the team a boost at the Junior Goodwill Championships. Given Gretzky's preeminent status to hockey in Canada, and the detrimental role of U.S. interests in Canadian hockey development programs, his presence as inspiration for Team USA has histrionic connotations.[31] In the fictive world of *D2*, however, Disney supersedes Gretzky's symbolic value for Canadian hockey, deploying him as icon of upmarket consumer sport and symbol at large of transnational capital and culture. *D2* performs a similar sleight of hand with Team Russia, the former Olympic and World champion, as the Ducks in the guise of Team U.S.A. defeat the Russian contingent to connote the unraveling of the Soviet Union and its hockey programs.[32]

Against Team Iceland, the underdog Ducks literally strip off their U.S.A. jerseys in the Junior Goodwill championship game, revealing Disney Duck uniforms in which they proceed to win the gold medal. Having accomplished their goal, Charlie Conway skates with the American flag alongside the rest of the team in Ducks jerseys, and the musical score celebrates their victory by declaring them champions. The Ducks' chant "We're on our way to Hollywood" and "U.S.A. and we're going all the way" earlier in the movie, also synergizes the project of nationalism with Disney's business mandate. In one fell swoop, then, *D2* equates investment in the Disney brand with the national interest. The film's plot line and the team's jersey changes symbolize the post–Cold War reorganization of the world stage in the early nineties by way of global markets and the influence and growing power of the transnational corporation. The Company in short order deploys its trademark to allude to the nation through a form of brand nationalism that in the era of globalization celebrates the expansion and influence of corporations headquartered in the United States.[33]

D3 moves the franchise forward by anteing up the stakes for the Ducks, who have traded the sparkling Bombay for taskmaster Orion. The new coach, who first appears via a close-up of his skates as a metonym for autocratic power, wastes no time in announcing an alternative direction for the squad: "We're here for one reason and one reason only. It starts with a "W": to work," even as the Ducks' mantra continues to be: "We don't really practice per se … we have fun." Bombay's exhortation about working hard to overcome obstacles in the first two *Mighty Ducks* movies also transforms into Orion's more cautionary directive: "Don't be careless but don't be too careful either. That's how you attack life even when you don't think you have any control." Although the game remains in its role as training ground for life, the fierce challenges posed by the Social Darwinist transnational marketplace, coupled with the junior varsity status of the Ducks who face imminent adulthood, now shifts the emphasis on play for play's sake to a perspective that openly valorizes success.

Still, consonant with Disney's emphasis on the young's benevolent ebullience, the players, led by Charlie, unabashedly rebel against the new coach's injunctions, resisting their new Eden Hall Warriors moniker and holding onto their Ducks jerseys and identity. Even though the Ducks are now teens, their resistance falls in line with Disney's foregrounding of youngsters' perspectives over that of adults.[34] The genre also reinforces the democratic impulse,[35] and given that coach Bombay had failed to evoke respect in autocratic mode, Orion's dictates only serve to entrench the squad's resistance. Unable to move forward, the team soon loses their motivation to play along with their scholarships, and Gordon must return to defend their position and rescue the outfit, reaffirming the squad's brand as Ducks. As the contingent goes up against a second set of all-white, all-male bullies in the guise of the senior varsity team and find themselves with their backs against the wall, one of the wary players notes that it will take a "miracle" to win, an allusion to the underdog U.S. triumph over the Soviet team at the 1980 Olympics dubbed the "Miracle on Ice."[36] The film also trots out NHL Mighty Ducks star Paul Kariya who in the locker room confirms that, "Size isn't everything in hockey…. Speed and determination." In short order, the Ducks come out on top and retain their Disney identity, recapitulating the annexation of the athlete's physique and performance by the corporation's brand.

TV movies *H-E-Double Hockey Sticks* (Miller, 1999) and *Den Brother* (Taylor, 2010) showcase many of the motifs fronted in *The Mighty Ducks*, such as play for play's sake, keeping self-centeredness in check, and giving social others the opportunity to share in the fruits of success. Their main protagonists, Delaware Demons ace Dave Heinrich (Matthew Lawrence) and Hounds whiz Alex Pearson (Hutch Dano) are star forwards who are so self-absorbed with dreams of glory that they spend little time with significant others. They're also flashy players and puck hogs, which make them ripe for just punishment. In line with the Disney family entertainment template, both characters also attain redemption thanks to significant downsizing and the intercessory agency of the child's benevolent tricksterism.

The youngest player ever in contention for the Stanley Cup, Dave Heinrich fails to accomplish masculine success at the film's outset because his experience must encompass the fraught arena of gender relations and accommodate the emotional needs of figure skater partner Anne (Tara Spencer-Nairn). His commitment to her entails spending time with kid brother Lewis (Shawn Pyfrom), who looks up to the budding star, and longs to show him his "Lewis Left Over," a clever maneuver designed to confound the opponent, to no avail. On account of his self-centeredness, Dave promptly becomes a target for the forces of the underworld. A young, brash demon named Griffelkin (Will Friedle), who also deems himself a "solo act," is sent on a mission to trick the ace into signing over his soul. Griffelkin befriends Lewis, enabling himself a way into the locker room to negotiate his target's soul in return for winning the Stanley Cup. As the team goes on a winning streak, Dave begins spending time with Lewis and Griffelkin also finds himself prone to sentimentality and besieged by an intense desire to help his target due to bouts of Human Attachment Syndrome (HAS).

The twist in the plot arrives as Hell's chief honcho, "Ms. B" or Beelzebub (Rhea Perlman), who frowns on the proceedings, promptly has Dave traded to the last place Annapolis Angels. On Griffelkin's counsel, Dave begins passing the puck giving teammates a shot to shine, and the Angels soon find themselves in the playoffs facing the Demons. But just as Annapolis ties the final game, Ms. B. shows up and puts Dave out of commission with a brutal check from an opponent. With his protégé out of the game, the young demon, who can hardly skate, must take his place and thanks to young Lewis' trademark "Left Over," he confounds the Demons, fans on the puck, and scores to win the game.

Because Dave and Griffelkin are aspects of the same character in their embodiment of an over-confident, lone wolf masculinity, they transform into "good guys" at the same pace and set up the expectation that both will partake from the final goal-scoring of the sports genre. The clobbering that Dave suffers in short order allows room for the trickster ist maneuvering and goal dispersal seen in *The Mighty Ducks* trilogy, which enables Griffelkin to partake in the moment of attainment. Given Griffelkin's friendship with Lewis, the young demon's move by proxy also allows the boy in on the goal, actualizing the Disney precept that the child's benevolent tricksterism ultimately leads to the good of the adult.

The film's critique of the athlete's absorption into his occupational role to the exclusion of relationships is a staple of family fare designed to teach children lessons about honing upstanding character and moral citizenship. Hockey in these films operates as a social leveler that habituates young recalcitrant to the ways of the homosocial brotherhood, and as Buma notes, to suggest "male collectivism as the rationale for individual effort."[37] Indeed, family fare at large exhibits this didactic emphasis. Non-Disney film *Airborne* (Bowman, 1993), for example, draws up its high school protagonist Mitchell Goosen (Shane McDermott) in much the same way: as a surfer and inline skater from California who is also a pacifist and a loner. To help check his individualist tendencies, Mitchell is transplanted to the Midwest when his parents garner a six-month long grant for a stint at the National Zoological Institute in Australia, and upon cousin Wiley's (Seth Green) insistence, joins in a high school hockey game. Predictably, he runs into the team's bullies but ultimately allies with them to defeat the rival high school's squad, the Preps, in a downhill race. By film's end, Mitchell becomes the embodied reconciliation of the surfer's individualism and the hockey player's group orientation.

Just as the individualist mythology clashes with the collective aspect of hockey and must be exorcised in line with the augmented didacticism of the sports film and family fare, professionalism in this genre combination amounts to the game's very corruption. However, Luc Robitaille's and Paul Kariya's cameo appearances in *H-E-Double Hockey Sticks* to model the NHL as pinnacle of the game for young viewers contravenes this directive. Although in line with Disney's penchant for promoting its commercial interests, NHLer cameos disavow the reality that elite-level hockey is far more individualistic than appears, and national leaguers must hone highly competitive instincts and adhere to the prerogatives of professionalism to accomplish career success.[38]

The idea of play for play's sake appears less discordant in *Den Brother*, whose central protagonist Alex Pearson, a star scorer and captain of his high school hockey team, is set on the All-Stars team. Predictably, however, he reiterates the Disney motif of the hockey player who must uncover the right balance between his pursuit of individual goals and accountability to social and familial others. Not a reprobate sort, but merely a callow, if enterprising youth, Alex must also learn to keep his self-promoter instincts in check. He makes a grand entrance *sans* teammates in showman form, and as the coach lets him know he has crossed the line, Alex protests that "this is good for everyone, it's advertising, the crowd gets information." For his efforts, he garners a two-week suspension and after one too many times of skipping house chores, he is also charged by his busy professor-dad (Maurice Godin) to look after kid sister Emily (G. Hannelius) so he will learn to be answer to others.

Since the Bumble Bee troop that Emily is part of is facing termination right before Camporee for lack of a Den Mother, the children press Alex to do the honors and summarily dress him up in costume for the impromptu role of Mrs. Zamboni. The dual punishment of suffering a suspension and donning a feminizing get-up are not unlike Derek Thompson's downsizing from reigning goon to wimpy Tooth Fairy and second fiddle to rookie Mick "The Stick." However, Alex, while brawny, is not endowed with Derek's hyper-masculine physique, and the Mrs. Zamboni duds risk enfeebling his masculinity. The film must consequently reassure the Disney Channel's young audience that, although a wily gamesman, Alex is hardly effete or foppish. Teaching Emily and friends hockey fundamentals, he makes a point of noting the athlete's gritty determination: "You give a hundred percent. You never back off. You never back down." He also conveys the hockey player's muscularity when he tells love interest Matisse (Kelsey Chow) that in hockey, bumping against someone is a form of greeting.

While Alex helps with the many tasks the children must perform to qualify for attendance, true to his irrepressible character, he also wrecks their chances when at a bake sale held at the hockey rink he inserts himself into the lineup during a crucial game in Mrs. Zamboni attire. To atone for his misdeeds, he asks an elderly neighbor to serve as Den Mother for the girls and with his two-week suspension over, he also returns to the team reformed. Rather than hogging the puck during the game, he creates the necessary distraction on the ice, enabling teammate and best friend Danny "Goose" Gustavo (David Lambert) to score and make the All-Star squad. With that move he sacrifices his chances at his cherished goal, but he is long past his self-absorption, having offered Goose the captain's badge. As it happens, Emily's troop wants Alex back as Den Brother at Camporee and he obliges, but after donning his Mrs. Zamboni costume, a rival Den Mother objects to the exercise and sends her husband to stop the teen's involvement. The husband turns out to be the referee who ousted Alex from the game prompting his suspension, but upon seeing the teen in the feminizing get-up, he is moved by his changed ways, and on the spot offers him a berth on the All-Stars team. Alex accepts the position providing he can work around his Bumble Bee responsibilities.

Critiques of the athlete's self-absorption to the exclusion of relationships are a staple in Disney hockey-themed films, because self-interest smacks of professionalism, which in children's fare amounts to the game's very corruption. Although Alex notes in different segments of the film that "becoming a great hockey player is the most fun thing in the world" and "hockey is not about winning and losing, it's about challenging yourself," the greater part of the plot amplifies that he is afflicted by a self-serving gamesmanship that contravenes the sports ideal. Because the only acceptable form of gamesmanship in Disney films is the benevolent tricksterism of the child, central protagonists who happen to be beset by this condition are configured as suffering from a psychological block or dysfunction, which they must urgently remedy to maintain the integrity of the family unit, or its surrogate, the team. Happily, and much like Dave Heinrich, Alex reforms to reassure the audience that the individualist mythology and the Social Darwinist aspects of sport have been contained.

Den Brother's critique of commercialism appears deceptively heartfelt since Disney remains synonymous not only with the commodification of children's culture but that of the culture at large.[39] Though by the time the TV movie saw its Disney Channel broadcast, the Company had exited the NHL fray, hockey remained part of the Company's portfolio of youth sports by way of its resort properties and film production arm.[40] Because popular film texts are rife with contradictions, upholding sports tenets and family film conventions while simultaneously disavowing them, Disney is able to veil its commercial injunctions by speaking to core values in U.S. culture, such as the balance between individual and communal objectives, the importance of staples like childhood, family, and friendship, and the primacy of meritocratic self-betterment encapsulated by the ideals of Middle America. While navigating the masculinity minefield by drawing up athletes through the same inoffensive referents of 1990s family fare, the Company's synergistic talent stands out for the way it fuses its distinctive brand of watchable upmarket spectacle with mainstream American values, so that hockey is produced and perceived in the context of commodified entertainment and audiences do not question the role of the corporation in the process.

Hockey in Canadian Family Fare: *Ronnie and Julie, MVP: Most Valuable Primate, Slap Shot 3: The Junior League* and *Sticks and Stones*

The conglomeratization of the film industry in the 1990s greatly expanded markets, and paved the way for co-productions and culturally hybrid products that banked on family entertainment for marketable content. Migration of Hollywood production to Canada, particularly to Canadian Western provinces, procured great advantages for the capital-intensive movie-making business since generous film incentives and a weaker Canadian dollar presented industry players with the prospect of compounded returns. As Hollywood studios opted for location-shooting in large Canadian cities, in particular Vancouver, B.C., Canadian film companies also took to producing and co-producing mock-ups of Hollywood features with an eye on the American entertainment market, blurring the specificity of Canadian locales.[41] Transnational film market economics thus began to erase the boundaries between Hollywood and non–Hollywood, commercial and non-commercial film, creating a hybrid cultural space not entirely Canadian or American.⁴² Family entertainment, with its easy-to-understand, spectacle-driven, emotional subject matter, and broad audience address also lent itself well to Canadian film culture, which is highly proficient in American genres. Not unexpectedly, production companies based out of Canada aimed their hockey-themed family-driven content not just at domestic audiences but at the entire North American film market. Given Disney's preeminent role as one of the top global entertainment conglomerates, Canadian producers that looked to the Company for distribution also enhanced the transborder appeal of content through co-production of popcorn films that reaffirmed genre conventions.

The B.C. made-for-television co-production *Ronnie and Julie* (Spink, 1997)⁴³ is a prime example of films that activate various plot and character motifs to enhance their transborder marketability. The movie takes advantage of the earlier pairing of actors Joshua Jackson and Margot Finley in Disney's *D3: The Mighty Ducks* to channel the archetypal story of Romeo and Juliet into a propitious outcome through the hockey player-figure skater motif. It also deploys various models of masculinity for much the same reason, as Ronnie (Jackson), the hockey star of his Verona high school team, portrays a sensitive type in his relationship with up-and-coming figure skater Julie (Finley), going as far as to import one of her signature figure skating moves to score the winning tally at the championship game. Ronnie is able to cross over to a sport that is known for its female glitz because the film establishes his masculine credentials in the introductory scenes. Much as in *The Cutting Edge* (Glaser, 1992), which in the opening scene amplifies U.S. hockey Olympian Doug Dorsey's (D.B. Sweeney) virile allure through a casual liaison with a pretty woman because he will have to cross over into pairs figure skating, at practice Ronnie appears distracted by the presence of the school's hottest girl. Seeing the teen's absent-mindedness, another player takes a shot at him and lands him on his rear. But Ronnie shakes it off, heads for the net, and scores. After the goal, he spots high school bully Tim Capell (Brad Payne) and his cohorts threatening cousin Marty (Billy O'Sullivan), and instantly moves to intervene by throwing down his helmet and gloves as if preparing for a fight. Towering over the bullies and bumping them slightly, he boldly orders them to scram. The sequence summarily introduces the hockey player as a rugged heterosexual male who is unafraid to engage in fisticuffs to defend weaker others.

Ronnie has a decidedly robust bent that shows him physically venting his frustrations more often than the staple Disney protagonist. After Arthur Capell (Tom Butler), father of his love interest and chief opponent in mom Elizabeth's (Terry Garr) mayoral race, finds out about the affair between the teens, he grounds his daughter. Quarantined from Julie, Ronnie takes his frustrations out on the ice and an extended game sequence depicts him punching out an opponent as he is checked against the boards, mowing down a second player, and upending yet a third player as he advances toward the net. Ronnie, however, also learns to pick his fights, and in the championship game between his new and old teams, he refuses to engage rival Paul Reese (Jade Pawluk) the film's villain and assistant to Capell. As Reese's mantra illustrates—"If you're not on the winning team, you're nothing"—he sees winning as an end-all be-all in politics and in hockey, and displays the sinister makeup of the Disney bully on and off the ice.

In contrast, Ronnie's masculinity is neither vicious nor unscrupulous, but consistent with that of the film's rival coaching figures, who vigorously espouse an old-fashioned physicality that is neither menacing nor dishonorable. Verona's coach Chuck (Marcus Turner) extols his charges by invoking the traditional ties between sport and the battlefield: "Gentlemen, in my day the game of hockey was not just a game. It was war!" Lawrence's Russian coach Peshlov (Zinaid Memisevic), whom the film introduces by way of his players' machine-like drills accompanied by a slightly nefarious musical score that alludes to his Soviet roots, addresses his team by yelling, reminiscent of longtime Soviet national coach Viktor Tikhonov's tactics. Peshlov also wastes no time informing his charges: "Your job is to stop the puck with your face if you have to." The championship game, however, does not reveal him as an authoritarian figure, but as a studious, convivial coach who encourages his players by observing that a 1–0 deficit hardly constitutes a dent and the team can still win the game. Although impassioned, neither coach is cynical or underhanded like Hawks coach Jack Reilly in *The Mighty Ducks*, making room for various images of hockey robustness that bolster the film's status as a hybrid cultural product.

Ronnie and Julie's first meeting behind the scenes at a mayoral press conference is lighthearted as Julie teases that figure skating is "real skating," and, in turn, Ronnie retorts: "And hockey isn't real skating? Maybe you'd like to try it sometime." After Julie attends one of Ronnie's games, the pair next meet on a pond in a secluded area of the woods that has a distinct Disney-like fairytale aura and helps solidify their relationship. Ronnie shows Julie a few hockey maneuvers, which she immediately repurposes into a spinning move that enables her to score a quick surprise goal. Her movement recalls the spin-shoot-and-score play of Ducks Tammy Duncan in *The Mighty Ducks* films. Following their first meeting on the pond, Ronnie successfully tries out the spin-and-score move in practice, which he eventually deploys to avoid a check and score the winning tally in the final game, while Julie ecstatically spins in place to the approval of her figure skating coach. The playful spinning motif that occurs throughout the plot, and the theme song, "Something Happened to My Heart," captures the wonderment of falling in love and the intense quality of the teens' bond. Ronnie's crossing-over operates as a form of tricksterism, mimicking the cloaked maneuvering wielded in *The Mighty Ducks* films to score goals. The strategy proves that he exhibits the pliability of the new nineties male in gender relationships, which because of potentially feminizing figure overtones, he must counteract with the characteristic tough muscularity of the Canadian hockey protagonist, a category of robustness that contrasts with the skill-driven, offensive mindset of Ducks captain Charlie Conway, the character Joshua Jackson plays in the Disney trilogy.

To keep the teens apart, mom Elizabeth gives her approval to have Ronnie transferred to Lawrence high school. While separated their performances suffer, albeit the parents sell it as something their children must do for their own good. Taking their cue from the feuding families in *Romeo and Juliet*, Elizabeth Monroe and the elder Arthur Capell fail miserably in their boundary-setting roles, resembling the dysfunctional family heads of Canadian canonical film. Family fare leaves the performative ground to children and young adults who must make sense of their own predicaments, and the film also makes clear that Ronnie and Julie are justified in pursuing their relationship particularly as love enhances their athletic talents. Illustrating the genre's concern with the stability of the family unit and its emphasis on happy outcomes, the film must also bypass the tragic denouement of its Shakespearean antecedent. Arthur and Elizabeth finally admit to prioritizing their own selfish political agendas and allow Ronnie and Julie see each other again. The ending invokes the expectation of an optimal resolution through an intertextual motif, emulating the actors' pairing in *D3*. *Ronnie and Julie* is a classic example of family entertainment, which strives to appeal to both Canadian and

American film markets in its depiction of hockey masculinities, its concern with the family unit, its support for its young protagonists' wishes and objectives, and its Disneyesque visual and textual motifs.

The B.C. production *MVP: Most Valuable Primate* (Vince, 2000) also depicts hockey's small-town roots, but negotiates those referents to produce a narrative distinctive of its Northwestern Canadian bearings. Made with the assistance of Film Incentive B.C. and recipient of the province's Film and Video Tax Credit program, *MVP: Most Valuable Primate* emerged as one of a handful of locally-produced films touted by the Canadian Association of Film Distributors and Exporters (CAFDE) as evidence that with appropriate marketing and support by critics, Canadians were willing to "leav[e] home and pay ... to see ... [a] movie."[44] A film set for distribution by Disney's Buena Vista arm, it features an American protagonist who is whisked to the province's interior and finds success by helping his team reach the championship finals.[45]

MVP: Most Valuable Primate begins with the career path of Steven Westover (Kevin Zegers), leading scorer of his California high school team, taking a questionable turn upon his family's liberation to Nelson, British Columbia. The film depicts Steven through the formula of the smaller, fleet-of-foot pacifist American star player who confronts archetypical Canadian hockey toughness. Intent on making his way to the professional ranks, the Nelson Nuggets are not Steven's idea of the perfect career move: "No one's going to scout the worst Junior B hockey team on the planet!" Adding insult to injury, stronger, more physical Canadian players continually manhandle him on the ice. "Welcome to Junior B hockey! No time to celebrate," an opponent snidely remarks after Steven scores a goal. Younger sister Tara (Jamie Renée Smith), an intelligent child with hearing disabilities, also has problems trying to acclimate to the new social setup. Into this alien world comes Jack (played by chimps Bernie, Louie, Mac), an ape with the IQ of a genius, who has been trained in sign language as part of a study of human-primate interaction at Southern California's Pueblo University. With head researcher Dr. Kendall (Lomax Study) dead of a heart attack and aided by janitor-friend Darren (Russell Ferrier), Jack heads for El Simian Nature Preserve to escape the clutches of Dr. H.F. Peabody (Oliver Muirhead), the cost-cutting English dean who threatens to ship Jack to a medical lab behind the backs of the college's alumni. Jack mistakenly gets off the train in Nelson and soon encounters Tara and Steven. Thanks to his expertise in sign language,[46] as well as a mean shot and superlative inline skating abilities, the young chimp gets off to a splendid start with the Westover children. In short order, he teams up with Steven, and as the duo rises to stardom, they take the Nuggets to the finals of the Harvest Cup in Vancouver. With the game won, Steven is set to start his professional career with the Mighty Ducks' farm team.

The unlikely story of a hockey-playing chimp, which smacks of calculated gimmickry in conflating mild animality with family sports fare, may be partly explained by producers' designs to negotiate distribution rights with Disney's Buena Vista arm. But it also well illustrates the transborder marketability of Canadian co-productions released at this time. The film's Nelson setting, for example, lends itself to multiple readings. When Nelson is described as "the end of the road for many," the town emerges in line with depictions of Canada that date back to 1907 Hollywood film and feature the generic wilderness of snow, mountains, and pine trees to which Pierre Berton refers in *Hollywood's Canada*.[47] This image highlights the North as backcountry and also accords with the unblemished natural surroundings that recur in Disney's post–World War II nature films,[48] one that, according to Mike Gasher, the B.C. Film Commission actively promotes to lure Hollywood production since it voids towns of cultural and social specificity.[49]

The transborder Northwest, however, also lends the Canadian small town referents that allude to frontier opportunity in line with "New World" ideas of the American origin myth. Nuggets coach Marlowe (Rick Ducommun) demonstrates the archetypal resourcefulness of frontier inhabitants when he allows Jack to join the team by donning fellow teammate Ribchimpski's jersey when he philosophically muses that "technically he's a chimp but the chimp is our closest relative." Nelson also partakes from the mythical West in the American imaginary in that it heralds the psychological start of a new life and allows Steven and Tara to find their successful mediations with the Northern environment by way of Jack's intercessory role.

Jack the Chimp in the Nuggets locker room in *MVP: Most Valuable Primate* (Keystone Entertainment/Photofest).

Given the Northwest's geographical bearings as a crossroads for multiple cultural influences, its not surprising that Nelson should draw on ideas of the West in the American and Canadian imaginaries. William Katerberg notes that while historians have insisted that the Canadian process of frontier expansion and settlement was quite different from that of the U.S., the frontier West's abundant resources equally spawned in Canadians and Americans confidence in the New World's distinctive vitality.[50] This shared function is activated as Nelson acts as jumping-off point for Steven's career prospects in Vancouver where the Nuggets reach the finals of the Harvest Cup, enabling the American teen's sports success story.

In much the same way Nelson's operates as vehicle for gauging and promoting the protagonists' future prospects, Jack's character and trajectory amplify his association with the Westover children. When he first lands in Nelson forlorn because of a miscalculation, Jack expresses Steven and Tara's dislocation in a similar way that Animal Daemons act as exteriorized souls by embodying the innermost feelings of the characters in *The Golden Compass* (Weitz, 2007). *MVP*'s depiction of Jack also draws on portrayals of chimpanzees as the good apes in the *Planet of the Apes* movies of the late sixties and early eighties. Eric Greene notes in his discussion of Donna Haraway's *Primate Visions* that the figure of the ape acts as bridge between civilization and wilderness in the narrative of science, and this portrayal has influenced pop culture constructions of apes. Popular fictions that revolve around ape characters, Greene suggests, investigate fundamental questions regarding "the worlds of 'origin' and 'destination'"—and constitute blueprints through which to reorganize human experience.[51] Jack's passage, therefore, is also an iteration of the journey embarked on by Steven and Tara.

MVP, however, also scripts Jack with a decided personhood that aligns with Disney's history of animal portrayals. The Westover children's geographical and psychological displacement echoes Jack's own sense of uprootment because he too has been forcibly pulled from familiar surroundings, and furthermore orphaned through the loss of surrogate father and head scientist Dr. Kendall. Jack has also grown up blended into an excessively structured and hyper-produced human environment that allows no interface with the outside world. His stranding in Nelson is a threat to his very survival because as an equatorial species he is not acclimated to the wintry harshness of the North. His hardship fittingly illustrates Chris Clarke's argument that in Disney's filmic anthropomorphizing of the wild, "animals ... [are] so thoroughly 'people' that wilderness resume[s] its traditional threatening role."[52] Jack has literally lost his frontier or forest heritage, which he will eventually regain in El Simian by way of his sojourn in Nelson. By dipping into hockey's roots in the frontier landscape of the North, Jack too will ultimately find his way back to his own simian roots.

Like the Westover children, then, Jack must adjust to his new surroundings and he does so in a way that takes advantage of Nelson's frontier-like opportunities for self-realization. It is no coincidence that he adapts his inline skating skills to pond hockey prior to his foray as a star of the Nelson Nuggets. *MVP* also aligns Steven and Jack by way of blinding speed and playmaking abilities to reaffirm hockey's transformation from a sport that subordinates the physicality that Steve encounters when he first sets foot on Nuggets ice to the goal-scoring spectacle that the Disney Company favors. Although in keeping with Disney films' penchant for gimmickry, Jack exhibits a marked trickster side, the young chimp also signals his predilection for the highly marketable game of skill and speed that Wayne Gretzky brought to L.A by way of a poster of the icon on his bedroom wall. Albeit Gretzky had been traded to the New York Rangers and ended his career there in 1999, his role in expanding hockey to the Sun Belt region endures. Not surprisingly, when a Nuggets old-timer fan first glimpses Jack on the ice, he remarks: "I think he's from California too!" The humorous sight of a Nuggets player knitting a sweater for Jack in appreciation of his skills also conveys the impact of the American sports marketplace on the Canadian juniors game.

The idea of an American protagonist fronting a Canadian film might lend weight to arguments about the difficulty of preserving domestic public culture in Canada.[53] *MVP*'s rank as the number one family film in Canada the first six weeks of its release, and one of the top ten films in the Greater Toronto Area (GTA) between 1994 and 2004, certainly attests to the notion that Canadian audiences readily accept American protagonists in stories beamed across the border as well as produced locally.[54] However, choosing an American protagonist for a Canadian-produced film that deals with a core symbol of Canadian identity cannot be construed as a zero-sum game—i.e., as a Canadian loss and an American gain. Transnational film market economics have promoted the emergence of new co-productions, erasing the boundaries between Hollywood and non–Hollywood as well as commercial and non-commercial film, creating a hybrid cultural space that is not entirely Canadian or American.[55] The very notion that an American protagonist acts as the driver of a hockey story produced in Canada might be less significant than the film's confirmation that hockey has become a source of vital storytelling in North America. By scripting a story around an American hockey protagonist and enhancing cross-border marketability, the movie actualizes CAFDE's call for "increased flexibility in Canadian content rules for feature films" and "competitive Canadian content that will appeal to Canadians."[56]

MVP's ending expresses producers' view of their participation in the North American film market economy, which takes into account Disney's prospective distribution of the film. Neither the journey that takes the Nuggets to the championship final nor the scoring of the final goal, typically the moment of glory for a franchise player, structures input from Steven or Jack.[57] Mirroring the male-female makeup of the Ducks and the benevolent tricksterism of the child favored by Disney, the film instead ascribes the crucial role to Tara, who impersonates Jack and wins the championship for the Nuggets. By deploying Disney's goal-dispersal signature, the film adopts a presentational technique that speaks to wider North American audiences, in the process promoting the interests of local B.C. players by facilitating the film's cross-border promotional potential. *MVP* illustrates in sterling fashion that producers can make use of hockey-centered family fare to appeal to regional, national, and international audiences in a way that accords with British Columbia's historical and economic ways of imagining place and constituting identity.

The third B.C.-filmed product in the roster, the Universal Home Entertainment *Slap Shot 3: The Junior League* (Martin, 2008), repurposes the popularity of the Hanson Brothers for family fare. The film starts out with a recap of the Hansons' cultural mark on the Charlestown community by its well-intentioned but absent-minded mayor (Leslie Neilsen). The mayor highlights the brothers' contributions recalling that their aggressive hockey style allowed the Chiefs to win the Federal Cup and rekindle in the demoralized town residents a passion for the game. He adds that after winning the lottery, the Hansons went missing and it took a ragtag team of orphans, whose 1950s-founded Newman Home for Boys[58] was threatened by ruthless developer Bernie Frazier (Linda Boyd), to track them down, bring them back into the game, and save their own tight-knit outfit. The orphans' oldest, main protagonist Riley Haskell (Greyston Holt), is well aware that Ms. Frazier will stop at nothing to take over the town with her posh "Frazier Point Golf Community Country Club and Spa" slated for "200 luxurious new homes … and 36 holes of golf," as she proudly announces on a TV promotional spot. Ms. Frazier also owns a first-class hockey arena that is home to the three-time champion Ice Hounds led by son and MVP goalie Kain (Ryan McDonell), who is predictably a chip of the old block. Although the popular mayor is the lone figure who stands between Ms. Frazier's nefarious plan and the orphans, he also goes missing when he sets out on a shamanic expedition to Peru.

Rick Baker (Adrian Hough), owner and manager of the former Chiefs arena where Riley works, and dad to love interest and hockey MVP Shayne (Emma Lahana), suggests the orphans join the Pennsylvania Junior league as an expansion team to re-instill the love of the game in Charlestown residents. The makeshift outfit, who plays daily pickup hockey with a ball in the Home's barn and attic, lack the proper training and the money to join the league but not the heart. Riley gets a whiff that the Hansons have opened a "Peace and Balance" franchise in town, and he sets out to curry their favor for sponsorship monies. The brothers, however, have adopted a non-violent Zen lifestyle complete with monk-like robes, and they balk at the proposal noting that hockey is "a dumb game where you bleed a lot." Riley prevails on them by making the case that the squad, which will feature "Salvation on Ice" hockey, will actively serve as advertisement for their Zen franchise. The Hansons provide the orphans with shiny gear, but the team's jerseys resemble Zen robes and their Zennovators moniker inspires little respect from both opponents and spectators. Fortuitously, the brothers wake up from their Zen-like slumber, pelted by food and containers at their jersey-retiring ceremony, and return to train the group in old-time hockey, help them defeat the Ice Hounds and keep their home.

Slap Shot 3 borrows widely from the repertoire, deploying motifs from *Slap Shot*, *Slap Shot 2*, *Youngblood*, *MVP: Most Valuable Primate*, and Disney's *The Mighty Ducks*, *H-E-Double Hockey Sticks*, and *Miracle*. Riley takes on both the leadership role of Reggie Dunlop in *Slap Shot*, and the mild masculinity of Canadian canonical film in his relationship with Shayne, a character that resembles Dean's love interest Jesse Chadwick in *Youngblood*. Although like Reggie, Riley is a proactive gamesman who will do anything to keep his orphan family intact, with the romantically dominant Shayne, he is indecisive, responding to her straightforward demands for a kiss by noting that those kinds of things "magically happen exactly at the right time" much like rainbows. Unable to disclose that he is effectively in charge of the Home's orphans, Riley unwittingly drives a frustrated Shayne to the arms of Kain. Like Jesse Chadwick who has a strong aversion to goon hockey, Shayne is unimpressed by the hard masculinity of the Hansons and their mini-me sons, even more so because of her stellar hockey skills. It consequently takes Riley the duration of the film to strike the right note with the shiny Shayne.

Riley's rival Kain is the star on a team that announcer Dickie Dunn, Jr. (Eric Keenleyside) describes as "every bit the monstrous machine that has dominated the region for many seasons." The Ice Hounds' red uniforms as well as their superior skills and circling strategies are reminiscent of the powerhouse Soviet teams of old, which Disney's feature *Miracle* visually reprises in like manner. In the stands, Shayne confirms the allusion when she says of the orphans' first game, "Maybe they can win; it will be like that Miracle on Ice." Sitting beside her dad Rick she reiterates that it will be a miracle if the team manages to get to the end of the game intact. Although more adept at the dating game than Riley, Kain's masculinity is ultimately too hard for Shayne's liking. During their scrimmaging bout, he comments on her physical appearance, objectifying her instead of recognizing her as an equal. It is no surprise that their connection is brief and she works to do him in by film's end. Kain has complete derision for Riley and his bully-clown game, taunting that he doesn't have the skills "to win a fair game." As an extension of his devilish mother, who is a twist on Chiefs owner Anita McCambridge in *Slap Shot* with more than a splash of Ms. Beelzebub in *H-E-Double Hockey Sticks*, Kain uses every bit of advantage to demoralize the underprivileged Riley at every opportunity.

For Riley and the orphans, border-crossing into goon territory is essential so that the squad can firm up their masculinity and have a chance against more skilled opponents. As orphans, the team must go on a journey to find their way home—literally to retain their Newman Home abode—and this journey goes through the Hansonian game. But to act as mentors, the Hansons themselves must return from their effete masculine stint as monk-like figures. Indeed, renouncing erstwhile pleasures such as fighting and gambling in favor of "peace, focus, clarity," the brothers have taken to advocate emptying the "mind of all distractions." The film makes clear, however, that the Hansons have taken on a misguided, docile role by way of the short-circuiting electrical fuses that form the backdrop of their jersey-retirement ceremony. As they counsel those in attendance to open to the cosmic energy through "Zen-ervation," a farcical term that represents the draining of their own primal vitality, the crowd's vexation reaches a crescendo. A beer can hits one of the brothers in the face, causing his head to pitch backward in slow motion. The accompanying dissonant musical tones, which recall a tense turning point in Japanese classical film, marks the Hansons' awakening as the brother on the receiving end of the hit tastes the blood spilling from his lip and flashes a zany smile. Reinvigorated, he rushes toward the stands, climbs over the glass, and pummels the culprit behind the container-hurling. Seeing their brother re-inhabit his old self, the other two look at each other and rush forth after him to take on the crowd with relish. Once home, the three burn their monk robes in a large cauldron, and with open cans of beer in hand, chant in unison: "We're baaaaaaaack!"

They are now set to mentor their young charges in the in-and-outs of old-time hockey, and, call up their own teenage sons—Toe (Trevor Chong), Dit (Willy Lavendel), and Gordie (Adam Klein), named after Toe Blake, Dit Clapper and Gordie Howe—to assist them. The practice primarily consists of brawling, spearing, tripping and other such fanciful drills. In a sequence reminiscent of *Slap Shot 2*, one of the junior Hansons dives straight at the camera as team members pummel, trip, and pile on him. As opposed to the circus-like choreographed performance that robs the Super-Chiefs of their masculinity, this hardy maneuver brings out the necessary fierceness and lack of restraint that increases the orphans' underdog chances, particularly as they have neither position nor status in the town. The Hansons reprise their trademark Daemon-like trickster selves, but also take on the role of exemplars, asserted at the tail end of *Slap Shot 2* when the brothers win the lottery and purchase the team to reclaim old-time hockey. Because the orphans lack the protective guidance of the father, which is pivotal to the sports genre, they are in dire need of surrogate father figures and the Hansons'

The Hanson Brothers, left to right: Jack (David Hanson), Steve (Steven Carlson) and Jeff (Jeff Carlson) do promotion for *Slap Shot 3: The Junior League* (AP/The Canadian Press/Chris Young).

sponsor role is insufficient, even though much like District 5 in *The Mighty Ducks*, the orphans become a bona fide team thanks to this support.

With the brothers fully inhabiting their surrogate role as fathers and coaches, the young Chiefs must do some border-crossing into bully territory, which the film depicts through a number of tilted shots, ice level camera sequences, and visual effects that augment speed while taking away the viewer's sense of bearings. As they firm up their masculinity, the Junior Chiefs must ultimately cross back into sportsman territory, and to that effect, the film must neutralize the Hansons' aggression by confining them to the sidelines—i.e., behind the bench. In irrepressible Daemon-like form, they repeatedly attempt to insert themselves into the game by hitting the referee over the head when he's not looking, tripping an opponent that skates by the bench, and squirting yet another with a water bottle. From the sidelines, these gestures are largely harmless and more in line with the benevolent tricksterism of the child in Disney films, which was meant to replace the Hansons' hyperphysicality and re-brand hockey as family entertainment. *Slap Shot 3*, which deploys the Hansons to fulfill a yearning for old-time hockey, must ironically also sanitize the brothers' signature by restricting them to gimmicks and containing their force-of-nature character in line with the new genre of family entertainment.

The purpose of popcorn films that speak to children and teens is to stress a moral angle, and *Slap Shot 3* delivers this message through the figure of former NHLer Mark Messier who appears in the hallway sporting a halo to impress on Riley and Kain the need to shed the cheap stuff. He instructs that a quality opponent propels a player to new heights, and "in the end, it doesn't matter who wins or loses … you've both earned the trust and respect of each other." The moral of the tale is to play the game with gusto but, in true sportsmanlike form, avoid straying into bully territory, a directive that the mayor reaffirms and the Hansons relay by through their injunction to "find … balance." However, after Messier delivers his missive, and the young duo have gone back to their respective locker rooms, the Hansons appear behind him casually munching on a snack. One of them queries Messier if he'd like to partake, and as he makes a move to join in, without losing a beat the brother retrieves the morsel with the remark: "I don't think so!" Apart from reiterating the Hansons' trickster signature, the move communicates to Messier that he is not one of their kind and that their Daemon-like character is nothing like the hockey code that the NHL icon lives by, regardless of the toughness of his game. Whereas as mentors of the young orphans, the Hansons must temper the game's rough edges, extolling the teens to find a happy medium between the pugnacious game and the sort of enfeebled play that only invites merciless pummeling, with a veteran NHL star the brothers see no need for such niceties. The Hansons are the embodiment of Hollywood's pre–Disney idea of hockey as a game of mayhem without protocol or rules, in contrast with Messier who as NHLer stands for a sturdy masculinity that embodies the codes of the Canadian game. With this humorous aside, the Hansons reclaim their force-of-nature stature as icons whose mark on the game is no less consequential.

Slap Shot 3 conveys hockey through numerous motifs of cultural convergence that evoke the game as a transnational product. Kevin Robins notes that globalization processes tend to rework old elements and draw on a locality's integration with world markets by interspersing change with continuity.[59] In much the same way, the film plays with the Hansons' iconic signature by blending continuity with change. The brothers represent a variant of hockey masculinity that connotes the populist pleasures of excess as a salve for depersonalized seventies sport, the objectification of the athlete, and the enfeeblement of men by big capital, which stripped males of their breadwinning role and their vigorous identity at a time of economic duress. Their incarnation in the second film serves much the same purpose but with increasing exemplary hues, as the Hansons are neutralized and absent for most of the story, but return to rescue hockey from the clutches of corporate-driven family entertainment.

Slap Shot 3 elevates the Hansons to full-fledged exemplary status, redrawing them as mentors, coaches, and father figures. However, the directives of family entertainment with its glitzy corporate spectacle advocate the underwriting of sport by hefty sponsorship monies and in short order remake the Hansons into stars in a genre whose referents the seventies original and the first sequel sharply critique. Only the Messier sequence reaffirms the brothers' distinctiveness as akin to a physical phenomenon outside human control, which is key to their transgressive and irreverent character. Still, the inclusion of the Hansons in family fare is doubtlessly meant to enhance the film's saleability in the North American entertainment market, as these rascal-icons remain popular with hockey connoisseurs on both sides of the border for conveying an authentic aspect of the game: the unmistakable potential for haphazard and unbridled violence despite the existence of codes that check aggression.[60] *Slap Shot 3*'s fusion of Disneyesque markers with Hansonian referents, which Disney sought to extirpate with its own brand of upmarket spectacle, also ultimately attest to the way family fare is able to blend well-known iconographies to appeal to both kids and adults in search of global audiences.

The CTV-aired *Sticks and Stones* (Mihalka, 2007), a family movie filmed in New Brunswick and Nova Scotia, procures yet another view of transborder hockey connections through the story of two peewee teams from Fredericton, New Brunswick and Brockton, Massachusetts.[61] The film's narrative center is Jordy Martin (Alexander de Jordy), a talent for the Fredericton Canadiens who along with pal Kyle "KP" Perkins (Scott Beaudin) looks to have a bright future in the game. Jordy's dad, Neil (David Sutcliffe), coaches the squad with a steady hand, while KP's dad, Craig (Mark Camacho), embodies the win-at-all-costs hockey parent who expects his son to go places.

On the other side of the border, the Brockton Boxers' young captain Michael Carver (Daniel Magder), who has the hallmark feisty intensity of the Massachusetts hockey player, hails from a patriotic military family whose dad, Peter (John Robinson), is state police, older brother and erstwhile hockey promise, Chris (Mark Trottier), has enlisted in the military, and mom, Anne (Lori Hallier), is stay-at-home, apple-pie neighborly. The relationship between Boxers head coach Al Bouchard (Richard Fitzpatrick) and the Carvers, as well as the yellow ribbons decking many of the homes in the working-class suburb of Boston on the eve of the Iraq War, make clear that the Boxers are part of a tight-knit community. When the Boxers arrive in Montreal, their bus lands in the midst of a fiery demonstration against the U.S. role in Iraq. The protestors, who carry signs in English and French that read "Kill Bush," "USA terrorists," and *"Non à la guerre,"* rock the vehicle and burn a U.S. flag forcing the intervention of police in riot gear. The peewees shake off the encounter, and like their Fredericton counterparts, are treated that evening to an NHL Canadiens-Islanders game. Their jitters return, however, as some attendees boo the U.S. national anthem, even as others frown on the hostile display. The following day the animosity continues unabated as adults in attendance at the Canadiens-Boxers game taunt some of the accompanying American parents and heckle the young team. The referee also stacks the deck by handing the Boxers nine consecutive penalties and none to the Canadiens, and coach Bouchard has no option but to pull his squad from the game and head back home. Fredericton celebrates the win in the locker room, but disturbed at the unfair treatment, Jordy pledges to make it up to the Boxers and goes all out planning a friendly game modeled on the Canada-Russia 1972 Summit Series.[62]

Although *Sticks and Stones* frames the story by way of Jordy's exemplary masculinity and his quest for friendly transborder ties, as a family film it also foregrounds the value of the family unit as a mirror of the nation. The narrative makes clear that Jordy's efforts are overlaid with worries over his parents' separation and that he clearly views the rapprochement between the Fredericton and Brockton teams as symbol of their prospective reunion. As he tells dad Neil, "someone just has to go first, someone just has to say they're sorry," conveying with urgency that dad must renew his efforts to get mom back. The family film is inherently conservative and expresses anxieties over the family's breakdown, which it implicitly blames on the absent mother and the social fallout resulting from women embarking on professional paths. Although clearly a parent who loves her son and looks after his wellbeing, mom Linda (Debra McCabe), who is offered a plum educator's position in Bathurst, also values her career prospects and communicates these priorities to Jordy: "The thing is, I have been working toward an offer like this my whole career. It's kind of a now or never thing for me." She sounds vague about her separation from Neil amplifying that dad hesitates to move the family as he has secured a coveted management position. But Jordy rightly gauges that the situation is serious.

The more educated and professionally aspiring Martins epitomize the hurdles of the modern-day family with their upwardly mobile, dual-working parent lifestyle. The close-knit Carver ensemble, in contrast, comes together when jeopardized by the deploy-

Sticks and Stones **movie poster (CTV/Photofest).**

ment of Chris to Iraq, as Jordy witnesses with longing when Anne invites him and Neil to stay for dinner on a visit to Brockton. *Sticks and Stones* thus reverses the notion that the U.S. as an embodiment of the values of modernity poses a threat not only to Canada's game but the viability of the nation as a differentiated political and cultural entity.[63] The Carvers effectively personify a nostalgic, almost mythical, version of the small-town family whose wholesome life is enmeshed in community, as seen in the introductory scenes when coach Bouchard personally drives Michael home from hockey practice to receive news of Chris' deployment. Brown notes that imagery of the small-town family has its origins in the Hollywood films of the 1930s and 1940s, which portray the family's grounding in community and the father's respected public profile within it as a way of furthering a romanticized vision of the U.S.[64]

Neil and Jordy's tensions with the KP-Craig Perkins team further exacerbate the differences between the Canadian and American contingents. While an unmistakable talent, KP is sorely lacking in the sportsmanship required by family fare because dad has forgotten that hockey embodies particular values that are just as important as a game's final tally and his son's statistics. Craig, who bears an uncanny resemblance to underhanded Hawks coach Jack Riley in *The Mighty Ducks*, goes as far as to summon a scout from the Notre Dame Hounds to assess KP and Jordy's prospects in the hopes of advancing the young duo's hockey careers. The scout frowns on KP's continual hotdogging during the Canadiens-Boxers game, and even as KP's actions evoke a reprimand from Neil, Craig appears to discern nothing amiss, instead playing up his kid's and Jordy's combined wizardry. Craig is also well aware that KP needs Jordy to help him pad his numbers in advance of a Quebec hockey assessment camp. He sabotages the youngster's attempts to invite the Boxers back to Fredericton because their prospective arrival conflicts with his presence at camp. When these efforts fail, Craig resorts to blaming Neil that "Your son is ruining his [KP's] career," to which the latter responds, "He's 12 years old. He doesn't have a career." Tensions between the two father-son teams add to the Martins' domestic instability and cultural rifts over the Iraq War to heighten the idea of Canada as a nation beset by social and political divisions.

Except for hockey, the Canadian families at first appear to have little in common with their southern neighbors, who seem invested in patriotic duty and institutional authority. Nonetheless, the film hints that hockey may just be the healing force that brings both sides together. Edits that show the mood in both buses as the contingents travel to Montreal for the hockey championship reveal the children's playful outlook. The teams' unexpected first meeting at the Bell Centre is also full of humorous innuendo. At the arena for the Canadiens-Islanders game, the peewees engage in a comical version of trash-talk. When Jordy asks Michael: "Ray Bourque or Nick Lidström?" Michael replies without hesitation: "Bourque." After some more strutting on both sides, Jordy asks again: "Jagr or Thornton?" This time Michael surprises him and his own teammates with another Boston powerhouse: "Cam Neely." Satisfied that the Brockton captain is suitably tough, Jordy and teammates nod their heads in approval and walk away promising to give the Boxers a fight for their money. The children's amusing masculinity display, which displaces hockey's aggressive warrior referents onto professional surrogates, amplifies the youngsters' playfulness because the lone game in the film will turn into a source of discord.

Sticks and Stones, however, also leaves little doubt that the Carvers stand as exemplars of social cohesion for the Canadian contingent, corroborating Eva Mackey's findings that Canadians regard American patriotism and social bonds bonds as a possible "solution to the problem of Canada's fragmented and even non-existent identity."[65] This longing for utopia in the form of the mythic small town aligns with sport's respect for traditional compacts and its desire to return to nostalgic origins. It also reflects Canadians' identification with the small town as a site for nurturing hockey talent and a mirror of the nation at large.[66] Clearly gleaning his priorities, Jordy acts in the spirit of the small town neighbor, and heals the rift with the Boxers by staging a weeklong Canada–U.S. Friendship event, ultimately persuading dad to do the right thing by mom.

Hockey-centered family fare is chiefly concerned with developing children into a form of social capital for the community. For this reason, it emphasizes the father-son link in sport and the role of the family as bulwark against social ills in line with the conservative values of the family and sports genres even as it cedes the performative ground to children. These movies also negotiate hockey's masculinity-honing capabilities in line with the sports film's didacticism, which serves to ground the work of citizenry and nationhood. Additionally, new family entertainment fare taps the tricksterism of the child to augment a film's mode of address and bring in global audiences consisting of both kids and kidults. This benevolent gamesmanship is also part and parcel of the genre's heightened visual spectacle, which delivers the game in sanitized form but by way of new camera angles that open up the ice and actors who can actually hold their own on skates. These movies blend motifs from antecedent films with assorted plot twists that amplify commercial potential. But they also short-circuit the multiculturalism espoused by the new family genre with the conservatism of the sports film in fielding token characters from diverse social backgrounds that readily cede the center of the narrative to young white males.

5

Hockey, Masculinity and Nationhood in Quebec Cinema

The hockey repertoire produced in Quebec, like the province's canonical films, touches profoundly on issues of national identity. Because Quebec cinema prioritizes difference from the Rest of Canada (ROC), hockey protagonists and their game preeminently dramatize Francophone national character. The commitment to express a distinct cultural identity in a vast North American continent where Anglophone cultures preside developed out of the province's close-knit relationship between image-making and the politics of independence.[1] Unlike Canada's larger concept of nationhood, which is articulated by way of legalistic referents, traditional French-nationalism premises the nation as an *ethnie*—as a kind of family who traces its roots to a common ancestry through which Francophones differentiate themselves from outsiders.[2] And although Quebec's governments and Parti Québécois have made inroads in articulating a more inclusive model of nationalism, this impression persists. The above paradigm also formulates the province as a small nation or *petit pays*, a stateless nation within a nation struggling to endure despite a history of colonization and disenfranchisement. The discourse of *petit pays* foregrounds the cultural memory of the Conquest—the defeat of the French by the English in 1759 on the Plains of Abraham—as responsible for furthering the subjugation of the Francophone spirit. It also stipulates the necessity of a politics of *survivance* through French-Canadian opposition to linguistic and demographic absorption into Anglophone culture.[3]

From the earliest days of New France, political elites and Church clergy advocated cultural preservation through rural ideals as the only alternatives to the Anglophone elite's economic and political ascendance in urban centers. The province's political and religious power base espoused with politics of *survivance* by way of the humble *habitant* doctrine, which idealized rural life through the figure of the farmer who managed to carve out a piece of productive land from the harsh Northern wilderness. This tradition encouraged accommodation as a form of resistance to assimilation, and exhorted citizens to embrace sacrifice, meekness, and devotion to work.[4]

Quebec's "deep past"—the era spanning Jacques Cartier's frontier explorations in the 1500s to 1759[5]—however, supports a model of masculinity that, unlike the conservative humble *habitant* ideology, prioritizes independence and resilience through the iconography of the *coureurs de bois*, *trappeurs*, and *voyageurs*. These figures, who operated outside the control of the French government and the Church in propelling the fur trade, endure as a fearless, defiant, and vital model of Francophone masculinity. Even though these pioneers hold a central role in Canadian nation-building, they also comprised an exclusive Francophone demographic. Carolyn Podruchny observes that the French language presided in the *voyageurs* and *coureurs de bois'* transient social space and that these individuals retained their French-Canadian identity even as some of their values converged with those of Aboriginal cultures.[6] And although there were differences within this group, the same audacious, enterprising spirit motivated their sense of identity. The licensed *voyageurs*, who ranged from *engagés* to small contractors, were effectively indentured servants who deployed their trade under the oversight of Anglophone bourgeois managers.[7] They differed from the *coureurs de bois*, who operated as unlicensed independent traders, and from former *voyageurs*, who remained in the *pays d'en haut* (up-country)[8] as freemen relying on their trading, trapping, hunting, fishing and other skills. The *voyageurs* nevertheless viewed their adverse circumstances as suitable to *faire l'Homme*—to making the man—and for honing a vigorous masculine identity by way of wilderness referents. These men prioritized courage, risk, and freedom, and a lived a bold, enterprising life in which cherished and durable horses, dogs, and canoes, as well as titillating liaisons with women took center stage. They also resorted to various forms of gamesmanship, controlling the pace at which they trapped, traded, and traveled, even making off with supplies and engaging in free trading to garner leverage and negotiate better working conditions. In appraising themselves as sturdier than their bourgeois handlers and their Aboriginal counterparts, and engaging in strategic gamesman tactics, the *voyageurs* accrued various forms of symbolic capital and pushed back against the master-servant relationship.[9]

In contrast to the submissive figure of the humble *habitant* who led a life informed by hard agricultural labor and the edicts of Roman-Catholicism, the *voyageurs* along with the *coureurs de bois* embodied a strapping, adventurous model of masculinity that has shaped Quebec national character and to this day remains useful in leveraging Francophone identity because of its heroic, apostate elements. Speaking to the staying power of Quebec's deep past, Jean Harvey notes that in the nineteenth century, French-Canadians continued to refer to themselves as the original *Canadiens* to associate themselves with the explorers and settlers of this era and set themselves apart from *les anglais* or "the English" in Canada. As Francophones took to the English(-Canadian) practice of sport, and hockey in particular, they also appropriated the game to express national identity and stage the Anglo-French rivalry.[10] Because the clergy exploited the meek, rural humble *habitant* ideal to control every aspect of the people's lives, including their leisure activities, and hockey in Quebec was not seen as part of this tradition since it was a cultural practice borrowed from the English, the sport stood out as the one symbol that rivaled the Church's central role in articulating Francophone identity. Scott Mackenzie notes that the power of the game in fashioning identity resided in upsetting the Church's exclusive hold on ceremony and tradition because of its ritualistic features and its nation-building potency.[11]

Throughout the 1960s Quiet Revolution (*Révolution tranquille*)—a period of political and social change in which the province secularized and articulated the desire for a distinct geopolitical future independent of Francophone minorities outside the province[12]–hockey, and in particular, the Montreal Canadiens, remained powerful symbols of French-Canadian identity. From its inception the Canadiens communicated its identity politics through the use of the French language, as numerous groups involved in the 1950s and 1960s project of identity rallied around the team as "porte-étendards of competing ... national projects," as

Jean Harvey documents.[13] Amy Ransom corroborates that to this day the province's pop culture artists link the club to the founding mythology of Quebec and stress that "a Canadiens fan is a true Quebecer."[14]

The cinema mirrors the game's durability and the significance of the Montreal Canadiens in expressing Quebec identity. Gilles Groulx's poetic documentary *Un Jeu si simple* (1964), produced by the National Film Board,[15] still serves as enduring paean to the game and to the formidable stature of the Canadiens. The piece opens with extensive newsreel footage of the squad at play at the Forum as the narrator affirms that hockey is our national sport (*"le hockey est notre sport national"*) watched by 1.5 million on TV and 14,000 at the arena. Zeroing in on Montrealers of all ages and both sexes intently focused on the proceedings, the piece portrays them watching the best in the world (*"les champions du monde"*)—the Canadiens battling the Detroit Red Wings, and later the Leafs, and unleashing their wizardry in vivid color. The introductory sequence underlines the intimate connection between the people and the game by philosophically musing that on account of familiarity, the game by nature eludes definition (*"il échappe à la description"*). The spectators—conveyed primarily in black and white close-ups and extra-wide shots—also depict the idea of a people rehearsing the rituals of nationhood. Above all, the sequence dexterously hints at hockey's dual character by effectively splitting the messages communicated by the narration and the cinematography. The voiceover relays the game's status as a national sport, while the visuals convey hockey as peerless symbol of the French-Canadian project of identity and nationhood. Decades later, Michel Brault amplifies the sport's significance for Quebec's project of identity in film by underscoring its long history as metonym for the city of Montreal. In an interview on his *Montréal vu par* (1991) entry, "*La Dernière Partie*" ("The Last Game"), Brault notes with a tinge of regret that because Montrealers have a habit of tearing down old buildings, the city he loves "no longer exists," and for this reason he chose to "show it … [by way of] the most 'Montreal' of activities—hockey."[16]

Because hockey is one of the few cultural symbols that express both a unified notion of Canadian identity and Quebec nationalism, it represents the nation as two very different projects. Whereas English-Canadian nationalism argues that Canada is a "fractured mosaic," a state without a shared symbolic culture,[17] French-Canadian nationalism draws on the "small nation" code to emphasize Quebec's history through meaningful struggle against a referent Other. Hockey's enduring link to the province's mythologized past, and its expedience in articulating a politics of resistance, also suggests that in film the game primarily amplifies Quebec's cinema of difference.

Quebec and the Montreal Canadiens: *The Mystery of the Million Dollar Hockey Puck* and *The Sweater*

The children's chase film, *The Mystery of the Million Dollar Hockey Puck—La Poursuite mystérieuse: $1,000,000 sur la glace* (LaFleur and Svatek, 1975), also known as *Pee Wee*,[18] expresses the Francophone romance with the Montreal Canadiens through the sojourn of Chicoutimi orphans Pierre Brunet (Michael MacDonald) and younger sister Catou (Angèle Knight), who set out to alert the team about an international diamond-smuggling conspiracy that threatens to implicate them and sully their reputation. A diehard Canadiens fans who plays hockey with gusto, Pierre overhears crooks Napoléon (Kurt Schlegl) and Belletête

(Jean-Louis Millete) at a flower shop scheming to smuggle into the U.S. a million dollars worth of diamonds in a hollowed out Canadiens puck they will place with the team's gear. To foil the crooks' scheme, Pierre tries first to alert the nuns about the plot. Seeing he is getting nowhere, he decides to take matters into his hands and head for the jeweler's shop in Quebec City where the infamous puck must be retrieved. In his haste, however, the youngster has left his wallet at the flower shop and the crooks, suspicious that he has overheard their plans, head for the orphanage to capture him. But Pierre and Catou manage to outfox them and stow away inside their van. The children are almost discovered and escape only with the help of an RCAF pilot who flies them to their destination where they get to the puck ahead of the crooks. The chase takes them through Quebec City's most recognizable locations and to the Winter Carnival, where they unsuccessfully try to catch the attention of Canadiens "Le Gros Bill" Jean Béliveau riding on one of the floats. After the crooks execute another clumsy attempt at pinning them down, Pierre and Catou are finally entrapped by an old lady who turns out to be the ringleader behind the fake puck scheme and who goes by the alias "the Boss" (Marthe Thiéry). Locked inside a room at the crook's sumptuous home, the children again manage to escape and take off by snowmobile en route to the Montreal Forum, where the Canadiens happen to be at play. Crawling around one of the arena's catwalks on his way to the announcer booth, Pierre drops the puck onto the ice where the team plays with it for a while. Upon reaching the media booth, he relays the details of the plot to Danny Gallivan, the voice of the Canadiens, and succeeds in convincing him. The crooks are arrested in short order and the grateful players gift Pierre with his own Canadiens jersey and take the children for a skate on home ice.

The Mystery of the Million Dollar Hockey Puck dramatizes the populist roots of Quebec nationalism by procuring a glimpse of the Canadiens' sturdy connection with the people as exemplified by young Pierre's resolve to warn the organization of the gang's nefarious activities. Pierre's commitment is such that even though the crooks give relentless chase, the boy never once takes off his Canadiens pullover nor does he waiver in the faith that, unlike authority figures such as the orphanage nuns or the police whom they approach about the conspiracy, the team will believe his story.[19] The imagery of children suggests the idea of a young Francophone project of identity that in the mid-seventies was still fresh and remained vulnerable. The children's representation as orphans is also revealing in that orphaning implies a sense of uncertain roots. Katharine Monk views the orphan as an allegorical motif for "dislocation and outsiderism," a palpable symbol for the perceived failure of nation-building.[20] Orphan imagery pointedly speaks to Quebecers' sense of uprootedness following secularization, which reconfigured identity by casting aside the humble *habitant* ideology espoused by the Church and the governing elites. At this time, however, nationalist fervor in the province also diminished owing to the October 1970 violent acts by the *Front de libération du Québec* (FLQ). The FLQ's actions alienated the core figures that had supported the province's political and cultural independence in the sixties,[21] producing profound changes in the expression of Quebec nationalism. Many in the province, particularly poets and visual artists, summarily reconsidered their allegiance and chose to restructure their political loyalties in support of the federalist vision of government.[22]

The film mirrors the aftereffects of these events by harmonizing Quebec nationalism with the federalist vision espoused by Prime Minister Trudeau. It speaks to the idea of Canada as comprised by two founding nations—Anglophone and Francophone—by distinctly splitting the use of language. Even though Pierre and Catou are Francophones, they communicate in English much like the rest of the characters. On the other hand, the film relays the French language, one of the primary symbols of Francophone identity,[23] visually through street placards and store signs as well as other pictorial signifiers of Francophone culture. The lone French expression heard in the film comes from one of crooks. Because the scoundrel is hiding inside the costume of a giant rabbit in hopes of ambushing Pierre and Catou during the Winter Carnival, the greeting registers as muffled and hardly intelligible. When expressed through language, then, the Francophone project of identity in *Million Dollar Hockey Puck* is one of cultural duality: in plain sight but essentially never heard.

Hockey Night in Canada announcer Danny Gallivan, who called Canadiens games for thirty years until his retirement at the end of the 1983–1984 season, is the sole figure in the film who believes the children's story and gives them credit for helping to foil the smugglers. As the voice of Canadiens hockey, he also gives the orphans a voice, although again, all dialogue takes place in English. This connection suggests that the budding yet still vulnerable secular Francophone project of identity is likely to find its most successful expression through the cultural industries: in Canadiens hockey and its media broadcasts, which Gallivan as *Hockey Night in Canada* play-by-play commentator represents. The sequence of Pierre reaching the announcer booth high in the confines of the Montreal Forum as the Canadiens score the game-winning tally suggests as much, reaffirming the sturdy link between team and people. Because orphaning implies a lack of family structure and uprootedness, the Canadiens provide Pierre along with the rest of the children at the orphanage, with a sense of belonging to a larger vital community.

The allegory of the family by way of orphan imagery also hints at the populist roots of Quebec nationalism, indicating that at a time of deep social transformation the people safeguarded the Canadiens' social standing and upheld the team as symbol of Francophone identity. In contrast to the violent character of hockey in English-Canadian and Hollywood films of the period, Canadiens hockey is skilled, gallant, and represented by marquee names who convey the team's Stanley Cup juggernaut status. *The Mystery of the Million Dollar Hockey Puck* also activates the link between the team and the people through visual framing of the Forum as the home of the Canadiens. The last fifteen minutes of the film, along with the rolling credits, take place within its confines, merging team and arena in a symbiotic relationship, unlike later films like the 2006 *Bon Cop, Bad Cop*, where the Montreal team connotes Québécois identity but arena sequences take place around the perimeters—in the bathroom and hallways—and the details of the rink are largely generic.[24] The film's visual appreciation of the Forum is also consistent with the chase genre's focus on cinematic attractions which allow for unadulterated moments of visual excitement that procure the filmic experience as a spectacle ride.[25] The crooks' pursuit of Pierre and Catou effectively takes the viewer through a tour of Quebec's principal monuments, a thrill ride that comprises the Winter Carnival and Canadiens hockey, which by their nature are the very embodiments of spectacle. The sequence that features icon "Le Gros Bill" Jean Béliveau on one of the parade floats also harks back to the roots of the first hockey tournaments held alongside the 1880s Winter Carnival. Since the festival was created, assembled, and managed entirely by Québécois who trace their lineage back to the original explorers and settlers of New France,[26] the sequence effectively interpolates the Canadiens in the long-time rituals of cultural self-valorization.

The Mystery of the Million Dollar Hockey Puck is also consistent with the period's movies in how it grounds Quebec identity. In his survey of Quebec films from 1968 to 1980, Michel

Pierre (Michael MacDonald, child, right) and Catou (Angèle Knight, child, left) in the Canadiens locker room in *The Mystery of the Million Dollar Hockey Puck* (Cinépix/Greg Dunning).

Houle notes that this repertoire is preoccupied with "protagonists from the popular classes" and the desire to "assert the specificity" of Quebecers through the image of the common people. He observes that these films also show an interest in Quebec subcultures—criminals, the destitute, and other marginal folk—which he explains as an outcome of the growing industrial structure of the economy and pressures from the CFDC to draw audiences to a cinema that insisted on depicting the commonplace.[27] As a popular movie produced by Cinépix with assistance of CFDC, *The Mystery of the Million Dollar Hockey Puck* showcases a similar focus on the common people as blueprint for French-Canadian identity. Even the purported heretics who seek to gain by sullying the lofty image of the Canadiens signal the team's high standing by way of the password required to obtain the puck with the embedded diamonds from the complicit jeweler: "I like a good hockey game"—"Yes, if the Canadiens are playing." If, as Houle suggests, imagery of the people works to consolidate Quebec identity at this time, *The Mystery of the Million Dollar Hockey Puck* also shows that the formula very obviously foregrounds the Canadiens' connection to the people in forging this identity.

Imagery of the Church in the film is also consistent with social changes in the province brought on by secularization. The Quiet Revolution was effectively a two-fold revolt against the repressive edicts of the Roman Catholic Church and the conservatism of political elites personified by the Maurice Duplessis government. Houle notes that during the 1940s and

1950s the Church exercised exclusive authority over health and social affairs, overseeing hospitals, orphanages, reform schools, and other such institutions, and the cinema similarly showed evidence of the clergy's ubiquitous presence in Quebecers' lives. During the Quiet Revolution clergy numbers saw a spectacular decline that mirrored the crumbling of Church power, and the filmmakers in like fashion effaced the clergy from the silver screen. *The Mystery of the Million Dollar Hockey Puck* symbolically articulates the fading influence of Roman Catholicism by prioritizing the children's urgent task. In the course of their sojourn, Pierre and Catou take refuge inside a church before they continue on their quest. This religious symbolism points to the Church as safe harbor at a time when the province was transitioning from its Catholic roots. The initiative the children show, which leads to their escape from the orphanage to warn the Canadiens, however, also entails disobeying the nuns' strict rules, and implies setting aside the mandates of the Church and its humble *habitant* directive. Pierre's independent instincts, which drive the children's undertaking, are consistent with the idea of rebellious resistance as the honorable choice in Quebec's mythical iconography. Because children's films typically endorse conservative values that uphold the sacrosanct status of the family, Pierre's actions also suggest that the Canadiens, not the nuns, are the children's true family, which underscores Quebec's questioning of the Church-state relationship during the 1970s. And although by film's end Pierre and Catou are set to return to the orphanage, the final sequences are of the children enjoying themselves on the ice in the company of the players, suggesting the Church's ultimate representation as emblem of the past.[28]

As an anglo-québécois production, *The Million Dollar Hockey Puck* also dramatizes changes in the expression of Québécois identity, which in the seventies inflected this identity with *americanité* at the expense of the province's French-European roots.[29] André Loiselle observes that this change, which formulated Quebecers as the French of North America, was propelled by Francophones' own aspirations for upward mobility fueled by the influence of American product on Canadian TV screens. This shift intersected with structural changes in the Canadian movie industry that emphasized commercial film production and placed less stress on the auteur-driven vehicles that traditionally bolstered Francophone identity in the cinema. Houle notes with some consternation that many of the films of the mid–1970s are neither French-language films nor theatrical releases, but commercial pictures distributed through the medium of TV or community circles linked to the National Film Board. Funding agencies' subsidy of commercial film at this time also sharply reduced the audience for Quebec film to an all-time low.[30]

A film that expresses French-Canadian identity through protagonists that only speak English nonetheless also renders this identity fragmentary. The distortion can be accounted for by way of the funding constraints of the period and impacted by the reality that Quebec's film industry was still in its "art film" phase. Producing a children's film in French therefore would not have been marketable. Whether or not it was the intention of the producers to field such a discourse regarding French-Canadian identity and the most French-Canadian of hockey teams, the Canadiens, *The Mystery of the Million Dollar Hockey Puck* emerges as a classic example of articulated tension between Francophone nationalism and federalism.[31] That is, the English-language focus of the film and the NHL referents of hockey tap Greater North American markers to contextualize Francophone identity and Quebec as part of the Republic of North America. The Canadiens, the Forum, *HNIC*'s Danny Gallivan, the Church, the Winter Carnival, as well as the masculinity of young Pierre and the link between the team and the orphans who represent the people, on the other hand, reprise hockey as part of the Francophone project of identity in line with Quebec's desire for a future as distinct geopolitical entity.

The NFB's children's animation piece[32] *Le Chandail* (Cohen, 1980), based on Roch Carrier's short story *Le chandail de hockey*,[33] also recapitulates the prominent place of the Canadiens in French-Canadian culture. The story opens with a picturesque sketch of the small town of Ste. Justine, Quebec, as Carrier, who narrates the piece, notes that when he was a boy, village life revolved around two mainstays: Sunday Mass and Saturday hockey broadcasts. The entire town is glued to the radio following the feats of the Canadiens—"the best hockey team in the world," as Carrier notes. The 10-year-old boy at the center of the story is no less of a diehard fan and when Maurice Richard scores, he holds up his Canadiens sweater to his chest and waltzes around in celebration. One day, mom notices that the sweater is ripped in several places and she digs up her Eaton's catalogue to order a new jersey for her growing boy. The department store, however, mishandles the order and sends a Leafs sweater instead. Distraught, the boy refuses to wear it, noting that he's always worn a Canadiens jersey, his friends are all Canadiens fans, and besides, the Leafs are always beaten by the Canadiens. But mom prevails noting that "Monsieur Eaton" will be insulted if the item is returned, and he won't secure another sweater until spring. Faced with the prospect of foregoing hockey for the entire winter, the boy relents and nervously wears his blue sweater to the weekly game.

As soon as he arrives at the rink, his teammates spot him and are on him like a small army, wearing their Canadiens number 9 red, white, and blue. Their faces in close-up fill the frame and show their patent displeasure. He is promptly relegated to the sidelines unable to see ice time. When finally there is an opening and he is able to join in, he is given yet another penalty. The boy's enraged face, his head growing larger, nostrils flaring, and face turning red, expresses his frustration: "*C'était trop! C'était injuste! C'est la persécution! C'est à cause de mon chandail bleu!*" ("It was enough. It was unjust. Persecution! All because of my blue sweater!") The blend of past and present tenses show that the episode is still fresh in Carrier's mind. The boy throws down his stick with all his might and it breaks with a clean "click!" As he bends over to try to put it back together, a purplish shadow washes over him. He looks up and two immense skates and legs up to the knees—a metonym for power—come into view surrounding his tiny figure. The large torso and small head of the parish priest fill the frame with the church in the distance, and as *le curé* admonishes that he cannot behave recklessly because he is wearing a blue sweater, the boy's reaction shot shows his small figure looking up ruefully, the ice scratched up all around him as if about to break.

The priest summarily sends the boy to the village church to pray for forgiveness. Once there, however, the youngster fervently asks God to send a hundred million hungry moths that will eat the Leafs sweater into oblivion. As he does, Maurice Richard magically appears in the vision and vigorously shakes hands with him. The icon's arm is powerful, hinting that he easily carries the dreams, the longings, and the vigor of the people. Two beams of light reaching from the church's tall windows converge on the boy and his idol, blessing the tacit pact between them and making clear that a Quebecer is forever, and uncompromisingly, a Canadien.

Much like *The Mystery of the Million Dollar Hockey Puck*, the story depicts the people safeguarding the Canadiens' cultural standing, and in so doing, reaffirms the connection between the game and Quebec nationalism. During the 1940s and 50s Maurice Richard was on a tear on Forum ice, and he symbolized the province's desire for independence. Because the Canadiens' rivalry with the Leafs alludes to Anglo-French antagonisms off the ice, the boy's comical entanglement as a matter of course activates his fierce resistance to subordinating Québécois identity to larger iterations of Canadianicity, much like the story's original title, "*Une abominable feuille d'érable sur la glace*" ("An abominable maple leaf on the ice"), implies. Maurice is the face of French-Canadian success after almost two centuries of repression and second-rate citizen status, and the boy cannot simply swap the symbol of this success—his Canadiens jersey—for "loser" Leafs status.

The Sweater derives its charm from the way the whimsical imagery interfaces with Carrier's narration. While in English, the author's French-Canadian accent lends color to the story, in French it contributes not only authenticity but cultural potency as it synchs up with the visual style and the musical motifs. Carrier is a consummate storyteller and his acting skills, which come through his well-nuanced narration, carry the story. The opening suggests a swift journey back into the past, as the houses, barns, trees, horse-drawn sleigh and other images that appear in the snowy landscape move toward the viewer and in fluid fashion change into one another accompanied by a folksy, rhythmic French musical tune. The images also flicker throughout and give the impression of looking at an old movie. Pastoral iconography of the benevolent Northern settlement invokes the pre–1960s role of the Catholic Church in promoting the cohesiveness and survival of French-speaking communities, even as Carrier makes clear that "[t]he hockey rink was more important than the school."[34]

The Mystery of the Million Dollar Hockey Puck and *The Sweater* bring up similar images of young boys whose hockey loyalties take precedence over conformity to Church rules. Given that the game in film in the 1970s is not associated with children's fare because of its violent complexion, the image of boys fiercely professing their allegiance to the Canadiens and rehearsing Quebecers' aspirations in their hockey rituals while symbolically rebelling against Church figures is no small gesture. Even though the Catholic nuns and priests who ran the schools and orphanages sought to hone upstanding citizens by inculcating Christian morals and spiritual values, by prioritizing the humble *habitant* doctrine they also endorsed allegiance to a form of servitude. After a long history of social and economic repression, Quebecers could only welcome success in the very public arena of hockey by way of Maurice Richard's premier status in the league and the Canadiens' multiple Stanley Cup triumphs. The children's fierce loyalties to the team, then, dramatize the people's rejection of the humble *habitant* doctrine and corroborate that early on the game rivaled religion's hold on Quebecers because of its powerful ritualistic and nation-building aspects. George Melnyk links Roch Carrier's exploration of identity in folk novels, along with and Michel Tremblay's *joual*-inflected plays, to the emergence of Quebec cinema and significant developments in other arts.[35] Imagery of boyhood, hockey and the Church in children's classics substantiate the emergence of a newly developing Francophone identity that, although fledgling, expresses buoyantly and irrepressibly in film.

Les Boys I, II, III, IV: Hockey, Identity and Commercial Success

If in the preceding two decades, Quebec cinema consolidates a distinct sense of nationhood, in the 1990s and beyond it resumes its focus on themes of resistance in keeping with the province's secular realities. Because Quebec film prioritizes cultural difference and Montreal hockey foregrounds this distinctiveness, hockey-themed movies also dramatize the game's potency in articulating the nationalist cause. A more secular, confident Quebec emerges at this time as globalization attenuates the province's isolationist tendencies, replacing them with a cosmopolitanism that also takes into account Quebecers' place in the world.[36] Although reaffirming the relationship between image-making and the politics of independence, hockey in film during the period also comments on the province's engagement with the Rest of Canada, North America, and the world.

The genre fare of the prior decades, typical of small emerging cinemas of the time, spoke to Quebec's insular concerns. As André Loiselle notes, there were advantages to this insularity, since Quebec's linguistic marginality in North America propelled the maturation of the cultural industries, and procured a large and sturdy audience base that would also allow Quebec filmmakers to participate in larger markets. The catalyst for genre diversity was the 1984 change in the CFDC's funding policy, which made possible the production of a motion picture industry that was commercially viable and in time culminated in cinematic powerhouse status.[37]

The success of Quebec cinema spurred the production of popular films that drew on hybrid French- and Anglo-Canadian as well as American motifs and production values.[38] Although international recognition for Quebec cinema served the entire industry because it extended Canada's repute beyond the documentary form, the quality of programming and the range of its film genres set Quebec apart from English-Canadian product. These two types of content also moved through distinct channels—theatrical releases and English-language television broadcasts, respectively—magnifying the gap between the directorial voices from both sides of the cultural divide, which according to George Melnyk, "either clashed with or completely bypassed the ... other."[39] Of the two cinemas, Quebec's surged because it found common ground with the cultural codes of North American popular cinema. A Miramax scout in attendance at the 2004 Toronto International Film Festival remarked that "If a film is Canadian.... I always ask one question to determine whether or not I'm going to make time to see it. Is it in French?"[40] In contrast, English-Canadian films endured as a cinema "conditioned to obscurity," populated by "desperate women ... [and] self-loathing men ... [who] plumb[ed] new depths of anti-heroism," as Brian Johnson notes.[41]

Unlike the crisis of confidence befalling English-Canadian cinema, Quebec was fast creating a flourishing movie-making industry that enhanced the province's standing in the international stage. Of the top ten Canadian box office hits between 1991 and 2001, six were Quebec comedic releases grossing approximately CAD 3.5 million.[42] From 2001 to 2005, the market share of French-Canadian films also rose from 8 to 26 percent during this time, a striking feat for a small national cinema.[43] Despite accounting for only 23 percent of the Canadian population, in the 2000s, Quebec customarily had a minimum of four productions in weekly top five Canadian film lists.[44]

The major hits that opened a path for success in the province's film market were comedies, since this genre, along with *policiers* or police dramas, enjoyed popular appeal and fit government agencies' funding guidelines.[45] Among cinematic fare that struck a resonant note with viewers, *Les Boys*, a co-creation of producer Richard Goudreau of Montreal's Melenny Productions and director Louis Saïa, and its first two sequels surged to a phenomenal success, grossing a stunning $17 million domestically. The Saïa-directed *Les Boys* (1997), *Les Boys II*

(1998), and *Les Boys III* (2001) ranked as the first, second, and third all-time highest grossing Canadian comedies, garnering Golden Reel Awards as well as Bobines D'Or for biggest Canadian box office draw of the year. *Les Boys* became the biggest domestic success of Canadian cinema, coming in second only to Canadian director James Cameron's *Titanic* (1997).[46] *Les Boys II* outsold all Canadian-produced films, and *Les Boys III* performed similarly, displacing the mega-hit *Harry Potter and the Philosopher's Stone* (Columbus, 2001) in its debut weekend. *Les Boys IV* (Mihalka, 2005), for its part, surpassed the CAD 4 million mark at the box office and held the number one spot in Quebec seven weeks in a row.[47] Director Érik Canuel underscored the films' significance in nurturing an audience for cinema in the province, adding that "after the success of films like *Les Boys*, people in Quebec were also willing to go and see the smaller, more artistic films."[48] The franchise helped propel the upward trend of Quebec cinema as it came together with the right ingredients: the widely acknowledged passion for the game, the attachment of Quebec's big entertainment names to the films, comedic appeal, and smart promotion.

In their introductory foray, the thirteen who gather each Monday for a game in a Montreal beer league must rescue coach Stan (Rémy Girard) when he manages to get himself $50,000 in debt with shadowy figure Méo (Pierre Lebeau). The gangster unleashes his goons and threatens worse should he not pay up, and with no recourse, the coach agrees to put his pub, *Chez Stan*, on the line. Les Boys must rally forth and defeat Méo's team of bullies in a hockey game to prevent the loss of the bar. In *Les Boys II* Méo has joined the team and heads overseas to take part in an international amateur competition in France's alpine village of Chamonix. The second installment exploits the differences between French and Québécois for humor and revels in the culture shock with which les Boys must contend. This sequel also showcases plenty of hockey action and when the team loses to the Ivory Coast squad in a typical turn of self-parody on ice, the players must regroup to save what's left of their pride. They fortuitously manage to get to the final and go up against the Moscow Sputniks in a burlesque rendition of the 1972 Summit Series. *Les Boys III* features Stan returning from his three-year sojourn in France after his affair with a French woman ends, to find competition close by in the form of glitzy sports bar *Les Champions*, headed by a wealthy club owner with a beer-league team. Although the newcomer lures many of Stan's charges with various offers, team members who stick by their coach show the others the meaning of friendship and loyalty. This installment features an exhibition game between Les Boys and the Canadian women's Olympic hockey team with expected histrionic results. In *Les Boys IV* the team must defeat the Toronto Barristers squad for the chance to play a select lineup of NHLers. To focus on the big match, Stan sequesters his players in the outskirts of the province for intensive training and team-building exercises that predictably backfire. Les Boys nonetheless succeed and go up against a Legends team comprised of Francophone NHL icons past and present, including Bossy, Bourque, Brodeur, Brunet, Gagné, and Lafleur, to whom Les Boys happily lose.

The *Les Boys* tetralogy features a cast of run-of-the-mill individuals whose masculinity has much in common with the loser-buffoon protagonist, an archetype that pokes fun at the blustery male ego. In contrast to the physically and mentally superior exemplar of the North who molds the external environment to suit his aims, Les Boys are a set of misfits who bumble the job all the way to the eleventh hour. Part of their popularity resides in the carnivalesque signature *Les Boys*' films share with *Slap Shot*, to which the franchise also relates intertextually. Both films feature actor Yvan Ponton, who plays French-Canadian forward Jean-Guy Drouin in the Charlestown Chiefs lineup and strapping gay lawyer and team ace Jean-Charles on the Les Boys bench. *Les Boys IV* also astutely references *Slap Shot* in a playful inversion of Quebec and American national myths that point to a rearrangement of core values.

Like the Hansons who are the blissful and oblivious embodiment of the hearty pleasures of the game, Les Boys personify an adolescent masculinity that prioritizes hockey over other aspects of life. Much as Roch Carrier's narrator in *The Sweater* recounts that growing up hockey was more important than church or school, in *Les Boys*, team members shamelessly exemplify that family and job rank a distant second or third to their hockey matchups. In the first installment, the high-ranking professionals on the team, lawyer Jean-Charles and surgeon François (Serge Thériault) both cut short their duties for the day, and to hurry off to the rink, accept a plea bargain and leave a dead patient on the operating table, respectively. Entrepreneur and playboy Bob (Marc Messier) and handsome car mechanic Mario (Patrick Labbé) also desert their sexually available partners to make it to the game. As Amy Ransom proposes, Les Boys are grown-up men but they effectively remain boys, and their trajectory is that of a Bildungsroman, which implies that the protagonists must grow up at some point.[49]

The father-son relationship that the franchise foregrounds as important—that of Stan and Leopold (Michel Charette)—also satirizes parenting as the coach scolds his son for not playing vigorously but matter-of-factly treats him like a child. Stan's badgering contravenes the romantic father-son bond in sport, which *Face Off* conveys through beginning and ending clips of the father on the pond as integral to the son's sports trajectory. Léopold's subpar hockey skills and discomfort with his size make the father-son project in sport all the more necessary yet in *Les Boys* it takes on farcical tones given Stan's daft parenting skills. If in film, male hockey protagonists must express agency in breadwinning roles, in heteronormative sexual relationships, and by living up to their fathering duties, none of it is in evidence when it comes to this group. Per story arc conventions that dictate that leading men develop and change by the end of the narrative, the protagonists inch their way toward maturity in various roles at some point in the four films, but also evince necessary backsliding as the built-in humor in their character types depends on reversals distinctive of the carnivalesque.

André Loiselle notes that popular Quebec comedies like *Les Boys* capitalize on the carnivalesque to subvert the good taste and propriety encoded in highbrow cultural forms and mock authority by throwing decorum out the window.[50] The object of the carnivalesque is to thumb the collective populist nose at norms of social conduct because these cultural codes represent power blocs' control over the so-called lower orders. Les Boys' reliance on robust physicality in winning contests, their use of insults and profanity—which prioritize oral culture and assume no separation between protagonist and spectator—and their comically grotesque expressions all dramatize populist transgressions centered on the body that, in turn, sanction pleasures otherwise repressed by the rigors of mundane life.[51]

Les Boys films also perform their carnivalesque function by contrasting protagonists' escapades with weighty sports values that entreat men to remain hardy and battle to the end, respect the primacy of team bonding, and absorb difference into the group. Playing it straight, the protagonists are hockey devotees who approach their matchups like a crusade, giving their all once on the ice much like the ideal sportsman. In the manner of the coach who expects utmost sacrifice and allegiance to the cause, Stan exhorts his charges in the first installment: "We've gotta have the puck tattoed on our hearts," and Les Boys invariably block shots and battle through to the end to come out on top. The motif of hockey as social leveler seen in many hockey-themed films also appears built into the *Les Boys* premise, as director Louis Saïa affirms during an interview designed to market the second sequel: "There's a feeling of crossing over lines.... You have a player on social security, a doctor, a lawyer—the lowest class to the highest class. They're brought together because of their shared passion for the game."[52] *Les Boys* films entwine the national-militaristic model of honing character through pain to the social leveler aspects of sport by way of working-class notions of manhood. In their 1999 study of fifteen- and sixteen-year-old Francophone boys' views of athletics, Suzanne Laberge and Mathieu Albert highlight that upper- and middle-class teens regard athletics as a platform for practicing leadership skills and gaining acceptance by a network of peers, whereas their working-class counterparts see sport as offering a chance to stage robust maleness.[53] *Les Boys'* courageous game in like manner prioritizes a working-class ethos that offsets gaps in talent with hard work to win games.

Much as they satirize the sports protagonist's agencies in various social roles, the squad's carnivalesque gamesmanship also makes a mockery of the sportsman's approach to the game. While technically the tricksterism of these characters recalls that of Disneyesque family entertainment since, as underdogs, Les Boys will use any advantage they can handle, most of the ruses these rogues deploy are taboo subjects in children's films. In the first installment, Julien (Roc Lafortune), a rocker notorious for his drug consumption, and momma's boy-realtor Ti-Guy put a cocaine high to good use during a game. *Les Boys II* also harnesses Julien's cocaine habit for buffoonish effect as he recalls the 1972 Canada-Soviet Summit Series and expresses befuddlement over the presence of a crocodile on the ice and players furiously swimming away from it. Because the Canada-Soviet 1972 series has been memorialized as a seminal triumph for the Canadian game with ongoing symbolism for both Anglophones and Francophones, Julien's cocaine high during an event that had most of the nation glued to the TV plays to supreme burlesque effect. *Les Boys'* transgressive signature parodies the sports genre's clichéd heroism, not only by downsizing the sportsman ideal, but also by making a mockery of hockey's relationship to both the projects of Canadian nationalism and French-Canadian identity. All the while, Les Boys reinscribe Francophone identity as authentic through populist, carnivalesque sensibilities that downsize refinement and uphold artlessness and naïveté.

The primacy of team bonding and absorption of difference into the group is particularly interesting as the *Les Boys* films draw up Jean-Charles, who is gay, as one of the most masculine, well-rounded, and skilled members of the squad. What's more, the rest of the team has no inkling of his homosexuality when the first film opens. As various studies on the marginalization of gay players make explicit, homosexuality remains controversial for infringing on the myth of dominant masculinity that ties sport to the project of nationalism.[54] Homosexuality also risks disrupting the sexualized hypermasculine's connection to the project of nationhood through the motifs of combat and war. Michael Buma discusses the idea of homosexuality as a threat in hockey novels by way of Eve Sedgwick's concept of "homosexual panic," a space of uncertainty between being a "man's man" and expressing "interest ... in men" that motivates the heteronormative policing of all-male relationships in modern Western cultures. He notes that most Canadian hockey novels seek to portray heterosexuality and homosexuality as discrete realities in order to facilitate marginalizing the latter.[55] Despite that populist sensibilities can align with heteronormative conventions, because *Les Boys* films spoof sports clichés of dominant masculinity, they also make allowances for different models of manhood on the playing field. *Les Boys*, for example, grants Jean-Charles, along with inexpert Leópold, crucial tallies that lead to winning the game to show that presumed marginality can be readily swapped for heroism. Even after Jean-Charles' outing, which occurs when boyfriend Pierrot (Guy Jodoin) shows up at the rink unannounced, the lawyer continues to be embraced as part of the lineup and is even looked to for leadership.

At the same time, the picture of Pierrot as a love interest amounts to nothing short of a maligned stereotype of homosexuality that portrays the character as a hysterical, hyperfeminine type that Hollywood film and TV typically harness for laughs to highlight the leading man's heterosexual allure. In short order, Pierrot embarrasses Jean-Charles with his melodramatic entrance at the rink, but all the more affirms the lawyer's virility as he scores the winning goal, which may be the point of the film since Pierrot's character will disappear in subsequent installments while Jean-Charles' status will increase. As Amy Ransom documents, several scenes in the tetralogy, like the one in the first film in which he intimidates gangster Méo for stocking his team with ringers during the final game, work to configure his character as physically assertive and sexually dominant.[56] What's more, judging by his professional status as barrister, Jean-Charles is hardly marginal but has all the makings of an alpha male, particularly given the working-class positions or unclear job status of several team members. Nonetheless, Pierrot's clownish characterization implies the existence of homosexual gradations, and Jean-Charles' masculinity is secured not only through sheer comparison with his partner, but by way of actor Yvan Ponton's intertextual referents to the muscularity of *Slap Shot*. As Ransom points out, Jean-Charles' homosexuality also at times appears acceptable to some team members largely on the basis that it not be continually on display. Thus, at his wedding to a much younger and attractive Christopher (Jean Petitclerc), Méo and Fernand (Paul Houde) express compunctions about the kiss between the two that culminates the wedding ceremony.[57] Although the carnivalesque is meant to display populist resistance to refinement and respectability, team members' sexist and racist responses can also be quite reactionary. With good reason, then, Loiselle notes that these films are difficult to gauge because they are simultaneously conservative and progressive.[58]

The *Les Boys* films' series of politically progressive avowals and reactionary disavowals of allegiance to the homosocial outfit likely mirror the disorientation of heterosexual white masculinity in the face of changing social norms and a traditional gender order in disarray, much like *Slap Shot* responds in carnivalesque fashion to the displacement of men from the workforce at a time of economic duress. Bill Marshall notes that euphoric game finales in the *Les Boys* films work to resolve tensions within the homosocial ingroup instead of staging the triumph of individual character as is common in the Hollywood sports film. For this reason, in these movies the utopian ending dramatizes masculinity striving to reassert itself in the face of social pressures.[59]

Les Boys films also affirm the conservatism of the genre by refusing to surrender the romance of the optimal outcome in line with Quebec film sports conventions. As Loiselle notes, the motif of the victorious Francophone underdog, which allegorizes the triumph of good over evil, remains at the heart of the Francophone North American Dream as one of the most potent national Quebec myths.[60] The franchise follows in the footsteps of popular movies post–1980, which poignantly dramatize that characters of French-Canadian origin can still succeed however marginal or unorthodox they or their lives happen to be.[61] *Les Boys'* nick-of-time triumphs emulate the sports genre's melodramatic staging of the feats of the bold exemplar not only to compensate for the increasing difficulty in living out these ideals, but to perform French-Canadianicity on the ice.

These films also uphold the sports film's nostalgia for an unproblematized, uniform model of masculinity and nationhood by forging a team that consists exclusively of white Francophone males despite the multi-ethnic character of Montreal. *Les Boys* succeed in reproducing the nation in this manner because they thrust into the game's spotlight many of Quebec's film and TV stars, among them a number of high-profile stand-up comics. The Legends team in *Les Boys IV* also frames the nation in much the same way: through a nostalgic signature that rehearses Quebec identity and nationhood through its NHL markers. Because the mythic aspect of hockey in the cinema has a prescriptive element that makes the case for particular realities, this image also expresses a yearning for an elite Quebec squad that competently represents the nation in international prestige hockey contests, particularly since Francophones participate as part of Canadian teams.[62]

Alongside the above pledge to the so-called mainstays of sport, masculinity, and nationhood, Les Boys' devilish lampooning of sacred myths simultaneously disrupts the formula of the hockey player ideal as faithful mirror of the project of citizenship and nationhood. *Les Boys II*, which takes the motley crew to an international amateur hockey competition in Chamonix, France, shreds any allegiance Quebec may still have to France as Mother country by inserting scenes in which characters affirm their French-Canadianicity vis-à-vis French or European identity. The subject matter of *Les Boys II* may have been framed by Quebecers' ongoing interest in France as referent Other through a concern with ancestral roots.[63] Surveys conducted in 1992 and 2000 Quebec's showed that media commentators, artists, social scientists, and the public at large were captivated by the subject of origins as encapsulated by the questions, "who are we?" and "where do we come from?"[64] Bill Marshall notes that while the 1759 Conquest of the French by the British has been interpreted as the "orphaning of Quebec," the France-Quebec relationship would remain informed by contradiction and conflict because France was not only colonial ruler but served as a potent model through which to resist cultural and demographic assimilation into English-Canadian culture.[65]

Les Boys II articulates Quebecers' search for origins by exploring the France-Quebec relationship in parodic form. The film mocks the cramped quarters and poor sanitary conditions of the French hotels where team members stay, inverting the France's core and Quebec's peripheral standing of earlier decades. Marshall notes that in the early 1960s the French-Canadian elite associated France with high culture and Quebec with underdevelopment as the province braced itself for modernization symbolized by American consumerism. With the subsequent framing of Québécois identity as Francophones of North America, the earlier paradigm suffered a reversal spurred by Quebecers' aspirations for upward mobility based on American models of economic advancement. *Les Boys II* mirrors this inversion by fashioning France as the backward party, lacking in the most basic amenities North Americans have come to expect.[66] In *Les Boys II* coach Stan also literally explores the French-Quebec relationship as he finds love with a local Frenchwoman and stays behind for three years while his charges return to Canada to resume their lives. The relationship flatlines, however, and Stan goes back to his bar and his friends in Montreal. *Les Boys III* implies that he has exhausted his exploration and a symbolic return to the past is insufficient in formulating a modern and robust Québécois identity.

On the hockey front, the amateur championships serve to spoof another national myth, the performance of Canada in the 1972 Summit Series (*la Série du siècle*) and to field questions of nationhood that may come as a surprise given the way Francophones regard hockey as an expression of French-Canadianicity. The crafty framing of the spoof occurs by way of a mishap that sees the team departing in search of more desirable accommodations and losing their gear to a huckster. With no recourse, team members are forced to don equipment that can pass for collectibles, which, in turn, serves to mark them as full-fledged Northmen, reminiscent of the forest figures of myth who dramatize vigorous masculinity and leverage nonconformism to convey Canadian distinctiveness. Ti-Guy's reference to *"mon Canada"* earlier in the film as a retort to an outsider's comments on Canadian politics, also serves notice that Les Boys will be playing with their federalist hats on.[67] When the Ivory Coast team makes its entrance, the stage is set as the captain pays his respect to the Canadians, professing that they are there to learn. Parodying the conceit that the Soviets attributed to the Canadians during the series, Ti-Guy replies matter-of-factly that they're in the right place. Faithful to the Summit Series script, Les Boys are summarily defeated and panic sets in, in a satire of Game One in Montreal where all hell breaks lose after the Soviets score six goals against the Canadians.

Subsequently, Les Boys, who as Québécois underdogs do not typically perform their on-ice identity by means of violence, proceed to make their way through the competition slashing, high-sticking, tripping and otherwise thumping opponents like consummate hockey bullies. As will be seen in the next chapter, the series was renown for the criticism the Canadian squad received for their violent hockey, to which the team responded with further retrenchment and worse violence as they held on to their conviction about the superiority of the Canadian game. *Les Boys II* spoofs in stellar form the team's use of physicality and distinctive nonconformism first insinuated through their outdated gear and Northmen imagery, one which the Summit Series elicited as a pointed tension since the Soviets complained repeatedly about the Canadians' refusal to play by the rules. Dramatizing the seminal confrontation of the series (Game Eight), in the final the Boys go up against the Moscow Sputniks, whom Méo refers to in characteristic oblivious form as *les communistes*, parodying Team Canada members' insistent references during the series about playing for "our way of life." This time around, *Les Boys II* depicts the Russian players much the same way Disney's 2004 film *Miracle* does: as the giants that they became coming into the 1980s, rather than the squads scarcely able to medal in hockey in Winter Olympics post–1992. The scheme also inverts Les Boys' bully status and reframes them as characteristic underdogs, much like happens in *Canada Russia '72*. To come out on top, Les Boys must switch tactics and beat their opponent at their highly cerebral and refined game. The 1972 series is known for introducing to the world stage a game never before seen in the West: a non-violent, intellectual style that adhered to the Soviet concept of play instated by coach Anatoli Tarasov.[68] Unlike Team Canada's continual assertions throughout the years that the Summit Series was a critical juncture for the Canadian game that they settled by winning,[69] Les Boys' tactical shift in the championship game, then, registers as an homage to the Soviets' innovative brand of hockey.

As a *petit pays*, Quebec has frequently trusted the cinema to reflect its sense of identity and national coherence, as well as its growing pains and successes. The tetralogy also juggles these issues as the first installment foregrounds serious political differences between the teammates that surface when Jean-Charles assails Fern for failing to vote in the 1980 Referendum and sinking Quebec's independence efforts. As expected, *Les Boys'* burlesque approach pokes fun at well-rehearsed themes of Quebec nationhood. The fourth installment laughs at Les Boys' guffaws by focusing on pillars of Quebec culture—core myths of *québécité* and secessionist aspirations. In preparation for their meeting with the NHL legends, Stan sequesters his charges in rural Quebec for intensive training far from the distractions of the city. The beauty of the secluded wilderness notwithstanding, in the middle of summer the area is infested with black flies and mosquitoes and the exercise soon turns into a fiasco. Instead of regaining their team spirit, the outfit breaks up in two and half of them get lost in the woods. On the way back to the city, the coach casually observes that if separation from Canada were in the cards, he would "give up this part of Quebec." Stan's farcical remark plays with secessionism to subvert the idea of the countryside as core symbol of Quebec's soul. Loiselle notes that in film the countryside exists as a serene space that provides respite to the urbanite's psyche and puts him back in touch with the traditional values of Quebec.[70] In film, therefore, the land endures as the spiritual and cultural container of the province's iconography and myths. Instead of invigorating, however, Les Boys' sojourn to the countryside proves more stressful and daunting than life in the city because the setting turns out to be completely alien to the protagonists. The expedition is, in any case, ill-conceived because Quebecers do not travel to rural areas for intensive sports training but for relaxation and spiritual renewal. The sojourn in short order transforms into another opportunity to stage the buffoonery of les Boys, who in attempting to rehearse Quebec's national myths prove themselves too modern to partake from authentic French-Canadianicity.

The image of the French confronting the English in hockey commonly calls up traditional rivalries that in Quebec discourse call for French-Canadians' vigorous pushback against English-Canadian dominance. As expected, *Les Boys IV* also takes a poke at this centerpiece of Quebec discourse. As Méo is entrusted with the pre-game locker room speech, he comically exploits the rhetoric of French-Canadian victimization against the Toronto Barristers team[71] through familiar imagery of *la Conquête*, the 1759 French defeat by the English on the Plains of Abraham, noting that the matchup will serve to avenge the stalwarts' lost honor. When he is sent to the penalty box he also mocks national tensions as he blurts out with relish: "For years we've been at a disadvantage in Quebec!" Méo's humorous statements convey that no element of *québécité*, not even the touchy Anglo-French rift, is off limits in keeping with the burlesque tone of the *Les Boys* films.

In Canada, Quebec's commercial cinema is held up as paragon of success for its ability to appeal to popular audiences. *Les Boys IV* not surprisingly also offers self-reflexive commentary about the province's achievement in this arena. At the wedding of Jean-Charles, Bob endeavors to explain his new job to Stan by attributing the opportunity to the exponential growth of film production in the province. Stan's reaction is to claim ignorance: "I wouldn't know. The last Quebec film I saw was *Slap Shot*." When Bob questions whether *Slap Shot* is not an American film, Stan calmly replies: "No, in my book Paul Newman spoke French." Stan's answer only serves to confirm Bob's point: "There you go. If Paul Newman is playing in a Quebec film, it means it's become big around here." Calling up the carnivalesque *Slap Shot* as a referent, Bob and Stan's humorous exchange plays with long-standing Canadian cultural nationalist rhetoric about the negative impact of the South-North flow of entertainment to acknowledge the international success of Quebec cinema while underscoring these characters as dimwits in good satirical form. In alluding to Hollywood's most popular hockey-themed movie as part of the province's film repertory, the repartee subverts Quebec's mapping as *petit pays* and embraces a notion of *québécité* that is more characteristic of the expansive American story to mirror the province's self-confidence as a cinematic powerhouse.

The comical subversion of the *petit pays* code is also in keeping with director Louis Saïa's vision in producing the films, which he broached in a 2001 interview: "[i]n Quebec, the attitude has been that we're born to lose. Stay low, stay small. We're not out to simply make money with these films ... we are out to get people into the cinemas."[72] Saïa's statement suggests that tropes such as the *petit pays* code may no longer suffice in summing up Quebec identity and nationhood. The makeup of a technologically advanced Quebec where the language of business is English and the existence of more bilingual and secular Francophone communities outside the province both work to downplay the old "stay-small, stay low" referents. And although Les Boys' Quebeckisms authenticate the films' reticence to strive for an audience beyond the province's boundaries, Quebec writers, producers, editors, and others whose talent draw audiences out to the theaters must also work in a global film marketplace that does not easily accommodate these types of high context tropes. As *Jesus of Montréal* (Arcand, 1989) producer Roger Frappier notes, "we cannot listen to the word 'globalization' for years and years without its having an effect" on the mindset of young film talent from Quebec.[73] Stan and Bob's droll exchange underlines that although Quebec continues to rely on its cinema to consolidate its sense of nationhood, dramatizing *québécité* may also have to take into account the province's role on the global stage.

Gina Freitag and André Loiselle point to the *Les Boys* comedies as part of one of two broad practices in Quebec cinema alongside the auteur voice. They note that this genre draws on the early twentieth century burlesque stage and prioritizes light political satire along with sexual innuendo to produce "conservatively subversive entertainment" and occasional insightful social commentary.[74] *Les Boys* films' parody of Quebec's cultural cornerstones hints that, more than sporadic revelation, these films may be signaling a subtle shift in core myths. The fourth installment's comical portrayal of the Boys' awkward fit with the province's backcountry pounces on the idea that Quebecers can feel at ease anywhere within the province. Loiselle addresses the topic with regard to the proliferation of popular horror movies as evidence of the fragmentation of Quebec as a nation. He observes that the rural in Quebec culture operates as safe harbor against "the foreign influences that threaten *pure laine* Québécois identity," particularly in Montreal, and the horror genre contravenes this convention by commonly locating characters in threatening rural settings, and depicting them as uneasy within their own nation.[75] *Les Boys IV* drives much the same point home but in parodic form to showcase the trademark dunce-like makeup of the protagonists.

Hockey-themed films pick up on unease about globalization and cultural hybridization by putting forward a nostalgic version of masculinity as a palliative for the traditional nation's fragmentation, confirming Gruneau and Whitson's observation that Canadians have reacted to globalization by attempting to hold on to high-profile symbols of cultural identity such as hockey.[76] Amy Ransom in like manner notes that the balancing act that characterizes the *Les Boys* tetralogy posits alternatives to dominant masculinity models while simultaneously reinscribing the traditional gender order.[77] In line with the hybrid motifs that characterize Quebec comedies, the *Les Boys* tetralogy plays with the Hollywood sport's heroic ideal and field characters that stand in contradistinction to English-Canadian understandings of the French-Canadian carnivalesque in canonical film.[78] In so doing, the characters in these films perform their French-Canadianicity by both reaffirming and disrupting the homogenizing narrative of sport, masculinity, and nationhood.

Il était une fois les Boys: *Les Boys* and the Family Genre

The fifth installment of the Les Boys franchise *Il était une fois les Boys—When We Were Boys* (Goudreau, 2013)—is a family film that operates as a prequel and recounts the beginnings of the friendship between high-schoolers Stan (Simon Pigeon), Bob (Samuel Gauthier), Jean-Charles (William Legault-Lacasse), Méo (Maxime Desjardins-Tremblay), Marcel (Derek Poissant), and Fern (Jassen Charron) who, along with hockey whiz Ben (Maxime Gibeault), play for the St.-Michel parish team the Aces (*les As*) and dream of winning the 1967 Christmas holiday championships (*le Tournois des Fêtes*).

As a family film that seeks to appeal to the largest audience possible, the prequel minimizes potentially offensive material and therefore lacks the carnivalesque tenor of the franchise. Nonetheless it also blends in intratextual and intertextual reversals, avowals and disavowals that interject *Les Boys*–kind of light satire and draw on burlesque cinema.[79] Typical of the franchise's mischievous plot twists, several of the actors that appear in the original les Boys re-emerge as the youngsters' family members—Yvan Ponton, Marc Messier, Luc Guérin, Rémy Girard, Michel Charette (in cameo)—coaches—Pierre Lebeau, Girard—and the town's chief of police—Roc Lafortune—either playing against type or rehashing familiar motifs.

Yvan Ponton, who depicts strappy gay lawyer Jean-Charles in the tetralogy, plays young Jean-Charles' dad, François Taillefert, a jolly homophobe who thinks that brains are consonant with queerness. When at the dinner table mom Micheline (Marie-Claude Michaud) gushes over her boy's superlative school grades positing that the family surely has an Albert Einstein in their midst, François cheerfully remarks whether Einstein wasn't gay and queries his son about the pretty girls he will dance with at the upcoming Aces' jersey-fundraising party. Young Jean-Charles who is a model student and straight-laced sort that responds with visible discomfiture to any actions that go against school regulations or parental injunction, reacts with noticeable alarm at his father's oblivious comments. Because the family genre does not typically delve into sexual themes, the newspaper that Stan hands Jean-Charles on the school bus, which sports a *"homosexuelle"* headline on the front page, serves as primary identifier that that the boy is gay.

Luc Guérin, who portrays sleazy Marcel in *Les Boys*, plays the young character's dad, Gérard Bilodeau, a faithful family man who, like the other parents, works at the town factory and alongside his wife babysits the neighbors young children for the much-needed extra dollars. The fifth installment reroutes the elder Marcel's deviance by contouring his young counterpart as a cross-eyed, naïve sort prone to goofy interjections and slapstick humor. The young Aces' goalie, Fern, is similarly drawn up as an ardent hockey fan who is always spotted wearing a Canadiens-colored toque, and whose hero is goalie Jacques Plante. Doting mom Lison (Sonia Vachon) appeals to her son's enthusiasm for hockey to camouflage the family's meager resources, cheerfully noting of the plain spaghetti dinner she serves the youngster before the evening match: "Jacques Plante ate that on game day." Dad Léo, played by the comic Laurent Paquin, makes his own attempts at supplementing the family's income by way of a gambling habit that has the debt collectors paying frequent visits to the home. Though young Fern never knows what kind of TV he will come home to, the Rivests parlay dad's weakness for the ponies as a chance to try out new furniture and appliances. At one point, Fernand's goalie gear suffers the same fate as the home's furnishings, and the film comically portrays his reaction through an external night shot of the house in which the lights turn on one by one, followed by the boy's anguished scream. Happily, dad retrieves the pads in time for Christmas. As with the Stan-Popold relationship, the prequel underscores the father-son arrangement for its humorous, dysfunctional effects, though in line with family genre conventions that articulate the family as sacrosanct, it also makes light of these parental flaws.

Il était une fois les Boys nonetheless also fields weighty concerns uncharacteristic of the genre by way of serious crises in the family lives of young Bob and Stan. Bob's dad, Denis Chicoine, played by Marc Messier in a part that is the very opposite of the ladies man he enacts in the *Les Boys* films, carries fourteen years of grief in his heart because of wife Rachel's (Joëlle Morin) brief infidelity early in their marriage. At the film's outset, he emerges as a distant, downcast character who pays little attention to his wife or son. Denis is never on site at practice or at games like the other parents, and when Bob gets home from a match, as usual he is working on his elaborate train set and barely looks up when the boy sarcastically relays about the final tally that they won 8–0, he scored 10 goals, and he has 200 goals in the season. Careless gossip deepens the festering wound and when head coach Jimmy (Pierre Lebeau) pays Denis a visit after Rachel's departure, he notes teary-eyed that although the separation only lasted a week, Bob's birth not long after entrenched his doubts about whether the boy is even his.

The absent father motif seen in *The Boy Who Drank Too Much*, *Youngblood*, *Mystery, Alaska*, as well as in *Breakaway* and in the Quebec film *Les Pee Wee 3D: l'hiver qui a changé ma vie* (discussed in a subsequent chapter), typically contours the missing or distant father as a figure who must surmount personal blocks and heal the breach between him and the son. In the hybrid sports film-family genre, this resolution commonly takes place following a family crisis that necessitates the mother's absence, whether temporarily or permanently, after which the father reassesses his place in his son's life and fills the gap. In this scheme, the father also takes up his traditional supportive role in his offspring's sports sojourn, precisely because the son has a need for him. Not surprisingly, after Rachel departs and a second crisis ensues that impacts the Aces at their core, Denis relays to Bob that he is there for him and grief-stricken, the boy embraces him father as he feelingly notes: "like father and son." Denis also hugs the boy tightly and softly echoes his words. Much to Bob's surprise, dad subsequently puts in an appearance at the championship game, where he cheers for his son more loudly than the other parents. There he also quickly reconciles with Rachel, mirroring not only the hallowed place of the family unit in the sport and family genres, but the foremost institutional role of the family in Quebec culture.

The other family crisis occurs early in the film when Stan's single mom Marie (Catherine Sénart) is sexually assaulted by factory manager Jean-Guy Rachette (Jeff Boudreault). Young Stan has lost his father early in life, and the Aces' assistant coach, Uncle Fred—played by Rémy Girard who also performs the part of coach Stan in *Les Boys*—does his best to fill the gap. As the family's lone breadwinner, Marie keeps the assault quiet for fear of losing her job until Stan overhears her confiding in Mrs. Rivest at the Christmas party. To make matter worse, Rachette is the coach of the Aces' chief opponent, the Stars *(les Étoiles)*, the parish's other bantam team stocked by the best players around and led by the factory owner's son Steve Madison (Trevor Momesso). As the film's villain, Rachette takes every opportunity to disrespect the tight-knit Aces along with their coaches and dads, and flaunts his team's superiority in line with how sport conflict functions as proxy for social conflict.

Young Méo comes to the rescue when he spots Stan's distress and draws the secret out of him. In short order the boys plot to take their revenge on Rachette. They zero in on his shiny, new Mustang, and come up with a ploy that tricks the manager into thinking he has run over a youngster. As Rachette gets out to check, Méo makes off with the vehicle, and after picking up his teammates, the young goon proceeds to sell the sports car to his contacts for a mere $200 to hit the evildoer where it hurts. Far from the dark gangster-like figure in the *Les Boys* films, Méo's hoodlum resourcefulness plays out to supreme advantage for the Aces, who like any high schoolers are bent on experimentation. He produces the first marijuana joint for the group, and works as security for the fundraising party. Though much smaller in size, he confronts two of the Stars who are intent on crashing the function and rescues Ben when attacked by the same gang. When the latter remarks on his pluck in light of a prospective beating, the stalwart Méo replies that a punch never finished off anyone. Finally, when Rachette is exposed for his wrongdoing in front of factory boss Mr. Madison during the final game, it is also Méo who is at the forefront of the unmasking.

Given that the sport and family genres advance the directive of honing boys into a form of social capital for the project of citizenship and nationhood, the film must put forth a fatherly figure who keeps Méo's wayward tendencies in check. Pierre Lebeau, who plays the shadowy Méo in the *Les Boys* films, and is serious and earnest as coach Jimmy, does the honors as a surrogate father who takes interest in his charges' personal lives. As noted, when he hears from young Bob that mom has left, he takes it upon himself to visit with Denis and makes clear he is fortunate to have the kind of wife and son he has, while he himself has missed out on such blessings by devoting himself to the care of his elderly mother. He also looks after young Méo—who has bounced from one foster home to another, made no friends, and learned little hockey—by allowing him on the team even though he has yet to learn to stop. He also teaches the young thug manners and makes sure he is not left behind when the others head for the Bilodeaus' Christmas party.

Méo's masculine sturdiness, independence, ruffian appearance, and trickster skills nonetheless prove highly adaptive to the youngsters as he acts with decisive courage and leadership when the moment calls for it. His character, which draws on the picaresque rogue who survives by his wits, harks back to sixties and seventies portrayals in Quebec film through marginal protagonists from the popular classes such as criminals and the destitute. When Ben taps Méo for the role of team enforcer, the youngster's outsiderism is also healed as he is fully incorporated into the group in line with the sport's promise of ideal brotherhood. Unlike the symbol of the orphan in *The Mystery of the Million Dollar Hockey Puck*, which infuses the idea of Quebec as a nation with instability, Méo's redressed outsiderism reimagines this project as a sturdy one in line with the franchise's explicit premise of hockey as a social leveler and unifying agent, consonant with Pierre Véronneau's view of the anthology as articulating "the myth of a consensual Quebec culture."[80] By redressing Méo's outsiderism, the prequel also attenuates the marginal motifs that Houle documents in earlier Quebec cinema in favor of the new family genre's preference for an enlarged socio-cultural context.

Similarly, *Il était une fois les Boys* reformulates imagery of the Church in *The Mystery of the Million Dollar Hockey Puck* through a satirical depiction of religious icons such as the parish church, the Christmas choir, and the parish priest by conveying Roman Catholicism's dimming influence among Francophones. The opening slow motion wide shot of the parish church's lit-up interior for Christmas Eve Mass gives it the appearance of a cathedral in all its bright opulence. The choir also boasts an operatic lead that enthralls churchgoers with a sublime performance that has young Marcel forgetting the solemnity of the proceedings and clapping energetically in response.

The satire of the Church's grand theatrical rituals underlines the oversized role of religious institutions in Quebecers' lives, and contrasts it with *le curé*'s or parish priest's (Francois Léveillé) earthly approach to his ecclesiastical duties. When Fern and Marcel, who are serving as altar boys for the Mass, approach with the water and wine needed to perform the Eucharist, the priest signals Fern to keep pouring the wine into the Chalice. When Marcel moves to offer the water, however, the priest waves him off, and as the boy naively queries whether he doesn't perform miracles, the priest answers that he won't that evening. *Le curé* also puts in an appearance at the Bilodeaus' Christmas party much to Gérard's discomfiture, and promptly engages in lascivious appreciation of Rachel's body, as he muses of her nursing duties at the town's hospital: "Considering all the time she spends in patients' rooms she must be really something," also adding for full effect that he's witnessed patients come back to life. When he interjects that in his visits to the hospital he hears gossip, Gérard and François, sitting on either side of the priest, simultaneously scurry off in disgust. The priest's comments recall the Church's exclusive authority over health institutions at the time, and parlay the clergy's ubiquitous presence in the life of the community as unwelcome. Given Quebecers' aspirations for social mobility during the province's period of secularization, the Church's outsized social role and wealth further insinuate the institution's designs on the people as fundamentally inimical to their interests.

This less-than-idyllic look at the Church's institutional role also makes clear that the prequel focuses its nostalgia principally on childhood through imagery of outside rinks, the wood shed in which the boys don their hockey gear warmed by the heat of a wood stove, and the vast snowy expanse that serves for skill practice and bonding time away from the adults. This imagery configures Quebec as a smaller and a less multiculturally diverse nation than present in line with the pastoral sublimity found in children's genres. Because the natural environment in Canadian cinema alludes to the characters, consonant with canonical conventions the film also shrinks the children's figures within the landscape at various points in the narrative to articulate them as products of the North. When two of the boys first head out to the big snowy expanse to meet the others, the film presents the landscape as vast and unpopulated and the youngsters as minuscule. Likewise, when the boys experiment with pot, the scene's concluding visual is a wide shot of the snowy icescape that relegates their shack, now much-reduced, to the far left of the screen, even as the teens' excited laughter is conveyed quite audibly. This pastoral imagery also veils that the Northern environment conceals dangers as much as it affords pleasures, and as the boys forget themselves in their play, they also let their guard down. When Ben goes to retrieve one of Marcel's wayward pucks, he falls through the ice and drowns despite his teammates' desperate efforts to rescue him. The priest's words at the funeral, that the power of Nature took Ben according to the wishes of God, bring little relief to the youngsters, contravening the cheery tone of nineties family entertainment by interjecting loss in line with the social realist observation of the North as an experience of survival in Canadian film.

Because family fare leaves the performative ground to young protagonists, the boys must resort to their Northern toughness to surmount their grief and win the championship game in the newly acquired yellow and red uniforms seen in the *Les Boys* tetralogy. With two periods gone, the Aces are down by one goal and poignantly miss their teammate Ben. Their spirits are dropping and their prospects for a comeback look grim. At this point, the prequel re-engages the fuse provided by sports film's final game and reconnects to the family entertainment genre by way of "Miracle on Ice" imagery. Coach Jimmy draws on coach Herb Brooks' speech in Disney's *Miracle* ("Great moments are born of great opportunity") to remind his squad that there is only one period left, and "in life some moments are more important than others," after which he quickly makes his exit. Jimmy's use of "Miracle" imagery, in turn, references his repartee with Fred before the first game, as he observes that he's getting set to "work miracles." When his slow-on-the-uptake assistant coach quizzically wonders why he has given up on the boys since he's talking about miracles, the coach fires back that he's alluding to teamwork: "Eleven hearts beating as one can wreak havoc, Fred.... Heart, heart."[81] Jimmy's use of "Miracle" imagery in his final speech summarily calls up the viewer's expectation that the teens will somehow regroup and win the game by one goal.

Young Bob provides the fuel for the fire as he announces to his teammates: "I saw Ben on the ice." Adding with great feeling that Ben is in their midst sitting next to them, that he was behind their swift skating, their passes, their goals, and even the deflections of the opponent's pucks in the first and second periods, he rallies the troops until the Boys are set for their comeback. He suitably ends his exhortation remarking that they will take the ice and win the game: "Not for Ben, but with Ben!" When the Aces tie the championship game on account of an unlikely wraparound goal by Marcel, dads François and Gérard also call up "Miracle" imagery, as the first queries whether they are not about to witness a miracle, and the second responds that it's not a miracle because the team can certainly win the game. Bob makes the final push by going behind the net, and as he comes out the other end, it is none other than Ben. His teammates spot him too as he drives to the net in slow motion, takes a pass, and scores a goal to the raucous cheers of those in attendance. When the Stars captain approaches Bob to congratulate him for the win and let him know that he played well even without Ben, the youngster pauses slightly confused and then goes along with the post-game rituals: "Without Ben? Ah, yes."

The film's humorous avowal and disavowal of "Miracle" imagery shows Quebec film practitioners' adroitness at playing with various intertextual hockey signatures. While cueing the viewer about the team's resurgence, characters ultimately downplay the idea of miracles as commentary on the stereotypical way family fare taps the "Miracle on Ice" triumph to speak to underdog protagonists who win in good moral form. This disclaimer and numerous references to dreaming, in turn, allow for the reassertion of the Francophone version of the sports dream through linkages to the Montreal Canadiens. As the film opens, the radio announcer highlights the team's 5–0 win against the Leafs with three tallies scored by captain Jean Béliveau. The children's bus at the film's outset also passes by a billboard with a picture of Béliveau extending the Canadiens best wishes for the Christmas season to frame the team as part of the community. When Béliveau's character puts in an appearance in full Canadiens gear as the children are stretched out on Fred's backyard rink looking up at the stars and talking about Ben, Fern catches a glimpse of him and remarks: "I must be dreaming." His teammates, in turn, chime in: "It's no dream." "Jean Béliveau." Fred watching from the home's interior with cousin Raymond (Michel Charette), who turns out to be the Forum's zamboni driver, also remarks in amazement about the presence of Jean Béliveau on his rink adding: "I must be dreaming!" to which Raymond responds with a chuckle that he's not dreaming because Béliveau is the real article. Ben's dreams of playing at the Forum and the boys musings about what it must feel like to win the Stanley Cup also underscore the Francophone Dream in sport to similar effect.

However, the final scene brings back the viewer around to the group's togetherness. The sequence portrays the six boys with their medals around their necks staring in silence at the river where Ben drowned. Following Bob's lead, they throw them in the water to honor their friend. As they repeat their rallying call, "One for all! All for one!" the lyrics echo their closeness and reaffirm their trademark togetherness. The scene ends with a boom shot of the vast snowy landscape, taking in the river to symbolize Ben's presence. In reaffirming the tight-knit character of the team in emblematic form, the film ultimately relegates other hockey iconography to the background, reasserting the foremost status of the *Les Boys* brand much in the way Disney films continually reference the Company's trademark.

Quebec's Hockey Icon and the Nation: *Maurice Richard/The Rocket*

The multiple Genie Award winner *Maurice Richard/The Rocket* (Binamé, 2005) pays homage to Quebec's most idolized hockey player, Maurice "The Rocket" Richard.[82] Known for his fiery brand of play and his penchant for scoring multiple goals per game, Richard played for 18 seasons with the Montreal Canadiens (1942–1960), topped the 20-goal mark—emblem of marquee status–14 consecutive seasons, and was the first player to score 50 goals in a season. Because of his thrilling game and his popularity in Quebec, Richard's suspension by the league in 1955 engendered a riot of unprecedented dimensions, which many saw as feeding directly into *la Révolution tranquille* and the election of the Parti Liberal's Jean Lesage, whose series of reforms led to the modernization of the province.[83]

The Rocket opens with the Richard Riot of March 17, 1955, and immediately segues to a socio-economic tableau of 1937 Montreal that depicts Quebec workers, among them steel mill machinist Maurice Richard (Roy Dupuis), as second-class citizens in an economy overseen by Anglophone managers and bosses. Richard witnesses the dismissal of a coworker and is discomfited by the incident. At the junior league's championship game, his Lafontaine Park coach, Paul Stuart (Mario Jean), gives a heroic pre-game speech and succinctly outlines Richard's itinerary: "This is about who you are!" Maurice's history of broken ankles, however, follows him to his first Montreal Canadiens camp. "He's not tough enough for big-time hockey," manager Tommy Gorman (Philip Craig) complains. But coach Dick Irvin (Stephen McHattie), with a yen for the exceptional and strapped by his club's bottom place standings, has already gauged the player's intensity and talent and blares, "I want Richard!" Maurice is signed by the team, but after scoring five goals and six assists he is out with a season injury, leading the Montreal press to lament that the organization has signed a dud that can be easily flattened. The following year, he waits in frustration to be called up, all the while fearing that his contract will be allowed to run out. When coach Irvin finally plays him, he begins a meteoric rise to national fame, becoming the league's top offensive player and helping Montreal win the Stanley Cup. He is now "the Rocket" filling up arenas across the league with an intense, fiery brand of play.

New York Times writer A.O. Scott notes in his brief review of the film that Maurice Richard's story is told "by means of a familiar melodramatic machinery."[84] Indeed, *The Rocket*

Maurice Richard (Roy Dupuis) faces the press in *Maurice Richard/The Rocket* (Palm Pictures/Photofest).

is one of the hockey repertoire's most melodramatic films in that it operates through two chief mechanisms: a passive female aspect, delivered through paroxysms of pathos like tears and laments as expressions of the hero's physical and mental suffering, and an active male aspect, which manifests through the "flight, rescue, chase or fight" that the hero deploys to exit and/or solve his dire situation, as Linda Williams argues.[85] These two poles with which the film expertly plays, besieges the audience with the melodramatic tension that it may be "too late" to salvage the situation, only to provide relief at the eleventh-hour at the sight of the hero's just redemption on account of his virtue.[86] *The Rocket* deftly weaves the high points of Richard's achievements with the low points of his unremitting suffering, taking viewers, both familiar and unfamiliar with his life,[87] on a rollercoaster ride of pathos and action.

In a six-team league dominated by English-speaking owners, coaching staff, players, and media, Maurice is attacked on multiple fronts, physical and psychological, public and private. The 1993 release *Net Worth* already hints at Richard's status as a target in the league in a scene in which Red Wings manager Jack Adams humiliates star forward Ted Lindsay for failing to contain the Montreal forward. *The Rocket* communicates this constant assailment by the league's goons through extensive melees in which Maurice's blood is repeatedly drawn. Even in scoring sequences designed to highlight Richard's superlative abilities and strength, such as one from the February 8, 1945, game in which Maurice makes his way to the net with only the goalie in sight, he literally carries notorious Red Wings goon Earl Seibert on his back, pointing to his feats in the context of repeated abuse by the league's thugs to keep him in check. Up-close elongated sequences in which the hero faces the goalie one-on-one and the crowd is obstructed from view are common in the repertoire to heighten the tension of the scoring moment and deliver the just-in-time redemption that he, his team, and the viewers seek. Despite the clear celebratory elements in the above sequence, it is also one of several such scenes in the film, which include the February 25, 1945, breaking of Joe Malone's record with a 45th regular season goal, and an eight-point game in the December 28, 1944, 9–1 Canadiens win against the Detroit Red Wings. These groundbreaking accomplishments attest to Maurice's star attributes, but they also underscore that he unjustly continues to be kept out of the scorer's list by the league.

The Rocket also contextualizes Maurice's five goals and three assists of December 29, 1944, by way of an entire day of moving house with the sole help of his brother-in-law and in the midst of an icy Montreal Winter. The moving sequence, which is bathed in cool, dark blue colors to convey the frigid conditions under which Maurice must climb up and down several flights of stairs, bypasses the explicit focus on NHL players' modest salaries and owner profiteering stressed in *Net Worth*. But it also has the effect of portraying Richard's virtual abandonment by both league and team. The magnificent scoring display that follows that evening not only highlights Richard's larger-than-life abilities and stamina but all the more calls attention to the prejudice wielded against him despite that he answers the call to revitalize the game, and save both his team and a league plagued by declining attendance and bordering on collapse.

In line with the melodramatic mode's dual use of action and pathos to underscore the hero's virtuous suffering, *The Rocket* depicts Maurice openly bursting out in tears in the locker room because of his mistreatment. The tearful scene is set up by a brutal sequence from the April 8, 1952, game against the Boston Bruins in which the player is once again struck from behind and knocked unconscious. Though nursing a serious injury above his eye, he manages to return and score another spectacular tally, which not only has spouse Lucille (Julie LeBreton) in tears in the stands and the crowd roaring, but brings team president, Senator Donat Raymond (René Gagnon), into the locker room to pay his respects: "It is the most beautiful goal that I've ever seen." Maurice's paroxysm of tears by way of deep, unrelenting sobs displays the suffering of his battered, laboring body and anguished mind, bringing the viewer to the realization that he is at breaking point. A rarity in the sports repertoire because it is associated with female expressions of pathos, crying, as Williams explains, is a significant aspect of melodrama that communicates "the feeling that something important has been lost [that also] implicates readers or audiences...."[88] It is also an aspect of melodrama that recurs when bringing "minorities to the forefront of the drama" as unique objects of sentiment.[89] In spotlighting Maurice's stoicism as well as physical and mental suffering in the face of unremitting violence, then, *The Rocket* addresses an audience beyond the national viewership and exposes them not only to Richard's victimization, but by proxy, that of Quebecers.

Maurice's pathos is also clearly on display in a scene that recapitulates a climactic incident in the March 13, 1955, Boston Bruins game. *The Rocket* and *Net Worth* distinctly portray a similar sequence in which the referee ties down the arms of the protagonist while he is brutally pummeled by an opponent. In *Net Worth*, the up-close pummeling is directed at the camera from the perspective of both protagonist and opponent. The scene underscores Ted Lindsay's exemplary durability in light of the game's rough complexion during the 1940s and 1950s. Focus on the athletes' laboring bodies accentuates the moral turpitude of owners and managers who profit from the spectacle of bloodshed but short-circuit players' demands for fair remuneration. *The Rocket*, on the other hand, captures the scene through a shot of Maurice's bloodied face after he receives a stick in the head that leaves him lying flat on the ice during the game. As the Bruins' Hal Laycoe slashes Maurice from behind and he moves to defend himself, the referee ties his hands in back, at which point Laycoe lays a punch on the Montreal icon's face. The sequence is set up so that it appears that the referee and the Bruin are acting in sync, and the close-up of Maurice captured in dark hues invokes the idea of saint-like suffering to communicate the pathos of his hardship. Sports films commonly augment the visual force of pain through the physical spectacle and *The Rocket* reinforces the poignancy of the player's suffering by way of powerful religious iconography that packs a punch in today's predominantly secular Quebec.

Although the film certainly portrays Maurice defending himself by returning punches and nailing referees, the visual underscoring of his blood sacrifice, as seen in the above scene, communicate Richard's plight in line with the inequity that is at the base of the melodramatic impulse, which, as Williams posits, is "structured upon the 'dual recognition' of how things are and how they should be."[90] The film in short order explains Maurice's victimization as founded in the English-speaking players inability to counter his formidable speed, strength, and talent with clean tactics. It also explains the league's underhanded stratagems to keep the player out of the spotlight as a categorical refusal to recognize a French-Canadian as the face of the league.

The highly melodramatic undertones of Maurice Richard's story in *The Rocket* can also be understood in the context of Quebecers' own oppressed condition under English-Canadian governance. The film dramatizes the province's emergence from the dark recesses of the Maurice Duplessis era (1936–1939 and 1944–1959)—a time now known as *la Grande Noirceur* ("The Great Darkness")—to a period that launched full-blown secularization and modernization. Rebecca Sullivan observes that Duplessis and the *Union Nationale* party championed French-Canadian distinctiveness by prioritizing religion over language. Duplessis upheld the Church's power in the social sphere and promoted the idea of Quebec as a rural, agrarian economy despite that it was moving toward secularization, industrialization, and rationalist business practices.[91] The era then stands for an old order that Quebecers must leave behind. And although Maurice always maintained he was only a hockey player, because his retirement coincided with the election of Jean Lesage who instituted reforms that led to the Quiet Revolution and modernization, *The Rocket* affirms that his sojourn is an allegory of the province's rise from underdevelopment and marginality to modernity.

In line with representations of the working class in Quebec-produced feature films, Maurice at first is reluctant to reprise the symbolic role of icon that is thrust on his lap. When he is first asked to give his view on the wrongs he witnesses against other Francophones, the player is diffident about offering his views. His Canadiens teammates scold him for his self-effacing ways, arguing that the approach works against forging a higher profile for French-Canadians in the league. Émile "Butch" Bouchard (Patrice Robitaille), in particular, chastises Maurice for being *"peu bavard"* and *"complètement docile"*—too low-key and meek—and exclaims in frustration that whereas Babe Ruth scores a handful of homers and brags that next time he'll hit twice as many, "What do you say? 'It's not me, it's my stick!'" Michel Houle notes that the standard image of the French-Canadian in films of the 1940s and 1950s is that of the "docile worker, resigned, traditionally gullible, who lets others take advantage of him, and whose life seems to be immutably ruled by age-old habits, dividing his time among work, tavern, Forum, and Mass."[92] The film very obviously casts Richard in the same mold, and as Bouchard's remark hints, the icon's reticence to assume the leadership role fitting of his rank appears to be motivated by his humble *habitant* acculturation.

Richard thus reifies the powerlessness and marginal status of Francophones in line with the historical context given that the Anglophone elite at the time maintained control of the state and the economy of the urban centers.[93] Although the social makeup of Quebec's working class was more complex than the film intimates since, as Loiselle explains, Anglophones comprised a visible segment of this demographic, the French-Canadian nationalist movement formulated its cause and that of the working-class as one and the same.[94] The film therefore implies that Richard initially fails as spokesperson for the nationalist cause because he is reticent to dispose with his "stay low, stay small" attitude. Unlike the working-class characters of earlier Quebec cinema, however, he also begins to sound and act more assertively. On breaking Joe Malone's record, he tells the announcer interviewing him: "I'm very proud of this 45th goal. I set a record that I believe brings honor to all French-Canadians." The presenter beams at his reversal and replies: "On behalf of all of us, I thank you." Maurice also publishes a letter in the press assailing NHL president Clarence Campbell (Ted Dillon) for allowing the unfair treatment of French-Canadian players. *The Rocket* then intimates that Richard begins to embody the role for which he was born, forging an independent path for the province through sheer will and fiery force and acting as symbol of Quebec's emergence as self-confident nation within Canada.

Actor Roy Dupuis, who has reprised the role of the Rocket three times,[95] and effortlessly pulls off Maurice Richard's fiery intensity, notes in the DVD extra that even as Richard remained a "simple" man, "hockey was the mainspring," the cornerstone for the cultural and political awakening of the province. Dupuis explains the reason behind the making of the biopic as a necessary homage to Richard: "We owed him a debt of gratitude" for his role as standard-bearer of *les petits Canadiens*. The concept of *petit pays* encompasses the idea of honorable struggle against a superior adversary in the context of multiple political reversals.[96] Richard's barber, Tony Bergeron (Rémy Bergeron), in like fashion counsels Maurice to stay in the game after his suspension by the league: "Since we never win out there, it's important for a French Canadian to win, even if only in sports." The final game, which integrates the Laycoe incident and ends with Maurice punching out the referee, also aptly encapsulates idea of fighting back against methodical oppression.

Knocking out the referee, however, also garners Richard a suspension for the rest of the season, and a riot unprecedented in the history of the NHL breaks out four days later. Because the display of unremitting prejudice against the player throughout the plot, the riot, which also opens the film, is now understood in terms of the series of injustices committed against him. Williams notes that that the agony that the victim-hero undergoes is all-important in supporting his moral legitimacy, for without this righteousness and innocence, a character's suffering would amount to mere heroism.[97] Although the film inserts Maurice's radio plea to stop the violence, the riot for this reason becomes an extension of Maurice's action to right the wrongs against Francophones.

Because of its melodramatic and eulogist bearings, *The Rocket* sidesteps any focus on Maurice Richard's temperament or inadequacies, which are common in social-realist canonical film. It also bypasses some of the actual events that led to the riot, such as crowd displeasure at NHL President Clarence Campbell's arrival at the Forum, his subsequent pelting with debris, as well as the ensuing vandalism,[98] likely because this imagery would take away from the long-suffering mien of Francophones that the film attempts to project and additionally sully Richard's virtuous suffering and heroism. Sidney Katz writes in "The Richard

Riot" that Campbell's decision to suspend Richard ignited the most devastating riot in Canadian sports history.[99] Yet the film hardly shows the scope of the violence and the vandalism on the streets but reveals it chiefly through a post-facto broadcast news report, in which the presenter underscores the incident as a racially-motivated struggle. Jean Harvey explains, however, that at the time suspending a player for the rest of the season was unprecedented, and fans in Montreal could only feel Richard was being targeted given that referees largely turned a blind eye to opponents' obstructive play. The anger that Montrealers expressed in the Richard Riot therefore was effectively a demonstration against their subordinate status and the control exerted by the Anglophone managerial class.[100]

Doug Beardsley notes that the hockey era of power forwards like Maurice Richard and Ted Lindsay was not one of goons or role players whose prime function was intimidating the opposition, but of all-around skilled players who could hold their own on the ice.[101] Richard himself noted about the rough play of the time, "If you know nothing else about the game I played, know about how violent the game was."[102] The NFB documentary *Of Sport and Men* (Aquin, 1961) depicts the Montreal icon as the very image of hardiness and virility as attested by his "joy of the attack" which warrants "every risk."[103] The Rocket's fiery temperament was also legendary and opposing teams set him off with insults like "[French] Pea Soup!" so he would swiftly find his way into the penalty box. Herbert Warren Wind observed in a 1954 report that Richard was "a good man to avoid" during a scoring slump when he was liable to pick arguments with referees and fights with opponents in a pointed display of "overly aggressive if fruitless hockey."[104] In contrast to the real Richard, who did not mind tough defensive tactics as long as they were above-board, in *The Rocket*, Maurice Richard emerges as a "redemptive, sacrificial hero for a modern secularized Quebec in-the-making," as Amy Ransom aptly observes.[105]

Richard's funeral of May 31, 2000, attested to the player's symbolic reach even among Quebecers who for the most part experienced the Rocket and his era as cultural myth. Ingrid Peritz and Tu Thanh Ha of *The Globe and Mail* observe that 75 percent of Quebecers who were present at the funeral were too young to have attended one of his games.[106] For most of those paying homage, then, Richard could only have been an abstract idea and his death an occasion that precipitated nostalgia for a bygone age. But for Quebecers, the 1940s and 1950s that Maurice Richard embodied were, according to Loiselle, "a time when all dreams were still possible ... [t]he nationalist aspirations of French Canadians were still legitimate, and the Quiet Revolution was still in the making."[107]

Because *The Rocket* is a celebration of Maurice Richard, producers must replicate a heroic narrative that articulates the triumph of the Francophone underdog in sport. In line with the biopic's directive to procure history as a linear, self-enclosed narrative,[108] the film leaves audiences with a moral message while painting an unproblematic, uncontested, and progressive picture of the historical record. The unambiguous, sequential structure of the biopic, coupled with the genre's emphasis on historical figures' legendary status,[109] harmonizes with the mythic aspect of Quebec nationalism which, according to media theorists, has made it difficult to challenge political discourse in the province even in the context of misconstrued premises.[110] Although *The Rocket* puts forth a view of recent history through the prism of Quebec's cultural myths, this portrayal is also consonant with the reality that French-Canadians can tap a separate stream of news and public affairs programming that shares little in common with the cultural discourse that English-Canadians regularly consume.[111] Ransom illustrates the specificity of hockey symbolism for Quebecers in her investigation of the Canadiens and the group Loco Locass' pop-rap "Le But (à la gloire de nos Glorieux)." She notes that the rappers link Maurice's fiery brand of play to the people's triumph on and off the ice to convey hockey as metaphor for Quebecers' greater struggle for sovereignty. Loco Locass' song also connects the Montreal Canadiens to the original *Canadiens*, tapping the ancestral history of Quebecers to articulate all Montrealers and Francophones as sharing in the same past and common destiny.[112]

The sports film is a popular genre that is less suited to the auteurial voice, and as such, it builds its message from the cultural reservoir of a people. Maurice Richard's representation in *The Rocket* in like fashion emphasizes common understandings of the player among Quebecers, which coach Irvin captures in his impassioned acknowledgment of Maurice as the greatest player that ever lived. Needless to say, the film leaves out Richard's own perspective of his role as a hockey player. Rick Salutin of *The Globe and Mail* addresses the player's hesitation over embracing a role outside the arena in noting that, "[i]t's hard enough for political leaders and heroes to carry the weight of their society's needs and hopes. But at least they applied for the role. The Rocket didn't ask for it, didn't want it, and probably didn't understand it."[113] In keeping with Quebec popular cinema's focus on the social and historical context,[114] the film nonetheless depicts the player's journey as symbolic of Quebecers' transformation from a long-suffering people seeking reprieve in the mandates of Church and harbor in the traditional family to emancipated citizens of a modern state. As Williams argues, the most relevant aspect of the melodramatic mode is the acknowledgment of virtue in a world where morality, righteousness and honor have been vanquished from sight.[115] Maurice Richard's journey and towering effort, then, stands as a metaphor for Francophones' arduous but triumphant struggle for cultural and political continuity.

Mending Canada's Cultural Divide: *Bon Cop, Bad Cop*

The popular film *Bon Cop, Bad Cop* (Canuel, 2006)[116] also recreates a fiery model of Francophone masculinity in a comedic feature of two cops who, as embodiments of the Anglo-French divide, must learn to work together to counter hockey's plundering by American vested interests. A mix of buddy-cop comedy and crime thriller, the film opens with an anxious call to a Montreal hockey radio show regarding the prospective sale and relocation of the Toronto Loyalists—a stand-in for the Leafs—to the U.S. The caller has it on good faith that the sale is all but wrapped up, and he balks at the prospect of his beloved team's relocation south and its permeation by the American model of entertainment: "cheap American crap" complete with mascots and cheerleaders, as he laments. The body of a hockey executive is soon discovered hanging from a billboard straddling the Quebec and Ontario borders. *Sureté du Québec* detective David Bouchard (Patrick Huard) and Ontario Provincial Police constable Martin Ward (Colm Feore) are forced by their superiors to team up on the case until the appropriate police jurisdiction is discerned. The killer (Patrice Bélanger) leaves a tattoo on his victim that provides clues about the reasons for the murders, all of which relate to the relocation of Canadian franchises or the trade of marquee Canadian players to U.S.–based teams. Another hockey-related murder follows: that of the first female hockey agent who represented a high profile player initially drafted by the Fleurs de Lys and subsequently traded to a Philadelphia team, a veiled reference to Eric Lindros' trade from the Quebec Nordiques to the Philadelphia Flyers. A third victim is found with a tattoo of a heart and a #99, an allusion to Wayne Gretzky's trade to the L.A. Kings.

The murders take place in the midst of the Holt Cup finals between the Toronto Loyalists and their archrival, the Montreal Patriotes, a surrogate for the Montreal Canadiens. When the detectives appear on a popular televised hockey show hosted by outspoken commentator Tom Berry (Rick Mercer)—a not-so-subtle proxy for Don Cherry on "Coach's Corner"—because the guest booked for the evening has not shown up, the killer realizes that the police are closing in on him. He threatens Bouchard over the phone and subsequently kidnaps his teenage daughter Gabrielle (Sarah-Jeanne Labrosse), and straps her to a chair with explosives. After exchanging league Commissioner Harry Buttman (Richard Howland)—NHL Commissioner Gary Bettman's double—for Gabrielle, Bouchard and Ward each take a turn at the derelict and deploy those same explosives to hasten his demise.

The film's prime visual metaphor suggested by the body of the murdered hockey executive straddling the Quebec-Ontario border points to two major elements of contention in Anglo-French divide: jurisdictional partitioning and hockey. The Anglo-French duality in Canadian film is a recurrent motif of madness that dramatizes the inability to resolve the gap between these identities, as Janice Kaye notes.[117] In *Bon Cop, Bad Cop*, the unhinged bilingual Québécois killer, who will stop at nothing to avenge hockey's appropriation, represents the national psyche frayed by the sale of teams and franchise players to American interests bent on stealing Canada's cultural symbols.[118] His choice of target, which includes figures of the

Detective David Bouchard (Patrick Huard, right) and Constable Mark Ward (Colm Feore) argue over the body of a hockey executive found straddling the Quebec-Ontario border in *Bon Cop, Bad Cop* (courtesy of Bon Cop, Bad Cop Productions, Inc./Park Ex Pictures/Kevin Tierney; photograph Atilla Dory).

French- and English-Canadian hockey community, also shows that the issue transcends the cultural divide. Michel Grossbut (Gilles Renaud)—a stand-in for Marcel Aubut—is criticized for the sale of the Quebec Nordiques to Colorado, as is Mr. Pickleton (Robert Jadah)—an alternate for Edmonton Oilers owner Peter Pocklington—who is assailed for exporting Wayne Gretzky to the L.A. Kings.

Bouchard and Ward are charged with healing this rift and take turns at expressing their agreement on the matter of hockey as common denominator in Canadian culture. Unlike in *Les Boys* where villain Méo dons the #99 jersey, Bouchard alludes to Gretzky as the greatest hockey player in the world. And when a journalist asks in French whether Buttman is trying to make a fool of French-Canadians when he fails to show up for a press conference, Ward replies in English that it isn't just the French but Canadians in general that the Commissioner appears to dislike. Because, as in *Sudden Death*, the plot threatens the protagonists' kids, the film suggests that the future of Canada's children is at stake as the national psyche comes unhinged by the plunder of hockey. Whereas Darren McCord in *Sudden Death* singlehandedly does away with Foss, Bouchard and Ward succeed in sending the villain to oblivion just barely, in line with Lee Parpart's argument about the less-than-dominant masculinity that characterizes male characters in Canadian film, stressing the need to form a united front to push back on American expansionist designs on the game.

If the threat from within looms as a matter of urgency, the threat from without is no less significant. The repartee between the Commissioner and the Texan magnate, Mr. Arbusto (Paul Stewart)—a witty play on U.S. President George W. Bush's name—who intends to make hockey "as Texas as a big American steak" echoes entertainment conglomerates' transformation of hockey into upmarket consumer sport during the 1990s and calls forth Innisian images of hockey as cultural staples targeted by unfettered cowboy capitalism. Buttman tells the Texan in a private teleconference call that he is doing great things for the sport, invoking the good of the game much in the way that league higher-ups do in *Net Worth*.

Because *Bon Cop, Bad Cop* very obviously draws on the 1990s Canadian crisis of identity associated with Disney's entry into the NHL, the migration of Canadian hockey franchises to the Sun Belt, as well as Fox's tampering with the game by inserting a red glowing puck in National league broadcasts, it suggests that this crisis is not over but ongoing. The film further buttresses the opposition between the crassly commercialized space of American entertainment and the organic roots of hockey in the Northern Canadian icescape through the presence of the beaver mascot at the Patriotes-Loyalists game, which conveys the Montreal-Toronto rivalry as a sporting tradition that legitimizes the Canadian stamp on the game. A Canadian national symbol prominently displayed both in the 1988 Calgary and 2010 Vancouver Winter Olympics, beaver iconography alludes to the vast Northern forests that Hollywood associates with Canada dating back to 1907 silent film.

Arbusto's allusions to hockey by way of a Texas-big steak call up not only insistent imagery of American influence in the NHL and exploitation of the game as a natural resource, but resonate with fears of U.S. annexation of the Canadian West as the "free space" conveyed in Frederick Jackson Turner's "Problem of the West," an essay that debates the idea of American progress with ramifications for the entire continent. The Montreal Canadiens colors on the sweater of the Patriotes' mascot additionally communicate to French-Canadians that hockey has populist relevance in Quebec and warns about the game's absorption by U.S. finance. Imagery of the crook that hides inside the mascot lying in wait to launch a potentially devastating attack is similar to that of *Sudden Death*, a film that dramatizes from NHL owners' perspective the destruction of small-market franchises due to escalating player salaries and inadequate infrastructure. Like the CBC documentary *Going South*, which enlarges on the idea of children as fallout from Canadian teams' relocation to the Sun Belt, *Bon Cop, Bad Cop* intimates that once again American finance is headed North to poach the very future of Canada's children.

To address the allegorical unhinging of the Canadian psyche by the Anglo-French duality, the film first focuses on traditional hockey rivalries through the Two Solitudes' history of political opposition.[119] Just as the Toronto Loyalists hint at English-Canada's historic links to England and the Monarchy, the Montreal Patriotes recall the Patriotes Rebellion of 1837–38, an armed conflict between French rebels who strove to drive out the British colonial power in the province. The rebellion failed, and with the arrest of the insurgents, Britain put in place measures to assimilate Francophones into British-Canadian culture. According to Bill Marshall, both the Rebellion and the subsequent ascendance of the Anglophone business elite in the province in time also contributed to the development of a nationalism that was chiefly inflected by populism.[120] By conveying Montreal hockey through the Patriotes rubric and its link to identity and nationalism, *Bon Cop, Bad Cop* communicates the foremost standing of the team as symbolic of Quebec's endurance as a nation.

The buddy-thriller genre features two cops, who must work together to solve a crime despite very different personalities and different ethnic or cultural backgrounds. One is levelheaded, "old school," and typically the senior partner. The other, considerably younger, is a non-conformist hothead. In *Bon Cop, Bad Cop*, the metaphor of two detectives forcibly bound together for a common cause accentuates the need for negotiation to institute a coalition of Canadian cultures based on the myth of two founding nations. In an essay on linguistic code-switching, Émilie Pelletier discusses a handful of passages from the film and observes that the detectives use their native tongue and shift to the other's language to negotiate dominance and extract support for their respective positions.[121] In response to Bouchard's request that Ward speak in French—"*au Québec on travaille en français*"—the constable answers that switching depends on the subject's mother tongue. Bouchard remains insistent, however, and Ward accedes but cites the Canadian Constitution's official language provision, noting that the remainder of Canada, with the exception of a few areas in New Brunswick, falls under his jurisdiction. Although the humorous negotiation tactics hint at compromise, in reality they amount to entrenched resistance on both sides. To shake the characters out of their ossified attitudes, the film structures events so that the partners are forced to elicit assistance from one another in alternating sequences. This framework suggests that if the two parties do not engage willingly in genuine negotiation and rapprochement, circumstances will propel them out of their intractable stances.

In the context of transacting leverage, however, the detectives also use discrete tactics. Although the film points to Ward as the more culturally sophisticated of the two because of his sojourn in Paris, his excellent French, and his turtleneck sweaters and suave demeanor, the constable also repeatedly castigates Bouchard by alluding to him as Francophone, and questioning when he crosses the line whether he does it "because you're ignorant, because you're lunatic, or just because you're French." Ward's exasperation with Bouchard's almost rugged insistence on doing things his way all the more calls to mind symbolism of the iconic independence and virile masculinity of the *voyageurs* and *coureurs de bois*, the romantic frontier

Mending Canada's Cultural Divide

figures of the North who operated outside the control of the government and Church in colonial times. Ward also bellyaches about Quebecers' historical resentment toward Anglophones. When he and Bouchard discuss the murdered female agent, Ward remarks that "some people still aren't over the Plains of Abraham," alluding to the 1759 Conquest of New France by Britain that triggered Anglicization and Francophone resistance.[122] In his passing comment, Ward implies that the Quebecers' sense of victimization is a throwback to another era and its continual emphasis remains inappropriate. In another scene, Ward turns a personal disagreement with Bouchard to a diatribe about national issues. When Bouchard balks at his partner's interest in ex-wife Suzie (Lucie Laurier), Ward lashes out: "You Quebecers are all the same.... *Je me souviens.* You're living in the past!" and emphasizes for good measure that it's high time French-Canadians got over it. Bouchard revealingly counters by reasserting the expediency of the Quebec's *petit pays* code and its politics of linguistic, cultural, and demographic resistance to assimilation into Anglo-Canadian culture: "At least we survived!" In other words, Bouchard does not respond to Ward's criticism by attacking Anglophones or the history of English governance, but by insisting on the very annoyances that irk his partner and noting that he's got rights.

In buddy-cop form, Bouchard and Ward are set up as characters with opposite traits, and as the junior, rebellious partner, the Francophone detective also takes on the role associated with heroics in the genre. With a highly individual, adventurous style, Bouchard thinks nothing of putting his body on the line and has the scars to prove it. In one of the more comical scenes in the film, Bouchard takes on Tom Berry, who as surrogate of Don Cherry,

David Bouchard (Patrick Huard, right) bloodied in the course of his duties alongside suave and clean-shaven partner Mark Ward (Colm Feore, left) arresting an unidentified miscreant in *Bon Cop, Bad Cop* (courtesy of Bon Cop, Bad Cop Productions, Inc./Park Ex Pictures/Kevin Tierney; photograph Atilla Dory).

complains about game arbiters who want to eradicate fighting and turn hockey into golf. Cherry is known for accusing Francophone players of a lack of grit and Bouchard's skirmish with Berry registers as a categorical rejoinder about French-Canadians' physical durability and vigorous masculinity.[123]

Bon Cop, Bad Cop's comical riposte extends to Eric Lindros, a rugged talent who was selected first in the 1991 NHL draft by the Quebec Nordiques but refused to play until the league traded him to the Flyers the following year. Amy Ransom notes that Quebec's media referred to this incident as the "Lindros Affair" and linked it to the constitutional debates that led up to the 1995 sovereignty referendum, and along with the Nordiques' relocation to Colorado, stoke "the fires of nationalist discontent."[124] Much the same had transcurred with Gretzky's trade to the L.A. Kings, which the media linked to the 1988 Free Trade Agreement and the 1988 Calgary Olympics in the context of Canada's "fate as a nation," as Steven Jackson indicates.[125] The national crisis that ensued with Gretzky's trade, deepened with the relocation of several NHL teams to the U.S. Sun Belt and led to fears about the Americanization of Canada, as noted earlier. *Bon Cop, Bad Cop*, however, makes no mention of Gretzky in this context, while in line with its French-Canadian lens, it alludes to the Lindros Affair as Bouchard notes about the player, who was prone to head injuries, that he is in the hospital with another concussion, suffered after hearing about his agent's death and summarily collapsing to the ground.

As the "bad cop" of the duo, Bouchard also exhibits a defiance that comically extends to police protocol. He respects neither the direction of traffic nor speed limits, disregards sidewalk boundaries and handicap parking spaces, and is quick to pull a gun and act on his own. He is the law unto himself if he can get away with it. Bouchard has all the makings of the American outlaw who sought to escape institutional control by moving West. *Paperback Hero* well illustrates that an outlaw-like behavior is misguided, because the idea of Canada as orderly and peaceable country presupposes the need for a police force. Bouchard's behavior, however, amplifies the carnivalesque humor in *Bon Cop, Bad Cop*, since albeit representing the law—the very police charged with safekeeping of order and peace in the land—the detective goes at his duties by thumbing his populist nose both at the norms of social conduct and institutional force. His daring, adventurous, physical style, which he also deploys in enforcing the law his own way, is in keeping with John Fiske's argument that the body and physical displays remain critical sites of social contestation between the elites and the people. As a hero in a Quebec film, Bouchard also hews to mythology that buttresses self-sufficiency and resilience: that of the *coureurs de bois* and *voyageurs* of Quebec's deep past, who operated outside the control of Church and government and remains valuable in leveraging Francophone identity through heroic, apostate elements.

Ward's physicality in *Bon Cop, Bad Cop*, in contrast, is appreciably less emphatic than that of his free-spirited partner and very much unlike that of the other figures in the English-Canadian hockey repertoire, which lend him an aura of supporting character at the start of the film. Even though like Bouchard, Ward is roughed up in the course of his duties, this "good cop" plays according to the rules and can hardly keep up with his partner who is in excellent physical shape. His yearning for a desk job, his cooking abilities, and his pant ironing imply a degree of domesticity that is congruent with his cerebral bent and seniority. Since the English-Canadian protagonist in popular or canonical film featuring destiny or decline-into-fall story arcs does not eschew physical exertion, although gallant and polished, Ward emerges as the more conservative of the two, a subdued personality when compared to Bouchard's outside-the-line disposition and sheer animal magnetism. Although *Bon Cop, Bad Cop* remains true to the buddy-cop genre, audiences in Canada likely sensed the uneven allocation of attributes, since albeit the film was promoted as a bilingual project suitable to both Francophone and Anglophone markets, 80 percent of its record CAD 13 million at the domestic box office was garnered in Quebec, and in French-Canadian language theaters.[126] The popularity of star Patrick Huard, who plays Ti-Guy in *Les Boys*, also likely contributed to the film's saleability in Quebec as Matthew Hays notes.[127]

Hockey in the Anglo-French binary is conspicuous for expressing opposition and difference, and to heal the national divide, *Bon Cop, Bad Cop* avoids formulating a winning side in the Holt Cup championships. Aside from mentions by radio announcers and Tom Berry's comments, the film does not even visually zero in on the Holt Cup finals, but conveys the game through a single generic long shot from high above the arena. To heal the Anglo-French divide, the film instead suggests conciliation through the trope of the family, a major institution of Quebec culture,[128] by recruiting the help of Bouchard's ex-wife Suzie, and Ward's sister, Iris (Sarain Boylan), who each fancies the cop from the other precinct. Iris' interjection "*Vive le Québec Libre!*" during an intimate scene with Bouchard—an allusion to French President De Gaulle's encouragement of Quebec independence during a 1967 visit to Canada—reiterates the mix of politics and sexuality that makes for subversive social commentary in Quebec film. And although the producers opted to edit out a take of Bouchard and Ward wearing each other's jerseys because of its excessively formulaic undertones, the film still

Left to right: David Bouchard (Patrick Huard) and Mark Ward (Colm Feore) inside the killer's lair with Commissioner Harry Buttman (Richard Howland) in tow (*Bon Cop, Bad Cop*, courtesy of Bon Cop, Bad Cop Productions, Inc./Park Ex Pictures/Kevin Tierney; photograph Atilla Dory).

delivers the happy ending in good Hollywood form as the four happily watch the playoffs in the living room. *Bon Cop, Bad Cop* articulates the characters coming-together as a symbol of the fit rather than dysfunctional Canadian family, a form of successful border-crossing that heals the unhinging of the nation by reconciling the duality of the Two Solitudes.

An announcement by Buttman at a press conference inserted at the end of the film, which makes clear that no more Canadian franchises will be relocated to the U.S., serves as a covenant with fans that Commissioner Gary Bettman reiterated in a 2009 interview with *Maclean's* Magazine in a case of life imitating art.[129] It nonetheless also registers as an addendum since the announcement appears in a reduced screen as the credits roll. The arrangement suggests that the central issue in *Bon Cop, Bad Cop* is not the plunder of the game by outside interests after all, but the resolution of the Anglo-French divide, a notion that Patrick Huard, the actor playing David Bouchard and the screenplay's co-writer, expresses in an interview when he notes that the "Québécois and English-Canadian[s] do indeed share a culture."[130]

The hockey-themed films in this chapter attest that the game continues to play an important role in how Quebecers perform their identity. This small but remarkable repertoire not only reaffirms the relationship between image-making and the politics of independence, but shows that these creatives pull at the Québécois collective heartstrings through mythically inflected touchstones: Quebec's romantic *coureurs de bois* and *voyageurs* past, *la Conquête*, English rule and the central role of the Roman Catholic Church and its humble *habitant* directive, *La Grande Noirceur, la Révolution tranquille* and the province's secularization, as well as Quebec as a *petit pays* and questions of secessionism. While Quebec film may play with the sports genre's intertextuality by alluding to Hollywood and (English-)Canadian game imagery, this repertoire is fundamentally concerned with hockey as expression of Francophone masculinity and identity. These films not only memorialize Quebec's hockey icons—Maurice Richard and the Canadiens, especially—but ponder history, revise cultural codes, rethink social norms and leverage nonconformism to convey distinctiveness through a populist "theater of resistance,"[131] a combination of physical resilience and a historically-inflected notion of defiance.

6

Hockey Biopics and the Nation

Sport and film share the cultural role of representing the ideal nation to its members, and sports biopics that allude to the feats of athletic exemplars and convey the nation as a sacred hub are especially potent as mythic constructs. The sports film is typically "character-driven and plot-driven," rather than sports-motivated, as Peter Guber notes.[1] As a subcategory of the sports genre, the sports biopic is designed to attract a wider demographic than just the sport fan. George Custen notes that biopics are marketed as "accessible versions of history" that implicitly promise viewers that no detail has been spared to deliver a "true portrait" or a person or event.[2] As dramas that recount historical endeavors about national exemplars and teams, sports biopics harmonize with the sports genre's viability as domestic repertoire. In speaking to a community's values, these films also stand out in the era of globalization with its emphasis on corporate brands, pervasive elements of leisure, and consumption-based identity.[3]

Canada's victory in the eight-game 1972 Summit Series tourney, an inaugural meeting between NHLers and Soviet national team, and the "Miracle on Ice," the U.S. triumph against the U.S.S.R. team in the 1980 Winter Games at Lake Placid, are hailed as mirrors of the essential character of the nation and for this reason are natural picks for hockey biopics. As unique televised contests that dramatize the longing for the feats of towering figures, these events speak to public nostalgia for the mythical masculinity modeled by team sports and its relationship to the nation.[4] The numerous documentaries and features designed to keep the memory of these victories alive show that they continue to widely resonate with audiences. For obvious reasons, hockey biopics feature influential coaches in central parts because these figures take on a nation-building role. They operate as acculturating agents, who speak to mythic ideals that hone exemplary masculinity in the service of citizenship and nationhood. Coaching icons also typically uphold the doctrine that pain builds character in keeping with sport's connection to warfare, much like military figures in war films borrow sports metaphors to motivate soldiers to take one for the team and execute the big win. The appearance of these coaches and the commemoration of these contests in biopic format are not unexpected given that historical figures and events are more believable in a nation-building capacity than fictional ones. As a mix of journalism and fiction, these works are also not definitive renditions but representations of producers' views of social actors, which amplify particular historical, political, and cultural angles of these events.[5]

The Memory Work of Allegiance: ABC's *Miracle on Ice* and Disney's *Miracle*

No hockey story speaks more intently to American audiences than the 1980 U.S. Olympic semifinal win over the U.S.S.R. in Lake Placid. The victory entered the pantheon of American sports stories as part of the Cold War,[6] and due to U.S. setbacks on the military front along with skyrocketing unemployment and stagflation, the win carried with it the hopes of American resurgence.[7] Although in the 1970s hockey was largely a regional sport, in Olympic competition the U.S. had attained a measure of success, scoring gold in the 1960 Squaw Valley Games and silver in the 1972 Sapporo Games. The Soviet record in hockey, however, included gold medals in every Winter Games since 1956, except for 1960 where the team garnered silver. Out of 35 confrontations between the U.S. and U.S.S.R., Soviet squads had claimed victory 34 times. Sports commentators expected the Soviets to take the 1980 Olympic gold, and the American victory in the semifinal game, as well as their eventual gold medal, came as an utter shock to the hockey world. Over thirty-four million viewers watched in amazement the unfolding events and the tape delayed broadcast of the semifinal garnered a 29.3 national rating, making it the highest-rated hockey game in U.S. broadcast history.[8]

The event's popularity[9] with American audiences has contributed to the making of two accounts: the ABC telefilm[10] *Miracle on Ice* (Stern, 1981) and the Disney feature *Miracle* (O'Connor, 2004). Both productions showcase the motif of men on a mission, which chronicles the heroic endeavors of male outfits common in the combat and sports genres and highlights the value differences of protagonists and opponents by underlining why and how these groups do battle. Because of the event's Cold War connection and the sports film's reprise of the heroic quest as a moral story, these films also deploy the idea of the U.S. as headspring for progress, which is built into the Westering myth and its march of civilization code.[11] However, their narratives also draw on distinct historical referents that shed light on producer choices in recalibrating the event into narrative form.

In *Miracle on Ice* a band of Olympic prospects clustered around a room waits for the arrival of coach Herb Brooks (Karl Malden). A Boston recruit says of the Minnesota and Wisconsin players that they make him uneasy. Moments later, his Minnesota counterpart refers to Easterners as "never leav[ing] concrete streets." The U.S. lineup is comprised by prospects who come from very different geographic and cultural backgrounds—from the large metropolis of Boston and the rural and mining areas of Minnesota and Wisconsin—which makes for cultural fissures on the bench. When a Massachusetts player during a subsequent bus trip is unable to differentiate between Minnesota's Iron Range and Minneapolis, he is accused of being ignorant about the rest of the country and advised to do away with the snobbery because he is "just as poor as your [goalie] Craig." Out of this fractioned bunch Brooks must mold a winning team. The outlook is not a promising one. Since the Cold War conflict formulated the U.S. and U.S.S.R. as polar opposites, to conform to the narrative demands of storytelling, the films must deploy the Soviet and home team's journeys in direct opposition.[12] That is, they must present the audience with a cohesive Soviet lineup and a U.S. hero in disarray. The theme of dissension on the U.S. bench implicitly lays out players' figurative passage towards the U.S. mythic ideal of *e pluribus unum*, the-one-in-the-many. *E pluribus unum* encapsulates the ideology of consensus, which, as Roger Fowler notes,

The 1980 U.S. Olympic hockey team celebrates their victory in the Soviet semifinal (Photofest).

"assumes, and in times of crisis actually affirms, that within the group, there is no difference or disunity in the interests and values of any of the population or institution."[13] The U.S. squad must come together to ritually unite a nation that finds itself divided by the culture wars of the previous two decades and in the doldrums due to a severe economic downturn and loss of political influence, thus highlighting the national biopics' preoccupation with the mythic ideal of unity to denote the solidity of the social project.

However, arguments among team members also focus on breadwinning issues. As in other seventies and eighties Hollywood films in the repertoire, players' conversations make clear that hockey is the sport of the working people, and athletes from upper- or middle-class backgrounds are the exception rather than the rule. Thus, at training camp in Colorado

Springs two players point to forward Rob McClanahan's (Ken Stovitz) expensive jeans and wonder "what's a rich kid doing playing hockey?"[14] In keeping with its televisual audience form of address, *Miracle on Ice* also foregrounds these concerns through familial discussions and characters' personal confidences as players weigh the benefits of turning pro to offset pecuniary woes. Jim Craig (Steve Guttenberg) tells his father that remaining amateur is costly for the family, and another player interrupts a discussion of the league's remunerative potential by reminding teammates of the necessity of an education in case their NHL prospects do not materialize. During the round-robin segment of the competition, as team captain Mike Eruzione (Andrew Stevens) sees his girlfriend off at the bus station, she justifies her early departure by stating that she cannot lose her job as his future as a hockey professional is unclear. In another poignant scene, Eruzione mulls the option of retiring prior to the Games to take a position as assistant coach on the national team with the hopes that it will translate into a college coaching job. Close friend and teammate Lester Auge (Jerry Houser) urges him to reconsider, noting that this is the chance of a lifetime for, although football and baseball are "big business" and offer great professional opportunities to the American athlete, the same cannot be said of hockey. Eruzione ultimately stays with the team to score the winning goal in the semifinal while Auge is cut from the squad early on. While reiterating seventies films' view of a hockey career as a job rather than a glamorous occupation, the scene also mirrors the status of the American player in the league coming into the 1980s when U.S. college stars seldom made it to the NHL except as role players.[15] *Miracle on Ice* thus features agents and player reps as allies who seek to extract the best possible outcomes for their charges.

Miracle, in contrast, makes no mention of players' socio-economic backgrounds, their concern with financial security, or the role of sports agents in their lives. Instead, the Disney feature plays up regional tensions between Eastern and Western college hockey divisions to amplify the idea of conflict within the ranks. When goalie Jim Craig (Eddie Cahill) informs Boston cohort Jack O'Callahan (Michael Mantenuto) that coach Brooks (Kurt Russell) has selected mostly marquee players from Minnesota and Boston for the Olympic roster, O.C. replies sarcastically that the recipe is certain to work. A fight between O'Callahan and Minnesota's Rob McClanahan (Nathan West) is also explained as unfinished business stemming from a college championship confrontation. The film downplays players' utilitarian reasons for joining the team likely because these mundane concerns tarnish the towering quality of the victory.[16] Indeed, *Miracle* from the very outset sets an exalted tone. While *Miracle on Ice* opens with visuals of U.S. prospects at their geographical enclaves accompanied by an Olympic-like soundtrack that evoke the idea of troops heeding the call to take up a mission, *Miracle* sets up the win through a large number of dissolves that recall disruptive events of the time and convey the historical period in which the story unfolds as deeply troubled. This material is relevant to apprise the viewer of the event's historical context. President Jimmy Carter's Crisis of Confidence speech,[17] which plays in the background at the film's outset and at Christmastime to highlight coach Brooks' emotionally arduous job in honing a national team, however, also equates the assignment of winning to the monumental task of solving a national crisis. *Miracle*'s framing of events, then, summarily sets up the need for the introduction of the hero whose feats will restore the ailing nation.

These opening sequences also make clear that whereas *Miracle on Ice* is the story of the U.S. players' journey to the gold, *Miracle* chronicles the quest of Herb Brooks, who valiantly sacrificed his personal life to take on a difficult national task, as director Gavin O'Connor observes.[18] Even though both films uphold Brooks' acculturating role, they paint a distinct picture of the coach's relationship with his players. By most accounts, Herb Brooks was a real-life gamesman, a thinking-man's coach who spied out loopholes in his charges' psychological makeup and devised teaching strategies accordingly. But in *Miracle on Ice* actor Karl Malden portrays the coach as a grump with high standards given to long-drawn speeches.[19] The players, in contrast, emerge as gamesmen *extraordinaires* who systematically challenge the coach's strategies and remain one step ahead of him as well as the media, happily feeding reporters what they want to hear. Mike Eruzione's character, in particular, displays great leadership in calling the coach on his locker room tactics. When Brooks chides the captain for not bearing up to the pressure of being singled out in front of the team, Eruzione retorts that he is indeed able to take the heat but that he and goalie Jim Craig are being used as scapegoats. Although American culture prizes self-reliance and individualism, the sports film, much like its combat counterpart, upholds a hierarchical structure and the need to sublimate self-interest to the goals of the larger outfit. Eruzione's character in *Miracle on Ice*, however, conveys the anti-establishment stance of seventies sports protagonists who systematically question the orders of superiors, once a credible and trustworthy source of institutional authority now transformed into suspect representatives of the power structure.[20] Eruzione's position in the TV movie also diverges from E.M. Swift's account that the coach's bond with his players was marked by nuance, and that he was closest to both the captain and the team's go-to-goalie, Jim Craig.[21] Because the film heroizes the players and retains their anti-authoritarian perspective, Eruzione's character personifies the fraying of the connection between coach and team, which persisted until the end. The coach in the ABC film therefore has his hands full with the skeptical lot he must develop into a team.

Miracle's players, on the other hand, resemble innocents both on and off the ice, trying to catch up to Brooks' machinations. Russell-Brooks keeps players on their toes, in particular, captain Mike Eruzione (Patrick O'Brien Demsey) whom he repeatedly tests and admonishes by noting that his game leaves much to be desired. Eruzione's character is affable but meek, as he readily admits his fear of getting cut, adding that every single member of the team is feeling the pressure. The team captain is aware of his precarious position and deeply afflicted by self-doubt as he treads cautiously around the coach. Herb's habit of keeping players in the dark about his intentions has the entire team on alert attempting to second-guess his next move. As the coach calls up Minnesota Gopher Tim Harrer (Adam Knight) and threatens to cut Eruzione, in a rare scene of quasi-rebellion that takes the form of a plea, the players oppose the move "because we're family!"[22] The metaphor of team as family speaks to the Disney brand because the company markets its products to the child and its mainstay, the family, and through this imagery, infuses media content with pastoral values. David Morley and Kevin Robins make clear that the idea has its political uses, since Disney routinely deploys iconography of the family as metaphor for national unity.[23] Silk, Schultz and Bracey extend this argument in expressly linking Disney's politicization of the 1980 victory to pressure from the George W. Bush Administration on major studios and TV networks to maintain a united front after the events of September 11, 2001. *Miracle*, as a result, props up a sporting discourse that bolsters a unified, patriotic, and militaristic vision of the past.[24] The emphasis on unity is also consonant with the film's enfeebling of players as "kids" who never rock the boat but routinely defer to their autocratic coach, consistent with Isabelle Freda and Rebecca Bell-Metereau's findings that characters of televisual and cinematic texts in the wake of 9/11 displayed marked "[p]olitical infantilization" and a subservient demeanor toward authority.[25]

The coaching role in this seminal U.S. hockey event must also speak to national audiences as a triumph of the pioneering spirit that forged the nation in line with the nation's origin myth, and *Miracle* follows suit by depicting Herb Brooks as a maverick innovator who goes over the heads of the USOC panel overseeing the selection process. Historian Richard Francaviglia notes that Walt "Disney depicted the western frontier as a place of individual initiative,"[26] and *Miracle* echoes this stance when Brooks acts alone in the certainty of his personal vision: "I'm not looking for the best players…. I'm looking for the right ones." When USA Hockey's Walter Bush (Sean McCann), speaking for the USOC panel, objects to the coach's strategy, Brooks remains adamant that he knows best what he needs to compete, noting that he has already chosen his prospects, having carefully studied film on each, talked to scouts and coaches, and personally trained many of them. Historian Stephen Hardy labels the scene the worst of *Miracle*'s distortions and explains that "Brooks skillfully employed coaches from both Eastern and Western divisions to help him select the team."[27] *Miracle*'s portrayal of the coach nonetheless synchronizes with the heroic masculinity of the western's protagonist who in riding alone exemplifies the American romance with independence and self-confidence.[28]

As a taskmaster, the coach must also acculturate his players to the martial values and the obligatory sacrifices of men on a heroic quest. In *Miracle on Ice*, Malden-Brooks embodies the attitude of a man on a sacred mission, as he addresses his players very much in line with destiny narratives, informing them that only twenty of them will have the honor of donning the U.S. Olympic colors: "It will be the best of you … the bravest, the ones who believe in themselves and can trust the other man and he, in turn, can trust you." His speech at the Olympic training camp in Colorado resonates with the essential traits needed for the task, and the coach insists that the assignment calls for full commitment: "This has got to be the only thing…. Not choices. This!" The coach also insists on working his players hard. He puts together a grueling five-month, 61-game schedule that a player rep describes as one that only the fittest can endure. But Malden-Brooks insists he wants no floaters on his team, commanding players in bellowing tones to hit their spots. The coach also fights to keep his charges from the press for fear that the media hype will instill in them a false sense of security by delving out star treatment. In the process he also leaves agents little room to market their players. As *Miracle on Ice*'s upbeat martial musical motif suggests, Brooks' vision of the national team is that of an entity singularly committed to the undertaking at hand.

Russell-Brooks in *Miracle* likewise reiterates the militaristic model of honing character, warning his charges to be ready to endure great pain for he will skate them harder than they ever have. He works to condition his team through long practices, and resembles a take-no-prisoners drill sergeant who decks out punishment for their lack of commitment. The coach reminds his players of the ideals that built the country, giving notice that he will not allow them to perform like average men because this approach will get them nowhere: "You have to be uncommon!" Russell-Brooks mirrors the ideals of the nation in a way that approximates the figure of the frontiersmen, who built the country with great effort and sacrifice and deployed military metaphors to refer to the coming of civilization.[29] *Miracle*'s recurrent visual iteration of work and forbearance take the form of numerous conditioning exercises that underscore players' Herculean exertion in meeting the coach's demands, conveying team members' physical suffering with great emotional force and convincingly heightening the audience's sense of the spectacle's arduousness. In the sports film, these hardship situations are necessary to hone not only specialized skills but attain goals and enable the defeat of the forces threatening the social macrocosm.[30] Not surprisingly, the U.S. squad gels during their European tour, not in reaction to their Norwegian opponent's play, but as a lesson learned when forced to do post-game drills called "Herbies." The Disney film conveys the sequence as a vital military exercise that ends when Eruzione blurts out in soldier-like manner, "Mike Eruzione, United States of America!" and communicates that the players grasp the coach's directive. The sequence implies that Brooks' strongman tactics encode trailblazing abilities that empower him to lead the team at a time of national crisis.

Miracle on Ice, for its part, draws up the classic team-gelling moment by way of an exhibition game against the Minnesota North Stars.[31] The young Americans are not only defeated but decidedly manhandled, and the announcers remark that the U.S. collegians must get used to the hard physicality of the NHLers.[32] After the end of the game Malden-Brooks tells his charges that a good lashing instills character,[33] and that they should consider how challenging the pros found the Russians. In the hallway Brooks informs wife Patti (Jessica Walter) about the evening's success in helping to cement the team. The film deploys the rugged NHL contact game as part of the team's learning curve, even though Soviet teams de-emphasized extreme physicality.

The ABC movie also hews to both political and sporting imagery of the Soviets coming into the 1980 Olympic. Early in the film, Malden-Brooks must solicit sponsorship funds from a company CEO to provide a stipend for his players. The coach pleads his case by arguing that while Soviet team members are subsidized by the state as officers in the Army, his charges cannot compete without corporate support, and it is Americans, not America, who send athletes to the Olympics. The TV movie frames the U.S.–U.S.S.R. Cold War binary as a contest between "We, the Nation" and "They, the State," which construes the state as a juridical concept, dreary and soulless, and the nation as a living, breathing entity that fosters a companionate feeling.[34] Malden-Brooks, however, also holds up the opponent as the benchmark against which he gauges his players' performance, reflecting news media reports of the coach's system as based on the principles of Soviet hockey.[35] He chastises his charges for being too prosperous, while the Russians "they're hungry … really hungry," admonishing that in the Soviet Union their lackluster performance would precipitate a trade to the "TransSiberian All-Stars." His view of U.S. players as unfocused, without zeal, and distracted by the accouterments of consumer society draws on Cold War media representations of the West as "an island of life and luxury,"[36] and of the Soviet Union as plagued by perennial shortages and economic problems, which made discipline and resourcefulness a necessity. The players, however, are full of admiration for their Soviet opponents.[37] At the Madison Square Garden exhibition game, as the U.S.S.R. squad scores yet another goal, Mike Eruzione queries his netminder whether he saw the tally, to which the latter replies that he was the one scored on. Eruzione nonetheless retorts: "Hey, sorry, Jimmy, class is class." Witnessing the repartee, Brooks expeditiously scolds his charges to stop admiring the Russians and start playing them, yet he also makes clear that playing the Soviet team is a matter of privilege that necessitates character: "You don't deserve a second crack at the Russians…. You've got no guts."

Even though *Miracle on Ice* alludes to "the Russians" or "the Soviets" close to three dozen times through players', agents', and coaching staff's comments, the Soviet presence in the film remains spectral, since the Soviets appear largely in archival footage embedded in the semifinal. That is, the outfit's shadow hangs over the story, but the viewer is only able to catch a glimpse of the CCCP uniform. The TV movie thus reiterates the Soviet Cold War image, consonant with opponents in the war genre, who are seldom seen.[38] The team's nebulous, shadowy quality also harks back to the obscure workings of the Kremlin, which spawned the emergence of Kremlinologists and Sovietologists who set out to decode the Soviet state's internal decision-making. Like many of the news reports of the time, then, *Miracle on Ice* explicitly links Soviet sporting superiority to the power of the state and its use of prestige athletic contests as instrument of foreign policy.

Miracle also paints a picture of the U.S. coach dedicated to the task of finding a way around Soviet excellence through his incessant review of game newsreels, even as wife Patti (Patricia Clarkson) warns that he may be pursuing an untenable goal. Russell-Brooks' view of the Soviet opponent, however, evokes none of the respect or admiration of Malden-Brooks or the U.S. contingent in the 1981 film. As he projects black and white footage of the Soviet team at play, Russell-Brooks methodically describes them as an unstoppable machine incessantly looking for the advantage, for the patch of ice where the pass can be redirected for the easy tally. The coach points to Boris Mikhailov, the world's best right wing, and his words hint at artistry as he calls attention to the fluidity and creativity of Soviet play. But as he does, a sense of the Soviets' coldly efficient brand of play also remains inescapable. The script underscores the stature of these giants as they fill the screen and scarcely celebrate the goal just scored. The constant circling, like the image of an assembly line, gets the attention of the U.S. squad. Brooks next lays eyes on goaltender Vladislav Tretiak and alludes to his perfect record in the last forty-two games. He advises his charges to keep the puck if they happen to score on Tretiak for it is bound to be a fluke. When a U.S. player notices the squad's unemotional approach and casually inquires whether they ever smile, without skipping a beat Jack O'Callahan's character answers that they're Russians and are liable to be shot if they smile.

The scene succinctly brings forth the many rehashed attributes of the Soviets and their continuum of über-teams, attributes which designated them as the West's mythic Shadow, a mysterious and scary outfit that blurred the line between state and sport. Russell-Brooks' quasi-angry remark that the team who manages to "take their game and ... shove it right back in their face" will win the day, adapts Herb Brooks' reliance on the principles of Soviet hockey by formulating it as an aggressive counteroffensive. Because the Cold War defined Soviet sporting superiority through the repressive power of the state, the statement also speaks to the march of civilization code as an inverted conquest, amplifying, as Richard White notes, that "[w]e ... do not plan our conquests.... We just retaliate against barbari[ty]."[39] The Soviets are not to be applauded but beaten and brought down to size, since as seen from *Miracle's* post–Soviet era perspective, their vanquished political system is unworthy of deference.

Unlike their spectral cast in the 1981 movie, in the post–Cold War *Miracle* the Soviets are also sketched as known entities. The players make a grand entrance at Madison Square Garden and tower over their U.S. counterparts. The script describes them as god-like looking down on mere mortals, the American collegians who dare find themselves on the same ice. Young Vladimir Krutov, Sergei Makarov, and Slava Fetisov, for whom the 1980 Olympics would be their first, receive no special mention. The U.S. players, after all, are up against a force of nature.[40] The Madison Square Garden sequence in *Miracle* also prominently features Soviet coach Viktor Tikhonov (Zinaid Memisevic), who, except for a medium shot in the archival footage of the semifinal, remains faceless in the 1981 TV movie. Tikhonov is first glimpsed barking orders to his players, reprising his reified role as symbol of the Soviet authoritarian state. Brooks glances at the opponent bench exchanging a short look with the Soviet coach. Herb next encounters Tikhonov at the Olympic village closely followed in semi-military formation by several of his players. The U.S. coach is in the midst of downplaying the political significance of his squad's victories, and as he passes the opponent coach, Brooks greets him as "Viktor," and mutters that someone is bound to beat the Soviet team. The scene is pivotal because aside from planting the prospect of the win, it shows that slowly but surely the Soviet squad is being brought down to size prior to the decisive encounter. Tikhonov is now "Viktor," a more personal form of address, and though reserved, the Soviet coach acknowledges the greeting.[41]

The films also render distinctly Herb Brooks' address to his players prior to the Olympic semifinal. The ABC movie depicts the scene in subdued tones as Malden-Brooks tells his players that they have earned their current standing. Urging them to remember the system they learned over the past several months, he tells them to skate with the Russians and play both a passing and checking game. Although he remarks that the Soviet team is ripe for the beating, he also strikes a cautious note warning his charges not to squander the lone opportunity they have been given or they will live to regret it. "You are born to be a player, each and every one of you. You were meant to be here. This moment is yours," he concludes. These lines form part of the core of the "Miracle on Ice" story and resonate with audiences because they are the fated call of the hero's journey, one which *The Boston Globe*'s John Powers would allude to on the twentieth anniversary of the win: "[t]his is no accident, Brooks told his players before they took the ice. This was fate."[42] Like the ABC film, the pre-game speech[43] in *Miracle* includes the coach's famous lines, but Russell-Brooks renders it as grand gesture, as he states: "Great moments are born of great opportunity." After reassuring his players that they were destined to be there, he emboldens them to seize the moment by forcefully relaying that the Soviets' time is "done." Unlike the muted tone of the TV movie, which because of its release in the midst of the Cold War's second phase mirrored that the ultimate outcome of the superpower contest remained in doubt, *Miracle* rehearses grander concepts to reproduce the victory as definitive, fitting in the context of the Soviet state's demise and the ensuing globalization of markets.[44]

To conform to its Cold War geopolitical bearings, *Miracle on Ice* conveys the semifinal game in a muted way by combining a small amount of reenacted bench shots with archival footage pre-selected to highlight U.S. goal-scoring.[45] Coach Tikhonov's replacement of Tretiak with backup goalie Vladimir Myshkin in *Miracle on Ice* takes the form of a matter-of-fact remark by Al Michaels, who makes quick note of the change. The film also bypasses any statements about the disarray on the Soviet bench, foregoing explicit mention of minor Soviet mistakes highlighted for drama in the full ABC game broadcast on the assumption that such errors were likely to evoke severe punishment by higher-ups.[46] *Miracle*, on the other hand, vividly represents the disarray on the opponent bench as the Ragnarok of the Soviet gods, marking Tikhonov's momentous pulling of Tretiak with Russell-Brooks' cheery remark, "Boys, he just put the best goaltender in the world on the bench." Although both films end the game with Al Michaels' signature countdown and classic call, "Do you believe in miracles?," the Disney film amplifies the emotional quality of the sequence as Herb Brooks notes about Tikhonov, "He doesn't know what to do!" and Donald Craig (Malcolm Stewart) hollers to his son, "Way to go, Jimmy!" *Miracle* also features dozens of carefully choreographed plays, bringing the audience on board by mixing re-dubbed broadcast commentary with proprietary bench dialogue.[47] The game takes a long 20 minutes, and is augmented through innumerable medium-to-close-up edits and special effects that blur the action, which, along with the considerable amount of activity within the shot, convey the U.S. players' battle as a rollercoaster ride.

The distinct endings of *Miracle on Ice* and *Miracle* also speak to the Cold War and post–Cold War contexts of the films. After Malden-Brooks leaves the bench in the TV movies he is never seen again, surrendering the stage to his players. *Miracle on Ice* therefore implies that with the U.S. victory clenched Herb's role is over. The coach is no longer useful to the story since the team has managed to earn the gold medal and unite the nation. The ending segments feature iconic moments that are now part of the discursive package of the event: the expression of team members' joy at the triumph, goalie Jim Craig wrapped in the U.S. flag and searching for his father in the stands, Mike Eruzione beckoning players to the gold medal platform, and the players' index fingers raised above their heads proclaiming "We're number one!" At the tail end of the movie, Al Michaels articulates the meaning of the game for the audience: "In proud recognition of their incredible performance at the 13th Olympic Games in Lake Placid this motion picture is dedicated to the 1980 U.S. Olympic hockey team. Here receiving their medals the members of that team." The film then identifies every player visually and verbally,[48] rendering the win as a commemoration of the triumph rather than a celebration of the collapse of the opponent. This muted portrayal is consistent with Cesar Torres and Mark Dyreson's assessment in *Cold War Games* that, with the absence of the U.S. and its allies from the 1980 Moscow Summer Games, "the East convincingly beat the West in the medal count, reinforcing the growing perception that communists had won the Olympic battle in the Cold War."[49]

The Disney film, for its part, reenacts the indelible moments following the win seen in the TV movie, but additionally inserts a highly emotional sequence that shows Russell-Brooks heading off to the locker room and privately expressing elation bordering on tears. As with the weeping scene in *Maurice Richard*, the sequence lets the viewer in on a very personal moment that humanizes the coach's character, but also underscores the melodramatic feel of the movie. Brooks also ends the account by appending the final game against Finland to the Soviet semifinal, noting that the U.S. team's win over the Finns rendered the miracle "complete." The coach belatedly recognizes that the event turned out to be far more than a hockey game, not only for spectators but for the players themselves, remarking on the image of twenty young men from disparate backgrounds standing in unison. With the statement "It was a lot more than a hockey game,"[50] *Miracle* makes short shrift of Herb Brooks' actual view of the match as a sporting competition, conferring on the win the mythic patina that producers sought all along. The Disney film not surprisingly bypasses the visual ID in *Miracle on Ice*, instead showcasing in the final credits the actors playing U.S. team members, bracketed by a short paragraph that updates players' professional status.[51] This format implies that it no longer matters who the 1980 squad was, but how the team and the triumph serve as symbols of the American spirit. As Brooks' final words intimate, rather than the sport of hockey, the semifinal contest, whose significance the film construes as analogous to a gold medal win, is the object of homage for its value to the nation. Unlike the commemorative stance of the 1981 telefilm, which hews closer to historical detail, *Miracle*'s triumphalism resonates potently because of its prolonged and decisive downsizing of the Soviet mythic image to amplify the oft-quoted argument that the U.S. won the Cold War.[52]

The historical win of the U.S. collegians took not only the Soviet team but hockey connoisseurs around the world by surprise. The U.S.S.R. squad outshot their U.S. counterpart 21–8 in the last two periods and 39–16 during the matchup. Besides having the fans on their side, the U.S. squad was fast, well coached, had a "hot" goalie in Jim Craig, and deployed a degree of physicality to contain their opponents in all their matchups, which none of the commemorations mention but newspaper photos and TV footage amply display.[53] On the other hand, the Soviets were well known for their powerhouse scoring abilities, modeled on the Stakhanovite politics of productivity, efficiency, and overachievement. The U.S. attainment for good reason persists in the annals of sport imbued with a mythological aura that resonates with the Hollywood sports film's promise of future prospects. The 1972 series between the Soviets and Canadians, on the other hand, albeit forecast as a sure victory for the latter, took on a different trajectory, shaking the nation to its core, and ending in a narrow escape that while still lionized, does not deflect the memory of the series' complexity.

Negotiating the Nation: *Canada Russia '72*

Canada Russia '72 (Peacocke, 2006)[54] dramatizes Team Canada's seminal triumph over the Soviet opponent in what is now known as the Summit Series. To this day, the event remains enshrined in Canadian popular discourse as "our defining moment,"[55] celebrated in numerous documentary pieces and cited as an example of Canadians' ability to hang tough in the face of almost certain defeat. Originally dubbed the Friendship Series, and played in the Canadian cities of Montreal, Toronto, Winnipeg, Vancouver and in Moscow, Russia, the September 1972 tournament staged the first-time meeting in the modern history of the game between a Soviet national team and Canada's marquee NHL players.[56] Three years earlier, Prime Minister Pierre E. Trudeau, who regarded Canadian amateur team losses to the Soviet Union as squandering the political capital that hockey offered, had laid the groundwork for reinstating the primacy of the Canadian game by passing an initiative that resulted in the formation of Hockey Canada. The newly formed organization—an alliance of universities, the Canadian Amateur Hockey Association (CAHA), the National Hockey League (NHL), the NHL Players Association (NHLPA), and the now defunct World Hockey Association (WHA)—sought to press the European-based International Ice Hockey Federation (IIHF) to jettison amateurism, which prevented Canadian professionals from taking part in international prestige contests. Although the effort did not immediately succeed, in 1969–1970 the IIHF authorized checking in the offensive zone.[57] The adjustment had the notorious impact of ratcheting up violence in the game, facilitating the emergence of new tactics, and lending greater focus to the contending playing-styles of national teams.[58] Trudeau's attempts to enact nation-building through elite-level hockey eventually coalesced in what would become a pivotally close contest between Canadian NHLers and their Soviet counterparts.[59]

Although the series was staged to reiterate the superiority of the Canadian elite professional, developments quickly suggested a prospective Canadian loss, which the team was able to avoid by the narrowest of margins, and it is this angle that the four-hour CBC-televised miniseries *Canada Russia '72* highlights. The film traces how the Canadian-Soviet hockey showdown devolved into a dead-on reflection of the Cold War, simultaneously exposing the Canadian project of sport and nationhood as assailable. It also displays the discord that

The Canadian and Soviet teams take the ice in *Canada Russia '72* (CBC Still Photo Collection; courtesy of Dream Street Pictures/Summit Films).

riddled the series from the start as Alan Eagleson (Judah Katz), impresario, agent, and executive director of the NHL Players Association (1964–1990), balks at the idea of pitting his headliners against their Soviet counterparts because of European referees' penchant to call a penalty on all checks. Eagleson relents, however, and brings on board 1969–1970 "Big Bad Bruins" coach Harry Sinden (Booth Savage), who, for his part, insists on recruiting onetime NHL enforcer and multiple Stanley Cup Montreal Canadiens winner John Ferguson (Mark Owen) for the job of assistant coach.

So sure of success are the Canadians that few see the making of a Soviet tidal wave coming. Striking a cautious note, Sinden initially warns his charges that despite the superiority of the Canadian game, all teams can be beat, even by this team of Russians. But his fears are assuaged by a scout's report that sizes up the Soviets as "a slow, poor-shooting team," and he muses that winning is not an issue and his only concern is with the number of goals the Canadians will score. Eagleson for good measure reminds Sinden that anything less than a complete sweep will be considered a national calamity. A voice of doom simultaneously arrives through the airwaves as a caller to radio talk show *Hot Topic* notes that Canadians are being hoodwinked as the Soviets purposely selected September for the eight-game contest knowing full well that the NHL training camps were yet to gear up.

The Russian squad, for their part, views the series as a critical juncture for their game. "Your attention, *tovarich*," legendary ex-player and acting coach Vsevolod Bobrov (Yuriy Sobeshchakov) tells his charges as he points to a newspaper cartoon of a schoolboy being lectured by a Canadian in hockey gear. Bobrov shows his team a newspaper write-up of the

1954 World Championships, when the Soviet team beat the Canadians 7–2, and advises that they are arrogant and not to give in to intimidation. By the time team captain Phil Esposito (David Beri) and company set foot on the ice in Montreal, it is too late. Although ahead by two goals, the Canadian team quickly cedes the lead in what would be a recurrent pattern of early successful starts and ultimate losses due to poor physical conditioning. In an effort to stem the Soviet tide, Wayne Cashman (Gerry Dee) and Bobby Clarke (John Bregar) urge teammates to "spear them" and "get 'em with the stick," but the Francophone players in the lineup quickly gauge the back-breaking task noting in their native French that Soviet passing is so extraordinary that they can't even get to the puck.

As the series moves along, the film shows how it tears the nation apart. Although some fans cheer the use of physical tactics to get the job done, others are bewildered, noting that it is not the losses that hurt, but the Canadians' shameful goon hockey. In Vancouver, the team is booed as they take the ice while the Soviets arrive to stentorian applause. Agitated by the adversarial display, Esposito admonishes fans in a post-game interview that the team tried their best to come up on top but the bad press and the jeers in their own building were demoralizing. Midway through the series dissension on the Canadian bench mounts. Goalie Ken Dryden (Gabriel Hogan) attempts to impress on Sinden that the Soviets can't be beaten with grinders. Players not seeing ice time also pack up their bags and take the next flight home. The Canadian press, for their part, continues to question the coaching staff's tactics, from Esposito's tackling of defenseman Alexander Ragulin to Bobby Clarke's "tapping" of Valeri Kharlamov's ankle in Game Six. Ferguson shoots back that it is a rough series and it is high time reporters got used to it. By the final game, however, 75 percent of Canadians are tuned in and 3000 are in Moscow rooting for their team. The eight-match contest comes down to the wire as Paul Henderson (David Alexander Miller), with 00:34 left, scores the final goal to win the series for Canada.

Much like the "Miracle on Ice" films, *Canada Russia '72* presents a squad in disarray and a nation pervaded by rift. The film expresses the project of unrealized unity as Canada's own are booed off the ice in Game Four by Vancouverites disgusted at their team's unsportsmanlike display. When Phil Esposito reprises his "To the people of Canada.... We came because we love Canada" speech, he continues to be ridiculed and pelted with water. In Toronto, a commentator on the TV program *Front Page Challenge* alludes to the shameful behavior by local fans as standard Vancouver fare, calling attention to the politically fragmented state of the Canadian nation. The team captain also dramatizes the problem of national unity as he articulates the feeling of being forsaken by the nation when he visits defenseman Wayne Cashman in his hospital bed after receiving an injury in the Swedish exhibition game prior to the Moscow segment of the series. Depicting the enforced isolation of fighting outfits in survival scenarios, Esposito reflects that the team has been deserted in the midst of the most significant hockey series in history, and it is now "us against the world."

The film calls on the sympathy of the viewer by tapping the melodramatic mode of the genre and portraying the virtuous suffering of the stoic players. As the Canadian squad find themselves on the receiving end of bloody confrontations and sneaky Soviet retaliation, they also experience abandonment by their public and harassment by the press and their government representatives. They likewise endure enfeebling of the ranks as players who see little ice time drop out, and the French-Canadians on the team frame the sense of estrangement that leads to their departure as akin to the Francophone player's outsider status in the league. In lieu of the sports film's fated call of the hero, which coach Brooks dramatizes in both "Miracle on Ice" films with his "destiny" rhetoric, the miniseries activates the survival motifs associated with the Canadian "loser" hero journey, as coach Sinden sums up the situation through imagery of looming disaster. Likening it to "being on a leaky rowboat," and urging anyone who is stultified by the fear of losing to abandon ship and avoid the potential shame that will come with a loss, he nonetheless admonishes that if they succeed, those that bailed out will have forfeited the win of a lifetime. The balancing of sports genre and canonical motifs that occurs throughout the plot thus deftly calls attention to the series' ambiguous and complex historical character.

Since the sports film revolves around the value of political unity to confirm the national project's solidity, *Canada Russia '72* amplifies this ideal through the motif of regained public trust and Francophones' reintegration into the team, as the Canadian squad starts down the path of redemption and notches up much-needed victories through hard work and sheer will. A caller also feelingly offers on *Hot Topic* that since the team has transformed into underdogs, they now have the support of the nation. The image of 3,000 Canadian fans in Moscow cheering their team and the federalist overtones of Yvan Cournoyer's (Louis-Philippe Dandenault) statement after the series-winning Henderson goal that "a nation has become a reality," likewise resolve the political unity question in line with the conventions of the sports genre.[60]

However, the project of social cohesion is hardly solvable and the miniseries conveys it through the skill vs. physicality problem, which mirrors the conflict between upper-class conceptions of sport as civilizing project and working-class ideas of identity by way of physical performance. The sports genre reaffirms the masculinity-as-toughness formula in line with old nationalistic form of sport. Thus, neither Sinden nor Ferguson, and certainly not captain Phil Esposito, renounce their views about hockey as people's game and mirror of the national character. Speaking of Team Canada's physical strategy, the coach adamantly states to the press, "We're Canadians. That's the way we play the game." Phil Esposito's cowboy boots, his pre-game comment to opponents, "lose, you Commie bastards," the cowboy hats the Canadians gift their Soviet counterparts during the Moscow leg of the series, as well as Leonard Cohen's lyrics, which speak about defying the rules, all play up the team members' maverick character. This frontier imagery, which Canadian cultural nationalism regards as a misguided Wild West ethos, contravenes ideas of Canada as peaceful, orderly nation, and the film's co-writer Malcolm MacRury acknowledges it as such in his comment that "[t]he Canadians were … very cocky and full of themselves. So, they were kind of the villains when the story begins."[61]

Taking its cue from the English-Canadian social-realist project, the film duly chastises players' and coaching staff's attitudes as maladaptive[62] but also shows Sinden and Ferguson under extreme pressure from both sides of the socio-cultural divide. When the coach hears criticism of his goon tactics on the radio, he blurts out in dismay that Canadians like to swallow their own. In the cab next to him, Ferguson is reassuring, and dismisses critics as "intellectuals" out of touch with the idea that "hockey's never been anything other than a street game." However, when External Affairs attaché Gabrielle Fournier (Sonia Laplante), a fictional character who dramatizes Canadian official views, criticizes the team's use of violent tactics in the Stockholm exhibition game, Sinden reaffirms the team's untenable position in noting that while the typical Canadian might not absolve the team for the loss of the series, "the intellectuals will never forgive us if we win."

In dramatizing hockey's cultural divide and opposing players' maverick masculinity to Canadian social norms, *Canada Russia '72* also displaces the fierce ideological conflict that the series evoked at the time. In the CBC telefilm, Frank Mahovlich (Jeff Roop) insists that Canadians are not merely up against a Soviet hockey squad but the Red Army, and that the Soviets' need to prove the superiority of their system means that Canada is playing for nothing less than "our way of life." *Canada Russia '72* intimates that his fears are excessive because they spring from his parents' experience with Soviet repression. In doing so, however, the miniseries partially de-historicizes the event by expunging the intensity that the Cold War contributed to the competition.

Summit Series documentaries, for example, make clear that for the players the contest exceeded the boundaries of mere sport and was akin to a war between communism and capitalism. In these pieces, Canadian team members also repeatedly voice the notion that letting a communist entity triumph on their watch would have enabled the U.S.S.R. to send the world the message that their political and social system were superior to that of Canada and other Western nations.[63] Unlike the American players under Herb Brooks who genuinely admired their Soviet opponents, Team Canada players saw themselves as fighting for the hearts and minds of all Canadians. Phil Esposito notes in the French-produced documentary *Les Grands Duels du Sport: Canada-URSS* (2004) that a handful of Canadian fans, who taunted during his post-game interview in Vancouver that the communists' game and their system were superior and it was high time he admitted it, precipitated his "To the People of Canada" address. In *September 1972* (1997) Wayne Cashman, in like fashion, elaborates that Canadian fans attacked the national team's style of hockey as outmoded and believed that the Russian style won matchups and constituted the new and ideal way of playing the game. In players' minds, then, defending the way Canadians played the game was commensurate with patriotism, and throwing in the towel would have amounted to an act of treason, since they believed that the Soviet establishment was sure to propagandize the triumph by trumpeting it as a win for their political system. Team members in these documentaries thus repeatedly underscore that they would have done whatever it took to win. *Canada Russia '72*, on the other hand, does not pay heed to the reasons for the NHLers' excessive physicality, not only because Canadian canonical film punishes hockey characters with a penchant for throwing their weight around, but because airing the players' perspectives risked opening yet another can of worms by exposing the irreconcilable ideological differences between the team's conservative, capitalist values and the nation's more liberal, progressive ideals.[64]

At the same time, because the series celebrates Canadians' persistence in the face of certain defeat, *Canada Russia '72* must also reaffirm this narrative in line the sports genre's dualistic structure, which defines protagonists by contrasting them with opponents. This approach plays out in the film's depiction of Philadelphia Flyers Bobby Clarke, whose motivated slash of forward Valeri Kharlamov's ankle in Game Six remains controversial. The film portrays it as further dividing the nation, as Attaché Fournier labels the play downright "vicious," and in response, assistant coach John Ferguson calmly observes that hockey is a rough sport and that all that matters is winning. In the locker room, Ferguson amplifies the reason behind the move when he takes a discomfited Paul Henderson to task, noting that Bobby's actions made his subsequent goal possible. Brett Kashmere in his essay film *Valery's Ankle* (2006) argues that the slash has been contained in Canadian social memory because it "enacts a shadow identity that is frustrated, aggressive and vengeful," an analogue persona of Canadian self-identity as "polite, peaceful and sportsmanlike,"[65] and *Canada Russia '72* strikes a congruent note by foregrounding Clarke's act as deplorable.

As the film denounces the shady character of the slash, however, it simultaneously softens the rebuke by providing alternative viewpoints of the incident. These perspectives come from Canada's opponent as Anatoli Tarasov's assistant coach Arkadii Chernishev (Sergei Nikolich) unceremoniously takes Valeri Kharlamov (Joel Cousins) to task, criticizing him for the "pampering" he receives as he sits out Game Seven with a broken ankle. When the coach comes across the injured forward watching the televised game with his wife, Chernishev asks whether he is on vacation, deriding his manhood by noting that his wife appears to be tougher than him. Tarasov (Eugene Lipinski), who is revered as the Father of Soviet hockey, also accuses that his foundational teachings have taken a backseat as Soviet teams focus on individual rather than collective performance, effectively taking a swipe at the power structure's star treatment of Kharlamov. The film's allusions to Serge Savard (Marc Savard) playing on a broken ankle also indirectly serve as commentary on Kharlamov's less-than-tough disposition, widening the discursive framework around Clarke's actions. At the end of the series, Tarasov congratulates the Canadian team for their courage, sealing the film's containment of the slash.

The above portrait of the opponent nevertheless transcends the melodramatic role of the Soviet villain in *Miracle* or its spectral Cold War rendition in *Miracle on Ice*. Unlike these films' views of the Soviets solely through the eyes of the U.S. team members or coaching staff, *Canada Russia '72* deploys the sports film's hero-opponent polarity by procuring close-up

Bobby Clarke (John Bregar, left) provokes Valeri Kharlamov (Joel Cousins) in *Canada Russia '72* (CBC Stills Photo Collection; courtesy of Dream Street Pictures/Summit Film).

views of both benches. The first glimpse of the Canadians is their locker room setup, and *Canada Russia '72* depicts the NHLers as supremely confident.[66] The camera bounces from one team member to another in pseudo-documentary style. The scene exudes excitement as players come in and out of the frame. The restless, upbeat mood also conveys the professional status, glamour, and untidy individuality of the elite NHLer. Assistant coach John Ferguson looks smooth as he enters the room in an all-white suit and expensive tie and casually greets his million-dollar recruits. At the Soviets' first practice, the camera also gives a snapshot of the Canadian team in the stands sneering at their opponents' tactics, unaware that the Soviets had a penchant for not showing their hand. The scene is photographed in warm colors despite the half-lit arena, and the NHLers give the impression of a disorderly, overconfident bunch chattering away like frat boys. Frank Mahovlich points a finger at the Soviet squad and gestures as if shooting a gun. Smoking a cigar, Phil Esposito chimes in the banter. As the Soviets gather around in a circle to a pass to a player in the middle, a third blurts out with derision: "Look a hockey game broke out!" prompting teammates to burst out in laughter. In short order the Canadians proceed to verbally harass Valeri Kharlamov gesturing and hollering that they have his number.

Out on the ice, the sounds are all of hockey—of sticks cleanly hitting pucks, net posts, and boards. When the noisy Canadians jeer at Kharlamov, the Soviet players silently look up at the stands. No words are exchanged as they continue their workout.[67] Despite the ominous-looking Aeroflot plane parked at the hangar and the heavy musical tones that introduce the team (associated with the U.S.S.R. in Cold War televisual texts), the menacing image is soon superseded by the squad's single-minded dedication to their craft. Their first appearance on the ice is likewise orderly, while the Canadians shift on their feet with obvious restlessness and freely assume various poses. As opposed to the jovial relationship between Team Canada players and coaching staff, the locker room scene shows the Soviet players gathering around their coach attentively listening to his injunctions. They too are in continual motion, but practicing training techniques unfamiliar to the West. In the locker room prior to Game Eight, goalie Vladislav Tretiak (Leo Vernik) prods teammates to avoid distractions and take up their drills as Tarasov advised. Attaché Fournier, for her part, provides running commentary that humanizes the Soviet team explaining that players as a rule have earned a higher education, like Vladimir Shadrin who teaches at university and Boris Mikhailov who has an engineering degree.

The film's representation incorporates post–Soviet era material that contributes to players' depiction as dedicated, virtuous athletes, while also revealing internal pressures from the Soviet state apparatus. Russian athletes are represented as victims of sorts operating within a system that demands results backed by harrowing punitive sanctions. After Game One, when a Canadian journalist asks Bobrov what he said to his team when they were down by a couple of goals, the interpreter relays that the coach warned they would be shipped to Siberia. Throughout the story Soviet players are also seldom heard and locker room scenes, shot in black and white, evoke archival footage of elite players training at facilities resembling barracks, which replay the idea of the U.S.S.R. as a stark military operation and recall the team's glacial all-work-no-play media image.

The Soviet side of the story is also told through the voice of institutional authority—coaches and officials—which calls up representations of the Soviet state in Cold War texts. The smooth Russian attaché and suspected KGB agent, Alexander Gresko (Daniel Matmor), assures players that Vancouver merits no sightseeing, even though he and coach Bobrov shortly after head to a downtown strip bar. With good reason, Esposito accuses the Soviet outfit of hypocrisy for pretending to be impervious to the lure of consumer goods and the Western lifestyle. Soviet officials also attempt to trick the Canadian team into replacing referees prior to the final game, adamantly stating that in Russia all disputes are to be adjudicated by them. Even though *Canada Russia '72* depicts the Canadians as paranoid, the Moscow segment of the plot corroborates popular perceptions of the U.S.S.R. as an autocratic state as Soviet police rough up a French-Canadian fan for blowing a horn during the game. Dissension within the Soviet sports power structure is also in evidence as Tarasov and Chernishev call attention to internecine bureaucratic conflicts by censuring official policies that propagandize the Soviet political system and commending the NHLers for their heart after the win. The coaches' critique summarily bolsters the idea that the Canadian contingent, for all their foibles, is on the right side of history.

The final game in *Canada Russia '72*, which in the sports film typically reaffirms the hero's future prospects, unfolds in line with the conventions of English-Canadian canonical film and refrains from displays of triumphalism and bravura. In the locker room scene preceding the final contest, Coach Sinden quietly informs the squad that only winning matters as the team can vindicate everything they represent by taking the series. The ensuing sequences cursorily enact the most dramatic points of Game Eight: Sinden's physical venting at the referees, Jean-Paul Parisé's (Jason Thibodeau) stick-raising and immediate expulsion from the match, Eagleson's so-called rescue by the Canadian players and the staff's vulgar gesturing at Russian goal judges, all markers that attest to the maverick character of the team. Much as with the negative aspects, the film also abridges the high points, including Phil Esposito's and Yvan Cournoyer's goals, supported by rare upbeat lyrics that synchronize with the team's comeback. With the game tied and as Gresko notifies Eagleson and the coaching staff that their side will be claiming victory should the game end in deadlock, the lyrics disappear signaling the urgency of the task at hand. As Paul Henderson scores and celebrations ensue, ending locker room sequences depict an utterly exhausted team and only a fleeting glimpse of Henderson post-goal.

Because biopics follow the directives of the melodramatic mode in underscoring the cost that protagonists undergo to attain their coveted goals, unlike the many documentaries about the event, the telefilm places Canadian players after the win in an empty, mostly dark Luzhniki ice rink, sitting or lying on the ice with beer in hand, as if attempting to take in the series in one fell swoop. The scene exudes relief rather than fist-pumping jubilation as Leonard Cohen's "Avalanche" plays in the background. Once again, the purported heroes resemble survivors of the ferocious Northern icescape who barely made it back from their experience of overwhelm. *Canada Russia '72*, however, goes further by coloring the Canadian team's quest with a sense of precariousness, buttressing the idea that Team Canada's sojourn was not the expected cakewalk, but a hard-won effort that exposed Canadian weaknesses in the game and had a compromised sense of integrity about it. Behind the cocksure, fierce façade of the coaching staff, hints of self-doubt emerge. "You know, we led this series for only 34 seconds," Ferguson tells Sinden behind closed doors at the end of the film.

Unlike Summit Series documentaries that embellish the final goal as the power of the hero to unite the fragmented nation by appending images of the flag, rooting fans, and statements by players about Canadian contributions to the game,[68] Ferguson's declaration in

Canada Russia '72 conveys the doubts about the superiority of the Canadian game that the contest amply exposed. The final locker room sequence, which features a CCCP player arriving with samovar in hand to congratulate the Canadian team and players reciprocating by expeditiously handing him a Canadian beer and toasting, "To Russia!" suggests a homage to the Summit Series for opening Canadian hockey to Soviet innovation. Indeed, the contest is widely credited for changing the course of the game, updating development and training methods, and refocusing play in teams of skill and artistry.[69]

While *Canada Russia '72* film commends the team for digging deep and coming up with a memorable last-minute win, it also features the characteristic ambiguity of Canadian canonical film toward hockey's history of physical excesses. Unlike the memory work of the Canadian-produced Summit Series documentaries, which is split between the Canadian and Russian versions of the event,[70] then, the miniseries appears to side with the Russian account, which frames the cross-pollination of strategy and technique[71] that resulted from the series as tantamount to progress in the sport. Although *Canada Russia '72* focuses on the history and politics of the Cold War and the part that Team Canada's NHLers played in it (wittingly or not), the squad's particular brand of hockey was popular chiefly in the 1970s. Contextualizing the status of the Canadian victory as precarious based on this variable alone is thus less important than what the team represents in social memory to reaffirm the relationship between sport and the nation. As noted, past contests with mythical resonance are functional in framing current events, all the more so if they are cast as media events. The stature of the Summit Series, much like that of the "Miracle on Ice," ensures that the contest will remain serviceable as reporters continue to tap tradition and call up its mythical ending to create excitement in upcoming elite Canada-Russia tournaments and memorialize the feats of the nation for future generations.

Coaching and Honing Character: *The Hounds of Notre Dame, Keep Your Head Up, Kid/Wrath of Grapes* and *Waking Up Wally: The Walter Gretzky Story*

In sport the coach's role is that of a teacher and a manager, a brains-and-guile position that requires assertiveness, good judgment, the ability to command attention, and superlative communications skills.[72] On men's team's coaching posts are protected male enclaves guided by orthodox social arrangements, and coaches see their jobs within the context of personal and professional advancement as these positions can confer social status and include hefty salaries, lavish housing, and other perks. In film, however, these issues may largely fade from the picture, as the coach harmonizes the virtues of sturdy physicality with respectability, responsible breadwinning, and Christian morality to hone young men into exemplars. Michael Buma discusses the power of the national manhood ideology in helping young males assimilate the values of self-control, courage, and self-sacrifice. He alludes to the role of coaches in hockey novels as largely supportive in helping young men fulfill their social utility function, one in which national unity and identity assume the foreground and take for granted the ability of men to influence the direction of the nation.[73] While films like *Maurice Richard* and *Net Worth* depict coaches in professional hockey as enforcing ownership's dictates, or at the very least as scheming sorts, iconic coaches in film can also be benevolent paternal figures who take on the part of the surrogate father when the protagonist's real father has gone missing literally or symbolically. Whether they assume taskmaster attributes to promote the production of fit, virile males that articulate the social standing of the nation or are natural-born teachers who know how to nurture the love of the game, the coaches in this section are entrusted with honing exemplary masculinity as an important form of social capital and perform their role with relish.

The Hounds of Notre Dame (Zalen, 1980), set in 1940s Saskatchewan, features a day and a half in the life of Canadian icon Father Athol Murray,[74] the larger-than-life Catholic *Père* who for decades headed the College of Notre Dame.[75] A political activist with decidedly conservative views, the chain-smoking, hard-drinking Murray was no run-of-the-mill priest, but a colorful teacher who brought to life chemistry, poetry, and history, and sought to provide children of both sexes and of all social backgrounds with the grounding of a classical education. The film largely underscores the *Père*'s oversight of male children and teens in hockey roles and underscores the role of the game as masculinity training in the service of citizenship and nationhood at a challenging time in Canadian and world history.

A gamesman coach *extraordinaire*, whose instruction methods involve not showing his hand, keeping charges on their feet, and getting them to earn their stripes, Murray's (Thomas Peacocke) approach is clearly visible in his acculturation of Ron Fryer (David Ferry), a young upstart who arrives at the school literally ditched by his well-to-do parents (Jim Brock and Ginny Bast), who are a loss about controlling his rebellious temperament. Ron makes clear he has no intention of mixing with the school's student body whom he labels "a bunch of plow jockeys," and he wastes no time in informing Murray that he can do nothing for him. He refuses to perform kitchen duties, takes over a youngster's bunk bed without conferring with shed mates, and professes to only eat delicacies, a laughable posture given the children's food staples of porridge, boiled eggs, and bread. He also makes the ultimate transgression in French class when he disrespects the teacher, Mother Thérèse (Frances Hyland), by refusing to speak other than "in white." The Sister sees through the teen's frustration with languages, and gently prods in French that he can surely manage a reply if he takes his time, but Ron yells that he will not be forced: "This is a free country! You can't make me talk like a Pea Souper!" In a show of bravura, the teen throws his books down on the floor, gets up from his desk and assumes a threatening stance.

The viewer next glimpses a pack of older kids carrying Ron off to the outhouse, intent on pitching him into its smelly depths. Murray puts in an appearance in the nick of time and halts the prospective exercise in vigilante justice. In a light mocking tone that Ron fails to detect, the *Père* apologizes for the students' uncouth behavior and notes that they are mere country boys unused to civil ways of enforcing the lay of the land. With great astuteness, Murray proceeds to give Ron a way out by enlisting him in the hockey team, noting that several Hounds are under the weather and they need reinforcements for a crucial game against arch-opponent Moose Jaw. Ron thinks of hockey as a "dumb game," but when the *Père* disguises his request in terms of much-needed help, the hotshot acquiesces. Little does the teen suspect that he is in for a consummate lesson in humility. At the short practice before the evening's meal, Murray advises his charges not to overexert themselves but to have fun. As he gets set to drop the puck, he suddenly utters a curious statement in feigned irked puzzlement: "Where's that stupid penguin?" In the distance a nun in hockey skates makes her way toward the group, her habit flapping in the wind. She takes to the ice hurriedly, and promptly perches herself in front of Ron ready for the faceoff. In utter bewilderment, the teen looks around glancing at his teammates but detects no sign that anything is amiss. The nun slaps her stick on the ice surface motioning him to refocus, and as Ron looks in the nun's eyes, she gives him a wink along with a sly smile. Ron realizes the figure standing in front of him is none other than head student Bob Cormack (Phil Ridley) in disguise, but before he can get his bearings, Murray drops the puck, and "the nun" summarily takes off with it, not before upending the young rogue.

The short scrimmage that ensues turns out to be a front for Ron's repeated rear-ending and re-training in the lessons of respect and self-effacement. He takes no less than five hearty hits from the dexterous, wily "nun" who appears from nowhere just as he is struggling to his feet. Murray and the other Hounds laugh at the merry show of expertise by Cormack and at Ron's futile attempts at preventing the onslaught. On his stomach and wincing, Ron finally declares his surrender, promising to apologize to Sister Thérèse. Although the North is hardly a friendly associate, acting according to rhythms independent from the protagonists' aims, in the above scene the ice is solid, the sky is blue, and the sun is out. The sequence unfolds through medium and close-up shots that convey the pond as a safe harbor for the *Pere*'s re-training of Ron in line with the needs of the school and the nation at this time and consonant with the sports genre's didacticism.

Athol Murray's view of hockey as training tool for nation-building is consistent with the muscular Christian ethos of 19th century English public schools, which envisioned sport as instrument for honing students into leaders by redirecting their unbridled impulses through physical activity.[76] According to the edicts of muscular Christianity, organized sport and abundant exercise habituated students to prolonged exertion with a view to withstanding adversity. Athletic pursuits also acclimatized youngsters to the virtues of self-control, inculcated respect for the edicts of authority and honed team-building and leadership skills.[77] In *Hounds*, muscular Christianity serves as a corrective for three constants: the fierce Prairies Winter, the yet-to-recover Depression-ravaged province, and the specter of World War II. In his pre-game speech at a dinner hosting Bishop Williams (Barry Morse), the *Père* observes in dramatic fashion: "We live in a world filled with adversity. Like that climate outside, like the Depression, like the war," presses on his charges the need to welcome adversity as the "test of a man." Murray reminds the students that they were not crushed by the Depression despite their meager meals of boiled dandelions and rancid meat for they foraged for necessities and proved themselves resourceful. He points to Hitler's war as the larger test yet for its potential to take every bit of Canadian resolve to defeat. But he professes his confidence in the Hounds' ability to stop the Hitlerian forces at the town's edge should the Huns land on Canadian shores, because adversity is nothing but "a bone for the Hounds to chew on." With the same theatrical eloquence, the *Père* deftly segues to the upcoming hockey game, cheering that the Hounds will easily put away the Moose Jaw players, "those Huns in Canuck uniforms." After Murray manages to shake up all those in the room, the team files out to pile into the truck set for the evening's match in Regina.

The hockey showdown displays the intensity of small town rivalries as the relentlessly partisan crowd boos the young Hounds with a ferocity that is hardly a match for the level of play. Although the Notre Dame program is well known for placing more than a hundred players in the NHL and on Canadian international teams, *Hounds* depicts the school in continuing development, and the hockey game is an opportunity to reveal the young players' heart despite their shortened bench. The camera allows the viewer to gauge the developing play through sequential medium shots, but the edits convey the *Père*'s charges trying their utmost, fumbling, and failing to score largely because half of the contingent is unwell. Consistent with the coach's archetypal taskmaster attributes, Murray pushes his students to the limit to dramatize the athlete-warrior's call to honor his duties. He lambastes team members as "weak-kneed, hollow-chested, [and] a simpering bunch of mothers' little darlings." Punctuating the diatribe with swears, he emphasizes that the game against Moose Jaw is not a mere match-up and that the team cannot simply roll over and quit just because they have the measles, least of all "the German measles!" Exhorting the troops by means of Christian muscular referents, Murray conflates hockey with the war front as a proving ground for warrior masculinity in the service of nationhood, citizenship, and God.

As Murray's gamesman instincts had gauged about Ron's leadership qualities, the teen, now a full-fledged member of the team, takes on a foremost role in the game. When he receives a serious cut in the head that merits a hospital visit, he shrugs it off as a few stitches, leading to interest from Moose Jaw coach Scottie Patterson (Frank Germann) for his plentiful "guts." Ron, however, scoffs at the offer, noting that he will not play for a "bunch of sissies." After he is taken out of the game, the valiant team is nonetheless unable counter the opponent's offensive even with Cormack's inestimable talents. The Hounds' school song takes on playful parodic overtones as Murray resorts to donning his priest's collar as last resort. The downtempo connotes deflating enthusiasm, surging only momentarily as Murray inserts the team's good luck charm, young Terry Caldwell (Dale Heibein), into the lineup to no avail. The Hounds lose the game and the forlorn players trudge into the locker room and hurl their equipment onto the floor, heartbroken at having failed their coach. But with the same gushing feeling, Murray blurts out that the squad did not fail him but gave him everything they had and showed their guts: "You're goddamned heroes, every one of you!" The game sequences illustrate that rather than concerned with the play-to-win impulse, which in children's fare amounts to the corruption of the game, Murray's exhortations and chastisement are designed to extract proof of his students' assimilation of the lessons of muscular Christianity.

But the team's efforts hardly end after the hockey game. Headed home after a brief stop for burgers, a savage blizzard blocks the group's way forward and the contingent is forced to abandon their truck and trek in the ferocious storm the endless half a mile to the nearest train station for help. Once there, poetry teacher Tom Howard (Larry Reese), a mild-mannered sort but no less a discerning educator, makes the case for giving the exhausted boys a break and waiting until morning to move forward. But Murray remains unconvinced for the truck contains the much-needed coal that the school urgently needs for cooking and heating. Despite that the group only manages to secure shovels, they heroically trudge back to dig out the vehicle stuck in the snow with Murray's adversity speech echoing in the howling wind. When Ron expresses doubts about heavenly protection by referring to the many who succumb to blizzards on a regular basis, the formidable stature of this teacher-coach once again comes into view as he derides those who perish as "a bunch of quitters." As the group treads slowly back to the truck mercilessly whipped by the wind, Murray, carrying young Terry and singing a cheerful song, also holds up the rear. He coordinates the maneuver to get the truck unstuck, pushing with the others as Tom drives the vehicle forward freeing it from the ice's jaws. Once again, Murray's valiant exhortations and yeoman strength help get the group out of their quandary and they make it back home to the grateful cheers of those waiting for them. While addressing the North as a site for survival, then, the *Père*'s success reorganizes the harsh Northern environment as a locus for Christian Canadians to deploy their hardiness.

In addition to illustrating Athol Murray's leadership, the blizzard sequence marks him as a man of the people and as partaking from their sturdy muscularity. Murray's preference for simple garb, in the form of a long-sleeved gray T-shirt worn underneath a red plaid shirt, succinctly communicates that despite his political and educational pedigree,[78] the *Père* is at heart an unaffected man. Because he lives his Christian principles, and his priestly outfit represents conformity with the bureaucratic directives of the Church, Murray also dons it only on formal occasions, as suggested by the parodic game sequence when he put on his collar to try and help the team win. These setups are scant and come across as mimicry, comedic rehearsals that mock the Church's hard and fast rules. Janice Kaye notes that mimicry has a history in the Canadian visual media that dates back to the 1950s and 1960s, and commonly signals the disruption of the power of subjugating forces by expressing resistance to assimilation.[79] Peter Morris also observes that Canadian film has a preference for realist protagonists who lean toward the picaresque to denote the careful scrutiny of the outer world.[80] The impish hero who survives by his wits in the midst of corruption is a sure fit to the *Père*'s picaresque gamesman tactics, not only in acculturating recalcitrant students but vis-à-vis higher-ups.

In the film's opening sequence, as Murray is set to give a speech to raise money for the school, he takes off his priest's outer garments and summarily rails against communist forces in Europe and the work of Canada's social democratic party, the Co-operative Commonwealth Federation Party (CCF), prompting Bishop Williams to walk out.[81] When Williams pays his unruly underling a visit to remind him of his promise to keep a low profile, Murray replies meekly that he was only trying to raise money for the school. Williams counters that the Liberal Party can hardly be his only source of assistance, noting that many an influential Roman Catholic in the town has thrown their support behind the CCF and that the party might well win the next election. Provoked, a now furious Murray denounces the "bloody socialists," even as the Bishop tries to reason with him about the province's new realities. Failing to get anywhere, Williams next resorts to threatening removal, but Murray remains undaunted noting that if he wishes to do so, and in fact he is able to, "his Grace" will have to do just that. Williams takes his leave in disgust, and it is up to Mother Thérèse, ever the voice of reason, to convince him to stay for dinner. A subsequent scene in which Williams consumes the best of the chicken meal to the obvious discontent of the student body makes amply clear that the Bishop enjoys the perks of his social standing and that Murray's subversion is a matter of integrity.[82]

In the tradition of English-Canadian cinema, *Hounds* also refuses to circumvent the *Père*'s imperfections, however, playing with Murray's personality by way of his gamesman referents to denote him as a passionate Catholic priest who espouses restraint even though he himself cannot temper his cigarette addiction and enjoys sneaking a "little drink" at all hours of the day. In a humorous scene in which he catches teacher Lila Petrie (Lenore Zann) smoking, he chides her noting that the school has a rule against those kinds of things even as a cigarette hangs from his own lips and smoke engulfs half his face. When Lila retorts in so many words that he is being hypocritical, Murray exonerates himself by arguing that he is not a woman, while she is a "delicate creature" whom students look up to. Next to Lila, teacher Tom tries hard to suppress his laughter much like the other students in the room. As the *Père* proceeds to exit the room he mutters to Cormack that "sometimes they catch you out." Murray's feet of clay, which align with the picaresque hues of Canadian cinema in deploying comedy and farce in the service of social realism, then, only serve to call attention to his humanity.

Canadian film's social-realist hues also discourage the triumphalist idea of mission by downplaying the adamant show of authority of Hollywood genres,[83] and as with its refusal to articulate characters without flaws, *Hounds* hesitates to make resolute winners out of its principal protagonist. Even as Father Athol Murray saw the task of honing citizens in the context of a young Canada charged with negotiating her national destiny,[84] the film delves the *Père* blow after blow, the last of which comes toward the finale when he hears of Cormack's enlistment in the Navy to fight Hitler's surge in Europe. While *Hounds* drops numerous visual hints that include framing Cormack in dark close-ups whenever the matter of the war comes up to portend his enlistment, Murray suspects nothing of the head student's plans. In the tradition of films that conflate exemplary sportsmanship with good citizenship, Cormack nonetheless must travel the story arc from his position as student leader and hockey talent to exemplary citizen, and he heeds Prime Minister Mackenzie King's radio exhortations to Canadian boys to "save Christian civilization from disaster." Murray's view of the war as a pressing matter that will cost the dearest of Canadian resources comes full circle when he loses Cormack. And although the head student's enlistment in the Navy is a logical conclusion of the *Père*'s muscular Christian directive, his loss comes as an enormous blow. The film's depiction of Murray by way of the guiding philosophy of *Luctor et Emergo*—of struggling and moving forward, surviving and pressing on with life's goals—then, is only fitting. By elegantly conforming to the prerogatives of Canadian cinema's social-realist leanings, *Hounds* confirms that Athol Murray was not only an enthusiastic hockey coach, but a spiritual leader who in trying times took on the task of honing students for the work of citizenry and nationhood.

Another example of the coach's national acculturation role emerges in the Don Cherry biopics, *Keep Your Head Up, Kid* and *Wrath of Grapes*. Cherry has left an indelible mark on hockey in Canada injecting his colorful and outspoken entertainment personality into the national discourse by way of his weekly stint on "Coach's Corner." Although some dismiss his views as so archaic they border on the ludicrous, others applaud his populist stance. Consonant with his #7 standing in the all-time lineup of great Canadians, he is also a staple in literature and film. Jason Blake counts Don Cherry among the top four icons in hockey fiction alongside Maurice Richard, Paul Henderson (for his last-minute goal in the Summit Series), and Bobby Orr.[85] Cherry is also present in the cinema of hockey, and as in literary fiction, he figures as supporter of the robust game. The coach embraces an old-fashioned code of masculinity that pays homage to hockey as expression of Canada's frontier heritage, emphasizing physical sturdiness, steadfastness, and mutual respect on the ice, and the biopics show that Don learns to be a coach as a journeyman in the minors, where he gleans that the role amounts to "being a leader of men." As a coach, Cherry takes his leadership cues from military heroes, particularly from Commander of the British Navy Admiral Horatio Nelson, whom he regards as ruthless but fair. He also models his role on his own formative experience with coaches as well as from the life injunctions passed on by his father. From dad, the young Don learns to stand his ground and to defend those in need of help. From his favorite coaches—Barrie

Flyers Hap Emms and Punch Imlach—he learns training smarts, as well as dexterity and a firm hand in keeping despots like Eddie Shore at bay. If there is one constant in Cherry's world, it is the concept of fairness and the complementary virtue of integrity.

Predictably, as a coach Cherry also prioritizes tough guys, corner players with a pugnacious streak. These proclivities make him a player's coach and a fan favorite on the one hand, and a headache for management who routinely balks at foregoing top picks for grinders and fighters, on the other. From his sixteen-year experience in the minors, Don understands that those players are the hard workers and non-quitters of the league, and he deploys them astutely to win games. Recalling the enforcer's respect-exacting and strategic deterrent roles after a fight scene involving Robert "Battleship" Kelly (Tom Anniko), he notes that having "the heavyweight champ on your bench" helped reroute opponents' view of his team. But he also affectionately mentors these players to higher ground. In a touching scene on the team bus, the coach urges Kelly to make use of his intimidating stature and carve out some space around the net in order to start putting pucks in the net. "The tough guy that can score, that's what the NHL wants," Don exhorts, counseling the young man to avoid getting himself pigeonholed.

Cherry vows to treat his charges like he would have wanted to be treated, but he also shows a firm hand, "let[ting] them know who was in charge," as he notes, when he is promoted to coach of the Boston Bruins. Not unlike coach Harry Sinden who in *Canada Russia '72* employs the metaphor of a leaky boat as his team struggles to find its footing, Cherry deploys imagery from *The Story of the British Navy* by Frank Cox, to impress on his NHLers that a team is like a ship that cannot fully function unless everyone on board pulls his weight. He also works on trades until he fashions the ideal team, sparing no star in the process and putting the fear of God into players by making clear they risk being shipped out with the next trade winds if they refuse to play his way. "I want teams to cringe when they come into the Garden. We gotta be mean," Cherry tells team manager Harry Sinden (Ian Tracey) prior to a tempestuous trade. As coach of the Boston Bruins, he remains ever complimentary of Bobby Orr (Gerry Mawhinney), who as a two-way defenseman would lead the league with 135 points, but he also castigates NHLers as big-headed and lazy. As a player in the minors he had marveled at the notion that National Leaguers "had new socks, fresh underwear, new everything, every day." But up close he realizes that they are qualitatively different, some of them

Don Cherry (Jared Keeso) behind the Boston Bruins bench in *Wrath of Grapes* (courtesy of Tim Cherry/Five for Fighting/Entertainment One Television/CBC Still Photo Collection).

drifters living a life of luxury as opposed to the hard-working minor leaguers who could ill-afford concussions for fear of being replaced. *Keep Your Head Up, Kid* frames Cherry's realization through a blurry shot of players' reflections cast on the glass, an image that merges with the crowd in the stands. The players engaged in a game are in soft focus symbolically fusing with fans who do not see them clearly for what they are: weak, coddled, and without heart, rather than the men of steel they're purported to be.

As with his coaching stint in the minors, Cherry soon begins to rely on the proverbial tough guys, choosing John Wensik (Bryan Clark) instead of the leading scorer of the American League, and insists on sending down to the minors a first draft pick in return for protecting American Mike Millbury. Despite butting heads with Sinden, he propels the Bruins to the top of the Adams Division and remains well liked by fans. He also goes all out for his team, showing his penchant for gamesmanship when he accuses *HNIC* producer Ralph Mellanby (Gordon Tanner) of Canadian bias for not showing Bruin fights. Surprised, Mellanby states that it's CBC policy to avoid showing fights, but Cherry shoots back that the network wants his opponent, the Montreal Canadians, to win. A smiling Mellanby quickly catches on to the ruse, as Cherry's voiceover explains that "Nothing motivates a team like an us-against-the-world mentality." Like Sinden's speeches in *Canada Russia '72*, Cherry's are short and straight-to the point, but also punctuated with a slam of the fist. Cherry's theatrics garner him results, and he takes his team to Game Seven of a second Stanley Cup championship. Although a too-many-men penalty costs him a final shot at the Cup, he leaves Boston still popular with fans, and he receives a standing ovation upon his return to the Garden as coach of the Colorado Rockies much to the dismay of Bruins management.

Don Cherry on the set of the CBC's *Hockey Night in Canada* (CBC Still Photo Collection).

As a media icon in "Coach's Corner," Don Cherry also takes the temperature of the nation in good populist form. On one occasion, he replays a fisticuffs incident between heavyweights L.A. Kings Marty McSorley and Toronto Leafs Wendell Clarke to honor a request from firefighters on duty at the Maple Leaf Gardens, but not before getting in a jab that "the sensitive types, they don't like me showing fights." In his role as provisional commentator of the 1987 World Junior Ice Hockey Championships in Czechoslovakia, Cherry also vociferously defends the Canadian team involved in the "Punchup in Piešt'any," arguing they were set up by the Russian coach who had nothing left to lose since his team was already out of contention. Although commentator Brian

Williams (Rory O'Shea) maintains that the Canadian squad behaved like a "bunch of hoodlums," public opinion proves the coach right as post-show Williams is besieged by callers and heckled as a communist, and he comically finds himself turning to Don and Rose for refuge.

Cherry's support of Canadians for coaching posts and NHL berths also comes across as a patriotic duty, except that the roster rarely includes Francophones. In *Wrath of Grapes,* Cherry castigates Pittsburgh Penguins captain Mario Lemieux for being a floater. Alluding to Lemieux as a one-zone guy who plays like "it's industrial hockey at one in the morning," Cherry incites panic in the production room, drawing ire from the CBC Board and the Francophone press who accuse him of anti–French sentiment and of bullying French-Canadian players. Don, for his part, complains to Rose that he doesn't pick on Lemieux because he's French, but because of his game, and laments that it's politically incorrect to criticize Francophone players because of their cultural background. To add insult to injury, Cherry grumbles that their names have to be pronounced according to "some stupid handbook," and as always, he reiterates he's not changing anything. Rose, the voice of reason in Cherry's life, sarcastically counters that indeed, why should he change a thing, since it's not like he owns anything to producer Ralph Mellanby. Mellanby might well lose his job, but that's his problem, she underlines. A flamenco motif underscores their humorous ripostes as a spirited dance, as Rose ultimately finds a subtle way around Cherry's intransigence.

The sequence highlights Cherry's insistence on voicing his opinions without a filter as highly controversial because of Mario Lemieux's stature in Quebec rivals Wayne Gretzky's in English-Canada. Alluding to David Adam Richards' comments in *Hockey Dreams,* Jason Blake reiterates Mario Lemieux's cultural standing in Canada through his superlative teamwork with Wayne Gretzky in the 1987 Canada Cup against the Soviets, which solidified the notion of a united Canada on and off the ice. Blake stresses that this symbolism amounts to a valuable variant of nation-building that is rare in Canadian social discourse and is perceived by the public as accomplishing far more than political rhetoric.[86] With reason, then, Cherry's exclusion of marquee Francophone players is seen as disloyal because it reinforces the Canadian political and cultural divide.

The coach's decision to revert to tried-and-true antics, kick up a storm and play up the frontier, cocksure persona in his second year of "Coach's Corner" also communicates eccentric mischief, and points to an element of showmanship in his feather-ruffling exercises.[87] Cherry's grappling with CBC honchos hints at an Athol Murray–like figure as he insists on bucking the rules and opposing "pinkos" in high places, even as his principled rebelliousness also lands him in hot water with superiors. Although CBC higher-ups accuse him of dividing the country and contravening the pubcaster's mandate, like Bishop Williams in *Hounds,* they also come across as humorless bureaucrats with jobs that entail a great deal of political pandering. Cherry, in any case, does not appear likely to change his demeanor any more than Athol Murray changed his opinion about the CCF or curtailed his views to please his superiors.

Cherry's allegiance to hockey as Anglophone project, however, also reifies Canada's makeup by way of the mythic masculinity of the Northern exemplar and hint at the principles of muscular Christianity in action as they intersect with the national project. In *Wrath of Grapes,* for example, he prefaces his support of the U.S. surge in Iraq with "God bless England," and bemoans that Canada only promised "a little moral help" because it amounts to "fifty years of pride down the drain." As Murray does in *Hounds,* then, Cherry extends masculinity training in hockey to the war front as a logical outcome of sport's link to militarism, nation-building, and foreign policy.

The coach's contributions in the realm of entertainment—as an original, colorful and home-grown figure that is instantly recognized as such—is also significant from a nation-building perspective, though he may not conform to the image of Canadians abroad. Given the amount of American-originated programming consumed by Canadians on a daily basis, Cherry's bequest to the nation is not small. Doubtlessly, he is also interested in holding forth about playing hockey his way and speaking primarily to English-Canadian boys, rather than to Francophones, girls and women, or multicultural and international others. Whether privately Cherry is inflexible about these views or not, the idea of hockey as a *Canadian*-Canadian game is synonymous with his brand.[88] Because the English-Canadian hockey film repertoire largely supports a similar idea, it may also mean that Don Cherry in some respects may also be the loudest, most reliable, voice in the shed.

A different kind of national coaching figure emerges in *Waking Up Wally: The Walter Gretzky Story* (Bennett, 2005). Based on Walter Gretzky's biography by the same name, *Waking Up Wally* tells the story of the elder Gretzky's stroke and difficult journey to recovery. The telefilm sets the tone of the narrative in a sequence that features Wally (Tom McCamus) teaching his oldest the way to the net: "See? ... where the puck's going, Wayne, not where it's been." The movie next segues to the stroke, prompting the entire family to gather in the hospital from far and wide, unsettled about the doctor's prognosis. Wally's odds of recovering from surgery are slim, but when he does come out of his deep coma, he is faced with learning the basics, from buttoning his shirt to tying his shoes correctly. Stoic wife Phyllis (Victoria Snow) and solicitous daughter Kim (Tara Spencer-Nairn) debate whether he should be back home, but Chinook Hospital's Rehab therapist Ian Kohler (Matthew Edison) warns that stubborn Wally is a handful and won't be easy to oversee. The patient is finally released after he re-acquires the skills to get dressed and comb his hair, but once home, he refuses to get out of bed, despite Phillys' pleas. At wit's end, she calls Ian back to work with Wally on an outpatient basis.

The vicissitudes of having Wally at home fall largely on Phyllis and Kim, as Wally is not only unable to join in mundane conversations and customary rituals with family and friends, but reacts with great emotional frustration, taking off at a moment's notice when he confuses what he sees in his mind's eye with his day-to-day realities. Wally's memory is so muddled he merges past and present, and cannot tell that the vivid episode of a child almost drowning in the lake is not of younger son Brent, but part of his own childhood. Worse, the Wally that emerges from the coma turns out to be someone the family doesn't always recognize, as attested by his first sentences in Ukrainian. As Phyllis soon comes to grasp, the Wally she must let back into her life and into her bed is a brand new man. Eventually, Kim and Ian figure out that the elder Gretzky needs to get back to coaching youngsters to recover not only his memory but regain his zest for life. Thanks to help from an AAA coach who heads a team of nine-year-olds, Wally is persuaded to take on the assistant coach's role and then tricked to take over when the head coach is nowhere to be found prior to the championship game. After wavering for a moment, Wally steps up to the plate, fine-tuning the lineup and extracting a win for the team. From that point, he is set on a firm path to recovery, albeit the journey is hardly an easy one as he continues to show fits and starts. Still, he can now dispense with Ian, although the therapist surprises him by transforming into his son-in-law as his relationship with Kim has become a genuine love partnership.

The tragedy in *Waking Up, Wally* is that Walter Gretzky, the father of Canada's icon Wayne Gretzky, one of the most globally recognized hockey players of all time, cannot remember any of his son's accomplishments, let alone his own seminal input as coach. Even more tragically, he appears to have little interest in remembering. Wayne (Kris Holden-Reid) is hardly absent from the film, but for all intents and purposes, in Wally's world he all but remains a young boy still learning the craft. The introductory lyrical sequence of father and son out on natural ice reverberates visually and textually throughout *Waking Up Wally*. The same series of shots of young Wayne intercepting the puck behind the net and putting it inside the goal repeats as Wally is taken to the hospital in an ambulance. The film picks up the motif yet again as Ian takes Wally to see an L.A. Kings game in Toronto to jog his patient's memory. In the locker room with Wayne, Wally expresses frustration that he can't remember attending any of his son's games. Wayne is gently reassuring, advising him not to worry about the past and prodding him to focus on what's ahead. He intelligently segues to Wally's lessons on the pond: "Remember the rule you taught us?" Wally flashes back on young Wayne going after the puck and recalls: "Where it's going." As Wayne prompts, "not..." Wally has another flashback of the introductory sequence in which the puck hits the board, and thinks back: "where it's been." The recollection is a small yet meaningful triumph in the context of the film's memory work of Wally's coaching contributions to Wayne's career. The fourth reference occurs at the end of the film, during Wayne's April 18, 1999, retirement ceremony. Wayne looks at his father in the stands and acknowledges him with a warm gesture. The camera pans down to his hockey boots as he skates off and dissolves into another pair of skates worn by a young Wayne in a toque carrying the puck around the net and tucking it in goal. As the youngster comes around the net and toward the camera in slow motion he looks straight into the lens. The edit segues back to Wally in the stands smiling as he acknowledges the recollection.

Because Walter Gretzky grounds himself in memories of childhood—primarily of coaching Wayne, but also his other offspring—the metaphor of children in the film serves dual directives. It is symbolic of starting over and it also refers to his coaching legacy as it points to his early work with Wayne. Moreover, his renewed and quite dynamic relationship with children reveal Wally as a natural-born coach who understands what youngsters need as hockey players better than their own parents. He frowns on the senseless drills that frustrate a child, and laments that humdrum exercises will only turn off a kid's enthusiasm. His uppermost instincts are to find the child a puck: "You need a puck if you're gonna learn to play hockey." He also dispenses the same advice he gave Wayne as a boy: "See that? Look at where he's going." Despite his difficulty in relating to adults, Wally sees the ice well and gives his young charges short but accurate guidance, recognizing when he needs to juggle the lineup as well as when to call a time out. The sequence that leads to the winning goal at the AAA Brantford-Niagara game recalls the introductory setup, capturing a similar behind-the-net goal-tucking moment without sound effects of the puck, blades, ref, or crowd that again harks back to his early coaching of Wayne. From the bench Wally prompts the player to take the shot, and as the youngster scores, it's clear that this is Wally's goal, and that the coach who had a hand in honing Wayne Gretzky's play is back. But the new Wally also comes to embody the soul of the game. Spying out a downcast young Niagara player that he encounters on the way out of the rink, he observes: "Little guys like you oughta have a reward for working hard." To pick up the child's spirits, he invites both teams to his home to see Wayne's memorabilia

196   6. Hockey Biopics and the Nation

Waking Up Wally: The Walter Gretzky Story movie poster (CBC/Photofest).

displayed in the basement, an occasion that prompts a gleeful parent to note: "This is better than winning the All-Ontario Championship."

The impromptu visit reroutes the sadness behind a preceding long scene in which Wally recognizes none of Wayne's paraphernalia, each of which memorializes an important record-breaking moment: a first Stanley Cup, an Edmonton Oilers jersey marking a third Stanley Cup win, pucks commemorating an NHL hat trick at the age of 18, 50 goals in 39 games, and the icon's 1,000th career point at 23. The room is chock full of such items, a virtual museum documenting Wayne's accomplishments, which Wally is intent on carting off to a AAA peewee auction. As Phyllis reads the caption on each item in a bid to help him remember, Wally insists that he wasn't there. A basement full of nine-year-old hockey players and their parents in short order rescues the family tragedy that is Walter Gretzky's memory loss, transforming it into an opportunity to revitalize Wally's life and that of many others. With the room brimming with people, Phyllis gazes at her husband smiling warmly as one of Wally's pals remarks that the fellow standing before them does not look anything like the old friend they used to know.

The film also textually relays through surrogates that Wally has been doing the work of citizenry and nationhood in honing athletes as exemplars. Kim alludes to Wally's coaching work multiple times noting that dad instilled in her and her brothers the duty to develop their talents to the fullest. A Christmastime scene in which the four Gretzky siblings engage in a game of shinny in the vast snowy expanse denote them as products of the Northern environment and its wintry rituals. Phyllis fills in Wally's hockey background noting that he played Junior with Woodstock, and went to Junior-A tryouts with the Toronto Marlies. She adds that he was too small to make the cut but scored as many goals as the others, confirming Wally's affinity and suitability for the game. Don Cherry also vets his contributions to hockey on "Coach's Corner" when he recalls a strenuous trip he took with Bobby Orr to the player's hometown of Parry Sound for a skate-athon in the deep freeze of winter, and seeing Wally, he realized he had driven down all by himself. As Jason Blake notes, "[b]eing praised by Cherry on Hockey Night in Canada or … is a very public stamp of approval for a certain type of hockey and a sure way of establishing, or accentuating, one's masculine image."[89] Cherry's salute thus reframes Wally as the embodiment of the Nordicity myth who boasts the necessary mental and physical attributes to thrive in the harsh Canadian winter, and hence, to coach the game.

Part of the task of confirming Walter Gretzky's indelible mark on hockey entails memorializing son Wayne. The film recruits "Coach's Corner" other icon, Ron MacLean, to perform the homage at the player's retirement ceremony. MacLean confirms Wayne's status in the hockey pantheon by reiterating his moniker as the Great One, citing his record-breaking work in Edmonton, and summing his talents as "that amazing gift to see the ice." His retirement ceremony, which the film depicts through an unobtrusive mix of real footage and reenactment, celebrates his accomplishments with the promise that "I will remember you," sung by Canadian Sarah McLachlan. Two of Wayne's powerful statements, in turn, emboss Wally's contributions to hockey: "'Everything I have I owe to you," a dedication by the icon after his first Stanley Cup win, and "Hey, dad, nobody knows me better at a game of hockey better than you," the player's salute to his father as he takes the ice prior to the start of his retirement ceremony.

In short order, *Waking Up Wally* enshrines in Canadian filmic memory the father-son link in sport by formulating Wayne Gretzky as one of Canada's hockey greats and articulating Wally's legacy to the nation as seminal coaching influence in his son's game. The film champions the Gretzky father-son relationship by continually looping the father's work back to the son, as well as referring to the son's imprint on the game and the culture through the father's early coaching. The textual circuitry that *Waking Up Wally* establishes between the two, while nonsequential, centers on visionary development of uncommon talent. The film links the concepts of memory and seeing—in the mind's eye and on the ice—to reaffirm the imaginary narrative of the nation through the Gretzky family history. Wayne Gretzky's very public life and work have served as repository of the nation's history and identity, as attested by media linkages between his L.A. Kings trade and the 1988 Canada–U.S. Trade Agreement, along with his role as 2002 Team Canada Manager.[90] Wally's memory loss and the urgent project of its recovery that *Waking Up Wally* depicts, then, operates as cautionary tale about the ramifications of forgetting Wayne Gretzky's achievements as in doing so a significant aspect of contemporary Canadian culture stands to be lost.

Sport's distinct association with masculinity and its sturdy link to the work of citizenry and nationhood relay the successes of men's teams as proxy for the elevated status of the nation. Sports that have a grounding in a specific historical tradition and are privileged as national become opportunities for self-assertion during moments of national angst, while expressing nostalgia for an idealized past.[91] In the era of globalized cinema in which co-productions tend to place subjects and themes in a broader context and historical traditions are perceived to be on the losing end, certain films are important in representing the nation, including its successes and anxieties.[92] Sports biopics that memorialize seminal athletic triumphs and notable coaches remain compatible vehicles for foiling the perceived erosion of political sovereignty activated by globalization processes. The project of identity that the above sports biopics reaffirm owes itself to the cultural specificity of the figures and events depicted, which makes them difficult to appropriate for global consumption. Characteristic of the sport and combat genres' easy fit and the way romantic metaphors of the warrior integrate hockey's high contact aspects to uphold male heroism, these films also convey the notion of men on a mission. Principal protagonists in these films nonetheless also emerge as maverick personalities, intimating that unusual vision necessitates bucking authority. This combination of militarism and nonconformism is also characteristic of how frontier referents in the sports film allow for the interplay of cultural and countercultural values.

7

Hockey, Race and Sexuality

Hockey in film expresses nostalgia for nationalistic sport and its connection to traditional masculinity. Michael Messner notes that this model of identity articulates ascendance by virtue of what it is *not*—"not-gay, not-black ... and not-immigrant."[1] Cultural integration and the ongoing hybridization of cultures certainly offer the prospect of articulating national citizenship free of reference to "culture, race, sexual preference and gender," as Eva Mackey observes.[2] However, much as Leonard and King assert of sport in film, the genre also dramatizes an ideological project designed to expunge or smooth over social rifts in the postmodern state.[3] Hence, hockey's mythic signature and its association with dominant masculinity may conversely reaffirm the sport's traditional linkages. Indeed, the nostalgic filter of hockey in the cinema tends to limit the kinds of protagonists and narratives fielded because this traditional lens perpetuates identity as an ahistorical, mythical construct. Few films therefore feature hockey protagonists who hail from a non-white racial background or a non-heterosexual orientation. When these representations do occur, they are valuable for their potential to contest traditional hierarchies. And although these films depict social tensions and rifts in the cultural fabric of the nation, to some degree cultural minorities' value referents also interface with the norms of the dominant culture.[4] Examining portrayals of the handful of ethnic and gay characters in leading hockey roles, then, may serve to clarify the extent to which this imagery fits with the hockey ideal, its model of masculinity, and its connection to the nation, and to what degree it chafes against its inflexibility.

Ethnicity and the Hockey Protagonist: *The Love Guru* and *Breakaway/The Speedy Singhs*

The Love Guru (Schnabel, 2008) spoofs hockey as an eminently white male Canadian sport by fashioning a black American as captain of the Toronto Maple Leafs, an Original Six team. The protagonist in question is Darren Roanoke (Romany Malco), a franchise player whose game haplessly falls apart because of romantic troubles with wife Prudence (Meagan Good). Leafs owner Jane Bullard (Jessica Alba) offers a $2 million reward to anyone who can help solve Roanoke's relationship problems in time for the Stanley Cup finals against the L.A. Kings. Guru Pitka (Mike Myers), an American-born holy man raised in India who is intent on wresting the top guru title from Deepak Chopra, hears about the reward and decides to tackle the task. Complicating matters for Pitka, Prudence has a fondness for amply gifted

Kings Québécois goalie Jacques "Le Coq" Grande (Justin Timberlake). If the guru succeeds, however, Oprah Winfrey's producers promise to have him on the show and catapult him to celebrity.

In keeping with the film's satirical bent, the story's characters are configured in caricaturesque mold. Coach Punch Cherkov (Verne Troyer) is an irascible sort whose diminutive stature cannot command the respect required of his post. Jane Bullard wants her team to win the Cup after a decades-long drought solely to put an end to the taunts and jeers of fans. *Hockey Night in Canada* announcer duo Trent Lueders (Jim Gaffigan) and partner Jay Kell (Stephen Colbert), for their part, lampoon sports broadcasts' straight play-by-play man and oddball color commentator. Pitka too is a fame-seeking clown with notorious coward and bully tendencies who panders to Hollywood's fascination with cults. As a wise guy who seeks to profit from his own cleverness, Pitka is nonetheless also a timid, gutless sort who lacks the nerve to confess his feelings of love to Bullard.[5] Although she reciprocates the sentiment, she is not apprised of Pitka's abstinence vow and the chastity belt that guards it, and thinks he is simply not interested. Because the guru also lacks the advantage of Pastor Dan Parker (John Corbett) in *Raising Helen* (Marshall, 2004), who offsets the feminizing effects of his man-of-the-cloth role by playing goal in the local church league, Pitka resorts to fights and skirmishes that reinforce his masculine fitness but all the more spoof the holy man's calling.

An extension of Pitka's character, Roanoke struggles with the same issues of gutlessness and enfeeblement. Dubbed "the Tiger Woods of hockey," the club's star is hailed in the media as the future of the game for his potential to deliver a brand new fan demographic, which the film spoofs by way of an overhead shot of black teens playing pickup hockey on a basketball

Guru Pitka (Mike Myers, left) counsels Darren Roanoke (Romany Falco) in the Leafs locker room (*The Love Guru*, Paramount/Photofest).

court. Although he dresses like a rap star and travels with an entourage, Darren's macho cockiness is also a façade since he lives in perpetual fear of his stern, disciplinarian mother Lillian (Telma Hopkins), who reenacts the black sitcom's competent but bossy parent disaffected by her offspring's life choices. Roanoke's rivalry with Jacques Grande exacerbates the captain's sexual inadequacies for the goalie's legendary gifts extend to his physical attributes. This rivalry dramatizes the motif of dueling black and Latin sensualities by spoofing not only depictions of the black athlete's superior physical aptitudes, but also the formidable stature of the hockey player in film.[6]

Grande, like Chiefs goalie Denis Lemieux (Yvon Barette) in *Slap Shot*, butchers English to farcical effect. But unlike his Charlestown counterpart, who specializes in masochistic rituals, the L.A. netminder typifies Francophone romantic passion in Hollywood film augmented by an amusing weakness for Celine Dion. Grande's dual Quebec–L.A. signature and his sabotage of the Leafs captain also represent both the Anglo-French sports opposition and hockey's shift to Sun Belt meccas, which reprocess recurring Francophone-Anglophone and U.S.–Canada doubled tropes in English-Canadian film.[7] Grande's "Le Coq" moniker, a play on the goalie's sexual prowess and swagger, is also inscribed in all his prized possessions: the gates leading to his sumptuous estate, the hood and license plate of his trendy car, and the bottom of his luxurious pool. His moniker is even conveyed by his striking guard-rooster. Grande's humorous branding obsession not only inverts the exemplar's self-effacement and witty comments on the franchise player's commodification, but also sums up professional sport's upmarket metamorphosis and the game's distancing from its small-town roots.

Because Roanoke's sexual inadequacies and self-worth issues are the mirror opposite of Grande's braggadocio, Pitka has his hands full getting his pupil back on his feet. In keeping with the film's satire of hockey as an atavistic sport, the guru's teachings are also delivered in good carnivalesque fashion. As part of Roanoke's therapy, Pitka instigates an attack by the opposition and suggests the player take it. Roanoke protests noting that, "I'm a hockey player and that's what hockey players do, they fight!" But the guru insists he abstain. Then just as quickly, and with a roll of the dice, he pronounces it all arbitrary and tells Darren to go out and fight anyone and everyone. The captain predictably goes after goalie Grande and pummels him mercilessly, garnering a two-game suspension. The contest promptly devolves into a brawl, which plunges coach Cherkov into the proceedings to Pitka's delight. Announcer Trent Lueders pronounces the obligatory caveat that "this is not how you play hockey," while color man Jay Kell makes clear that he relishes the mayhem. Hockey's atavistic image is reiterated in game broadcasts, which open with pugnacious Kings and Leafs logos who go at each other and recall the brawling NHL team logos in Fox Channel's nineties telecasts. The hockey player's pugnacity is also rehashed in a pub fight sequence that spoofs the barroom brawls of the Old West to allow Roanoke and Pitka to bond through violence in keeping with the western's Code of Honor. The film plays up the game's carnivalesque excess at every turn, both celebrating and satirizing the hockey player's frontier image in good Hansonian form.

The final matchup also features pointed absurdities in Pitkaesque fashion. As Darren is set to take the game-ending penalty shot, and he freezes when Grande reminds him of his affair with Prudence, Pitka interrupts the contest by riding in atop two Asian elephants. Following his teacher's advice that pleasant distractions release emotional pain, he prods the pachyderms to mate and succeeds in breaking the player's trance. Once recovered, Roanoke must make his move to help the Leafs win the Cup. Before he takes the game-ending penalty shot, Pitka approaches him to gauge whether he has assimilated the lessons of self-worth and probe what he will do if he is unable to score. The captain confidently replies that whatever happens, he will remain a hero to himself, after which he shoots the puck high into the air and scores on Grande to clinch the Cup for the Leafs.

Taking his own teachings to heart, the guru also relinquishes his obsession with claiming the top spot from Deepak Chopra and in the manner of the canonical film protagonist contents himself with second-best status, returns to India, and entreats his teacher, Guru Tugginmypudha (Ben Kingsley), to release him from the bonds of his chastity belt.[8] To his surprise, the contraption turns out to be unlocked, and he is freed to pursue his love for Bullard. The two of them magically don Indian garb, and with respective entourages, engage one another in Bollywood-style dance and song. While the characters disavow the need to win at all costs, in line with the sports genre's melodramatic conventions, they are also granted their most cherished wishes based on their substantial exertions.

The film's blend of English-Canadian and Hollywood motifs also illustrate that film markets are no longer constrained by well-delineated borders.[9] As is true of the *Les Boys* tetralogy, which combines the sports genre's conventions with French-Canadian burlesque sendups of hockey masculinity to scoff at social conduct guidelines, *The Love Guru* lampoons standard parameters of masculinity in the game through cultural and racial stereotypes that disrupt the moral and aesthetic order and make the film's intent difficult to appreciate.[10] The farcical ongoings during matchups also spoof hockey's potential for the unexpected and celebrate physical excess, subverting the highly controlled environment of upmarket entertainment to convey the sport as people's game.[11] *The Love's Guru* carnivalesque version of hockey and its Mike Myers-esque signature also lend themselves to intricate readings that, much like the *Les Boys* films, make the film difficult to interpret in any definitive way. For example, the team's success, which mirrors Myers' own diehard support for the Leafs, acts as nostalgic wish-fulfillment and argues for hewing to childhood referents as one of the last bastions of individual memory and locality at a time when social identity is no longer contained by the nation-state's boundaries.[12] A shot of Myers as himself cheering in the stands after the Leafs' win suggests as much, and confirms that, in keeping with the fan-spectator's role in the carnivalesque, he is granted the space to engage in critique or mockery.[13] The idea of a black American Leafs superstar who reifies the never-ending corporate search for new markets also potentially advances this commentary because it is incompatible with the project of nostalgic hockey for dislodging the sport from its traditional Canadian poles.

However, NHL hockey is neither just a referent of communal practice and identity nor a corporate venture but a complex arrangement subject to the interplay between cultural nationalism and corporate influence.[14] The Leafs in like manner are both nostalgic significators of region (Toronto) and nation (Canada), and a corporate brand involved in complex relationships with the community and wide-ranging partnerships with other teams and corporate entities, including Hollywood studios and marquee actors.[15] The league's endorsement of the film and its extensive collaboration with Paramount Pictures during production and marketing were also based on Mike Myers' involvement, as NHL Deputy Commissioner Bill Daly's comments about the actor confirm: "We're thrilled that he wanted to do this movie, at least in part, because he thought it would be a positive thing for the … [NHL]."[16] The existence of these relationships, the fluidity of sports and film markets, and Mike Myers' own positive opinions about multiculturalism suggest that instead of a wholesale critique of the game's disconnection from Canadianicity, *The Love Guru* comments on the blurred and complicated alignments of present-day elite-level hockey.[17] Because Myers' personal experience and preferences inform his cinematic work, these complex arrangements also speak to the actor's own dual signature as a Canadian with a transnational Hollywood star brand.[18]

The Telefilm-funded *Breakaway/The Speedy Singhs* (Lieberman, 2011) presents a variation on the non-white hockey protagonist by offering an Indo-Canadian perspective on hockey that contests the sport's default status as *Canadian*-Canadian. The film's protagonist is Rajveer Singh (Vinay Virmani), a 21-year-old Canadian-Sikh talent frustrated with his athletic prospects. Raj's traditional father, Darvesh (Anupam Kher), is a man of deep conviction who believes that honest work at younger brother Sammy's (Gurpreet Guggi) successful trucking venture will teach his son accountability. Uncle Sammy, for his part, relays to his nephew that if he proves himself worthy, he also stands to inherit his profitable company. But the young man's heart is set on hockey, and he dreams of playing in the NHL and scoring impressive breakaway goals with the Leafs. Although Raj merely goes through the motions at his uncle's workplace, he shows flair and creativity with his teammates who are turban-wearing Sikhs, and, like him, are all surnamed Singh. Raj's dad, however, finds his son's predilection for hockey disturbing. He dubs the sport one of the many "stupid inventions by [the] white man," primarily because it is not cricket, a sport that "India rules." Dad and son's divergent views about the game are only the tip of the iceberg, for Raj has also cut his hair and symbolically moved into Canadian society, as a teammate confirms in noting that "he is always dreaming of hot white chicks." Raj's courting of law student Melissa (Camilla Belle), former NHLer Dan Winters' (Rob Lowe) off-limits younger sister, deepens the estrangement between father and son. Raj, however, has his heart set on both hockey and Melissa, and he will not be dissuaded from either quest.

The Singhs' first encounter with the reigning champs of the Hyundai Cup—the all-white Hammerheads—is tantamount to a showdown marked by pointed racial overtones. Dismissing the players' derogatory remarks, Raj appeals to the Hammerheads coach to give him a shot, showing he can handle the puck with the best of them. But the coach retorts that he's got all the players he needs, and sarcastically adds: "I'll make sure there's a ticket for you when they play in the finals." Dan Winters, who serves as the rink's janitor, watches the proceedings with interest and remarks to Melissa that "this Indian" is "not half bad," while also wincing at the team's lack of physical durability. After the snub, Raj talks his teammates into entering the Hyundai Cup as the Speedy Singhs, and persuades Winters to coach them as an experiment of sorts, even though he must also pretend to stay away from hockey in keeping with his father's admonitions. To complicate matters, cousin Reena's (Noureen DeWulf) yuppie fiancé, Sonu (Russell Peters), who vies for the family business and sees Raj as a rival, arrives on the scene in short order. When Raj approaches Uncle Sammy as key sponsor, Sonu predictably advises against the scheme. Sammy nonetheless reconsiders when he learns that his support will increase the visibility of his company and engender goodwill in the Indo-Canadian community.

The first practice shows that the Singhs have a long way to go to claim contender status, even as Raj is clearly the playmaker of the lot. Dan's first order of business is to toughen up the players so they can give themselves a shot at the title. But when he arranges a practice against their archrivals, his charges are less than ready, and the Hammerhead goons predictably elbow and bully their way around the ice. Realizing they need help, Raj recruits a burly player from the working-class sport of *kabadi* to serve as enforcer. When the first game of the contest arrives, Raj repurposes Sonu's underhanded maneuvering to his advantage and tricks his parents into believing that he'll be off on his first trucking assignment to New York City. In on the ruse, Uncle Sammy encourages his nephew, and though the Speedy Singhs lose their first game, they soon climb their way to the top of the ranks. When they are set to meet the Hammerheads, the latter lodge a safety complaint because Raj's turban-wearing teammates will not wear regulation helmets for religious reasons. The Speedy Singhs stand to be disqualified from the competition if the players will not relent, which as devout Sikhs, they will not do. After Raj comes up with the idea of fashioning Sikh warrior helmets into hockey headgear, the game is back on track, and as the fated day arrives the whole community shows up in support. The contest comes down to a one-goal differential, and Raj performs the breakaway of his dreams scoring a showy goal to win the championship. He makes amends with his father shortly after and caps off the win by sealing his romance with Melissa.

Because of Raj's small build and his playmaking abilities, *Breakaway* parlays his masculinity and game through multiple allusions to *Youngblood*. In a scene in which the player ends up on the receiving end of a hard hit, the coach lets him know he will pull him the moment he sees evidence of a concussion, but the hotshot retorts: "If you can catch me!" The playful assertion recalls Dean's confidence in his playmaking abilities when countering dad Blane's and brother Kelly's assumption that his small size will be a liability: "They'll never catch me!" *Breakaway* also links Raj and Dean through poetic training scenes that configure skill-honing through the athlete's single-minded dedication to his craft. A romantic

Breakaway movie poster (Screen Media Films/Photofest).

sequence of Raj in a hoodie, and as fast as a bullet skating laps around a rink bathed in soft haze, recalls images of Dean in a misty rink practicing shots on net backlit by the lights of the zamboni. The film also intertextually connects Rob Lowe's character Dan Winters to his earlier incarnation as Dean Youngblood in a scene in which the coach wears a Mustangs #10 T-shirt that references the team name and jersey number that the young protagonist wears in the 1986 film. Lowe's presence in *Breakaway* serves as a consistent reminder of his role twenty-five years earlier, which the actor acknowledges when he notes in an interview that the top is "my little nod to my first film for those who care."[19]

Story originator Vinay Virmani confirms the link between both films in referring to *Youngblood* as "one of my favorite sports films of all times."[20] *Youngblood*, however, is more than just a cherished movie since not only does it mediate the masculinity and game of *Breakaway*'s main protagonist, but lends force to commentary about hockey's gatekeeping by vested interests. *Youngblood* challenges the normative physicality of the Canadian culture of hockey by configuring the American player in Canadian junior leagues as a symbolic little brother who must go up against the Canadian older brother's heavyweight ideal of masculinity. *Breakaway* reiterates similar commentary but parlays *Youngblood*'s critique of Canadian hockey into a racial issue. Although the Bombers are merely cheapshotting villains who threaten the social mobility of the skilled protagonist, a working-class American, the Hammerheads augment their physical excess with racism, threatening the Canadian ideal of multiculturalism and disrupting hockey's potential to serve the project of citizenship and nationhood. As one of them yells when contesting ice time for practice, "We're waiting for you snake-charmers to get off the ice." Both Bombers and Hammerheads are bullies, but the latter are also bigoted and disloyal to Canada's cultural value of tolerance, and in melodramatic form, all the more merit deposing from the top ranks. Raj's teammates, however, also play a role in their own bullying by ceding the hockey turf to the Hammerheads. As one of them notes, "They're bigger, they're faster, they're stronger" … "Well, they're whiter." The players hold no illusions that their cultural traditions make them anything but outsiders, and they matter-of-factly concede in Punjabi that, "ice hockey is a white man's game." It is up to Raj, then, to convince them of the contrary.

Hewing to family entertainment conventions, *Breakaway* prioritizes hockey through skill rather than violence and addresses audiences by way of an enlarged socio-cultural context.[21] Thus, although Raj recruits Nikku Hussein (Ali Hassan) from the scrappy sport of *kabadi* to serve as enforcer, the move backfires because it lands the tough guy in the penalty box and costs the Speedy Singhs the game. When coach Winters notes that inserting Nikku into the lineup got the team "some much-needed respect and … showed that we belong," Raj disputes the move, countering that respect can only be garnered by scoring. The captain's insistence about answering the opponent's aggression with skill is consistent with family fare's notion that brute force is the exclusive preserve of the villain, particularly since the Hammerheads' physical excess operates as proxy for keeping Canada's social minorities from the game.[22]

While articulating the skill-vs.-physicality dialectic of the game in Canadian film, *Breakaway*'s objection to physical force is based on how it preserves hockey as an all-white enclave. Rather than resorting to hockey brawls or a single decisive physical encounter to vanquish the opponent as in *Youngblood*, *Breakaway* dramatizes peaking racial tensions in a key fight at a Toronto bar, the site of Sonu's stag party and the same outlet where Reena is holding her bachelorette party. Two Hammerhead bullies, also at the bar, put the moves on Reena and Melissa to instigate a fight. Raj takes the bait and throws the first punch followed by the rest of the players, and an all-out brawl promptly breaks out and lands the team in jail. Since the Singhs refrain from brawling to set themselves apart from the Hammerheads, the film must somehow reinforce the players' sturdy masculinity off the ice. However, given that physical excess also stands for the villain's racist proclivities, just as with Nikku's recruitment, the fight backfires as Melissa chides Raj for protecting not her but his ego, and Reena thinks twice about marrying Sonu for failing to control his drinking. Coach Dan, angry at Raj for enmeshing his kid sister in the proceedings, also strips him of the captain's "C" and prompts the whiz to walk off the team. The fight also exposes the Singhs as nothing less than bully-clowns, a mirror image of the Hammerheads whose game and character they deride. What's more, the exercise in macho showmanship borders on the absurd as Nikku and other members of the group reveal that they, rather the Hammerheads, put the obnoxious Sonu out of commission during the fight. The film links the sporting and social realms by pronouncing physical excess as consistent with the game's exclusive white male referents and the hard masculinity of the Hammerheads. On both of these fronts, bully expressions contravene the Singhs' project of identity, which prioritizes masculinity by way of self-restraint and pliant engagement with female partners.

To articulate a warrior masculinity that is consistent with hockey's heroic referents and Sikh culture, Raj fights for his right to field a team without sacrificing players' religious priorities. He notes of the Sikh warrior hockey helmets: "Our ancestors wore these into battle centuries ago, and now you guys are going out to protect the pride of our community, only this time the battle's on ice," an exhortation that is musically amplified by martial drum rhythms. Coach Winters' pre-game speech also establishes the Singhs' attainment in line with Canada's idea of multiculturalism: "Tonight you can show the entire country that you belong. Yes, you look different and all that stuff. But if you go out there, if you do what I know you could do, then the only real difference is that Singhs are champions, and they're not." The coach's speech alludes to Canada's tolerant narrative of nationhood and pays homage to hockey as an integrating force.

The final game reiterates the national narrative by way of multiple ice-level medium shots of spectators—of both sexes and all ages—dressed in saris and other colorful attire enthusiastically cheering for their team. Medium shots follow the play both at ice-level and from the stands to capture fans' POV and immerse the viewer in the Indo-Canadian communal experience of hockey. The film conveys the contest by emphasizing the authentic, small-town feel of the game in tight-knit communities as an alternative to the corporate-driven spectacle. Much like frontier pond hockey infuses new blood into the NHL in *Mystery, Alaska*, Raj's fantasies of playing for the Leafs suggest that Indo-Canadian participation can play a central role in revitalizing the professional game. The Indo-Canadian community's solemn singing of "O, Canada" at the start of the championship matchup mobilizes the notion of belonging to dual cultures and configures the hockey team as part of this commitment. The Speedy Singhs' social functionality in representing the Indo-Canadian presence in the game, then, is not unlike that of les Boys in expressing a desire to render Quebec visible as a nation by way of an all-Québécois team. Vinay Virmani's comment that young South Asians expressed excitement about having a team (and a jersey) to rally around[23] suggests as much.

The story of the Speedy Singhs is a narrative of both cultural difference and integration that exposes the problems that arise during the acculturation process. Virmani underlines that many of the actors in *Breakaway* are schoolmates with whom he used to play hockey and who faced similar difficulties, such as friction with parents, the helmet dilemma, and other race-related issues. Speaking to the problem, Eva Mackey argues that although multiculturalism as both policy and myth celebrates Canada's myriad cultures, it also defines minority groups against a core white Anglophone heritage and subordinates them to the culture of "'real' and 'authentic' Canadians, who tolerate and even celebrate the 'color' and 'flavor' of multicultural 'Others.'"[24] *Breakaway* both acknowledges and challenges this peripheral status by foregrounding hockey's centrality as cultural practice of identity and arguing for Indo-Canadian participation in like manner.

The above two films put forward hockey exemplars whose cultural and ethnic backgrounds contravene the all-white indicators of the archetype. In keeping with minorities' necessary interface with the dominant culture's values, these films also stress aspects of martial masculinity that are consistent with popular conceptions of hockey. Darren Roanoke in *The Love Guru* proves his suitability for the sport by readily partaking from the pleasures of excess.[25] The Singhs' Sikh warrior helmets in *Breakaway*, while asserting cultural difference, also speak to the courageous manhood that hockey celebrates. Even though Roanoke's acrobatic leaps subtly hint at the athleticism of the basketball player and the Singhs' Sikh warrior helmets tamper with the realism of hockey in film, these motifs communicate a cultural desire to belong to a game that narrowly prescribes identity through the mythology of the heroic white male. However, while *The Love Guru*'s satirical representation of hockey comments on the blurred and complicated alignments of elite-level hockey in the age of globalization, *Breakaway* advances the idea of a nation within a nation to articulate the place of Indian-Canadians in the game.[26]

Sexuality and the Hockey Protagonist: *Perfectly Normal, Breakfast with Scot, Grown Up Movie Star* and *The Sheldon Kennedy Story*

In his overview of sports fiction themes, Glenn Cummins observes that if explorations of male sexuality in film and literature are scant, portrayals of patent homosexuality are downright rare.[27] The hockey repertoire is no exception given that in the movies the game is synonymous with muscular virility and films are more likely to censure or poke fun at the hockey player's violent or buffoon-like ways rather than risk representing him through androgynous traits that might not respond to firming. *Perfectly Normal* (Simoneau, 1991) traverses uncommon ground in fashioning a hockey protagonist who evokes the mild male leads of Canadian canonical film. The character in question, Italian-Canadian Renzo Parachi (Michael Riley), works at a beer factory and plays goal for the plant's Tate Titans team. On his nights off he also drives his father's cab to earn extra cash. On cab duty, he picks up American Alonzo Turner (Robbie Coltrane), a smooth talker who turns out to share Renzo's Italian ancestry and love of opera. Alonzo wastes no time in capitalizing on Renzo's hospitality and quickly takes over his apartment. When Renzo hints that it is time he moved on, Alonzo contests the breadth of the goalie's aspirations and ridicules his plans to build a house on plot of land outside the city as "tiny little fizzy dreams." Belittled, Renzo takes Alonzo in as a lodger, but the latter predictably ends up paying no rent. Instead, he cajoles his roommate to invest in a theatrical restaurant he plans to christen La Traviata and to oversee as head chef. One evening when the two are talking opera, Alonzo catches sight of a dollar bill about to slip out of a record sleeve, money that Renzo's defunct mother has left tucked away in the opera collection. Intent on digging out more cash, Alonzo maneuvers his prospective business associate out of the room and sends him off on his date with love interest Denise (Deborah Duchene). While Renzo is away, the rascal ransacks the room and thinks of skipping town, but ends up calling prostitute friend Gloria (Elizabeth Harpur) for a rendezvous. When the goalie returns from his date, Alonzo presents him with the stash and proposes he invest it in the restaurant.

In the midst of the chaos brought on by Alonzo's appearance, Renzo slowly disengages from the game. Nemesis Hoblisch, a.k.a. Hopeless (Eugene Lipinski)—an unhinged coworker and the Titans' reigning goon—does his best to sabotage Renzo's work at the plant, hobbling him during a game and also sending supervisor-coach Charlie Glesby (Kenneth Welsh) to the hospital. Away from his coworkers and team, Alonzo prevails all the more on Renzo, locating a suitable place for the restaurant and enlisting his help in overhauling it with high theatrical detail. He also hires a motley crew who will dress as opera characters and sing for customers in drag. Once Alonzo has roped Renzo in, he delivers his *coup de grâce*, proposing a floorshow in which his business partner will sing a high-pitched aria as the Druid priestess in Bellini's *Norma* while he naturally takes on the sturdy male lead. Despite his protestations, Renzo is no match for wily Alonzo who works him over by insisting he "find the pearl" in this prospect and protect his investment. Fortuitously, Charlie makes a partial recovery in time to return to the bench against archrival Eastern Clay. Relieved and recovered from his own injuries, Renzo returns to the team to the reassurance of best pal Duane (Jack Nichols). At dinner with Alonzo, Renzo attempts to turn down the opera role by arguing he has an important hockey game coming up. But Alonzo counters that the show will begin late in the evening and he can easily manage both.

After the Titans eke out a victory, Renzo quietly slips out of the locker room and heads for the restaurant. The team promptly finds out about the floorshow, and to celebrate their triumph against Eastern Clay, they vote to crash the performance instead of going to the local strip bar. The hockey outfit arrives at the busy restaurant where they are escorted to the bar, and as the curtains open, they catch sight of their goalie dressed as a priestess feelingly singing away in falsetto tones. A sense of shock washes over the group but it promptly turns into fascination for Denise and Hopelesss. True to his goon stature, Hopeless soon starts a fight by punching a noisy customer who detracts from his enjoyment of the performance. As an all-out brawl breaks out, Alonzo, who is being pursued by investigators for past wrongdoings in Florida, takes advantage of the disturbance to slip out the back door and get on the bus back to the U.S. Renzo, now wig-less, continues to sing away but as Denise lands in his arms in the melee, he seizes the chance and passionately kisses her. The next day the papers hail both Renzo's show against Eastern Clay as "powerful" and the restaurant's "superior food" and "magnificent performance," handing him wins on both fronts.

As a courteous, shy, sexually reticent sort living a sensible life, Renzo is the paragon of mild masculinity, and his goaltending similarly favors economy of movement over spectacular flair, a sensible game that gets the job done. The boards of the rink where he plays, the ice surface, and players' uniforms are unmarked by advertisement, and when Renzo first takes the ice a Canadian flag is visible in the background, denoting him as a perfectly sober Canadian. Alonzo, on the other hand, is the proverbial American Other, and everything that Renzo is not. As the goalie immerses himself in his pre-game rituals, Alonzo in the stands confuses the warm-up with the game proper and boisterously cheers his partner's performance until one of the fans in attendance informs him the contest has yet to start. Alonzo's large buffoon-like behavior and his Florida background are reminiscent of *Going South*'s newbie fans who boisterously applaud the game's premium on spectacle but understand little of the sport's intricacies. A showman at heart, Alonzo does not shirk with embarrassment at his *faux pas*. Indeed, when Renzo accuses him of taking over other people's lives in a subsequent scene, Alonzo passionately defends his outlook noting that on the contrary, "I try to bring them color and excitement. And they would just as soon live their dull and drab little lives." Audacious, quick on the uptake, and opportunistic, Alonzo is also persuasive in a huckster kind of way. He towers over Renzo's slim frame, and even after shedding his light-colored Florida outfit, always wears ruby red or royal blue as opposed to Renzo's drab overalls and sensible clothes. He pairs the sumptuous meals he cooks with wine, which injects refinement into Renzo's mundane life as defined by the industrial, vapor-filled beer factory where he works. Alonzo also exhorts the goalie to own his uniqueness for "God made only one of you," chiding him for his self-effacement and prodding him to mirror in his endeavors both his "Roman elegance" and "rugged yahoo" sensibilities.

Although Alonzo and Renzo share a fondness for European high culture, the film defines them largely through oppositions. Janice Kaye addresses the Alonzo-Renzo relationship through the dualized symbolism of the masculine-colonizer and the feminine-colonized. If Renzo represents Canada, the dynamic recalls Eva Mackey's argument that the country is often defined as marginal and gendered in relation to the U.S. on account of the force of "American cultural imperialism" and other colonial legacies.[28] Alonzo also exhibits all the makings of the male colonizing force when he lets Renzo know that the gown he has hung outside the goalie's closet door, "would go beautiful with your eyes.... Pluck your eyebrows, the world has never seen a more beautiful Norma." Because of this feminization and the goalie's donning of the Norma costume, Kaye assesses Renzo's identity in *Perfectly Normal* as an archetype of transgressive masculinity. She argues that Canadian film's preference for the anti-heroic allows for the reassertion of the repressed homoerotic, which *Perfectly Normal* corroborates by establishing the Hopeless-Renzo relationship as a latent homosexual connection. This relationship is reaffirmed through the accompanying "Romeo and Juliet" musical score of Russian composer Sergei Prokofiev and by director Yves Simoneau's gay identity, which also consistently informs his work.[29]

Perfectly Normal certainly sketches Renzo's masculinity as rather anomalous for a hockey player. The introduction hints that Renzo is unusual when, after attending his mother's funeral, he stands in the middle of the rink where he plays hockey and falls backward as if making a save, softly uttering that he hardly knew her. The rink caretaker, who spots Renzo in the recumbent position, yells out a pert "Hey!" to get him off the ice, mumbling to himself, "Strange guy." In a subsequent scene, Renzo appears in a tilted shot at the factory where he works spraying cold water on the conveyor belt's beer bottles to distinguish his masculinity from that of Charlie and his coworkers, who after work hurry off to check out the new girl at the strip bar while Renzo demurs in favor of driving his father's cab for the extra cash. A second tilted shot frames Renzo in the hallway approaching his apartment where, it turns out, Alonzo has hung the beautiful sequined gown outside his bedroom closet door for his prospective female role in *Norma*. Though Renzo is horrified when he finds out about his business partner's scheme, calling him a pervert and accusing him of turning his apartment into a brothel, he nevertheless accedes to play the role. And even though he keeps his operatic performance from his hockey teammates, in the final analysis he also he embraces the part wholeheartedly.

However, even as the hockey repertoire configures highbrow art and theatrical performance as transgressions into femaleness, *Perfectly Normal* also grants Renzo some leeway in his performance of gender identity by virtue of his netminder role, which in the repertoire allows for all manner of eccentricity in line with the goalie's individual preferences. As the concept of the goaltender brotherhood denotes, in popular culture the goalie is the team's quintessential odd duck, because in standing alone to face the opposition he has the room to articulate a quirky individuality. While Renzo's goalie aspect also ostensibly allows cover for the repressed homoerotic, *Perfectly Normal* simultaneously attenuates his crossover into drag by configuring his game and that of his team at variance with the traditional dichotomy of art (skill) vs. toughness (physicality). Instead, the film merges both aspects of the game through medium shots of players checking and upending one other in slow motion to the flow of non-diegetic classical music, an approach that is consonant with the visual poetry of the art film.[30] This representation of hockey as both tough and artistically skillful does not detract from instinctive and straightforward aspects, unlike its disfiguration as a circus act in *Slap Shot 2* or the unusual sight of hockey players singing and dancing in *Score*. Hence, by endorsing the sport as a hybrid cultural space that conflates artistry and toughness, *Perfectly Normal* also bolsters Renzo's character as a blend of "highbrow" artistic sensibilities and understated "lowbrow" toughness and self-effacement that mark him as perfectly Canadian.

Much as *Keep Your Head Up, Kid* and *Wrath of Grapes* deploy extremely violent characters to attenuate Don Cherry's unsentimental view of his hockey role, *Perfectly Normal* draws up Renzo's teammates as characters who, though embodying the sturdy masculinity of the hockey player, also come off as wanting because of their working-class attributes. Coach Charlie, a surrogate father figure, is a theatrical sort who is given to mixing Shakespearean-speak with mundane hockey exhortations about "kicking butt." Despite his lively histrionic persona and gamesman hues, Charlie is also inadequate as a coach, unable to harness his squad's talents to beat arch-nemesis Eastern Clay. His coaching counterpart sees through the ruse letting him know, "you've got a mouth ... but I've got a team." Charlie only secures a win over Eastern Clay after his nurse, Mrs. Hathaway (Patricia Gage), gives the squad a scolding. Similarly, Renzo's socially well-adjusted friend Duane, although handsome, sexually proficient, and suitably tough, shows he lacks foresight when he observes he would readily fritter away any fortune that should come his way. Team goon Hopeless, for his part, comes off as a buffoon who is unable to transcend his role even when mesmerized by Renzo's artistic rendition in *Norma*. Indeed, he scores the winning goal against Eastern Clay by accident and with his forehead, confirming that he is a witless dunce. Although the entire hockey outfit is initially transfixed by the liminality offered by *La Traviata*, players and coach bring the hockey arena to the artistic space with a brawl that subsumes the floorshow and wrecks the exotic setup that had transported their mundane lives. Only the women in the film, Denise and Mrs. Hathaway, grasp the high art aspect of the performance. The women belong to the strong lineup of heroines in Canadian canonical film, who channel their assertiveness appropriately and allow for an enlarged and non-judgmental outlook on the human experience. Kaye makes the case that because hockey in film rigidly dramatizes heterosexuality, breaking away from it may evoke laughter.[31] Clues of Hopeless' attraction to Renzo also come across comically as they straddle bully-clown territory. Although the cover for the men is that hockey players, at least these hockey players, are too working-class and daft to appreciate the subtleties of high art, the brawl also confirms that hockey masculinity is inflexibly heterosexual and overly invested in toughness to incorporate artistic sensibilities.

Having dared to publicly acknowledge his love of opera in full drag, and going where his more heteronormative working-class persona dare go, Renzo emerges with a more confident, decisive voice as a successful hockey goalie and entrepreneur that plays a part in communal life by procuring the liminal experience of La Traviata. Indeed, even though Alonzo acts as the motivating force to shake Renzo out of his dull life, in the end the goalie commits fully to the project, telling his business partner when he is on the verge of giving up on the endeavor that "they [the patrons] need to have this place." When circumstances expose Alonzo as running from the law because of his previous failed restaurant venture, he gets on the bus back to the U.S., and as he reads a report on the Titans-Eastern Clay game, he proudly points out Renzo's picture to a nearby passenger: "That's my brother." The sequence summarily inverts the prosperous older brother-frustrated little brother dynamic, revealing Renzo's life as more successful than that of the fugitive Alonzo.

If *Perfectly Normal* ventures out of the hockey player's comfort zone by dualizing Renzo's masculinity through his hockey identity and his artistic leanings, the same flexibility is not present in sports dramas that acknowledge the presence of gays on the bench, since these characters emerge in typical closeted mode and struggle to come to terms with partnering preferences. The conflicted hockey protagonist of *Breakfast with Scot* (Lynd, 2007) is Eric McNally (Tom Cavanagh), an intimidating former Leafs player who, because of a career-ending injury at a charity exhibition game, repurposes himself as a sports hockey commentator for the fictional Canadian Sports Network (CSTN). McNally is in a long-term partnership with the team's lawyer, Sam (Ben Shenkman), who cares for him during his five-year recovery. But both men keep the relationship secret for fear that it will cost Eric his new job. Just as the hockey tough is taking his first productive footsteps into broadcasting, a charming 11-year-old boy by the name of Scot Latour (Noah Bernett) comes into the partners' lives. Scot is the surrogate son of Sam's brother, Billy (Colin Cunningham), a free spirit who for a number of years was in a close relationship with Scot's mother, Julie, but is now living a playboy's life in Brazil. With Julie dead of a drug overdose, Sam and Eric are persuaded by Child Services to take care of the young boy until Billy flies up from South America to fetch him. Eric clearly dreads the idea of a having a youngster on the verge of adolescence in the house and reminds Sam that he cannot take further disruptions to his life. The die is nonetheless cast and the downcast, displaced young boy soon arrives at the couple's doorstep. A quick look at the plastic bag containing his belongings promptly reveals that it is full of suspicious items: numerous colorful boas, a singing hairbrush, a pink poodle belt, and several fanciful scarves. Scot appears to have all the makings of flamboyance as he dresses in girls' clothes, puts on his mother's makeup, and thinks nothing of kissing boys as often as girls. Eric, in particular, is scared stiff about Scot's meanderings into femininity not only because he "doesn't know much about being a boy," but because, as he poignantly confesses to coworker Nula (Jeananne Goossen), he is terrified that Scot will make him gay.

To Sam's chagrin, his partner soon sets out to socialize Scot if only for self-preservation's sake. He locks the young boy's necklaces, bracelets, and brooches—mementos of his deceased mother—inside an old toolbox that he tucks away in a corner of his own bedroom. He also takes him to a game of pickup hockey at the neighborhood rink where the youngster can witness for himself appropriate male behavior. After the game, Scot takes to the ice to show Eric his own skating abilities, spinning and jumping like a figure skater, and querying whether "it's good enough for hockey." Ecstatic, Eric immediately signs up the youngster with the local peewee team. Coach Bud Wilson (Graham Greene) recognizes the former Leaf and expeditiously taps him for the role of assistant coach. Neighborhood bully Ryan Burlington (Dylan Everett) is also on the team, but promptly becomes Scot's good friend and takes on the role of protector. When the police apprehend Ryan for stealing goalie Joey Morita's (Alexander Franks) brand new skates, Scot is petrified at the thought of taking the ice without protection. Eric reassures his young charge that he does not need an enforcer to look out for him and gives him a brief lesson in self-defense. But as Scot catches sight of Ryan in the stands on his first game, the youngster panics and heads straight for Morita, a schoolmate and erstwhile close friend who is also gay, bloodying him for turning Ryan in. Furious and embarrassed, Eric throws Scot out of the game. In the parking lot he has a serious argument with Sam, who blames him for teaching the boy to fight. Teary-eyed, Scot blurts out that he took up hockey to please them both for he never seems to do anything right. When Sam checks in on him, Scot's jersey is on the floor and the young boy is curled up in bed crying himself to sleep. Eric, for his part, is on the couch, confirming that Scot's masculinity training has become a major point of contention for the partners.

At Christmastime, with Billy set to retrieve Scot, Eric and Sam throw the boy a goodbye party with neighborhood friends in attendance. When Billy shows up with a new prospective mom, Sam and Eric realize he is unsuitable for the role of surrogate father and that he is there to claim the insurance money Julie has left for her son's rearing. Scot, for his part, is also hesitant to go but it takes a poetic plea from Eric for the youngster to venture that he wants to stay. Billy has no option but to relent and Scot settles down with his newfound family for good. The rolling credits confirm that Scot has taken up hockey again while retaining a feminine identity off the ice, and Eric and Sam have come out of the closet at work and the hockey tough has made peace with his gender orientation.

From the outset, *Breakfast with Scot* establishes Eric McNally as an unsentimental, harsh contender who thinks nothing of brushing off kids' requests for autographs and brutally running into teammates at the Leafs' White and Blue charity game. Although a likeable sort, Eric is gay, and his masculinity contravenes the essence of the hockey archetype since the ideal does not accommodate the marginal gender identity of queer men. Because hockey is consonant with hardiness, however, the film must also leave no doubt about McNally's suitability for the game. The viewer's first glimpse of the hockey tough comes by way of a medium upward tilted close-up as he files out onto the ice. When a young fan holds out his picture professes him to be his hero, Eric brusquely shoves it to the side with his stick, while his teammates happily take the time to sign the children's leaflets and photographs. The sound effects recall the boot marching of an army and the musical score soon turns into a sturdy flamenco motif as McNally runs into every player in sight to the protests of teammates. He is just as ruthless in the corners and against the glass as he is in the middle of the ice, and by this point the viewer is left without a doubt that Eric McNally is the very embodiment of the hockey archetype.

Because his reputation as a hockey tough precedes him, the former Leaf is highly recognized for his exploits both on the job and about town. A high profile European player whom Eric is set to interview greets him by asking whether he's still "slamming them around" and reiterates his admiration for his bruiser and penalty-taking abilities. A customer at a retail store, where Scot tries on coats while complaining about the drab colors, pokes fun of the boy as a sissy, but when Eric confronts him, he is stunned: "You are Eric McNally. You played for the Leafs. You were a great fighter till you got injured in that practice. Now you're on TV." Eric looks him in the eye and quietly but firmly reiterates that he's still a "decent fighter," sending the man scrambling for the door. Coach Wilson greets Eric with similar admiration citing his Game Seven overtime goal in the 2000 playoffs semifinal. The official refereeing Scot's first game also appraises him in like manner to humorous effect. The public at large mirrors back the side that McNally has unproblematically projected for years, and he strives to keep this image intact.

Because the hockey archetype outlines a masculinity that is the very opposite of so-called low-ranking effeminacy, Eric chokes at the thought of identifying himself as gay. He instructs young Scot to "watch the twirling" while enjoining him not to speak about his private life in public, because he works in a sport-related field and prospective interviewees would not accede to talk to him "if they knew that I was, that I'm a ... ." In an amusing scene, Nula reassures Eric he's not "gay-gay-gay-gay," which Eric reassured acknowledges with a thank you. In a conversation with Sam, Eric also hints that Scot might "be gay, gay-gay," and expresses relief that they're both off the hook because the youngster was obviously that way before his arrival. Eric also makes the case that he is only gay with friends and family, but not when he's out in the world at large, construing his homosexuality as a costume that he can put on or take off at will depending on the circumstances. He is not a gay hockey player, because being a hockey player precludes being gay. Eric is gay only with his inner circle, while resolutely non-gay as an ex-NHLer.

He also wrestles with Scot about his split identity. Scot is a bright lad but still young enough that he doesn't understand the big fuss about gender identity, or even grasp what the word "gay" means anything other than not being liked. Seeking to glean how Eric elucidates his setup, the youngster unwittingly pushes the hockey tough to define himself past his mental acrobatics. In the supermarket, Scot innocently asks how Eric keeps track of who knows he is gay and who doesn't. Eric fumbles the answer noting that he is not gay, then that he is, but not "just gay," while reconsidering that he is "just gay," leaving doubts about how exactly he configures his sexual identity. Outside the store, Scot presses on, querying what Eric did early on, since he probably did not want anyone else to know that he was "not 'just gay.'" Eric's reply is quite revealing: "I didn't do anything. I played hockey." Hockey resolves any doubts about Eric's manhood because he has reached the pinnacle of the game and his masculinity needs no further redressing.

Although winsome, Eric is first and foremost preoccupied with his macho image, much like Bobby Barbato in *Touch and Go*, who resists fatherhood because his masculinity is "pre-paternal, still bound up in its own narcissism," as Stella Bruzzi observes of the (single) athlete's gender identity in film.[32] Eric is also hesitant to take on the role of father and does so out of fear that Scot will expose his gay lifestyle. Because he remains invested in the game, he seizes the opportunity to use hockey to re-masculinize the youngster. He welcomes Ryan's input because the young ruffian plays the game with enforcer relish and struts the bravado off the

Eric McNally (Tom Cavanagh) coaches young Scot Latour (Noah Bernett, left of Cavanagh) and his peewee team in *Breakfast with Scot* (courtesy of Mongrel Media).

ice. Ryan even comments to Nula's face when she's babysitting Scot that she's attractive, a remark that Eric's coworker regards with utter bewilderment. Eric is intent on re-making Scot to his own image, and he embraces sturdy Ryan's help in this acculturation. When Eric watches a game with Scot and Ryan, he takes great pleasure in pointing out hockey tactics and mentoring the children in a surrogate father role without Sam's input.

Eric is the masculine party in the relationship, hardly affectionate or expressive, indeed almost reluctant, and frequently appearing with folded arms near his life partner. As the caring, nurturing sort, Sam is charged with tutoring Scot in appropriate shows of homosocial affection, gradations of hugs that exclude kissing. Although he takes on the house chores, Sam is also no pansy, proving he can resort to physical punishment when the occasion calls for it. In a repartee with Billy during the Christmas party, the younger brother tells Sam that he and Eric are lucky because they are gay and they will never get stuck with an ex-girlfriend's kid. When Sam chides him for not attempting to help Julie out with her drug problem, Billy replies that he was not going to get involved and ironically be the one contracting AIDS. Upon hearing the callous remarks, Sam takes off after Billy intent on giving him a trouncing that is narrowly avoided because of Eric's prompt intercession.

Sam also voices concern over Eric's attempt to remake Scot by taking away his jewelry, signing him for hockey practice, and teaching him to brawl. Although Eric firmly believes that the youngster is courting retaliation for his effeminate response from a school bully, Sam deems that rigidly binding Scot's identity does him a disservice because it stunts his innate joy. The film does not always make clear whether Scot is gay or simply going through an androgynous phase that need not conform to mainstream modalities, but it also leaves no doubt that the child is ill-suited to becoming tough Eric's mini-me. Although an expression of protective instincts, Eric's desire to socialize Scot to the hockey player's manly ways is in part self-serving, a projection of his own fears that mirrors his split between his public and his private personas. As Eric admits his profound love for the child, he also learns to relax into his own masculinity, which includes both full embrace of his partnership with Sam and his sports identity.

The credits segment in scrapbook format shows Eric in front of the Hockey Hall of Fame with Scot and Sam. Scot, for his part, appears in dual masculine and female aspects alongside his peewee team and with Don Cherry, as well as in feminine garb in childlike self-portraits. Friends Ryan and Joey, who represent facets of the boy's masculine and feminine identities, also prominently feature in the album. The final picture, a Christmas card that features a shot of Sam, Eric, and Scot with the caption "The Latours," humorously amplifies that young Scot has socialized Eric and Sam as parents and facilitated their coming out of the closet as a couple.

Breakfast with Scot makes the case that gender identity is fluid and complex and that young Scot is entitled to stake a claim on the game by expressing an unguarded identity, whether in its female or male aspects. In a moving scene, Scot in his hockey jersey lovingly caresses his favorite charm bracelet before giving it away to his neighbor Mildred Monterossos (Fiona Reid). Mildred re-gifts the bracelet to the boy at Christmas to signal the recovery of his feminine side. The film, on the other hand, does not provide a full view of Eric and Sam's relationship except by opposing Sam's ease with his gender identity to Eric's hard hockey masculinity and closeted status. The narrative structure also leaves the resolution of Eric's inner conflict until the very end, and spends most of the time tracking the difficulties of navigating his problematic identity, even as it makes for an entertaining, well-drafted story, and contributes realistic complexity to the hockey player's characterization in film. Above all, however, *Breakfast with Scot* captures with humor the strain imposed by the inflexible masculinity of the hockey ideal on gay athletes whose sporting identities continue to be foregrounded in public even after retirement.

Grown Up Movie Star (Maggs, 2009) also features a former NHLer's stressful exploration of his sexuality. The man in question is Ray (Shawn Doyle), a single dad to 14-year-old Ruby (Tatiana Maslany) and 11-year-old Rose (Julia Kennedy). After wife Lillian (Sherry White) walks out on the family intent on fulfilling her acting dreams, Ray finds himself in over his head with restless Ruby, a precocious teen who wants to follow in mom's footsteps. Other than putting food on the table, the hockey tough appears thoroughly at a loss about childrearing. He chastises Ruby for smoking, but his censure falls on deaf ears since his daughter knows he himself smokes. He also attempts to restrain her sexual explorations, but since Ray is engaged in a similar itinerary, he has no credibility in that arena either. Although the tough man attracts women like bees to the honey, a visit to the high school hockey rink reveals that his thoughts are elsewhere and that his love interest is none other than gym teacher James (Steve Cochrane). Ruby catches the two in a compromising pose after the adults believe the children have gone to bed, and Ray, perturbed, ends the affair. When next morning Ruby makes light of the liaison, since she does not see it as aberrant, Ray slaps her across the face. But there is not much he can do to control his daughter. At wit's end Ray begs his own father (Andy Jones) for help, and dad acquiesces but only for a week.

The children also have a surrogate uncle, Stuart (Jonny Harris), who suffered a mysterious accident and is now wheelchair-bound. He is a photographer and Ruby suggests he use her as model so she can repurpose her headshots into a Hollywood career, and he can also catapult into fame alongside, oblivious that she is walking into dangerous territory. When Ruby is not with Stuart, she courts trouble in school with Will (Mark O'Brien), an American teen from Colorado, whom she does her best to seduce. While looking for his daughter who is on a date with Will, Ray comes across James who insists on helping him track her down in the dark of the night. The two soon forget about Ruby and resume the affair. The next morning, however, Ray gets a wind that someone has been taking provocative pictures of his daughter. When he finds out Stuart is behind the photos and further transgressions, he sets fire to his house. The cops arrive just in time and cart Ray off to prison, where a teary-eyed Ruby entreats him to keep his desire for revenge in check. Seeing his distraught daughter, the hockey tough realizes he cannot kill Stuart because he would leave his children destitute. After serving a short jail time he is reunited with his family to start a new life.

Much as *Breakfast with Scot*, *Grown Up Movie Star* draws up the gay NHLer as a harsh, sort that leaves no doubts about his suitability for hockey. The introductory scene depicts Ray with Ruby and Rose at his construction job in the midst of a Newfoundland wintry landscape. When the girls find a small animal in the snow and bring it to dad, he unceremoniously kills the creature with the smack of a hammer. The kids let out a scream and Ruby protests that only a psychopath behaves in such a way. But Ray shoots back that they will not be visiting him at the site again, and admonishes Stuart, who is taking pictures of the landscape and the family, to put down the camera or folks around town will assume he is "some kind of fruit." The scene portrays Ray's masculinity so narrowly that it allows neither for refined artistic pursuits nor for soft, nurturing expressions.

Even when Ray makes an honest attempt at bonding, however, his efforts prove humorously inadequate. He manages to coax his young daughter Rose into a game of shinny in the family home's driveway and the scene starts out with an archetypal close-up of the blade on a moving a ball which denotes the national passion for the game. But soon it turns into its parodic rendition, as Rose, dressed in goalie attire that is one size too big for her makes no attempt to block dad's shot. Instead, she whimpers that she wants to go inside and watch an episode of the Disney Channel's *Hannah Montana*. When Ray insists that she is a natural, taking another shot which his daughter actively avoids and which he dresses up as "Good evasion, Rose!," the youngster nonchalantly walks off to watch her TV series. Ray pleads with her for another five minutes to no avail, cutting a sorry figure in the context of empowering the father-daughter bond in sport. Ray tragicomically

Former hockey star Ray (Shawn Doyle, facing) with love interest James (Steve Cochrane) in *Grown Up Movie Star* (courtesy of Mongrel Media/ Laurie Lynd/Paul Pope; photograph Ken Woroner).

has nothing to offer his daughters other than hockey, but the youngsters only have a hankering for Disneyland, Hollywood dramas, and mainstream American entertainment.

Out of ideas on how to restrain Ruby's rebelliousness and sexual exploration, Ray brings in his own father to help. Granddad is an old-timer who served in the Canadian military and excuses Ray for not following in his footsteps only because the NHL happened to require his services. He sees the parenting of children as women's purview and matter-of-factly advises his son to find himself a wife. He also instructs Ray to punish his wayward daughter the old-fashioned way: with a belt. Needless to say, granddad's hard warrior masculinity does not sit well with Ruby. Although he insists that Ray is a hero, as attested by a highway sign welcoming visitors to the town, Ruby retorts that it is "a waste of a good sign." Granddad also considers serving in the military as on par with playing in the NHL, while Ruby regards enlisting as a baby-killing exercise. The old man frowns on gays in the military and contextualizes Ray's early gay proclivities as something he straightened out with physical punishment. Ray's own view of his gay identity resembles Eric McNall's in that he is clearly in love with a man yet at the same time deeply conflicted because hockey toughness allows only for heterosexuality. He derides photography as the pursuit of "fruits" because of its artistic implications, even though Stuart's picture-taking sessions with Ruby embody the consummate transgressive male gaze. Ray also laughs at Will's pink pants, and instantly assuming he is gay, addresses him as his daughter's "little gay boyfriend." Ruby chastises dad for his bigotry, appalled that despite his own leanings, he adjudicates for himself the right to discriminate against anyone with colorful pants or an artistic bent. As opposed to family film *Breakfast with Scot*, which scantily depicts any physical affection between Eric and Sam and renders their outing through stills, *Grown Up Movie Star* spends more time visually depicting the physical relationship between Ray and James, which works to check the notion that homosexuality is acceptable chiefly because of its invisibility. This visual representation all the more calls attention to Ray's absurd bigotry as a clear displacement of his own inability to accept his homosexuality because he deems it incompatible with his hockey identity.

The Sheldon Kennedy Story (Bailey, 1999), an account of NHLer Sheldon Kennedy's (Jonathan Scarfe) recovery from sexual abuse at the hands of bantam and junior coach Graham James (Robert Wisden), also illustrates players' conflation of homosexuality with sexual deviance and demonstrates that young hockey players' acculturation with respect to gender and sexuality starts early. The film shows the coach's transgression as a veritable act of hostage-taking that affects Sheldon throughout his life. In a disturbing scene in which he entraps the youngster, and forces him to stay at his home, James assaults him by brandishing a loaded shotgun, warning: "I've got the power. You will do what I say." The teen suffers the assault as well as teammates' taunts in silence, but as he grows older and stronger, he takes his frustrations out on the ice. When an opponent goads him during the faceoff, greeting, "Hey sweetie…. Homo!" Sheldon mercilessly beats him to a pulp at the first opportunity. In obvious pain, the player yells that he is crazy but the enraged Sheldon carries on with the thrashing as the crowd cheers and Graham James watches from the bench in sinister delight. The scene amplifies the beating from various angles as well as through sound effects that magnify the thumping and the opponent's painful cries, conveying the teen's assault as nothing short of transgressive. James' enjoyment of Sheldon's venting, however, also makes clear that the player resorts to violence in a desperate attempt to reclaim some measure of power, consistent with Sabo and Jansen's argument that the sporting arena operates as cultural theater where men seek to redress the victimization they experience in the social milieu.[33] The policing of heterosexuality that the opponent's abuse reveals also aligns with the "homosexual panic," which regards homosexuality in the locker room as a threat that must be disposed of through marginalization.

The abuse weighs on Sheldon's performance with the Calgary Flames and he is soon unable to focus on his game. A poignant image captures both his torment and predicament. As the Flames find themselves down by 3–0 to the Detroit Red Wings, the camera zeroes in on a goalie mask painted in red and hanging next to a hockey stick framed by a dark background. There are eyes on the mask, but no mouth. The mask hangs in such a way as to suggest itself as a dark presence, the ghost of a past that still has power because it cannot be spoken. As an ominous musical motif plays in the background, the announcer makes clear that the fans are not happy with Sheldon's performance. The powerful image conveys that the player's bondage will hold until he is able to speak out. James, however, reminds him of the peril of going public after he hears that the player is moving to press charges. Querying what terms would best describe their involvement, he taunts: "The battered wife syndrome? No. Stockholm Syndrome? No. The answer is in fact, they were hhhot for each other." Before taking his leave, he admonishes: "Don't forget to tell the cops about the good times." Sheldon's suffering is such that the judge's words in uttering the coach's conviction come as a relief: "The accused was a father figure, a mentor, and a coach; in the eyes of his young players, he controlled their lives." The press is instructed to keep the defendant's name concealed, but the player decides to grant an interview to impress on kids the need to tell on coaches' transgressive behavior, and with that courageous act his healing begins.

The scant few English-Canadian movies that deal with homosexuality recapitulate that gay identity is so disturbing to the hockey player that it borders on dysfunctional homophobia even when the character is queer. *Perfectly Normal* conveys the repressed homoerotic by activating the mild masculinity of canonical film protagonists, displaying it in what amounts to a form of drag, but also displacing homosexual attraction into violence. Films that deal with homosexuality head-on also show that the hockey archetype's profile is so narrow that artistic endeavors like a fondness for opera, theatrical costuming, photography, and a lone instance of donning pink pants renders an individual suspect, because, as discussed, artistry is deemed incompatible with the masculine hockey project for the way it subverts men's performance on the playing field and feminizes it as a form of ornamentality. In these films, the continual threat of violence, acts of brutality, and even cruelty toward small animals figure as part of the continuum of toughness that the gay hockey player resorts to in order to displace the threat of feminization. As Mike Buma suggests in discussing Messner and Sabo's work on homosexuality in sport, because homoeroticism projects a narcissistic focus on the male body, the use of violence implies a rebuttal of homoerotic tendencies.[34] While these films do not de facto bundle masculinity with heterosexuality,[35] they nonetheless make patently clear that homosexuality in professional sport remains difficult to negotiate because of the hockey player's powerfully heteronormative acculturation.

Yvan Ponton's rendition of Jacques Mercier in *Lance et compte*'s spinoff telefilm *Le Moment de vérité* (Martin, 1991) procures a similar look at homosexuality as taboo subject in the game when the character, a former coach for the Leafs and the (fictitious) National team, discovers son Jimmy (Robert Brouillette) in the embrace of another man and proceeds to beat both up before they manage to escape.[36] Jacques is shaken to the core by the abrupt revelation and runs to the bathroom to throw up. When wife Judy (Ilana Linden) finds him in a state of shock, Jacques angrily refers to Jimmy as *her* son, tersely conveying that homosexuality can instantly fracture the father-son bond because of the sports father's expectations of virility. As Amy Ransom notes in her analysis of *Lance et compte*, the series reflects very little change both in the hockey industry and in Quebec society despite efforts by government to promote inclusiveness in the game.[37] Jean-Charles' character in the *Les Boys* films appears progressive in comparison for the way the tetralogy stages his virility as that of an alpha male.[38]

The characterization of gay protagonists in the repertoire presupposes a hierarchy of identities, and suggests that because the project of sport is so intricately bound with national character, it must relegate to the background alternative expressions of individuality. Alluding to the archetype's intractability, Michael Robidoux notes that because hockey mythically dramatizes Canadian history and character, the sport does not always speak to social identity in positive ways.[39] Because sport links to default configurations of the nation as heterosexually male, the sports film stages homosexuality as deviant and outside of professional athletics, disavowing that gay or heterosexual preferences have no relationship to sports aptitude since the entertainment marketplace values athletic skills and durability regardless of sexual orientation.[40]

A very different look at homosexuality in the hockey arena is offered by Swedish TV drama *Kronjuvelerna—The Crown Jewels* (Lemhagen, 2011)—whose hockey star Petterson-Jonsson (Björn Gustafsson) fantasizes of kissing a black player from another team.[41] In a humorous take on the hockey player's propensity for brawling, Jonsson-Petterson heads straight for his man in what looks to be a bout of fisticuffs, but as the opponent-cum-love interest drops his gloves and readies himself for a fight, Petterson-Jonsson leans over and kisses him. Dumbfounded, the opponent stops in his tracks but promptly gives in to his desires and the two passionately embrace and stop the hockey game. A dream sequence that expresses Petterson-Jonsson's yearning to out himself, the scene has carnivalesque connotations for its disruption of the status quo, summoning the laughter that transgressions of hockey's inflexible heterosexuality commonly call forth. The sequence thus expresses homosexuality as a destabilizing act that subverts the hockey player's toughness.[42]

The power of the *Kronjuverlerna* scene, and any scene that depicts homosexual desire between athletes, rests in making visible a taboo subject by subverting the routine displacement of homosocial tensions into violence. The gay hockey protagonists in *Breakfast with Scot* and *Grown Up Movie Star*, in particular, have assimilated the locker room's injunctions about homophobia as incompatible with the project of heterosexual brotherhood that sport promises, and thus must embark in a journey that assists them in coming to terms with their identity however imperfectly. These films depict the struggle as heartfelt and with dollops of satire that draw on Canadian film's penchant for producing sendups of masculinity. Despite the difficulty in navigating non-normative identities in sport, the presence of the above characters in the repertoire spells progress in the social project of integration because depictions of homosexuality in sports narratives remain altogether sparse.

8

The Women's Game

Mainstream sports discourses dichotomize maleness and femaleness by reifying men's sports attainment as the standard, and women's as sub-par in comparison. This assumption normalizes the gender order as naturally occurring, leaving out that differences between male and female physiques are relative and do not exist in absolute extremes.[1] Sports media programming and film fare nonetheless routinely naturalize the gender order by prioritizing male direction and limiting female agency in sport.[2] Studies suggest a correlation between the kinds of programming that the industry produces and the gender of the talent who create and promote this content, as well as the audience this content targets.[3] The objectification of women as well as the ascendant position of male characters in televisual and film content also corroborate that U.S. media programming is overwhelmingly male-driven and male-subservient, and the sports film as a male action genre serves this demographic.[4] Canadian producers, who often play with Hollywood genre conventions technically have a better shot at inverting this paradigm, given that Canadian canonical film is less invested in shows of male dominance. Yet the task is also a difficult one since hockey romanticizes male competence and masculinity's connection to the nation.[5] Mary Louise Adams speaks to this point in her argument that naturalizing hockey as central element of Canadianicity distracts from the idea that "the hockey that really counts is undeniably men's hockey."[6]

Case in point, during the 2010 Vancouver Winter Olympics reports on both sides of the border reiterated that the Games would not be considered a success unless Canada won men's hockey gold.[7] A 2011 NBC Nightly News feature about the semi-professional Canadian Women's Hockey League in like manner underlined women's decision to play for the so-called love of the game with pizza as their sole reward for winning.[8] The report implied that women's hockey is not marketable, not unexpectedly given that corporate sponsorship and media invest in men's elite-level sport and air amateur athletic events, many of which showcase women's competition, only sparingly. Despite the rise of two women's pro leagues,[9] reports of this kind ensure that female athletes do not receive the exposure of their male counterparts, trapping them in a vicious cycle of insufficient remuneration and curtailed prospects.

Mirroring sports broadcast values, female characters in sports films that feature male athletic exemplars for the most part occupy passive spectating roles. Deborah Tudor notes that non-athletic female leads in the genre are confined to dispensing emotional support and demonstrating self-abnegating behaviors toward male characters, because the heroic male protagonist embodies the values of the social order.[10] Although plots in which female protagonists play hockey are not missing, the ratio of male-female hockey characters is quite lopsided and exemplifies high-contact sports as the stronghold of robust males. These films, however, are also significant in that they offer a glimpse of women's participation in the game—as players, coaches, and owners—and reveal the extent to which the cinema sanctions or discounts their agency.

Forging a Path for Women in the Game? *Hockey Night, Ice Angel, Go Figure, Chicks with Sticks,* National Lampoon's *Pucked* and *Les Pee Wee 3D: L'hiver qui a changé ma vie*

Richard Gruneau and David Whitson comment on the problems that faced girls and women in the game during the 1970s and 1980s and note that despite improved opportunities, traditional attitudes that frown on girls competing on boys teams remained in place.[11] The CBC telefilm *Hockey Night* (Shapiro, 1984) broaches this subject and parlays it as a critique of outmoded male practices and ideologies. Teenage goalie Cathy Yarrow (Megan Follows) assumes the controversial role when she is whisked to Parry Sound, Ontario, after mom Alice (Gail Youngs) decides to restart a teaching career following her divorce. A former goalie for the two-time city champs Scarborough Hawks, Cathy has a stellar record as a divisional finals MVP and boasts close to a dozen regular-season shutouts and a goals-against-average of 2.1, as she relays to All Stars bantam minor hockey coach Willy Leipert (Rick Moranis). After sizing up her skills, Leipert formally recruits Yarrow as starter goalie for his all-boys team. Her teammates initially balk at having a girl in the lineup, but Cathy quickly gains their respect as well as their allegiance, including that of up-and-coming scoring whiz Spear Kozak (Yannick Bisson). Business interests and the media, however, appear more reticent. Despite prior lip service about supporting every kid who wants to take part in the community's youth hockey programs, lumber tycoon and team sponsor Bill Moss (Henry Ramer) balks at Cathy's insertion in the lineup and moves to get her dropped before the championship game against top opponent North Bay. Spear and his teammates hold up the game to have Cathy reinstated, and as Moss acquiesces under duress, her expertly goaltending helps the underdog All Stars take the championship.

To illustrate the long climb faced by women and girls, *Hockey Night* stresses the premier status of the men's game by calling attention to widespread concern about Soviet ascendance in hockey. A caller to Bum Johnston's (Maury Chaykin) radio show urges reconnaissance of Soviet training methods by sending coach Leipert and several of the better players to the U.S.S.R. Johnston cites their use of innovative scientific technique sarcastically noting that the Russians can train chickens to live under water. He also argues that if acquiring such feats entails interfering with individual choice the price is not right as most Canadians would not be comfortable with such coercion: "Let's face it, how would you feel if the government told you that your five-year-old had to go to play hockey?" Johnston foregrounds Soviet repression but describes Cathy's prospects in patronizing terms, noting that although she can tell her gear apart, the women's movement is now "old business," and "I don't see too many ... [girls] playing for the New York Islanders." About Cathy's teammate and romantic interest Spear Kozak, Johnston enthusiastically observes that he is an "[up-and-] comer." Although comparable in skill, Bum disparages Yarrow while upholding Kozak's status as power forward.

Johnston also argues against mixed teams by painting a picture of girls "chok[ing] under pressure" and unending lawsuits by parents who seek to have them reinstated when teams drop them from the lineup.

Moss' counsel Kevin McLeod (Robin Ward) informs Leipert that although Cathy is legally entitled to be part of the All Stars, informally the company discourages female participation because it lowers the level of play and because of parents' touchiness about co-ed teams. Moss, for his part, urges Leipert to drop Cathy and notes, "It's nothing personal against the girl.... It's for the sake of the game." Later he bellyaches over pressure from the Chamber of Commerce regarding his Lumberettes' prospects against North Bay as well as increasing queries from parents demanding tryouts for their daughters. When Leipert retorts, "So what?" Moss argues he will not negotiate Cathy's position on the team and threatens to drop his sponsorship of the All-Stars, jeopardizing their game against North Bay. The film augments business interests' bias by way of a sequence in which coach Leipert takes the team on a two-mile run around the hilly town's perimeter. Cathy and Spear soon outdistance the others, and as the extremely fit goalie is set to beat the team ace to the finish line, she lets up in the final moments to avoid embarrassing him. Spear notices and chides her for it. Cathy's superlative fitness is nevertheless clear, a potent symbol of her commitment to the game. Her appreciable aptitudes and dedication in short order expose the hostility of big sponsors and the media as sheer chauvinism, and designate the plight of girls access to hockey as nothing short of an ideological struggle.[12]

Cathy's bigoted treatment also assumes significance in view of lumber, construction, and other industries' historical support of regional sports. Gruneau and Whitson note that early on the magnates of these industries were drawn to amateur sports because they mirrored their own entrepreneurial spirit and procured a superior platform for expressing a commitment to public culture.[13] The film shows the sponsor's role in honing children as a form of social capital, as Moss exhorts team members to remember they represent the community as All Stars. Spear Kozak's assertion that "When I'm seventeen I'm supposed to be in the NHL" also illustrates industry's part in helping develop young talent for elite-level hockey. Because this sponsorship favors boys while discouraging the dreams of girls, Moss' lofty encouragement about working hard and attaining something of value as community exemplars leaves little doubt that the game that matters is men's hockey. *Hockey Night* signals the subordinate status of females in the game by way of Cathy's move from a larger urban center, where she honed her skills, to the hometown of NHLer Bobby Orr where, without all-girl teams and thanks to the provincial mindset of local sponsors and media, her participation becomes a matter of public debate.

The archetypal motif of the father's link to the game also conveys Cathy's cheerless situation. The father's presence in *Hockey Night* is felt throughout the story but never visually noted. Nevertheless, it assumes significance because of Cathy's continual mention. Although dad was her first coach, he now lives across the country in Vancouver and for all intents and purposes remains largely inaccessible. Mom Alice praises Cathy for making the team as evidence of her favorable adjustment but she takes no active part in furthering her daughter's trailblazing role in the community. Indeed, Alice appears distracted by her teaching duties and engrossed with dating eligible prospects who foreground the father's absence all the more since they have no interest in hockey. The film's father-daughter bond in sport by way of "presence-through-absence" is reminiscent of a similar motif in 1940s Hollywood cinema that poignantly expresses the daughter's psychological need for her father.[14] In a decade where the recuperation of fatherhood is a central theme in the cinema, the absence of dad in Cathy's life corroborates that the cultural battle for women and girls enfranchisement in the game is a lonely one.

Addressing the topicality of the CBC's dramatic content during the 1980s, Mary Jane Miller observes that they reveal less certainty about "who women are and what they can or should do," but films like *Hockey Night*, which deal with hockey's value system, still speak to matters of enduring social concern.[15] The film explores these anxieties by depicting the pros and cons of embedding Cathy in an all-boys team in a game against a rugged opponent. The rough-and-tumble Midland Nationals go at the All Star goalie during most of the game, a strategy that backfires because it gets them out of position and allows Spear to score. The opponent's harassment, however, continues unabated throughout the game and when one of their starring players purposely catches the back of Cathy's head with his stick, she grabs him by the ankles and takes him down in short order. Cued in by a teammate, Spear goes after the unsportsmanlike player and promptly gets himself—and Cathy—thrown out of the game. Aggravated, the goalie lets her teammate know, "Don't do me any favors, ok?" as Johnston from the media booth calls attention to the official's questionable call by observing that, "she was provoked."

The scene is invaluable in underscoring Cathy's commitment, durability, and skill, since despite continual harassment the opponent is unable to throw her off her game. The young Nationals also clearly view Cathy as the All Stars' weak link because she's a girl. This intimidation, enabled by codes that allow players the discretion to deploy physical tactics, therefore also registers as a form of gatekeeping that preserves hockey as all-male enclave. Because hassling the goalie automatically prompts swift retaliation, the opponent's borderline actions also relieve the All Stars of their most valuable player. Although reaffirming Cathy's suitability for the game, the scene poignantly captures the quandaries experienced by girls who play on boys teams, as they are targeted by unsportsmanlike opponents and unduly burdened by teammates' actions that nonetheless hew to the game's normative codes.

Cathy Yarrow (Megan Follows) in goal for the All Stars in *Hockey Night* (CBC Still Photo Collection).

Cathy's heroic endurance in pressure-cooker situations all the more underscores Moss' unethical actions to drop her from the team in time for the North Bay matchup because he clearly views hockey as a preeminent stage for male performance that also reflects on his business. As he adamantly tells coach Leipert: "I'm running a business here ... and when people see Mr. Lumber's All Stars on the ice they think about my biz and that's the name of the game." The young players in stark contrast display a clear moral compass argue for boycotting the long-awaited matchup. Declaring, "screw North Bay!" and remarking that Cathy "is really good" and Moss' actions are "not fair," the players endearingly contend that if they refuse to play, Moss "will give us all the girls we want." At the arena, Spear goes missing just as Moss is set to introduce him to VIPs. He is off to fetch Cathy and returns in time for the faceoff, halting the proceedings by rallying his teammates: "Where's the game?" "In the head!" "Who are we?" "Number one!" Down to the wire and anxious about losing face, Moss accedes to let Cathy back on to the team amid the crowd's cheers, enabling the All Stars to win the crucial game.

Hockey Night airs the pressures on young hockey players by parents and influential community leaders who expect them to go places while upholding outworn masculinity norms that counter those very prospects. The squad's decision to publicly demonstrate their allegiance to their teammate and jeopardize their place in the tournament also shows hockey's acculturating force in honing youngsters as genuine form of social capital in ways unaccounted for by their inflexible elders. The film gives ample evidence that girls can play hockey with the best of them, but it also argues that because the institution of sport preserves the values of the dominant gender regime and upholds males as the standard, changes must be spearheaded with their help. Cathy's eventual triumph announces that through progressive forces like visionary coach Willy Leipert and the rest of her teammates, there is hope for girls fullfledged participation in the game. The closing lyrics reinforce the sentiment by exhorting teens to take a stand and take these efforts to their conclusion.

Deborah Tudor notes that in the cinema women characters have often been "reduce[d] to the body" as locus for male desire. To offset these expectations, she suggests re-imagining the female physique's potential, even though sport privileges assumptions about the body that reproduce the gender order.[16] *Ice Angel* (Erschbamer, 2000) takes a stab at this refiguration in its depiction of a male hockey player who dies before his time and returns to the material plane in the body of a female figure skater. The TV movie's hockey protagonist is Matt Clark (Aaron Smolinski), who as a star forward and captain of an up-and-coming Team USA, is counting on a good run alongside his buddy, goalie Ray (Thomas Calabro). Matt is a rugged type who has no trouble cutting to the chase. He prods teammates to dig deeper by telling them they're playing "like a bunch of pansies!" and like the storied tough guy, he drinks his early morning raw egg and juice libation straight from the blender. During the U.S.–Czech Olympic matchup, however, a wayward puck that hits him in the head and leaves him for dead. Soon he finds himself in an in-between place where he is promptly told that he is not supposed to be there. To Matt's disbelief, an angel named Allan (Brendan Beiser) has botched the job and taken the wrong man. In order to fulfill Matt's Olympic promise, the best Heaven can do is send him back in the body of Sarah Bryan (Nicholle Tom), a Games-bound figure skater who has hit her head while skating. There is only only caveat: Matt can have contact with loved ones, including girlfriend Danielle (Judy Tylor), only if they come across him on their life path.

When Matt wakes up in the hospital as Sarah, she promptly informs Alan that she will shred his wings for the blunder. Once home, and to the chagrin of her parents, Sarah continues to reach for the beer can, the milk carton, and the cigar case, and wears hockey pads and a helmet to figure skating practice, complaining that she's "been drafted into the froo-froo army." Taking spill after spill in repeated attempts at a double-toe loop, she ignores coach Parker's (Alan Thicke) instructions, and brusquely lets him know that she needs no help in finding her bearings when it comes to "this stupid sport." Through sheer persistence, Sarah manages to regain her footing and make the team as well as befriend rival competitor Tracy (Tara Lipinski). At the Games she comes across Ray, as well as Danielle, who much to her surprise, is pregnant. Crushed, Sarah immediately suspects Ray, but she discovers that the child is Matt's. Touched and reassured, she attends the U.S.–Russia game with Danielle, but quickly gauges that the U.S. team, sidelined by the loss of Matt, is struggling. Unable to contain herself, Sarah bursts into the locker room and rallies the troops, urging Ray to step up to the plate and take over the team's reins, in turn spurring Team USA to rally in the third period and win the gold. Having seen to her former team's success, Sarah must now land the formidable triple axel. She tells herself that if a team was able to score four times in a single period, she too can perform the feat required of her. She does so, instantaneously letting go of her former identity to finally and fully inhabit her female body and embark on a new life.

Ice Angel showcases the oppositional aspects of sport in film by depicting the hockey player-figure skater pairing through clichéd gender representations. Figure skaters are a "Barbie convention," while hockey players "are the ones who never evolved." In this universe of opposites, hockey is a "Neanderthal" sport fraught with danger while figure skating is replete with catty women who do not value friendship. Admonishing his charges to avoid hockey as a cross-training exercise, coach Parker warns about its dangers, drawing a blank on Sarah Bryan's own "almost" fatal accident. Matt/Sarah nonetheless deploys team-building strategies during a rollerblade game to bond with other figure skaters, galvanizing their competitive energies, and beating a street hockey team made up of young men. Replaying gender stereotypes, the film assigns hockey the role of fostering peer friendships, the kind of team-gelling that popular film depicts as absent in figure skating.[17] Sarah bridges the stereotypical image of the glamorous, hyper-feminized figure skater and the traditional macho image of the hockey player to update gender roles for young audiences in and out of the sports arena.[18]

In keeping with the intertextuality of sport in film, *Ice Angel* also depicts hockey through its dual Hollywood film signatures, portraying Matt as a tough man and the U.S. team through "Miracle on Ice" referents that communicate that the squad will score an unexpected last minute goal. Miracle imagery surfaces in the hospital the moment Matt regains consciousness as Sarah when the nurse exclaims: "It's a miracle!" Although a Czech player takes Matt out of the game—likely a proxy for the Czech's 1998 Nagano Olympics gold victory—and in Heaven the forward adamantly states that he wishes to come back as an American and not as a "lousy Czech," the final U.S. game in which the Americans score four goals tellingly comes against the Russian team. *Ice Angel* intertextually references the four tallies the 1980 U.S. team scored on the Soviets to defeat them in the Lake Placid semifinal.[19] The film also reiterates a number of motifs that are part of "Miracle on Ice" lore: the countdown to the game's end, the crowd roaring "USA! USA!" and the final call by the announcer: "It's a miracle!" Matt/Sarah's comment "I know what it's like to be cut short of an Olympic dream," also recalls coach Herb Brooks' own termination from the 1960 U.S. hockey lineup.

Sarah Bryan (Nicholle Thom, center), Nancy Kerrigan (left) and Tara Lipinski (right) ready for a game of rollerblade hockey (*Ice Angel*, ABC Family/Photofest).

Although Matt's expertise would have naturally inclined Sarah to search out opportunities in the women's game, *Ice Angel*'s focus on Olympic figure skating preempts this possibility. Indeed, the movie appears to take its cue from the 1998 Nagano Olympics where Tara Lipinski, who plays Sarah's nemesis, took the gold for the U.S. in women's figure skating. Although men's hockey did not make it into the medal round, the Nagano Olympics inaugurated women's hockey competition in which the U.S. captured gold. The hockey–figure skating theme suggests that the Miracle motif in the picture both operates as a form of wish fulfillment and confirms the preeminence of men's hockey. *Ice Angel*'s choice of these two sports is also not surprising given the interrelationship between sports cinema and sports broadcasts. Indeed, Olympic figure skating has consistently drawn good ratings on U.S. TV networks and during men's hockey competition commentators invariably look back on the "Miracle on Ice" victory. Although in the sports film these stereotypes indicate that athletes from these two sports have nothing in common but the ice as work domain, in fielding a hero who experiences gender dysphoria, *Ice Angel* ultimately enacts a magical reconciliation that synthesizes gender roles and suggests the need for hardier female protagonists.

The Disney Channel movie *Go Figure* (McDougall, 2005) expresses a similar theme by way of a young protagonist who must cross over into hockey to actualize her figure skating dreams. Fourteen-year-old ace Katelin Kingsford (Jordan Hinson), who is bent on landing the #1 spot at U.S. Nationals, knows that the way to the top goes through renowned coach Natasha Gobermann (Cristine Rose). Although Katelin has no way to finance her lessons, she remains adamant about sticking to her master plan: "I have to train with her. She's Russian." Natasha, who affectionately dubs her young charge "Sputnik" for her energetic approach to the sport, pulls some strings and secures a scholarship for Katelin at Buckston Academy where she coaches. The catch is that the young prospect must join the women's Eagles hockey team as part of the deal. Despite the formidable task, Katelin remains undaunted: "They're just girls, except bigger, meaner, with unconditioned hair. I can do this." Still, she must keep her identity as a figure skater secret since only the hockey coach is in on the ruse and her teammates sneer at "twirl girls." Struggling to balance tough hockey and figure skating schedules, and victim of a prank staged by one of her figure skater rivals, Katelin goes home disheartened. There she figures she is not a quitter and, still in her hockey jersey, decides to "kick some ice" and return to Buckston to her newfound friendships. Faced with the option of taking part in her Olympic figure skating qualifier and contesting the East Coast hockey championship, Katelin votes with her feet to help her hockey teammates. Chagrined, Natasha urges Katelin to reconsider: "This is your shot…. And what you do with it will define you for the rest of your life." The hockey game over, Katelin arrives barely in time to take part in the competition, and in her hockey skates makes it onto the women's national figure skating squad in front of her cheering hockey teammates.

Go Figure targets the nine-to-fourteen-year-old 'tween demographic by way of the Disney Channel's blend of comedy, fantasy, and preteen angst.[20] The film emphasizes the protagonist's charm principally through her figure skater attributes since the sport approximates athletics' traditional function in honing female grace, poise, and decorum. As in other Disney films, hockey in *Go Figure* is synonymous with teamwork and an augmented social identity, and during her hockey itinerary, Katelin must surmount the shadow aspects of figure skating's hyper-glamourized ideal. Teammate Ronnie (Amy Halloran), a gritty player of large build and gruff demeanor, at first questions Katelin's status as a bona fide hockey player because she regularly shies away from brawling. She suspects her of being a member of the "twirl girl" club, who make it difficult for women hockey players to secure respect. Once Katelin integrates into the team, however, she insists on engaging in the rough-and-tumble aspects of the sport by tussling with opponents and blocking for other players. *Go Figure* thus reaffirms an unambiguous element of grit in configuring female players and mirrors hockey's role in producing durable females. Of the hockey roster, however, the hardier but still charming Katelin models the female athletic standard of femininity. Although her figure skating competitors are catty and spiteful, Ronnie's excessive female masculinity as a hockey player also strays from the ideal. And while roommate Hollywood Henderson (Whitney Sloan) helps the young figure skater adjust to the game, she is also fashioned as distant from the female athletic norm because of her keen interest in new age subjects and the latest fads. Teammate Mojo (Tania Gunadi), a comically superstitious player of Asian descent who resembles a similar character type in baseball films, also borders on the picturesque.

Although Katelin never loses her likeability, the message in *Go Figure* is that, despite her dedication, she succeeds because she leaves behind her unsociable tendencies. Family fare often frowns on young characters all-work-no-play attitude because it borders on athletic professionalization and veers away from the idealized realm of "pure sport." Talented male hockey protagonists in Disney films who suffer from similar narcissism have their weaknesses redressed by coaches and/or teammates who uphold standards of sporting conduct that contain these excesses. In popular film, however, figure skating operates as a carrier for individual goals and teammates are an oxymoron. Fictive coaches like Natasha, for their part, are not overly concerned with the social trappings of team sports because they prioritize excellence in technique and aesthetic performance to help their charges garner top grades. Writers must thus devise ruses to switch figure skating characters into teams sports, however temporarily, to have them hone their social skills and help mold them into social capital for the community. Douglas Brode notes of Disney film values that, "when dealing with society, community loyalty is far more valuable than rugged individualism." In Disney fashion, however, the hero must also achieve "success in ... [his or her] own mind, and ... [his or her] own terms."[21] Hence, at the film's outset Katelin firmly states that she's not headed to Buckston Academy to make friends but to skate. By the end of the movie, she delights in having changed her ways and become part of a larger endeavor—"a family," as she notes—while her main figure skating rival remains personally stunted by cutthroat competitive instincts.

Conforming to the didactic Disney sports film formula, the protagonist earns her figure skating victory because of her superior moral standing and retains the newfound friendships derived from her social hockey experience. Like Sarah Bryan in *Ice Angel*, Katelin's character performs a bridge function to upgrade gender norms by incorporating a measure of toughness to contemporary ideals of femininity, even as both films ultimately configure their main protagonists as figure skaters. In keeping with the Disney Company's business interests in youth hockey,[22] the Disney Channel's "Follow Your Dreams" segment, featured during an airing of the film,[23] also showcases a teenager who plays hockey and relays to viewers that girls hockey is the fastest growing sector of the game as attested by the availability of college scholarships. In underscoring the existence of new opportunities for women and girls in the sport, this segment operates as addendum to the film, and conveys that girls should and, indeed, are playing hockey in greater numbers.

Chicks with Sticks/Hockey Mom/Anyone's Game (Skogland, 2004) breaks ground by recognizing the women's game after a decades-long uphill climb. The movie secured production rights after the Canadian women's hockey gold at the 2002 Salt Lake Winter Olympics[24] and it develops its main theme through the figure of foiled Olympic hockey prospect Paula Taymore (Jessalyn Gilsig). One of her biggest fans, her bouncy seven-year-old boy Stewart (Andrew Chalmers) queries whether she will ever play again, relaying that he expects mom to demolish the opposition. Brother Ross (Kevin James) once in a while recruits Paula to play incognito on a recreational league men's team, but she must deal with crank comments when exposed: "Two minutes for shopping!" Taunted by the male players, Paula takes on a dare to compete against the all-male Chiefs squad and issues a call to "any woman over the age of 18 that lives 200 miles within this table." Sifting through unruly, unfocused, and mismatched prospects, Paula finally puts together a contender team, the Black Widows raises $86,000 to confirm countrywide support for the women's game. She must subsequently deal with getting fans in the stands and sponsors on board, while battling treachery in the ranks and backhanded tactics on the men's side. On game day, the Black Widows beat the Chiefs with a decisive 6–4 and scores the $140,000 cache on the line, giving Paula the green light to take the women's game pro.

Paula opens the story as "somebody who's good at something but didn't quite get there,"[25] in the words of screenwriter Don Truckey,[26] but she also manages to carve a second chance at the game. Her journey, however, is also full of fits and starts, since she must counter misperceptions of women's hockey as inherently inferior to the men's game. When she is interviewed on a radio show, a caller offers that women do not have the upper body strength to effectively compete against men, and Paula quickly rectifies the misconception by adding that women have successfully worked around this issue, and indeed, "some people consider women's hockey to be a different game...." She refutes assumptions about the inherent superiority of the larger, more muscular male physique and notes that "the female is better suited to power skating," "we play a thinking game," and "plenty of Hall-of-Famers are no bigger than us...." Paula's arguments reaffirm hockey as a precinct where skill rather than size rules the day. When a player brings in one of Wayne Gretzky's first sticks from his tenure in Sault Ste. Marie to boost the team's confidence, the act reclaims the game in the same manner.

Chicks with Sticks also recapitulates many of the unpalatable dynamics depicted in *Hockey Night*. On the fateful day, the Chiefs turn up dressed as the Hanson Brothers to send the message that hockey is a man's game. But they soon find themselves trying to stave off a defeat, and the captain warns his teammates to ratchet up their game or they will lose to "a bunch of bugs." Subverting *Slap Shot*'s homage to old-time hockey as populist resistance against the machinations of power blocs, *Chicks with Sticks* depicts the Chiefs as bullies who deploy aggression to keep women in marginalized positions in the sport. The film also displaces formulaic notions of female athleticism as adversely affected by nature,[27] by fashioning the women's approach as beyond the terse sensibilities of the male contingent. As Paula directs her squad in meditative relaxation techniques prior to the contest, the men who are spying on them are addled and attribute her unorthodox approach to the influence of a Black Widows player who is a self-described Wiccan. The women's strategies are also informed by the power of meaningful relationships as well as by skill rather than retaliation, even as they uphold the evolution of women's hockey into a more robust game.

Chicks with Sticks organically fashions females at the center rather than at the periphery of the sport by drawing up characters that combine skill with a measure of grit. Because landscape typically alludes to characters in Canadian film, the small town of Okotoks, Alberta, authenticates the women's game as an organic cultural form. The neighborliness of small Western communities who help Paula and her team garner much-needed funds also suggests that the authenticity of women's hockey rests in its non-corporatized roots. And although the hockey prospects of *Chicks with Sticks* first emerge as scatterbrained, unfocused, and less-than-competent athletes, inflecting the team-building process with the sabotaging of women by women usually seen in stories about female athletes,[28] ultimately they succeed in demonstrating the viability of the women's game.

Paula, the film's dramatic focus, embodies the attractive Venus type[29] who is both energetic and competent, even as her character walks a type rope between self-abnegation and self-realization. As the *Hockey Mom* U.S. title suggests, Paula's parental role is an important aspect of her identity, and her son's entreaties that she take up the game partly account for her re-entry into competitive hockey after her divorce. Aaron Baker, however, regards the role of mothering as limiting the discursive scope of women in sports by endorsing the preservation of so-called feminine attributes that entail support for the goals of familial and social others like mates and offspring.[30] Deborah Tudor makes a similar argument in noting that in film those very aspects keep female leads in subordinate positions. Paula's character nonetheless is also informed by a decisive agency. Her ready dismissal of love interest Steve Cooper (Jason Priestley), when he expresses doubt in the Black Widows' ability to beat the Chiefs, also underscores her faith in the women's hockey project.

Although *Chicks with Sticks* certainly advances the idea that women can and should displace assumptions of hockey as male purview, it also validates females participation in the game by way of NHL iconography. Steve Cooper reconsiders his doubts about a Black Widows victory, and presents Paula with a mock of the Stanley Cup as a memento of her first win with her pro team. Allusions to Wayne Gretzky, which connote the rebirth of NHL hockey after the physical game of the seventies, also tap national league iconography even while pointing to intelligent tactics and superlative talent. In referencing the men's game to validate women's sports participation,[31] however, the script fails to link Paula's Black Widows to the history of women's hockey in Canada. Although sidelined from the game's institutional framework, women's history of participation is almost as deep as the men's.[32] Julie Stevens and Carly Adams observe that even as the women's game never reached the mythic status of men's hockey, early female hockeyists successfully sketched a trajectory of their own in Eastern metropoles and colleges as well as on Western and small Northern town teams.[33] The struggle of women in the game, then, is to effectively return home, as Paula does, and reconstitute fully as part of the Canadian cultural landscape.

If *Hockey Night* and *Chicks with Sticks* advance the women's project in hockey, National Lampoon's *Pucked* (Hiller, 2006) checks its progress by contouring female athletes as atavistic and hypersexualized. As the National Lampoon franchise suggests, the film parodies the women's game by subverting female athleticism and refiguring it as male sexual fantasy. The protagonist who does the honors is lawyer-turned-drifter Frank Hopper (John Bon Jovi) who lives off his sister's handouts and one day hits on the idea of starting a women's league. Modeling his World Wide Women's Hockey League enterprise on pro-wrestling and the WNBA, he surmises that "there are millions of hockey fans out there!" and that his venture is sure to serve this demographic. Even though his presentation to prospective investors fails miserably, he finds a way to realize his dream thanks to the torrent of unsolicited credit cards that arrive in the mail. This, after all, is the mid–2000s when even babies and dogs become proud cardholders. Armed with a hefty credit line, Frank and best friend Carl (David Faustino) refurbish an old arena and in short order prepare for tryouts.

Rather than the skilled athletes of *Chicks with Sticks*, the players in *Pucked* can hardly wait to hit the ice to start a fight. As one of the prospects notes: "Ice Capades.... I've done that. No fun. I'm dying to knock the shit out of somebody." Although invariably feisty, the women also resemble female models and pinups, because as Frank notes, "men love to watch [beautiful] women beat the heck out of each other." To bring home the point that his players "are going to be beautiful," he dubs the two starter teams Foxes and Swans. Since these characters are not actual hockey players, they must be suitably foul-mouthed so that their speech connotes the feistiness of the hockey player and her repertoire of abilities. Blonde player Danielle (Danielle James) spoofs French-Canadian women in the game as lusty bombshells, the equivalent of oversexed Québécois goalie Jacques "Le Coq" Grande in *The Love Guru*. She counters the coach's suggestion to move quicker and make better use of her stick with a nasty rejoinder: "I'll shove it up your ass, fatso!" Like *Chicks with Sticks* and *Go Figure*, *Pucked* also inserts into the mix a tough, masculine female player—forward Wendy Delvecchio (Dot Jones)—on whom the team heavily depends to win games. Confused for a man at first blush, she turns out to be Frank's idea of a real hockey player, the only team member that can skate, puckhandle, and shoot. She is also purportedly easily dented, however, as she makes clear that despite being all muscle, she is "very feminine" and in need of a man. Frank manages to retain her services by fixing her up with diminutive Carl, and the partners get the inaugural league game off to a good start. As expected, a fight between the Swans and Foxes breaks out almost immediately,

Prospects show up for hockey tryouts in National Lampoon's *Pucked* (National Lampoon Productions/Photofest).

plunging the referees into the proceedings and calling forth seventies imagery of police visiting the locker room as the cops arrive soon after. Their target, however, is Frank, whom the credit card industry has been tailing and plans to make a symbol of consumptive excess. In the end, however, he successfully handles his own defense and keeps the league afloat thanks to his players' credit cards.

A satire of hockey that is little more than a succession of fights and diatribes, *Pucked* falls flat given its depiction of players as nasty and oversexed. The film reiterates the idea of hockey as a zany excuse for brawling, while underscoring the foremost status of the male spectator's gaze in women's sport. Frontal shots of female fans baring their chests at the Hansons in *Slap Shot* metamorphose into a frontal slow motion shot of a bare-chested player hitting the glass in a fantasy sequence. The intertextual reference to *Slap Shot* in *Pucked* subverts the idea of hockey as legitimate arena for female athletic performance by objectifying the female body and inverting women's agency. The film's repurposing of nudity also disfigures hockey to such an extent that it is little more than a violent, sexual spectacle preeminently designed for male consumption.

Hockey in *Pucked* is, after all, merely an addendum, a blue-collar sideshow of fights between women in provocative, pseudo-athletic outfits to entertain the viewer until the moral of the story arrives: an indictment of the finance industry for creating a credit bubble that peaked between 2006 and 2008 with serious consequences for the domestic and global economies. The film's finale, which signals the Foxes' and Swans' desire to perpetuate their disenfranchisement, communicate that women are eager participants in haphazard schemes that disempower their agency by settling for suspect jobs. Frank's ideas of women's hockey resemble Claremont's plans in *Slap Shot 2* to grow a sporting empire by appending the bodies of athletes to the sale of tickets and luxury boxes, except that the former lacks the mogul's resources or network. Although women's hockey in *Pucked* is essentially a gimmick to call attention to protracted credit card abuse, the film's ending suggests that women's active role in pimping themselves out amounts to a sound business decision, an idea that the Super-Chiefs ran with and did not turn out so well, and which the original *Slap Shot* actively protests through Ned's strip tease finale.

Pucked, however, is also consistent with the rest of the hockey repertoire in affixing a pioneering stamp on the women's game. The film dramatizes Americans' prerogative to actualize enterprising ideas, even as the protagonist's notion of women's hockey amounts to its very corruption. Thus, Frank unabashedly underlines that "dreamers built this country" and "all your dreams can come true." In his mind, then, the potential for the league is endless, consonant with the idea of Westering as a limitless project. Along with a franchise of "beautiful women that can really play," he fantasizes about television contracts, team merchandise, and other derivative businesses that hold the Turnerian promise of wealth but in Turnerian form also guarantee nothing. Although by film's end Frank reiterates his intention to see the new league through, his plans to keep it going have a tentative feel and lend weight to a remark by a prospective investor at the film's outset: "This is worst than the guy who tried to sell us mall-wrestling." Even as the film aligns women's hockey with imagery of dreaming, the capitalist enterprise, and the American story of social and material ascendance, much like the 2011 NBC Nightly News feature that spotlights women athletes playing hockey for pizza, *Pucked* ultimately communicates that women's hockey is not marketable.

The Quebec popular movie *Les Pee Wee 3D: L'hiver qui a changé ma vie—The Pee Wees 3D: The Winter that Changed My Life* (Tessier, 2012), a film that garnered over CAD 1 million at the box office,[34] features a protagonist who draws on the strong female leads of Canadian film and recovers *Pucked*'s buffoonish characterization of women in the game. The protagonist in question is Julie Morneau (Alice Morel-Michaud), a young goalie who plays for the all-boys Lynx team in a small Quebec town and dreams of becoming the first female netminder to win the Quebec World Hockey Pee Wee Tournament. To accomplish her objective, she calls on the services of hockey whiz Janeau Trudel (Antoine-Olivier Pilon), who upon his mother's death moves into the neighborhood with dad Carl (Normand Daneau). Janeau's impressive skills, in turn, spark the anger and jealousy of team captain Joey Boulet (Rémi Goulet), who is under pressure from dad Luke (Claude Legault), a former Philadelphia Flyers prospect, to score flashy goals.

A determined, strappy, and charming Katelin-like figure who despite her diminutive stature does double duty as the team's head and heart, Julie keeps order in the ranks and prevents the squad's pickup games from devolving into fights. On occasion savvier than coach Mike Boulanger (Guy Nadon), Julie boasts an impressive female toughness that far outstrips that of her teammates. She instructs Janeau to put on an attitude commensurate with his stellar talents and once on the team, keeps the pressure on him just enough by humorously signaling that she's watching his every move. She also calls Joey, who is intent on teaching Janeau "who is boss," as he puts it, on his heavy-handed tactics and takes on masculinity training of backup goalie Éric (Gabriel Verdier), who in sendup form is afraid of incoming pucks. Like the proverbial coach entrusted with preparing charges for their mission by honing character through pain, she leads four other players in Éric's desensitization drill, as she calls it, and before the puck-firing starts exclaims with utter conviction: *"Le hockey n'est pas un pays démocratique. Le hockey c'est la guerre!*" ("Hockey is not a democratic realm/arena. Hockey is war!"). Before evening practice, she also humorously reminds mom Sylvie (Édith Cochrane) to avoid major shows of affection at the rink.

Her role as squad leader is relevant in that both Janeau and Joey, the team's best players, have "missing mothers"—the former's has passed on, and the latter's is being kept out of the loop through subterfuge—and their respective dads do not operate with the steadiness of the archetypal father in sport. Carl, still grieving from the death of his wife, is too feeble a character to provide any emotional support for Janeau and take up mom's place in the game. Luke, for his part, is overly hard and stultifying a masculine figure who also teaches Joey all the wrong lessons. He chides his son that what he does reflects on him, and yells that he must not spend an extra second lying flat on the ice like a wimp. He also interferes with team gelling by prodding Joey to prove to everyone that he is the captain. Like Craig in *Sticks and Stones* who, concerned with son K.P.'s stats, celebrates his puck-hogging and hotdogging displays without discerning that anything is amiss, Luke instills in Joey the very individualist mindset that the augmented didacticism that the sport and family genres seek to expunge. He promotes the professionalization of youth play, which family fare equates with the game's very corruption, by offering his son $10 for each tally and $50 for a hat trick. He also conducts skating drills in his backyard, trains Joey like a boxer, and invests in six weeks of hockey summer camp, including one month at Don Cherry's school in Toronto, to mom Line's (Sophie Prégent) utter dismay. Like Craig, Luke has lost touch with the reality that Joey is just a peewee. The film's very mention of Don Cherry, whose imprint communicates a decided stout masculinity, conveys that Carl and Joey are on the wrong track, since in Quebec films Cherry consistently shows up as a *bête noire* and as anti–Francophone.

When Julie is sidelined and forced to rest because of an encounter with a much larger opponent during the tournament's first qualifying game, Joey stoops to lower depths by relaying to the opponent during a faceoff that Janeau has a weak ankle, an injury he himself caused. The opponent naturally exploits the advantage by delving out a couple of slashes and taking Janeau out of the game. Joey next proceeds to steal the puck from another teammate during a breakaway to score and send the Lynx to the tournament. In good didactic form, the film renders the puck-lifting maneuver through a slow motion medium close-up, and the ensuing celebration aurally by way of the sole echoing cheers of Joey on center ice and dad Carl in the stands to convey their misguided attitude and the shock of those present. Joey's lack of sportsmanship prompts a melee on the ice as the miffed teammate accuses him of dastardly behavior and the hotshot punches him in return. A parallel scuffle breaks out in the stands as the teammate's dad takes on Luke when he refuses to acknowledge his son's bad behavior. As the crowd boos, to coach Mike's mortification, one of the moms on the opponent bench yells: "A bunch of losers! And they get to go to Quebec instead of us!" When coach Mike gets a wind of Joey's subterfuge and his reasons for acting up, he bans Luke from practices and subsequent games much to the tough guy's chagrin.

As expected, Julie is impatient about getting back on the ice and resents the enforced rest despite the concussion she is nursing. Before leaving for Quebec City, Janeau impresses on her that her health is more important than the tournament, but she insists her injury is not serious, all the while aggressively bouncing a rubber ball against the wall in frustration. Intent on seeing her dreams come to fruition, when the doctor's call arrives Julie picks up the phone and fakes her mother's voice, and subsequently convinces her to drive her to

Quebec City. The film intimates that Julie's attitude is reckless but that the Lynx need her help in the finals against a far superior Russian team straight out of Disney's *Miracle* and headed by another coach named Viktor with the same bad attitude. As one of the Lynx despondently notes while taking in the *Colisée* after their first off-ice meeting with the Russian opponent: "Without Julie, there's no way."

Julie and mom arrive with Carl in tow just in time for the final, but with Éric in net the Lynx are outscored by several goals. During the second intermission, in a sendup of Coach Brooks' speech in *Miracle*, Mike tells his charges how proud he is of their effort but that the opponent is too strong and it is not the end of the world. When Joey interjects that there is still a period of play left, the coach rehearses the sport-as-fun formula and counsels his charges to enjoy themselves, leaving the peewees disconcerted. Once the coach effectively goes missing, the film sets the stage for Julie's re-entry into the game. Young Éric stands up and pronounces to the team that she should take over: "Julie, let's go, man!" But a downcast Julie confesses she cannot play because she has not yet healed and exhorts: "Listen guys, I'm here. I'm with you. But it's your game. It's your game, Eric, your tournament. You've gotten us this far. Go all the way." Janeau also chimes in that he wants to hear the crowd roar: "We can score five goals in a period. I've done it before." When the rest note that the Russians are always on him, he counters that they can take advantage of their strategy and urges: "We can't end this here. We can't stop dreaming. Not now!" After a rallying cry, the squad files out as Julie encourages: "*Allez-y!*" ("Go forth!").

As soon as the locker room door shuts, Julie breaks down in tears over her unrealized dreams. She casts a forlorn figure that the camera renders with poignancy as she sits alone with her back against the cold locker room wall. In short order, however, she is back on the bench and when she overhears the coach placing Janeau and Joey on the same line she perks up. Once the Lynx tie the game and the Russian coach calls a time out, Julie rallies the troops with the chant: "Go, let's go!" Taking a page out of Disney's *Miracle*, the assistant coach happily remarks to coach Mike: "Viktor is panicking." Much like Russell-Brooks, Mike also encourages: "They're nervous, boys. Keep it up!" The Lynx predictably end up taking the game and the tournament title, and as they do, Janeau glimpses his mom in the crowd smiling, and immediately after Carl approaches the glass and tells his son that he did a great job. In "Miracle on Ice" fashion, the team gathers around Julie and comes together in celebration. As they have their pictures taken, they also have their index fingers up in the air to signal "We're number one!"

Like *Pucked*, *Les Pee Wee* fields imagery of dreaming from the very outset. When Julie feelingly tells Janeau about playing in the Pee Wee Worlds, she notes: "*C'est mon rêve*" ("It's my dream"). Janeau however resists the call of the hero's journey and sarcastically replies, "Dreams are fun. Don't give up." When Janeau and Carl have an argument about dad not making the tournament because of work duties, Janeau lets him know that he no longer hopes for anything. When Carl arrives at the arena in time for the final, he entreats his son to keep dreaming, "because when you win, that's dreams coming true." Janeau's locker room rally to his teammates about not giving up and truncating their dreams mid-game shows he has assimilated his father's directives.

While in line with the Francophone Dream in sport the film gives the Lynx the win in "Miracle on Ice" form, Julie's own Manon Rhéaume–like[35] dreams summarily come to naught as shown by her dejection in the locker room scene. The exceedingly didactic *Les Pee Wee*, whose sportsmanship directives and concussion cautions border on public announcement ads, thanks to mid-range camera framing and actors mode of address, certainly ensure that Julie will be kept on the sidelines. Her removal, however, is also a letdown because she carries the emotional force of the film due in large part to Alice Morel-Michaud's superlative acting skills.[36] Nonetheless, the sports genre typically signals the weight of protagonists by way of their goal-scoring displays and *Les Pee Wee* amply reiterates that the hero of the film is Janeau, not Julie, not only because he nets all the important tallies, but because the film displays his hockey wizardry at length. In one involved sequence, the camera conveys his artistry by allowing the viewer in on his skating and puck-carrying skills through framing at mid-leg level, and follows with wider shot lengths that abundantly display his goal-scoring abilities. Upbeat musical scores also accompany these sequences to convey Janeau's star quality. None of Julie's skills are featured even remotely in like manner despite that the film deploys doubles for game sequences. Her limited representation calls to mind Jason Blake's observation that women and girls in real life shinny games and in depictions of hockey are typically "stuck in goal—in the game, but not of it."[37] Since Julie is replaced in the tournament matches by the backup goalie she helped train, her removal further nuances her statement to her teammates "it's your game," as a heavy-hearted acknowledgment that hockey is a male preserve.

Her absence from the Pee Wee Worlds also comes across as regressive in light of Cathy Yarrow's starring role in the championship game twenty-eight years earlier, given that Julie no longer has to contend with the opposition of parents, sponsors, and the media. As one of the hardiest females in the repertoire, Julie is not only skillful but strong, as coach Mike notes when he reassures his peewees after her injury: "Julie is tough; everything will be ok." However, as with the opponent's harassment of Cathy in *Hockey Night*, Julie's concussion also occurs at the hands of a player who is twice her size, and reiterates the predicament of girls playing on boys' teams since unsportsmanlike adversaries see them as a weak link. Much like Spear Kozak in *Hockey Night*, Janeau also goes after the opponent who fells his goalie, and he too is thrown out of the match in line with the game's normative codes, further communicating the idea of girls on boys teams as a potential liability. Although a brief clip of a speedy female forward for a Philadelphia team (ultimately defeated by the Lynx) asserts that girls can and do compete with their male counterparts, *Les Pee Wee*'s sidelining of its female goalie ultimately makes short shrift of the Lynx's heartfelt remark: "Without Julie, there's no way."

Not coincidentally perhaps, Julie, much like Cathy, also has a "missing father" who is never mentioned in the film, but whose function cannot be superseded by mom Sylvie despite their close relationship. Because coach Mike, like Neil in *Sticks and Stones*, is charged with gatekeeping duties aimed at weeding out brawling and other unsportsmanlike displays, his team function does not substitute for that of the archetypal father in sports. In drawing up an exceedingly self-determined and self-reliant character in Julie, *Les Pee Wee* does not see fit to address this familial gap like *Hockey Night* does, but it matters nonetheless as Janeau's insistent complaints about dad's absence from games, even when mom was alive, pointedly show. As with *Hockey Night*, then, the father's absence, and the film's appending of Julie's (unrealized) dream to her male teammates' victory recapitulates that the cultural battle for girls enfranchisement in the game is not yet won.

The great number of family films with hockey protagonists attests that this is a marketable genre that blends well with the sports film because it depends on familial-type inclusion and provides athletic role models for 'tween girls. Films lend a pioneering cast to women's hockey drawing it up as full of heady potential given the inroads made by female Olympians in recent decades and increasing opportunities for young girls. At the same time, these movies quickly abridge women and girls' trajectories in the game, leaving serious doubts about their future prospects, particularly in the professional circuit.

Even though the cinema of hockey makes the case that girls and teens should play hockey, these characters also largely appear in supportive or minor roles. Much as *Les Pee Wee*'s sidelining of goalie Julie in the tournament games, numerous other films draw up alluring protagonists who help carry the narrative but see little ice time. In *Slap Shot 3*, the expert Shayne Baker is a multiple MVP who goes after what she wants, and just like Paula Taymore, does not tailor her responses to please either of her suitors, Riley Haskell or goalie Kain Frazier. When Riley playfully teases her to stop putting pucks in net and drop her stick, she dares him to come take it from her, taking a shot that ricochets back and whizzes dangerously past his face. Similarly, when Kain taunts her that he has the record for the lowest goals against in the state's history, she answers nonchalantly: "That's funny … I've scored the most goals in Pennsylvania history." During scrimmage, Frazier stops all of Shayne's shots, but he gets a workout the likes of which he never expected, and she has the last say, beating him during the championship final where it does the most damage. Despite Shayne's stellar skills, which are superior to the entire junior Chiefs roster, the film inserts her as subterfuge at the tail end of the final, much like *MVP: Most Valuable Primate* does with Tara Westover to help the Nelson Nuggets win the Harvest Cup while older brother Steven takes Jack, the Chimp, to El Simian reserve. *D2: The Mighty Ducks* also inserts the team's backup goalie, Julie "the Cat" Gaffney (Colombe Jacobsen), in the final minutes of the game and confines her largely to a picturesque role. *The Ducks* trilogy, much like *Ice Angel* and *Go Figure*, also configure female hockey characters as figure skaters, harking back to early notions of femininity in which sport was designed to nurture grace and lady-like dispositions in girls and women.[38]

The repertoire repeats this treatment with female characters in ownership and coaching roles. *Slap Shot*'s dismal portrayal of owner Anita McCambridge is a veiled assessment about women who head sports teams. Aaron Baker notes that the film's representation of Ms. McCambridge does not mirror how women owners manage teams, and instead gives a glimpse of the business of sport as operated by men. Baker interprets her portrayal as a backlash on the women's movement for its repercussion on men's lives.[39] When McCambridge reaffirms her decision to sell the team, Reggie responds by blurting out that her son will grow to be a "faggot" to express his vexation at the idea that a woman owner with no genuine connection to the sport should so callously dispose of her property. If McCambridge is heartless, *Slap Shot 3*'s Bernie Frazier, owner of the Binghamton Ice Hounds, is fiendish. A red-haired, Luciferian figure—"a devil … in a suit," as the town's mayor observes—Frazier deploys "anything-goes, no-holds-barred" tactics to take over the Hansons' large-acreage home and bring her close to full ownership of Charlestown.

Jesse Dage in *Slap Shot 2* is also largely wasted as Super-Chiefs coach, since she must deploy her appreciable skills and knowledge of the game's history to trick her charges into respecting her authority. The film builds up Dage's credibility only to neutralize her when she effectively turns into the head of a circus team and remains in a dead end job as far as her goals to coach an NHL team are concerned. By film's end, she acknowledges her situation for what it is and resigns her position, typifying Martha Wilkerson's observation that "[w]omen who aspire to coaching positions tread on sacred soil" by encroaching on conventional social arrangements.⁴⁰ Jesse winds up as captain Sean Linden's romantic partner to buttress Tudor's argument that, in relegating women to supporting roles vis-à-vis male others, the sports realm operates as a proxy for the social order. *The Rhino Brothers* likewise deflects the potentially empowering role of a hockey mom-turned-coach who is well versed in the game's intricacies. Ellen Kanachowski's (Gabrielle Rose) appreciable knowledge of hockey tactics successfully reroutes son Stefan's (Curt Bechdholt) minor hockey prospects. The catch is that Ellen is set up as a largely dysfunctional figure who uses her son's attainment to stave off feelings of inadequacy about her unlived life. Because Stefan is facing burnout and wants out of professional hockey, her expertise amounts to a virulent form of entrapment that casts her son in the role of casualty.

Although the repertoire invokes images of women and girls exploring sporting frontiers, hockey operates largely to ascribe grit and determination to female characters, much as it does with male characters in feminizing situations. TV movies *Santa Baby* (Underwood, 2006) and *Holiday In Handcuffs* (Underwood, 2007) epitomize this arrangement as Christmas-themed romantic comedies designed for the North American televisual market. In the first film, Santa's daughter Mary Clause (Jenny McCarthy) takes shots on net flanked by majestic mountains that signal her North Pole roots. As a headstrong woman who is intent on modernizing her father's business, she is also in the wrong relationship with a smooth corporate type. Childhood friend Luke Jessup (Ivan Sergei), who harbors a longtime crush for Mary and whom the film points to as the right partner, is the sensitive, mild masculine type who cannot dig up the courage to propose. He approaches her as she is venting her frustrations by taking shots on net much like the standard vexed male hockey protagonist, a setup that communicates Luke must "man up" if he expects to stake a claim on her.

In the second film, protagonist Trudie Chandler (Melissa Joan Hart) engages on a one-on-one with prospective love interest David Martin (Mario Lopez) to denote her Northern small-town roots and convey that the two have something special in common. David is a virtual stranger whom Trudie kidnaps to pass off as beau to her unsuspecting family after her real boyfriend breaks up with her. As an artist who appears to do nothing right in the eyes of her kin, Trudie's hostage taking is an act of desperation that takes a fortuitous turn given that David is in a dysfunctional relationship with a spoiled princess type. Although David and Trudie are a better fit, because she feminizes her prospective partner by taking him by force, the film must rescue his masculinity by having him soundly beat her at "hockey." In a subsequent scene his appeal grows when Trudie accidentally walks in on him and sees his shirtless, muscled body. Starring recognizable U.S. female actors, these Canadian productions are prime examples of how popular film and TV movies deploy hockey imagery to reference strong but alluring females and set them apart from the so-called average woman.

Women in hockey roles, above all, communicate the desirability of hardier females as a form of social capital. Family fare, in particular, conveys that girls and teens should play the game for the very same reason that parents deploy sport to instill in male offspring the skill and confidence that will serve them in the competitive marketplace. However, because women and girls in hockey roles are the exception rather than the rule and typically see little ice time, the occurrence of so many characters in subordinate positions, truncated career paths, and villainous roles suggest that females in the game are still struggling to emerge from under the influence of the men. The women's trajectory mirrors *USA Today* sports journalist Christine Brennan's comments that "[w]e as a Western culture have decided we want women and girls to play sports, not so much to become pro athletes, but to learn life lessons and become better people and leaders."[41] The unveiling of hockey histories at all levels assumes greater urgency in retrieving the women's game from the sidelines, a project of rediscovery without which the regime of contemporary sports representation cannot be fully contextualized. To offset Hollywood's impression of hockey-playing females as exotic or unusual, women and girls must also take on weightier athletic roles and emerge from their peripheral position in the sports film repertoire.

9

The Hockey Spectacle in Film

Hockey epitomizes the kind of high-octane performance that speaks to popular expectations of spectacle. Jay Coakley observes that the sport spectacle privileges the heroic over the aesthetic aspect of athleticism by foregrounding daring, tenacity, and rugged style over expert technique and artistic ability.[1] These values inscribe sport as the purview of warriors and emphasize athletic exploits' larger-than-life aspects. Although producers typically view sports-themed movies as dramas that relegate the athletic contest to the background, the great part of sports films feature matchups, and those with budget flexibility, especially those of the 1990s and beyond, depict contests as elaborate rollercoaster rides that highlight the visual and aural aspects of spectacle.

The sports film's penchant for spectacle is compatible with hockey in the movies in several ways. Spectacle enlarges the prospective audience by working primarily on the viewer's body, which hockey enhances based on viewers expectations of its kinetic allure.[2] Spectacle also does away with the separation between performer and audience by emphasizing the festival-like feel of viewing the sport in the movies as a celebratory break from the mundane, which, in turn, aligns with hockey's many carnivalesque representations.[3] In expediting the viewer's immersion in the media experience, spectacle also distracts from implausible narrative premises by accentuating the sensual aspects of entertainment, particularly significant to the project of hockey in family fare. No less importantly, spectacle amplifies the heroic elements of athleticism that are useful in alluding to hockey as part of the male action genres.[4]

The Grammar of Hockey in Film

Audiences who are habituated to watching sports at stadiums or on TV typically bring their assumptions of sports to the movies, and film practitioners must meet these expectations in their productions. David Rowe observes that "the politics of the popular" that sports in the media epitomize incorporate "elements of sports discourse ... couched in visual and verbal languages whose grammar and syntax, vocabulary and framing ... allow ... myths to do their work on the emotions, and [enable] ideologies to represent [particular] interests...."[5] Mythic imagery in the sports film has an insistent quality that both frames and resolves problems in normative ways to promote distinct configurations of reality. Jeff Hopkins argues that cinematic imagery does not merely reproduce or reflect back people and places to viewers, but is carefully constructed to create an "impression of reality" through the quick succession of iconic gestures. The power of the cinematic image lies in its capacity to blur the borders between the real and the imaginary and distort subjects and their social worlds, even more so if the particulars of the ideologically based production process are also rendered inscrutable and otherworldly.[6] Joshua Meyrowitz's typology of media literacy addresses several ways of decoding the value systems embedded in the movies and other media products. The first entails taking up themes, motifs, character roles, behavioral patterns, narratives, plot lines, and genres, and examining them for both manifest and latent messages. The questions pertinent to this analysis focus on content patterns as well as on correspondences between media portrayals and real life subjects. The second centers on production factors—the interface of cinematography or videography, sound/music, editing, etc.—and analyzes how manipulation of these elements relays content to influence public perception of places, events, people, and cultural practices.[7] The third looks at media formats' fixed features to gauge the specific form information takes and a particular medium's reach. This chapter considers content and the mechanics of its delivery jointly, and much as Rowe suggests, as a "grammar" whose thematic elements and technical aspects convey the ideological messages behind the hockey spectacle in the cinema.[8]

Because audiences draw their primary ideas of sport largely from television broadcasts, one of the ways film practitioners meet audience expectations is by affecting a particular sport's authenticity on screen. Writing about the pressures on the genre from developments in media technologies, Bruce Babington underscores that the larger screens and sharp color of high definition TV as well as HD sports coverage's multiple-camera placements, ever-expanding array of shooting angles, close-ups, and extreme slow motion replay effects have made for increased expectations that audiences in the 1950s, who only had access to real sport matches through newsreels, would never have insisted on.[9] The question of realistically deploying a sport is no small matter since a central feature of genre is its regime of believability. As Geoff King notes, genres establish the contractual parameters between filmmakers and audiences over the types of events that must express with a degree of verisimilitude and neither viewers nor critics take such breaches lightly.[10] It is the power of the verisimile image that obscures the boundary between the real and the imaginary, and therefore the realism with which an actor portrays a sports role appears to be the key variable for why a sports film succeeds or falters with audiences.[11] Hollywood producers, ever preoccupied with portraying sport with believability, must therefore identify actors who can pull off the role with self-assurance, and as in the case of *Miracle*, have gone as far as casting hockey players with some acting ability after repeatedly attempting the opposite to mixed reviews. Hiring doubles for involved hockey sequences and inserting NHLers in bit parts also conflate the fictional with the real to validate the "authenticity" of hockey in film. *Face Off, The Mystery of the Million Dollar Hockey Puck, Maurice Richard, Les Boys IV, Sudden Death,* and most Disney hockey movies feature recognizable National League athletes in cameo roles.

Because hockey in the cinema uses to advantage television's own economic and cultural relationship with sport, filming techniques strive to emulate televised sports' broadcasts and their multiple-angle views of the action. Establishing game setups typically open with exterior and interior shots of the arena combined with ambient sounds and announcer approaches to coverage. To propel the match, a film may segue from wide shots of the impending action to medium shots of players primed for the face-off as well as close-ups of sticks hitting the puck. Cutting from wide shots to medium shots and close-ups builds tension and excitement due to the contrast in point of view. Because the hockey spectacle in film is about electrifying movement, assertive gestures, dramatic counter attacks, and decisive goal-orientation, producers deploy varying shot lengths, camera movement, editing rhythms, and visual effects, accompanied by sound effects and non-diegetic music, to satisfy viewers' expectations of the sports experience. Alongside intensity of emotion, the spectacle's visual and auditory discourse must communicate kinetic feel because hectic pace conveys hockey as a high-gear performance.

Indeed, the hockey spectacle entertains by immersing audiences in the kinetic experience of the game while delivering its ideological message below the viewer's conscious threshold. The message is that hockey is the purview of daring, muscular men and as such it exalts the male body and upholds the values of dominant masculinity. These values highlight risk-taking, resolve, the tactical use of force, tolerance for pain and injury as well as embed the work ethic into the athlete's physique.[12] Sequences that articulate the forward's contributions dramatize the exemplar's heroic feats by amplifying his goal-orientation. Thunderous hits and brawling additionally magnify the tough workmanlike attributes of defensemen, putting muscles on display in the service of teamwork. Goaltending shots also amplify the fearless countenance of the goalie who, as the last and lone line of defense, must stand up to persistent strikes from the opponent bench. To relay the athlete's commitment and sacrifice, films may also deploy sequences that are not part of the game proper but portray a player nurturing his dream and honing the special skills needed to accomplish his task. Historical films, for their part, may make use of archival footage to either problematize or reaffirm the relationship between masculinity and nationhood depending on whether the hockey protagonist is rejected as a social outcast or held up as a paragon of the national character. Children and teen fare, on the other hand, blend hockey's play aspect with masculinity training, while discouraging the excessive use of force by moralizing about sportsmanship and teamwork in keeping with the genre's didactic tendencies.

Goal-Orientation

Susan Sontag theorizes that seeing through a camera bolsters the viewer's aesthetic awareness while stimulating the desire to commodify the subject.[13] Hockey in film disavows this commodification by way of the realist aesthetic and by representing the protagonist's goal-orientation and triumph as an allegory for social mobility. The toiling, deserving athlete who succeeds in his objectives, ratifies the ideological project of the market and instills faith in free enterprise, competitiveness, and meritocracy.[14] The goal-scoring moment expresses the potent populist fantasy of triumphing against all obstacles and garnering social and material ascendance as a result. In light of the ideological implications of the game-clinching moment, skillful playmaking, although aesthetically pleasing, must also ultimately deliver the victory since the sports film regards finesse that does not translate into favorable outcomes as effete playmaking. For similar reasons, despite the acceptability of the draw in actual games, hockey games in film do not usually end in a tie.

Given that the hockey protagonist is typically a dark horse battling dire odds, films take their time to deploy the peak moment of attainment to amplify the drama and spectacle of the game, quite in contrast with the realities of an actual matchup where a goal may materialize without buildup or even haphazardly. The pinnacle goal-scoring moment *par excellence* is the game-winning penalty shot, and because of its dramatic overtones, films grant it to a character who suffers excessive physical punishment or unjust broadsiding. In *Youngblood*, the durable Dean is the object of systematic harassment by enforcer Racki and his Thunder Bay team, and the game-winning moment must articulate the redemption of the small-framed, fleet-footed protagonist who vanquishes the hockey heavyweight with his scoring touch. The film draws out Dean's penalty shot by upping the tension to breaking point and conveying the action entirely in slow motion. With ten seconds left in the game, the rookie assumes his place in front of the puck. Three sets of POV shots of the teen glancing at his father and brother in the stands, at Racki and his teammates on the bench, and at girlfriend Jesse in another part of the rink, paired with his own tense reaction set up the exceedingly long sequence. Three additional sets of medium and close-up shots of the Thunder Bay goalie staring at the Mustangs rookie who nervously looks back at him communicate to the audience that the faceoff resembles the shootout of the western. As he takes off, Dean quickly circles to gain momentum, and without losing a beat, kicks the puck with his skate onto his blade. No less than twenty edits follow, including side shots of significant others in the stands and sundry views of the ever-nearer goalie and of Dean advancing toward the goal past a sign that reads: "Voice of the Mustangs." The rookie finally passes the puck in between his legs onto his forehand and shoots, beating the goalie by scoring top shelf. After four more close-ups, the puck lands flat inside the net, at which point the red light goes on and Dean and the crowd erupt in cheers. Although the sequence's slow motion contravenes Dean's purported signature speed, it heightens the suspense by playing up the melodramatic hues of the confrontation. The stirring ending operates as payback for the hero's suffering while communicating that, despite unremitting physical attack, his game must be one of difference.

Paying homage to *Youngblood*, *Breakaway* offers a similar variation on the scoring moment. As Raj Singh makes his way to the net on a breakaway, he has flashbacks of coach Winters ripping the captain's "C" off his jersey, of love interest Melissa warning about quitters, and of arguments with his dad over never watching him play, as well as of childhood memories of the elder Singh expressing hopes that his son will one day make him proud. Side shots of the audience intently watching the proceedings, including dad praying in the stands, amplify Raj's trajectory to the net. Behind the goal, the camera captures the puck bouncing in and Raj erupting in celebration. Following the formula of the sports film, non-diegetic music accompanies the entire sequence.

Slap Shot 3, which also widely alludes to *Youngblood*, grants the game-winning goal to Alex Gorall (Tyler Johnston), the Junior Chiefs' skilled forward who has quietly endured punishment for a crime he did not commit. Alex starts out much like Dean, gaining momentum and kicking the puck onto the blade of his stick with his skate. Similar side shots of the goalie, of significant others, and of the announcer booth magnify the tension as the teen makes his way to the net in slow motion. When he reaches the goalie, he does a flip of the puck from behind a leg, lifts it and scores. After putting the puck in the net, Alex erupts in celebration and his teammates leave the bench to mob him. The forlorn, bent-over goalie motif in *Youngblood* recurs by way of a tilted shot of villain Kain Frazier sitting flat on the ice and ripping his equipment off in frustration.

Mirroring the sports genre's intertextuality, the above films refer to one another down to specific moves. *Youngblood* operates as an antecedent in pitting a skilled underdog against a larger, meaner opponent who represents an outdated model of masculinity. These films also make use of slow motion to elongate the metaphorically potent moment. This tactic is not motivated by the linear events of classical realism. Rather, as Linda Williams posits of these "just in time" moments, slow motion speaks to the melodramatic mode's directive that it might not be too late to rescue the suffering hero and inscribe virtue and forthrightness into the affairs of men by way of his deeds.[15] The use of slow motion also has the effect of making objects appear larger in scale, exalting the protagonist's efforts by articulating the goal as resulting from skill and never as fluke or by-product of luck, which are common in hockey. The elongated sequence also typically showcases the hero's vindication by incorporating views of family and friends who witness his attainment.

Needless to say, sequences like the above have little to do with the way spectators in the arena see the game. These final setups, which are part of the aesthetic realism of hockey in film, do not reproduce the game, but mimic some of its features to heighten narrative tension and amplify the spectacle of sport. Glenn Cummins makes clear that the various empirical theories that deal with the role of suspense and arousal in fictional narratives[16] substantiate that these conditions contribute to viewer gratification, particularly in the case of films that are able to escalate the range and magnitude of thrills.[17] The vividness of audiovisual media counters potential frustration over clichéd subjects by producing the intense mood-altering response that viewers seek in action genres. These stirring, elongated sequences contribute to viewer satisfaction and deliver the film's ideological message about high-minded underdogs who justly, and in the nick of time, attain their cherished objectives.

Films may also opt to divvy up roles and augment the hockey spectacle through the scorer's skillful touch and the enforcer's show of strength. In those cases, protagonists embody the athlete's goal-orientation through puck-handling skills, skating ability, and signature moves that lead to goals while defensemen provide a supportive role. The lighting in these sequences reproduces the spotlight of big metropolitan arenas that call attention to the athlete's highly marketable game. *Score: A Hockey Musical* fashions main protagonist Farley Gordon as someone who chooses not to exercise the requisite mean streak dictated by the "hockey code," a system that Coach Donker illustrates in accounting for the arch-opponent Devils' top dog status as "cheapshot artists" who would tear out their mother's hearts and sell it for peanuts on Ebay. Because Farley's debut is preceded by a brawl that has a numbing effect on both benches, the initial scoring sequences that display his talents are short—of three cuts each—yet sufficient to demonstrate that the teen is a natural talent who has the power to invigorate the game.

The second contest is more involved and features fourteen edits that showcase both the scorer's and defenseman's contributions. The segment starts out with a close-up of the puck on a blade, followed by a medium close-up of skates and lower legs in a breaking maneuver. An upward pan reveals Farley as the puck-carrier. The teen's rush to the net predictably results in a goal, and the sequence is executed slowly but in real time to showcase Farley's dexterity. As he stickhandles with ease, a back-of-the-net medium shot shows him scoring top shelf on the goalie. Subsequent segments intercalate the defenseman's contributions, as Moose in a close-up, bumps an opponent and enables Farley to take the puck. A medium close-up once again shows the big defenseman expeditiously moving in on opponents and crushing them against the boards while Farley looks on at the display. Moose checks yet another player to rescue a teammate, and the glass reflection broadcasts that the play results in another goal, with Farley barely celebrating. The sound of a loud thump in short order reveals Moose behind yet another pounding move that ends up with the hapless victim lying flat on the ice. The sequence concludes with a medium close-up of the teen rushing toward the net with the puck and another look at a second top-shelf goal that strikes the goalie's bottle to the raucous delight of the fans.

Farley's plays above all feature his superlative skill, grace, and clean game, which mark him as the best expression of the national project. These segments also amplify his character by means of a whistling tune that communicates his no muss, no fuss natural scorer signature and fosters in the viewer the expectation of more goals. Subsequent goal-staging scenes are not as elaborate but also not entirely minimalistic and, as in the first game, take on average three edits to perform. Moose's contributions, however, pale in comparison, unfolding in the context of large buffoon-like bashing that, while making space for the scorer's display of wizardry, conveys little of the specialization associated with the defensive role. This arrangement bolsters the film's message that the enforcer's function on the team is largely subsidiary to the scorer's talents.

Goon underscores the same division of labor but communicates precisely the opposite message by saluting the grimy but heroic work of the enforcer. The film sets up the defenseman's heroization by first calling attention to the scorer's star attributes. More than any other protagonist in the repertoire, hockey virtuoso Xavier Laflamme has the skills of an artist and multiple sequences in the film showcase his inestimable gifts. Xavier's introduction arrives courtesy of Coach Rollie Hortense, who calls enforcer Doug Glatt into his office to explain that his services are needed to protect someone who is "a hundred percent pure natural talent."

Farley Gordon (Noah Reid) cheered by teammates in *Score: A Hockey Musical* (courtesy of Mongrel Media/Michael McGowan).

The introductory clip of Laflamme begins with a medium close-up that shows lower legs in hockey gear speedily curving around one end of the ice with a whoosh. A slight upward pan reveals Laflamme in a medium shot taking the pass from a teammate and carrying the puck up the ice. He spins acrobatically, easily avoiding the incoming defenseman. A split-second cut demonstrates he has no trouble repeating the move. Third and fourth edits of the player's lower legs in medium shots vary the angle of the rush, giving way to a wider shot of Laflamme further up the ice. Yet another medium shot shows him going in on net as the puck rolls into the corner. Two additional medium shots, also rendered by way of split-second cuts, track the player's legs behind the net and subsequently on the side, after which he tucks the puck right past the goalie's pads scoring a pretty goal. The sound of the crowd bursting in cheers is heard almost as if in waves, and a middle shot displays Laflamme on his knees sliding on the ice in celebration. Another quick medium shot locates the player behind the net, followed by a cut of closer length that shows him coming out toward the camera and scoring yet another tally, his expert deflection punctuated by the sound of the horn. Celebrations ensue and a medium shot of Laflamme gesturing as if riding a horse, alongside teammates holding their sticks aloft, conveys his masterful performance as masculine potency. The sequence ends with a shot that, photographed from behind, elongates the play and reiterates Laflamme's many contributions. Not surprisingly, the player goes second in the draft. The dizzying and seamless array of shots and the quick edits augmented by sound effects display the scorer masterfully wielding his craft and adroitly convey the excitement of hockey in the big leagues as consummate spectacle.

The game against the Quebec Victoires displays Laflamme's star quality in similar fashion. The home crowd boos him fiercely for having purportedly deserted Quebec by plying his craft with an Anglophone team. After the establishing wide shot of the rink, the camera follows the whiz through medium lateral shots as well as from behind, amplifying his speed and skill as he makes his way toward the opponent's net. A total of nine edits track him up the ice as he skates from one end of the rink to the other to score an easy tally. Enforcer Doug Glatt follows from behind and after the goal attempts a high-five. But Laflamme merely stares at him and skates on by. As the rest of the team gathers around him to celebrate, the forward gives the Francophone crowd a finger while the spectators continue to heckle him. The sequence highlights that Xavier is an individualist, a playmaker who can take the puck to the net all by himself. He is not beholden to tribe or squad because his superlative skills can carry the day

Xavier Laflamme (Marc-André Grondin) takes a breather in *Goon* (courtesy of No Trace Camping/Entertainment One).

and retaliate where it hurts most. A second set of ten edits displays his balletic moves in much the same way, focusing on his skating legs as he dances up the ice. However, on this try all of Laflamme's artistry comes to naught as he is taken out of the play by a brutal hit when Doug hesitates for a split second and leaves him unprotected. Much as the introductory clip exemplifies, Laflamme's small size makes him a target of other teams and requires the services of someone who will protect him at all times. *Goon* in short order makes clear that the spectator is able to experience the aesthetic pleasure engendered by the star forward's skill and artistry in large part because of the vital support and wholehearted commitment of the enforcer.

Toughness

Since the hockey player projects an aura of physical strength and durability which the media commodify for public consumption, much of the spectacle of hockey in film has to do with the glamorization of mastery and heroization of sacrifice and pain. Jay Coakley notes that the commodified sports product and its promotional rhetoric favor the sort of depictions of masculinity that encourage shows of dominance. These demonstrations of power, which showcase thunderous hits rendered in slow motion heightened by sound effects, sell the sports product of major leagues, including the NHL's.[18] In hockey, moves that entail the risk of physical injury are especially prized for their spectacular quality. Skirmishes, all-out brawling, and blow-by-blow exchanges are also popular with fans because they epitomize the macho aspect of the hockey culture while exercising a cathartic effect on audiences. Theories of catharsis suggest that the brawling spectacle enables viewers to vicariously take part in the proceedings and vent vexations accumulated in the course of day-to-day activities hostile behavior that may erupt in social situations outside the rink.[19] Forceful actions can therefore function as a socially useful escape valve by ritualizing violence through surrogates that dramatize the frontier masculinity of the exemplar.

In film, the aggressive displays of force and grit that form part of the hockey player's exemplary physical masculinity are easier to choreograph than the superlative skill of the star forward. Staged pummeling, over-the-shoulder camera shots, and slow motion editing can create the expectation of the hit in the viewer's mind, simultaneously invoking the prerequisite endurance of the male athletic body as well as the player's commitment to his craft. In a real hockey game, fighting stops the action proper and works to release pressure, although it can arguably provoke retaliatory actions. The kinetics of spectacle in film integrates brawls as part of the hockey action to code the game as high contact and heighten dramatic tension. Brawling can take place at any point in the story depending on the film's message. In *Slap Shot*, it occurs haphazardly and in every segment in which the Hansons appear to satirize the violent game of the seventies. In *The Deadliest Season*, the crucial fight occurs at midpoint so the remainder of the story can focus on the trial of protagonist Gerry Miller to assess his role in furthering the sport's excesses. *Youngblood* leaves the sequence until the end to deliver the message that putting stock in fighting expresses outdated masculinity norms.

Producers may also opt to harness sequences that connote the game's high contact edges to magnify the emotional intensity of the hockey spectacle. A smashing sequence in *Tooth Fairy*, which focuses on both players' and spectators' perspectives of the hit, amplifies defenseman Derek Thompson's forceful hit on an opponent at ice level. A subsequent shot from the rafters reveals fans flinching as shattered glass flies their way in slow motion. The tilted shot of the smashed glass communicates hockey's power to upend the viewer's bearings, as an approaching tooth catapults upward toward the camera accompanied by announcer remarks and crowd roars that celebrate the hit. The sequence summarily conveys Derek Thompson's "tooth-collector" moniker through the power of his bruising actions. Even though in *Tooth Fairy* Thompson's character has lost his scoring touch due to an injury, the choreography conveys the protagonist's physical mastery and hockey as a sport of eminent force, mirroring director Michael Lembeck's laudatory remarks that "[i]t was breathtaking to be on the ice with the cameras down low and feel the sheer power of what these guys do."[20]

Spectacular hits that send an opponent flying through the air are relatively rare in real hockey contests, because such outcomes depend on any number of variables. But in film, producers can easily choreograph these acrobatic sequences. One such setup, which appears in a promotional L.A. Kings video, also occurs in *Tooth Fairy*. The sequence consists of several edits that elongate Derek's hit on an opponent, flipping him in the air, and sending him crashing onto the ice. The edits slow both the defensive tactic and the spill, prolonging them as a source of viewing pleasure in keeping with the aesthetics of hockey in the cinema. Choreographed sequences like the above spill in *Tooth Fairy* resemble a similar sequence in *Miracle* (between recruits from rival colleges Jack O'Callahan and Rob McClanahan) for good reason. Twentieth Century Fox called on the services of Mayhem Pictures producers Mark Ciardi and Gordon Gray as well as choreographer Mark Ellis, all of whom worked on *Miracle* years earlier. These sequences show that studios build on ideas of hockey as spectacle by drawing on the contributions of experienced talent, thereby habituating the viewer to a particular visual grammar of hockey in the movies. Given that big-budget sports films have increasingly partaken from the textual narrative of the action film, these sequences also reiterate the prerequisite thrills expected of the sports experience in the genre.

Toughness also embosses hockey with a patina of work while reclaiming it as Canadian popular cultural form, a valuable signature in view of the game's immersion in the global entertainment marketplace. A paean to the enforcer, *Goon* employs high-profile American actors in central roles to heighten cross-border marketability, while presenting the game as quintessentially Canadian through the tough man's heavy workmanlike physicality. The big fight between Doug Glatt and Ross Rhea is nested within the final game, but as it occurs shortly after Doug's yeoman-like performance against the Minutemen—where he blocks the net with his face—it plays out as part of his continuum of sacrifice. Doug not only has not had an opportunity to recover, but has suffered further bruising at the hands of Eva's ex-boyfriend to comically atone for the couple's break-up. The ensuing fight is about endurance, courage, unsanitized violence, and most of all, about communicating the enforcer's codes. The sequence takes the viewer from Glatt's interaction with Rhea in the penalty box to their exit, which is marked by opening bolts on either side that elevate the tension of the prospective confrontation. As the fighters take their positions, refs and teammates clear the ice, and realizing the long-awaited spectacle is imminent, the audience comes to its feet with a roar. Many of the shots that follow are over-the-shoulder and a blur, but the sound effects that amplify the loud face-thumping continue even through crowd reaction shots and elongate the ferocity of the fighting spectacle. The pounding, which occurs in quick successive outbursts that frame the enforcer's workmanship as a boxing match, also registers as part of the kinetic experience of hockey in film. The extended sequence punctuates Doug's heroic performance with

Turandot's "Nessun Dorma," a musical passage that heralds the prospect of the protagonist's victory and likely gives a wink to *Perfectly Normal*'s use of opera since *Goon* widely alludes to other hockey-themed films. The bloodied tooth sequence that opens the film also brackets its finale and acts as a retort to *Tooth Fairy*'s use of sanitized effects.

Goon's cinematographic staging of violence engages the viewer in a rollercoaster ride of close-up shots and diegetic sound that adjoin the bloodiest limits of the enforcer's role. Fighting that is relegated to the end of the narrative has a similar function as the goal-scoring moment, and films may deploy it to frame the opponent's categorical vanquishing. Both *Youngblood* and *Goon* nest a film-ending fight within a game to corroborate the physical durability of the protagonist and augment dramatic tension while communicating different messages about hockey's ideal of heavyweight masculinity. In an era in which the upmarket commodification of sport has purged the least savory aspects of hockey in film, the extensive fights in *Goon* recuperate masculinity by amplifying the ferocity of the sports spectacle.

Perfectly Normal is unique in the repertoire for its refusal to express the traditional dichotomy between skill and physicality. The film deploys slow motion and non-diegetic operatic scores to process hits, spills, crashes, and other elements of play that convey the required athletic durability of the hockey player through the aesthetics of toughness. Although goalie Renzo Parachi favors sensible efficiency over flair and flamboyance, his teammates go all out, enhancing the proceedings by way of collisions that send opponents flying through the air in slow motion. *Youngblood* also makes prolific use of slow motion to call on viewer sympathies right before the impending attack and enhance identification with the protagonist. In *Perfectly Normal*, however, the aesthetic of toughness does not perpetrate physical harm but evokes appreciation for the hockey player's workmanship as a form of art. Although team goon Hopeless sustains a slight injury to the forehead in a play that turns him into the game's unwitting hero, the wound registers as a modest payback for his continual sabotaging of Renzo, and as a humorous motif that communicates that the character's hard head can take it. The aesthetics of tough play in *Perfectly Normal* also serves to downplay pain and injury to convey players as stalwart sorts who embody the frontier durability of the Northern exemplar.

The (Lesser) Role of Goaltending

Sports broadcasts commonly refer to actions that unfold near the net as peak moments of tension and showcase the goalie's pivotal role as the team's last line of defense. In actual games, netminders can play a spectacular defensive function that leads to celebrated wins and attests to the powerhouse abilities of the role. The cinema, however, has not figured out a way of portraying the goalie's athleticism with flair, adequate drama, or yeoman-like effort, likely because of theatrical conventions and the medium's limitations. Unlike game broadcasts where viewers follow the developing play mostly in wide shots all the way to the net, movies do not always provide a sense of the evolving play because they cut up the action to bring in the viewer up-close to the proceedings. In addition, the build-up of excitement in sports broadcasts is of a different order than in film because real hockey games do not script the action, while sports films stage their pinnacle moments to grant protagonists their cherished objectives. Game-clinching episodes are furthermore designed to enlarge the body and physical performance of the scorer, and perforce diminish the goalie's role. Portraying the netminder's defensive actions with the poise and brilliance that the part deserves also entails choreographing out-of-the-ordinary plays that are difficult to stage because of the reactive quality of the role. Even actual goalies may find these sequences difficult to render with flair given the disparities between staging a play for film and the ebb and flow of real games.

Still, salient goalie roles are not missing in the repertoire, as shown by Denis Lemieux in *Slap Shot*, Jacques "Le Coq" Grande in *The Love Guru*, Renzo Parachi in *Perfectly Normal*, Ray in *Ice Angel*, Greg Goldberg in *The Mighty Ducks* franchise, Julie Morneau in *Les Pee Wee 3D*, Cathy Yarrow in *Hockey Night*, Felicity Corelli (Juliette Marquis) in *Chicks with Sticks*, Marco Melchior in *Goon*, Fernand in the *Les Boys* films, and Kain Frazier in *Slap Shot 3*. Films that confer the role narrative force position the goalie in line with popular culture's perception of the player as an independent, self-reliant sort who suitably embodies the individualist mythology. Cathy Yarrow in *Hockey Night* dramatizes the trailblazer qualities necessary to push against the barriers of tradition and carve out space for women in the game. Renzo Parachi's mild masculinity and love of opera also capitalize on the goalie's self-sufficiency to defy conventional representations of the hockey player in film. Films frequently mobilize the goalie role to meet the cinema's need for eccentric or picturesque types because the player's image in popular culture is that of an odd duck who is borderline compulsive about his gear and whose training and skills set him apart from teammates.

The recurrence of quirky Francophone goalies in the repertoire, while highlighting Quebec's long history of producing iconic players for the role, reiterates the popular vision of the archetype as personified by Denis Lemieux's comical masochistic pre-game rituals and farcical butchering of English language in *Slap Shot*. Movies sometimes dispense with the Francophone angle and simply feature the netminder as a peculiar sort whose antics resemble the benevolent tricksterism of the child. Although unimaginative, this characterization is expedient when creators wish to pay homage to *Slap Shot* and position their work as part of the repertoire. Conversely, the goalie may amplify a team's makeup possibly as a way to mark the position's importance and compensate for the cinema's inability to detail it with adequate flair during action sequences. The more malevolent or machine-like, whacky, hodgepodge, fragmented, unfocused, timid, jocular, or working-class the team, the more

L.A. Kings goalie Jacques "Le Coq" Grande (Justin Timberlake) in *The Love Guru* (Paramount Pictures/Photofest).

pointedly the goalie will magnify those qualities, and likely with a twist in keeping with the unconventional aspects of the character.

These limited approaches unquestionably fail to do the netminder role justice. The primary impetus of film to foster the kinetics of cross-ice movement with an eye on procuring thrill rides for viewers certainly works to sideline the goaltender's contributions. The critical symbolism of the final goal-scoring moment and hockey's association with toughness also designate the goalie's role as subservient to the spectacle provided by the scorer and his skill and the large defensive moves of enforcer types who help the scorer attain his objectives.

The Dream and the Work Ethic

Popular narratives allude to playing hockey for the love of the game in a way that evokes the child's archetypal passion. Hockey drills and practice exercises contravene the child's archetypal play, but they are necessary to show characters developing the special skills needed for the task in line with the conventions of the sports film and action-adventure genres. Training sequences or montages also display the athlete's commitment to his objectives to validate his success. Because workouts can be boring to the viewer, films commonly serve them up poetically, conveying these sequences through angles that underscore the athlete honing his craft, taking shots on net, skating around the rink, and doing numerous drills with the help of props. When the story zeroes in on an individual rather than a team, sequences may also depict the athlete taking shots on net by himself, as occurs in *Face Off, Tooth Fairy, The Boy Who Drank Too Much* and *Keep Your Head Up, Kid*. One or more long shots may also downsize his image as he casts a lonely figure in the rink. This physical diminishment communicates that the game is larger than the individual, and the medium shots that follow allow the viewer to witness the character's steely will in working toward his dream and measuring up to the ideal.

In *Youngblood* this poetic sequence has the feel of a daydream accomplished in large part through the use of soft lighting. Skating around a dark foggy rink with the zamboni lights on, Dean rehearses his skills and expresses his dedication to the quest. The scene pictures the dream for the audience's benefit and conveys the romance of the sojourn fueled by individual passion. The film aesthetically highlights Dean's physical movements by way of medium shots, and as the teen propels puck after puck into the net by the zamboni lights, booming sound effects also textually enlarge his actions. Positioned behind the net, the camera further amplifies the rookie's skill-honing by capturing the puck as it goes into the goal and promising an optimal outcome to the protagonist's quest.

In *Miracle*, working-the-dream sequences also register poetically through well-choreographed drills. The team's practices include a number of dissolves that feature close-ups of skates hard at work kicking up snow against the surface of the ice, properly spaced circular skating around the rink, and line drills that encompass as many players as the director can comfortably get in the shot. These drills procure the sense of a collective unit at work honing the special skills for the task at hand. Except for the initial confrontation between O'Callahan and McClanahan that takes the form of an elongated spill, none of these sequences feature conflict expressed through disjointed movements to reassure the audience that the players are on the same page preparing for their national mission.

A similar honing-the-craft, working-the-dream moment emerges in *Go Figure* when protagonist Kaitlin Kingsford reaches a pressure cooker point in the plot, psychologically and physically squeezed between the figure skating and hockey worlds. On an evening when all her peers are out partying, she practices maneuvering around cones, skating on one leg, and spinning as a way of adapting figure skating moves to her narrow hockey repertory. As she focuses on her drills, the coach's right-hand man, Spencer (Jake Abel), spots her and queries what she is doing. Spencer, who believes Kaitlin does not belong on the team because she does not have the chops for hockey, is quite touched by her show of dedication. But she retorts with a one-on-one dare that will soon put an end to his criticism of her lousy hockey technique. With a spinning move that takes her through the air, she easily puts the puck in the net, finishing off the maneuver by skating along the boards. Sitting flat on the ice, Spencer remarks that he is quite impressed by the exercise, but she quickly reminds him of his promise to never say a word to her again. Because the film does not confer on Kaitlin the hockey championship but grants her the figure skating title, the scene shows that she is set on solidifying her resolve, and that by doing so, she fortifies her female masculinity consonant with the way the women's hockey repertoire works to depict sturdier females while truncating their hockey sojourns.

In *Keep Your Head Up, Kid* and *Wrath of Grapes*, the multiple practice sequences portray Don Cherry's hardworking and long-suffering journey through the minors. In these movies there is less focus on poetic drills in favor of a workman-like feel. The practice sequences alongside the players' yeoman-like contributions during games and his senseless punishment at the psychopathic Eddie Shore's hands all highlight Cherry's tough defender outlook as a working-class exemplar. These scenes also serve to stage Don's struggle to both support his family and retain his berth on the bench in a way that departs from the routine romanticization of hockey as a dream occupation.

Another version of the dream motif, repurposed as a traumatic, career-truncating episode, occurs at the outset of *D2: The Mighty Ducks* to set up the protagonist's second chance at fulfillment. The sequence intercuts a lyrical shot of young Gordon Bombay on the pond with scenes of him in the minors augmented by scoring and celebration. The poetically rendered childhood scene, shot in hues that communicate wistful nostalgia, emphasizes the importance of the pond and the father, and the subsequent slow motion clip of the opponent knocking over Gordon as he grabs his knee in pain, dramatizes the end of the dream. The sequence contrasts the uncomplicated joys of childhood play with the realities of professional hockey. The scene also serves to reassure the viewer that despite obstacles, Gordon's formative experience will come into play and guide the Ducks' ship away from the intimidator role. After the initial vicissitudes, the coach exhorts his charges during the championship game that they are not goons and that they must stay true to themselves. The final scene brackets the film with the same romantic feel of the introductory childhood sequence as the Ducks sing around a poetic campfire "We are the champions." In poetically repurposing the truncated dream motif through the Ducks' victory and augmenting the virtues of the sportsman as the recipe that makes for a winning team, *D2* emphatically depicts Gordon's quest as a story of redemption.

The Use of Archival Footage

Bruce Babington notes that staging sports action in biopic or historical narratives typically necessitates the insertion of doubles in sequences that demand superior athletic performance. Producers may also use film or TV archival footage and employ a mix of simulated sequences and archival footage to amplify the authenticity of the narrative.[21] Motion pictures that incorporate archival footage to reinforce historical context do so as a way of reassuring audiences of their realism while veiling that cinematic representations are always staged for consumption. When films opt to insert footage that chronicles events from the past, they re-contextualize the original's meaning to accord with the story's premises. *Face Off* deploys Leafs and other NHL team footage to augment the plot's believability and bring home the message that the league's capitalist mandate and hierarchical setup militate against the athlete-worker's wellbeing. Decades later, these sequences, which are the only 35mm NHL footage in existence, communicate nostalgia for a bygone era and recapitulate the game as part of Canadians' heritage.

Hockey biopics that dramatize past historical events and foremost figures may also make use archival footage if it suits their narrative needs. *Miracle on Ice*, which originally aired on ABC, repurposes 1980 Olympic hockey game footage owned by the network to commemorate the squad's accomplishment. Producers likely found it less costly and more historically compelling to edit segments of this footage into the story rather than completely recreate play. As noted, these long archival sequences of the team's journey to the gold produce a documentary feel that bolsters the film's historical referents and reminds the audience of the thrill of the journey while keeping an eye out for ratings.

Miracle's use of archival shots, on the other hand, provides historical color,[22] while advancing a different perspective of the win. The film's introductory scene makes use of news footage to set the story in a troubled period of U.S. history. A series of dissolves reduces two decades comprising the Nixon Presidency and the Carter era to crisis points and watershed developments through which the film frames the 1980 win. This imagery alludes to youth's role in the Save the Earth movement, planes dropping bombs in Vietnam and anti-war protestors, Women's Liberation Movement posters, Soviet military parades, the Munich Olympics and Olga Korbut, the 1972 U.S.S.R. defeat of the U.S. basketball team, Watergate, silicon chips, the first man on the Moon, Gerald Ford sworn in as U.S. president and rising inflation, Saigon falling, disco fever and streaking, the U.S. Bicentennial, Jimmy Carter's inauguration, long gas lines and rationing, Elvis Presley's death, the first test tube baby, Love Canal and Three-Mile Island, and finally, Jimmy Carter at the Oval Office giving his Crisis of Confidence speech. This newsreel footage serves to enlarge the historical setting expedient, in particular, for young viewers who did not experience the era. However, these dissolves also close down the interpretation of the event so that it is understood in the context of the Cold War and the U.S.–U.S.S.R. superpower contest, domestic unrest, economic hardship, radical technological changes that created disorientation and as segments of Jimmy Carter's July 1979 speech imply, a national crisis of confidence.

Through this introductory sequence, the film fashions history much in the way Misia Landau describes its manufacture: "as a series of critical moments and transitions" that once translated into narrative, formulate "individual events that had been conceived of as merely successive … as 'turning points,' 'crises' or 'transitions.'" Once set up through the lens of crisis, these events can take on "fall and redemption" or "empire and decline" connotations.[23] *Miracle*'s "crisis of confidence" focus likewise develops the 1980 story of the win as an American fall and redemption story. This historical footage, which extends two decades into the past and far exceeds the context of the Games, represents citizens as long-suffering to underscore the importance of the victory. The newsreel footage by its very nature also underlines the very act of looking back and advertises the film's post–Cold War perspective, which in turn facilitates a reading of the event as consonant with the U.S. winning the Cold War. *Miracle on Ice* and *Miracle*'s distinct framing of the story mirrors commentators Cold War and post–Cold War perspectives of the win. Although following the victory reporters lauded the team's success in the context of its legacy for U.S. hockey,[24] media discourse subsequently reframed the triumph as responsible for the about-face in morale between the superpowers.[25] And although director Gavin O'Connor did not intend to emphasize the Cold War aspect of the victory,[26] the above use of archival footage hindered this aim.

The insertion of archival matter in feature films, then, is hardly a seamless exercise, and in the case of game footage it is particularly perilous since contests embody the aesthetics and norms of TV broadcasts. Game footage additionally encodes very specific historical and cultural referents that can make its use decades later quite risky. Margaret MacNeill, for example, points out that Canadian hockey broadcast values commonly naturalize cultural ownership of the game.[27] In addition, early Canadian NHL footage is tied to CBC's *Hockey Night in Canada* broadcasts, which emphasize hockey's nation-building role.[28] Because of the limitations and historical referents of game footage, then, filmmakers must gingerly handle this material in their biographical accounts.

Gross Misconduct's use of black and white *HNIC* archival sources with dramatic enactments to augment Brian Spencer's character showcases the perils of joining this footage together. To critique Spencer's bully masculinity as well as the brutal game of the seventies, the film moves back and forth between game footage of the player and of the actor playing him. The archival material amplifies Brian's speed and skill and the brutal tactics of his Chicago Blackhawks opponent. After taking the punishment a couple of times, Spencer finally has enough and takes him on in the corner to the fans' delight. Both the archival footage and the reenactment communicate the player's formidable strength as he picks up the Chicago player and flips him over. But because the archival material does not stress Spencer's play as overreach but as consistent with the seventies game, the actor enlarges these actions with borderline moves. In one brief filler shot, Spencer, the actor, pulls the opponent down from behind, and in a subsequent sequence puts up his hand to signal that the fight is done. When the opponent lets down his guard he gets in a punch in the face with his bare fist. These actions are rendered in medium shots and medium-close-ups as well as in vivid color to bring Spencer's brutality to the viewer. Brian the Boy, directly addressing the viewer, interjects that he was never the relaxed sort, but rather someone who always experienced intense feelings, whether deep affection or great loathing, all of which have suited his inherently violent makeup as a hockey player. The youngster outlines the fighter's code and stresses the imperative of protecting goalie and scorers like kin, adding that if an opponent crosses the line, he will hunt him down to inflict damage.

The statement fleshes out the guidelines that rule the physical game in a way that legitimates the contributions of the heavyweight ideal of masculinity. But the boy's words also hint at predatory instincts. Michael Messner critiques the shadow role of sport in acculturating boys and teens to violence so that later in life they have no compunctions about physically harming others.[29] *Gross Misconduct* depicts Spencer's character in like manner by linking his violent play to his actions off the ice in a sequence in which he savagely beats a man who damages his car. The brutal and sinister quality of the dramatic enactments paired with the nostalgic overtones of the *HNIC* theme song that opens the broadcasts deftly reframe the national game as preeminent theater of transgression. In embellishing Spencer's play, however, the film also contradicts the perspective of the original game footage and the HNIC's long tradition of showcasing hockey as a symbol of the national character. Although the CBC is well known for its incisive look into the ethics of professional hockey, NHL game broadcasts also commonly shore up the expression of masculinity through pain, pugnacity, and bloodshed in keeping with hockey's dramatization of Canada's frontier heritage.[30] *Gross Misconduct*'s use of archival footage to articulate Brian's deviant masculinity consequently treads a fine line between sober critique and outright reinscription of his play as a breach of the social order.

Brian Spencer (Daniel Kash) about to land a punch on a Chicago Blackhawks opponent but is being held back by the referee in *Gross Misconduct* (CBC Still Photo Collection).

The above hockey biopics illustrate that archival footage primarily serves to buttress a film's message regardless of the extent to which the connection disfigures the intent of the original. Because in this genre historical footage serves the visual spectacle, the dramatic aspects of the display militate against historical complexity. Even though sports biopics are traditionally marketed as truthful and accessible portraits of the past,[31] and historical audio-visual sources supposedly enhance a film's credibility, the insertion of archival footage may also register as an imperfect exercise and render these portrayals as eminently fictionalized accounts.

Overview

The grammar of hockey in film shows the extent to which films reiterate conventions and build on one another textually (thematically and stylistically) to naturalize particular perspectives of sport. These conventions may distort the game by injecting fantasy sequences that heighten the spectacle, but they also point to connections between film technologies and ideologies. The profuse use of close-ups and medium shots in these films is designed to attach the viewer to the main protagonist, because "[s]hot framing draws on the culturally patterned used of interpersonal distances in real life interactions," as Joshua Meyrowitz explains."[32] Camera movement and special effects also play with time and space to simulate rapid motion. Choreographed moves that may prove difficult during an actual game, amplified by split-second edits that compress time and create the effect of lightning-swift progress up the ice, likewise may contribute the impression of agility and call attention to the mastery of the scorer, as occurs with Laflamme's introductory clip in *Goon*. However, in these movies, focus on the minutiae of playmaking such as stickhandling and footwork is typically brief and not visually dissociated from the scorer, at least not for more than a couple of shots. Action sequences thus promote just enough appreciation of individual skill since lingering may contribute to effete playmaking and feminization if it does not communicate progress toward the goal in line with the sport spectacle's emphasis on the heroic over the aesthetic.

For much the same reason, and unlike actual games, these movies usually showcase little on-ice banter between teammates because it detracts from the ritual display of heroism. Teammate interactions, particularly in new family fare, are relegated to sequences that, while effectively operating as masculinity-training sessions, chiefly convey the "fun" of brotherly bonding that characterizes these all-play, no-work features. In *Slap Shot 3*, as noted, the Hansons bring in offspring Dit, Toe, and Gordie to help tutor the orphans in the particulars of the rugged game period. They incorporate drills that feature jabbing, tripping, pummeling, spearing, slamming against the boards, as well as grabbing an opponent by the jersey and pulling it overhead, all to upbeat music.

Similarly, the rollerblade game in *D2*, which is designed to metamorphose the Ducks into astute, sharp-witted sorts who can hold their own against rival Team Iceland, feature tilted shots and quick cuts accompanied by a hip-hop motif that showcase the squad's transformation.

Exchanges between protagonists and opponents during the game are also scarce and occur chiefly to reaffirm the malicious character of the rival and relay that the protagonist is in a Manichean struggle. Michele Aaron discusses the content of Hollywood action genres (to which the sports film is related),[33] as embodying the pleasures and politics of self-endangerment. The assumption of risk is embedded in the protagonist's very audacity to embark on an impossible assignment and in his sheer disregard of loved ones' cautionary injunctions about the obstacles likely to be encountered as well as the serious consequences of failure.[34] Hence, in *Miracle* Patti relays to husband Herb her concern that "you are chasing after something you didn't get, that you may never get," even as Brooks counters that he set out to coach the U.S. team since he stopped playing, and that this is something he must do for her as well as for the kids. Judge Walter Burns in *Mystery, Alaska* likewise cautions that the New York Rangers will surely shatter any illusions Mystery has about its game, while son Birdie overrides his admonishment by announcing that he's ready to play the professionals.

This sense of self-endangerment lies not only in the ritual testing of the hero, but in the potential strain to his relationships, even as these relationships are the reason why he undertakes the journey in the first place. Dancyger and Rush underscore the centrality of relationships to the sports protagonist's wellbeing, and add that only melodramas and gangster movies feature more emphasis on family.[35] Glimpses of significant others during the hero's peak moment of attainment, such as pertinent sequences in *Youngblood*, *Miracle*, *Breakaway* and *Il était une fois les Boys*, therefore do not function as mere cutaways, but convey the idea of loved ones witnessing the hero's attainment in line with the mythic codes of the genre. Family symbols of support are also noteworthy because "[t]he hero of the motion picture culture is not a 'heavy' figure noted for great physical strength and moral courage, nor the 'lighter' figure of print known for intellectual cunning and strategy, but rather a figure of 'face'—an image that [culturally] unifies..." as Lance Strate observes.[36]

The goal-clinching moment, as noted, has a formulaic quality that confirms self-endangerment as "a managed affair" and "one that lies at the heart of the medium's potential [and prestructured] conservatism,"[37] as Michele Aaron argues of the action genres. The soundtrack, nonetheless works to camouflage the clichéd character of storylines by appealing to the emotions and helping audiences decode filmic sequences in specific ways. Timothy Scheurer observes that musical motifs in the heroic sports genre are drawn from "classical (especially post–Romantic) music literature, light-classical music, and classic Hollywood genre films" and suffused with "driving rhythms, dramatic intervallic leaps ... and soaring [or ascending] melodic patterns" that reinforce the lofty status of protagonists in the dramatic finales.[38] The *Miracle* sequence in which the U.S. players head out for their meeting with the Soviet team boasts similar upbeat martial rhythms and helps package the twenty minute-long match as a heroic mission, consistent with the epic quality of the confrontation in the Disney film. In contrast, *Canada Russia '72* favors dialogue, which reduces the need for sound effects in keeping with its documentary-like tone. The miniseries' televisual form of address also allows the audience in on characters' personal confidences and behind-the-scenes deliberations. The songs—"Signs" and "Absolutely Right" by Five Man Electrical Band, "Evil Grows" by The Poppy Family, "One Fine Morning" by Lighthouse, "Oh, What A Feeling" by Crowbar, and "Avalanche" by Leonard Cohen, in addition, nuance the characters' journey (nostalgically) to connote the contest as a quintessential seventies Canadian event.

The game in film is increasingly being depicted through fast cuts, tilted angles, shot lengths that create maximum contrast and other effects that emulate the fast-pace of the sports environment and recreate the feeling of confused bearings in the viewer. The key difference between the hockey spectacle in pre- and post-nineties films is unquestionably the dizzying array of action-packed sequences that mirror the information-filled environments to which young audiences are habituated. *Les Pee Wee*'s 3D technology, for instance, harnesses digital effects that realistically convey pucks flying at the viewers face (rather than toward the goal as occurs in *D2*), and camera work that frames the game in richer, more compelling ways.

While spectacle certainly underlines the kinetic allure of hockey in line with the sensibilities of the heroic, films increasingly also veil that the main thrust of this representation is to commodify the athlete alongside the cultural practice of the game and its landscape-related myths. *The Mighty Ducks* trilogy, *Slap Shot 3*, and *Breakaway*, for example, all showcase game-winning tallies that feature advertising in the background and make short shrift of sporting ideals as antithetical to commercialism. The Disneyesque fairy tale setups in which the protagonists of *Ronnie and Julie* and *MVP: Most Valuable Primate* play pond hockey are also infused with a faux aesthetic that reeks of sentimentality and mirrors the way "places are used ... [to] reflect ... [particular] ideologies," as Stuart Aitken and Leo Zonn note .[39]

Emphasis on spectacle also has the effect of downplaying hockey's link to the roots of the game in a way that corresponds with changes in sports consumption at hockey arenas. Brian Kennedy notes that the spectacle of hockey has evolved from watching a simple game to a full-fledged "sports experience." While matchups are still important, they are served up in a standard way night after night because the focus is on the brand and the time fans spent inside the arena to expose them to the entire franchise.[40] It is no surprise, then, that since the 1990s, the repertoire also features less and less visual imagery that explicitly emphasizes the sport's connection to Nature.[41] The effect is a whitewashing of landscape's central role in honing autochthonous sports practices, echoing John Beebe's objection to the media circus that descends on the town for the Rangers game in *Mystery, Alaska*. "We agreed to a game of pond hockey, on open ice; no one in a rink playing on a box, boards, blue lines, referees."

Spectacle in film nonetheless has succeeded in habituating viewers to a particular visual grammar (and vision) of hockey that remains culturally salient because of its "visceral appeal" as dreamscape or "world where dreams come true," as Dancyger and Rush note.[42] Ever-evolving technologies that link to how the sports spectacle in film lines up with changing expectations of the sports experience are also capable of procuring the cathartic effect that viewers expect from the aesthetics of self-endangerment that informs hockey in the movies. Even when fettered by stock characters, clichéd story lines, and repetitive stylistic motifs that convey particular ideologies about sport, masculinity, and the nation, then, the genre is sure to continue to procure the thrill ride that fans expect of hockey as a high contact, brisk masculine game with a high probability for the unexpected.

Conclusion

The films in this volume confirm that hockey player's representation coincides with pop culture's portrayal of athletes in high-contact sports as powerful, physically resilient specimens.

The three national cinemas not only specify who plays the game—(overwhelmingly) heterosexual white men and boys—and in what way—with toughness, determination, and resilience—but why this imagery appears insistently throughout the entire repertoire: because of cultural codes and sports genre norms that show a predilection for the heroic and reaffirm hockey as a quintessential male game. In amplifying the spectacle of male bodies by way of the sports genre's realist aesthetic, these cinemas also reify the relationship between masculinity and the nation through the power of muscularity. This representation, as noted, is not unexpected given that on the one hand, the hockey player mythologizes the robust resourcefulness that made possible North America's frontier-opening and relays this virility as necessary symbolic capital. On the other, the hockey athlete embodies the rebelliousness, individualism, resistance to authority, and violence that distinguished male occupational cultures on the frontier.[1]

The tension dramatized by the hockey player's frontier characterization also resonates with the structural aspect of genres, which continually opposes cultural to countercultural values.[2] As a particularly didactic format, the sports film prioritizes self-restraint and social adjustment in line with the directives of the civilizing process. Because Hollywood film and Canadian popular fare make allowances for sport's populist features by articulating athletic conflict as social conflict and siding with the everyman's aspirations for social mobility, the visual spectacle also commonly incorporates shows of physical suffering that prompt the allegiance of the viewer and justify awarding characters the boon in good melodramatic form (*Youngblood*, *Sudden Death*, *Maurice Richard*). Transgressions of the game's stated rules by way of gamesmanship or tricksterism are also common in uneven field-of-play situations to help underdog characters secure their goals (*The Mighty Ducks* films, *H-E-Double Hockey Sticks*, *MVP: Most Valuable Primate*, *Ronnie and Julie*, *Slap Shot 3*, *Les Pee Wee*). Gamesmanship and tricksterism, however, may also express counterculturally when characters disrupt social checks in good carnivalesque form even as they dramatize hockey as the people's game (*Slap Shot*, *Happy Gilmore*, *Les Boys* films).

Unlike the Hollywood sports film genre, which takes note of the athlete's exertions to grant him the windfall, the English-Canadian-produced hockey repertoire that draws on canonical motifs provides for no such outcomes on the grounds that life is arduous and does not guarantee risk-takers big payoffs (*Face Off, The Hounds of Notre Dame*). This theme is common in narratives that dramatize the transgressive aspects of masculinity (*Paperback Hero*, The *Last Season, Gross Misconduct*). English-Canadian cinema, with its mix of canonical and popular motifs also fields sendups of masculinity that allow picaresque characters (*Hounds*, the Don Cherry biopics, *Waking Up Wally*) to transgress the rules and go about the game in their own way likely because they serve the project of citizenship and nationhood. The English-Canadian repertoire for this reason accounts for slightly more diverse outcomes that, in turn, mirror Canadian film's support for heterogeneity and difference.

Quebec hockey-themed films, which blend Hollywood and Canadian canonical motifs and characterization, feature both heroic archetypes and sendups of masculinity to relay that most men are hard-pressed to emulate the athletic ideal though they continue to be judged by it (*Les Boys* films). Characterization of the French-Canadian protagonist may also blend fiery appeal and roguish hues that tap the carnivalesque by activating resistance consonant with mythic ideas of Francophone heroism (*Bon Cop, Bad Cop*). Protagonists who play the sport in the above films also put the body on the line to articulate hockey as people's game.

With respect to themes, the three national cinemas insistently express a concern with the commodification of the game through arrangements that prove injurious to the athlete, the sport's upmarketization, the alienation of traditional constituencies, as well as the Americanization of the Canadian game (*Face Off, Slap Shot, The Deadliest Season, The Last Season, Gross Misconduct, Net Worth, Slap Shot 2, No Sleep 'til Madison, Bon Cop, Bad Cop*).

The English-Canadian repertoire also registers an insistent anxiety with whether hockey is best expressed by the scorer's speed and skill or the tough man's physical prowess (*Face Off, Score: A Hockey Musical, The Last Season, Canada Russia '72, Keep Your Head Up, Kid/ Wrath of Grapes, Goon, Breakaway*). These films plainly do not fall on the same side of the cultural divide, one that by all accounts appears dubious since hockey requires both dexterity and grit. Still, hockey players in Canada are developed in a system that allows for physical excess, which Canadian nationalism deems a degraded form of the game. Films that take to task physical excess also discount the athlete-worker's laboring body because they emphasize myths of cultural nationalism that stress national unity and downplay class-based distinctions.[3]

Quebec cinema, which deals mostly with Francophone national culture, in contrast, does not feature the skill-physicality duality that preoccupies English-Canadian film because the ideal embodies the resilience and durability of the Northern exemplar. These films also feature protagonists who resort to violence only on rare occasions (*Les Pee Wee, Les Boys II*). Quebec films may nonetheless make space for physical retaliation when justified, particularly when protagonists push back on political oppression. *Youngblood* and *Maurice Richard* both condemn the use of systemic violence in the game but the latter film does so by activating the political overtones of physical force in Quebec cinema.

Family entertainment movies also express a noted preoccupation with the professionalization of the children's game as corruption of the play impulse (*The Mighty Ducks* trilogy, *H-E-Double Hockey Sticks, Den Brother, Sticks and Stones, Les Pee Wee*). In line with the augmented didacticism of the sport and family genres, these movies point to hockey as masculinity training, but they also express the need for adequate restraints to mold the young into a form of social capital. Hockey in family fare preeminently helps young protagonists with lone wolf personalities and boastful tendencies hone a more functional mindset. Even protagonists preoccupied with their athletic objectives to the detriment of social and familial ties are taken to task for their so-called selfishness. These films validate the curbing of individualistic leanings as Social Darwinist excess because the team as ideal is premised on the sacredness of communal bonds by way of allegiance and interdependence. Disney films pay homage to the same pastoral values in conflating sports competence with moral character, but also insistently reference the NHL as the site of pinnacle hockey in line with the Company's corporate synergistic mandate.

Based on the range of characters, and furthered by Hollywood's reliance on family entertainment with its lack of socio-specificity and its mass audience address, the repertoire of the last two-and-a-half decades also proclaims that hockey is no longer just a white male sport and that the rink must accommodate increased diversity. Because toughness is intrinsic to the archetype, protagonists from diverse ethnic backgrounds nonetheless also draw on warrior referents to reaffirm their suitability for the game (*The Love Guru, Breakaway*). Gay protagonists may also reprise the exemplar's ruggedness with extreme harshness (*Breakfast with Scot* and *Grown Up Movie Star*) as proof that they have what it takes to play the game, even the repertoire has not solved the dilemma of accurately portraying how to be gay and a male hockey player because of the archetype's inflexibility.

Because of its frontier referents, the cultural practice of hockey also expedites the production of hardier women and girls who as resilient exemplars operate as a form of social capital (*Ice Angel, Go Figure, Les Pee Wee*). Although this repertoire faintly expresses the argument that women's hockey is a different game (*Chicks with Sticks*), males who represent the gender regime consistently surface as foils for these characters, and most of these pictures naturalize the value of grit to push back on their influence (*Hockey Night, Go Figure, National Lampoon's Pucked, Les Pee Wee*). Furthermore, these films also largely field heterosexual characters in line with the feminine ideal, and suggest deviance through secondary characters with so-called masculine traits.[4] The repertoire also features white women and girls in main roles, and is conspicuous for a virtual lack of hockey-playing women of color even in secondary roles. Women's hockey in film also displays very narrow themes that fail to bring up the increasing use of physical tactics to legitimate female participation in the game, labor and recruitment issues, women's history of competition, and how the women's game mirrors regional and national character. The scarcity of female hockey characters, their narrow characterization, and the limited subject matter all suggest that women and girls cannot hope to upstage their male counterparts preeminent position in the game.

The repertoire's profuse imagery of fathers and sons bonded together under the auspices of sport also ratifies the game as male preserve. The many fathers, father-coaches, and coaches who serve as surrogate fathers (*Hockey Night, The Hounds of Notre Dame, Miracle on Ice, Youngblood, The Mighty Ducks* trilogy, the *Les Boys* tetralogy, *Mystery, Alaska, Miracle, Keep Your Head Up, Kid/Wrath of Grapes, Waking Up Wally, Perfectly Normal, Breakfast with Scot, Les Pee Wee*) hone their charges into exemplary citizens. Whether in central or peripheral roles, these characters largely perform a guiding function, since the nurturing aspect of fatherhood checks the articulation of strong masculinity, which retains a robust connection to physicality and the narcissistic focus on the male body, as Stella Bruzzi notes.[5] For this reason, fathers who occupy the center of the narrative as athlete-stars are also rare in the repertoire (*Touch and Go*). The scarcity of father-daughter (*Hockey Night, Go Figure*) and mother-son combinations (*Les Pee Wee, The Rhino Brothers, Slap Shot 3: The Junior League*) in like manner is in keeping with the orthodox character of social setups in hockey-themed films.

In the context of heteronormative relationships, male protagonist in the hockey repertoire are prompted to be pliant with female partners in line with "New Man" directives, which downplay physical aggression and promote a more conciliatory stance. Nonetheless, significant others repeatedly show up primarily in key supporting roles that promote men's attainment (*Mystery, Alaska, The Mighty Ducks, The Last Season, Paperback Hero, The Deadliest Season, Miracle, The Tooth Fairy* et al.). Only *Ice Castles* inverts this prescription through a disillusioned seventies protagonist who exits the game to dedicate himself to the career of his figure skater girlfriend. In cases when the partner is an athlete, as in the above film, females commonly take on the role of figure skaters, a sport that encapsulates desirable femininity while replicating the experience and glamour of athletic performance. Few movies even hint at romantic relationships between hockey-playing males and females (*Hockey Night, Slap Shot 2, Slap Shot 3*) likely because these scenarios require setting up a scheme that both upholds women's place in the game and relegates them to subsidiary status. Regardless of the extent to which motion pictures update the status of women/girls and cultural minorities in the game, then, the cinema of hockey behaves as it if were a strain to treat its cast of characters with any degree of social complexity.

Consistent with the game's male focus, Anglo- and French-Canadian-produced repertoires also noticeably deploy the NHL rubric to configure their protagonists as top athletes and to mark regional and national identity. Over 90 percent of Quebec films and 80 percent of English-Canadian films feature references to NHLers past and present, the league, and/or its teams to denote Canadian competence in the game even in dramas where league owners, coaches, and players do not escape untainted. Although *Net Worth* and *Maurice Richard* show the volatile nature of professional hockey and star players' mistreatment by the league's upper echelon during the 1940s and 1950s, the Anglo- and French-Canadian repertoires also deploy Original Six markers to point to historical rivalries and denote the game in "traditional" enclaves (i.e., Toronto, Boston, Detroit, New York, Chicago, and Montreal). Jason Blake notes that for Canadians this era evokes a time when "stars were rarely traded, money seemed less part of the game, and hockey life was sweet."[6] Thus, Original Six markers romanticize the game in line with the genre's ideological project and signal protagonists masculine allure by denoting the authenticity of their game.

Quebec cinema also overwhelmingly signals Francophone competence in the game by way of the Montreal Canadiens, only occasionally calling up Quebec Nordiques (*Bon Cop, Bad Cop*) and Notre Dame hockey referents (*The Hounds of Notre Dame, Sticks and Stones*). The Canadiens' primary role in configuring Québécois distinctiveness in the cinema is consistent with the team's historical significance in the province. Amy Ransom observes that from its inception the Canadiens original moniker—*le Club de hockey canadien*—conveyed the team's symbolic force in relaying French-Canadian identity and mobilized Anglo-French rivalries to bring Montrealers indifferent to the game into the stands.[7] The entire hockey repertoire deploys the Canadiens, Montreal hockey, and NHLers like Maurice Richard, Jean Béliveau, and Guy Lafleur as distinctive of Francophone culture and identity. Canadiens and Montreal referents in film also dramatize traditional Anglo-French hockey rivalries most frequently versus the Leafs, but also against the Boston Bruins, the Detroit Red Wings, and Chicago professional teams (the Don Cherry biopics, *Net Worth*, and *Touch and Go*, respectively).

The practice of signaling regional and national identity by way of NHL markers, while commonplace, also has problematic implications because it enmeshes capital in the manufacture of character, which, in turn, militates against the notion of hockey as the organic expression of a people. This practice also creates a convoluted web of significations about identity that are difficult to disentangle. For example, in the English-Canadian repertoire the generic NHL imprint (as opposed to that of specific teams) reinforces the *Canadian*-Canadian connotations of the game to formulate a federalist vision of Canadianicity and to field concerns about sovereignty and unity. Case in point, *Canada Russia '72* examines the way in which the Summit Series negotiates national character through the game of Canada's NHLers and articulates the team's triumph as a (hard-won) victory for the Canadian game, and hence, all Canadians. Drawing on the NHL to manufacture identity also makes the act of divvying up the league into positive and negative aspects—as a long-time symbol of Canadian athletic competence and character and as degrading American big business—a nonsensical exercise.

The responsibility for creating this cultural knot lies with league owners who from the very outset sought to associate their corporate interests with the good of the game and with the welfare of communities in Canada. Echoing Amy Ransom's observations about the way in which the Canadiens organization drew Francophones into the stands, Gruneau and Whitson point to a similar practice across the league. They note that when the struggle between amateur and professional leagues subsided, game programs, newspaper and magazine articles, as well as *Hockey Night in Canada* features and interviews, insistently reiterated the link between the NHL and local communities until the idea that the league constitutes the preeminent Canadian form of hockey was ingrained as sensible and natural. This acculturation was so effective that for some, "the production of 'made in Canada' NHLers remains an important and even patriotic task."[8] Tapping NHL markers to activate national or regional identity harmonizes communal and corporate interests much like *Mystery, Alaska* and new family fare imply. The practice of fielding critiques of the hockey business, while hesitating to contest the league's standing in the culture, illustrates that despite that Canadian popular fare and canonical film feature dissimilar conventions, much like Hollywood genres, they also mesh ideologically by resolving contradictions in dominant ways.

The repertoire as a whole also alludes to another Original Six team, the Boston Bruins, as often as the Leafs and Canadiens to refer to hockey as an American regional sport.[9] These references acknowledge that both in Canada and the U.S., Boston is well recognized for its hockey tradition, not unexpectedly since the NHL arrived in the city in 1924 and the game has a strong footing in the state. Historian Stephen Hardy documents that by the time "Montreal hockey" was adopted in the 1890s, the sport had been well established and "[i]n Boston at least, hockey quickly shed its 'Canadian' veneer. It was 'our' game as much as anyone else's."[10] Needless to say, references to the Bruins call up the same problematic of inserting capital in the manufacture of regional Northeast identity. However, this practice does not impact the framing of U.S. identity in the same way as it does that of English- or French-Canadian character because NHL hockey is only one of four major sports in the American entertainment marketplace alongside NFL football, MLB baseball, and NBA basketball. In addition, only forty-five percent of films in the Hollywood repertoire make explicit allusions to the NHL, its icons, or its teams, and several of those references appear in Disney films released during the Company's Ducks tenure. The Hollywood repertoire also depicts slightly more diverse forms of men's hockey that include elite level and minor professional, college, junior, high school, organized beer league, pond and asphalt hockey.

The above differences and the greater range of men's hockey depictions make clear that the game in Hollywood film does not require National League indicators to communicate the protagonist's physical superiority likely because merely playing the sport relays this message to audiences. Moreover, alternative iconographies, such as the 1980 "Miracle on Ice" victory, exist to communicate the American imprint in the game. Although NHLers have taken part in Olympic competition since the 1998 Nagano Games, U.S. TV networks continue to memorialize the U.S. triumph during Winter Games hockey matchups, framing American teams as underdog entries to hike up interest. The three national cinemas also deploy "Miracle" markers in keeping with the intertextuality of the sports genre to allude to underdog protagonists who attain success in good moral order (*D2: The Mighty Ducks, Ice Angel, Slap Shot 3, Goon, Sticks and Stones, Il était une fois Les Boys, Les Pee Wee*).

Given the significance of the "Miracle on Ice" in the U.S. history of the game, and the ease with which these referents convey particular types of characters and contexts in film, it is perhaps little surprise that the repertoire features no representations of U.S. Women's Olympic hockey despite American teams' stellar record, particularly since upholding men's foremost place in the game entails depicting women's status as subsidiary. Because of the sports film's intertextuality and the way that family fare insistently references the "Miracle on Ice," the three national cinemas across four decades also depict the Soviets/Russians as chief rivals, not unexpectedly given the superlative record of Soviet national teams and the history of Canadian and American rivalries with this Cold War foe.[11]

In keeping with Hollywood's popular view of hockey, the impish Hanson Brothers epitomize the game's propensity to devolve into mayhem.[12] Although in film the Philadelphia Flyers' (Broad Street Bullies) also denote physical excess, because of their Cup-winning history the Flyers are neither underdogs nor anti-establishment. The Hansonian brand is more versatile as it both lampoons and validates the hockey player's frontier masculinity with singular political innuendo. Aaron Baker addresses the role of nostalgic sports movies and figures as a response to the threats posed by women and non-whites and the pressures exerted by an "increasingly corporatized sports world that makes self-determination harder to portray plausibly."[13] The Hansons, in like manner, represent the people's ability to thwart the schemes of vested interests and remain nostalgic referents of old-time hockey in the repertoire.

It is a testament to the Hansons' staying power that *Slap Shot*'s popularity endures despite that Ned's striptease preempts the final scoring sequence that expresses the tantamount promise of the sports film in American myth through the protagonists' future prospects. As noted in the introductory segment, the disruption of this myth, which correlates with breaks in genre conventions, can signal a crisis or turning point in the culture's values. *Slap Shot* certainly registers this juncture in the context of the seventies' anti-heroic masculinity. *Les Boys*' parodic losses to women and ethnic teams from countries where hockey is not indigenous also parlay this crisis by amply communicating men's difficulty in living up to the standards of mythical masculinity. The uncertain prospects of protagonists who challenge systemic forces and the staging of male insecurity by way of the bully and bully-clown blueprints also underline that masculine success by way of the traditional sports project is anything but guaranteed.

The Hanson Brothers' own temporary banishment in *Slap Shot 2* and their effacement as Zenovators in *Slap Shot 3*, in addition, convey family entertainment's attempts at expunging Hansonian markers in the context of an increasing framing of sport under corporate aegis. Indeed, the displacement of objectionable subject matter from family fare has had the effect of narrowing the discourse around hockey in the three North American cultures, with few films boasting the bite of motion pictures and TV movies of the seventies and eighties, and fewer even coming close to the satirical depth of *Slap Shot*. As nostalgic embodiments of old-time hockey, the Hansons represent both the potential for mayhem and the disruption of the social order. Because the carnivalesque offers the prospect of rescuing the insecure project of dominant masculinity, the Hansons appear to function as a magical solution to this "crisis" by serving as powerful (and nostalgic) symbols of redress.[14]

The nostalgic arrangement of hockey in film foregrounds protagonists in masculinity-testing situations because sport remains one of the last bastions for staging white male heroism, and furthermore, groups against which the culture defines the archetype continue to demand access to the traditional masculine enclave that the game represents.[15] The three national cinemas' ongoing rehearsal of the nostalgic hockey archetype, with its emphasis on toughness and its compulsory link to national character, then, appears to articulate cultural desires and fantasies as well as fears and anxieties over whether the heroic muscular archetype remains as ascendant as ever. Because many groups look to hockey to express social affiliation and identity, these motion pictures show that, much as in real life, the game in the cinema is in a constant state of negotiation. It is therefore only in the context of conflict and contradiction, as well as in the interface between art, commerce, and politics that the nostalgic hockey archetype in the three North American cinemas continues to transact its cultural standing.

Filmography

Airborne. Dir. Rob Bowman. Icon Entertainment International and Icon Productions. 1993.
Blades and Brass. Dir. William Canning. National Film Board of Canada. 1967.
Bon Cop, Bad Cop. Dir. Érik Canuel. Park Ex Pictures, Sortie 22 Inc., Alliance Atlantis Vivafilm, Telefilm, 2006.
The Boy Who Drank Too Much. Dir. Jerrold Freedman. Company Four and MTM Enterprises. 1980.
Les Boys. Dir. Louis Saïa. Melenny Productions, Telefilm Canada, Gouvernement du Québec et al. 1997.
Les Boys II. Dir. Louis Saïa. Melenny Productions. 1998.
Les Boys III. Dir. Louis Saïa. Melenny Productions. 2001.
Les Boys IV. Dir. George Mihalka. Melenny Productions. 2005.
Breakaway. Dir. Robert Lieberman. Breakaway Productions, the Canadian Broadcasting Corporation (CBC), Telefilm Canada, Caramel Films, Don Carmody Productions. 2011.
Breakfast with Scot. Dir. Laurie Lynd. Scot Pictures, Mongrel Media. 2007.
Canada Russia '72. Dir. T.W. Peacocke. Dream Street Entertainment, Trailer Park Productions. 2006.
Chicks with Sticks. Dir. Kari Skogland. Earth to Sky Pictures, The Nightingale Company. 2004.
The Cutting Edge. Dir. Paul Michael Glaser. 1992. Interscope Communications. 1992.
D2: The Mighty Ducks. Dir. Sam Weisman. Walt Disney Pictures, Avnet/Kerner Productions. 1994.
D3: The Mighty Ducks. Dir. Robert Lieberman. Walt Disney Pictures, Avnet/Kerner Productions. 1996.
The Deadliest Season. Dir. Robert Markowitz. Titus Productions. 1977.
Den Brother. Dir. Mark L. Taylor. The Disney Channel. 2010.
"La Dernière Partie." *Montréal vu par*. Dir. Michel Brault. Atlantis Films Limited and National Film Board of Canada. 1991.
The Dilemma. Dir. Ron Howard. Universal Pictures, Spyglass Entertainment. 2011.
Do You Believe in Miracles? The Story of the 1980 US Hockey Team. Dir. Bernard Goldberg. Home Box Office. 2001.
The Duke of West Point. Dir. Alfred E. Green. Edward Small Productions, United Artists. 1938.
Face Off. Dir. George McCowan. Canadian Film Development Corporation, Agincourt Productions Limited. 1971.
The Game That Kills. Dir. D. Ross Lederman. Columbia Pictures. 1937.
Gay Blades. Dir. George Blair. Republic Pictures. 1946.
Go Figure. Dir. Francine McDougall. Disney Channel et al. 2005.
Going South. First broadcast April 14, 1994, by the Canadian Broadcasting Corporation (CBC) and produced by Allen Abel.
Golden: The Hobey Baker Story. Dir. Paul Lally. New Hampshire Public Television. 2004.
Goon. Dir. Michael Dowse. Entertainment One, No Trace Camping, Caramel Film, Don Carmody Productions, Inferno Pictures, 2011.
Les Grands Duels du Sport. Hockey sûr glace: Canada–URSS. Dir. Serge Laget. Ethan Productions. 2005.
Gross Misconduct. Dir. Atom Egoyan. The Canadian Broadcasting Corporation (CBC). 1993.
Grown Up Movie Star. Dir. Adriana Maggs. The Harold Greenberg Fund, Pope Productions, Mongrel Media. 2009.

Happy Gilmore. Dir. Dennis Dugan. Universal Pictures, Brillstein-Grey Entertainment, Robert Simonds Productions. 1996.
H-E-Double Hockey Sticks. Dir. Randall Miller. Walt Disney Television, Big W Productions. 1999.
Here's Hockey. Dir. Leslie Mcfarlane. National Film Board of Canada. 1953.
The Hockey Champ. Dir. Jack King. Walt Disney Productions. 1939.
Hockey Homicide. Dir. Jack Kinney. Walt Disney Productions. 1945.
Hockey Match on the Ice. Dir. William Heise. Edison Manufacturing Company. 1898.
Hockey Night. Dir. Paul Shapiro. The Canadian Broadcasting Corporation (CBC) and Martin-Paul Productions. 1984.
Holiday in Handcuffs. Dir. Ron Underwood. Alberta Film Entertainment, Hand Cuff Productions. 2007.
Hot Ice: The Anatomy of Hockey, Canada's National Game. Dir. Irving Jacoby. Canadian Government Motion Picture Bureau. 1940.
The Hounds of Notre Dame. Dir. Zale Dalen. Pere Films. 1980.
Ice Angel. Dir. George Erschbamer. Fox Family Films, Shavick Entertainment. 2000.
Ice Castles. Dir. Donald Wrye. Columbia Pictures Corporation. 1978.
Idol of the Crowds. Dir. Arthur Lubin. Universal Pictures. 1937.
Idols of the Game, TBS, November 30, 1995.
Il était une fois les Boys. Dir. Richard Goudreau. Melenny Productions. 2013.
Is Commercialism Ruining Canadian Sport. National Film Board of Canada. 1955.
It's a Pleasure. Dir. William A. Seiter. International Pictures, RKO Radio Pictures, MGM/UA Pictures. 1945.
Jack Frost. Dir. Troy Miller. Warner Bros. 1998.
Just Friends. Dir. Roger Kumble. Just Friends Productions, Cinerenta, Inferno. 2005.
Keep Your Head Up, Kid: The Don Cherry Story. Dir. Jeff Woolnough. 5 for Fighting Productions, Blue Coach MB Productions, E1 Entertainment, CBC Television. 2010.
King of Hockey. Dir. Noel M. Smith. Warner Brothers. 1938.
Kronjuvelerna. Dir. Ella Lemhagen. Filmlance International AB, Sveriges TV, Film i Väst and Svenska Filminstitutet (SFI). 2011.
The Last Season. Dir. Allan King. The Canadian Broadcasting Corporation (CBC). 1986.
The Love Guru. Dir. Marco Schnabel. Paramount Pictures et al. 2008.
Love Story. Dir. Arthur Hiller. Paramount Pictures. 1970.
Lovers in a Dangerous Time. Dir. May Charters, Mark Hug. Fruitstand Loft Films, White Goat Productions. 2009.
Maurice Richard. Dir. Charles Binamé. Cinémaginaire Inc. 2005.
The Mighty Ducks. Dir. Stephen Herek. Walt Disney Pictures, Touchwood Pacific Partners, Avnet/Kerner Productions. 1992.
Miracle. Dir. Gavin O'Connor. Walt Disney Pictures, Mayhem Pictures, Pop Pop Productions. 2004.
Miracle on Ice. Dir. Steven Hilliard Stern. Filmways Television, Moonlight Productions. 1981.
Le Moment de vérité. Lance et compte. Dir. Richard Martin. Communications Claude Héroux, Téléfilm Canada, Télé-Métrople, et al. 1991.
MVP: Most Valuable Primate. Dir. Robert Vince. Keystone Family Productions, Film Incentive B.C. et al. 2000.
Mystery, Alaska. Dir. Jay Roach. Hollywood Pictures, Baldwin/Cohen Productions, Rocking Chair Productions. 1999.
The Mystery of the Million Dollar Hockey Puck. Dirs. Jean LaFleur, Peter Svatek. Cinépix. 1975.
National Lampoon's Pucked. Dir. Arthur Hiller. National Lampoon Productions. 2006.
NBC Nightly News. "A League of Their Own: Ladies Hit Ice, Go Pro." Aired Feb. 2011. http://www.nbc.com/news-sports/msnbc-video/a-league-of-their-own-ladies-hit-ice-go-pro/.
Net Worth. Dir. Jerry Ciccoritti. The Canadian Broadcasting Corporation (CBC). 1995.
No Sleep 'til Madison. Dirs. David Fleer, Eric Moe, Peter Rudy. Modern Ping Pong. 2002.
Of Sport and Men. Dir. Hubert Aquin. National Film Board of Canada. 1961.
Paperback Hero. Dir. Peter Pearson. Agincourt International. 1973.
Les Pee Wee 3D: L'hiver qui a changé ma vie. Dir. Érik Tessier. Christal Films. 2012.

Perfectly Normal. Dir. Yves Simoneau. BSB, Byalistock & Bloom Limited, Ontario Film Development Corporation, Telefilm Canada. 1991.
Raising Helen. Dir. Garry Marshall. Touchstone Pictures et al. 2004.
The Return of the Bling (American Dad). Dir. Joseph Daniello. Fox Broadcasting Company. 2010.
The Rhino Brothers. Dir. Dwayne Beaver. Rhino Brothers Film Co., Film Incentive B.C. et al. 2001.
Ronnie and Julie. Dir. Philip Spink. Showtime Networks, Evergreen Entertainment, Vidatron Entertainment Group. 1997.
Santa Baby. Dir. Ron Underwood. "Mary Christmas" Filmproduktions, Alberta Film Entertainment. 2006.
Score: A Hockey Musical. Dir. Michael McGowan. Mongrel Media, Telefilm Canada. 2010.
September 1972. Prods. Rob MacAskill, Ian Davey. CTV National Television Network. 1997.
The Sheldon Kennedy Story. Dir. Norma Bailey. Alberta Filmworks, Sarazin Couture Productions. 1999.
Slap Shot. Dir. George Roy Hill. Universal Pictures, Kings Road Entertainment. 1977.
Slap Shot 2: Breaking the Ice. Dir. Steven Boyum. Universal Home Entertainment. 2002.
Slap Shot 3: The Junior League. Dir. Richard Martin. Universal Studios Home Entertainment Family Productions, Refrain Productions, Movie Central Network. 2008.
Soul of a Nation. Episode VII. *Hockey: A People's History.* Warner Home Video. 2006.
Sticks and Stones. Dir. George Mihalka. Cirrus Communications, Dream Street Pictures, CTV. 2008.
Sudden Death. Dir. Peter Hyams. Universal Pictures, Imperial Entertainment, Signature Pictures. 1995.
Summit on Ice. Dir. Robert MacAskill. Canadian Broadcasting Corporation (CBC). 1996.
The Sweater. Dir. Sheldon Cohen. National Film Board of Canada. 1980.
13 Going on 30. Dir. Gary Winick. Columbia Pictures and Sony Pictures Entertainment. 2004.
Tooth Fairy. Dir. Michael Lembeck. Twentieth Century Fox Corporation. 2010.
Touch and Go. Dir. Robert Mandel. Kings Road Entertainment. 1986.
Waking Up Wally: The Walter Gretzky Story. Dir. Dean Bennett. Accent Entertainment Corporation, Alberta Filmworks, Canadian Broadcasting Corporation (CBC). 2005.
White Lightning. Dir. Edward Bernds. Monogram Pictures, Allied Artists. 1953.
Wrath of Grapes: The Don Cherry Story II. Dir. Jeff Woolnough. 5 for Fighting, Entertainment One, Pier 21 Films, CBC. 2012.
Youngblood. Dir. Peter Markle. The Guber-Peters Company, United Artists. 1986.

Chapter Notes

Preface

1. See, for example, the dearth of hockey movies in Marc Harvey Zucker and Lawrence J. Babich's *Sports Films: A Complete Reference* (Toronto: Macmillan, 1987); Jeffrey H. Wallenfeldt, ed., *Sports Movies: A Review of Nearly 500 Films* (Evanston, IL: Cinebooks, Inc., 1989); Judith A. Davidson and Daryl Adler, *Sport on Film and Video. The North American Society for Sport History Guide* (Metuchen, New Jersey: The Scarecrow Press, Inc., 1993); Wyndham Wise, ed., *TAKE ONE's Essential Guide to Canadian Film* (Toronto: University of Toronto Press, 2001); Randy Williams, *Sports Cinema 100 Movies: The Best of Hollywood's Athletic Heroes, Losers, Myths, and Misfits* (Pompton Plains, New Jersey: Limelight Editions, 2006); Ronald Bergan, *Sports in the Movies* (New York: Proteus, 1982); Ray Didinger, *The Ultimate Book of Sports Movies* (Philadelphia, PA: Running Press, 2009); Laurel Zeisler, *Historical Dictionary of Ice Hockey* (Lanham, Maryland: Rowman and Littlefield, 2015). The comprehensive hockey film database maintained by the Society for International Hockey Research (SIHR) gives a better glimpse of the extent to which hockey has been part of cinematic storytelling.

2. Demetrius W. Pearson, Russell L. Curtis, C. Allen Haney, and James J. Zhang, "Sports Films: Social Dimensions Over Time, 1930–1995," *Journal of Sport and Social Issues* 27, no. 2 (2003), 152.

3. Steven A. Riess, *Sports in America from Colonial Times to the Twenty-First Century: An Encyclopedia* (New York: Routledge, 2015), 350.

4. See, for example, the "Top 10 Hockey Movies" 10-plus minute Mojo.com this promotional video showcasing Hollywood, English-Canadian and Quebec hockey movies: http://www.youtube.com/watch?v=mWCkYfx6ydA.

Introduction

1. See EA's "NHL 13" *Our Game* at http://www.youtube.com/watch?v=iqMQHMxYyVA.

2. Researchers define dominant, traditional or hegemonic masculinity as a configuration of practices that naturalizes the political, social, and cultural ascendance of a category of men (white, heterosexual male) and their power over women, working-class men, cultural minorities, immigrant groups, and gays. Michelle Helstein notes that sporting cultures like hockey's, which prioritize "strong, aggressive, forceful, space-occupying movements," are the ones most apt to link to national identity construction. Moreover, the concept of dominant masculinity is so totalizing that it configures the practice of sport by women as either contrary to "real" sport or to "real" womanhood. See Michelle Helstein, "Producing the Canadian Female Athlete: Negotiating the Popular Logics of Sport and Citizenship," *How Canadians Communicate III: Contexts of Canadian Popular Culture*, eds. Bart Beaty, Derek Briton, Gloria Filax, and Rebecca Sullivan (Edmonton, AB: Athabasca University Press, 2010), 243–4. For more on dominant masculinity, see R.W. Connell and James W. Messerschmidt, "Hegemonic Masculinity: Rethinking the Concept," *Gender & Society* 19, no. 6 (2005): 838, 841, 852.

3. Michael A. Messner, "Still a Man's World? Studying Masculinities in Sport," *Handbook of Studies on Men and Masculinities*, eds. by Michael Kimmel, Jeff Hearn, and R.W. Connell (London: Sage, 2005), 314.

4. Messner, "Still a Man's World?," 314.

5. Jay Coakley, *Sports in Society, Issues and Controversies* (Whitby, ON: McGraw-Hill Ryerson, 2004), 12.

6. Stella Bruzzi, *Bringing Up Daddy: Fatherhood and Masculinity in Post-War Hollywood* (London: BFI Publishing, 2005), xvi, xvii.

7. Harry M. Benshoff and Sean Griffin, *America on Film: Representing Race, Class, Gender and Sexuality at the Movies* (Oxford: Wiley-Blackwell, 2004), 263.

8. Ralph Donald, "From 'Knockout Punch' to 'Home Run': Masculinity's 'Dirty Dozen' Sports in American Combat Films," *Film & History* 35, no. 1 (2005), 20; Messner, Still A Man's World?," 317, 320.

9. Donald F. Sabo and Sue Curry Jansen, "Prometheus Unbound: Constructions of Masculinity in Sports Media," *Mediasport*, ed. Lawrence A. Wenner (London: Routledge, 1998), 209.

10. Deborah V. Tudor, *Hollywood's Vision of Team Sports: Heroes, Race, and Gender* (New York: Garland, 1997), 80.

11. Joseph Maguire, "Sport, Identity Politics, and Globalization: Diminishing Contrasts and Increasing Varieties," *Sociology of Sport Journal* 11 (1994), 310.

12. Michael Buma, *Refereeing Identity: The Cultural Work of Canadian Hockey Novels* (Montreal: McGill-Queen's University Press, 2012), 43.

13. Amy Ransom, *Hockey, PQ: Canada's Game in*

Quebec's Popular Culture (Toronto: University of Toronto Press, 2014), 6.

14. Hollywood production meets 70–80 percent of global demand in TV and feature film content. See Scott Robert Olson, *Hollywood Planet: Global Media and the Competitive Advantage of Narrative Transparency* (London: Routledge, 1999), 23; Seán Crosson, *Sport in Film* (London: Routledge, 2013), 49.

15. Bart Beaty in "Not Playing, Working: Class, Masculinity, and Nation in the Canadian Hockey Film" examines gender and class themes in a handful of Canadian-produced films. Jeremy Michael Ward looks at *The Mighty Ducks* films in connection with Disney's entry into the NHL. Michael Silk, Jamie Schultz, and Brian Bracey in "From Mice to Men: Miracle, Mythology and the 'Magic Kingdom'" tackle Disney's *Miracle* from historical and ideological perspectives. Janice Kaye's "Perfectly Normal, Eh? Gender Transformations and National Identity in Canada" explores director Yves Simoneau's film from the standpoint of the American-Canadian relationship and as expression of aggressive and mild (latently homosexual) masculinity. In her Ph.D. thesis Kaye also discusses *Bon Cop, Bad Cop* in "Certain Tendencies in Canadian Cinema" as commentary of the relationship between Canada's Two Solitudes. Bill Marshall in *Quebec National Cinema* considers *Les Boys* films as a utopian version of white Francophone masculinity. André Loiselle in "Subtly Subversive or Simply Stupid: Notes on Quebec Popular Cinema" zeroes in on the comically rebellious aspects of the characters in the *Les Boys* tetralogy in line with the simultaneously conservative and progressive markers of Quebec popular cinema's light satire. As noted, Amy Ransom in *Hockey, PQ: Canada's Game in Quebec's Popular Culture* delivers an in-depth analysis of Québécois masculinity in the *Les Boys* franchise and feature films *Maurice Richard* and *Bon Cop, Bad Cop* as reflections of Francophone identity and their relationship to Quebec as a nation.

16. Rick Altman, *Film/Genre* (London: BFI, 1999), 18, 23.

17. Michael Hewitt, "Best Picture? Says Who?" *The Orange County Register*, February 23, 2013, accessed February 24, 2014, http://www.nbcnews.com/id/50917358/ns/local_news-orange_county_ca/t/best-picture-says-who/.

18. Sports producers made the above comments at The Octagon/Street and Smith's *SportsBusiness* World Congress of Sports, Sports and Entertainment/Sport in Cinema and TV event held in Newport Beach, California, March 3–5, 2004 in interviews with *SportsBusiness Journal* reporter Joe Oliver. A month prior, on February 6, 2004, Disney had debuted its hockey movie *Miracle* with great success. The film garnered USD 64 million on a production budget of USD 28 million. For more on the above, see Joe Oliver, "Sports and Cinema: Experts Discuss What Works on Screen, at Box Office," *SportsBusiness Journal*, March 1–7, 2002, 53; for *Miracle's* box office numbers, see "Miracle (2004)," *The Numbers: Where Data and the Movie Business Meet*, accessed March 20, 2014, http://www.the-numbers.com/movie/Miracle-The-(2004)#tab=box-office.

19. Playwright and filmmaker Eric Henry Sanders points out that the controversies about reading genres in the academic community are partly due to film theorists' approaches. He notes that locating a movie with particular iconographies and themes and positing it as a historical antecedent for another with similar characteristics in order to extrapolate theoretical foundations about a particular genre, only lead to caveats about the stability of said format. Film theorist Daniel Chandler, for his part, also cautions about casting about for an ideal, unadulterated concept of genre, because practitioners and the public may make sense of a film in one way while critical theorists may do so in another. Chandler cites Robert Stam's framework for sorting out films according to literary forms (comedy, melodrama), budget (blockbusters), story content (the war film), location (the western), racial identity and sexual orientation (Black and Queer cinema, respectively), as well as media formats (the musical). He also alludes to David Bordwell's outline of genres, which includes classification by period or country, director, producer or marquee actor, and by audience or subject matter (teen flicks and family films). Chandler also alludes to Stephen Neale's argument about viewing genres as fundamentally historically-grounded concepts. For more on the subject, see Sanders' revision of the western, Jason Landrum's take on how horror and science fiction films destabilize traditional genres, and Seán Crosson's discussion of genre. Eric Henry Sanders, "The Plot Genre Revolution: Or, Why the Western Isn't a Genre," *Bright Lights Film Journal*, April 16, 2015, accessed July 8, 2015, http://brightlightsfilm.com/the-plot-genre-revolution-or-why-the-western-isnt-a-genre/#.VdYrfFrF_dk; Daniel Chandler, "An Introduction to Genre Theory," accessed July 8, 2013, http://visual-memory.co.uk/daniel/Documents/intgenre/; Stephen Neale, *Genre* (London: British Film Institute, 1980), 464; Robert Stam, *Film Theory* (Oxford: Blackwell, 2000), 14; David Bordwell, *Making Meaning: Inference and Rhetoric in the Interpretation of Cinema* (Cambridge: Harvard University Press, 1989), 148; David Landrum, "Rethinking Genre Theory," *The Journal of Cinema and Media*, 48, no. 1 (2007): 109–111; Crosson, *Sport in Film*, 26, 49, 50, 55.

20. Emma Poulton and Martin Roderick, "Introducing Sport in Films," *Sport in Society* 11, no. 2 (2008): 107–116.

21. Garry Whannel, "Winning and Losing Respect: Narratives of Identity in Sport Films," *Sport in Society* 11, no. 2 (2008): 195–208.

22. Glen Jones, "In Praise of an 'Invisible Genre'? An Ambivalent Look at the Fictional Sports Feature Film," *Sport in Society* 11, no. 2 (2008): 117–129.

23. Bruce Babington, *The Sports Film: Games People Play* (New York: Columbia University Press, 2014), 10.

24. Babington, *The Sports Film*, 4, 6.

25. Crosson approaches his reading of the sports film through the lens of post-structuralism, in particular, through Roland Barthes' view of the media's mythologizing of sport as a transcendental endeavor that conceals the economic gain derived from these images. He also draws on Rick Altman's work on genre and David Rowe's definition of the sports film. See Crosson, *Sport and Film*, 27–8, 60–5; Roland Barthes, "The Tour the France as Epic," *The Eiffel Tower and Other Mythologies* (New York: Hill and Wang, 1979), 67; Altman, *Film/Genre*; David Rowe, "If You Film It, Will They Come?—

Sports on Film," *Journal of Sport and Social Issues* 22, no. 4 (1989): 350–9.

26. Ken Dancyger and Jeff Rush, *Alternative Scriptwriting: Beyond the Hollywood Formula* (London: Focal Press), 92–4.

27. Babington, *The Sports Film*, 27.

28. Crosson notes that the sports film's repetitive aspect diminishes the importance of any ending, while nonetheless procuring a ritualistic enjoyment of the hero's testing and obstacle-negotiation. Crosson draws on Altman's work on genres for his discussion. Crosson, *Sport in Film*, 62–4.

29. As examples of works that deal with mythological constructs, Elfriede Fürsich cites James Carey's *Media, Myths, Narratives: Television and the Press*, Jack Lule's *Daily News, Eternal Stories: The Mythological Role of Journalism*, and Daniel Berkowitz's "Suicide Bombers as Women Warriors: Making News Through Mythical Archetypes." Elfriede Fürsich "In Defense of Textual Analysis: Restoring a Challenged Method for Journalism and Media Studies," *Journalism Studies* 10, no. 2 (2009): 238–252.

30. For more on myth and genres' similarities, see George Wead and George Lellis, *Film: Form and Function* (Houghton, Mifflin and Co., 1981), 206. For the prescriptive aspects of myth, see Eric Greene, *Planet of the Apes as American Myth* (Hanover, New Hampshire: Wesleyan University Press), 11.

31. Richard Slotkin argues that just as the continual use of particular genres calls attention to the culture's most profound anxieties and pervasive public concerns, major ruptures in genre development also point to a crossroads in the values and organization of a culture. Richard Slotkin, *Gunfighter Nation: The Myth of the Frontier in Twentieth-Century America* (New York: Atheneum, 1992), 8.

32. Films in the hockey repertoire have elements of the war or combat film, the western, the blockbuster action film, the sitcom and its dysfunctional family motif, the musical, the romantic comedy, family entertainment, the buddy-cop thriller, the road movie, the genre parody, as well as film fare that delves into racial/ethnic issues and sexual identity.

33. Dancyger and Rush, *Alternative Scriptwriting*, 92–4.

34. As an area of research, hockey is in a distinctly privileged position with respect to the amount of scholarly work in the social sciences, media, literature, folklore, kinetic studies and other fields that has has gone into investigating its various aspects. In referring to Andrew Holman's perspective on interdisciplinary hockey scholarship. Michael Buma notes that, because of the amount of work in this area, it is now possible to speak of "hockey studies." Buma, *Refereeing Identity*, 24; Andrew Holman, Introduction to *Canada's Game: Hockey and Identity*, ed. Andrew Holman, 7.

35. Although these archetypes encapsulate cultural and historical premises that were relevant at the time of their inception, they remain important because they continue to promote a sense of common culture as well as to make tangible the "imagined nation." These archetypes, which also ground the origin myths to which hockey is linked, are nonetheless simply models or representations that cannot definitively pinpoint the birthplace of the game in North America. *On the Origin of Hockey*, for example, makes a persuasive case for hockey's connection to the "stick and ball games" of England. Indeed, Charles Darwin himself referred to being "very fond of playing at hocky on the ice in skates" in his letter to son William. For more, see Carl Gidén, Patrick Houda, and Jean-Patrice Martel, *On the Origin of Hockey* (Stockholm and Chambly: Hockey Origin Publishing, 2014), 48–49. For more on archetypes, see Slotkin, *Gunfighter Nation*, 6; Benedict Anderson, *Imagined Communities: Reflections on the Origin and Spread of Nationalism* (London: Verson, 1989).

36. André Légaré, "Nunavut: The Construction of a Regional Collective Identity in the Canadian Arctic," *Wicazo Sa Review* 17, no. 2 (2002): 69–71.

37. National scripts operate as mythic constructs by formulating the nation as a sacred hub and attributing a quality of transcendence to the territory over which the nation-state has sovereignty. See Anthony D. Smith, *National Identity* (Reno: University of Nevada Press, 1991), 4.

38. Susan Kollin, *Nature's State: Imagining Alaska as the Last Frontier* (Chapel Hill: University of North Carolina Press), 73.

39. Although in myth, the westerly advance of the frontier appears linear, the process was geographically and culturally complex. For more on this process, see Patricia Nelson Limerick, "The Adventures of the Frontier in the Twentieth Century," *The Frontier in American Culture*, ed. James R. Grossman (Berkeley: University of California Press, 1994), 67–102; Richard White, "Frederick Jackson Turner and Buffalo Bill," *The Frontier in American Culture*, ed. by James R. Grossman (Berkeley: University of California Press), 1994, 7–66. For a comparison of Canadian and American realities of frontier development, see Lorry W. Felske and Beverly Jean Rasporich, "Challenging Frontiers," *Challenging Frontiers: The Canadian West*, ed. Lorry W. Felske and Beverly Jean Rasporich (Calgary, AB: University of Calgary Press, 2004), 1–11.

40. The environmental determinism that supported historians' interpretations of Canadian and American identity drew from Baron de La Brede et de Montesquieu's (1689–1755) ideas on geography, climate, and natural barriers as central determinants of behavior and cultural character.

41. Donald Worster, "Two Faces West: The Development Myth in Canada and the United States," *One West, Two Myths: A Comparative Reader*, ed. Carol L. Higham and Robert Thacker (Calgary: University of Calgary Press, 2004), 26.

42. Eva Mackey, *The House of Difference: Cultural Politics and National Identity in Canada* (Toronto: University of Toronto Press, 2002), 30, 42.

43. The *coureurs des bois* initially represented French-Canadian culture, but in time they transformed into icons of North American frontier masculinity. Brian Martin notes that over the centuries these early explorers, as well as the trappers (*trappeurs*) and loggers (*bûcherons*) that built Quebec, became symbols of bold masculinity in the North American popular imaginary. As an example, he cites Paul Bunyan whose iconic lumberjack roots lie in the timberlands of Quebec. Brian Martin, "Cultural Formations, North America," *Interna-

tional Encyclopedia of Men and Masculinities, ed. Michael Flood, Judith Kegan Gardiner, Bob Pease, and Keith Pringle (New York: Routledge, 2007), 116.

44. Michael Robidoux, "Historical Interpretations of First Nations Masculinity," *The International Journal of the History of Sport* 23, no. 2 (2006): 272.

45. Robidoux, "Historical Interpretations of First Nations Masculinity," 275.

46. Harold E. Innis, *The Strategy of Culture* (Toronto: University of Toronto Press); Peter Morris, "In Our Own Eyes: The Canonizing of Canadian Film," *Canadian Journal of Film Studies* 3, no. 1 (1994), 39. Government committees of the late 1920s repurposed Innis' ideas to advocate public control and subsidies of the cultural industries: broadcasting, film, music and other arts. Cultural studies scholar Jody Berland notes that to this day Innis' work, known to have pioneered the field of dependency theory, remains highly influential in Canadian intellectual and artistic circles, extending into "Literary Theory, Politics, Feminism, and Cultural Studies." Jodie Berland, "Marginal Notes in Cultural Studies in Canada," *University of Toronto Quarterly* 64, no. 4 (1995), 518.

47. William H. Katerberg, "A Northern Vision: Frontiers and the West in the Canadian and American Imagination," *The American Review of Canadian Studies* 33, no. 4 (2003): 551, 556; Matthew Evenden, "The Northern Vision of Harold Innis," *Journal of Canadian Studies* 34, no. 3 (1999): 178.

48. David Noble, *The End of American History: Democracy, Capitalism and the Metaphor of Two Worlds in Anglo-American Historical Writing* (Minneapolis: University of Minnesota Press, 1985), 6, 19.

49. Frederick Jackson Turner titled his 1893 paper "The Significance of the Frontier in American History."

50. Frederick Jackson Turner, *The Frontier in American History*, ed. Harold P. Simonson (New York: Frederick Ungar, 1963), 342.

51. Frederick Jackson Turner, "The Problem of the West," *The Atlantic Monthly* (September 1896), accessed August 4, 2006, http://www.theatlantic.com/past/docs/issues/95sep/ets/turn.htm.

52. Slotkin, *Gunfighter Nation*, 34, 59.

53. Slotkin, *Gunfighter Nation*, 30.

54. Sheila McManus, "Making the Forty-Ninth Parallel: How Canada and the United States Used Space, Race, and Gender to Turn Blackfoot Country into the Alberta-Montana Borderlands," *One West, Two Myths: A Comparative Reader*, eds. Carol L. Higham and Robert Thacker (Calgary: University of Calgary Press, 2004), 111.

55. Catherine Gouge, "The American Frontier: History, Rhetoric, Concept," *Americana: The Journal of American Popular Culture* 6, no. 1 (Spring 2007), accessed November 9, 2007, http://www.americanpopularculture.com/journal/articles/spring_2007/gouge.htm.

56. Writers like Zayne Grey, whose sixty western novels cemented representation of the rugged individualist cowboy, and Owen Wister, who in *The Virginian* (1902) set the standard for the frontier archetype, contributed to popular perceptions of the mythological West.

57. Unlike Turner who conceptualized frontier-opening as a democratic, non-heroic, and chiefly agrarian process, Roosevelt formulated it as a heroic sporting contest against Indian tribes in which the superior side had triumphed for the benefit of mankind. Michael Oriard notes that in *The Winning of the West* (1885–1894) Roosevelt linked athleticism to frontier-opening, synthesizing the Western sporting myth and advancing the "Myth of National Origins and Future Destiny." Michael Oriard, *Sporting with the Gods: American Sports Fiction, 1868–1980* (Chicago: Nelson-Hall, 1982), 20–1, 23.

58. Theodore Roosevelt, *The Theodore Roosevelt Cyclopedia*, 581–2.

59. Theodore Roosevelt, "At the Harvard Union, February 23, 1907," *Presidential Addresses and State Papers: January 16, 1907 to October 25, 1907*, volume VI, 1164–1181 (New York: The Review of Reviews Company, 1910, Kessinger Publishing's Rare Reprints): 1166. The author thanks Len Kotylo, President of the Society for International Hockey Research, for this reference cited in "The Roots of Hockey's International Appeal" (paper presented at the Canada & The League of Hockey Nations Conference, Victoria, British Columbia, Canada, April 19–21, 2007).

60. Clay Motley, "Fighting for Manhood: Rocky and Turn-of-the-Century Antimodernism," *Film & History* 35, no. 2 (2005): 61.

61. Holly Allen, "Heroism," *American Masculinities*, ed. Bret E. Carroll (Thousand Oaks, CA: Sage: 2003), 206; J.A. Mangan and James Walvin, *Manliness and Morality: Middle Class Masculinity in Britain and America 1800–1940* (Manchester: Manchester University Press, 1987).

62. Motley, "Fighting for Manhood," 60.

63. For more on the subject, see Ann Douglas, *The Feminization of American Culture* (New York: Farrar, Strauss and Giroux, 1998).

64. Joane Nagel, "Nation," *Handbook of Studies on Men and Masculinities*, eds. Michael Kimmel, Jeff Hearn, and R.W. Connell (London: Sage: 2005), 400. Jim McKay, Toby Miller, Geoffrey Lawrence, and David Rowe also note that modern sport emerged at the intersection of diverse political and social ideologies, such as muscular Christianity, physical education in the school curriculum, gymnastics and physical culture movements, French neoclassical classicism as it fused with diplomacy articulated in Baron Pierre de Coubertin's version of the Greek Olympics, imperialist militarism and its conflation of sport and war, and the white supremacy ideologies of Eurocentrism and Social Darwinism. The authors also note that the decline of absolute monarchy, the rise of parliamentary democracy, as well as the arrival of global capitalism, with its industrializing and urbanizing influences, also expedited modern sport's development. Jim McKay, Toby Miller, Geoffrey Lawrence and David Rowe, *Globalization and Sport: Playing the World* (London: Sage, 2001), 39–40.

65. Stacy Lorenz and Geraint B. Osborne, "'Talk About Strenuous Hockey': Violence, Manhood, and the 1907 Ottawa Silver Seven-Montreal Wanderer Rivalry," *Journal of Canadian Studies* 40, no. 1 (2006): 129–30.

66. Oriard, *Sporting with the Gods*, 14.

67. John Fiske, *Understanding Popular Culture* (New York: Routledge), 57–60.

68. Norbert Elias and Eric Dunning, *The Quest for Excitement: Sport and Leisure in the Civilizing Process* (Oxford: Basil Blackwell, 1986), 49; David McArdle,

From Boot Money to Bosman: Football Society and the Law (London: Cavendish, 2000), 6.

69. Daniel S. Mason and Gregory H. Duquette, "Newspaper Coverage of Early Professional Hockey: The Discourses of Class and Control," *Media History* 10, no. 3 (2004): 170.

70. Lorenz and Osborne argue, however, that there was no hard dividing line between middle-class and working-class sporting values. Lorenz and Osborne, "Talk About Strenuous Hockey," 29; McArdle, *From Boot Money to Bosman*, 5–6.

71. See Stephen Hardy's comments in the documentary *Golden: The Hobey Baker Story* (2004).

72. Stephen Hardy, "Long Before Orr," *The Rock, the Curse, and the Hub: A Random History of Boston Sports*, ed. Randy Roberts (Cambridge: Harvard University Press, 2005), 245–51.

73. While the proponents of amateurism attacked professional leagues for prioritizing winning over fair play as well as for furthering gambling and match-fixing, the real reason for the friction appeared to be the fierce competition for top players. Mason and Duquette, for instance, make clear that newspaper coverage of the IHL frowned on the new league's "openly commercial and professionalized" status, and resented "the loss of elite canadian players to the USA...." Mason and Duquette, "Newspaper Coverage of Early Professional Hockey: The Discourses of Class and Control," 168–70. See also Ernie Fitzsimmons, "Early Pro Leagues," *Total Hockey*, ed. Dan Diamond (Scarborough, ON: Total Sports Publishing, 2000), 32; Michael McKinley, *Hockey: A People's History* (Toronto: McClelland & Stewart, 2006), 47.

74. Lorenz and Osborne, "'Talk About Strenuous Hockey,'" 12.

75. Hardy, "Long Before Orr," 255.

76. Richard Gruneau and David Whitson, "Upmarket Continentalism," *Continental Order? Integrating North America for Cybercapitalism*, ed. Vincent Mosco and Dan Schiller (Lanham, Maryland: Rowman and Littlefield, 2001), 240–1.

77. Lorenz and Osborne, "'Talk About Strenuous Hockey,'" 129–30. Andy Holman documents that by the 1890s Canadian hockey grew noticeably more violent as players privileged the physical encounter at the expense of puckhandling, passing, skating, and scoring skills, and this version of the game promptly became the national standard. Andrew Holman, "Playing in the Neutral Zone: Meanings and Uses of Ice Hockey in the Canada–U.S. Borderlands, 1895–1915," *The American Review of Canadian Studies* 34, no. 1 (2004): 38. See also Anthony E. Rotundo, *American Manhood: Transformations in Masculinity from the Revolution to the Modern Era* (New York: BasicBooks, 1993).

78. Robert G. Hollands, "Masculinity and the Positive Hero in Canadian Sports Novels," *Arete* IV, no. 1 (1986): 79.

79. Hollands, "Masculinity and the Positive Hero in Canadian Sports Novels," 79.

80. Hollands cites Sheldon Ilowite's *Centerman from Quebec* (1972) as an example of this kind of characterization. Robert G. Hollands, "English-Canadian Sports Novels and Cultural Production," *Not Just a Game: Essays in Canadian Sports Sociology*, ed. by Jean Harvey and Hart Cantelon (Ottawa: University of Ottawa Press, 1998), 221.

81. Jason Blake, *Canadian Hockey Literature: A Thematic Study* (Toronto: Toronto University Press, 2010), 9, 42, 79.

82. Buma, *Refereeing Identity*, 43, 146, 150.

83. Hollands, "Masculinity and the Positive Hero in Canadian Sports Novels," 79–80.

84. Michael Oriard notes that both of these archetypes loom large as prime symbols of the American experience. Michael Oriard, *Dreaming of Heroes: American Sports Fiction, 1868–1980* (Chicago: Nelson-Hall, 1982), 47, 48.

85. Slotkin, *Gunfighter Nation*, 61.

86. Robert Ray, *A Certain Tendency of the Hollywood Cinema, 1930–1980* (Princeton: Princeton University Press, 1985), 36; Garry Whannel, "No Room for Uncertainty: Gridiron Masculinity in North Dallas Forty," *You, Tarzan: Masculinity, Movies and Men*, ed. Pat Kirkham and Janet Thumim (London: Lawrence and Wishart, 1993), 202.

87. The CBC's multi-part documentary *Hockey: A People's History* (2006) expresses the intimate connection between the nation's genesis and the game: "We witnessed a nation that was created when the game was created."

88. Kristi Allain outlines these elements in Canadian media's construction of the hockey archetype as personified by NHL star Sidney Crosby and bolstered by *Hockey in Night in Canada*'s Don Cherry. Kristi Allain, "Kid Crosby or Golden Boy: Sidney Crosby, Canadian National Identity, and the Policing of Hockey Masculinity," *International Review for the Sociology of Sport* 46, no. 2 (2010): 8–9. For a discussion of the ways in which the beer industry capitalizes on the hockey player's self-affirming masculinity, see Robert E. Seiler, "Selling Patriotism/Selling Beer: The Case of the 'I Am Canadian!' Commercial," *American Review of Canadian Studies* 32 (Spring 2002): 45–66.

89. Richard Gruneau and David Whitson, *Hockey Night in Canada: Sport, Identities and Cultural Politics* (Toronto: Garamond, 1993), 191.

90. Linda Williams cites Peter Brooks' discussion of melodrama as reference. See Linda Williams, "Melodrama Revised," *Refiguring American Film Genres*, ed. Nick Browne (Berkeley: University of California Press, 1998), 59; Peter Brooks, *The Melodramatic Imagination: Balzac, Henry James, Melodrama, and the Mode of Excess* (New Haven: Yale University Press, 1976).

91. Misia Landau notes that the "humble origins" motif recurs in myth and folklore. Misia Landau, "Human Evolution as Narrative," *American Scientist* 72 (1984): 265.

92. Neil Sinyard, "Sporting Screen," *Film and Filming* 330 (1982): 15.

93. Williams, "Melodrama Revised," 58.

94. Williams, "Melodrama Revised," 48, 75, 78.

95. Marjorie D. Kibby, "Nostalgia for the Masculine: Onward to the Past in the Sport Films of the Eighties," *Canadian Journal of Film Studies* 7, no.1 (1988): 17.

96. Janice Kaye lists a number of distinctive features of Canadian canonical film, including films originating in the Tax-Shelter Era and those funded by Telefilm, which deploy similar conventions and rupture generic

storytelling in line with Canadian producers' desire to put forth narratives quite unlike those of their American counterparts. Kaye labels these features "narrativus interruptus" and enumerates them as follows: inscrutable accounts of events, aimless plots, characters without apparent connection to the narrative, unpleasant central protagonists, arbitrary violence, inversion of the classical narrative structure which does not augur the story's denouement, and scant happy endings, among others. She adds that rather than unrelentingly advancing the story, directors also often disrupt the narrative pace to make expressly metaphoric or individual statements. See Janice Kaye, "Certain Tendencies in Canadian Cinema: Temporary Insanity and the National Tax-Shelter Masquerade" (Ph.D. diss., University of California, Los Angeles, 2008), iv, 29.

97. Jim Leach, *Film in Canada* (New York: Oxford University Press, 2010), 154.

98. Andra McCartney discusses Northrop Frye's *Bush Garden* and his notion of the North as untamed and threatening because of its overwhelming character. Frye describes the same sense of overwhelm in looking southward toward the United States because of the country's military and political power. As opposed to the pastoral, small town ideas of Canada that motivate the East-West gaze of the country, Frye associates the North-South gaze with a "romantic," nationalist, and "exploratory" tendency in the Canadian imaginary as articulated by the *voyageurs* legacy. In Frye's view, then, the explorer identity embodied by the *coureurs de bois*, *trappeurs* and *voyageurs* of the Nordicity myth is decidedly adventurous and heroic. However, film researchers who uphold canon conventions also interpret Frye's and Atwood's views of the North as an experience of overwhelm, and as central in motivating the "weak" or "loser" Canadian hero in the cinema. See, for example, Kass Banning, "Conjugating Three Moments in Black Canadian Cinema," *North of Everything: English-Canadian Cinema Since 1980*, ed. William Beard and Jerry White (Edmonton, AB: University of Alberta Press, 2002), 93. For more on the above discussion, see Andra McCartney, "Sounding Places: Situated Conversations Through the Soundscape Compositions of Hildegard Westerkamp," (Ph.D. diss., York University, 1999); Northrop Frye, *The Bush Garden: Essays on the Canadian Imagination* (Toronto: Anansi, 1971).

99. Margaret Atwood, *Survival: A Thematic Guide to Canadian Literature* (Toronto: Anansi, 1972), 35–6.

100. Peter Urquhart, "1979: Reading the Tax-Shelter Boom in Canadian Film History" (Ph.D. diss., McGill University, 2004), 194. Eva Mackey speaks to the same premise in underlining that the wilderness of the North and its climate are two constants in mythic representations of Canada vis-à-vis more influential countries. See Eva Mackey, *The House of Difference*, 40, 48.

101. Canadian film as defined by the canon is considered highbrow or art cinema.

102. Hart Cantelon, "Have Skates, Will Travel: Canada, Europe and the Hockey Labour Market," *Artificial Ice: Hockey, Culture and Commerce*, ed. Richard Gruneau and David Whitson (Toronto: Broadview Press, 2006), 215–36.

103. Cultural nationalist critics also insist that Canadian film must enrich cultural life by trading on Canadian social contexts, backdrops, and themes. See Urquhart, "1979: Reading the Tax-Shelter Boom in Canadian Film History," 194.

104. Gruneau and Whitson, *Hockey Night in Canada*, 143.

105. Buma cites Garry Whannel's discussion of heroism as disrupted and democratized by modern technologies with sport filling the gap. He also calls attention to the profusion of anti-heroes in literature and film, which according to Patricia Hughes-Fuller, is warranted by "The Death of the (Humanist) Subject" and the rise of postmodernity. Buma, *Refereeing Identity*, 187–8; Patricia Hughes-Fuller, "The Good Old Game: Hockey, Nostalgia, Identity" (Ph.D. diss., University of Alberta, 2002), 108; Garry Whannel, *Media Sport Stars: Masculinities and Moralities* (London: Routledge, 2002), 40.

106. Linda Robertson, "A Perfect Ending for Canada's Games," *Bradenton Herald*, February 28, 2010, accessed March 1, 2011, http://www.bradenton.com/2010/02/28/2093178/a-perfect-ending-for-canadas-games.html.

107. Lee Parpart, "The Nation and the Nude: Colonial Masculinity and the Spectacle of the Male Body in Recent Canadian Cinema(S)," *Masculinity: Bodies, Movies, Culture*, ed. Peter Lehman (New York: Routledge, 2001), 176.

108. A November 2010 news article underlines that while hockey is the Canadian passion, it has also failed to hit the mark in English-Canadian film. Gayle MacDonald, "Offside: Why Can't English Canada Make a Hockey Film That Scores at the Box Office?," *The Globe and Mail*, November 12, 2010, accessed January 15, 2011, http://m.theglobeandmail.com/arts/film/offside-why-cant-english-canada-make-a-hockey-film-that-scores-at-the-box-office/article1314011/.

109. Tim Edensor, *National Identity, Popular Culture and Everyday Life* (Oxford: Berg, 2002), 17.

110. Williams, "Melodrama Revised," 53, 82.

111. See King and Leonard's discussion of Marjorie Kibby's and Mary Louise Adams' work for more on cultural minorities' contestation of hockey as a white, male cultural space. Richard C. King and David J. Leonard, *Visual Economies Of/In Motion* (New York: Peter Lang, 2006), 4; Mary Louise Adams, "The Game of Whose Lives? Gender, Race and Entitlement in Canada's National Game," *Artificial Ice: Hockey, Culture and Commerce*, eds. Richard Gruneau and David Whitson (Peterborough, On: Broadview Press, 2006), 71–84.

112. Ryan Diduck makes these arguments in his discussion of the popular Canadian TV series *The Trailer Park Boys*. Ryan Diduck, "From Back Bacon to Chicken Fingers: Re-Contextualizing the 'Hoser' Archetype," *Offscreen* 10, no. 1 (2006), accessed June 5, 2007, http://www.offscreen.com/index.php/phile/essays/hoser_archetype/.

113. Urquhart notes that the argument mirrors Innisian anxieties in envisaging the Canadian economy as branch plant of American corporations. Urquhart, "1979: Reading the Tax-Shelter Boom in Canadian Film History," 194–8.

114. André Loiselle, "The Decline ... and the Rise of English Canada's Quebec Cinema," *Self Portraits: The Cinemas of Canada Since Telefilm*, eds. André Loiselle and Tom McSorley (Ottawa: Canadian Film Institute, 2006), 49, 63–4; Pierre Véronneau, "Genres and

Variations: The Audiences of Quebec Cinema," *Self Portraits: The Cinemas of Canada Since Telefilm*, eds. André Loiselle and Tom McSorley (Ottawa: Canadian Film Institute, 2006), 93. See also, Peter Urquhart, "Film Policy/Film History: From the Canadian Film Development Corp. to Telefilm Canada," *Self Portraits: The Cinemas of Canada Since Telefilm*, eds. André Loiselle and Tom McSorley (Ottawa: Canadian Film Institute, 2006), 20, 23.

115. André Loiselle, *Cinema as History: Michel Brault and Modern Quebec* (Toronto: Toronto International Festival Group, 2007), 52.

116. Because movie-making is a collective enterprise, not every individual involved in the production of a hockey-themed film is a fan of the game. Story originators such as scriptwriters and sometimes directors and producers, however, appear to be hockey enthusiasts, or at least harbor particular views of the sport that they bring to bear on their work. Films that revolve around a hockey protagonist, in any case, contribute to cementing distinct perspectives of the sport in popular culture, and to that extent occupy a position in cultural debates about the game.

117. Seán Crosson notes that sports films, albeit popular genres, are not vehicles for making directors a name as they rehearse similar themes and have narrow aesthetic significance. Since cinema studies is concerned with the aesthetic and artistic value of motion pictures, this bias may also explain why scholars from this field have hesitated to take on the study of the sports film. For more on the sports film's functional aspects, see Crosson, *Sport in Film*, 28.

118. Like the notion of genres, Canadian film also remains a contested construct, since some theorists argue for defining the concept through canon conventions, while others make the case for integrating popular film and regional cinemas into the notion. See, for example, Lee Parpart's discussion of Canadian cinema in "The Nation and the Nude," 175.

119. Fürsich, "In Defense of Textual Analysis." Noel Brown also advises that an analysis of popular family fare that does not take into account the larger historical, corporate, and technological contexts of film production and reception remains fragmentary because the evolution of the cinematic product affects the way audiences view and consume it. Peter Urquhart, for his part, advocates linking texts to the prevalent social issues of the day in noting that despite differences in the way that audiences and film critics read films, viewers do not typically interpret these narratives in haphazard ways. Urquhart, "1979: Reading the Tax-Shelter Boom in Canadian Film History," 131; Noel Brown, "Hollywood, the Family Audience and the Family Film, 1930–2010" (Ph.D. diss., New Castle University, 2010), 45.

120. Véronneau notes that Canadian film scholars are mainly trained in art history and literary studies, and lack any basic knowledge of social science concepts and methodologies. Véronneau, "Genres and Variations," 93–4.

121. See *Hockey Match on the Ice* at http://www.youtube.com/watch?v=gmEaUIc1F5s.

122. Riess, *Sports in America from Colonial Times to the Twenty-First Century*, 345.

123. See *King of Hockey* at http://www.youtube.com/watch?v=6gd_UqfLhqw.

124. See *The Duke of West Point* at http://www.youtube.com/watch?v=PvDzDkGu9yo.

125. Christopher E. Gittings, *Canadian National Cinema: Ideology, Difference and Representation* (New York: Routledge, 2002), 34.

126. The NFB is a federal film agency mandated with producing and distributing film material that portrays Canada to Canadians and other nations. It absorbed the Canadian Government Motion Picture Bureau in 1941. See the NFB's website at http://www.nfb.ca.

127. See *Here's Hockey* at: http://www.youtube.com/watch?v=AD_wpNz3QmA.

128. See *Blades and Brass* at: http://www.youtube.com/watch?v=z3NPVJXqgrM.

129. *Ice Hockey World Special*, "Ice Hockey Films," 10.

130. Zeisler, *Historical Dictionary of Ice Hockey*, 218.

131. John Wayne's statement is quoted in Scott Eyman, *John Wayne: The Life and Legend* (New York: Simon & Schuster, 2014). *Idol of the Crowds* was released two years before the actor's breakout role in *Stagecoach* (Ford, 1939). For more, see James Hughes, "John Wayne's Forgotten Movie," *Slate.com*, June 5, 2014, accessed August 6, 2015; "Ice Hockey Films," *Ice Hockey World Special: 60th Anniversary* (December 1995), 9. http://www.slate.com/blogs/browbeat/2014/06/05/idol_of_the_crowds_celebrate_the_nhl_s_stanley_cup_finals_by_revisiting.html.

Chapter 1

1. R.W. Connell, "Globalization, Imperialism, Masculinities," *Handbook of Studies on Men and Masculinities*, eds. Michael Kimmel, Jeff Hearns, R.W. Connell (London: Sage, 2005), 74.

2. John Branch, "Derek Boogard: Blood on the Ice," *New York Times*, December 4, 2011, 4.

3. Valerie Walkerdine, "Video Replay: Families, Films and Fantasy," *Formations of Fantasy*, eds. Victor Burgin, James Donald, and Cora Kaplan (London: Methuen, 1986), 172.

4. Norbert Elias and Eric Dunning, *The Quest for Excitement: Sport and Leisure in the Civilizing Process* (Oxford: Basil Blackwell, 1986), 49.

5. John Fiske, *Understanding Popular Culture*, 2nd ed. (New York: Routledge, 2010), 57–8.

6. Gruneau and Whitson, *Hockey Night in Canada*, 110.

7. Parpart, "The Nation and the Nude," 176–7.

8. Katherine Monk, *Weird Sex & Snowshoes and Other Canadian Film Phenomena* (Vancouver: Raincoast Books, 2001), 139.

9. Tobias Stark, "The Pioneer, the Pal and the Poet: Masculinities and National Identities in Canadian, Swedish & Soviet Ice Hockey During the Cold War," *Putting It on Ice. Vol II: Internationalizing Canada's Game*, ed. Colin D. Howell (Halifax, Nova Scotia: Gorsebrook Research Institute, 2001), 41–2.

10. Bart Beaty, "Not Playing, Working: Class, Masculinity, and Nation in the Canadian Hockey Film," *Working on Screen: Representations of the Working Class in Canadian Cinema*, eds. Malek Kouri and Darrell Varga (Toronto: University of Toronto Press, 2006), 119, 125.

11. Doug Beardsley, *Country on Ice* (Toronto: Paperjacks, 1988), 133.

12. Beardsley recounts that "Fred Shero, the Philadelphia Flyer coach who built an NHL championship based on such tactics once said: "To beat Boston, you do the same thing to Orr that Clarke did to Kharlamov. Break his ankle." Beardsley, *Country on Ice*, 134.

13. See Crawford, Scott, A.G.M., "The Sport Film—Its Cultural Significance," *Journal of Physical Education, Recreation and Dance* 59, no. 6 (1988): 46.

14. Gruneau and Whitson, *Hockey Night in Canada*, 110.

15. Managed by the Canadian Film Development Corporation (CFDC), the CCA enabled investors to deduct from their taxes sixty per cent of the funds slated for film subsidy, a greater amount than allowed for charitable contribution deductions. In 1975, the CCA was raised to 100 per cent to aim at an annual average production of seventy feature films, resulting in a colossal 708 features, double the number produced in the preceding five decades and only half of which were released. The subsidies behind the CCA films aimed to replicate Hollywood's profit-making models, and succeeded in producing prodigious numbers of films. Critics, however, derided most of these productions as a cinema of failure. For more on the CCA, see George Melnyk, *One Hundred Years of Canadian Cinema* (Toronto: University of Toronto Press, 2004), 13–14, 113; Martin Knelman, *This Is Where We Came In: The Career and Character of Canadian Film* (Toronto: McClelland and Stewart, 1977), 97.

16. Janice Kaye notes that conventions that disrupt generic storytelling were especially prominent in the films of this period in both large budget and smaller productions, but they also occur subsequently. Kaye traces the roots of the Canadian loser archetype to the 1967 policies of the CFDC, an agency designed to grow Canadian film and boost the production of a national mythic tradition. Kaye, "Certain Tendencies in Canadian Cinema," iv, 29.

17. Kaye makes clear that this psychological characteristic first became evident with the emergence of contemporary notions of Canadian identity in the 1960s. Kaye, "Certain Tendencies in Canadian Cinema," 112–4.

18. Robert Fothergill, "Coward, Bully or Clown: The Dream-Life of a Younger Brother," Reprinted in *The Canadian Film Reader*, eds. Seth Feldman and Joyce Nelson (Toronto: Peter Martin Associates, 1977), 235, 243.

19. Fothergill, "Coward, Bully, or Clown," 238–9.

20. Beaty, "Not Playing, Working," 120.

21. Patrick Lowe, "Paperback Hero Review," *Canuxploitation! Your Complete Guide to Canadian B-Film*, nd, accessed February 10, 2008, http://www.canuxploitation.com/review/paperback hero.html.

22. Gerald Horne, "Interpreting Prairie Cinema," *Prairie Forum, the Journal of the Canadian Plains Research Center* 22, no. 2 (Fall 1997), accessed October 12, 2011, http://members.shaw.ca/horne/prairiecinema.html.

23. Ronald Tranquilla, "Ranger and Mountie: Myths of National Identity in Zane Grey's *The Lone Star Ranger* and Ralph Connor's *Corporal Cameron*," *Journal of Popular Culture* 24, no. 3 (1990): 74, 78; Dick Harrison, *Unnamed Country: The Struggle for a Canadian Prairie Fiction* (Edmonton: University of Alberta Press, 1977).

24. The economic decline experienced by the Prairie region that the film depicts was a result of the Canadian economy's integration with that of the U.S. During the 1970s both nations were plagued by an energy crisis, skyrocketing inflation, and labor unrest that threatened social and political destabilization. Bruce Kidd and John Macfarlane regard the decline of amateur hockey in Canada as an adverse by-product of this integration. Malek Khouri and Darrell Varga, "Introduction," *Representations of the Working Class in Canadian Cinema*, eds. Malek Khouri and Darrell Varga (Toronto: University of Toronto Press, 2006), 78; Darrell Varga, "The Image of the 'People' in the CBC'S *Canada: A People's History*," *Representations of the Working Class in Canadian Cinema*, eds. Malek Khouri and Darrell Varga (Toronto: University of Toronto Press, 2006), 78; Bruce Kidd and John Macfarlane, *The Death of Hockey* (Toronto: New Press, 1972), 18–9.

25. Eli Mandel, "Images of Prairie Man," *A Region of the Mind: Interpreting the Western Canadian Plains*, ed. Richard Allen (Regina: Canadian Plains Research Centre, 1973), 28; Douglas R. Francis, "Regionalism, Landscape, and Identity in the Prairie West," *Challenging Frontiers: The Canadian West*, eds. Lorry W. Felske and Beverly Jean Rasporich (Calgary: University of Calgary Press, 2004), 38.

26. Tranquilla, "Ranger and Mountie," 75.

27. Tranquilla, "Ranger and Mountie," 75.

28. Katerberg points out that historians have interpreted the Canadian frontier experience as an orderly development following the British North America Act's mandate of "peace, order, and good government." He makes the case that, in deploying the Royal Canadian Mounted Police to maintain the rule of law in the Dominion's outposts, Canadians effectively deterred the gunplay culture that characterized American frontier experience. See Katerberg, "A Northern Vision," 545.

29. Kaye alludes to Tom Hedley's argument that Canadian imagination and identity, while shaped by the myths of the land—its vastness and distance—is also informed by the country's institutions. Kaye, "Certain Tendencies in Canadian Cinema," 113; Tom Hedley, "Colossus from the North," *Documents in Canadian Film*, ed. Douglas Fetherling (Peterborough, ON: Broadview Press, 1988).

30. Wes D. Gehring, "Black Humor," *Handbook of American Film Genres*, ed. Wes D. Gehring (New York: Greenwood Press, 1988), 179–80.

31. Peter Harcourt, "Speculations on Canadian Cinema," *Queen's Quarterly* 111, no. 2 (2004): 237–51.

32. Patricia Hunt makes a similar point about the motivating force behind Prairie literature in her argument that secular figures like the Royal Canadian Mounted Police operate as symbols of order and civilization whose main function is to rein in the unruly masculine. Patricia Hunt, "Contrasting Images of Garden in Canadian and American Literature," *American Studies* 23, no. 1 (Spring 1982): 44.

33. Although the novel makes clear that Batterinski ingests the rat poison that ends up taking his life by mistake, the film implies that this life-ending event is part and parcel of his unraveling.

34. Joseph Maguire applies this typology to Canadian hockey players on European teams. Alongside pioneers, he alludes to: (a) settlers, who choose to remain in the culture where they dispense their labor; (b) mercenaries, who play the role of "hired guns" and are driven by short-term profit; and (c) nomads, whose primary intent is to embark on a cosmopolitan sojourn as non-assimilated outsiders. Joseph Maguire, "Blade Runners: Canadian Migrants, Ice Hockey, and the Global Process," *Journal of Sport and Social Issues* 20, no. 3 (1996): 336, 338–9.

35. Elite-level hockey in Finland took on professional status in 1975 with the instatement of the *Suomen Mestaruus Liiga* (SM-liiga). Although Finnish players Jari Kurri and Esa Tikkanen were key members of the 1980s multiple-Stanley Cup-winner Edmonton Oilers, according to NHL correspondent Bill Meitzer, Finnish national teams did not achieve contender status in the international game until a decade and a half later. Since 1988, however, Team Finland has been the most consistent Olympic hockey medalist of the top-tier nations, winning silver at the 1988 Calgary and 2006 Torino Games, and bronze at the 1994 Lillehammer, 1998 Nagano, 2010 Vancouver, and 2014 Sochi Winter Games. Finnish luminary Teemu Selänne garnered the MVP title in Sochi for the 24 goals he scored in six Olympic tournaments, including the 1992 Albertville and 2002 Salt Lake Winter Games. He also won the Stanley Cup in 2007 with the Anaheim Ducks. Although a small nation, Finland is known for having a well-rounded bench as well as for its consistent success in goal. For more, see Bill Meitzer, "Hockey World Remembers Marjamaki," *NHL.com*, May 30, 2012, accessed May 31, 2012, http://www.nhl.com/ice/news.htm?id=633253; Dan Rosen, "Selanne Ends International Career with Memorable Win," NHL.com, February 22, 2014, accessed February 23, 2014, http://www.nhl.com/ice/news.htm?id=706060; Chris Koentges, "The Oracle of Finnish Hockey: How a 70-Year-Old Finnish Goalie Coach Is Transforming a Global Sport," *The Atlantic*, March 2014, accessed April 20, 2014, http://www.theatlantic.com/magazine/archive/2014/03/the-puck-stops-here/357579/.

36. Mary Jane Miller, *Turn Up the Contrast: CBC Television Drama Since 1952* (Vancouver: University of British Columbia Press/CBC Enterprises, 1987), 257.

37. Gruneau and Whitson, *Hockey Night in Canada*, 182.

38. Richard Gruneau and David Whitson, "Introduction," *Artificial Ice*, 9.

39. Joseph Maguire, "Globalization: Critical Concepts in Sociology," *Sociology of Sport Journal* 11 (1994): 398–427, reprinted in *Globalization: Critical Concepts in Sociology*, ed. Roland Robertson and Kathleen E. White (London: Routledge, 2002), 298.

40. Michael Buma notes that the novel requires fans to look in the mirror and examine how their behavior feeds the use of violence by players like Batterinski. The film, however, places the responsibility squarely on the player's shoulders. See Buma, *Refereeing Identity*, 196.

41. Maguire, "Blade Runners," 348.

42. Beaty, "Working, Not Playing" 129.

43. Paul Gross echoes this view when he notes in an interview that, "Brian was the raw edge of the Canadian soul." See Victor Dwyer, "Hockey's Hell-Raiser: Spinner Spencer Battled on and Off the Ice. Gross Misconduct," *Maclean's*, March 1, 1993, accessed May 12, 2007, http://www.paulgross.org/ grossmis.htm.

44. The center-margins view obscures Western provinces' pride in placing players in the NHL regardless of their foibles and failures. As Beaty maintains, it also refrains from calling attention to Toronto's advantaged position over the rest of the nation, focusing instead on U.S. economic and cultural control of Canadian resources. Christine Ramsay similarly points to this Toronto-centric bias in her discussion of *Goin' Down the Road* (Shebib, 1970), arguing that the film amplifies its protagonists' marginality vis-à-vis "Toronto's status at the centre of Canada's social and personal identity and economic prosperity." See Beaty, "Not Playing, Working," 125; Ramsay, "Canadian Narrative Cinema from the Margins: 'The Nation' and Masculinity in Goin' Down the Road," *Canada's Best Features: Critical Essays on Fifteen Canadian Films*, ed. Eugene Waltz (Amsterdam, New York: Rodopi, B.V., 2002), 112.

45. Beaty, "Not Playing, Working," 129.

46. Eva Mackey refers to Carl Berger's discussion of Canada's Northernness in amplifying muscular fitness, vigor, and moral value, and the U.S.'s Southernness in denoting effeminacy, wantonness, and infirmity. Mackey, *The House of Difference*, 30; Carl Berger, "The True North Strong and Free," *Nationalism in Canada*, ed. Peter Russell (Toronto: McGraw-Hill, 1966), 4; Carl Berger, *The Sense of Power: Studies in the Ideas of Canadian Imperialism 1867–1914* (Toronto: Toronto University Press, 1970), 129.

47. A decade after the broadcast of *Gross Misconduct*, Paul Gross reiterated the problematic role of U.S. financial interests in the game: "Hockey is political ... it is hard to take hockey in this country since we think of it as our game, but it's largely owned by others." Cynthia Amsden, "Canadian Comedy, Eh? Paul Gross's Men with Brooms and Steve Smith's Red Green's Duct Tape Forever," *TAKE ONE* (June–Sept. 2005), accessed January 30, 2006, http://www.finadarticles.com/p/articles/mi_m0JSF/is_50_14/ai_N14704669/.

48. Anne Swardson, "Canada's Big Chill: Hockey Heads South to Seek Fortune in America," *International Herald Tribune*, 20. Monique Tchofen calls attention to the link between globalization processes and the unhinged characters in Egoyan's films, noting that these instabilities arise because they disturb a sense of "home, place, [and] self." Tschofen, "Repetition, Compulsion, and Representations in Atom Egoyan's Films," *North of Everything: English-Canadian Cinema Since 1980*, eds. William Beard and Jerry White (Edmonton: University of Alberta Press, 2002), 174.

49. Gruneau and Whitson maintain that the debate about whether hockey is best served by skill and speed or toughness and competitive force intensified with the Philadelphia Flyers' use of aggression, and elicited "high-profile commentaries, reports, and commissions." Richard Gruneau and David Whitson, "Introduction," *Artificial Ice: Hockey, Culture and Commerce* (Toronto: Broadview Press, 2006), 6.

50. Victoria Elmwood notes that the Beadle & Adams dime novels "reinvoked the trope of the frontier and the eighteenth century separation between East and West as an organizing contrast at the core of American values." See Victoria Elmwood, "'Just Some Bum from

the Neighborhood': The Resolution of Post-Civil Rights Tension and Heavyweight Public Sphere Discourse in *Rocky* (1976)," *Film & History* 35, no. 2 (2005): 51.

51. Walkerdine, "Video Replay," 173.

52. Geoff King argues that while the subject matter of Hollywood film does not show evidence of simple historical progression, "[s]ome [movies] ... seem more directly to be products of a social context," and sixties and seventies films convincingly mirrored the *Zeitgeist* of the times. Sixties cinema, however, produced a mere 43 sports movies, since film practitioners did not deem the format suitable for the radical commentary of social and political institutions put forward by the social projects of the era. It therefore fell to the sports cinema of the seventies to enact the same intense questioning of public myths. With the Hollywood studio system gone, niche films were aimed at younger and more educated audiences, and the nonconformist political views and lifestyles of America's youth soon found their way into cinematic story lines. Influenced by political, social, and institutional trends, themes showcased rebellion, alienation, and cynicism as Hollywood sought to appeal to this large viewer demographic. For more on the subject, see Pearson et al., "Sports Films: Social Dimensions Over Time," 150; Leonard Quart and Albert Auster, *American Film and Society Since 1945* (Santa Barbara: Praeger, 2001), 73; Geoffey King, *New Hollywood Cinema*, 7, 51; Richard Slotkin, "Gunfighters and Green Berets: The Magnificent Seven and the Myth of Counter-Insurgency," *Radical History Review* 44 (1989): 44.

53. Slotkin, *Gunfighter Nation*, 556. The 1972 *Surgeon General's Report* also provided evidence that screen violence exacerbated youth and children's aggressive behavior. The reports were followed by the 1975 National PTA resolution demanding that networks lower the amount of violent content in TV programming and advertising.

54. Hilary Findlay enumerates McMurtry's 1974 findings on the causes of violence in amateur hockey as follows: "(1) the influence of professional hockey with its emphasis on winning and use of violence as a tactical instrument to achieve that goal; (2) a rule structure (in professional and amateur hockey) which not only tolerates violence but encourages its use by rewarding those who excel in physical intimidation and also makes reciprocal violence inevitable; (3) the lack of any proper definition of the purpose and objectives of amateur hockey; (4) the failure of referees to apply existing rules, and the inconsistency and lack of support for referees from fans, coaches and players; (5) the failure of coaches to control players, and the emphasis on winning games rather than instilling the true value of sport and skill development; (6) the lack of respect by players for rules and officials; and (7) the undue pressure from parents, fans and coaches with over-emphasis on winning." See Hilary A. Findlay, "Violence in Sport: Policy Consideration for the Amateur Sport Organization" (paper presented at the Symposium "Sports Management: Cutting Edge Strategies for Managing Sports as a Business," August 2002).

55. Slotkin, *Gunfighter Nation*, 634.

56. Joan Mellen, *Big Bad Wolves: Masculinity in the American Film* (New York: Pantheon Books, 1977), 293–4.

57. Tudor, *Hollywood's Vision of Team Sports*, 185.

58. Kibby, "Nostalgia for the Masculine," 17.

59. Timothy E. Scheurer, "The Best There Ever Was in the Game: Musical Mythopoesis and Heroism in Film Scores of Recent Sports Movies," *Journal of Popular Film and Television* 32, no. 4 (2005): 158, 165.

60. Don Gillmor calls attention to the systemic use of violence in the Canadian juniors game by pointing to the crowded emergency wards of the Prairie region. Gillmor, "Hockey: The Great Literary Shutout," *The Walrus* 2, no. 1 (2005), 92.

61. Gruneau and Whitson, *Hockey Night in Canada*, 189; Beaty, "Not Playing, Working," 120.

62. Robin Finn, "Triumph Opened Doors," *New York Times*, February 19, 1990, C5.

63. Mike Machnik, "1972 Silver Medal Team Gathers to Launch Book, Celebrate Accomplishment," *College Hockey News*, February 16, 2006, accessed March 10, 2006, http://www.collegehockeynews.com/news/2006/02/16_striking.php.

64. This motif, which taps the heroic masculine project by way of the father, farming, and sport, also recurs in baseball literature and in eighties Hollywood baseball films. See Michael Oriard, *Dreaming of Heroes: American Sports Fiction, 1868–1980* (Chicago: Nelson-Hall, 1982), 7.

65. Beaty, "Not Playing, Working," 119, 120, 126.

Chapter 2

1. Fiske alludes to Mikhail Bakhtin's idea of the carnivalesque as occasions when the voices of the popular speak with stentorian force and overturn the norms of the mundane. He explains that the carnivalesque dramatizes popular participation in the sporting spectacle in prescribing no separation between spectators and the agents of disruption. John Fiske, *Understanding Popular Culture*, 2nd ed. (New York: Routledge, 2010), 41–2, 56, 162; Mikhail Bakhtin, *Rabelais and His World* (Cambridge: Massachusetts Institute of Technology Press, 1968), 7; Tony Bennett, "Hegemony, Ideology, Pleasure: Blackpool," *Popular Culture and Social Relations*, eds. Colin Mercer and Janet Woollacott (Milton Keynes and Philadelphia: Open University Press, 1986), 148.

2. E.A. Williams notes that in the Bakhtinian framework, the Rogue, the Clown, and the Fool are agents *par excellence* of the carnivalesque. These character types effectively epitomize a continuum of ingenuousness based on the extent to which they represent the author's perspective. While the rogue is the closest to the author in recognizing his role as an agent of the carnivalesque, clown and fool characters do not appear to grasp that they function as satirical cultural archetypes. Both the clown and the fool, however, are not "of this world" and thus have special prerogatives in satirizing mainstream culture. The clown in film, however, is also defined distinctly without the lack of agency of the Bakhtinian archetype. Wes Gehring refers to film clowns as part of the personality comedian genre. He lists five aspects of this archetype: incompetence, lack of orthodoxy and an outsider status, that parody the traditional hero; a nomadic nature with links to the picaresque hero; team interaction, required for the character to bounce his humor off someone else; reliance on physical and visual

humor; and the *shtick* for which the actor or comedian's screen persona is known. For more, see Wes D. Gehring, "Clown Comedy," *Handbook of American Film Genres*, ed. Wes D. Gehring (New York: Greenwood Press, 1988), 195–204; E.A. Williams, "Bakhtin and *Borat*: The Rogue, the Clown, and the Fool in Carnival Film." *Philament* 20 (2015): 110, 112.

3. Gehring, "Clown Comedy," 193.
4. Fothergill, "Coward, Bully, or Clown," 237.
5. Hughes-Fuller, "Am I Canadian?," 29.
6. The Hanson Brothers are U.S.-born players from Minnesota and Wisconsin who played professional hockey for over a decade. Their popularity as burlesque impersonations of the game's mayhem has endured in blockbuster films and comedies. *Sports Illustrated* confirmed the appeal of the brothers by placing them on the cover of its "Where Are They Now?" July 2007 issue with the caption: "30 years later, a beloved sports movie lives on, thanks to three bespectacled goons." See Austin Murphy, "The Hanson Brothers. Goons Forever," *Sports Illustrated*, July 16, 2007, 107.
7. Nancy Dowd based the character of Syracuse Bulldogs' Oggie Oglethorpe on NHL defenseman Bill Goldthorpe, who, according to Adam Proteau of *The Hockey News*, was one of the "most intimidating men to play pro hockey." Goldthorpe developed his game in Thunder Bay, Ontario. See Adam Proteau, "Goldthorpe Legend Inspired *Slap Shot*," *The Hockey News*, September 7, 2004, 36.
8. Scott Martelle, "As Fiction Fodder, Ice Hockey's Not a Natural," *Los Angeles Times*, May 28, 2003, E1.
9. Aaron Baker, *Contesting Identities: Sports in American Film,"* (Urbana: University of Illinois Press, 2003), 93.
10. Jay Coakley, *Sports in Society: Issues and Controversies* (Whitby, ON: McGraw-Hill Ryerson, 2004), 79.
11. Kibby, "Nostalgia for the Masculine," 17; Janet Riblett Wilkie, "The Decline in Labor Force Participation and Income, and the Changing Structure of Family Economic Support," *Journal of Marriage and the Family* 53 (February 1991): 113.
12. Baker, *Contesting Identities*, 92.
13. Murphy, "The Hanson Brothers. Goons Forever," 106.
14. John Dizikes, *Sportsmen and Gamesmen* (Boston: Houghton-Mifflin, 1981), 39.
15. Oriard, *Sporting with the Gods*, 16.
16. Oriard explains that even though American sports fans frowned on outright illegal moves, they praised coaches who routinely spotted loopholes and tweaked rules, and such "smart play" became the basis for "scientific" football. Oriard, *Sporting with the Gods*, 15.
17. Motley, "Fighting for Manhood," 62.
18. Baker, *Contesting Identities*, 108.
19. Baker, *Contesting Identities*, 108; Peter Roffman and Jim Purdy, *The Hollywood Social Problem Film* (Bloomington: Indiana University Press, 1981), 64; Slotkin, *Gunfighter Nation*, 22.
20. Baker alludes to Eve Kosofsky Sedgwick's work on the western's Code of Honor as a conduit for expressing affect in homosocial bonding rites. Brian Baker, *Masculinity in Fiction and Film: Representing Men in Popular Genres 1945–2000* (London: Continuum, 2006), 135.

21. Slotkin, *Gunfighter Nation*, 145.
22. Oriard, *Sporting with the Gods*, 15–7.
23. Oriard, *Sporting with the Gods*, 8.
24. For more on seventies sports cinema's antiheroic protagonists, see Scheurer, "The Best There Ever Was in the Game," 157.
25. Catherine Gouge observes that while Turner privileged the use of material power by communal institutions rather than by the corporation and the state, the frontier merely offered the prospect of economic return, and for plenty of individuals opportunity was hard to come by. See Gouge, "The American Frontier."
26. Slotkin, *Gunfighter Nation*, 145–6.
27. Don Gillmor remarks that despite *Slap Shot*'s critique of violence in minor league hockey, the Hansons have assumed nothing short of mythic status. Gillmor, "Hockey: The Great Literary Shutout."
28. Richard Harrison, "Hockey as Canadian Tragic Theatre—And Slap Shot as Comedy's Reply" (paper presented at the Hockey Conference "Putting It on Ice IV: Visioning and Re-Visioning Hockey's Arena," London, ON, June 18–20, 2014), 12–13.
29. Babington, *The Sports Film: Games People Play*, 60.
30. Gehring, "Clown Comedy," 192.
31. The cinema echoed the commodification of athletes in the early 1990s by implementing product placement as an additional stream of income. *Happy Gilmore* in like manner features products from sports manufacturers (Wilson, Golf Digest, Top-Flite golf balls, Odyssey clubs), NHL club paraphernalia (Boston Bruins gear), beverages (Pepsi, Michelob, Heineken, Budweiser), restaurants (Subway, Sizzler) and even telcoms (Bell Atlantic and AT&T).
32. Sandler's early comedies, like *Happy Gilmore* and *Billy Madison* (Davis, 1995) feature boorish, juvenile characters that appeal to young audiences. His later work—*Mr. Deeds* (Brill, 2002), *Spanglish* (Brooks, 2004), *50 First Dates* (Segal, 2004), *Just Go with It* (Dugan, 2011)—however, has evolved toward romantically accented themes.
33. Gehring, "Clown Comedy," 189.
34. Babington, *The Sports Film*, 58.
35. The super-sizing of the hockey goon by way of The Rock's musculature says much about the way Hollywood looks upon the game, since producers attached the hockey aspect to his character following his casting as the Tooth Fairy. According to Mark Ciardi, "It was very important to make a portion of Derek's life really masculine and sports-oriented, and from this came the idea of making him a hockey player." Tim Nasson, "'The Tooth Fairy': Behind the Scenes," *Wild About Movies*, accessed March 11, 2012, http://www.wildaboutmovies.com/behind_the_scenes/thetoothfairy-behindthescenes/.
36. While in the past English-Canadian films expressed highbrow views in line with the favored perspectives of state-sponsored cultural nationalism, Catherine Murray notes that Canadians have increasingly balked at granting national elites license "to define, regulate, and finance ... [Canadian] uniqueness," opting instead to decide for themselves what they consume. Hockey nonetheless persists as a popular cultural form for expressing identity, and as David Whitson confirms, hockey-related

content on the CBC remains one of the viable ways through which Canadians claim membership in national life and through which Canada is set apart from other nations. The cultural nationalist highbrow perspective of hockey, which in the past has defined physicality as contravening the CBC's mandate for high-merit programming, also appears to have ceded ground to popular tastes. Rick Groen notes in a 2010 *Globe and Mail* article that while the debate about whether hockey is best expressed through skill or hyperphysicality continues to resonate throughout the Canadian arts and cultural institutions, Telefilm and the CBC managers have increasingly turned to mainstream themes and perspectives rather than to the highbrow subject matter common in past content. The bully-clown characters of Canadian film in this section are compatible with the above developments. See Catherine Murray, "Wellsprings of Knowledge"; David Whitson, "Hockey Night in Canada: Cultural Institution of 'Niche Sport'?" (paper presented at the Opening Plenary Session, Canada & the League of Hockey Nations, Victoria, B.C., April 19–21, 2007); Rick Groen, "Tiff's High-Shticking Breakaway," *The Globe and Mail*, September 3, 2010, accessed April 8, 2012, http://www.theglobeandmail.com/arts/awards-and-festivals/tiff/tiffs-high-shticking-breakaway/article1379451/.

37. For more on the enforcer's role, see Branch, "Derek Boogaard: Blood on the Ice," 4.

38. James M. Collins, "The Musical," *Handbook of American Film Genres*, ed. Wes D. Gehring (New York: Greenwood Press, 1988), 275.

39. Aaron Baker, *Sport Films, History, Identity, Journal of Sport History* 25, no. 2 (1998): 217–33; Stephen Neale, "Masculinity as Spectacle," *Screening the Male: Exploring Masculinities in the Hollywood Cinema*, eds. Steven Cohan and Ina Rae Hark (London: Routledge, 1993).

40. *Score* made approximately CAD 250,000 at the box office, while its production and cost several million. See Gayle MacDonald, "Offside: What Can't English Canada Make a Hockey Film That Scores at the Box Office?," *The Globe and Mail*, November 12, 2010, accessed January 14, 2011, http://m.theglobeandmail.com/arts/film/offside-why-cant-english-canada-make-a-hockey-film-that-scores-at-the-box-office/article1314011/.

41. Gruneau and Whitson, *Hockey Night in Canada*, 191.

42. Peter C. Phan, "The Wisdom of Holy Fools in Postmodernity," *Theological Studies* 62 (2001): 737–8.

43. Phan, "The Wisdom of Holy Fools in Postmodernity," 749.

44. Jay Baruchel describes this scene in *Goon* through imagery of the veteran gunslinger whose time is drawing to a close, and the newcomer, a younger rival who is set to depose him. Colin Covert, "'Goon' Is All Brawl," *The Star Tribune*, March 30, 2012, accessed April 10, 2012, http://www.startribune.com/entertainment/movies/144925515.html?refer=y.

45. John Branch makes this very statement about the enforcer. See Branch, "Derek Boogaard: Blood on the Ice," 4. For more on the Ace of Spades, see Herb Friedman, "The Death Card," accessed February 17, 2012, http://www.psywarrior.com/DeathCardsAce.html.

46. *The Globe and Mail*, "Jay Baruchel Talks About Goon," CP Video, February 24, 2012, accessed February 28, 2012, http://www.theglobeandmail.com/arts/arts-video/video-jay-baruchel-talks-about-goon/article548791/.

47. After the deaths of former NHLers Rick Rypien, Wade Belak, and Derek Boogaard during the summer of 2011, news reports and sports theme-driven TV programs like HBO's *Real Sports with Bryant Gumbel* underscored the high price that the enforcer position exacts. The deaths included two suicides. More deaths attributed to the role have occurred since then. For more on the deadly repercussions of taking on the enforcer's role, see James Mirtle, "Did Hockey Kill Todd Ewen?," *The Globe and Mail*, October 29, 2015, accessed October 30, 2015, http://www.theglobeandmail.com/sports/hockey/was-todd-ewens-death-caused-by-his-nhl career/article26987457/.

48. As of 2015, teams have reduced the number of fights per season by underscoring skill alongside toughness. Brawling nonetheless remains essential to professional hockey because of its policing function. See Branch, "Derek Boogaard: Blood on the Ice," 4.

49. For Baruchel's take on *Goon*, see Mark Olsen, Indie Focus: 'Goon' is a hockey comedy 'for Canadian kids'," *Los Angeles Times*, March 25, 2012, accessed March 31, 2012, http://articles.latimes.com/2012/mar/25/entertainment/la-ca-indie-focus-20120325.

50. Rachel Fox, "He Shoots, He Scores: Michael Dowse and Jay Baruchel Talk Goon and the Canadian Conundrum," accessed April 7, 2012, http://gordonandthewhale.com/he-shoots-he-scores-michael-dowse-and-jay-baruchel-talk-goon-and-the-canadian-conundrum/. A sequel, *Goon 2: The Last of the Enforcers*, also written by Jay Baruchel and starring Seann William Scott is scheduled for release in 2016. See Pat Bradley, "Jay Baruchel: Hockey Film Sequel Goon 2 to Start Filming This Summer," NESN.com, April 11, 2015, accessed June 30, 2015, http://nesn.com/2015/04/jay-baruchel-says-goon-sequel-goon-2-starts-filming-this-summer/.

51. Doug's ability to repurpose his skills and the closing credits' title song "Work with What You Got" also pay homage to resourcefulness at a time of high job accretion for working-class males that also impacted the twenty-something demographic. In Baruchel's words, "Doug is about … finding what you are good at … [and] doing what you need to do in a given time." *Goon*'s statement is timely as the Recession of 2007–08 decimated the jobs of twenty-somethings at a rate two to three times greater than older adult positions. Although the Canadian economy fared better than that of the U.S., where the percentage of the American participating workforce tumbled its lowest point since 1980, the country's unemployment rate in May 2012 remained close to 8.5 percent. See Derek Thompson, "No Country for Young Men (Or Women)," *The Atlantic*, November 8, 2011, accessed April 12, 2012, http://www.theatlantic.com/business/archive/2011/11/no-country-for-young-men-or-young-women/248124/; Tony Dokoupil, "Dead Suit Walking: If This Isn't the Great Depression, It Is the Great Humbling. Can Manhood Survive the Lost Decade?," *The Daily Beast*, April 17, 2011, accessed April 5, 2012, http://www.thedailybeast.com/newsweek/2011/04/17/dead-suit-walking.html; Kyle Leathers, "'Goon', 'Hit Somebody' Two Upcoming Hockey Movies to Watch For," *NESN.com*, November 8, 2010, accessed

November 21, 2010, http://nesn.com/2010/11/goon-hit-somebody-two-upcoming-hockey-movies-to-watch-for/. For Canadian employment statistics, see: "Canada Employment Rate, 1999–2015," http://www.tradingeconomics.com/canada/unemployment-rate.

52. The broadcast garnered an audience of 1.5 million, turning into the highest-rated telefim in the pubcaster's history. Don Cherry's son, Timothy, wrote and executive-produced the first installment and Andrew Wreggitt penned the second.

53. Hardy, "Long Before Orr," 253.

54. By his own admission, after he retired from minor hockey the first time around Cherry felt deep embarrassment about his poor job prospects. As he noted in an interview, "I couldn't get a job sweeping floors." See Cherry's comments in Vinay Menon, "The Wonderful, Unlivable Life of Don Cherry," *Moneyville.Ca*, May 29, 2011, accessed June 9, 2012, http://www.moneyville.ca/article/998677—the-wonderful-unlivable-life-of-don-cherry.

55. Parpart, "The Nation and the Nude," 176.

56. Kristi Allain describes Cherry's vision of hockey masculinity as follows: the hockey player must be able to give and take hits, avoid embellishment and subterfuge, and assume a well-groomed, self-effacing, and courteous demeanor off the ice. For more, see Allain, "Kid Crosby or Golden Boy," 7, 472.

57. Consonant with the populist carnivalesque, Cherry's views need not be progressive, but can be actively reactionary, reining in the perceived excesses of liberalism and political correctness. Likely because his views are eminently populist, his popularity also remains high. He edged out Wayne Gretzky on the CBC's list of all-time Greatest Canadians.

Chapter 3

1. Only in prestige sports competitions like the Olympics do national markers take precedence, particularly since the U.S. has had a series of successes in both men's and women's hockey.

2. Hollands, "English-Canadian Sports Novels and Cultural Production," 81.

3. During the sixties and early seventies, social reformists and radical feminists the world over offered a critique of capitalism that opposed cultural nationalism to commodity culture. North American activists defined their political identity against the dictates of the market, proffering a progressive analysis of social inequalities and reappraising core national myths. For more on the subject, see Paulla Ebron, *Performing Africa* (Princeton, NJ: Princeton University Press, 2002); 208–9; *The Economist*, "Endless Summer," April 28, 2007, 73.

4. Hollands, "English-Canadian Sports Novels and Cultural Production," 215.

5. Hughes-Fuller, "Am I Canadian?," 32.

6. Felske and Rasporich, "Challenging Frontiers," 7.

7. Hughes-Fuller, "Am I Canadian?," 29.

8. Hollands notes of the novel on which *Face Off* is based that it constitutes only a pseudo-critique of the league's cartelization, since in Canada professional sport, sports merchandising companies, and the publishing industry feature a strong American presence and depend on U.S. markets for profitability. Hollands also cites Kidd and McFarlane's work, which makes the case that the novel activates only a partial critique of the NHL because it romanticizes the period in which the story unfolds as that of gentlemen-players and owners, and discounts elite hockey's near-monopoly since World War II. Hollands only discusses the novel and not the film, but his argument about the book's tepid criticism of the league remains pertinent. It is also significant that the film was produced with the cooperation of the NHL. Owners' consent, then, may convey that the project did not contravene their interests likely, since Billy ultimately returns to the bench. At the same time, *Face Off* stands out because it fields issues that are not broached in the repertoire post-1990s. For more, see Hollands, "English-Canadian Sports Novels and Cultural Production," 218; Hollands, "Masculinity and the Positive Hero in Canadian Sports Novels" 81; Kidd and Macfarlane, *The Death of Hockey*, 58.

9. *Going South* was produced by Allen Abel for the CBC's *Primetime News* slot.

10. The portrait of Queen Elizabeth in Winnipeg's NHL arena with which the CBC piece represents the city's hockey tradition nonetheless also alludes to the country's colonial past, and in Innisian form conveys the message of Canadian staples harvested for the benefit of foreign metropoles. This reading may not have been intended by the producer since the Nordicity myth in part stresses ties to Britain, the Mother Country, to differentiate Canada from the United States. For more, see Mackey, *The House of Difference*, 30, 42.

11. In 1996 the FCC passed the Telecommunications Act, which convulsed the media playing field by enabling main actors from one sector of the industry to provide services in another and promoting mergers and consolidations previously forbidden under antitrust provisions of federal law. The Telecommunications Act also enabled networks to increase ownership of more than a dozen television stations across the nation. See Kathleen Fitzpatrick, "Network: The Other Cold War," *Film & History* 31, no. 2 (2001): 34; King, *New Hollywood Cinema*.

12. In the late 1980s, the NHL secured deals with SportsChannel for up to 100 games, as well as with ESPN, not yet part of the Disney infrastructure, for 33 games a season. SportsChannel served large U.S. markets and had a comparatively small subscriber base of about 10 million viewers, but it provided the league with increased revenue. After the deal with SportsChannel expired in 1992, the NHL expanded brand presence in the large U.S. metropolitan centers by way of TV contracts with Fox for the abridged 1994–1995 season, and ESPN in 1998. As part of an economic restructuring, the league also created a commissioner post in 1993 filled by former National Basketball Association senior vice president Gary Bettman, and embarked on another wave of expansion and relocation to match the ongoing demographic shift to the American West and South. The NHL considered relocation necessary because of tripling player salaries between 1980 and 1994 and a drop in the value of the Canadian dollar, both of which made it difficult for small Canadian markets to continue fielding profitable teams. From 1991 onward, the league added or relocated a total of 12 teams in a wave of expansion that

spanned a decade. The first wave began with the San Jose Sharks (1991–92), the Ottawa Senators and the Tampa Bay Lightning (1992–93), the Anaheim Mighty Ducks and the Florida Panthers (1993–94). Expansion was followed by a number of relocations: The Minnesota North Stars reemerged as the Dallas Stars (1993–94) in Texas, the Quebec Nordiques as the Colorado Avalanche (1995–96) in Colorado, the Winnipeg Jets as the Phoenix Coyotes (1996–97) in Arizona, and the Hartford Whalers as the Carolina Hurricanes (1997–98) in North Carolina. A final wave of expansion brought on board the Nashville Predators (1998–99), the Atlanta Thrashers (1999–2000), the Minnesota Wild and the Columbus Blue Jackets (2000–2001). By the end of 2001, the NHL had a total of 6 Canadian- and 24 U.S. teams. The league's restructuring strategies occurred alongside the building of new arenas complete with luxury boxes and new corporate and marketing partners, shifting the game up-market in pursuit of the affluent consumer. A steep increase in indoor rink construction and youth development programs, spurred in part by the popularity of inline skating, also benefited newly minted elite-level teams in places where hockey had barely had a foothold. In 2016, the NHL granted a new franchise to Las Vegas, the Vegas Black Knights, and passed over Quebec City's bid. The new team would be iced in time for the 2017–2018 season. For a more detailed discussion of the NHL's 1990s expansion strategies, see Daniel S. Mason, "Expanding the Footprint?— Questioning the NHL'S Expansion and Relocation Strategy," *Artificial Ice: Hockey, Culture and Commerce*, eds. Richard Gruneau and David Whitson (Peterborough ON: Broadview Press, 2006), 181–200; Gruneau and Whitson, Upmarket Continentalism," 247, 251. For more on the NHL's 2016 expansion, see Dan Rosen, "Las Vegas awarded NHL franchise," *NHL.com*, June 22, 2016, accessed June 23, 2016, https://www.nhl.com/news/nhl-expands-to-las-vegas/c-281010682.

13. Commenting on the changing face of professional hockey Don Cherry voiced his vexation in noting that "[T]He Canadian influence is definitely slipping," despite that "[I]t's our religion … [and a] lot of people resent it." South of the border, numerous media reports defined team relocation from Canada to the U.S. on a similar standard. An April 1994 *Washington Post* article argued that the potential move of Canadian teams to U.S. cities placed Canada's dual position as ancestral birthplace of hockey and chief producer of the game's elite professionals in jeopardy. Bill Knight, "New Ice Age: Canada's Sport Making Strides South of the Border," *Seattle Post-Intelligencer*, May 31, 1994. D6; Swardson, "Canada's Big Chill," 7, 20.

14. Daniel S. Mason, "'Get the Puck Outta Here!': Media Transnationalism and Canadian Identity," *Journal of Sport and Social Issues* 26, no. 2 (2002): 162, 144.

15. Mason observes that Fox's strategy made sense in the context of the network's long-term investment in regional sports, since professional hockey was a stellar platform, superior to football and basketball, in delivering the highly desirable 18–34 male demographic that sponsors sought. Fox negotiated a five-year $155 million contract with the NHL starting with the 1994–95 season. Mason, "'Get the Puck Outta Here!,'" 145.

16. Margaret MacNeill makes clear that packaging the game is hardly a neutral exercise, since cultural codes dislodge a considerable part of the material reality of a hockey game from the screen. She amplifies that the long-time use of particular cultural codes in hockey broadcasts have also extended "the myth of cultural ownership … to the broadcast industry." See MacNeill, "Networks: Producing Olympic Ice Hockey for a National Television Audience," *Sociology of Sport Journal* 3 (1996): 111–12.

17. Political pressures over Quebec's status within Canada in the form of three national referenda escalated the sense of a looming Canadian crisis and fears about the splintering of the nation-state. See Mackey, *the House of Difference*, 14, 145, 150.

18. Swardson, "Canada's Big Chill," 20.

19. Knight, "New Ice Age," D1.

20. Norris died in 1952 and Lindsay's scoring contributions continued well after his passing. Lindsay's plans to start a Players Union, which he scaled down to a Players Association, were fully deployed after Norris' death.

21. Ted Lindsay helped the Detroit Red Wings win four Stanley Cups in the 1940s and 1950s.

22. Lindsay was traded to the Chicago Blackhawks as direct result of his efforts to form the NHL Players Association.

23. Gruneau and Whitson, "Introduction," *Artificial Ice*, 10.

24. NHL owners were able to circumvent laws against the formation of cartels because corporate ownership allowed their interests to remain undisclosed.

25. Despite the creation of the Major League Baseball's Players Association in 1953, the staunchly anti-communist McCarthyist period of the 1940s and late 1950s exacerbated NHL players' doubts about forming a union for fear of risking their careers as leftist agitators. In Canada, sympathizers of the Left were also under threat of surveillance by the RCMP. On the above, see, for example, CBC, "The Red Scare," n.d., accessed February 12, 2013, http://www.cbc.ca/history/EPISCONTENTSE1EP15CH1PA2LE.html; Matthew S. Wiseman, "Origins of the Cold War—The Canadian Perspective," February 25, 2013, accessed February 28, 2014, http://www.mattwiseman.ca/origins-of-the-cold-war-the-canadian-perspective/; Jennifer Anderson, "Propaganda and Persuasion in the Cold War: The Canadian-Soviet Friendship Society, 1949–1960" (Ph.D. Diss., Carleton University, 2008).

26. Beardsley, *Country on Ice*, 143.

27. Beaty, "Not Playing, Working," 118–9.

28. Lindsay's efforts finally bore fruit in June 1967 when owners learned that the newly formed Players Association was seeking certification from the Canadian Labour Relations Board.

29. Robert Berry and William B. Gould, *Labor Relations in Professional Sports* (Boston: Auburn House Publishing, 1986), 3.

30. Gruneau and Whitson, "Upmarket Continentalism," 244.

31. Berry and Gould, *Labor Relations in Professional Sporsts*, 4.

32. Bruzzi, *Bringing Up Daddy*, xi.

33. Bruzzi, *Bringing Up Daddy*, 77.

34. The film's allusion to Canadian NHLers as labor

harks back to Canada's framing as branch plant of the U.S. It also erases the country's visibility in multiple high-profile international arenas, including the Canadian state's middle power internationalism policy that dates back to early post-World War II, which has facilitated the nation's actions in international affairs by way of multilateral channels. See Prosper Bernard, Jr., "Canada and Human Security: From the Axworthy Doctrine to Middle Power Internationalism," *The American Review of Canadian Studies* 36, no. 2 (2006), 233–4, 255.

35. John C. Lyden, *Film as Religion: Myths, Morals, and Rituals* (New York: New York University Press, 2003), 142.

36. Slotkin, *Gunfighter Nation*, 351.

37. Thomas Sobchack, "The Adventure Film," *Handbook of American Film Genres*, ed. Wes D. Gehring (New York: Greenwood Press, 1988), 14.

38. See Mario Lemieux's and NHL Commissioner Gary Bettman's comments in *The Sun Sentinel*, "Around the League," December 21, 2006, accessed January 17, 2007, http://articles.sunsentinel.com/2006-12-21/sports/0612201221_1_penguins-options-million-arena.

39. David Ingram notes that personalizing the issues wrought by corporate entities through individual conflict emotionally engages the viewer but prevents recognizing the need for effective political action. See David Ingram, *Green Screen: Environmentalism and Hollywood Cinema* (Devon: University of Exeter Press, 2000), 4.

40. The groundbreaking ceremony for the Pittsburgh Penguins' new Consol Energy Center was held on August 14, 2008 with the opening scheduled for the start of the 2010–2011 season.

41. Gouge, "The American Frontier."

42. Kollin, *Nature's State*, 73.

43. For a fitting definition of pond hockey, see Charles McGrath, "The Game as It Should Be Played: On a Pond, in the Cold," *International Herald Tribune*, February 16. 2004, 1.

44. In 1890 the U.S. Census Bureau declared the frontier closed because a moving western line could no longer be seen on its demographic maps. The line had been pushing outward since 1790 but was no longer visible. Thomas Jefferson's assertion, that the vast open spaces of America would take a hundred generations to fill, took about 80 years according to Bureau data. Turner vetted the Bureau's findings and projected that the closing of the frontier would have deleterious effects on the nation.

45. Susan Kollin, *Nature's State*, 5.

46. As David Ingram makes clear in his discussion of Erik Davis' essay on indigenous imagery, Hollywood film largely deploys diversity through picturesque characters that are "short on information." Ingram, *Green Screen*, 58–9; Davis, "Review of *Ferngully*," 10.

47. Ingram, *Green Screen*, 45.

48. Bruzzi, *Bringing Up Daddy*, xii.

49. Buma, *Refereeing Identity*, 186.

50. Ingram, *Green Screen*, 31.

51. Kollin, *Nature's State*, 5.

52. This motif appears to allude to the controversial proliferation of Walmart stores during the 1990s.

53. McGrath, "Pond Life."

54. Gruneau and Whitson, "Upmarket Continentalism," 236.

55. *Mystery, Alaska* harnesses Disney's long-time tradition of Wild West storytelling founded on Walt Disney's (1901–1966) original directive to construct the fictive space as a place "dedicated to the ideals, the dreams and the hard facts that have created America." Historical geographer Richard Francaviglia documents that Walt drew on Frederick Jackson Turner's late nineteenth century vision of the frontier West as inspiration for his work because the mogul saw it as the revitalizing agent of the American spirit. Walt himself was known for his strong pioneering instincts, and introduced the first film-TV combined effort on record, which allowed the ABC network to broadcast feature films made by the Disney studio. The program named *Disneyland* (1954–2008) linked to the Disneyland Park by way of four iconic entertainment precincts: Frontierland, Fantasyland, Adventureland, and Tomorrowland. Revolving around the idea of Westering as the national journey, Frontierland was also Walt's favorite, an enclave whose management he personally oversaw. See Leonard Mosley, *Disney's World: A Biography* (New York: Stein and Day, 1985), 221; Richard Francaviglia, "Walt Disney's Frontierland," *Western Historical Quarterly* 30, no. 2 (1999): 167; Jon Lewis, "Movies and Growing Up ... Absurd," *American Cinema of the 1950s: Themes and Variations*, ed. Murray Pomerance (New Jersey: Rutgers University Press, 2005), 136.

56. Peter Donnelly, "The Local and the Global: Globalization in the Sociology of Sport," *Journal of Sport and Social Issues* 20, no. 3 (1996): 246.

57. Producer Peter Rudy accounts for the film's subject matter in noting that he and co-producer Erik Moe played high school and college hockey together, and upon moving to California held on to their "obsession with small-town Wisconsin hockey programs." See Jim Lundstrom, "'Friends' Hockey Film Puts Wisconsin Up Front," *Appleton Post-Crescent*, April 19, 2004, accessed April 20, 2006, http://nosleepthemovie.com/lundstrom.html. Cinema Libre Studio, a progressive outlet formed to counteract the effects of media consolidation, distributed the film.

58. Stuart C. Aitken and Christopher Lee Lukinbeal, "Dissasociated Masculinities and Geographies of the Road," *The Road Movie Book*, eds. Steven Cohan and Ina Rae Hark (London: Routledge, 1997), 351, 354.

59. Wendy Everett refers to Tim Corrigan's work in discussing the road movie's four elements. See Wendy Everett, "Lost in Transition: The European Road Movie, or a Genre 'Adrift in the Cosmos,'" *Literature/Film Quarterly* 37, no. 3 (2009): 165–75; Tim Corrigan, *A Cinema Without Walls: Movies and Culture After Vietnam* (New Brunswick, NJ: Rutgers University Press, 1991).

60. See Mason, "'Get the Puck Outta Here!'" 141, 154.

61. Kimmel, "Globalization and Its Mal(E)Contents: The Gendered Moral and Political Economy of Terrorism," *Handbook of Studies on Men and Masculinities*, eds. Michael Kimmel, Jeff Hearn, and R.W. Connell (London: Sage Publications, 2005), 415.

62. Connell, "Globalization, Imperialism, and Masculinities," 76–8.

63. Kimmel, "Globalization and Its Mal(E)Contents," 419.

64. Romano and Dokoupil discuss the erosion of

exclusive male spaces at work as well as feminists' and progressives' calls for men to take on more involved parenting roles and assume occupations formerly reserved exclusively for women as prompting a segment of the male demographic to revert to seasoned models of manhood for self-preservation. Not surprisingly, much like its 1977 predecessor, *Slap Shot 2* preceded yet another Rocky sequel, *Rocky Balboa* (Stallone, 2006), which brought in audiences nearly 75 per cent male. For more about the social pressures faced by men, see Andrew Romano and Tony Dokoupil, "Men's Lib," *Newsweek*, September 27, 2010, 44.

65. In contrast to the standard media images of corporate owners as suspect, the press nunaced Lemieux and Gretzky's mediating roles as beneficial to all parties: owners, athletes and fans.

66. Gruneau and Whitson, "Upmarket Continentalism," 262.

67. In an interview about the changing face of NHL game attendance, David Whitson underscores the fallout of corporations' underwriting of sport, noting that as teams have sought to fill seats with season ticket holders and more affluent patrons, "lunch bucket fans" have been increasingly unable to afford tickets to live hockey games. Television networks, which pay a hefty price for the rights to broadcast games and other media that profit from a close working relationship with sports leagues, nonetheless routinely reiterate commonsense assumptions about the corporate underwriting of sport. This emphasis conceptualizes the fan as affluent enough to afford game attendance at local arenas and purchase team paraphernalia and corporate partner products, further alienating hockey's traditional constituencies. For Whitson's interview, see Bill Graveland, "White Collar Workers Replacing Traditional Blue Collar Fans in NHL," October 30, 2003, accessed October 31, 2003, http://www.canada.com/components/printstory/printstory.asp?id=6EA434F3-8899-4E11-93C0-547F8756F241.

Chapter 4

1. Scheurer, "The Best There Ever Was in the Game," 158.

2. Bruzzi, *Bringing Up Daddy*, 109.

3. Noel Brown notes that the family film originated in the 1930s and was inflected with a moral tinge as a way to speak to middle-class audiences. Brown, "Hollywood, the Family Audience and the Family Film, 1930–2010," 2.

4. Landon Y. Jones, *Great Expectations: America and the Baby Boom Generation* (New York: Coward McCann and Geohegen, 1980), 1–2.

5. Brown alludes to articles from *The Los Angeles Times*, *The Chicago Tribune*, *The Christian Science Monitor*, and *Readers Digest* as key actors in pleading for the production of more family fare to counteract the rampant violence and sexuality of seventies Hollywood movies. Brown, "Hollywood, the Family Audience and the Family Film, 1930–2010," 27.

6. Scheurer, "The Best There Ever Was in The Game," 158, 165.

7. Unlike the new family fare of the 1990s, which focuses attention on the hockey journey of children and young teens, *Touch and Go* highlights Bobby Barbato's personal journey, one that comprises a stellar hockey career as a star forward of an elite professional team along with the perks of a swank lifestyle and numerous superficial sexual liasons. The film amplifies the theater of the adult male body through sequences of Barbato jogging and lifting weights. This emphasis, in turn, brands the hockey hotshot as an unsuitable specimen for fatherhood since "[M]acho fathers or fathers preoccupied with their bodies ... in hollywood ... [films] ... tend ... to be deficient paternal role models," as Stella Bruzzi notes. So that he does not turn into "an ex-jock who knows everything about hockey and nothing about anything else," as love interest Denise tersely remarks, Barbato must also learn to ground himself in familial relationships while continuing to pursue his career goals. As he tellingly muses to a teammate, "All I am is hockey. that's pretty fucking scary, man." An unusual comment for an athlete, Barbato's statement shows the renewed interest in family values after the cultural upheaval of the preceding decades. Michael Keaton plays a similar character who must fully assume his fatherhood role in the family film *Jack Frost* (Miller, 1998). Although as Jack, he encourages son Charlie's (Joseph Cross) hockey proclivities, he is also preoccupied with his music career and skips the youngster's hockey game because of an important engagement that takes him out of town. Jack must reconnect with Charlie, teach him hockey strategy on the pond, and he succeeds in mending the relationship. Although both *Touch and Go* and *Jack Frost* emphasize the father-son bond in sport, the first film fields adult themes, puts on display Barbato's muscular physique, and much like in seventies film, makes use of expletives that hike up the realism of the narrative, quite in contrast with the sanitized values of new nineties family fare. For more on masculinity and fatherhood, see Bruzzi, *Bringing Up Daddy*, 129–30, 132; Peter N. Stearns, *Be a Man! Males in Modern Society*, 2nd ed. (New York: Holmes and Meier, 1990), 198–201.

8. Kevin Allen, "Hockey in America: American Hockey: The State of the Game," *Total Hockey*, ed. Dan Diamond, 85–7. 2nd ed. (Scarborough, ON: Total Sports Publishing, 2000), 85.

9. Charles McGrath, "Rocking the Pond," *The New Yorker*, January 12, 1994, 42.

10. Jeremy Michael Ward, "Disney, the Mighty Ducks, and the National Hockey League," (master's thesis, University of Illinois at Urbana-Champaign, 1997), 85.

11. The NHL had lost viewers in 50,000 homes between 1992 and 1993. Vicki Contavespi, "Bad Blood on the Ice." *Forbes*, January 31, 1994, n.p.

12. Staci D. Kramer, "Hockey's TV Message Still Mixed," *Multichannel News*, May 24, 1999, vol. 20, issue 22, 38. For more on Disney Company holdings, see Ward, "Disney, the Mighty Ducks, and the National Hockey League," 79–81.

13. Brown, "Hollywood, the Family Audience and the Family Film, 1930–2010," 17–8.

14. Jeremy Schickel, *The Disney Version: The Life, Times, Art and Commerce of Walt Disney* (Chicago: Elephant Paperbacks, 1997), 316.

15. Ward, "Disney, the Mighty Ducks, and the National Hockey League," 71.

16. Ward, "Disney, the Mighty Ducks, and the National Hockey League," 84.

17. Steven Riess notes that *The Mighty Ducks* was a key film in helping to launch "the growth of the family sports film," thanks in part to a strong DVD market. Riess, *Sports in America from Colonial Times to the Twenty-First Century*, 350.

18. In true Disney form, *The Mighty Ducks* movies were also developed with systematic product placement in mind, capitalizing on the Company's unique capabilities for cross-promotion. Linda Fuller documents that prior to making *The Mighty Ducks*, Disney Studios entered into multiple licensing and cross-promotional agreements, particularly with hockey equipment makers whose products were featured in a number of close-ups. Disney likewise struck agreements with fast food franchises as well as with soft-drink giant Coca Cola, among other corporate players. The imaginary Ducks team also appeared in cereal Wheaties' box cover upon the film's theatrical release. In time *The Mighty Ducks* generated a TV cartoon series "The Mighty Ducks," placed on ABC Saturday's morning block after Disney's 1995 buyout of Capital Cities/ABC, plus a derivative feature-length animation film, *Mighty Ducks the Movie: The First Face-Off* (Barruso, Murphy, Peters, and Sung, 1997). Attendant media acquisitions that turned Disney into the third largest media corporation in the world allowed the company to further synergize its holdings and showcase *Mighty Ducks* films on the Disney Channel opposite team match-ups on ABC. The Anaheim Ducks' 2003 Stanley Cup run, for example, spurred TV announcers into repeated references to *Ducks* features, making for the ultimate in cross-promotion of team and films. For more, see Linda K. Fuller, "We Can't Duck the Issue: Imbedded Advertising in the Motion Pictures," *Undressing the Ad: Reading Culture in Advertising*, ed. Katherine Toland Firth (New York: Peter Lang, 1998), 121.

19. As J.P. Telotte observes, Disney blurred the boundaries of the real and the cinematic by fashioning a hybrid product that incorporated multiple media formats and merging entertainment, publicity, and education. J.P. Telotte, *Disney TV* (Detroit: Wayne State University Press, 2004), xii, 79.

20. Bettman countered allegations about hockey violence by downplaying the role of fighting as tangential, stating that "[T]he game is not violent. It's physical," and redirecting the attention to news sports wraps for highlighting misperceptions of the sport. He also stressed the need to educate U.S. audiences about the subtleties of the game. See Knight, "New Ice Age," D6.

21. Bellamy and Schultz, "Hockey Night in the United States? The NHL, Major League Sports, and the Evolving Television/Media Marketplace," 166.

22. McGrath, "Rocking the Pond," 44–45.

23. For *The Hockey Champ*, see http://www.youtube.com/watch?v=-9A3XD70SsA

24. For *Hockey Homicide*, see http://www.youtube.com/watch?v=E1-YL9S53bk.

25. Brown, "Hollywood, the Family Audience and the Family Film, 1930–2010," 10, 17–18, 305.

26. Baker, *Contesting Identities*, 12.

27. The nineties "New Manhood" model downplayed physical aggression in favor of men's engagement with feminism by way of a more emotionally committed and conciliatory stance toward partners. It also redressed social norms that fashioned men as competent performers in the workplace to the detriment of their personal relationships. See Susan Jeffords, "Can Masculinity Be Terminated?," *Screening the Male: Exploring Masculinities in the Hollywood Cinema*, eds. Steven Cohan and Ina Rae Hark (London: Routledge, 1993), 259; Ward, "Disney, the Mighty Ducks, and the National Hockey League," 61.

28. Bruzzi, *Bringing Up Daddy*, xv.

29. Ward, "Disney, the Mighty Ducks, and the National Hockey League," 73.

30. J. Robert Craig documents that in 1992 Disney made over USD 7 billion in sales of licensed athletic apparel featuring the virtual and real Ducks Wild Wing "Hockey Mask" logo. By the second season, Mighty Ducks merchandise ranked first in sales among all NHL teams. For more, see J. Robert Craig, "From Triumph of the Will to the Mighty Ducks of Anaheim: Riefenstahl Rocks by the Pond." *Popular Culture Review*, vol 8, no. 1 (February 1997), 118.

31. Wayne Gretzky's hiring as General Manager of Team Canada in the 2002 Olympics illustrates that, whatever his marketable flexibility as a transnational star, in international competition Gretzky is, and always will be, uncompromisingly Canadian.

32. *D2*'s dramatization of the Ducks' triumph over Russia mirrored Team Russia's inability to qualify for the medal-round of Olympic hockey competition in the 1994 Lillehammer Winter Games for the first time since the U.S.S.R.'s 1956 entry into the Olympics. North American and European media reports framed this failure as proof of the unravelling of former Soviet hockey programs and the country's loss of superpower status. See, for example, Russia's representation in CTV and CBC broadcasts of the 1994 Winter Olympics Finland-Russia bronze-medal hockey matchup in Lillehammer, Norway in Iri V. Cermak, "Seeing Red: Images of Soviet and Russian Hockey in U.S. and Canadian Olympic Broadcasts" (Ph.D. diss., University of Washington, 1996), 169–224.

33. Eisner's comments on the fall of the U.S.S.R that, "It may not be such an exaggeration to appreciate the role of the American entertainment industry in helping to change history," reaffirmed Disney's "brand nationalism" in like fashion. Michael Eisner, "Planetized Entertainment," *New Perspectives Quarterly* 12, no. 4 (1995), 9; Henry A. Giroux, *The Mouse That Roared: Disney and the End of Innocence* (Lanham: Rowman & Littlefield,) 28.

34. Family entertainment also aims its content at the "kidult" and, in so doing, counts on the infantilization of society in the face of complex realities. For more on this social trend, see Frank Furedi, "The Children Who Won't Grow Up," *Spiked Online*, July 29, 2003, accessed April 14, 2013, http://www.spiked-online.com/Articles/00000006DE8D.htm.

35. Brown notes that the ideological populism of family entertainment films cannot be disconnected from foundational U.S. precepts, which foreground the values of "freedom, individualism, political superiority, the importance of family and community, and ... meritocratic self-advancement." Family entertainment's emphasis on ideological populism, then, constitutes both a draw and

a potential obstacle to increasing the global audience since, in consuming these films, viewers have to buy into Hollywood's branded rendition of America. Brown, "Hollywood, the Family Audience and the Family Film, 1930–2010," 40.

36. Given Disney's synergistic strategies, it is not unexpected that the company also reprised the bankable story of the 1980 win in its 2004 feature *Miracle* as a metaphor for the U.S. Cold War victory over the U.S.S.R.

37. Buma, *Refereeing Identity*, 185.

38. For more on the ethos of hockey professionalism, see Michael Robidoux, *Men at Play: A Working Understanding of Professional Hockey* (Montreal: Mcgill-Queen's University Press, 2001).

39. Janet Wasko, "The Magical-Market World of Disney," *Monthly Review*, April 2001, accessed April 18, 2006, http://www.findarticles.com/p/articles/mi_m1132/is_11_52/ai_74410355/.

40. Disney sold its Mighty Ducks of Anaheim team in February 2005 to Henry and Susan Samueli.

41. With a proven production infrastructure in place and boasting a wide array of desirable shooting locations well into the decade, British Columbia turned into a premier production center that consistently attracted foreign production projects because of its ability to deliver, in the words of B.C. Film Commissioner Susan Croome, "The Best Value for a Producer's Dollar." Mike Gasher explains that Hollywood's role in the B. C. film industry was not new and dated back to 1970 when the provincial government had chosen to market the region to Hollywood companies as a way to grow and diversify the economy, in part because Canadian federal film agency biases favored Quebec and Ontario talent. Gasher notes that Hollywood runaway production of the 1990s and 2000s functioned in the context of traditional resource-extraction, as projects were typically drawn up, funded, and finished outside Canada, and re-imported for consumption into the Canadian regions. He also makes the case that assessing the B.C. film industry solely based on staple economics is insufficient in judging the influx of Hollywood production into the province, since localities were able to develop and nurture a domestic pool of filmmakers. Increasing runaway Hollywood production also allowed Ontario and Quebec to become part of an international circuit of film production. In 2000, Quebec, Toronto, and B.C. generated almost CAD 3 billion, with B.C. at the forefront of production activity due in large part to a surge of 49 per cent in foreign location shooting. The Canadian Association of Film Distributors and Exporters (CAFDE) supported the rising profile of TV and film production in Canada and its transformation into one of the Canadian economy's sturdiest industries. For more, see Mike Gasher, *Hollywood North: The Feature Film Industry in British Columbia* (Vancouver, B.C.: University of British Columbia Press, 2002), 22, 67–9, 134–6, 143; Samantha Yaffe, "Production Still Booming," *Playback*, March 5, 2001, accessed February 6, 2006, http://www.playbackonline.ca/articles/magazine/20010305/Productions.html?word=2001&word=Production&word=booming.

42. David L. Pike, "Canadian Cinema in the Age of Globalization," *CineAction*. September 22, 2001. http://www.encyclopedia.com/doc/1G1-84194432.html; Lewis, "The End of Cinema as We Know It and I Feel..."

and "I Feel...: An Introduction to a Book on Nineties American Film," *The End of Cinema as We Know It: American Film in the Nineties*, ed. Jon Lewis (New York: New York University Press, 2001), 3.

43. *Ronnie and Julie* was produced as part of Showtime's "Contemporary Classics" youth movie series.

44. Canadian Association of Film Distributors and Exporters (CAFDE), "A Review of Canadian Content Criteria in the 21st Century" (brief presented to the Department of Canadian Heritage, May 31, 2002), accessed May 15 2006, http://www.pch.gc.ca/progs/acca/progs/cc21c/archives/docs/cadfe.htm).

45. Although *MVP: Most Valuable Primate* secured distribution with Disney, the Company relegated the film to the direct-to-video market. Warner Brothers subsequently picked it up for theatrical release. Gasher, *Hollywood North*, 135, 140.

46. Jack's expertise in sign language also replicates chimpanzees' superior tool-making and communication aptitudes seen in Jane Goodall's *Specials*. See Cynthia Chris, *Watching Wildlife* (Minneapolis: University of Minnesota Press, 2006), 66; Donna Haraway, *Primate Visions: Gender, Race, and Nature in the World of Modern Science* (New York: Routledge, Chapman & Hall, 1989).

47. Pierre Berton, *Hollywood's Canada: The Americanization of Our National Image* (Toronto: McClelland & Stewart Limited, 1975), 16–7.

48. Alexander Wilson, *The Culture of Nature: North American Landscapes from Disney to the Exxon Valdez* (Cambridge, MA: Blackwell, 1992), 18–9.

49. Gasher, *Hollywood North*, 112–13.

50. Katerberg, "A Northern Vision," 545–6.

51. Greene, *Planet of the Apes*, 3–4, 9.

52. Chris Clarke, "Nature by Design: How Disney's Treatment of Animals Has Altered Our Sense of the Wild and Cleared the Way for Environmental Decline," *New Internationalist* 308, December 1998, accessed September 14, 2006, http://www.newint.org/issue308/nature.html.

53. See Frederick Fletcher, "Media and Political Identity: Canada and Quebec in the Era of Globalization," *Canadian Journal of Communication* 23, no. 3 (1998), accessed June 10, 2006, http://www.cjconline.ca/index.php/journal/article/viewArticle/1049/955; Liss Jeffrey, assisted by Fraser McAninch,"Private Television and cable," *The Cultural Industries in Canada: Problems, Policies, and Prospects*, ed. Michael Dorland (Toronto: James Lorimer, 1996).

54. Seventy-five percent of programming consumed by Anglophone Canadians originates in the United States. Jeffrey, "Private Television and Cable," 227; Paul Rutherford, *The Making of the Canadian Media* (Toronto: McGraw Hill-Ryerson, 1978), 265.

55. Pike, "Canadian Cinema in the Age of Globalization."

56. Canadian Association of Film Distributors and Exporters (CAFDE), "A Review of Canadian Content Criteria in the 21st Century."

57. Steven's decision hints that younger generations are bestowed the larger task to preserve the natural world and that other objectives must be carefully weighed against this assignment. However, typical of popular film, the movie disavows the commodification of Nature that the so-called sport-loving chimp character dramatizes,

a motif that recurs in the *MVP* franchise—the theatrical release *MVP 2: Most Vertical Primate* (Vince, 2001) and the direct-to-video *MXP: Most Extreme Primate* (Vince, 2003). Young chimps Bernie, Louie, and Mac, who played Jack in the first film, were also taken on a month-long tour of NHL arenas to publicize the flick during game intermission shows.

58. *Slap Shot 3*'s Newman Home for Boys motif gives a wink to Paul Newman's character Reggie Dunlop in *Slap Shot* to denote his central gamesman role in protecting players against the machinations of management and ownership, and by proxy, empowering the town's disenfranchised residents.

59. Kevin Robins, "What in the World's Going On?," *Productions of Culture/Cultures of Production*, ed. Paul du Gay (London: Sage, 1997), 12.

60. The Hansons are bankable figures in both the U.S. and Canada. Steve Carlson, who plays one of the brothers, indirectly alludes to their marketability in noting that, "Most Canadians are kind of disappointed ... [to learn we're not Canadian]. But it's ok. We love Canadians because they're huge hockey fans.... We're just not one of you." See Chris Johnston, "Hanson Brothers Return for Slap Shot 3 Movie," *The Canadian Press*, November 25, 2008, accessed April 18, 2012, http://www.thestar.com/entertainment/movies/article/542905—hanson-brothers-return-for-slap-slap_shot_3_movie.html.

61. The film is based on the real-life efforts of Brian Johnson, a hockey parent in Fredericton, New Brunswick.

62. In choosing to model his Canada–U.S. Friendship event on the 1972 Summit Series, Jordy in *Sticks and Stones* reiterates the memory of series in line with the values of family entertainment: as a symbol of rapprochement between the Canadian and Soviet teams. While the series was far more controversial, the film must uphold the didacticism and lack of objectionable subject matter associated with sport in the new family genre.

63. Canadian hockey novels, in contrast, reiterate the notion of the U.S. as icon of modernity and as threat to the viability of the Canadian small town, and hence, to Canada as a whole. For more, see Buma, *Refereeing Identity*, 38, 43.

64. Brown, "Hollywood, the Family Audience and the Family Film," 119, 131–2.

65. Mackey, *The House of Difference*, 145.

66. Michael Buma encounters many of the same motifs in Canadian hockey novels. See Buma, *Refereeing Identity*, 38, 64.

Chapter 5

1. Historians argue that the roots of the industry's success lie with Quebec's "Quiet Revolution" of the 1960s. The resulting secularization of society and the control of the economy by Quebecers for the first time in Canada's history resulted in a cinema in which both political and cultural goals intersected. George Melnyk points out that by end of the decade almost fifty French language features had been released both by independent producers and in collaboration with the National Film Board of Canada. See Scott Mackenzie, *Screening Quebec: Québécois Moving Images, National Identity, and the Public Sphere* (Manchester: Manchester University Press, 2004), 2; George Melnyk, *One Hundred Years of Canadian Cinema* (Toronto: University of Toronto Press, 2004), 126; Yves Lever, *Histoire Générale Du Cinéma Au Québec* (Montréal: Boreal, 1995).

2. Mackenzie, *Screening Quebec*, 16; Mackey, *the House of Difference*, 154.

3. Paul C. Adams, "The September 11 Attacks as Viewed from Quebec: The Small-Nation Code in Geopolitical Discourse," *Political Geography* 23 (2004): 773, 768.

4. Sullivan, "Work It Girl! Sex, Labour and Nationalism in *Valerie*," *Working on Screen: Representations of the Working Class in Canadian Cinema*, eds. Malek Khouri and Darrell Varga (Toronto: University of Toronto Press, 2006), 99; Max Nemni, "Forum: Canada in Crisis and the Destructive Power of Myth," *Queen's Quarterly* 99, no. 1 (1992): 223, 225.

5. Adams, "The September 11 Attacks as Viewed from Quebec," 774.

6. Carolyn Podruchny, *Making the Voyageur World: Travelers and Traders in the North American Fur Trade* (Lincoln: University of Nebraska Press, 2006), 12.

7. Podruchny amplifies that after the French and Indian War of 1763, the fur trade that operated out of the Montreal area was restructured primarily under the direction of English, Scottish, and American managers, with only a few Francophones in the ranks. Podruchny, *Making the Voyageurs World*, xi.

8. The *pays d'en haut* refers to riverine areas where Francophones from the St. Lawrence carried out their trapping and trading operations. Podruchny, *Making the Voyageurs World*, xii.

9. Podruchny, *Making the Voyageurs World*, ix, 9, 14.

10. Harvey, "Whose Sweater Is This? The Changing Meanings of Hockey in Quebec," *Artificial Ice: Hockey, Culture and Commerce*, eds. Richard Gruneau and David Whitson (Peterborough, ON: Broadview Press, 2006), 34–5.

11. Mackenzie, *Screening Quebec*, 134.

12. Jane Moss, "The Drama of Identity in Canada's Francophone West," *The American Review of Canadian Studies* 34, no. 1 (2004): 81.

13. Harvey, "Whose Sweater Is This?," 49, 41.

14. Nonetheless, as Amy Ransom notes, the Canadiens' cultural makeup has always been ethnically diverse, and the total of Francophones drafted per season never exceeded 2.63 to 2.38 players. For more, see Amy Ransom, "*Lieux de mémoire* or lieux du dollar? Montreal's Forum, the Canadiens, and Popular Culture," *Quebec Studies Journal* 51 (Spring/Summer 2011): 27, 29, 36; Amy Ransom, "Language and Gender Politics in the Québec Television Series *Lance Et Compte*," *Ice Hockey in Quebec—The Same but Different?*, eds. Jason Blake and Andrew C. Holman. Forthcoming, 280; D'Arcy Jenish, *The Montreal Canadiens: 100 Years Of Glory* (Toronto: Anchor Canada, 2009), 50; Bob Sirois, *Discrimination in the NHL: Quebec Hockey Players Sidelined* (Montreal: Baraka, 2010), 87–88.

15. To view "*Un Jeu si simple*," see http://www.onf.ca/film/Un_jeu_si_simple/

16. Michel Brault's "*La dernière partie*" portrays Quebecers' gender divide in the game. The story opens with

two protagonists, diehard hockey enthusiast, Roger, and his wife, Madeleine, at a hockey rink. For years Roger has wanted his wife to attend the Saturday game but Madeleine is not a fan. Unbeknownst to him, she is also set to walk out on him because they have become estranged and she can no longer take it. At the rink as a last ditch effort, Madeleine grows all the more lonely as Roger focuses on the match. Filled with grief, she takes her leave and when her husband catches up to her in the hallway, she explains the reasons for her departure. Even as he hears his wife's grievances, his eyes stray to the match on the TV monitor. The final shot is of Roger, alone in his living room asleep in an armchair and in front of his TV. Next to him is an old photograph of a hockey team. Brault's "Montréal vu par" contribution conveys hockey as a preeminent site for expressing Francophone males' sense of belonging and females' sense of exclusion. Brault's piece, which was released on the 350th anniversary of the city of Montreal, depicts, much like the fading of the old Montreal, the fading of French culture's constants—marriage and the family—at a time when many women have chosen divorce rather than remaining in unhappy unions. For more on Brault's brief interview, see "Montreal vu par..." *Contemporary Canadian Film and Literature* (Fall, 1999), accessed August 12, 2012, http://www.eng.fju.edu.tw/canada/vu_par.html.

17. Parpart, "The Nation and the Nude," 188.

18. The film is also marketed as *The Littlest Canadian* and *Un Million Sur La Glace.*

19. Pierre's gutsy determination despite his young age has resonances in children's hockey literature as archetypically Francophone. In *Centerman from Quebec: A Hockey Story* (1972), the central protagonist is a French-Canadian boy who plays on a New York peewee team. As a spirited player who manages to raise his team's level of play, Sheldon never loses his fiery temperament and passion for the game despite hurdles. See Hollands, "English-Canadian Sports Novels and Cultural Production," 221.

20. Monk, *Weird Sex & Snowshoes,* 156.

21. Melnyk makes clear that the growth of Quebec's filmmaking industry originated in the Francophone project of identity with artists as the movement's core figures. See Melnyk, *One Hundred Years of Canadian Cinema,* 143.

22. Loiselle, *Cinema as History,* 105.

23. Loiselle, *Cinema as History,* 52.

24. The lack of Forum imagery in later films is likely the result of the Canadiens' 1996 move to the Molson Centre (renamed the Bell Centre in 2002), which has not inspired the same identification, because it lacks the history of the Canadiens' multiple Stanley Cup runs. For more, see Ransom, "Lieux de mémoire or lieux du dollar?," 21, 36, 39.

25. For more on the cinema of attractions, see John Gunning, "The Cinema of Attraction: Early Film, the Spectator, and the Avant Garde," *Wide Angle* 6.2 (1986): 68–9.

26. Houle, "Themes and Ideology in Quebec Cinema."

27. Houle adds that the marginal motifs seen in the French-Canadian films of this period are in part an offshoot of the displacement of the mundane by the gruesome and weird. See Houle,"Themes and Ideology in Quebec Cinema."

28. Mackenzie, *Screening Quebec,* 163.

29. Loiselle, *Cinema as History,* 123.

30. Mackenzie, *Screening Quebec,* 161. 173.

31. The tension between nationalism and federalism also expresses Québécois identity in the cinema. Mackenzie, *Screening Quebec,* 8, 161.

32. See the French version of "The Sweater" at http://www.youtube.com/watch?v=shyFWU8pCjs and the English version at http://www.youtube.com/watch?v=EgydkfnUEi8.

33. The short story was published in *Les Enfants Du Bonhomme Dans La Lune* (1979), translated as *The Hockey Sweater and Other Stories* (1979) by Sheila Fischman.

34. Tamara Tarasoff, "Capturing Customers: Roch Carrier and the *Hockey Sweater,*" *Before E-Commerce— A History of Canadian Mail-Order Catalogues.* Canadian Museum of Civilization Corporation, 2004, accessed March 19, 2013. http://www.civilization.ca/cmc/exhibitions/cpm/catalog/cat2208e.shtml.

35. Melnyk, *One Hundred Years of Canadian Cinema,* 124, 143.

36. Adams, "The September 11 Attacks as Viewed from Quebec," 769.

37. André Loiselle, "Popular Genres in Quebec Cinema: The Strange Case of Horror in Film and Television," *How Canadians Communicate III: Contexts of Canadian Popular Culture,* eds. Bart Beaty, Derek Briton, Gloria Filax, and Rebecca Sullivan (Edmonton, AB: Athabasca University Press, 2010), 142–3.

38. Loiselle, "Popular Genres in Quebec Cinema: The Strange Case of Horror in Film and Television," 142. Bill Marshall, *Quebec National Cinema* (Montreal: McGill-Queen's University Press, 2001), 185.

39. Melnyk, *One Hundred Years of Canadian Cinema,* 144–5.

40. Matthew Hays, "TV Nation: The Answer to English-Canadian Cinema's Woes? The Boob Tube, of Course (POV)," *TAKE ONE,* December 4, 2004, accessed April 3, 2007, http://www.accessmylibrary.com/coms2/summary_0286–18386265_ITM

41. Brian Johnson attributes the dismal state of English-Canadian film to a bureaucratic process that allows distributors to pick up publicly-funded films, cede broadcasters TV rights, and facilitate a one-time and largely symbolic release. Other critics blame policies dating back to the 1920 meant to offset the continentalizing effects of American content and create an English-Canadian cinema that stands out from Hollywood product, for promoting a cinema without an audience. Maurie Alioff argues that the repertoire of art-circuit releases that few Canadians have been willing to see has more to do with the creation of a "maverick," nonconformist film culture than it does with reflecting national identity on film. Brian Johnson, "English Canadian Films: Why No One Sees Them," *Maclean's Magazine,* April 17, 2006, accessed May 14, 2007, http://www.thecanadianencyclopedia.com/index.cfm?PgNm=TCE&Params = M1ARTM0012964; Maurie Alioff, "O Canadian Film, We Stand on Guard for Thee. Peter Rowe's Popcorn with Maple Syrup and Jill Sharpe's *Weird Sex and Snowshoes,*" *TAKE ONE* (Sept.–Dec. 2004), accessed May 18, 2006,

http://findarticles.com/p/articles/mi_0JSF/is_47_13/ai_n6219967/?tag+content;col1.

42. Melnyk, *One Hundred Years of Canadian Cinema*, 258.

43. Véronneau, "Genres and Variations: The Audiences of Quebec Cinema," 117; Loiselle, "Popular Genres in Quebec Cinema," 143.

44. In the 1990s, Quebec films' screen time had achieved a high of ten percent as opposed to English-Canadian cinema's routine one percent. In the 2000s, Canadian features in English accounted for only one percent of the English-Canadian box office, which also did not reflect Toronto and Montreal's multi-billion dollar movie industry. The trend continued into 2011, as seven out of top ten high-grossing Canadian films were French-Canadian movies. The astounding leverage of Quebec cinema did not happen overnight, according to former Canadian Minister of Heritage Liza Frulla, since despite early subsidies, "[C]ertain scripts weren't 'there' yet," and "[t]he American blockbuster would come in and take all the screen space." Federal cultural funding agency Telefilm Canada and the Quebec-funded Société de développement des entreprises culturelles (SODEC), provided financial support for Quebec filmmakers in the 1990s resulting in a prolific industry proficient in a variety of genres. Box office receipts in the province also benefited from Hollywood's less guarded stance toward Quebec's indigenous production. See George Melnyk, "Book Review Essay: Reflections on Canadian Cinema," *American Review of Canadian Studies* 35, no. 1 (2005): 145–49; Fox, "He Shoots, He Scores: Michael Dowse and Jay Baruchel Talk Goon and the Canadian Conundrum"; Melnyk, *One Hundred Years of Canadian Cinema*, 143; Marcus Robinson, "SODEC anchors Quebec's new wave," Page 17. *Playback Magazine*, November 21, 2005, accessed May 18, 2007, http://www.playbackmag.com/articles/magazine/20051121/sodec.html?word=Les&word=Boys&word=II.

45. Marshall, *Quebec National Cinema*, 185.

46. Cynthia Amsden, "Canadian Comedy, Eh? Paul Gross's Men with Brooms and Steve Smith's Red Green's Duct Tape Forever," *TAKE ONE* (June-Sept. 2005), accessed September 30, 2006, http://www.finadarticles.com/p/articles/mi_m0JSF/is_50_14/ai_N14704669/.

47. In Quebec, a film with a budget over CAD 4 million is hard-pressed to see production without backing from Telefilm Canada or from SODEC. On average, Quebec's motion pictures acquire seventy-five percent of their budget from government sources such as Telefilm, SODEC, and tax credits, as is true of English-Canadian films, which also require national and regional subsidies. *Les Boys*, however, garnered CAD 7 million in earnings and succeeded in gaining commercial success without SODEC funding. It also only tapped CAD 600,000 in Telefilm Canada monies for marketing. Etan Vlessing, "Industry Addresses Funding Crisis," Page 20. *Playback Magazine*, August 29, 2006, accessed March 29, 2007, http://www.playbackmag.com/articles/magazine/20060821/funding.html.

48. Matthew Hays, "Drôle Patrol. *Bon Cop Bad Cop* Attempts to Unite Canada—In Laughter," cbcnews.ca, August 17, 2006, accessed June 8, 2011, http://www.cbc.ca/arts/film/boncop.html.

49. Ransom, *Hockey, PQ*, 117.

50. André Loiselle, "Subtly Subversive or Simply Stupid: Notes on Popular Quebec Cinema," *Post Script-Jacksonville* 18, no. 2 (Winter/Spring 1998): 76.

51. Fiske, *Understanding Popular Culture*, 42, 67–72.

52. Matthew Hays, "Shooting for a Hat Trick: Director Louis Saïa on the Eagerly Anticipated Les Boys 3." *Montreal Mirror*, November 21, 2001, accessed March 15, 2006, http://www.montrealmirror.com/ARCHIVES/2001/112901/film4.html.

53. Suzanne Laberge and Albert Mathieu, "Conceptions of Masculinity and of Gender Transgressions in Sport Among Adolescent Boys: Hegemony, Contestation, and Social Class Dynamic," *Men and Masculinities* 1, no. 3 (1999): 243–267.

54. For more on homosexuality and sport, see Messner, "Still a Man's World"; Donald F. Sabo "The Politics of Homophobia in Sport," *Sex, Violence, and Power in Sports: Rethinking Masculinity*, eds. Michael A. Messner and Donald F. Sabo (Freedom: Crossing, 1994): 101–112; Brian Pronger, *The Arena of Masculinity and the Meaning of Sex* (New York: St. Martin's Press, 1990).

55. Eve Kosofsky Sedgwick, *Between Men: English Literature and Male Homosocial Desire* (New York: Columbia University Press, 1985), 3; Buma, *Refereeing Identity*, 179, 195.

56. Ransom, *Hockey PQ*, 132.

57. Ransom, *Hockey PQ*, 134–5.

58. Loiselle, "Subtly Subversive or Simply Stupid," 83.

59. Marshall, *Quebec National Cinema*, 203–4.

60. Loiselle, *Cinema as History*, 52.

61. André Loiselle, "Look Like a Worker and Act Like a Worker: Stereotypical Representations of the Working Class in Quebec Fiction Feature Films," *Working on Screen: Representations of the Working Class in Canadian Cinema*, eds. Malek Khouri and Darrell Varga (Toronto: University of Toronto Press, 2006), 223.

62. Quebec independence proponents scored a victory in 2010 by negotiating with Hockey Canada the ability to field a separate team in the Quebec Cup, an international competition that hosted national squads from France, Italy and Switzerland, which some in the Quebec media hailed as a breakthrough in a 30-year struggle. See Peter Rakobowchuk, "Quebec Gets Go-Ahead for a Separate Hockey Team," *The Canadian Press*, November 12, 2010, accessed November 15, 2010, http://news.ca.msn.com/canada/cp-article.aspx?cp-documentid=26325860; Sidhartha Banerjee, "Quebec Gets Own Hockey Team in International Tournament," *The Globe and Mail*, November 12, 2010, accessed November 15, 2010, http://www.theglobeandmail.com/news/national/quebec-gets-own-hockey-team-in-international-tournament/article1314351/.

63. Loiselle, *Cinema as History*, 153.

64. Serge Cantin, "Crise de la mémoire collective. Pour sortir de la survivance," *Le Devoir*, August 14, 1999, A9; Loiselle, *Cinema as History*, 153.

65. Marshall, *Quebec National Cinema*, 75.

66. Marshall, *Quebec National Cinema*, 74–5, 77, 79.

67. See Andrew Holman's discussion of how Quebecers regarded the 1972 series and the overconfidence of the Francophone press, which much like its Anglophone counterpart, took it for granted that the Canadians would easily come out on top. Numerous voices in

Canada nonetheless also hailed the Soviets' novel approach to the game. Amy Ransom alludes to Jerry Trudel's assertion that through their keenly honed strategies, the Soviets had demonstrated that "intelligence has its place even in hockey." See also Amy Ransom's detailed discussion of this part of the film. For more, see Andrew Holman, "Les Russes et nous: The 1972 Summit Series and the Birth of Hockey Sovereignty in Quebec," *Coming Down the Mountain: Rethinking the 1972 Summit Series*, ed. Brian Kennedy (Hamilton, ON: Wolsak and Wynn, 2014), 109–125; Trudel, quoted in Simon Richard, *La Série du siècle. Septembre 1972* (Montreal: Hurtubise, 2002), 95–6; Ransom, *Hockey PQ*, 148–150.

68. Alluding to the Soviet style of hockey, Anatoli Tarasov described Moscow's CSKA team and the Soviet national squad of the mid-1960s as "Cement[ing] ... the same highly creative understanding of hockey ... [and the] pursuit of the intellectual game." He credits three players, in particular—Konstantin Loktev, Alexander Almetov, and Veniamin Alexandrov—for instituting and popularizing the "intuition game"; that is, playing with the instincts required "to guarantee the highest synchronicity of action." For Anatoli Tarasov's thoughts on Soviet hockey, see his posts in"Twenty Years of Soviet Hockey—1962–1982," *Hfboards*, re-posted July 3, 2015, accessed July 7, 2015, http://hfboards.hockeysfuture.com/showthread.php?t=565254&page=4.

69. For more on the documentaries of the series, see Iri Cermak, "Media Retrospective of the Summit Series," *Coming Down the Mountain: Rethinking the 1972 Summit Series*, ed. Brian Kennedy (Hamilton, ON: Wolsak and Wynn, 2014), 210.

70. Loiselle cites Gillian Helfield's work on Quebec's rural tradition in film, and notes that the countryside trope solidified in the 1960s after the province's transformation into a predominantly urban culture. See Loiselle, "Popular Genres in Quebec Cinema," 145; Gillian Helfield, "Cultivateurs d'images: Albert Tessier and the Rural Tradition in Québécois Cinema," *Representing the Rural: Space, Place, and Identity in Films About the Land*, eds. Catherine Fowler and Gillian Helfield (Detroit: Wayne State University Press, 2006), 61.

71. The franchise's fourth installment also pokes fun of Les Boys' English-Canadian rivals by fashioning them as a team of Anglophone lawyers, the Toronto Barristers, who arrive by charter bus dressed in suit and tie. The team of barristers recalls the 1990s Americanization of the game, which saw the relocation of the Quebec Nordiques to Colorado, and precipitated accusations in Canada that American lawyers and accountants were changing the face of hockey and stripping it of its Canadian mystique. *Toronto Sun* writer Al Strachan, for example, expressed this very concern noting that hockey was transforming into a "bottom-line operation concerned with TV and making money." Because of these referents, the film's jab at the Anglophone team by way of barrister imagery has the effect of configuring Les Boys as a (French-Canadian) people's team. *Bon Cop, Bad Cop*, released a year after *Les Boys IV* also deals with the game's Americanization, suggesting that the topic remains relevant. For Al Strachan's comments, see Swardson, "Canada's Big Chill," 20.

72. Hays, "Shooting for a Hat Trick: Director Louis Saïa on the Eagerly Anticipated Les Boys 3."

73. Murray Whyte, "Where Films in English Can Seem a Cultural Betrayal," *New York Times*, September 17, 2000, accessed July 25, 2010, http://www.nytimes.com/2000/09/17/movies/film-where-films-made-in-english-can-seem-a-cultural-betrayal.html.

74. Gina Freitag and André Loiselle, "Tales of Terror in Quebec Popular Cinema: The Rise of the French-Language Horror Film Since 2000," *American Review of Canadian Studies* 43, no. 2 (2013), 191.

75. Loiselle, "Popular Genres in Quebec Cinema," 148. See also, Freitag and Loiselle, "Tales of Terror in Quebec Popular Cinema," 196–7.

76. Gruneau and Whitson, "Introduction," *Artificial Ice*, 14.

77. Ransom, *Hockey, PQ*, 156.

78. Loiselle notes that English-Canadian understandings of the French-Canadian carnivalesque in part derive from the standard set by Michel Tremblay's characters, which has the effect of rendering *Les Boys* as "shapeless successions of stupid skits without an ounce of cultural value," and disavows that these movies can carry as much potent social and political commentary as their canonical counterparts. Loiselle, "*The Decline ... and the Rise of English Canada's Quebec Cinema*," 65, 68.

79. See, for example, Elizabeth Lepage-Boily, "Il était une fois Les Boys: La Critique dure à assumer," *Cinoche.com: La Référence Cinéma Au Québec*, December 5, 2013, accessed September 15, 2015, http://www.cinoche.com/films/il-etait-une-fois-les-boys/critiques/la-critique-dure-a-assumer.html. For references to the film's commercial aspects and product placement, see Michator, "Il était une fois Les Boys," *Cinémasculin: Paradis de l'action*. January 14, 2014, accessed September 18, 2015. http://cinemasculin.com/?s=il+était+une+fois+les+Boys&searchsubmit.x=0&searchsubmit.y=0.

80. Véronneau notes that this myth was encouraged by the parti Québécois in power when the first three films saw their release. See Véronneau, "Genres and Variations," 114.

81. Coach Jimmy's line about heart also resembles Herb Brooks' film-ending lyrical remark in Disney's *Miracle* about the image of twenty young men from disparate backgrounds standing in unison.

82. *Maurice Richard/The Rocket* was nominated for 14 Prix Jutra, Quebec's cinema version of the Oscars. It garnered over CAD 4 million at the Quebec box office, with earnings outside the province totaling a remarkable CAD 1 million. Subsequent DVD sales landed the film in the top 20 slot from its September 19 release through the week of 2–8 October 2006. See Johnson, "English Canadian Films: Why No One Sees Them"; Mark Dillon, "Rocket's Release Noble but Risky," Page 11. *Playback Magazine*, April 17, 2006, accessed September 18, 2006, http://www. playbackmag.com/articles/magazine/20060417/comment.html?11; Hays, "Drôle Patrol."

83. Touted as the face of French-Canadian nationalism, the Richard Riot ignited tensions between Quebec and English-Canada. An English-Canadian resident of Westmount commented in a letter to the editor that the province was wreaked with nationalism and that French-Canadians were attempting to banish English-Canadians from the province. For more, see Sidney Katz, "The

Richard Hockey Riot," reprinted in "Maurice 'Rocket' Richard. Three Perspectives on Hockey's Most Electrifying Performer," *Total Hockey*, ed. Dan Diamond (Scarborough, ON: Total Sports Publishing, 2000), 158; Beardsley, *Country on Ice*, 134.

84. A.O. Scott, "Film in Review. the Rocket: The Legend of Rocket Richard. a Hero of Hockey," *New York Times*, November 30, 2007, accessed August 30, 2015, http://www.nytimes.com/2007/11/30/movies/30rock.html?_r=0.

85. Williams, "Melodrama Revised," 58.

86. Linda Williams, "Melancholy Melodrama: Almodóvarian Grief and Lost Homosexual Attachments," *Melodrama! The Mode of Excess from Early America to Hollywood*, eds. Frank Kelleter, Barbara Krah, and Ruth Mayer (Heidelberg: Universitätsverlag, 2007), 355.

87. Amy Ransom notes that Richard's account is based on well-known chapters of Richard's life. For more, see Ransom, *Hockey, PQ*, 28–9.

88. Williams, "Melodrama Revised," 70.

89. Williams, "Melancholy Melodrama," 355.

90. Williams, "Melodrama Revised," 48.

91. Rebecca Sullivan argues that even prior to the 1959 death of Duplessis and the Parti Liberal's rise to power, entrepreneurs in Quebec set out to lobby the government for reforms of the Church-controlled education system to facilitate the entry of a more suitable workforce into the province's emerging new economy. Sullivan, "Work It Girl!," 98–99, 101, 103.

92. Houle, "Themes and Ideology in Quebec Cinema."

93. Harvey, "Whose Sweater Is This?," 31.

94. The English-speaking boss seen in the opening scenes of *Maurice Richard* is a politically expedient cliché that aligns with the image of the Anglophone managerial class in working-class cinema. For more on the working class in film, see Loiselle, "Look Like a Worker and Act Like a Worker," 220, 231–2; Houle, "Quelques aspects idéologiques et thématiques du cinema Québécois," 152.

95. Roy Dupuis also played Richard in the TV series *Maurice Richard: Histoire d'un Canadien* (1999), as well as in an episode of *Heritage Minutes*, a collection of short depictions of Canadian history's leading figures, where he reenacted Maurice Richard's 5 goals and 3 assists of December 29, 1944.

96. Adams, "The September 11 Attacks as Viewed from Quebec," 790.

97. Williams, "Melodrama Revised," 62.

98. Dillon, "Rocket's Release Noble but Risky."

99. Katz, "The Richard Hockey Riot," 57.

100. Harvey, "Whose Sweater Is This?," 38.

101. Beardsley, *Country on Ice*, 143.

102. Richard's statement quoted in Lawrence Scanlan, *Grace Under Fire: The State of Our Sweet and Savage Game* (New York: Penguin, 2002), 199. See also Brian Kennedy, "Whatever Happened to the Organ and the Portrait of Her Majesty? NHL Spectating as Imaginary Carnival," *Now Is the Winter*, eds. Jamie Dopp and Richard Harrison (Hamilton, ON: Wolsak and Wynn, 2009), 162.

103. For more on Richard's image in *Of Sport and Men*, see Brett Kashmere's analysis in "*Valery's Ankle*: Supporting Documents and Notation," 40. For the documentary see http://www.nfb.ca/film/of_sport_and_men.

104. Herbert Warren Wind, "Fire on the Ice," *Sports Illustrated*, December 6, 1954, reprinted in "Maurice 'Rocket' Richard. Three Perspectives on Hockey's Most Electrifying Performer," *Total Hockey*, ed. Dan Diamond, 2nd ed. (Scarborough, ON: Total Sports Publishing, 2000), 157.

105. Ransom, *Hockey PQ*, 38–9.

106. Ingrid Peritz and Tu Thanh Ha, "Rocket Inspires Thunderous Applause: Luminaries at Funeral Rise in Final Tribute," *The Globe and Mail*, June 1, 2000, reprinted in "Maurice 'Rocket' Richard. Three Perspectives on Hockey's Most Electrifying Performer," *Total Hockey*, ed. Dan Diamond, 164–5. 2nd ed. (Scarborough, ON: Total Sports Publishing, 2000), 165.

107. Loiselle, "Look Like a Worker and Act Like a Worker," 225–6. See also, Harvey, "Whose Sweater Is This?," 42–3.

108. George Custen, "Making History," *The Historical Film: History and Memory in Media*, ed. Marcia Landy (New Brunswick, NJ: Rutgers University Press, 2001), 69; Robert A. Rosenstone, "The Historical Film," *History and Memory in Media*, ed. Marcia Landy (New Brunswick, NJ: Rutgers University Press, 2001), 56.

109. Carolyn Anderson, "The Biographical Film," *Handbook of American Film Genres*, ed. Wes D. Gehring (New York: Greenwood Press, 1988), 335.

110. Frederick Fletcher, "Media and Political Identity: Canada and Quebec in the Era of Globalization," *Canadian Journal of Communication* 23, no. 3 (1998), accessed August 5, 2006, http://www.cjconline.ca/index.php/journal/article/viewArticle/1049/955; Nemni, "Canada in Crisis and the Destructive Power of Myth."

111. Fletcher, "Media and Political Identity."

112. Ransom, "Lieux de mémoire of lieux du dollar?," 26–7.

113. Salutin, "A Little Paean to Hockey," *The Globe and Mail*, June 2, 2006, A19.

114. Sullivan, "Work It Girl!," 99.

115. Williams, "Melancholy Melodrama," 355; Brooks, *The Melodramatic Imagination*, 56–80.

116. *Bon Cop, Bad Cop* won the 2007 Genie Award for Best Picture.

117. Kaye, "Certain Tendencies of Canadian Cinema," 212–4.

118. The killer in *Bon Cop, Bad Cop* peculiarly speaks with an accent in both English and French, denoting someone who is unhinged from both Anglo- and French-Canadian cultural moorings.

119. Érik Canuel states in an interview that while the idea for the film was not original, the script's political overtones drew him to the project. See Hays, "Drôle Patrol: *Bon Cop Bad Cop* Attempts to Unite Canada—In Laughter."

120. Bill Marshall notes that this variety of nationalism had no link to Quebec's own Francophone elites. Besides the Patriotes Rebellion, Scott Mackenzie lists other historical political events that inform Québécois identity: the Duplessis era (1939–59), la Revolution tranquille (1960–65), the October Crisis (1970), the Parti Québécois election (1976), the Referendum on Sovereign Association (1980), the Repatriation of Canadian

Constitution and Charter of Rights and Freedoms (1982), the Oka Crisis (1990), and the Second Referendum on Sovereignty (1995). See Marshall, *Quebec National Cinema*, 5; Mackenzie, *Screening Quebec*, 8.

121. Pelletier, "'Right Language, Wrong Words!' L'Alternance de code comme élément participant de la négociation," *Commposite.Org* 11, no.1 (2008), accessed May 11, 2011, http://commposite.org/index.php/revue/article/view/55.

122. Gittings, *Canadian National Cinema*, 104.

123. Bouchard's ruggedness resembles depictions of Francophone players as physically tough customers unafraid to engage in fisticuffs. See, for example, *Touch and Go*, where American star Bobby Barbato tangles with Montreal defenseman Goulet. Canadian indie film, *Goon*, co-written by proud Montreal native Jay Baruchel, also draws up Quebec players and fans as fierce contenders.

124. Ransom, *Hockey, PQ*, 76.

125. Steven Jackson, "Gretzky, Crisis, and Canadian Identity in 1988: Rearticulating the Americanization of Culture Debate," *Sociology of Sport Journal* 11 (1994): 439. See also Steven Jackson, "Sport, Crisis, and Canadian Identity in 1988: A Cultural Analysis," (Ph.D. diss., University of Illinois at Urbana-Champaign, 1992).

126. From a box office total of $13 million, *Bon Cop, Bad Cop* earned $2.5 million outside Quebec. Randy Duniz, "Bon Cop: A How-To for Successful Canadian Movies," *InterActra* (Winter 2007): 8–10.

127. Hays, "Drôle Patrol."

128. Leach, *Film in Canada*, 101.

129. *Macleans*, "The Interview: Gary Bettman. NHL Commissioner Gary Bettman on Canada, on the 'Covenant' with Fans, Gretzky and on Trying to Do the Right Things."

130. Patrick Huard interview with Alexandra Shimo. Quoted in Kaye, "Certain Tendencies in Canadian Cinema," 249.

131. Podruchny, *Making the Voyageur World*, 14. This defiant signature also calls to mind the figure of *l'homme fort québécois*, the hyper-masculine strong man, who, as Katherine Ann Roberts notes, in the "symbolic economy" of 1960s Quebec allegorically offset the affront of English-Canadian colonization. See Katharine Ann Roberts, "Continental Drift: Negotiating Male Performance in Canadian and American Cinema from the Late Sixties," *American Review of Canadian Studies* 29, no. 1 (March 2009): 16–28.

Chapter 6

1. See Peter Guber's interview in Oliver, "Sports and Cinema," 53.

2. Custen, "Making History," 69.

3. David Whitson and Donald Macintosh, "The Global Circus: International Sport, Tourism, and the Marketing of Cities," *Journal of Sport and Social Issues* 20, no. 3 (1996): 289, 291.

4. Daniel Dayan and Elihu Katz, *Media Events: The Live Broadcasting of History* (Cambridge: Harvard University Press, 1992), 21, 27; Kibby, "Nostalgia for the Masculine," 17.

5. As Merja Ellefson and Eva Kingsepp note, many plots can be fashioned from the same event, and how a story is told is what ultimately imparts the meaning behind a text. Merja Ellefson and Eva Kingsepp, "The Good, the Bad and the Ugly: Stereotyping Russia the Western Way," *News of the Other: Tracing Identity in Scandinavian Constructions of the Eastern Baltic Sea Region*, ed. Kristina Riegert. *Northern Perspectives* 6 (2004): 204.

6. The superpower conflict that informed the 1980 U.S. hockey victory reframed almost every aspect of American society—from sports to education, science and popular culture—in the context of the American struggle against communism. In a 1995 interview, former head of ABC Sports, Roone Arledge spoke about the usefulness of the Cold War framework, noting that, "Americans who knew nothing about canoeing would watch a Russian and an American compete against each other.... Watch [how] their athletes came to blows in the sports arena." Reflecting on geopolitical changes decades later, former NBC Chairman of Sports and Olympics Dick Ebersol noted that "[S]o much of the instant success of the Olympics in the 1960s, 70s, and 80s was tied up in the existence of the iron curtain.... It gave the Olympics its greatest rivalries: East versus West, USA versus the Soviet Union, stars and stripes versus hammer and sickle." Acknowledging the degree to which the geopolitical context has affected sports broadcasts, Ebersol concluded that "[I]n the past, you could rely on the color of the uniform, however unfair that was." For more on the Cold War and its effect on American life, see Nick Gillespie, "The New Cold War: American Cultural Identity After September 11"; TBS, *Idols of the Game*; Mike Wise, "NBC'S Ebersol Puts His Games Face On, Comes Up a Winner," *The Washington Post*, August 28, 2004, C01.

7. Since the "Miracle on Ice"' mythically resonates with the American origin story, media outlets found it expedient to reprocess the event two decades later in connection with the developments of September 11, 2001. The 1980 U.S. hockey team also appeared as the surprise cauldron-lighters in the Opening Ceremony of the 2002 Winter Olympics in Salt Lake City, which featured a eulogy to victims of September 11 by way of the World Trade Center flag and a tribute to pioneers of the American West. News media characterized the team's appearance as suitable given their significance as symbol of "American tenacity" and "resolve and renewal," apt in invoking a "feel-good air" for a nation in need of a morale boost. The team's appearance reinforced their signature as compatible with the foundational American story, corroborating Robert A. White's argument that when national challenges arise, whether resisting enemy assault or overhauling an economy in shambles, a community resorts to symbols that speak to origin stories to buttress national solidarity. John Powers, "A Memory Relighted: At Winter Games, Symbols of Resolve and Renewal," *The Boston Globe*, February 9, 2002, accessed February 10, 2002, http://www.boston.com/daily globe2/040/nation/Amemory relightedP.shtml; John Crumpacker, "Ceremony a Tribute to American Tenacity," *The San Francisco Chronicle*, February 9, 2002, A1; Phil Coffey, "80 U.S. Team Adds Feel-Good Air to 2002 Olympics," February 9, 2002 (accesed February 9,

2002), NHL.com, http://www.nhl.com/olympics2002/usa/1980_torch020902.html; Robert A. White, "Television as Myth and Ritual," *Communication Research Trends* 8, no.1 (1987): 2.

8. Ratings showed that 34.2 million viewers in the U.S. watched the tape delay broadcast of the 1980 U.S.-Soviet semifinal.

9. The "Miracle on Ice" has also spawned comedic twists. In *The Dilemma* (Howard, 2011), bachelor Ronny Valentine (Vince Vaughn) finds out that Geneva (Wynona Ryder), wife of best friend Nick Brannen (Kevin James), is having an affair and he struggles to break the news to him. When Nick is chosen for a puck shoot challenge at a Chicago Blackhawks game, Ronny, in the stands, spots him and parlays Coach Herb Brooks' final speech to his players in Disney's *Miracle* into much-needed inspiration. Nick predictably scores and wins the big prize rescuing his battered masculinity. *American Dad*'s "Return of the Bling" episode (Daniello, 2010), for its part, plays with the heroic character of the 1980 U.S. victory as CIA agent Stan Smith (Seth Macfarlane), who has his own display of heroes to memorialize the team alongside Ronald Reagan, finds out that Roger, the alien from Area 51 he harbors in his home (also voiced by Macfarlane), had a hand in the contest's outcome as steroid-using goon Chex LeMeneux. Hijinks ensue and Stan attempts to chase down Roger to retrieve his gold medal and return it to the IOC.

10. The three-hour TV movie *Miracle on Ice* aired March 1, 1981 on ABC and was released theatrically in 1989. It also received a mention in E.M. Swift's "A Reminder of What We Can Be," a substantial piece on the U.S. team published in *Sports Illustrated*'s December 1980 issue.

11. Michael Vlahos argues that the religious connotations of the march of civilization code, which support the belief that Americans "serv[e] a higher calling," derive from Protestantism and center on "mission, service, sacrifice, [and] restraint." The 1980 triumph resonated with the Westering myth because sports confrontations during the Cold War operated as proxy for successes on the geopolitical front. Patricia Nelson Limerick notes that the narrative of the frontier as an arduous but triumphant and morally justified conquest made "a nearly perfect match ... to direct and motivate the American public," in the government's all-out offensive against communism, and in successfully allegorizing U.S. containment of Soviet forces. See Michael Vlahos, "The End of America's Post-War Ethos," *Foreign Affairs* 66, no. 5 (1998): 1092; Limerick, "The Adventures of the Frontier in the Twentieth Century," 82; Adams, "The September 11 Attacks as Viewed from Quebec," 769–70.

12. Stephen Cohen notes that North American media defined the U.S.S.R. as the very antithesis of the U.S. ideal: a crisis-ridden, corrupt colossus with a stagnant economy controlled by a bureaucratic elite who governed over pessimistic, disgruntled citizens. In his 1946 "long telegram" to the State Department, George F. Kennan of the U.S. Embassy in Moscow noted that the Soviet Union was on a political path that was inherently "unnatural," and for this reason, it had "within it the seeds of its own decay." Kennan maintained that the Soviet leviathan's demise was inevitable and would not be protracted. Before its predicted dissolution, however, the U.S.S.R. expeditiously morphed into a superpower whose sporting excellence explicitly operated as instrument of foreign policy, a point that both "Miracle on Ice" movies reiterate. For more, see Stephen Cohen, "Soviet State and Society as Reflected in the American Media," *Nieman Reports* (Winter 1984): 25–28; Roger Chapman, "George F. Kennan as Represented by Chuck Jones: Road Runner and the Cold War Policy of Containment (1949–1980)," *Film & History* 31, no.1 (2001): 41; George Kennan, "The Sources of Soviet Conduct," *Foreign Affairs* 25, no.4 (1947): 580.

13. Roger Fowler, *Language in the News: Discourse and Ideology in the Press* (New York: Routledge, 1993), 49.

14. The TV movie's depiction of players as working-class athletes mirrors accounts in which the team is compared not only to the Soviet team's elite ensemble of Merited Masters of Sport, but also to U.S. skiers and figure-skaters. For example, Richard Lipsky quotes a print news article that references the team as "Blue-collar athletes, the working-class heroes of the Winter Olympics.... [T]heir dirty blood-stained uniforms stand out amid the expensive ski attire and sequined figure skating outfits." Richard Lipsky, *How We Play the Game* (Boston: Beacon Press, 1981), 147.

15. Patrick Lethert, "NCAA Hockey Today," *Total Hockey*, ed. Dan Diamond, 2nd ed. (Scarborough, ON: Total Sports Publishing, 2000): 99.

16. Disney's *Miracle* downplays team members' working-class backgrounds and pecuniary woes likely because this description counters hockey's refurbished nineties image as upmarket sport through which the Company appealed to its consumer demographic.

17. Jimmy Carter gave his address to the nation in July of 1979. HBO's documentary *Do You Believe in Miracles?* (2001) first inserted Carter's Crisis of Confidence Speech into its rendition of the 1980 victory, and *Miracle*, which is based on the HBO documentary's narrative structure, does much the same.

18. Director Gavin O'Connor explains that he chose to parlay *Miracle* as "A character study of the man Herb Brooks," who put his family life on hold in pursuit of a long-cherished dream. Lucas Aykroyd, "Lights, Camera, Action! Miracle on Ice Hits the Big Screen," *IIHF Newsletter* 7, no. 5 (2004), 5, accessed July 7, 2004, http://www.iihf.com/news/ IIHF_Vol7No5.pdf.

19. This one-dimensional rendition of Herb Brooks precludes any focus on the coach's intelligence, sense of humor and exceptional powers of observation. The unfortunate depiction may have to do with Brook's reputation coming into the 1980 Lake Placid Games as a strict, maverick taskmaster disliked by his players and ill-disposed toward reporters. Karl Malden, for example, remarked with disapproval that Brooks could have ventured an occasional smile during one of the less intense games. Malden also wondered how, after working over the course of seven months to attain a cherished dream, Herb could have simply walked away after the team clinched the victory against the Soviet team. The opinion of the coach voiced by the actor was consistent with that of reporters who did not know how to appraise Brooks' tactics and accused that he was hard on his players and routinely refused to divulge to the press what he

had said during intermissions. Mike Eruzione, however, stated in a 2006 interview that Brooks' coaching style was common during the late 1970s, an era of "Vince Lombardi–type coaches." E.M. Swift, "A Reminder of What We Can Be," *Sports Illustrated*, December 22–29, 1980, 34; Gerald Eskenazi, "Americans Tie Swedes, 2–2, on Goal in Last 27 Seconds," *New York Times*, February 13, 1980, A22; *USA Today*, "What Makes Miracles? Work," February 20, 2006, 4B.

20. Motley, "Fighting for Manhood," 62.

21. Swift recounts that Brooks had amiable relationships with Mike Eruzione, who displayed the leadership and diplomatic qualities expected of a team captain, as well as with Jim Craig, who was unconventional in typical goalie form, and he used his connection to both players to smooth out relations with other team members. Swift, "A Reminder of What We Can Be," 41–2.

22. By no means did all news outlets use the concept of team as family in their reports. A number of newspapers underscored Jim Craig's and coach Brooks' statements about players as a family that came together to achieve a cherished goal. Other outlets, however, continued to emphasize dissension. Gerald Eskenazi, for example, reported that players from the Eastern college division, all hailing from Boston, at times grumbled about Brooks' Western college division emphasis, specifically about his placement of eight University of Minnesota athletes on the 20-player Olympic roster. See Lipsky, *How We Play the Game*, 147; Gerald Eskenazi, "U.S. Hockey Using Its Youth Well," *New York Times*, February 18, 1980, C5.

23. David Morley and Kevin Robins, "Spaces of Identity: Communications Technologies and Reconfiguration of Europe," *Screen* 30, no. 4 (1989): 142.

24. Silk, Schultz and Bracey note that a mere couple of months after the September 11 attacks, president Bush's political advisor Karl Rove called a meeting with over three dozen leading film and TV executives, including Disney's then President and COO Robert Iger, to confer over strategies that supported the U.S. war on terror. See Michael Silk, Jamie Schultz and Brian Bracey, "From Mice to Men: Miracle, Mythology and the 'Magic Kingdom,'" *Sport in Society* 11, no, 2 (2008): 283, 289; *The History Commons*, "Context of 'After September 11, 2001: Rove, White House Officials Press Entertainment Executives to Produce Government Propaganda," nd, accessed February 8, 2010, http://www.historycommons.org/context.jsp?item=a91101govtpropaganda.

25. Isabelle Freda, "*Survivors* in the *West Wing*: 9/11 and the United States of Emergency," *Film and Television After 9/11*, ed. Wheeler Winston Dixon (Carbondale: Southern Illinois University Press, 2004), 242; Rebecca Bell-Metereau, "The How-To Manual, the Prequel, and the Sequel in Post 9/11 Cinema," *Film and Television After 9/11*, ed. Wheeler Winston Dixon (Carbondale: Southern Illinois University Press, 1994), 142.

26. Francaviglia, "Walt Disney's Frontierland as an Allegorical Map of the American West," 181.

27. Stephen Hardy, "Miracle," Reviews of Books and Films, *American Historical Review* 109, no. 3 (2004): 944.

28. Although the above sequence is not based on fact, Brooks expressed similar views thirteen years later in his advice to then NHL Pittsburgh Penguins coach Eddie Olcyk, who wistfully relayed after the coach's sudden passing: "one of the last things Herbie said to me was, 'Always remember that you're American-born — you can do it and do it your way.'" Joe Starkey, "'Miracle' Coach Touched Millions. Herb Brooks: 1937–2003. Mastermind behind 1980 Olympic Triumph Shaped U.S. hockey," *The Hockey News*, August 26, 2003, 13; John Oliver Robertson, *American Myth, American Reality* (New York: Hill and Wang, 1980), 6.

29. Nash, *Wilderness and the American Mind*, 27.

30. Sobchack, "The Adventure Film," 9–10.

31. A 1980 U.S. player noted in a *New York Times* interview that the team-gelling moment occurred in December of 1979 during an international tournament at the Olympic Arena in Lake Placid. He added that except for the Canadian entry, the U.S. squad beat all participants in the B-team tournament, and that these victories enabled team members to believe in the possibility of an Olympic win. See Eskenazi, "U.S. Hockey Using Its Youth Well," C1.

32. Canadian-born hockey analyst Bill Clement observed about the criticism of the American player at the time that "They weren't tough enough, couldn't score when they had to, and couldn't win big games for you," adding that this view began to alter after 1980. Jamie Fitzpatrick, "Miracle on Ice: The Legacy," About.com, nd, accessed June 12, 2006, http://proicehockey.about.com/cs/miracleonice/a/miracle_legacy.htm.

33. In news accounts Brooks was repeatedly quoted as opposing the goonery of the average NHLer. Swift relays that players were forced to remain disciplined and not retaliate, a move typically considered un-American. Ruggedness, for all intents and purposes, was part of the Canadian game since Brooks emphasized stickhandling, passing, and speed. As Eskenazi remarks, "Brooks did not want behemoths, who merely clobbered opponents, but instead opted for players who were top skaters and proficient passers." See Swift, "A Reminder of What We Can Be," 37.

34. Crawford M. Young, "The National and Colonial Question and Marxism: A View from the South," *Thinking Theoretically About Soviet Nationalities*, ed. Alexander J. Motyl (New York: Columbia University Press, 1992), 78.

35. Eskenazi, "U.S. Hockey Using Its Youth Well," C1; Gerald Eskenazi, "The Balance of Power: Ice Hockey," *New York Times*. February 10, 1980, WO6.

36. Brian McNair, *Images of the Enemy: Reporting the New Cold War* (London: Routledge, 1988), 34.

37. Lawrence Martin recounts that a number of U.S. players had profound admiration for the Soviet national team, who had trounced NHL squads on various occasions. Wisconsin-born college star and scoring virtuoso Mark Johnson, son of well-loved Pittsburgh Penguins coach Bob Johnson, lionized the Russian players and had once ordered jerseys with Russian names on the back, including one for himself that featured Soviet veteran Vladimir Petrov. Martin notes that Brooks' own game was modeled on strategies of his personal hero and father of Soviet hockey, Anatoli Tarasov. Lawrence Martin, *The Red Machine* (Toronto: Doubleday Canada Limited, 1990), 184.

38. Dancyger and Rush, *Alternative Scriptwriting*, 90.

39. White, "Frederick Jackson Turner and Buffalo Bill," 27.

40. Joe Starkey of *The Hockey News* invokes precisely such imagery when he recounts that at one point Brooks, pretending he was lost, surreptitiously made his way onto the U.S.S.R. team bus so he could "get a close-up look at this mysterious force." Starkey, "'Miracle' Coach Touched Millions," 12.

41. *Miracle*'s balancing act around the figure of Coach Viktor Tikhonov resembles portrayals of Team Russia after the Soviet Union's dissolution. 1994 CBC Olympic hockey broadcasts during the Lillehammer Winter Games, for example, included a special feature of a congenial Tikhonov at home in Russia, while game commentary retained elements of the coach's Cold War image likely for dramatic purposes. Tikhonov's friendliness in the 1994 broadcasts corroborates Ray Ratto's assertion that the Russians "only became people when they joined the National Hockey League." NBC broadcast coverage of Tikhonov, however, reverted to the old Cold War image during the 2002 Salt Lake Games, in all likelihood because Herb Brooks had been appointed as coach of the U.S. team and the network hyped the contest as another prospective "Miracle on Ice." During matchups and in features, Tikhonov was also negatively compared to 2002 Team Russia Coach Slava Fetisov, who was one of the first Soviet players to defect from the U.S.S.R. and join the NHL. During the NBC Russia-Finland, MSNBC Russia-Belarus, and NBC Russia-USA Round Two games, as well as MSNBC Russia-Czech Republic quarterfinal, commentators stressed that coach Tikhonov had appropriated for himself the gold medal of the 1992 Unified Team's backup goalie, Nikolai Khabibulin, and it took Fetisov's intervention to restore it to its rightful owner in 2002. On balance, then, North American media have retained the image of Tikhonov, deceased November 24, 2014, as a hardline coach, and the one figure most intimately associated with Soviet rule. *Miracle*'s depiction of the Soviets as an entity to be toppled likely borrows from U.S. Olympic hockey broadcasts' decades-long portrayal of Coach Tikhonov, consonant with the melodramatic mode's rationale for handing losses to less-than-virtuous characters. For more on the Soviet Union's image in the media, see Iri Cermak, "Seeing Red: Images of Soviet and Russian Hockey in U.S. and Canadian Olympic Broadcasts," (Ph.D. diss., University of Washington, 1996), 169–224; Ray Ratto, "All We Needed Was a Miracle," *ESPN.com*, February 23, 2005, accessed February 24, 2005, http://www.espn.go.com/gen/miracle/ ratto.html; and Iri Cermak, "The Long Shelf Life of the Cold War: U.S. and Canadian Images of Russian Olympic Hockey at the Salt Lake Winter Games" (paper presented at the meeting of the Sport and Media Working Section of the International Association for Communication Research, IAMCR, Leipzig, Germany, January 17, 2004).

42. Powers, "Miracle on Ice," C2.

43. The speeches in both films obliterate the line "[L]et's have poise and possession of the puck," which Brooks attached to the end of his address. The final line, included in 1980 *Hockey News* and *Washington Post* reports, turns the speech into a more mundane article, and both films likely delete it because having poise and possession of the puck is a sport-specific reference that does not resonate with non-hockey fans in the U.S. See *The Hockey News*, "USA Wins Gold!," March 7, 1980, 3; Dave Kindred, "Born to Be Players, Born to the Moment," *The Washington Post*, February 23, 1980, A1.

44. The defeat of the Soviet team in *Miracle* harks back to global media reports during the 1994 Lillehammer Olympics in Norway which qualified Russia's inability to win the gold medal as evidence of the country's loss of geopolitical stature. Even before the Lillehammer Games, press reports about agreements between Russian hockey teams and NHL franchises, as well as about the subsequent influx of former Eastern bloc players to North American leagues, co-existed side-by-side media framing of Yeltsin's Russia as another "Wild West." This terminology pointed to an opening for American interests to enlarge their influence in the former foe's political and economic affairs. These developments suggested that, in subsuming countries that had remained outside the Western sphere of influence for decades, globalization had further extended the American frontier, which had originated with the first settlement of North America in 1607, to the entire world, as Tim Flannery posits. See Tim Flannery, *The Eternal Frontier: An Ecological History of North America and Its Peoples* (New York: Atlantic Monthly Press, 2001), 353.

45. The film includes these sequences because of ABC's ownership of Olympic footage, and Disney's purchase of ABC on August 1, 1995. Back in 1981 *New York Times* had commented on the network's move to tell the "Miracle on Ice" story as an astute synergistic move, "a model of merchandising" that allowed ABC to repeatedly cash in on the victory since it had originally helped garner record ratings. Disney's purchase of ABC further amplified these synergies. See John J. O'Connor, "More Mileage from an Olympics Victory," *New York Times*, March 1, 1981, accessed February 2, 2005, http://www.nytimes.com/1981/03/01/arts/tv–view–more-mileage-from-an-olympics-victory-by-john-jo-connor.html.

46. For a more detailed analysis of ABC and CTV broadcasts of the 1980 U.S.–Soviet semifinal, see Cermak, "Seeing Red: Mediasport Discourses of Soviet Olympic Hockey."

47. To blur the distinction between the actual game and *Miracle*'s script, producers tapped Al Michaels to insert a reference to the Conehead line which did not exist in ABC broadcast of the game: "And here we go. The second period is under way. The Conehead line out for the United States." Juggling between archival footage of the semifinal and the film's script also produced an error in continuity. With the game 3–2 in favor of the Soviet team, young center Vladimir Krutov had gone into the box, leading to a goal by U.S. forward Mark Johnson that tied the game 3–3. The film, however, confers the penalty on veteran center Vladimir Petrov yet also attaches Al Michaels' commentary from the ABC archival footage, which subsequently alludes to Krutov's expired penalty: "So the Americans, just as the penalty to Krutov was about to expire, scored and tied the game. 3–3 the United States and the Soviet Union." This error illustrates that *Miracle*'s producers were not fully aware of how infrequently the Soviet team took penalties. In confusing young Krutov with veteran Petrov, the film also reaffirms the image of the Soviets as a monolithic entity.

48. The only other text that visually and verbally identifies each U.S. player on the 1980 team is Swift's "A Reminder of What We Can Be."

49. Cesar R. Torres and Mark Dyreson, "The Cold War Games," *Global Olympics: Historical and Sociological Studies of the Modern Games*, ed. Kevin Young and Kevin B. Wamsley (New York: Elsevier, 2005), 77.

50. Steve Hardy makes clear that even as the victory was of no consequence in the international or domestic political arenas, as evidenced by Carter's loss of a second presidential term and the Soviets' eventual exit from Afghanistan years later, films typically offer more than a team-building account because audiences favor exalted narratives at the expense of the historical record. When asked about the Soviet advance into Afghanistan and the American boycott of the Moscow Summer Olympics, Herb Brooks, for his part, stated in a post-game interview that his players did not view their victory as a political statement nor did he see any politics from the part of the Russians. Hardy, "Miracle," 944; Kindred, "Born to Be Players, Born to the Moment," A1.

51. The only visual identification in *Miracle* is of Herb Brooks.

52. Joanne Sharp makes the case that the United States' Cold War policy of Soviet containment was fundamental to American identity and resembled a "moving frontier," one whose role was not unlike that of the frontier in American originary narratives of western expansion. Not surprisingly, Leonard Shapiro at the time described the win as "The most important U.S. victory in the history of this country's participation in international hockey." Post-Cold War media reports since also speak about the meaning of the triumph as responsible for the about-face in morale between the superpowers. See for example, Bruce Newman, "Movie Review: Against All Odds: 'Miracle' Gets the Hockey—And Politics—Right," *Mercury News*, February 6, 2004, accessed February 7, 2004, http://www.mercurynews.com/mld/mercurynews/entertainment/eye/7889795.htm; Joanne P. Sharp, "Reel Geographies of the New World Order: Patriotism, Masculinity and Geopolitics in Post-Cold War American Movies," *Rethinking Geopolitics*, eds. Gearóid Ó Tuathail and Simon Dalby (London: Routledge, 1998), 152; Leonard Shapiro, "U.S. Shocks Soviets in Ice Hockey 4–3," *The Washington Post*, February 23, 1980, D1.

53. *New York Times* writer Gerald Eskenazi highlights the impact of the U.S. team's physicality as a defensive strategy. Underscoring Brooks' brand as American hockey, "more intuitive than the conventional style of the National Hockey League," Eskenazi notes that it nonetheless incorporated "body contact [which] took its toll of the Finns as it did on the other American opponents and perhaps that is why the Americans were able to bounce back repeatedly in the third period." Gerald Eskenazi, "U.S. Squad Captures Gold Medal," *New York Times*, February 25, 1980, C4.

54. Shot on a $7.8 million budget, the miniseries was jointly funded by the CBC, the Canadian Television Fund, Lions Gate Films and New Brunswick Film, as well as provincial tax credits. It was entirely filmed in New Brunswick, Canada.

55. Dave Ebner, "Our Defining Moment in Hockey to Be a TV Movie: 1972 Summit Series Drama Inspired by the Success of the 2004 Disney Movie Miracle," *The Globe and Mail*, January 12, 2005, R1.

56. Although the NHL did not have jurisdiction over Team Canada, as Richard Harrison notes, the league's corporate politics impinged on the squad's very makeup. Roy MacSkimming, for example, relays that when the NHL President Clarence Campbell found out that the WHA's Bobby Hull would likely join the team, he warned that the NHL would prevent its players from participating, particularly given that a number of team owners were considering lawsuits against the new league for poaching its players. U.S. interests controlled thirteen out of sixteen NHL franchises, in any case, and some were less than overjoyed to send their labor force to Canada. Although the movie does not broach the subject at length, Eagleson does make passing reference to the NHL paying players healthy sums not to jump to the WHA. See Richard Harrison, "Canadian Iliad: The Summit Series as Canadian Epic Poem," *Coming Down the Mountain: Rethinking the 1972 Summit Series*, ed. Brian Kennedy (Hamilton, ON: Wolsak and Wynn, 2014), 79; Roy MacSkimming, *Cold War: The Amazing Canada-Soviet Hockey Series of 1972* (Vancouver, B.C.: Greystone Books, 1996), 16.

57. Markku Jokisipilä, "Maple Leaf, Hammer and Sickle: International Ice Hockey During the Cold War," *Sport History Review* 37 (2006): 42.

58. Tobias Stark notes that these changes came about even prior to the IIHF ruling. Stark, "The Pioneer, the Pal and the Poet," 41–2.

59. Trudeau viewed the 1972 contest as propitious for a Canadian-Soviet rapprochement, which in turn allowed him to pursue his "third option," a politics of independence from American foreign policy. The tournament also facilitated agreements of an economic nature. Marina Joukova writes that the first game in Montreal was conducive to finalizing an accord for Canadian wheat sales that the Soviet government coveted. Despite Team Canada's 7–3 loss to the Soviet team, Trudeau's reported "good mood" enabled both parties to hash out the details of the new compact before the game was over. Joukova, "Players Didn't Know They Were to Make History," Faceoff.com. August 25, 2002, accessed February 20, 2002, http://www.faceoff.com/news/20020825/020825117177.html.

60. The statement resonates politically with the low 37 per cent voter support for secession in polls taken during Canada's 2006 federal election. The film, however, does not touch on how the series deepened Quebecers' desire to field their own national team in international competition. For more on the subject, see Holman, "Les Russes et nous," 109–125.

61. William Houston, "Summit Series Movie Doesn't Paint Rosy Picture," *The Globe and Mail*, March 21, 2006, S3.

62. Producers' research gave viewers a look at moments in the series that have been papered over the decades. Tim Elcombe also recounts that coming into the series players' already suffered from a bad reputation. They got flak for demanding payment for playing, and their image took another dive when they switched their name to "Team 50"—for the number of players, management and staff on the team—in response to booing by fans in Vancouver after Game Four. MacSkimming likewise relays that Sinden wondered whether the players would do their utmost to win given that their motivation in the Stanley Cup's playoffs was the pot of gold

waiting at the end of the line. For more, see Tim Elcombe, "Reflections on Canadian Moral Nation-Making on the Occasion of the Summit Series Seventy-Fifth Anniversary," *Coming Down the Mountain: Rethinking the 1972 Summit Series*, ed. Brian Kennedy (Hamilton, ON: Wolsak and Wynn, 2014), 288; MacSkimming, *Cold War*, 23.

63. In *Summit on Ice* (MacAskill, 1996), Phil Esposito, Serge Savard, Red Berenson along with Alan Eagleson make clear that the series was nothing less than a war against communist Russia and that players were engaged in a battle of beliefs.

64. For more see Cermak, "Media Retrospectives of the Summit Series."

65. Kashmere, "*Valery's Ankle*: Supporting Documents and Notation," 33–4. See also, Brett Kashmere, "Lessons from *Valery's Ankle*," 239–256. Doug Beardsley echoes a similar argument in noting that the sport enacts the shadow or "demonic side of the collective Canadian psyche," and that the boundary that separates passion from violence is "a thin red line." Canadian Prime Minister Stephen Harper likewise acknowledges in a *Sports Illustrated* interview that although Canada's citizens are thought of as pleasant, peaceable, and just, Canadians play the game with aggression and these traits must be taken into account when discussing the national character. See Doug Beardsley, "Where There's Ice, There's Hockey," *New York Times*, February 27, 2005, 11. For Stephen Harper interview, see Michael Farber, "Canada's Leader on Canada's Game," *Sports Illustrated*, February 8, 2010, accessed February 9, 2010, http://sportsillustrated.cnn.com/vault/article/magazine/MAG 1165562/index.htm?eref=sisf.

66. Brian Kennedy discusses NHLers' sense of superiority vis-à-vis the Soviets as not only grounded in skill but in their status as NHL (business) professionals. Harry Sinden's own statement that the Canadian team wanted to win not because of pride of nation but because they sought above all to "[U]phold ... personal reputations as the greatest hockey players in the world..." speaks to the same point. Indeed, many of the Summit Series documentaries visually and textually underscore the idea of Canadians as products of the Northern landscape and their status as premium NHL commodity. As Kennedy notes, Westerners insisted that the Soviets were professionals, not the amateurs that they made themselves out to be. Nonetheless, they also did not have the professional status that NHLers ascribed to themselves. Since NHL professionalism has a distinctive business aspect that Soviet hockey did not share, their players also could not compete as commodities. Therefore, in Cold War media depictions they were referred to either as representatives of the Soviet sport and military complex or as students of the game consistent with the way coach Anatoli Tarasov saw hockey as an intellectual project. Ray Ratto's statement that the Soviets only became human—i.e., acceptable to West—when they joined the NHL (and became commodities), therefore rung true on many levels. For more, see Brian Kennedy, "Unintentional Epic: Ken Dryden's Struggle with Words and the Myth of Team Canada," *Coming Down the Mountain: Rethinking the 1972 Summit Series*, ed. Brian Kennedy (Hamilton, ON: Wolsak and Wynn, 2014), 264–265. See Sinden's statement in Paul Henderson with Jim Prime, *How Hockey Explains Canada: The Sport That Defines a Country* (Chicago: Triumph, 2001), 107. See also Ratto, "All We Needed Was a Miracle." For Cold War media texts on the Soviet hockey image, see Cermak, "Seeing Red: Images of Soviet and Russian Hockey in U.S. and Canadian Olympic Broadcasts." For an interesting iconography of hockey heroes, see also "Touchstones to Look Back On," chapter five in Brian Kennedy, *My Country Is Hockey: How Hockey Explains Canadian Culture, History, Politics, French-English Rivalry and Who We Are as Canadians* (Edmonton, AB: Argenta, 2011).

67. Other texts confirm that the Soviet contingent was always well prepared and the coaching staff assiduously studied their opponents. Roy MacSkimming notes that when Sinden and Ferguson got together with their Soviet counterparts for a few rounds of vodka prior to the series, they found out their opponent had in-depth knowledge of each player on the Team Canada roster. Soviet team members' depiction in the movie as dutiful students continually honing their skills likely draws from Canadian media assumptions of the era that they were coming to Canada to learn from the pros. Both Andrew Holman and Brian Kennedy note that in Quebec and the Rest of Canada, the belief was that the Soviets would readily succumb to the imposing Canadians and lose by most if not all games. "They came here to learn, they will learn," wrote *The Montréal Matin*'s Pierre Gobeil. *The Globe and Mail*'s Dick Beddoes also announced that if the Canadian national squad did not roll over the Soviets he would cut up his newspaper column and eat it mixed in with borscht at the doorstep of the Soviet embassy. Alexander Kubyshkin also recounts that Soviet higher-ups did not believe their team would win the series and instructed the players not to panic but lose gracefully. For more, see MacSkimming, *Cold War*, 16; Andrew Holman, "Les Russes et nous," 114–115; Pierre Gobeil referenced in Richard Simon, *La Série Du Siècle: Septembre 1972* (Montreal: Les Éditions Hurtubise, 2002), 82; Brian Kennedy, "Confronting a Compelling Other and the Nostalgic (Trans)Formation of Canadian Identity," *Canada's Game*, ed. Andrew Holman (Montreal: McGill-Queen's University Press, 2009), 50; Alexander Kubyshkin, "Hot Ice During Cold War: Soviet Reflections on Summit Series 1972," *Coming Down the Mountain: Rethinking the 1972 Summit Series*, ed. Brian Kennedy (Hamilton, ON: Wolsak and Wynn, 2014), 183–184, 188.

68. See, for example, *Summit on Ice, September 1972* (MacAskill, 1997) and *Hockey: A People's History* episode *Soul of a Nation* (MacAskill, 2006).

69. See Ken Campbell, "What Was a Bigger Moment: 1972 or 1980? Do You Believe in Miracles?," *The Hockey News*, Great Debates Special Issue, 2004, 69. Richard Lehman, "Do the Young People Still Believe? The Rise and Shift of Mythic Tradition," *Coming Down the Mountain: Rethinking the 1972 Summit Series*, ed. Brian Kennedy (Hamilton, ON: Wolsak and Wynn, 2014), 306–308.

70. See Cermak, "Media Retrospectives of the Summit Series," 209–10.

71. Michael Buma, "Pluralism and the 1972 Summit Series," *Coming Down the Mountain: Rethinking the 1972 Summit Series*, ed. Brian Kennedy (Hamilton, ON: Wolsak and Wynn, 2014), 56; Brian Kennedy, "Confronting

a Compelling Other and the Nostalgic (Trans)Formation of Canadian Identity," *Canada's Game*, ed. Andrew Holman (Montreal: McGill-Queen's University Press, 2009), 44–62.

72. Martha Wilkerson, "Explaining the Presence of Men Coaches in Women's Sports: The Uncertainty Hypothesis," *Journal of Sport and Social Issues* 20, no. 4 (1996): 414.

73. Buma analyzes a 2007 Nike TV ad that features the Canadian national men's hockey team. See Buma, *Refereeing Identity*, 99, 145–6.

74. Screenwriter Ken Mitchell's portrayal of Athol Murray in *The Hounds of Notre Dame* is a condensation of the *Père's* character and his decades-long work. Hounds got 9 Genie nominations in 1981 and garnered Tom Peacoke the Best Actor award. For more see, Evelyn Ellerman, "Hounds of Notre Dame Commentary," *Canadian Film Online*, nd, accessed September 10, 2012, http://film.athabascau.ca/commentary/hounds-notre-dame-comentary.

75. The school was founded in 1920 by the Catholic order, The Sisters of Charity of St. Louis, whom Murray joined in 1927. Ellerman, "Hounds of Notre Dame Commentary."

76. The term "muscular Christianity" first appeared in the novels of Victorian writer Charles Kingsley in the 1850s, and was subsequently popularized by the British press. Alister McGrath notes that leading lay figures in the Protestant tradition adopted the concept of muscular Christianity as a tool in transforming middle-class English public school students into manly exemplars of the nation. See Alister McGrath, *Christianity's Dangerous Idea: The Protestant Revolution—A History from the Sixteenth Century to the Twenty-First* (New York: HarperOne, 2007), 369; John W. Derry, *A Short History of 19th Century England* (New American Library: Mentor, 1963), 201–6.

77. McArdle, *From Boot Money to Bosman: Football Society and the Law*, 4; John Hargreaves, "The Body, Sport and Power Relations," *Sport, Leisure and Social Relations, Sociological Review Monograph 33*, eds. John Home. David Jary, and Alan Tomlinson (London: Routledge and Kegan Paul, 1986), 143. Margaret Marsh views muscular Christianity as the ecclesiastical form of Theodore Roosevelt's cult of masculinity. Alister McGrath also underlines muscular Christianity's influence in the athletic programs of the College of Notre Dame in Indiana. Although in discrete time frames, muscular Christianity impacted Catholicism as much as it did Protestantism. McGrath, *Christianity's Dangerous Idea*, 371; Margaret Marsh, "Suburban Men and Masculine Domesticity, 1870–1915," *American Quarterly* 40, no. 2 (June 1988): 165–186. See also Gerald Roberts, "The Strenuous Life: The Cult of Manliness in the Era of Theodore Roosevelt" (Ph.D. diss., Michigan State University, 1970).

78. An erudite educator, fluent in English and French, and well versed in Latin, Athol Murray was also the grand nephew of Canada's first Prime Minister John A. Macdonald.

79. Kaye, "Certain Tendencies in Canadian Cinema," 223–4.

80. Morris, "In Our Own Eyes," 39.

81. The CCF was founded in August 1932 by Canada's Western provinces' and Ontario's farm and labor organizations as a way of advancing a socialist party platform. See *The Quebec History Encyclopedia*, "The Co-Operative Commonwealth Federation," at: http://faculty.marianopolis.edu/c.belanger/quebechistory/encyclopedia/Co-operativeCommonwealthFederation-CCF-CanadianHistory.htm.

82. School president Terry O'Mally notes that Murray had a profound respect for "free government, family rights, individual liberty, property rights, [and] freedom of education." O'Malley, "Father Athol Murray and the Hounds of Notre Dame," Introduction by Jerry W. Bird, n.d., accessed September 9, 2012, http://www.airhighways.com/notre_dame.htm.

83. Parpart, "The Nation and the Nude," 176.

84. O'Malley, "Father Athol Murray and the Hounds of Notre Dame."

85. Blake, *Canadian Hockey Literature*, 4, 114.

86. Blake, *Canadian Hockey Literature*, 168.

87. The coach's eye-catching brand is illustrated by his high Edwardian collar shirts and his flamboyant suits, which in *Wrath of Grapes* he fashions from curtain material to Rose's dismay.

88. When Don Cherry was interviewed about his opinion on the concept of a gay Leaf player in *Breakfast with Scot*, a film made with the blessing of the NHL and the team, he noted with a chuckle that while he is aware that Commissioner Bettman aspires to fashion "a kinder, gentler league," the concept was "too much." Cherry, however, also appears in the credits sequence of said film with his arm around young protagonist Scot, who retains a strong dual male-female identity in the film. See Randy Starkman, "Movie Features Gay Leaf," *Free Republic*, November 24, 2006, accessed April 10, 2012, http://www.freerepublic.com/focus/f-news/1743583/posts.

89. Blake, *Canadian Hockey Literature*, 114.

90. In Canada, Gretzky's export was met with cries of treason and accusations of selling out the game. Critics also contextually aligned the trade with the Canada–U.S. Free Trade Agreement as evidence of further North American structural economic integration. See Jackson, "Sport, Crisis and Canadian Identity in 1988: A Cultural Analysis."

91. Maguire, "Sport, Identity Politics, and Globalization," 309.

92. Andrew Higson, *Waving the Flag: Constructing a National Cinema in Britain* (Gloucestershire: Clarendon Press, 1997), 7.

Chapter 7

1. Messner, "Still a Man's World?," 314.

2. Mackey, *The House of Difference*, 142. See also Adams, "The Game of Whose Lives?" and King and Leonard's discussion of Marjorie Kibby's work. King and Leonard, *Visual Economies Of/In Motion*, 4.

3. King and Leonard, *Visual Economies Of/In Motion*, 4.

4. Coakley, *Sports in Society*, 310.

5. In Fothergill's Bully, Clown and Coward scheme, the Coward is a faint-hearted character who cannot reciprocate his partner's love. Fothergill, "Coward, Bully, or Clown," 237.

6. Pop culture closely identifies blacks with the body and the white Québécois goalie's one-up-manship

in this arena amplifies the spoof. See Coakley, *Sports in Society*, 292–3; Fiske, *Understanding Popular Culture*, 79.

7. For more on recurrent themes in Canadian cinema, see Kaye, "Certain Tendencies in Canadian Cinema," 112.

8. The film's intertextual reference to Ben Kingsley's *Gandhi* (Attenborough, 1982) is quite carnivalesque.

9. Pike, "Canadian Cinema in the Age of Globalization," 3, 6.

10. Despite Myers' cheeky comedic approach, delivered via catchphrases and punctuated by the teeth-baring grin synonymous with his brand, the film's tasteless antics engendered disparaging reviews about the obscene and ill-advised character of the material. See, for example, A.O. Scott, "Just Say 'Mariska Hargitay' and Snicker," *New York Times*, June 20, 2008, accessed April 5, 2011, http://www.nytimes.com/2008/06/20/movies/20guru.html; Peter Morris, "There's Little to Love in Myers's 'Guru,'" *The Boston Globe*, June 20, 2008, accessed April 6, 2011, http://www.boston.com/ae/movies/articles/2008/06/20/theres_little_to_love_in_myerss_guru/. The $62 million film also did poorly at the box office garnering $32 million domestically and $8 million worldwide.

11. For more on the NHL's control of social conduct in its arenas, see Kennedy, "What Ever Happened to the Organ and the Portrait of Her Majesty?," 167.

12. Jane Bullard's character references Harold Ballard's Leafs ownership and the team's 1962, 1963, 1964 and 1967 championship victories, in turn, ratifying the wish-fulfillment element in the movie.

13. Myers' Guru Pitka is the archetypical Bakhtinian rogue in that the audience understands that through his character Myers is laughing at the status quo in carnivalesque form. As E.A. Williams notes, the roguishness of the rogue becomes even clearer when the biographical author of a text performs in this text. See Williams, "Bahktin and Borat," 116.

14. A number of theorists have noted that any changes to sports and cultural practices cannot be solely judged in one-directional ways. Lawrence Wenner argues that corporate directives typically co-exist alongside supranational, national, community, industry, and individual levels of decision-making, all of which interact with one another to expedite globalizing trends in sport and media. Kevin Robins also notes that old and new aspects of cultural forms are experienced distinctly by social groups in line with gender, ethnicity, and age differences, and in accordance with a particular locality's integration with world markets. See Lawrence Wenner, "One More '-Ism' for the Road: Dirt, Globalism, and Institutional Analysis." *Journal of Sport and Social Issues* 20, no. 3 (1996): 236–7; Robins, "What in the World's Going On?," 12.

15. Steve Maich notes that the Leafs are the most lucrative feature of a 1.5 billion dollar conglomerate that includes the Toronto NBA Raptors, the AHL Toronto Marlies, a pro soccer team, as well as the Air Canada Centre. Steve Maich, "Why the Leafs Stink," *Macleans. Ca*, April 2, 2008, accessed May 10, 2011, http://www.macleans.ca/canada/national/article.jsp?content=20080402_25296_25296&page=1.

16. For more, see *The SportsBusiness Daily*, "NHL Helpful in Filming Process of 'The Love Guru,' Opening Friday," June 20, 2008, accessed May 14, 2011, http://www.sportsbusinessdaily.com/Daily/Issues/2008/06/Issue-189/Leagues-Governing-Bodies/NHL-Helpful-In-Filming-Process-Of-The-Love-Guru-Opening-Friday.aspx.

17. In a 2008 interview, Myers expresses amazement at the idea that he "Live[s] in a country that views itself not as a melting pot, but as a salad bowl that has a ministry of multiculturalism and they have a multicultural channel and at two o'clock in the morning i get to see Indian movies." Myers' friendly associations with Kanye West, an American-born rapper, singer, and record producer whom the film pictures cheering for the Leafs' victory next to Myers and uttering: "I love hockey!" corroborates the multicultural composition of present-day fans. See Rebecca Murray, "Mike Myers Spreads Some Love with 'The Love Guru': Mike Myers Discusses the Origin of Guru Pitka," About.com, June 11, 2008, accessed May 13, 2011, http://movies.about.com/od/theloveguru/a/lovegurumm61108.htm.

18. In the October 1, 2005 *Saturday Night Live* backstage sequence, Myers made light of the consequences of appearing with Kanye West in a September 2005 telethon for Katrina Hurricane victims. West criticized President George W. Bush for his ineffectual response to the catastrophe, and Myers poked fun at his own complicity in the matter, noting that in case the Feds revoked his American citizenship, "I still have my Canadian citizenship to fall back on. I'm a Canuck!" See the video at Jordan Sargeant, "October 1: Backstage with Mike Myers," May 16, 2013, accessed June 17, 2014, http://www.spin.com/2013/05/kanye-west-snl-saturday-night-live-history-videos/130516-kanye-mike-myers/. Myers also appears in a Leafs jersey alongside fellow Canadian Ryan Gosling on the December 6, 2015 episode of *Saturday Night Live* jesting about Canadian staples such as winter, tuques, and beer, and singing a Canadian Christmas song next to the mascot of Quebec's Winter Carnival, the Bonhomme de Neige. See CBC, "SNL's Mike Myers Outs Ryan Gosling as Canadian," December 6, 2015, accessed December 10, 2015, http://www.cbc.ca/news/canada/newfoundland-labrador/ryan-gosling-mike-myers-saturday-night-live-1.3353019. See also, *The Daily Mail*, "Mike Myers Crashes the SNL Stage During Host Ryan Gosling's Opening Monologue … 20 Years After Departing the Show's Cast," December 6, 2015, accessed December 10, 2015, http://www.dailymail.co.uk/tvshowbiz/article-3347988/Mike-Myers-crashes-SNL-stage-host-Ryan-Gosling-s-opening-monologue-20-years-departing-s-cast.html.

19. Gayle MacDonald, "With Breakaway, Rob Lowe Continues His Search for the Canadian Identity," *The Globe and Mail*, SSeptember 28, 2011, accessed April 19, 2012, http://www.theglobeandmail.com/news/arts/movies/with-breakaway-rob-lowe-continues-his-search-for-the-canadian-identity/article2182177/.

20. Jim Slotek, "Father, Son Team Up for 'Breakaway,'" *Toronto Sun*, September 28, 2011, accessed April 19, 2012, http://www.torontosun.com/2011/09/28/father-son-team-up-for-breakaway. In the same article, Vinay's father, Ajay Virmani, who helped produce the film, relays Rob Lowe's statement to his son: 'I'm Old blood now. You're Youngblood.'"

21. Although hockey does not sell in all global

markets, the family film does, and not surprisingly producers emphasized the feel-good, family-oriented angle of the genre in promoting the film. *Breakaway* director Robert Lieberman also helmed *D3: The Mighty Ducks*. See Slotek, "Father, Son Team Up for 'Breakaway.'"

22. The film dramatizes the polarity of the protagonist's superlative skill coming up against the villain's brutality even though hockey necessitates becoming the sort of player that others dare not cross, and respect is also subject to continual negotiation. See Emma Poulton and Martin Roderick's discussion of the theme in Garry Whannel's article about sport in films. Poulton and Roderick, "Introducing Sport in Films," 111.

23. Slotek, "Father, Son Team Up for 'Breakaway.'"

24. Mackey, *The House of Difference*, 2, 145, 153.

25. Physical excess can also operate as a form of gatekeeping that deters multicultural others from participating in hockey contests, and to that extent it can also appear to be incompatible with cultural life. Because both hockey and multiculturalism mythologize Canadian identity, the Canadian culture of hockey's focus on toughness is no doubt problematic to Canada's official heritage of tolerance. *Breakaway*, which airs this issue, not unexpectedly garnered praise from Prime Minister Stephen Harper and government dignitaries at Parliament Hill, where it received a special screening. For more, see *Mybindi.com*, "Breakaway Receives Rave Reviews on Parliament Hill," October 6, 2011, accessed April 30, 2012, http://www.mybindi.com/articles/breakaway-receives-rave-reviews-on-parliament-hill; Ken Eisner, "Breakaway Is a Window into Modern, Multicultural Canada," September 28, 2011, accessed May 10, 2012, http://www.straight.com/movies/breakaway-cinematic-window-modern-multicultural-canada.

26. *The Love Guru*'s and *Breakaway*'s respective representations of hockey as ethnic projects also parallel the way these films deploy Bollywood-like sequences in their narratives. *The Love Guru*'s grotesque renditions of Indian food and burlesque song-and-dance sequences, as well as the sight of Guru Pitka atop two mating Asian elephants in the seventh game of the Stanley Cup finals have little in common with *Breakaway*'s authentic reveling in traditional culture, or the portrayal of the Singhs' game, which takes them to the top ranks of the Hyundai Cup. In *Breakaway*, the visual force of the Indo-Canadian community at the arena connects the hockey celebration to the rich visual texture of the film's lively Bollywood song-and-dance sequences, the aesthetic pleasures of Indian food, the beauty of Indian décor, and the vividness of the wedding festivities, which open with jocular Sonu's arrival on an elephant. *Breakaway* portrays Bollywood sequences consonant with its national cinema designation—as a distinct and unified expression of Indian nationhood—in line with Kevin Robins' argument that Bollywood "Represent[s] a defensive and protective response to the disruptions of global modernity," by expressing 'out of difference' with globalization. Myers' interpretation, which includes a tacky interlude between Pitka and Bullard and their respective entourages accompanied by nonsensical lyrics, on the other hand, highlights the very globalizing processes that Bollywood is meant to offset, because these spoofs are filtered primarily through the actor's creative impulse and transnational entertainment brand. For more on Bollywood, see Crosson, *Sport and Film*, 151; Wimal Dissayanake, "Issues in World Cinema," *World Cinema: Critical Approaches*, eds. John Hill and Pamela Gibson Church (Oxford: Oxford University Press, 2000), 145–6; Robins, "What in the World's Going On?," 33.

27. Glenn R. Cummins, "Sports Fiction—Critical and Empirical Analysis," *Handbook of Sports and Media*, eds. Arthur A. Raney and Jennings Bryant (Mahwah, N.J.: Lawrence Erlbaum Associates, 2006), 204.

28. Mackey, *The House of Difference*, 9–10.

29. Kaye, "Perfectly Normal, Eh?," 77–8; Kaye, "Certain Tendencies in Canadian Cinema," 235.

30. Babington describes the art film as disconnecting narrative cause from effect, foregrounding elliptical narration, advancing vague motivations and endings, and obscuring the difference between "objective realism and subjective interpretation." He notes that because audiences resist these conventions, the art film also often deploys a realist aesthetic blended with visual poetry. This blend is seen in some of *Perfectly Normal*'s hockey sequences. See Babington, *The Sports Film*, 22.

31. Doane, "Film and the Masquerade: Theorising the Female Spectator," *Film Theory and Criticism*, 4th ed., eds. Gerald Mast, Marshall Cohen and Leo Braudy (New York: Oxford University Press, 1992), 758–772; Kaye, "Perfectly Normal, Eh? Gender Transformation and National Identity in Canada," *Canadian Journal of Film Studies* 3, no. 2 (1994): 77.

32. Bruzzi, *Bringing Up Daddy*, 134.

33. Sabo and Jansen refer to the work of James McBride and his study of men's projection of their disenfranchisement onto female others, in particular. But the concept is also suitable to contexts in which men are victimized by male others by way of feminization tactics. Sabo and Jansen, "Prometeus Unbound," 210; James McBride, *War, Battering and Other Sports: The Gulf Between American Men and Women* (Atlantic Highlands, NJ: Humanities Press, 1995).

34. Buma, *Refereeing Identity*, 179; Michael Messner and Donald F. Sabo, *Sex, Violence and Power in Sports Rethinking Masculinity* (Freedom, CA: Crossing Press, 1994), 96–8.

35. In airing divergent conceptions of the hockey player, the cinema is ahead of genres like the hockey novel. For comparison, see Buma's analysis of homosexuality in in his "Homosocial Dressing Room" chapter. Buma, *Refereeing Identity*, 218–263.

36. The original 1991 telefilm *Le Moment de vérité* can be found at: http://www.youtube.com/watch?v=5Ae5_3sMhJU.

37. Ransom, *Hockey PQ*, 19, 85.

38. Jean-Charles depiction in *Les Boys* films may mirror that in secular Quebec homosexuality is becoming part of identity exploration, even as the hockey ideal also appears quite intractable in the sports film. For more, see Martin, "Cultural Formations, North America," 116; Marshal, *Quebec Cinema*, 119–20.

39. Robidoux, "Imagining a Canadian Identity Through Sport: A Historical Interpretation of Lacrosse and Hockey," *Journal of American Folklore* 115, no. 456 (Spring 2002): 209.

40. Although no gay NHLer has publicly come out of the closet, players' attitudes in the culture may not be

as inflexible as portrayed in the cinema, since in the course of their job activities, teammates get to know one another as individuals, and such individuation rarely withstands permanent objectification and marginalization. Boston Bruins' defenseman Shawn Thornton, expressed as much in a 2012 interview, noting that a certain amount of policing by players curtails out-of-line behavior and preserves an atmosphere of affability in the locker room. He remarked that having a gay teammate would not be an issue for him, and while acknowledging that instances of homophobia do happen during games, he also stated that the league clamps down on them. When asked whether he was concerned about speaking out on the topic, Thornton laughed and made clear he had the ability to stave off potential hazards. As Thornton mentions, the league has also made efforts to check homophobia, and in April 2013, owners teamed up with "You Can Play" for this purpose. Keeping homosexuality under wraps and pretending that all professional athletes are straight is undesirable because it advances the notion that sports leagues must forgo their top picks simply because of sexual orientation, a prerequisite that market economics imposes on no other profession or trade. A number of media reports have nonetheless made the case that homosexuality remains difficult to discuss in pro sports, let alone acknowledge, as evidenced by talented players who have opted out of sports careers for fear of harassment and retaliation. Former hockey goalie Brendan Burke, son of Leafs General Manager Brian Burke, and NFL player Michael Sam both left on the table promising futures in their respective sports. Burke came out to an ESPN journalist in 2009. He died in a car accident in 2010. For more on homosexuality in professional sport, see Jim Lopata, "The Bruins Shawn Thornton Talks About What If a Teammate Was Gay," *The Boston Globe*, April 11, 2012, accessed May 15, 2012, http://www.boston.com/lifestyle/blogs/bostonspirit/2012/04/the_bruins_shawn_thornton_talk.html; Michael Pearson, "NHL Partners with Advocacy Group to Stamp Out Homophobia," CNN.com, April 11, 2013, accessed May 4, 2013, http://www.cnn.com/2013/04/11/us/sports-nhl-tolerance; Mary Rogan, "Out on the Ice," *GQ*, December 20, 2010, accessed December 10, 2012, http://www.gq.com/story/brian-burke-nhl-gay-players-athletes; Les Carpenter, "David Denson's Huge Leap Conceals Pro Sports' Problem with Gay Players," *The Guardian*, August 17, 2015, accessed August 25, 2015, http://www.theguardian.com/sport/2015/aug/17/david-denson-gay-michael-sam-pro-sports.

41. See the scene discussed in *Kronjuvelerna* at http://www.youtube.com/watch?v=7La_Rv9rT-E.

42. For a discussion on the threats posed by homosexuality's visibility, see Ransom's examination of Michael William Saunders' take on homosexuality in the horror genre. Ransom, *Hockey*, PQ, 133; Michael William Saunders, *Imps of the Perverse: Gay Monsters in Film* (Westport: Praeger, 1998), 2.

Chapter 8

1. Michael Messner argues that there is greater variation among men's physiques than there is between men and women, since plenty of women have greater athletic aptitude—strength, speed and/or agility—than a good deal of men. Messner, "Still a Man's World?," 316.

2. Coakley, *Sports in Society*, 451, 437. The gender order in sport also lags behind the workplace achievements and social gains of women over the past several decades. In a September 2010 *Newsweek* article Andrew Romano and Tony Dokoupil remark on the inroads made by women noting that their numbers in college and graduate school have surpassed that of men, and that females now out-earn their male counterparts by 8 percent. In contrast, men have retained top rates in homelessness, alcoholism, suicide, and criminality. They argue that flexible gender roles have freed women from social expectations and improved job prospects, while inflexible male paradigms have conversely resulted in men's decline. Columbia University's Sylvia Hewlett argues, however, that women's gains are limited, for while females account for 60 percent of college graduates in the U.S. and for 34 percent of middle-level ranks, only 5 percent are top earners and barely 3 percent attain Fortune 500 CEO positions. See Romano and Dokoupil, "Men's Lib," 43–4; Sylvia A. Hewlett, "A Final Push Can Break the Glass Ceiling," *The Financial Times*, November 16, 2010, accessed December 2, 2010, http://www.fit.com/cms/s/0/186d2054-f1ba-11df-bb5a-00144feab49a.html.#axzz1CHZ4X79W.

3. As of 2011 women made up only 16 percent of Hollywood directors and writers, and stories about women have comprised approximately a quarter of U.S. content. Jennifer Siebel Newsome presented these findings in 2011 to the California Commission on the Status of Women. A 2015 Sundance Institute and Women in Film Studies study also found that there are 15.24 male directors for every female director working in Hollywood feature film. Speaking to this issue, director Chelsea McMullan noted in a *Globe and Mail* interview that even though viewers want to hear from other sources, "There aren't as many women in creative roles of power in the film industry." She stated that although viewers want to see material from different sources, "[P]art of the problem is that people in positions of power still want to see themselves represented in the cinema." See L. Smith, Katherine Pieper, Marc Choueti et al., "Exploring the Careers of Female Directors: Phase III" (Los Angeles: Annenberg School for Communications, & Journalism, University of California, 2015), accessed July 2, 2015, http://www.sundance.org/pdf/artist-programs/wfi/phase-iii-research---female-filmmakers-initiative.pdf; McMullan interview in Laura Beeston, "Film, Fashion and the Female Gaze," *The Globe and Mail*, September 1, 2015, L2.

4. Media producers view male-targeted content as more valuable because it draws both male and female demographics. Women also still comprise a minority sports spectatorship—nearly 25 percent to men's 75 percent of ESPN's viewership.

5. Reporting to the Commission on the Status of Women on research about gender issues in the media, actor Geena Davis noted that industry leaders believe the number of women who can fill various production positions in Hollywood is more than adequate. She also observed that producers typically regard widely acclaimed films like the soccer-themed *Bend It Like Beckham* (Chadha, 2002) as a fluke rather than as indicator

of the potential for more women-centered stories that appeal to a wide audience base. Davis elaborated that the lack of incentive to follow up on these trends and to promote gender balance stands in the way of creating a larger repertoire with memorable women protagonists. See Geena Davis, "Startling Research on the Gender Message in Media," Report to the Commission on the Status of Women, the California Channel, January 17, 2011.

6. Adams, "The Game of Whose Lives?" 78.

7. Karolos Grohmann, "Take Medals Monkey Off Our Back, VANOC Urges Athletes," *Reuters*, February 9, 2010, accessed February 10, 2010, http://www.canada.com/sports/2010wintergames/Take+medals+monkey+back+VANOC+urges+athletes/2541556/story.html; Abrahamson, "Canada: Ready for Its Olympic Moment," *NBC Olympics*. February 12, 2010, accessed February 12, 2010, http:www.nbcolympics.com/news-features/news/newsid=411448.html#canadas+moment+arrived.

8. NBC Nightly News, "A League of Their Own: Ladies Hit Ice, Go Pro."

9. The National Women's Hockey League (NWHL) was established in 1999 with two divisions, which subsequently split into three, and remained in operation until 2007. In 2007 also, the Canadian Women's Hockey League (CWHL) opened its doors to the public. It remains in operation with five teams. The National Women's Hockey League was reborn in 2015 and currently comprises four teams.

10. Tudor, *Hollywood's Vision of Team Sports*, 185.

11. Gruneau and Whitson note that the most publicized court case of the 1980s involving mixed play was the dispute between Justine Blaney and the Ontario Hockey Association (1986–87). For more see Gruneau and Whitson, *Hockey Night in Canada*, 170–1.

12. Gruneau and Whitson, *Hockey Night in Canada*, 169–170, 172. The authors argue that the issue of girls playing on boys' teams recurrently comes up in the 9–13 age category where girls and boys do not yet display conspicuous physical disparities in size and strength. Cultural assumptions about men's purported physical and performative superiority, however, have also distracted from the reality that among males and females of any given age there is a wide spectrum of athletic skills, including speed, coordination and strength.

13. Gruneau and Whitson, "Upmarket Continentalism," 238.

14. Bruzzi, *Bringing Up Daddy*, 9, 10.

15. Miller, *Turn Up the Contrast*, 257.

16. Tudor, *Hollywood's Vision of Team Sports*, 84, 188.

17. See for example, *Go Figure*, *Ice Princess* (Fywell, 2005) and *The Cutting Edge* (Glaser, 1992).

18. The film denotes the abilities needed for elite-level hockey and figure skating as virtually interchangeable.

19. Resonating with popular belief, *Ice Angel* procures the impression that the Americans clinched the gold medal in their February 22, 1980 semifinal win, much like Disney's *Miracle* appends the win against Finland to the U.S.-Soviet contest. HBO's *Do You Believe in Miracles?* (2001) corrected this widespread inaccuracy by making explicit that the victory against the Soviets did not automatically lead to Olympic gold, and indeed, because of the round robin structure of the tournament back then, a loss against the Finns would have left the U.S. team without a medal.

20. According to Disney Channel Worldwide President Rich Ross Levin, the cable network is aimed at the 'tween demographic who "didn't have a lot of places to go for entertainment media." See Levin's interview in Gary Levin, "Disney Finds Place for Tweens. TV Channel Relies on Wholesome Content," *USA Today*, October 27, 2005 2D.

21. Douglas Brode, *From Walt to Woodstock: How Disney Created the Counterculture* (Austin: University of Texas Press, 2004), xiv.

22. Even after the sale of the Mighty Ducks of Anaheim in February of 2005, Disney retained an interest in youth hockey by way of its Wide World of Sports property and California Disney Ice facility.

23. The segment aired February 8, 2006.

24. *Chicks with Sticks* was originally titled *Paula's Power Play*.

25. Marc Glassman, "Don Truckey Scores Again," *Writers Guild of Canada*, Spring 2004, accessed March 10, 2006, http://www.writersguildofcanada.com/magazine/articles/truckey.html.

26. The film's depiction of interest in women's hockey echoes the increasing numbers of registered female players in Canada from 7,321 in 1980 to 61,177 in 2003. Hockey Canada, "Registration Report."

27. Sabo and Jansen, "Prometheus Unbound," 203.

28. See, for example, *A League of Their Own* (Marshall, 1992), in which sibling tensions between talented catcher Dottie Hinson (Geena Davis) and team pitcher Kit Keller (Lori Petty) end up costing the Rockford Peaches the championship.

29. Paula's character is emblematic of the change in Canadian film's characterization of females. Katherine Monk submits that while the dominant woman motif endures, it has been recently updated by way of young, physically attractive, self-reliant, and good-natured protagonists. See Monk, *Weird Sex and Snowshoes*, 131.

30. Baker, *Contesting Identities*, 77.

31. Appending the women's game to the men's also mirrors mainstream media assumptions that males produce the nation and females reproduce merely this identity. Hockey's default construction as male preserve also aligns with the 8:1 ratio of male-female participation in organized hockey in Canada. See Julie Stevens, "Women's Hockey in Canada: After the 'Gold Rush,'" *Artificial Ice: Hockey, Culture and Commerce*, eds. Richard Gruneau and David Whitson (Peterborough, ON: Broadview Press, 2006): 85–100. For more on male performance as representation of the nation, see Tamar Mayer, "Gender Ironies of Nationalism: Setting the Stage" (London: Routledge, 2000), 18.

32. Gruneau and Whitson, *Hockey Night in Canada*, 191.

33. Julie Stevens and Carly Adams, "An Examination of Women's Sport Governance Issues: A Case Study of an Ontario Girls' Minor Hockey Association." Paper presented at International Conference on "Canada & the League of Hickey Nations." Victoria, B.C., April 19–21, 2007. The study makes clear that women's hockey also featured rugged tactics and routine fights, both of which were seen as deviant in the context of Victorian notions of femininity.

34. Canadian Broadcasting Corporation (CBC), "Quebec Films Bust at Box Office in 2012. Only *Les Pee*

Wee 3D and *Omertà* Made More than $1M." January 9, 2013, accessed September 3, 2015, http://www.cbc.ca/news/arts/quebec-films-bust-at-box-office-in-2012-1.1301478.

35. Manon Rhéaume was the first Quebec-trained female goalie to dress for an NHL (exhibition) game in 1992 and play in an entire pre-season NHL matchup in April 1993. A silver Olympic medalist and gold medalist at the IIHF Women's World Championships, she signed a contract with the Tampa Bay Lightning and also spent several years in the minors playing for various teams. Her record by all accounts remains historic. For more, see http://video.nhl.com/videocenter/console?id=186401.

36. Alice Michel-Moreau was nominated for the Canadian Screen Awards' category of Actress in a Supporting Role.

37. Blake, *Canadian Hockey Literature*, 89.

38. Coakley, *Sports in Society*, 79–80.

39. Baker, *Contesting Identities*, 144.

40. Wilkerson, "Explaining the Presence of Men Coaches in Women's Sports," 415. Geoffrey Gerson also examines the role of the old boys network and pinpoints a number of causes for the declining number of women's head coaches in Division I college hockey. He notes that individuals hired to coach women's hockey are male because the athletic director is male and has relationships primarily with male assistants. Men also coach women's hockey even without experience because often this is the only way to have the program approved. In addition, assistant coaching positions are appealing to men because of the entrenched status of males as head coaches. Finally, female athletes also prefer male coaches both in the U.S. and Canada because men's hockey coaches are regarded as the standard and female athletes demand and enforce the standard, particularly since they sit on school search boards. Geoffrey Jeffrey Gerson, "Women Coaches in Canadian and American College Ice Hockey: An Oral History" (paper presented at the Hockey Conference "Putting It on Ice IV: Visioning and Re-Visioning Hockey's Arena," London, ON, June 18–20, 2014).

41. Christine Brennan made these statements in response to IOC President Jacques Rogge's warning that women's teams would have to improve or risk having women's hockey eliminated as an Olympic sport only a mere seven Winter Games after its introduction. In contrast, he expressed support for having NHLers at the Sochi Games in 2014, noting that NHL participation would provide fans with the highest entertainment value and help the game grow around the world. Christine Brennan, "Jacques Rogge's Ioc No Advocate for Women Athletes," *USA Today*, February 24, 2010, accessed February 11, 2010, http://www.usatoday.com/sports/columnist/brennan/2010-02-24-IOC-women_N.htm. See also, Agence France Press (AFP), "Rogge Warns Women's Hockey to Improve or Exit," February 25, 2010, accessed February 26, 2010, http://www.ctvolympics.ca/hockey/news/newsid=52298.html#rogge+warns+womens+hockey+improve+exit.

Chapter 9

1. Coakley, *Sports in Society*, 401, 204.
2. Noel Brown refers largely to the movie-going experience, but larger TVs and the increasing blending of the televisual medium with digital platforms also allows for full immersion at home. Brown, "Hollywood, the Family Audience and the Family Film," 267–8.

3. Fiske, *Understanding Popular Culture*, 69.

4. Williams, "Melodrama Revised," 56, 60, 68.

5. David Rowe, *Sport, Culture and the Media: The Unruly Trinity*, 2nd ed. (Berkshire, UK: Open University Press, 2004), 112.

6. Jeff Hopkins, "Mapping of Cinematic Places, Icons, Ideology, and the Power of (Mis)Representation," *Place, Power, Situation and Spectacle: A Geography of Film*, ed., Stuart C. Aitken and Leo E. Zonn (Rowman and Littlefield, 1994), 48–49. 47–68.

7. Joshua Meyrowitz, "Multiple Media Literacies." *Journal of Communication* (Winter 1998): 97–103. Meyrowitz refers to media as a language and its production variables as a grammar. This chapter takes a more comprehensive view of grammar with respect to the sports genre.

8. A media studies orientation is vital in this chapter because film studies typically considers every movie as a unique creative endeavor. While genre attempts to pinpoint common topics and approaches to film, it also has a convoluted aspect and tends to focus on thematic and structural aspects (i.e., narrative, subject matter, characterization, setting, iconography) that nevertheless do not procure an in-depth look at the ideological component of the stylistic techniques deployed in film. Analysis of this kind is also virtually inexistent with respect to hockey. This chapter therefore addresses how the thematic and technical aspects of the game in film convey its ideological message.

9. Babington, *The Sports Film*, 50.

10. See King, *New Hollywood Cinema*, 121.

11. *Against the Ropes* (2004) director Charles S. Dutton reaffirms the emphasis on realistically portraying sport in film noting that "[W]hen you do a sports movie right, it's great ... but when they're bad, they're godawful. People have high expectations, particularly when it's a sport they love." Writer-director Robert Towne of *Personal Best* (1982) and *Without Limits* (1998) is also blunt about the prospect of bringing a sports-themed production to the big screen: "There's no point in doing a sports film if the sports sequences don't look right." For more on directors' priorities in depicting the sports film, see Jack McCallum, "Reel Sports: Hollywood Trends Come and Go, but Sports Movies—Clichéd, Corny, Sometimes Downright Comical—Are Never Out of Fashion. Just Don't Call Them Sports Movies." *Sports Illustrated*, February 5, 2001, 102; Scott Bowles, "Hollywood Bringing Sports Themes Off the Bench," *USA Today*, February 19, 2004, 1D.

12. Messner, "Still a Man's World?," 320.

13. Susan Sontag, *On Photography* (Harmondsworth: Penguin, 1977), 111.

14. Baker, *Contesting Identities*, 5.

15. Williams, "Melodrama Revised," 74.

16. Cummins cites the works of Vorderer, Wulff, Friedrichsen, Zillmann, and Carroll in theorizing that suspense is vital in arousing viewer emotions because it drives audiences to dread an all but assured ruinous outcome for the protagonist. See Cummins, "Sports Fiction—Critical and Empirical Analysis," 212–3. Vorderer,

Peter, "Toward a Psychological Theory of Suspense," *Suspense: Conceptualizations, Theoretical Analyses, and Empirical Explorations*, eds. Peter Vorderer, Hans J. Wulff, and Mike Friedrichsen (Mahwah, NJ: Lawrence Erlbaum Associates, 1996): 223–254; Hans J. Wulff, "Suspense and the Influence of Cataphora on Viewers' Expectations," *Suspense: Conceptualizations, Theoretical Analyses, and Empirical Explorations*, eds. Peter Vorderer, Hans J. Wulff, and Mike Friedrichsen (Mahwah, NJ: Lawrence Erlbaum Associates, 1996): 1–18; Mike Friedrichsen, "The Problems of Measuring Suspense," *Suspense: Conceptualizations, Theoretical Analyses, and Empirical Explorations*, eds. Peter Vorderer, Hans J. Wulff, and Mike Friedrichsen (Mahwah, NJ: Lawrence Erlbaum Associates, 1996): 329–346; Dolf Zillmann, "The Psychology of Suspense in Dramatic Exposition," *Suspense: Conceptualizations, Theoretical Analyses, and Empirical Explorations*, eds. Peter Vorderer, Hans J. Wulff, and Mike Friedrichsen (Mahwah, NJ: Lawrence Erlbaum Associates, 1996): 199–231; Noël Carroll, "The Paradox of Suspense," *Suspense: Conceptualizations, Theoretical Analyses, and Empirical Explorations*, eds. Peter Vorderer, Hans J. Wulff, and Mike Friedrichsen (Mahwah, NJ: Lawrence Erlbaum Associates, 1996): 71–91.

17. Cummins, "Sports Fiction—Critical and Empirical Analysis," 213. Cummins also alludes to the work of Allen Guttman, Dolf Zillmann, and Bryant, Zillmann, and Raney in confirming that depictions of violence can change a viewer's state of mind. See Allen Guttmann, "The Appeal of Violent Sports," *Why We Watch: The Attractions of Violent Entertainment*, ed. J.H. Goldstein (New York: Oxford Univ. Press, 1998): 7–26; Dolf Zillmann, "Mechanism of Emotional Involvement with Drama," *Poetics* 23 (1994): 33–51; Jennings Bryant, Dolf Zilmann, A. Raney, "Violence and the Enjoyment of Media Sports," *MediaSport*, ed. Lawrence A. Wenner (London: Routledge, 1998): 252–265.

18. Coakley, *Sports in Society*, 208.

19. Cummins, "Sports Fiction—Critical and Empirical Analysis," 211; Peter Vorderer and Silvia Knobloch, "Conflict and Suspense in Drama," *Media Entertainment: The Psychology of Its Appeal*, eds. Jennings Bryant and Peter Vorderer, (Mahwah, NJ: Lawrence Erlbaum Associates, 2000): 59–72. See also Jason Blake's discussion of catharsis in *Canadian Sports Literature*, 92–97.

20. Nasson, "The Tooth Fairy: Behind the Scenes."

21. Babington, *The Sports Film*, 50–51.

22. E.M. Swift explains the newsreel footage at the start of the film as "a necessary historical backdrop … [for] [p]eople younger than 30 [who] have little familiarity with the America of that era." Swift, "Miracle, the Sequel," 75.

23. Landau, "Human Evolution as Narrative," 268.

24. The 1980 win bolstered U.S. hockey by increasing player numbers at the collegiate and junior levels in both the women's and men's games. As Ray Ratto indicates in an article on the 20th anniversary of the win, the victory generated a 230 percent boost in total hockey registration numbers since 1980, and a 530 percent increase in women's hockey alone. Coach Brooks, however, did not concur that the U.S. hockey victory was without precedent as has commonly been portrayed in the media. See Ratto, "All We Needed Was a Miracle"; Finn, "Triumph Opened Doors," C5.

25. See, for example, Newman, "Movie Review: Against All Odds: 'Miracle' Gets the Hockey –And Politics– Right."

26. In an International Ice Hockey Federation (IIHF) interview, O'Connor underscored that he did not wish to stress "[t]he Cold War tensions that plagued the world in 1980." Lucas Aykroyd, "Lights, Camera, Action! Miracle on Ice Hits the Big Screen," *IIHF Newsletter* 7, no. 5 (2004): 5, accessed July 7, 2004, http://www.iihf.com/news/ IIHF_Vol7No5.pdf.

27. MacNeill, "Networks: Producing Olympic Ice Hockey for a National Television Audience," 111.

28. Along with the National Film Board, the CBC was charged with the directive of generating representative works that showcased both national diversity and national unity. Hockey broadcasts date back to the network's inception, on radio from 1931 onward and on television from 1952. By 1960, these broadcasts reached 3.5 million English-Canadian and 2 million French-Canadian homes. See Beaty, "Not Playing, Working," 123–4; Harcourt, "Speculations on Canadian Cinema."

29. Michael Messner, *Taking the Field: Women, Men, and Sports* (Minneapolis: University of Minnesota Press, 2002), 465.

30. Gruneau and Whitson, *Hockey Night in Canada*, 187–8; Kristi Allain, "'Real Fast and Tough': The Construction of Canadian Hockey Masculinity." *Sociology of Sport Journal* 25, no. 4 (December 2008): 464.

31. Baker, *Contesting Identities*, 8; Cummins, "Sports Fiction—Critical and Empirical Analysis," 203.

32. Meyrowitz, "Multiple Media Literacies," 101.

33. Dancyger and Rush, *Alternative Scriptwriting,*.

34. Michele Aaron, *Death and the Moving Image: Ideology, Iconography, and I* (Edinburgh: Edinburgh Press, 2014), 17–18.

35. Dancyger and Rush, *Alternative Scriptwriting*, 94.

36. Lance Strate, "Heroes: A Communication Perspective," *American Heroes in a Media Age*, eds. Susan J. Drucker and Robert S. Cathcart (New York: Hampton Press, 1994), 43.

37. Michele Aaron, *Death and the Moving Image*, 18.

38. Scheurer, "The Best Ever There Was in the Game," 160.

39. Stuart C. Aitken, and Leo E. Zonn, eds. "*Re-Pre*senting the Place Pastiche." In *Place, Power, Situation and Spectacle: A Geography of Film* (Lanham, Maryland: Rowman and Littlefield Publishers, Inc., 1994), 5, 8, 17.

40. For more on spectating changes at hockey arenas, see Kennedy, "Whatever Happened to the Organ and the Portrait of Her Majesty?," 158–164.

41. Of nineties films and beyond, *Gross Misconduct, Mystery, Alaska, Slap Shot 2, Waking Up Wally, Il était une fois les boys* and *The Sheldon Kennedy Story* mark the connection between the wild open spaces of the North and West and institutional hockey in much the way earlier films like *Face Off, The Last Season,* and *Youngblood* do.

42. Joshua Meyrowitz speaks to the same point in making the case that portrayals of subjects in "less replicative media" enable greater idealization than in media with a "[h]ighly replicative" component, which have a demystifying effect. See Joshua Meyrowitz, *No Sense of Place: The Impact of Electronic Media on Social Behavior* (New York: Oxford University Press, 1985),

272–275; Dancyger and Rush, *Alternative Scriptwriting*, 76–77.

Conclusion

1. This duality mirrors the frontier masculinity of the *coureurs de bois* and *voyageurs*, who carved their own destinies outside the powerful reach of the state and Church in the myth of the North. Similarly, in the myth of the West, the process of frontier-opening through which hockey mythically expresses the romance of open spaces and the prospect of social mobility in the American imaginary, allowed pioneers, frontiersmen and even outlaws the possibility of escape from institutional control. As a sanctuary for the metropolitan power structure, the frontier offered enterprising sorts the prospect of material ascendance. This is not to say that prevailing masculinity ideals of the time did not exercise a mediating influence. Richard Slotkin notes that the true American of the myth, while succeeding in freeing himself from the control of metropolitan regimes and its social mores governed by class and privilege, had also overcome the savagery of the wild. In Canada too, as noted, the nineteenth century Anglophone elite (business class) upheld masculinity models that drew on ideas of the Dominion as peaceable kingdom. The RCMP buttressed the regime of law and order by helping to oversee the country's process of expansion and settlement by operating as proxy for British authority. Slotkin, *Gunfighter Nation*, 11, 30.

2. See Crosson's discussion of how genres, including the sports film, deploy opportunities for countercultural expression for the audience's enjoyment. Crosson, *Sport and Film*, 61.

3. Beaty, "Not Playing, Working," 132.

4. Judith Alguire's novel *Iced*, in contrast, features lesbian hockey players.

5. Bruzzi, *Bringing Up Daddy*, 117, 132.

6. Blake, *Canadian Hockey Literature*, 216.

7. Ransom, "Lieux de mémoire or lieux du dollar?," 23; Brian McFarlane, *The Habs* (Toronto: Stoddart, 1996), 5–6; Bill Legrand, "Those Old Montreal Maroons," *The Montreal Canadiens: A Hockey Dynasty*, ed. Claude Mouton (Toronto: Van Nostrand Reinhold, 1980), 14–17.

8. Gruneau and Whitson, *Hockey Night in Canada*, 132–3, 163.

9. The Boston Bruins, much like the Leafs, receive seven mentions in the repertoire, while Boston college hockey receives three additional references. The Montreal Canadiens follow closely with six mentions, most of them made in the Francophone repertoire.

10. Steve Hardy notes that by the 1890s hockey was well established in the high schools and colleges and developed a sizeable support base in Massachusetts. Hardy, "Long Before Orr," 269, 272.

11. A total of fifteen movies (*Miracle on Ice, Hockey Night, D2: The Mighty Ducks, Les Boys II, Ronnie and Julie, Ice Angel, Slap Shot 2, Miracle, Go Figure, Sticks and Stones, Canada Russia '72, Goon*, the Don Cherry biopics, *Les Pee Wee 3D*) allude to the Russians/Soviets by name, by way of its long-time coach Viktor Tikhonov, his mannerisms or physical resemblance, or by proxy, through references to the team's red uniforms, players' larger physical size to denote superior status, fearsome "machine-"like circling, iron-willed-discipline, and so-called arrogance. Some films draw up Russians as teammates to denote their now standard presence at the elite, minor, and junior league levels. Specific references to Soviet opponents that summon memory of the "Miracle on Ice" as well as of the Summit Series tend to position the sports film as North American content.

12. During the 2008 NHL Winter Classic NBC paid homage to the Hansons by sending one of its announcers to humorously tangle with fans in the stands.

13. Baker, Contesting Identities, 143.

14. The primacy of the hockey archetype in film is also consistent with similar trends in media content. Augie Fleras and Shane Michael Dixon call attention to the wide array of TV reality programming that extols the re-masculinized heroic in line the values of virility and toughness (*Ax Men, Ice Road Truckers, Deadliest Catch, Sandhogs*). Fleras alludes to a similar dynamic in proliferating documentary film and television depictions of extreme sports. This so-called unscripted content spotlights masculinity-testing against natural forces by way of narrow escapes, heart-stopper situations, and injuries that resemble media coverage of high-contact sports like hockey and football. It also mirrors the way media frame conventional masculinity as "real and authentic ... and expressed through action" in contrast to the symbolic work of "the liberal and elite," as Fleras and Dixon amplify. Fleras and Dixon argue that the reassertion of working-class muscularity is consistent with the emergence of the new knowledge-based economy and the decline of manual labor jobs, pointing to the similar dynamics that oversaw the emergence of "strenuous manhood" in response to the late nineteenth and early twentieth centuries' "crisis of masculinity." Shows that depict the remasculinization of the heroic also foreground boldness, staying power, competitiveness, and independence, implying the regulation of dominant masculinity in accordance with the needs of the marketplace. Augie Fleras and Shane Michael Dixon, "Cutting, Driving, Digging, and Harvesting: Re-Masculinizing the Working-Class Heroic," *Canadian Journal of Communications* 36 (2011): 581, 583, 585–6, 592.

15. Sara Gee argues that media content that speaks to mythical (warrior) representations of the hockey player by way of physical superiority, fearlessness, heterosexuality, and power over women encourage men to (re-) claim their rightful space in the game and in society and fight off the encroachment of social others who express alternative versions of identity. Kibby, for her part, posits that nostalgia expresses a form of agitation over changed circumstances and that the genre's depiction of dominant masculinity operates as a salve for the passing of valued benchmarks while allowing for adjustment to new situations and beliefs. See Sara Gee, "Mediating Sport, Myth, and Masculinity: The National Hockey League's 'Inside the Warrior' Advertising Campaign," *Sociology of Sport Journal* 26 (2009): 594; Kibby, "Nostalgia for the Masculine," 26–7.

Bibliography

Aaron, Michele. *Death and the Moving Image: Ideology, Iconography, and I.* Edinburgh: Edinburgh Press, 2014.

Abrahamson, Alan. "Canada: Ready for Its Olympic Moment." *NBC Olympics.* February 12, 2010. http:www.nbcolympics.com/news-features/news/newsid=411448.html#canadas+moment+arrived (accessed February 12, 2010).

Adams, Mary Louise. "The Game of Whose Lives? Gender, Race and Entitlement in Canada's National Game." In *Artificial Ice: Hockey, Culture and Commerce,* edited by Richard Gruneau and David Whitson, 71–84. Peterborough, Ontario: Broadview Press, 2006.

Adams, Paul C. "The September 11 Attacks as Viewed from Quebec: The Small-Nation Code in Geopolitical Discourse." *Political Geography* 23 (2004): 765–95.

Agence France-Presse (AFP). "Rogge Warns Women's Hockey to Improve or Exit." February 25, 2010. http://www.ctvolympics.ca/hockey/news/newsid=52298.html#rogge+warns+womens+hockey+improve+exit (accessed February 26, 2010).

Aitken, Stuart C., and Christopher Lee Lukinbeal. "Disassociated Masculinities and Geographies of the Road." *The Road Movie Book,* edited by Steven Cohan and Ina Rae Hark, 349–70. New York: Routledge, 1997.

Aitken, Stuart C., and Leo C. Zonn. "Re-Presenting the Place Pastiche." In *Place, Power, Situation and Spectacle: A Geography of Film,* edited by Aitken, Stuart C. and Leo E. Zonn, 3–26. Lanham, Maryland: Rowman and Littlefield, 1994.

Alioff, Maurie. "O Canadian Film, We Stand on Guard for Thee: Peter Rowe's Popcorn with Maple Syrup and Jill Sharpe's *Weird Sex and Snowshoes.*" *TAKE ONE* (Sept.–Dec. 2004). http://findarticles.com/p/articles/mi_0JSF/is_47_13/ai_n6219967/?tag+content;col1 (accessed May 18, 2006).

Allain, Kristi. "Kid Crosby or Golden Boy: Sidney Crosby, Canadian National Identity, and the Policing of Hockey Masculinity." *International Review for the Sociology of Sport* 46, no. 2 (2010): 3–22.

———. "Real Fast and Tough: The Construction of Canadian Hockey Masculinity." *Sociology of Sport Journal* 25, no. 4 (December 2008): 462–481.

Allen, Holly. "Heroism." In *American Masculinities,* edited by Bret E. Carroll, 205–7. Thousand Oaks, CA: Sage Publications, 2003.

Allen, Kevin. "Hockey in America." "American Hockey: The State of the Game." In *Total Hockey,* edited by Dan Diamond, 85–7. 2nd ed. Scarborough, Ontario: Total Sports Publishing, 2000.

Altman, Rick. *Film/Genre.* London: BFI Publishing, 1999.

Amsden, Cynthia. "Canadian Comedy, Eh?: Paul Gross's Men with Brooms and Steve Smith's Red Green's Duct Tape Forever." *TAKE ONE* (June–Sept. 2005. http://www.finadarticles.com/p/articles/mi_m0JSF/is_50_14/ai_N14704669/ (accessed September 30, 2006).

Anderson, Benedict. *Imagined Communities: Reflections on the Origin and Spread of Nationalism.* London: Verso, 1989.

Anderson, Carolyn. "The Biographical Film." In *Handbook of American Film Genres,* edited by Wes D. Gehring, 331–351. New York: Greenwood Press, 1988.

Anderson, Jennifer. "Propaganda and Persuasion in the Cold War: The Canadian-Soviet Friendship Society, 1949–1960." Ottawa, Canada: unpublished doctoral dissertation, 2008.

Atwood, Margaret. *Survival: A Thematic Guide to Canadian Literature.* Toronto: Anansi, 1972.

Aykroyd, Lucas. "Lights, Camera, Action! Miracle on Ice Hits the Big Screen." *IIHF Newsletter* 7, no. 5 (2004). http://www.iihf.com/news/ IIHF_Vol7No5.pdf (accessed July 7, 2004).

Babington, Bruce. *The Sports Film: Games People Play.* New York: Columbia University Press, 2014.

Bahktin, Mikhail. *Rabelais and His World.* Cambridge: Massachusetts Institute of Technology Press, 1968.

Baker, Aaron. *Contesting Identities: Sports in American Film*. Urbana and Chicago: University of Illinois Press, 2003.

———. "Sports Films, History, and Identity." *Journal of Sport History* 25, no. 2 (1998): 217–33.

Baker, Brian. *Masculinity in Fiction and Film: Representing Men in Popular Genres 1945–2000*. New York: Continuum, 2006.

Banerjee, Sidhartha. "Quebec Gets Own Hockey Team in International Tournament." *The Globe and Mail*, November 12, 2010. http://www.theglobeandmail.com/news/national/quebec-gets-own-hockey-team-in-international-tournament/article1314351/ (accessed November 15, 2010).

Banning, Kass. "Conjugating Three Moments in Black Canadian Cinema." In *North of Everything: English-Canadian Cinema Since 1980*, edited by William Beard and Jerry White, 84–99. Edmonton, Alberta: The University of Alberta Press, 2002.

Barthes, Roland. "The Tour De France as Epic." In *The Eiffel Tower and Other Mythologies*. Translated by Richard Howard. New York: Hill and Wang, 1979.

Beardsley, Doug. *Country on Ice*. Toronto: Paperjacks, 1988.

———. "Where There's Ice, There's Hockey." *New York Times*, February 27, 2005.

Beaty, Bart. "Not Playing, Working: Class, Masculinity, and Nation in the Canadian Hockey Film." In *Working on Screen: Representations of the Working Class in Canadian Cinema*, edited by Malek Kouri and Darrell Varga, 113–33. Toronto: University of Toronto Press, 2006.

Beeston, Laura. "Film, Fashion and the Female Gaze." *The Globe and Mail*, September 1, 2015.

Bell-Metereau, Rebecca. "The How-to Manual, the Prequel, and the Sequel in Post 9/11 Cinema." In *Film and Television After 9/11*, edited by Wheeler Winston Dixon, 142–62. Carbondale: Southern Illinois University Press, 1994.

Bennett, Tony. "Hegemony, Ideology, Pleasure: Blackpool." In *Popular Culture and Social Relations*, edited by Colin Mercer and Janet Woollacott, 135–54. Milton Keynes and Philadelphia: Open University Press, 1986.

Benshoff, Harry M., and Sean Griffin. *America on Film: Representing Race, Class, Gender, and Sexuality at the Movies*. Oxford, UK: Wiley-Blackwell, 2004.

Berger, Carl. *The Sense of Power: Studies in the Ideas of Canadian Imperialism 1867–1914*. Toronto: University of Toronto Press, 1970.

———. "The True North Strong and Free." In *Nationalism in Canada*, edited by Peter Russell, 3–26. Toronto: McGraw-Hill, 1966.

Berland, Jody. "Marginal Notes in Cultural Studies in Canada." *University of Toronto Quarterly* 64, no. 4 (1995): 514–25.

———. "Politics After Nationalism, Culture After Culture." *Border/Lines* 38–39 (1995): 104–9.

Bernard, Prosper, Jr. "Canada and Human Security: From the Axworthy Doctrine to Middle Power Internationalism." *The American Review of Canadian Studies* 36, no. 2 (2006): 233–61.

Berry, Robert, and William B. Gould. *Labor Relations in Professional Sports*. Boston: Auburn House Publishing, 1986.

Berton, Pierre. *Hollywood's Canada: The Americanization of Our National Image*. Toronto: McClelland & Stewart Limited, 1975.

Blake, Jason. *Canadian Hockey Literature*. Toronto: University of Toronto Press, 2010.

Blumenthal, Sydney. *Our Long National Daydream*. New York: Harper & Row, 1988.

Bordwell, David. *Making Meaning: Inference and Rhetoric in the Interpretation of Cinema*. Cambridge, MA: Harvard University Press, 1989.

Bowles, Scott. "Hollywood Bringing Sports Themes Off the Bench." *USA Today*, February 19, 2004.

Bradley, Pat. "Jay Baruchel: Hockey Film Sequel Goon 2 to Start Filming This Summer." *NESN.com*, April 11, 2015. http://nesn.com/2015/04/jay-baruchel-says-goon-sequel-goon-2-starts-filming-this-summer/ (accessed June 30, 2015).

Branch, John. "Derek Boogard: Blood on the Ice." *New York Times*, December 4, 2011. http://www.nytimes.com/2011/12/05/sports/hockey/derek-boogaard-blood-on-the-ice.html?pagewanted=all&_r=0 (accessed February 14, 2012).

Brault, Michel. "La Dernière partie." *Montreal vu par…* (1991) *Contemporary Canadian Film and Literature* (Fall, 1999). http://www.eng.fju.edu.tw/canada/vu_par.html.

Brennan, Christine. "Jacques Rogge's IOC No Advocate for Women Athletes." *USA Today*, February 24, 2010. http://www.usatoday.com/sports/columnist/brennan/2010-02-24-IOC-women_N.htm (accessed February 25, 2010).

Brode, Douglas. *From Walt to Woodstock: How Disney Created the Counterculture*. Austin: University of Texas Press, 2004.

Brooks, Peter. *The Melodramatic Imagination: Balzac, Henry James, Melodrama, and the Mode of Excess*. New Haven, CT: Yale University Press, 1976.

Brown, Noel. "Hollywood, the Family Audience and the Family Film, 1930–2010." Newcastle, UK: unpublished doctoral dissertation, 2010.

Brunelle, Michel. "Rocket Knock-Out." *Moebius* 86 (2000): 21–24.
Bruzzi, Stella. *Bringing Up Daddy: Fatherhood and Masculinity in Post-War Hollywood.* London: BFI Publishing, 2005.
Bryant, Jennings, Dolf Zillmann, and Arthur A. Raney. "Violence and the Enjoyment of Media Sports." In *MediaSport*, edited by Lawrence A. Wenner, 252–265. London: Routledge, 1998.
Buma, Michael. "Pluralism and the 1972 Summit Series." In *Coming Down the Mountain: Rethinking the 1972 Summit Series*, edited by Brian Kennedy, 45–63. Hamilton, ON: Wolsak and Wynn, 2014.
_____. *Refereeing Identity: The Cultural Work of Canadian Hockey Novels.* Montreal and Kingston: McGill-Queen's University Press, 2012.
Burnside, Scott. "The Biggest Mouth in Sports." *ESPN.com*, nd. http://sports.espn.go.com/espn/eticket/story?page=doncherry (accessed August 20, 2012).
Campbell, Ken. "What Was a Bigger Moment: 1972 or 1980? Do You Believe in Miracles?" *The Hockey News*, Great Debates Special Issue, 2004.
Canadian Association of Film Distributors and Exporters (CAFDE). "A Review of Canadian Content Criteria in the 21st Century." Brief Presented to the Department of Canadian Heritage. May 31, 2002. http://www.pch.gc.ca/progs/acca/progs/cc21c/archives/docs/cadfe.htm (Accessed May 15, 2006).
Canadian Broadcasting Corporation (CBC). "Quebec Films Bust at Box Office in 2012. Only Les Pee Wee 3D and Omertà Made More than $1M." *CBC.ca,* January 9, 2013, http://www.cbc.ca/news/arts/quebec-films-bust-at-box-office-in-2012-1.1301478 (accessed September 3, 2015).
_____. "The Red Scare." n.d., http://www.cbc.ca/history/EPISCONTENTSE1EP15CH1PA2L.html (accessed February 12, 2013).
_____. "SNL'S Mike Myers Outs Ryan Gosling as Canadian." December 6, 2015. http://www.cbc.ca/news/canada/newfoundland-labrador/ryan-gosling-mike-myers-saturday-night-live-1.3353019 (accessed December 10, 2015).
Cantelon, Hart. "Have Skates, Will Travel: Canada, Europe and the Hockey Labour Market." In *Artificial Ice: Hockey, Culture and Commerce*, edited by Richard Gruneau and David Whitson, 215–236. Toronto, Ontario: Broadview Press, 2006.
Cantin, Serge. "Crise de la mémoire collective. Pour sortir de la survivance." *Le Devoir*, August 14, 1999.
Carp, Steve. "NHL to Meet Again Next Week on Las Vegas Expansion." *Las Vegas Review-Journal*, January 14, 2016. http://www.reviewjournal.com/sports/hockey-vegas/nhl-meet-again-next-week-las-vegas-expansion. (accessed January 14, 2016).
Carpenter, Les. "David Denson's Huge Leap Conceals Pro Sports' Problem with Gay Players." *The Guardian*, August 17, 2015. http://www.theguardian.com/sport/2015/aug/17/david-denson-gay-michael-sam-pro-sports (accessed August 25, 2015).
Carrier, Roch. *The Hockey Sweater and Other Stories.* Translated by Sheila Fischman. Toronto: House of Anansi Press, 1979.
Carroll, Noël. "The Paradox of Suspense." In *Suspense: Conceptualizations, Theoretical Analyses, and Empirical Explorations*, edited by Peter Vorderer, Hans J. Wulff, and Mike Friedrichsen, 71–91. Mahwah, New Jersey: Lawrence Erlbaum Associates, 1996.
Cermak, Iri. "The Long Shelf Life of the Cold War: U.S. and Canadian Images of Russian Olympic Hockey at the Salt Lake Winter Games." Paper presented at the meeting of the Sport and Media Working Section of the International Association for Communication Research (IAMCR), Leipzig, Germany, January 17, 2004.
_____. "Media Retrospectives of the Summit Series." In *Coming Down the Mountain: Rethinking the 1972 Summit Series*, edited by Brian Kennedy, 193–215. Hamilton, ON: Wolsak and Wynn, 2014.
_____. "Seeing Red: Images of Soviet and Russian Hockey in U.S. and Canadian Olympic Broadcasts." Seattle, WA: unpublished doctoral dissertation, 1996.
_____. "Seeing Red: Mediasport Discourses of Soviet Olympic Hockey." Seattle, Washington: Canadian Studies Center, Henry M. Jackson School of International Studies, University of Washington, 1997.
Chandler, Daniel. "An Introduction to Genre Theory." July 05, 2000. http://visual-memory.co.uk/daniel/Documents/intgenre/.
Chapman, Roger. "George F. Kennan as Represented by Chuck Jones: Road Runner and the Cold War Policy of Containment (1949–1980)." *Film & History* 31, no.1 (2001): 40–3.
Chris, Cynthia. *Watching Wildlife.* Minneapolis: University of Minnesota Press, 2006.
Clarke, Chris. "Nature by Design. How Disney's Treatment of Animals Has Altered Our Sense of the Wild and Cleared the Way for Environmental Decline." *New Internationalist* 308 (Dec. 1998). http://www.newint.org/issue308/nature.html.
Coakley, Jay. *Sports in Society: Issues and Controversies.* Whitby, ON: McGraw-Hill Ryerson, 2004.
Coffey, Phil. "80 U.S. Team Adds Feel-Good Air to 2002 Olympics." February 9, 2002. NHL.com. http://www.nhl.com/olympics2002/usa/1980_torch020902.html (accessed February 9, 2002).
Cohen, Stephen. "Soviet State and Society as Reflected in the American Media." *Nieman Reports* (Winter 1984): 25–28.

Collins, James M. "The Musical." In *Handbook of American Film Genres,* edited by Wes D. Gehring, 269–284. New York: Greenwood Press, 1988.
Connell, R.W. "Globalization, Imperialism, and Masculinities." In *Handbook of Studies on Men and Masculinities,* edited by Michael Kimmel, Jeff Hearn, and R.W. Connell, 71–89. London: Sage Publications, 2005.
———, and James W. Messerschmidt. "Hegemonic Masculinity: Rethinking the Concept." *Gender & Society* 19, no. 6 (2005): 829–59.
Cook, Pam. *Screening the Past: Memory and Nostalgia in Cinema.* New York: Taylor and Francis, 2005.
Corrigan, Timothy. *A Cinema Without Walls: Movies and Culture After Vietnam.* New Brunswick, NJ: Rutgers University Press, 1991.
Covert, Colin. "'Goon' Is All Brawl." *The Star Tribune,* March 30, 2012. http://www.startribune.com/entertainment/movies/144925515.html?refer=y (accessed April 10, 2012).
Craig, J. Robert. "From Triumph of the Will to the Mighty Ducks of Anaheim: Riefenstahl Rocks by the Pond." *Popular Culture Review* 8, no. 1 (February 1997): 111–120.
Crawford, Scott A.G.M. "The Sport Film—Its Cultural Significance." *Journal of Physical Education, Recreation and Dance* 59, no. 6 (1988): 45–9.
Crosson, Seán. *Sport and Film.* New York: Routledge, 2013.
Crumpacker, John. "Ceremony a Tribute to American Tenacity." *The San Francisco Chronicle,* February 9, 2002.
Cummins, R. Glenn. "Sports Fiction—Critical and Empirical Analysis." In *Handbook of Sports and Media,* edited by Arthur A. Raney and Jennings Bryant, 198–218. Mahwah, NJ: Lawrence Erlbaum Associates, 2006.
Custen, George. "Making History." In *The Historical Film: History and Memory in Media,* edited by Marcia Landy, 67–97. New Brunswick, New Jersey: Rutgers University Press, 2001.
The Daily Mail. "Mike Myers Crashes the SNL Stage During Host Ryan Gosling's Opening Monologue ... 20 Years After Departing the Show's Cast." December 6, 2015. http://www.dailymail.co.uk/tvshowbiz/article-3347988/Mike-Myers-crashes-SNL-stage-host-Ryan-Gosling-s-opening-monologue-20-years-departing-s-cast.html (accessed December 10, 2015).
Dancyger, Ken, and Jeff Rush. *Alternative Scriptwriting: Beyond the Hollywood Formula,* 4th ed. New York: Focal Press, 2007.
Davis, Erik. Review of *Ferngully. Village Voice,* April 22, 1992.
Davis, Geena. "Startling Research on the Gender Message in Media." Report to the Commission on the Status of Women, the California Channel, January 17, 2011.
Dayan, Daniel, and Elihu Katz. *Media Events: The Live Broadcasting of History.* Cambridge: Harvard University Press, 1992.
Derry, John W. *A Short History of 19th Century England.* New American Library: Mentor, 1963.
Diduck, Ryan. "From Back Bacon to Chicken Fingers: Re-Contextualizing the 'Hoser' Archetype." *Offscreen* 10, no. 1 (2006). http://www.offscreen.com/index.php/phile/essays/hoser_archetype/.
Dillon, Mark. "Rocket's Release Noble but Risky." Page 11. *Playback Magazine,* April 17, 2006. http://www.playbackmag.com/articles/magazine/20060417/comment.html? (accessed September 18, 2006).
Dissayanake, Wimal. "Issues in World Cinema." In *World Cinema: Critical Approaches,* edited by John Hill and Pamela Gibson Church, 143–150. Oxford: Oxford University Press, 2000.
Dizikes, John. *Sportsmen and Gamesmen.* Boston: Houghton Mifflin, 1981.
Doane, Mary Ann. "Film and the Masquerade: Theorising the Female Spectator." In *Film Theory and Criticism,* 4th ed., edited by Gerald Mast, Marshall Cohen and Leo Braudy, 758–72. New York: Oxford University Press, 1992.
Dokoupil, Tony and Rick Martin. "Dead Suit Walking: If This Isn't the Great Depression, It Is the Great Humbling. Can Manhood Survive the Lost Decade?" *The Daily Beast,* April 17, 2011. http://www.thedailybeast.com/newsweek/2011/04/17/dead-suit-walking.html (accessed April 5, 2012).
Donald, Ralph. "From 'Knockout Punch' to 'Home Run': Masculinity's 'Dirty Dozen' Sports in American Combat Films." *Film & History* 35, no. 1 (2005): 1–28. http://128.220.160.198/journals/film_and_history/v035/35.1donald.pdf (accessed October 12, 2012).
Donnelly, Peter. "The Local and the Global: Globalization in the Sociology of Sport." *Journal of Sport and Social Issues* 20, no. 3 (1996): 239–57.
Douglas, Ann. *The Feminization of American Culture.* New York: Farrar, Strauss and Giroux, 1998.
Duniz, Randy. "Bon Cop: A How-To for Successful Canadian Movies." *InterACTRA* (Winter 2007): 8–10.
Dwyer, Victor. "Hockey's Hell-Raiser: Spinner Spencer Battled on and Off the Ice. Gross Misconduct." *Maclean's,* March 1, 1993. http://www.paulgross.org/ grossmis.htm.
Dyer, Richard. "Introduction to Film Studies." In *Film Studies: Critical Approaches,* edited by John Hill and Pamela Church Gibson, 1–8. Oxford: Oxford University Press, 2000.
Ebner, Dave. "Our Defining Moment in Hockey to Be a TV Movie: 1972 Summit Series Drama Inspired by the Success of the 2004 Disney Movie Miracle." *The Globe and Mail,* January 12, 2005.
Ebron, Paulla. *Performing Africa.* Princeton, NJ: Princeton University Press, 2002.

The Economist. "Endless Summer." April 28, 2007, 73.
Edensor, Tim. *National Identity, Popular Culture and Everyday Life.* Oxford: Berg, 2002.
Eisner, Ken. "Breakaway Is a Cinematic Window into Modern, Multicultural Canada." September 28, 2011. http://www.straight.com/movies/breakaway-cinematic-window-modern-multicultural-canada (accessed May 10, 2012).
Eisner, Michael. "Planetized Entertainment." *New Perspectives Quarterly* 12, no. 4 (1995): 9.
Elcombe, Tim. "Reflections on Canadian Moral Nation-Making on the Occasion of the Summit Series' Seventy-Fifth Anniversary." In *Coming Down the Mountain: Rethinking the 1972 Summit Series*, edited by Brian Kennedy. Hamilton, ON: Wolsak and Wynn, 2014: 279–301.
Elias, Norbert, and Eric Dunning. *The Quest for Excitement: Sport and Leisure in the Civilizing Process.* Oxford: Basil Blackwell, 1986.
Ellefson, Merja, and Eva Kingsepp. "The Good, the Bad and the Ugly: Stereotyping Russia the Western Way." In *News of the Other: Tracing Identity in Scandinavian Constructions of the Eastern Baltic Sea Region*, edited by Kristina Riegert. *Northern Perspectives* 6 (2004): 203–22.
Ellerman, Evelyn. "Hounds of Notre Dame Commentary." *Canadian Film Online*, nd. http://film.athabascau.ca/commentary/hounds-notre-dame-comentary (accessed September 10, 2012).
Elmwood, Victoria A. "'Just Some Bum from the Neighborhood': The Resolution of Post-Civil Rights Tension and Heavyweight Public Sphere Discourse in *Rocky* (1976)." *Film & History* 35, no. 2 (2005): 49–59.
Eskenazi, Gerald. "Americans Tie Swedes, 2–2, on Goal in Last 27 Seconds." *New York Times*, February 13, 1980.
———. "The Balance of Power: Ice Hockey." *New York Times.* February 10, 1980.
———. "U.S. Hockey Squad Captures Gold Medal." *New York Times.* February 25, 1980.
———. "U.S. Hockey Using Its Youth Well." *New York Times*, February 18, 1980.
Evenden, Matthew. "The Northern Vision of Harold Innis." *Journal of Canadian Studies* 34, no. 3 (1999): 162–86.
Everett, Wendy. "Lost in Transition: The European Road Movie, or a Genre 'Adrift in the Cosmos.'" *Literature/Film Quarterly* 37, no. 3 (2009): 165–75.
Eyman, Scott. *John Wayne: The Life and Legend.* New York: Simon & Schuster, 2014.
Farber, Michael. "Canada's Leader on Canada's Game." *Sports Illustrated*, February 8, 2010. http://sportsillustrated.cnn.com/vault/article/magazine/MAG1165562/index.htm?eref=sisf (accessed February 9, 2010).
Felske, Lorry W., and Beverly Rasporich. "Challenging Frontiers." In *Challenging Frontiers: The Canadian West*, edited by Lorry W. Felske and Beverly Jean Rasporich, 1–11. Calgary: University of Calgary Press, 2004.
Findlay, Hilary A. "Violence in Sport: Policy Consideration for the Amateur Sport Organization." Paper presented at the Symposium "Sports Management: Cutting Edge Strategies for Managing Sports as a Business" Toronto: Centre for Sport and Law, Inc. August 2002. http://www.sportlaw.ca/articles/other/article9.html (accessed May 10, 2006).
Finn, Robin. "Triumph Opened Doors." *New York Times*, February 19, 1990.
Fiske, John. *Understanding Popular Culture.* 2nd ed. New York: Routledge, 2010.
Fitzpatrick, Jamie. "Miracle on Ice: The Legacy." *About.com.* (n/d) http://proicehockey.about.com/cs/miracleonice/a/miracle_legacy.htm (accessed June 12, 2006).
Fitzpatrick, Kathleen. "Network: The Other Cold War." *Film & History* 31, no. 2 (2001): 33–9.
Fitzsimmons, Ernie. "Early Pro Leagues." In *Total Hockey*, edited by Dan Diamond, 32–6. 2nd ed. Scarborough, Ontario: Total Sports Publishing, 2000.
Flannery, Tim. *The Eternal Frontier: An Ecological History of North America and Its Peoples.* New York: Atlantic Monthly Press, 2001.
Fleras, Augie. *The Media Gaze: Representations of Diversities in Canada.* Vancouver, B.C.: UBC Press, 2011.
———, and Shane Michael Dixon. "Cutting, Driving, Digging, and Harvesting: Re-Masculinizing the Working-Class Heroic." *Canadian Journal of Communications* 36 (2011): 579–597.
Fletcher, Frederick. "Media and Political Identity: Canada and Quebec in the Era of Globalization." *Canadian Journal of Communication* 23, no. 3 (1998): http://www.cjconline.ca/index.php/journal/article/viewArticle/1049/955.
Fothergill, Robert. "Coward, Bully, or Clown: The Dream Life of a Younger Brother." Reprinted in *The Canadian Film Reader*, edited by Seth Feldman and Joyce Nelson, 234–250. Toronto: Peter Martin Associates, 1977.
Fowler, Roger. *Language in the News: Discourse and Ideology in the Press.* New York: Routledge, 1993.
Fox, Rachel. "He Shoots, He Scores: Michael Dowse and Jay Baruchel Talk Goon and the Canadian Conundrum, February 23, 2012." http://gordonandthewhale.com/he-shoots-he-scores-michael-dowse-and-jay-baruchel-talk-goon-and-the-canadian-conundrum/ (accessed April 7, 2012).
Francaviglia, Richard. "Walt Disney's Frontierland as an Allegorical Map of the American West." *Western Historical Quarterly* 30, no. 2 (1999): 155–82.
Francis, R. Douglas. "Regionalism, Landscape, and Identity in the Prairie West." In *Challenging Frontiers: The*

Canadian West, edited by Lorry W. Felske and Beverly Jean Rasporich, 24–49. Calgary: University of Calgary Press, 2004.

Freda, Isabelle. "*Survivors* in the *West Wing*: 9/11 and the United States of Emergency." In *Film and Television After 9/11,* edited by Wheeler Winston Dixon, 226–44. Carbondale: Southern Illinois University Press, 2004.

Freitag, Gina, and André Loiselle. "Tales of Terror in Quebec Popular Cinema: The Rise of the French-Language Horror Film Since 2000." *American Review of Canadian Studies* 43, no. 2 (2013): 190–203.

Friedman, Herb. "The Death Card." http://www.psywarrior.com/DeathCardsAce.html (accessed February 17, 2012).

Friedrichsen, Mike. "The Problems of Measuring Suspense." In *Suspense: Conceptualizations, Theoretical Analyses, and Empirical Explorations,* edited by Peter Vorderer, Hans J. Wulff, and Mike Friedrichsen, 329–346. Mahwah, NJ: Lawrence Erlbaum Associates, 1996.

Frye, Northrop. *The Bush Garden: Essays on the Canadian Imagination.* Toronto: Anansi, 1971.

Fuller, Linda K. "We Can't Duck the Issue: Imbedded Advertising in the Motion Pictures." In *Undressing the Ad: Reading Culture in Advertising,* edited by Katherine Toland Firth, 109–29. New York: Peter Lang, 1998.

Furedi, Frank. "The Children Who Won't Grow Up." *Spiked Online,* July 29, 2003. http://www.spiked-online.com/Articles/00000006DE8D.htm (accessed April 14, 2013).

Fürsich, Elfriede. "In Defense of Textual Analysis: Restoring a Challenged Method for Journalism and Media Studies." *Journalism Studies* 10, no. 2 (2009): 238–252.

Gasher, Mike. *Hollywood North: The Feature Film Industry in British Columbia.* Vancouver, B.C.: University of British Columbia Press, 2002.

Gee, Sara. "Mediating Sport, Myth, and Masculinity: The National Hockey League's 'Inside the Warrior' Advertising Campaign." *Sociology of Sport Journal* 26 (2009): 578–98.

Gehring, Wes D. "Black Humor." In *Handbook of American Film Genres,* edited by Wes D. Gehring, 167–187. New York: Greenwood Press, 1988.

———. "Clown Comedy." In *Handbook of American Film Genres,* edited by Wes D. Gehring, 189–143. New York: Greenwood Press, 1988.

———. "Populist Comedy." In *Handbook of American Film Genres,* edited by Wes D. Gehring, 125–208. New York: Greenwood Press, 1988.

Gerson, Jeffrey. "Women Coaches in Canadian and American College Ice Hockey: An Oral History." Paper presented at the Hockey Conference "Putting It on Ice IV: Visioning and Re-Visioning Hockey's Arena." London, Ontario, June 18–20, 2014.

Gidén, Carl, Patrick Houda, and Jean-Patrice Martel. *On the Origin of Hockey.* Stockholm and Chambly: Hockey Origin Publishing, 2014.

Gillespie, Nick. "The New Cold War: American Cultural Identity After September 11." *Reason Magazine,* December 2001. http://www.reason.com/news/show/ 28239.html.

Gillmor, Don. "Hockey: The Great Literary Shutout." *The Walrus* 2, no. 1 (2005): 88–93.

Giroux, Henry A. "Animating Youth: The Disneyfication of Children's Culture." *Socialist Review* 38 (1995): 23–55.

———. *The Mouse That Roared: Disney and the End of Innocence.* Lanham, Maryland: Rowman & Littlefield Publishers, 2001.

Gittings, Christopher E. *Canadian National Cinema—Ideology, Difference and Representation.* New York: Routledge, 2002.

Glassman, Marc. "Don Truckey Scores Again." *Writers Guild of Canada,* Spring 2004. http://www.writersguildofcanada.com/magazine/articles/truckey.html (accessed March 10, 2006).

The Globe and Mail. "Jay Baruchel Talks About Goon." *The Globe and Mail.* CP Video. February 24, 2012. http://www.theglobeandmail.com/arts/arts-video/video-jay-baruchel-talks-about-goon/article548791/ (accessed February 28, 2012).

Gouge, Catherine. "The American Frontier: History, Rhetoric, Concept." *Americana: The Journal of American Popular Culture* (1900–present) 6, no. 1 (Spring 2007): http://www.americanpopularculture.com/journal/articles/spring_2007/gouge.htm.

Graveland, Bill. "White Collar Workers Replacing Traditional Blue Collar Fans in NHL." *Canadian Press,* October 30, 2003. http://www.canada.com/components/printstory/printstory.asp?id=6EA434F3-8899-4E11-93C0-547F8756F241 (accessed October 31, 2003).

Greene. Eric. *Planet of the Apes as American Myth.* Hanover, New Hampshire: Wesleyan University Press, 1998.

Groen, Rick. "TIFF's High-Shticking Breakaway." *The Globe and Mail,* September 3, 2010. http://www.theglobeandmail.com/arts/awards-and-festivals/tiff/tiffs-high-shticking-breakaway/article1379451/ (accessed April 8, 2012).

Grohmann, Karolos. "Take Medals Monkey Off Our Back, VANOC Urges Athletes." *Reuters.* February 9, 2010. http://www.canada.com/sports/2010wintergames/Take+medals+monkey+back+VANOC+urges+athletes/2541556/story.html (accessed February 9, 2010).

Gruneau, Richard and David Whitson. *Hockey Night in Canada: Sport, Identities and Cultural Politics.* Toronto: Garamond Press, 1993.

———. "Upmarket Continentalism." In *Continental Order? Integrating North America for Cybercapitalism,* edited by Vincent Mosco and Dan Schiller, 235–64. Lanham, Maryland: Rowman and Littlefield Publishers, Inc., 2001.

———, eds. "Introduction." *Artificial Ice: Hockey, Culture and Commerce,* 1–25. Toronto, Ontario: Broadview Press, 2006.

Gumpert, Gary. "The Wrinkle Theory: The Deconsecration of the Hero." In *American Heroes in a Media Age,* edited by Susan J. Drucker and Robert S. Cathcart, 62–81. New York: Hampton Press, 1994.

Gunning, John. "The Cinema of Attraction: Early Film, Its Spectator and the Avant-Garde." *Wide Angle* 6.2 (1986): 63–70.

Guttmann, Allen. "The Appeal of Violent Sports." In *Why We Watch: The Attractions of Violent Entertainment,* edited by J.H. Goldstein, 7–26. New York: Oxford Univ. Press, 1998.

Haraway, Donna. *Primate Visions: Gender, Race, and Nature in the World of Modern Science.* New York: Routledge, Chapman & Hall, 1989.

Harcourt, Peter. "Speculations on Canadian Cinema." *Queen's Quarterly* 111, no. 2 (2004): 237–51. http://findarticles.com/p/articles/mi_hb4957/is_200406/ai_n18142058/ (accessed December 18, 2007).

Hardy, Stephen. "Long Before Orr." In *The Rock, the Curse, and the Hub: A Random History of Boston Sports,* edited by Randy Roberts, 245–272. Cambridge, Massachusetts: Harvard University Press, 2005.

———. "Miracle." Reviews of Books and Films. *American Historical Review* 109, no. 3 (2004): 943–4.

Hargreaves, John. "The Body, Sport and Power Relations." In *Sport, Leisure and Social Relations, Sociological Review Monograph 33,* edited by John Home, David Jary, and Alan Tomlinson, 139–59. London: Routledge and Kegan Paul, 1986.

Harrison, Dick, ed. *Unnamed Country: The Struggle for a Canadian Prairie Fiction.* Edmonton: University of Alberta Press, 1977.

Harrison, Richard. "Canadian Iliad: The Summit Series as Canadian Epic Poem." In *Coming Down the Mountain: Rethinking the 1972 Summit Series,* edited by Brian Kennedy. Hamilton, ON: Wolsak and Wynn, 2014: 65–90.

———. "Hockey as Canadian Tragic Theatre—And Slap Shot as Comedy's Reply." Paper presented at the Hockey Conference "Putting It on Ice Iv: Visioning and Re-Visioning Hockey's Arena." London, Ontario, June 18–20, 2014.

Harvey, Jean. "Whose Sweater Is This? The Changing Meanings of Hockey in Quebec." In *Artificial Ice: Hockey, Culture and Commerce,* edited by Richard Gruneau and David Whitson, 29–52. Peterborough, Ontario: Broadview Press, 2006.

———, Geneviève Rail, and Lucie Thibault. "Globalization and Sport: Sketching a Theoretical Model for Empirical Analyses." *Journal of Sport and Social Issues* 20, no. 3 (1996): 258–77.

Hays, Matthew. "Drôle Patrol. *Bon Cop, Bad Cop* Attempts to Unite Canada—In Laughter." *CBCnews.ca,* August 17, 2006. http://www.cbc.ca/arts/film/boncop.html (accessed June 8, 2011).

———. "Shooting for a Hat Trick: Director Louis Saïa on the Eagerly Anticipated Les Boys 3." *Montreal Mirror,* November 21, 2001. http://www.montrealmirror.com/archives/2001/112901/film4.html (accessed March 15, 2006).

———. "TV Nation: The Answer to English-Canadian Cinema's Woes? The Boob Tube, of Course (Pov)." *TAKE ONE,* December 4, 2004. http://www.accessmylibrary.com/coms2/summary_0286-18386265_ITM.

Hayward, Susan. "Framing National Cinemas." In *Cinema and Nation,* edited by Mette Hjort and Scott Mackenzie, 88–101. New York: Routledge, 2000.

Hedley, Tom. "Colossus from the North." In *Documents in Canadian Film,* edited by Douglas Fetherling, 204–214. Peterborough, Ontario: Broadview Press, 1988.

Helfield, Gillian. "Cultivateurs d'images: Albert Tessier and the Rural Tradition in Québécois Cinema." In *Representing the Rural: Space, Place, and Identity in Films About the Land,* edited by Catherine Fowler and Gillian Helfield, 48–64. Detroit: Wayne State University Press, 2006.

Helstein, Michelle. "Producing the Canadian Female Athlete: Negotiating the Popular Logics of Sport and Citizenship." *How Canadians Communicate III: Contexts of Canadian Popular Culture,* edited by Bart Beaty, Derek Briton, Gloria Filax, and Rebecca Sullivan, 241–258. Edmonton, Alberta: Athabasca University Press, 2010.

Henderson, Paul. *How Hockey Explains Canada: The Sport That Defines a Country.* With Jim Prime. Chicago: Triumph, 2001.

Hewitt, Michael. "Best Picture? Says Who?" *The Orange County Register,* February 23, 2013. http://www.nbcnews.com/id/50917358/ns/local_news-orange_county_ca/t/best-picture-says-who/.

Hewlett, Sylvia A. "A Final Push Can Break the Glass Ceiling." *The Financial Times,* November 16, 2010. http://www.fit.com/cms/s/0/186d2054-f1ba-11df-bb5a-00144feab49a.html#axzz1CHZ4X79W (accessed December 2, 2010).

Higson, Andrew. *Waving the Flag: Constructing a National Cinema in Britain,* Gloucestershire: Clarendon Press, 1997.
The History Commons. "Context of 'After September 11, 2001': Rove, White House Officials Press Entertainment Executives to Produce Government Propaganda,'" n.d., http://www.historycommons.org/context.jsp?item=a91101govtpropaganda (accessed February 8, 2010).
Hockey Canada. "Registration Report." Calgary, 2003.
The Hockey News. "TV Networks Adopt Wait and See Attitude." March 14, 1980.
_____. "USA Wins Gold!" March 7, 1980.
Hollands, Robert, G. "English-Canadian Sports Novels and Cultural Production." In *Not Just a Game: Essays in Canadian Sports Sociology,* edited by Jean Harvey and Hart Cantelon, 213–26. Ottawa: University of Ottawa Press, 1998.
_____. "Masculinity and the Positive Hero in Canadian Sports Novels." *Arete* IV, no. 1 (1986): 73–84.
Holman, Andrew. "Introduction." In *Canada's Game and Identity,* edited by Andrew Holman, 3–8. Montreal and Kingston: McGill-Queen's University Press, 2009.
_____. "Playing in the Neutral Zone: Meanings and Uses of Ice Hockey in the Canada–U.S. Borderlands, 1895–1915." *The American Review of Canadian Studies* 34, No. 1 (2004): 33–57.
_____. "Les Russes et nous: The 1972 Summit Series and the Birth of Hockey Sovereignty in Quebec." In *Coming Down the Mountain: Rethinking the 1972 Summit Series,* edited by Brian Kennedy, 109–125. Hamilton, ON: Wolsak and Wynn, 2014.
Hopkins, Jeff. "Mapping of Cinematic Places, Icons, Ideology, and the Power of (Mis)Representation." *Place, Power, Situation and Spectacle: A Geography of Film,* edited by Stuart C. Aitken and Leo E. Zonn, 47–68. Lanham, Maryland: Rowman and Littlefield, 1994.
Horne, Gerald, S. "Interpreting Prairie Cinema." *Prairie Forum, the Journal of the Canadian Plains Research Center* 22, no. 2 (Fall 1997): 131–151. http://members.shaw.ca/horne/prairiecinema.html (accessed October 12, 2011).
Houle, Michel. "Quelques aspects idéologiques and thématiques du cinema Québécois." In *Les Cinémas Canadiens,* edited by Pierre Lhermier, 150–152. Montreal: La Cinématèque québécoise, 1978.
_____. "Themes and Ideology in Quebec Cinema." *Jump Cut: A Review of Contemporary Media* 22 (1980): 9–14. http://www.ejumpcut.org/archive/onlinessays/JC22folder/QuebecFilm.html#6.
Houston, William. "Summit Series Movie Doesn't Paint Rosy Picture." *The Globe and Mail,* March 21, 2006.
Hughes-Fuller, Patricia. "'Am I Canadian?' Hockey as 'National' Culture." In *Culture and the State: Nationalisms,* edited by James Gifford & Gabrielle Zezulka-Mailloux, 25–39. Edmonton, Alberta: University of Alberta Press, 2002. http://www.arts.ualberta.ca/cms/ hughes.pdf.
_____. "The Good Old Game: Hockey, Nostalgia, Identity." Edmonton, AB: unpublished doctoral dissertation, 2002.
Hunt, Patricia. "North American Pastoral: Contrasting Images of the Garden in Canadian and American Literature." *American Studies* 23, no. 1 (Spring 1982): 39–68. https://journals.ku.edu/index.php/amerstud/article/viewFile/2614/2573 (accessed October 12, 2012).
Ice Hockey World Special. "Ice Hockey Films." 60th Anniversary Edition. December 1995: 1–36.
Ingram, David. *Green Screen: Environmentalism and Hollywood Cinema.* Devon: University of Exeter Press, 2000.
Innis, Harold E. *The Strategy of Culture.* Toronto: University of Toronto Press, 1952.
Jackson, Steven. "Gretzky, Crisis, and Canadian Identity in 1988: Rearticulating the Americanization of Culture Debate." *Sociology of Sport Journal* 11 (1994): 428–446.
_____."Sport, Crisis, and Canadian Identity in 1988: A Cultural Analysis." Urbana, IL: unpublished doctoral dissertation, 1992.
Jeffords, Susan. "Can Masculinity Be Terminated?" In *Screening the Male: Exploring Masculinities in the Hollywood Cinema,* edited by Steven Cohan and Ina Rae Hark, 245–62. London: Routledge, 1993.
Jeffrey, Liss, assisted by Fraser McAninch. "Private Television and Cable." In *The Cultural Industries in Canada: Problems, Policies, and Prospects,* edited by Michael Dorland, 206–56. Toronto: James Lorimer, 1996.
Jenish, D'Arcy. *The Montreal Canadiens: 100 Years Of Glory.* Toronto: Anchor Canada, 2009.
Johnson, Brian. "English Canadian Films: Why No One Sees Them." *Maclean's Magazine,* April 17, 2006. http://www.thecanadianencyclopedia.com/index.cfm?PgNm=TCE&Params=M1ARTM0012964 (accessed May 4, 2007).
Johnston, Chris. "Hanson Brothers Return for Slap Shot 3 Movie." *The Canadian Press,* November 25, 2008. http://www.thestar.com/entertainment/movies/article/542905—hanson-brothers-return-for-slap-slap_shot_3_movie.html (accessed April 18, 2012).
Jokisipilä, Markku. "Maple Leaf, Hammer, and Sickle: International Ice Hockey During the Cold War." *Sport History Review* 37 (2006): 36–53.
Jones, Glen. "In Praise of an 'Invisible Genre'? An Ambivalent Look at the Fictional Sports Feature Film." *Sport in Society* 11, no. 2 (2008): 117–129.

Jones, Landon Y. *Great Expectations: America and the Baby Boom Generation*. New York: Coward McCann and Geohegen, 1980.
Joukova, Marina. "Players Didn't Know They Were to Make History." *Faceoff.com*. August 25, 2002. http://www.faceoff.com/news/20020825/020825117177.html (accessed February 20, 2002).
Kashmere, Brett. "Lessons from *Valery's Ankle*." In *Coming Down the Mountain: Rethinking the 1972 Summit Series*, edited by Brian Kennedy, 239–256. Hamilton, ON: Wolsak and Wynn, 2014.
———. *Valery's Ankle*. Video Pool, 2006. http://www.videopool.org.
———. "*Valery's Ankle*: Supporting Documents and Notation." MFA written thesis, Concordia University, 2006.
Katerberg, William H. "A Northern Vision: Frontiers and the West in the Canadian and American Imagination." *The American Review of Canadian Studies* 33, no. 4 (2003): 543–64.
Katz, Sidney. "The Richard Hockey Riot." *Maclean's*. September 17, 1955. Reprinted in "Maurice 'Rocket' Richard. Three Perspectives on Hockey's Most Electrifying Performer." In *Total Hockey*, edited by Dan Diamond, 157–164. 2nd ed. Scarborough, Ontario: Total Sports Publishing, 2000.
Kaye, Janice. "Certain Tendencies in Canadian Cinema: Temporary Insanity and the National Tax-Shelter Masquerade." Los Angeles, CA: unpublished doctoral dissertation, 2007.
———. "*Perfectly Normal*, Eh? Gender Transformation and National Identity in Canada." *Canadian Journal of Film Studies* 3, no. 2 (1994): 63–80.
Kennan, George. "The Sources of Soviet Conduct.'" *Foreign Affairs* 25, no. 4 (1947): 566–82.
Kennedy, Brian. "Confronting a Compelling Other and the Nostalgic (Trans)Formation of Canadian Identity." In *Canada's Game*, edited by Andrew Holman, 44–62. Montreal: McGill-Queen's University Press, 2009.
———. *My Country Is Hockey: How Hockey Explains Canadian Culture, History, Politics, French-English Rivalry and Who We Are as Canadians*. Edmonton, AB: Argenta, 2011.
———. "Unintentional Epic: Ken Dryden's Struggle with Words and the Myth of Team Canada." In *Coming Down the Mountain: Rethinking the 1972 Summit Series*, edited by Brian Kennedy, 257–276. Hamilton, ON: Wolsak and Wynn, 2014.
———. "Whatever Happened to the Organ and the Portrait of Her Majesty? NHL Spectating as Imaginary Carnival." In *Now Is the Winter*, edited by Jamie Dopp and Richard Harrison, 155–169. Hamilton, Ontario: Wolsak and Wynn, 2009.
Khouri, Malek, and Darell Varga, eds. "Introduction." *Representations of the Working Class in Canadian Cinema*, 3–21. Toronto: University of Toronto Press, 2006.
Kibby, Marjorie D. "Nostalgia for the Masculine: Onward to the Past in the Sports Films of the Eighties." *Canadian Journal of Film Studies* 7, no.1 (1988): 16–28.
Kidd, Bruce, and John McFarlane. *The Death of Hockey*. Toronto: New Press, 1972.
Kimmel, Michael. "Globalization and Its Mal(E)Contents: The Gendered Moral and Political Economy of Terrorism." In *Handbook of Studies on Men and Masculinities*, edited by Michael Kimmel, Jeff Hearn, and R.W. Connell, 414–31. London: Sage Publications, 2005.
Kindred, Dave. "Born to Be Players, Born to the Moment." *The Washington Post*, February 23, 1980.
King, Geoff. 2002. *New Hollywood Cinema: An Introduction*. New York: Columbia University Press, 2002.
King, Richard C., and David J. Leonard. *Visual Economies Of/In Motion: Sport and Film*. New York: Peter Lang, 2006.
Knelman, Martin. *This Is Where We Came In: The Career and Character of Canadian Film*. Toronto: McClelland and Stewart, 1977.
Knight, Bill. "New Ice Age: Canada's Sport Making Strides South of the Border." *Seattle Post-Intelligencer*, May 31, 1994.
Koentges, Chris. "The Oracle of Finnish Hockey: How a 70-Year-Old Finnish Goalie Coach Is Transforming a Global Sport." *The Atlantic*, March 2014, http://www.theatlantic.com/magazine/archive/2014/03/the-puck-stops-here/357579/ (accessed April 20, 2014).
Kollin, Susan. *Nature's State: Imagining Alaska as the Last Frontier*. Chapel Hill: University of North Carolina Press, 2001.
Kotylo, Len. "The Roots of Hockey's International Appeal." Paper presented at the International Conference on "Canada & the League of Hockey Nations." Victoria, B.C., April 19–21, 2007.
Kramer, Staci D. "Hockey's TV Message Still Mixed." *Multichannel News* 20, no. 22 (May 24, 1999): 38.
Kubyshkin, Alexander. "Hot Ice During Cold War: Soviet Reflections on Summit Series 1972." In *Coming Down the Mountain: Rethinking the 1972 Summit Series*, edited by Brian Kennedy, 179–190. Hamilton, ON: Wolsak and Wynn, 2014).
Laberge Suzanne, and Mathieu, Albert. "Conceptions of Masculinity and of Gender Transgressions in Sport Among Adolescent Boys: Hegemony, Contestation, and Social Class Dynamic." *Men and Masculinities* 1, no. 3 (1999): 243–267.
Landau, Misia. "Human Evolution as Narrative." *American Scientist* 72 (1984): 262–268.
Landrum, Jason. "Rethinking Genre Theory." *The Journal of Cinema and Media* 48, no. 1 (2007): 109–111.

Leach, Jim. *Film in Canada*. New York: Oxford University Press, 2010.
Leathers, Kyle. "'Goon,' 'Hit Somebody' Two Upcoming Hockey Movies to Watch For." *NESN.com*, November 8, 2010. http://nesn.com/2010/11/goon-hit-somebody-two-upcoming-hockey-movies-to-watch-for/ (accessed November 21, 2010).
Leeden, Michael. "Standing Up to the Russian Bear." *The Reader's Digest* 116, no. 696 (1980): 72–3.
Legaré, André. "Nunavut: The Construction of a Regional Collective Identity in the Canadian Arctic." *Wicazo Sa Review* 17, no. 2 (2002): 65–89.
Legrand, Bill. "Those Old Montreal Maroons." In *The Montreal Canadiens: A Hockey Dynasty*, edited by Claude Mouton, 13–22. Toronto: Van Nostrand Reinhold, 1980.
Lehman, Richard. "Do the Young People Still Believe? The Rise and Shift of Mythic Tradition." In *Coming Down the Mountain: Rethinking the 1972 Summit Series*, edited by Brian Kennedy, 303–309. Hamilton, ON: Wolsak and Wynn, 2014.
Lepage-Boily, Elizabeth. "Il était une fois Les Boys: La critique dure à assumer." *Cinoche.com: La référence cinéma au Québec*. December 5, 2013. http://www.cinoche.com/films/il-etait-une-fois-les-boys/critiques/la-critique-dure-a-assumer.html (accessed 15 September 2015).
Lethert, Patrick. "NCAA Hockey Today." In *Total Hockey*, edited by Dan Diamond, 98–100. 2nd ed. Scarborough, Ontario: Total Sports Publishing, 2000.
Lever, Yves. *Histoire générale du cinéma au Québec*. Montréal: Boreal, 1995.
Levin, Gary. "Disney Finds Place for Tweens. TV Channel Relies on Wholesome Content." *USA Today*, October 27, 2005.
Lewis, Jon. "The End of Cinema as We Know It and I Feel…: An Introduction to a Book on Nineties American Film." In *The End of Cinema as We Know It: American Film in the Nineties*, edited by Jon Lewis, 1–8. New York: New York University Press, 2001.
———. "Movies and Growing Up .. Absurd." In *American Cinema of the 1950s: Themes and Variations*, edited by Murray Pomerance, 134–54. New Jersey and London: Rutgers University Press, 2005.
Limerick, Patricia Nelson. "The Adventures of the Frontier in the Twentieth Century." In *The Frontier in American Culture*, edited by James R. Grossman, 67–102. Berkeley: University of California Press, 1994.
Lipsky, Richard. *How We Play the Game*. Boston: Beacon Press, 1981.
Loiselle, André. *Cinema as History: Michel Brault and Modern Quebec*. Toronto: Toronto International Festival Group, 2007.
———. "The Decline … and the Rise of English Canada's Quebec Cinema." In *Self Portraits: The Cinemas of Canada Since Telefilm*, edited by André Loiselle and Tom McSorley, 55–92. Ottawa: The Canadian Film Institute, 2006.
———. "Look Like a Worker and Act Like a Worker: Stereotypical Representations of the Working Class in Quebec Fiction Feature Films." In *Working on Screen: Representations of the Working Class in Canadian Cinema*, edited by Malek Khouri and Darrell Varga, 207–34. Toronto: University of Toronto Press, 2006.
———. "Popular Genres in Quebec Cinema: The Strange Case of Horror in Film and Television." In *How Canadians Communicate III: Contexts of Canadian Popular Culture*, edited by Bart Beaty, Derek Briton, Gloria Filax, and Rebecca Sullivan, 141–159. Edmonton, Alberta: Athabasca University Press, 2010.
———. "Subtly Subversive or Simply Stupid: Notes on Popular Quebec Cinema." *Post Script-Jacksonville* 18, no. 2 (Winter/Spring 1998): 75–84.
Lopata, Jim. "The Bruins' Shawn Thornton Talks About What If a Teammate Was Gay." *The Boston Globe*, April 11, 2012. http://www.boston.com/lifestyle/blogs/bostonspirit/2012/04/the_bruins_shawn_thornton_talk.html (accessed May 15, 2012).
Lorenz, Stacy L., and Geraint B. Osborne. "Brutal Butchery, Strenuous Spectacle: Hockey Violence, Manhood, and the 1907 Season." Paper presented at the North American Society for Sports History (NASSH) Thirty-Third Annual Convention, Green Bay, Wisconsin, May 27–30, 2005.
———. "'Talk About Strenuous Hockey': Violence, Manhood, and the 1907 Ottawa Silver Seven-Montreal Wanderer Rivalry." *Journal of Canadian Studies* 40, No. 1 (2006): 125–56.
Lowe, Patrick. "Paperback Hero." *Canuxploitation! Your Complete Guide to Canadian B-Film*, nd. http://www.canuxploitation.com/review/paperbackhero.html (accessed February 10, 2008).
Lundstrom, Jim. "'Friends' Hockey Film Puts Wisconsin Up Front." *Appleton Post-Crescent*, April 19, 2004. http://nosleepthemovie.com/lundstrom.html (accessed April 20, 2006).
Lyden, John C. *Film as Religion: Myths, Morals, and Rituals*. New York: New York University Press, 2003.
MacDonald, Gayle. "Offside: Why Can't English Canada Make a Hockey Film That Scores at the Box Office?" *The Globe and Mail*, November 12, 2010. http://m.theglobeandmail.com/arts/film/offside-why-cant-english-canada-make-a-hockey-film-that-scores-at-the-box-office/article1314011/.
———. "With Breakaway, Rob Lowe Continues His Search for the Canadian Identity." *The Globe and Mail*, September 28, 2011. http://www.theglobeandmail.com/news/arts/movies/with-breakaway-rob-lowe-continues-his-search-for-the-canadian-identity/article2182177/ (accessed April 19, 2012).
MacFarlane, Brian. *The Habs*. Toronto: Stoddart, 1996.

MacGregor, Roy. *The Last Season.* Toronto: Macmillan, 1983.
Machnik, Mike. "College Hockey News: 1972 Silver Medal Team Gathers to Launch Book, Celebrate Accomplishment." *College Hockey News,* February 16, 2006. http://www.collegehockeynews.com/news/2006/02/16_striking.php.
Mackenzie, Scott. *Screening Quebec: Québécois Moving Images, National Identity, and the Public Sphere.* Manchester: Manchester University Press, 2004.
Mackey, Eva. *The House of Difference: Cultural Politics and National Identity in Canada.* Toronto: University of Toronto Press, 2002.
Maclean's Magazine. "The Interview: Gary Bettman. NHL Commissioner Gary Bettman on Canada, the 'Covenant' with Fans, Gretzky and on Trying to Do the Right Things." November 17, 2009. http://www2.macleans.ca/2009/11/17/the-interview-gary-bettman/ (accessed Dec. 10, 2010).
MacNeill, Margaret. "Networks: Producing Olympic Ice Hockey for a National Television Audience." *Sociology of Sport Journal* 3 (1996): 103–124.
MacSkimming, Roy. *Cold War: The Amazing Canada-Soviet Hockey Series of 1972.* Vancouver, B.C.: Greystone Books, 1996.
Maguire, Joseph. "Blade Runners: Canadian Migrants, Ice Hockey, and the Global Process." *Journal of Sport and Social Issues* 20, no. 3 (1996): 335–60.
———. "Sport, Identity Politics, and Globalization: Diminishing Contrasts and Increasing Varieties." *Sociology of Sport Journal* 11 (1994): 398–427. Reprinted in *Globalization: Critical Concepts in Sociology,* edited by Roland Robertson and Kathleen E. White, 295–329. London: Routledge, 2002.
Maich, Steve. "Why the Leafs Stink." *Macleans.ca,* April 2, 2008. http://www.macleans.ca/canada/national/article.jsp?content=20080402_25296_25296&page=1 (accessed May 10, 2011).
Mandel, Eli. "Images of Prairie Man. In *A Region of the Mind: Interpreting the Western Canadian Plains,* edited by Richard Allen, 201–9. Regina: Canadian Plains Research Centre, 1973.
Mangan, J.A. and James, Walvin. *Manliness and Morality: Masculinity in Britain and America 1800–1940.* Manchester: Manchester University Press, 1987.
Marsh, Margaret. "Suburban Men and Masculine Domesticity, 1870–1915." *American Quarterly* 40, no. 2 (June 1988): 165–186.
Marshall, Bill. *Quebec National Cinema.* Montreal and Kingston: McGill-Queen's University Press, 2001.
Martelle, Scott. "As fiction fodder, ice hockey's not a natural." *Los Angeles Times,* May 28, 2003. http://articles.latimes.com/2003/may/28/entertainment/et-martelle28.
Martin, Brian. "Cultural Formations, North America." In *International Encyclopedia of Men and Masculinities,* edited by Michael Flood, Judith Kegan Gardiner, Bob Pease, and Keith Pringle, 113–17. New York: Routledge, 2007.
Martin, Lawrence. *The Red Machine.* Toronto: Doubleday Canada Limited, 1990.
Mason, Daniel S. "Expanding the Footprint? Questioning the NHL's Expansion and Relocation Strategy." In *Artificial Ice: Hockey, Culture and Commerce,* edited by Richard Gruneau and David Whitson, 181–200. Peterborough Ontario: Broadview Press, 2006.
———. "'Get the Puck Outta Here!' Media Transnationalism and Canadian Identity." *Journal of Sport and Social Issues* 26, no. 2 (2002): 140–67.
———, and Gregory H. Duquette. "Newspaper Coverage of Early Professional Hockey: The Discourses of Class and Control." *Media History* 10, no. 3 (2004): 157–73.
Mayer, Tamar. "Gender Ironies of Nationalism: Setting the Stage." *Gender Ironies of Nationalism: Sexing the Nation,* edited by Tamar Mayer, 1–24. New York: Routledge, 2000.
McArdle, David. *From Boot Money to Bosman: Football, Society and the Law.* London: Cavendish Publishing Limited, 2000.
McBride, James. *War, Battering and Other Sports: The Gulf Between American Men and Women.* Atlantic Highlands, New Jersey: Humanities Press, 1995.
McCallum, Jack. "Reel Sports: Hollywood Trends Come and Go, but Sports Movies—Clichéd, Corny, Sometimes Downright Comical—Are Never Out of Fashion. Just Don't Call Them Sports Movies." *Sports Illustrated,* February 5, 2001.
McCartney, Andra. "Sounding Places: Situated Conversations Through the Soundscape Compositions of Hildegard Westerkamp." Toronto, ON: unpublished doctoral dissertation, 1999. http://beatrouteproductions.com/Andradiss.pdf.
McFarlane, Brian. *The Habs.* Toronto: Stoddart, 1996.
McGrath, Alister E. *Christianity's Dangerous Idea: The Protestant Revolution—A History from the Sixteenth Century to the Twenty-First.* New York: HarperOne, 2007.
McGrath, Charles. "The Game as It Should Be Played: On a Pond, in the Cold." *International Herald Tribune,* February 16, 2004.
———. "Pond Life." *Outside Magazine.* February 1997. Published online May 2, 2004. http://www.outsideonline.com/outdoor-adventure/Pond-Life.html?page=1 (accessed May 17, 2006).

———. "Rocking the Pond." *The New Yorker,* January 24, 1994.
McKay, Jim, Toby Miller, Geoffrey Lawrence, and David Rowe. *Globalization and Sport: Playing the World.* Thousand Oaks, CA: Sage Publications, 2001.
McKinley, Michael. *Hockey: A People's History.* Toronto: McClelland & Stewart, 2006.
McManus, Sheila. "Making the Forty-Ninth Parallel: How Canada and the United States Used Space, Race, and Gender to Turn Blackfoot Country into the Alberta-Montana Borderlands." In *One West, Two Myths: A Comparative Reader,* edited by Carol L. Higham and Robert Thacker, 109–32. Calgary: University of Calgary Press, 2004.
McNair, Brian. *Images of the Enemy: Reporting the New Cold War.* London: Routledge, 1988.
Meitzer, Bill. "Hockey World Remembers Marjamaki." *NHL.com,* May 30, 2012. http://www.nhl.com/ice/news.htm?id=633253 (accessed May 31, 2012).
Mellen, Joan. *Big Bad Wolves: Masculinity in the American Film.* New York: Pantheon Books, 1977.
Melnyk, George. *One Hundred Years of Canadian Cinema.* Toronto: University of Toronto Press, 2004.
———. "Reflections on Canadian Cinema." *American Review of Canadian Studies* 35, no. 1 (2005): 145–49.
Menon, Vinay. "The Wonderful, Unlivable Life of Don Cherry." *Moneyville.ca,* May 29, 2011. http://www.moneyville.ca/article/998677—the-wonderful-unlivable-life-of-don-cherry (accessed June 9, 2012).
Messner, Michael A. "Still a Man's World? Studying Masculinities in Sport." In *Handbook of Studies on Men and Masculinities,* edited by Michael Kimmel, Jeff Hearn, and R.W. Connell, 313–25. London: Sage Publications, 2005.
———. *Taking the Field: Women, Men, and Sports.* Minneapolis: University of Minnesota Press, 2002.
———, and Donald F. Sabo. *Sex, Violence and Power in Sports Rethinking Masculinity.* Freedom, CA: Crossing Press, 1994.
Meyrowitz, Joshua. "Multiple Media Literacies." *Journal of Communication* (Winter 1998): 96–108.
———. *No Sense of Place: The Impact of Electronic Media on Social Behavior.* New York: Oxford University Press, 1985.
Michator. "Il était une fois les Boys." *Cinémasculin: Paradis de l'action.* January 14, 2014. http://cinemasculin.com/?s=il+était+une+fois+les+Boys&searchsubmit.x=0&searchsubmit.y=0 (accessed 18 September 2015).
Miller, Mary Jane. *Turn Up the Contrast: CBC Television Drama Since 1952.* Vancouver, B.C.: University of British Columbia Press/CBC Enterprises, 1987.
Mirtle, James. "Did Hockey Kill Todd Ewen?" *The Globe and Mail,* October 29, 2015, http://www.theglobeandmail.com/sports/hockey/was-todd-ewens-death-caused-by-his-nhlcareer/article26987457/ (accessed October 30, 2015).
Monk, Katherine. *Weird Sex and Snowshoes: And Other Canadian Film Phenomena.* Vancouver, B.C.: Raincoast Books, 2001.
Morley, David, and Kevin Robins. "Spaces of Identity: Communications Technologies and Reconfiguration of Europe." *Screen* 30, no. 4 (1989): 10–35.
Morris, Peter. "In Our Own Eyes: The Canonizing of Canadian Film." *Canadian Journal of Film Studies* 3, no. 1 (1994: 27–44.
Morris, Wesley. "There's Little to Love in Myers's 'Guru.'" *The Boston Globe,* June 20, 2008 http://www.boston.com/ae/movies/articles/2008/06/20/theres_little_to_love_in_myerss_guru/ (accessed April 6, 2011).
Mosley, Leonard. *Disney's World: A Biography.* New York: Stein and Day, 1985.
Moss, Jane. "The Drama of Identity in Canada's Francophone West." *The American Review of Canadian Studies* 34, no. 1 (2004): 81–97.
Motley, Clay. "Fighting for Manhood: Rocky and Turn-Of-The-Century Antimodernism." *Film & History* 35, no. 2 (2005): 60–6.
Murphy, Austin. "The Hanson Brothers. Goons Forever." *Sports Illustrated,* July 16, 2007.
Murray, Catherine. "Wellsprings of Knowledge: Beyond the CBC Policy Trap." *Canadian Journal of Communication* 26, no. 1 (2001). http://www.cjc-online.ca/index.php/journal/article/viewArticle/1194/1132.
Murray, Rebecca. "Eddie Cahill and Jim Craig Talk About 'Miracle.'" *About.com.* January 26, 2004. http://movies.about.com/cs/miracle/a/mrclec012604.htm.
———. "Mike Myers Spreads Some Love with 'The Love Guru': Mike Myers Discusses the Origin of Guru Pitka." *About.com.* June 11, 2008. http://movies.about.com/od/theloveguru/a/lovegurumm61108.htm (accessed May 13, 2011).
Mybindi.com. "Breakaway Receives Rave Reviews on Parliament Hill." October 6, 2011. http://www.mybindi.com/articles/breakaway-receives-rave-reviews-on-parliament-hill (accessed April 30, 2012).
Nagel, Joane. "Nation." In *Handbook of Studies on Men and Masculinities.* Edited by Michael Kimmel, Jeff Hearn, and R.W. Connell, 397–413. London: Sage Publications, 2005.
Nash, Roderick Frazier. *Wilderness and the American Mind.* 4th ed. New Haven and London: Yale University Press, 2001.

Nasson, Tim. "'The Tooth Fairy': Behind the Scenes." *Wild About Movies.* http://www.wildaboutmovies.com/behind_the_scenes/thetoothfairy-behindthescenes/ (accessed March 11, 2012).

Neale, Stephen. *Genre.* London: British Film Institute, 1980.

———. "Masculinity as Spectacle." In *Screening the Male: Exploring Masculinities in the Hollywood Cinema,* edited by Steven Cohan and Ina Rae Hark, 9–19. London: Routledge, 1993.

Nemni, Max. "Forum: Canada in Crisis and the Destructive Power of Myth." *Queen's Quarterly* 99, no. 1 (1992): 222–39.

New, W.H. *Land Sliding: Imagining Space, Presence, and Power in Canadian Writing.* Toronto: University of Toronto Press, 1997.

Newman, Bruce. "Movie Review: Against All Odds: 'Miracle' Gets the Hockey—And Politics—Right." *Mercury News,* February 6, 2004. http://www.mercurynews.com/ mld/mercurynews/entertainment/eye/7889795.htm (accessed February 6, 2004).

Noble, David. *The End of American History: Democracy, Capitalism and the Metaphor of Two Worlds in Anglo-American Historical Writing, 1880–1980.* Minneapolis: University of Minnesota Press, 1985.

O'Connor, John J. "More Mileage from an Olympics Victory." *New York Times,* March 1, 1981. http://www.nytimes.com/1981/03/01/arts/tv-view-more-mileage-from-an-olympics-victory-by-john-jo-connor.html (accessed February 2, 2005).

Oliver, Joe. "Sports and Cinema: Experts Discuss What Works on Screen, at Box Office." *SportsBusiness Journal,* March 1–7, 2002.

Olsen, Mark. "Indie Focus: 'Goon' Is a Hockey Comedy for 'Canadian Kids.'" *Los Angeles Times,* March 25, 2012. http://articles.latimes.com/2012/mar/25/entertainment/la-ca-indie-focus-20120325.

Olson, Scott Robert. *Hollywood Planet: Global Media and the Competitive Advantage of Narrative Transparency.* London: Routledge, 1999.

O'Malley, Terry. "Letter from the President." In "Father Athol Murray and the Hounds of Notre Dame." Introduction by Jerry W. Bird. http://www.airhighways.com/notre_dame.htm (accessed September 9, 2012).

Oriard, Michael. *Dreaming of Heroes: American Sports Fiction, 1868–1980.* Chicago: Nelson-Hall, 1982.

———. *Sporting with the Gods: The Rhetoric of Play and Game in American Culture.* Cambridge: Cambridge University Press, 1991.

Parpart, Lee. "The Nation and the Nude: Colonial Masculinity and the Spectacle of the Male Body in Recent Canadian Cinema(s)." In *Masculinity: Bodies, Movies, Culture,* edited by Peter Lehman, 167–92. New York: Routledge, 2001.

Pearson, Demetrius W., Russell L. Curtis, C. Allen Haney, and James J. Zhang. "Sports Films: Social Dimensions Over Time, 1930–1995." *Journal of Sport and Social Issues* 27, no. 2 (2003): 145–61.

Pearson, Michael. "NHL Partners with Advocacy Group to Stamp Out Homophobia." *CNN.com,* April 11, 2013. http://www.cnn.com/2013/04/11/us/sports-nhl-tolerance (accessed May 4, 2013).

Pelletier, Émilie. "'Right Language, Wrong Words!': L'Alternance de Code Comme Élément Participant de la Négociation," 44–63. *COMMposite* 11, no.1 (2008). http://commposite.org/index.php/revue/article/view/55 (accessed May 11, 2011).

Peritz, Ingrid, and Tu Thanh Ha. "Rocket Inspires Thunderous Applause: Luminaries at Funeral Rise in Final Tribute." *The Globe and Mail,* June 1, 2000. Reprinted in "Maurice 'Rocket' Richard. Three Perspectives on Hockey's Most Electrifying Performer." In *Total Hockey,* edited by Dan Diamond, 164–5. 2nd ed. Scarborough, Ontario: Total Sports Publishing, 2000.

Phan, Peter C. "The Wisdom of Holy Fools in Postmodernity." *Theological Studies* 62 (2001): 730–52.

Pike, David L. "Canadian Cinema in the Age of Globalization." *CineAction.* September 22, 2001. http://www.encyclopedia.com/doc/1G1-84194432.html.

Podruchny, Carolyn. *Making the Voyageur World: Travelers and Traders in the North American Fur Trade.* Lincoln, Nebraska: University of Nebraska Press, 2006.

Poulton, Emma, and Martin Roderick. "Introducing Sport in Films." *Sport in Society* 11, no. 2 (2008): 107–16.

Powers, John. "A Memory Relighted: At Winter Games, Symbols of Resolve and Renewal." *The Boston Globe,* February 9, 2002. http://www.boston.com/dailyglobe2/040/nation/Amemory relightedP.shtml (accessed February 10, 2002).

———. "Miracle on Ice: The Luster Hasn't Faded from Americans' Shining Moment at Lake Placid Golden Memories." *The Boston Globe,* February 22, 2000.

Pronger, Brian. *The Arena of Masculinity: Sports, Homosexuality, and the Meaning of Sex.* New York: St. Martin's Press, 1990.

Proteau, Adam. "Goldthorpe Legend Inspired *Slap Shot.*" *The Hockey News,* September 7, 2004.

———. "Screen Shots: Don't Presume Canada's Place in the Hockey Order." *The Hockey News,* February 11, 2010. http://www.thehockeynews.com/articles/31484-Screen-Shots-Dont-presume-Canadas-place-in-the-hockey-order.html.

Quart, Leonard, and Albert Auster. *American Film and Society Since 1945,* 3rd ed. Santa Barbara, CA: Praeger, 2001.

Rakobowchuk, Peter. "Quebec Gets Go-Ahead for a Separate Hockey Team." *The Canadian Press*, November 12, 2010. http://news.ca.msn.com/canada/cp-article.aspx?cp-documentid=26325860 (accessed 15 November 2010).

Ramsay, Christine. "Canadian Narrative Cinema from the Margins: 'The Nation' and Masculinity in Goin' Down the Road." *Canada's Best Features: Critical Essays on Fifteen Canadian Films*, edited by Eugene Waltz, 3–24. Amsterdam, New York: Rodopi, B.V., 2002.

Ransom, Amy J. *Hockey, PQ: Canada's Game in Quebec's Popular Culture*. Toronto: University of Toronto Press, 2014.

———. "Language and Gender Politics in the Québec Television Series *Lance et Compte*." In *Ice Hockey in Quebec—The Same but Different?*, edited by Jason Blake and Andrew C. Holman. Forthcoming.

———. "*Lieux de mémoire* or *Lieux du dollar?* Montreal's Forum, the Canadiens and Popular Culture." *Quebec Studies Journal* 51 (Spring/Summer 2011): 21–39.

Ratto, Ray. "All We Needed Was a Miracle." *ESPN.com*. February 23, 2005. http://www.espn.go.com/gen/miracle/ratto.html (accessed February 23, 2005).

Ray, Robert. *A Certain Tendency of the Hollywood Cinema, 1930–1980*. Princeton, NJ: Princeton University Press, 1985.

Richard, Simon. *La Série du siècle. Septembre 1972*. Montreal: Hurtubise, 2002.

Roberts, Gerald. "The Strenuous Life: The Cult of Manliness in the Era of Theodore Roosevelt." East Lansing, MI: unpublished dissertation, 1970.

Roberts, Katherine Ann. "Continental Drift: Negotiating Male Performance in Canadian and American Cinema from the Late Sixties." *American Review of Canadian Studies* 29, no. 1 (March 2009): 16–28.

Robertson, John Oliver. *American Myth, American Reality*. New York: Hill and Wang, 1980.

Robertson, Linda. "A Perfect Ending for Canada's Games." *Bradenton Herald*, February 28, 2010. http://www.bradenton.com/2010/02/28/2093178/a-perfect-ending-for-canadas-games.html.

Robertson, Roland. "Globalization, Time-Space and Homogeneity-Heterogeneity." In *Global Modernities*, edited by Mike Featherstone, Scott Lash, and Roland Robertson, 25–44. London: Sage, 1995.

Robidoux, Michael A. "Historical Interpretations of First Nations Masculinity and Its Influence on Canada's Sport Heritage." *The International Journal of the History of Sport* 23, no. 2 (2006): 267–84.

———. "Imagining a Canadian Identity Through Sport: A Historical Interpretation of Lacrosse and Hockey." *Journal of American Folklore* 115, no. 456 (Spring 2002): 209–25.

———. *Men at Play: A Working Understanding of Professional Hockey*. Montreal: McGill-Queen's University Press, 2001.

Robins, Kevin. "What in the World's Going On?" In *Productions of Culture/Cultures of Production*, edited by Paul du Gay, 11–66. Thousand Oaks, CA: Sage Publications, 1997.

Robinson, Marcus. "SODEC anchors Quebec's new wave." Page 17. *Playback Magazine*, November 21, 2005. http://www.playbackmag.com/articles/magazine/20051121/sodec.html?word=Les&word=Boys&word=II (accessed May 18, 2007).

Roffman, Peter, and Jim Purdy. *The Hollywood Social Problem Film*. Bloomington: Indiana University Press, 1981.

Rogan, Mary. "Out on the Ice." *GQ*. December 20, 2010. http://www.gq.com/story/brian-burke-nhl-gay-players-athletes (accessed 10 December 2012).

Romano, Andrew, and Tony Dokoupil. "Men's Lib." *Newsweek*, September 27, 2010.

Roosevelt, Theodore. "At the Harvard Union, February 23, 1907." *Presidential Addresses and State Papers: January 16, 1907 to October 25, 1907*. Volume VI, 1164–1181. New York: The Review of Reviews Company, 1910. Kessinger Publishing's Rare Reprints.

———. *The Theodore Roosevelt Cyclopedia*, edited by Albert Bushnell Hart and Herbert Ronald Ferleger. 1949, 1989. Westport, CT: Greenwood Publishing Group. http://www.theodoreroosevelt.org/TR%20Web%20Book/Index.html (accessed January 15, 2007).

Rosen, Dan. "Las Vegas awarded NHL franchise," *NHL.com*. June 22, 2016. http://www.nhl.com/news/nhl-expands-to-las-vegas/c-281010682 (accessed June 23, 2016).

———. "Selanne Ends International Career with Memorable Win." *NHL.com*, February 22, 2014. http://www.nhl.com/ice/news.htm?id=706060 (accessed February 23, 2014).

Rosenstone, Robert A. "The Historical Film." In *The Historical Film: History and Memory in Media*, edited by Marcia Landy, 50–66. New Brunswick, New Jersey: Rutgers University Press, 2001.

Rotundo, E. Anthony. *American Manhood: Transformations in Masculinity from the Revolution to the Modern Era*. New York: BasicBooks, 1993.

Rowe, David. "If You Film It, Will They Come?—Sports on Film." *Journal of Sport and Social Issues* 22, no. 4 (1989): 350–9.

———. *Sport, Culture and the Media: The Unruly Trinity*, 2nd ed. Berkshire, UK: Open University Press, 2004.

Rutherford, Paul. *The Making of the Canadian Media*. Toronto: McGraw-Hill-Ryerson, 1978.

Sabo, Donald F. "The Politics of Homophobia in Sport." In *Sex, Violence, and Power in Sports: Rethinking Masculinity*, edited by Michael A. Messner and Donald F. Sabo, 101–112. Freedom: Crossing, 1994.

_____, and Sue Curry Jansen. "Prometheus Unbound: Constructions of Masculinity in Sports Media." In *Mediasport*, edited by Lawrence A. Wenner, 202–17. London: Routledge, 1998.
Salutin, Rick. "A Little Paean to Hockey." *The Globe and Mail*, June 2, 2006.
Sanders, Eric Henry. "The Plot Genre Revolution: Or, Why the Western Isn't a Genre." *Bright Lights Film Journal*, April 16, 2015. http://brightlightsfilm.com/the-plot-genre-revolution-or-why-the-western-isnt-a-genre/#.VdYrfFrF_dk (accessed Aug. 20, 2015).
Sargeant, Jordan. "October 1: Backstage with Mike Myers." May 16, 2013. http://www.spin.com/2013/05/kanye-west-snl-saturday-night-live-history-videos/130516-kanye-mike-myers/ (accessed June 17, 2014).
Saunders, Michael William. *Imps of the Perverse: Gay Monsters in Film*. Westport: Praeger: 1998.
Scanlan, Lawrence. *Grace Under Fire: The State of Our Sweet and Savage Game*. New York: Penguin, 2002.
Scheurer, Timothy E. "The Best There Ever Was in the Game: Musical Mythopoesis and Heroism in Film Scores of Recent Sports Movies." *Journal of Popular Film and Television* 32, no. 4 (2005): 157–66.
Schickel, Richard. *The Disney Version: The Life, Times, Art and Commerce of Walt Disney*. Chicago: Elephant Paperbacks, 1997.
Scott, A.O. "Just Say 'Mariska Hargitay' and Snicker." *New York Times*, June 20, 2008 http://www.nytimes.com/2008/06/20/movies/20guru.html (accessed April 5, 2011).
_____. "The Rocket: The Legend of Maurice Richard. A Hero of Hockey." *New York Times*, November 30, 2007, accessed August 30, 2015, http://www.nytimes.com/2007/11/30/movies/30rock.html?_r=0.
Sedgwick, Eve Kosofsky. *Between Men: English Literature and Male Homosocial Desire*. New York: Columbia University Press, 1985.
Séguin, Rhéal. "Aubut, Parizeau at Odds Over Bid to Save Nordiques." *The Globe and Mail*, May 18, 1995.
Seiler, Robert M. "Selling Patriotism/Selling Beer: The Case of the 'I Am Canadian!' Commercial." *American Review of Canadian Studies* 32 (Spring 2002): 45–66.
Shapiro, Leonard. "U.S. Shocks Soviets in Ice Hockey, 4–3." *The Washington Post*, February 23, 1980.
Sharp, Joanne P. "Reel Geographies of the New World Order: Patriotism, Masculinity and Geopolitics in Post–Cold War American Movies." In *Rethinking Geopolitics*, edited by Gearóid Ó Tuathail and Simon Dalby, 152–169. New York: Routledge, 1998.
Siebel Newsom, Jennifer. "Gender in the Media." Report to the Commission on the Status of Women. The California Channel, January 17, 2011.
Silk, Michael, Jamie Schultz, and Brian Bracey. "From Mice to Men: *Miracle*, Mythology and the 'Magic Kingdom.'" *Sport in Society* 11, no, 2 (2008): 279–97.
Sinyard, Neil. "Sporting Screen." *Film and Filming* 330 (1982): 15.
Sirois, Bob. *Discrimination in the NHL: Quebec Hockey Players Sidelined*. Montreal: Baraka, 2010.
Skalko, Sherry. "Learning to Believe in 'Miracle.'" *ESPN.com*. February 9. 2004. http://sports.espn.go.com/espn/page3/story?page=skalko/review.
Slotek, Jim. "Father, Son Team Up for 'Breakaway.'" *Toronto Sun*, September 28, 2011. http://www.torontosun.com/2011/09/28/father-son-team-up-for-breakaway (accessed April 19, 2012).
Slotkin, Richard. *Gunfighter Nation: The Myth of the Frontier in Twentieth-Century America*. New York: Atheneum, 1992.
_____. "Gunfighters and Green Berets: The Magnificent Seven and the Myth of Counter-Insurgency." *Radical History Review* 44 (1989): 65–90.
Smith, Anthony D. "Memory and Modernity: Reflections on Ernest Gellner's Theory of Nationalism." *Nations and Nationalism* 2, no. 3 (1996): 371–88.
_____. *National Identity*. Reno, Nevada: University of Nevada Press, 1991.
Smith, Stacy L., Katherine Pieper, and Marc Choueti with assistance from Ariana Case and Kathleen Walsh. "Exploring the Careers of Female Directors: Phase III." Los Angeles: Annenberg School for Communications, & Journalism, University of California, 2015. http://www.sundance.org/pdf/artist-programs/wfi/phase-iii-research—-female-filmmakers-initiative.pdf.
Sobchack, Thomas, and Vivian Sobchack. "The Adventure Film." In *Handbook of American Film Genres*, edited by Wes D. Gehring, 9–24. New York: Greenwood Press, 1988.
_____. *An Introduction to Film*. Boston, MA: Little, Brown & Co., 1980.
Sontag, Susan. *On Photography*. Harmondsworth: Penguin, 1977.
The SportsBusiness Daily. "NHL Helpful in Filming Process of 'The Love Guru,' Opening Friday." June 20, 2008. http://www.sportsbusinessdaily.com/Daily/Issues/2008/06/Issue-189/Leagues-Governing-Bodies/NHL-Helpful-In-Filming-Process-Of-The-Love-Guru-Opening-Friday.aspx (accessed May 14, 2011).
Stam, Robert. *Film Theory*, Oxford: Blackwell, 2000.
Stark, Tobias. "The Pioneer, the Pal and the Poet: Masculinities and National Identities in Canadian, Swedish & Soviet Ice Hockey During the Cold War." In *Putting It on Ice. Vol II: Internationalizing Canada's Game*, edited by Colin D. Howell, 39–44. Halifax, Nova Scotia: Gorsebrook Research Institute, 2001.
Starkey, Joe. "'Miracle' Coach Touched Millions. Herb Brooks: 1937–2003. Mastermind Behind 1980 Olympic Triumph Shaped U.S. Hockey." *The Hockey News*, August 26, 2003.

Starkman, Randy. "Movie Features Gay Leaf." *Free Republic,* November 24, 2006. http://www.freerepublic.com/focus/f-news/1743583/posts (accessed April 10, 2012).
Stearns, Peter N. *Be a Man! Males in Modern Society,* 2nd ed. New York and London: Holmes and Meier, 1990.
Stevens, Julie. "Women's Hockey in Canada: After the 'Gold Rush.'" In *Artificial Ice: Hockey, Culture and Commerce,* edited by Richard Gruneau and David Whitson, 85–100. Peterborough, Ontario: Broadview Press, 2006.
———, and Carly Adams. "An Examination of Women's Sport Governance Issues: A Case Study of an Ontario Girls' Minor Hockey Association." Paper presented at the International Conference on "Canada & the League of Hockey Nations." Victoria, B.C., April 19–21, 2007.
Strate, Lance. "Heroes: A Communication Perspective." In *American Heroes in a Media Age,* edited by Susan J. Drucker and Robert S. Cathcart, 15–23. New York: Hampton Press, 1994.
Sullivan, Rebecca. "Work It Girl! Sex, Labour and Nationalism in *Valerie.*" In *Working on Screen: Representations of the Working Class in Canadian Cinema,* edited by Malek Khouri and Darrell Varga, 96–112. Toronto: University of Toronto Press, 2006.
The Sun Sentinel. "Around the League." December 21, 2006. http://articles.sun-sentinel.com/2006-12-21/sports/0612201221_1_penguins-options-million-arena.
Swardson, Anne. "Canada's Big Chill: Hockey Heads South to Seek Fortune in America." *International Herald Tribune,* April 7, 1994.
Swift, E.M. "A Reminder of What We Can Be." *Sports Illustrated,* December 22–29, 1980.
Tarasoff, Tamara. "Capturing Customers: Roch Carrier and *The Hockey Sweater.*" *Before E-Commerce—A History of Canadian Mail-Order Catalogues.* Canadian Civilization Corporation, 2004, http://www.civilization.ca/cmc/exhibitions/cpm/catalog/cat2208e.shtml (accessed March 19, 2013).
Tarasov, Anatoli. Message posted in "Twenty Years of Soviet Hockey: 1962–1982." *Hfboards* (n.d.), re-posted July 3, 2015. http://hfboards.hockeysfuture.com/showthread.php?t=565254&page=4 (accessed July 7, 2015).
Telotte, J.P. *Disney TV.* Detroit: Wayne State University Press, 2004.
Thompson, Derek. "No Country for Young Men (Or Women)." *The Atlantic,* November 8, 2011. http://www.theatlantic.com/business/archive/2011/11/no-country-for-young-men-or-young-women/248124/ (accessed April 12, 2012).
Torres, Cesar R., and Mark Dyreson. "The Cold War Games." In *Global Olympics: Historical and Sociological Studies of the Modern Games,* edited by Kevin Young and Kevin B. Wamsley, 59–82. New York: Elsevier, 2005.
Tranquilla, Ronald. "Ranger and Mountie: Myths of National Identity in Zane Grey's *The Lone Star Ranger* and Ralph Connor's *Corporal Cameron.*" *Journal of Popular Culture* 24, no. 3 (1990): 69–80.
Tschofen, Monique. "Repetition, Compulsion, and Representations in Atom Egoyan's Films." In *North of Everything: English-Canadian Cinema Since 1980,* edited by William Beard and Jerry White, 166–183. Edmonton, Alberta: The University of Alberta Press, 2002.
Tudor, Deborah V. *Hollywood's Vision of Team Sports: Heroes, Race, and Gender.* New York: Garland Publishing, Inc, 1997.
Turner, Frederick Jackson. "The Problem of the West." *The Atlantic Monthly* (September 1896). http://www.theatlantic.com/past/docs/issues/95sep/ets/turn.htm.
———. "The Significance of the Frontier in American History." *Annual Report of the American Historical Association for the Year 1893.* Washington, D.C., Government Printing Office, 1894, 199–227.
———. *The Significance of the Frontier in American History.* Edited by Harold P. Simonson. New York: Frederick Ungar, 1963.
Urquhart, Peter. "Film Policy/Film History: From the Canadian Film Development Corp. to Telefilm Canada." In *Self Portraits: The Cinemas of Canada Since Telefilm,* edited by André Loiselle and Tom McSorley, 29–54. Ottawa: Canadian Film Institute, 2006.
———. "1979: Reading the Tax-Shelter Boom in Canadian Film History." Montreal, Quebec: unpublished dissertation, 2004.
USA Today. "What Makes Miracles? Work." February 20, 2006.
Van Dijk, Teun A. *News Analysis.* Hillsdale, New Jersey: Lawrence Erlbaum, 1988.
Varga, Darrell. "The Image of the 'People' in the CBC's *Canada: A People's History.*" In *Representations of the Working Class in Canadian Cinema,* edited by Malek Khouri and Darrell Varga, 73–91. Toronto: University of Toronto Press, 2006.
Véronneau, Pierre. "Genres and Variations: The Audiences of Quebec Cinema." In *Self Portraits: The Cinemas of Canada Since Telefilm,* edited by André Loiselle and Tom McSorley, 93–127. Ottawa: Canadian Film Institute, 2006.
Vlahos, Michael. "The End of America's Post-War Ethos." *Foreign Affairs* 66, no. 5 (1998): 1092–1107.
Vlessing, Etan. "Industry Addresses Funding Crisis." Page 20. *Playback Magazine,* August 29, 2006. http://www.playbackmag.com/articles/magazine/20060821/funding.html (accessed March 29, 2007).
Vorderer, Peter, "Toward a Psychological Theory of Suspense." *Suspense: Conceptualizations, Theoretical Analyses,*

and Empirical Explorations, edited by Peter Vorderer, Hans J. Wulff, and Mike Friedrichsen. Mahwah, NJ: Lawrence Erlbaum Associates, 1996: 223–254.

———, and Silvia Knobloch, "Conflict and Suspense in Drama." In *Media Entertainment: The Psychology of Its Appeal*, edited by Jennings Bryant and Peter Vorderer, 59–72. Mahwah, NJ: Lawrence Erlbaum Associates, 2000.

Walkerdine, Valerie. "Video Replay: Families, Films and Fantasy." In *Formations of Fantasy*, edited by Victor Burgin, James Donald, and Cora Kaplan, 172–74. London: Methuen, 1986.

Ward, Jeremy, M. "Disney, the Mighty Ducks, and the National Hockey League." Master's thesis, University of Illinois at Urbana-Champagne, 1997.

Warren-Wind, Herbert. "Fire on the Ice." *Sports Illustrated*, December 6, 1954. Reprinted in "Maurice 'Rocket' Richard. Three Perspectives on Hockey's Most Electrifying Performer." In *Total Hockey*, edited by Dan Diamond, 153–157. 2nd ed. Scarborough, Ontario, Total Sports Publishing, 2000.

Wasko, Janet. "The Magical-Market World of Disney." *Monthly Review*, April 2001. http://www.findarticles.com/p/articles/mi_m1132/is_11_52/ai_74410355/ (accessed April 28, 2006).

Wead, George, and George Lellis. *Film: Form and Function*. Boston: Houghton, Mifflin and Co., 1981.

Wenner, Lawrence. "One More '-Ism' for the Road: Dirt, Globalism, and Institutional Analysis." *Journal of Sport and Social Issues* 20, no. 3 (1996): 235–8.

Whannel, Garry. *Media Sport Stars: Masculinities and Moralities*. London: Routledge, 2002.

———. "No Room for Uncertainty: Gridiron Masculinity in North Dallas Forty." In *You, Tarzan: Masculinity, Movies and Men*, edited by Pat Kirkham and Janet Thumim, 200–11. London: Lawrence and Wishart, 1993.

———. "Winning and Losing Respect: Narratives of Identity in Sport Films." *Sport in Society* 11, no. 2 (2008): 195–208.

White, Richard. "Frederick Jackson Turner and Buffalo Bill." In *The Frontier in American Culture*, edited by James R. Grossman, 7–66. Berkeley: University of California Press, 1994.

White, Robert. A. "Television as Myth and Ritual." *Communication Research Trends* 8, no.1 (1987): 1–6.

Whitson, David. "Hockey Night in Canada: Cultural Institution of 'Niche Sport'?" Opening Plenary Session paper presented at the Canada & the League of Hockey Nations, Victoria, B.C., April 19–21, 2007.

———, and Donald Macintosh. "The Global Circus: International Sport, Tourism, and the Marketing of Cities." *Journal of Sport and Social Issues* 20, no. 3 (1996): 278–95.

Whyte, Murray. "Where Films in English Can Seem a Cultural Betrayal." *New York Times*, September 17, 2000. http://www.nytimes.com/2000/09/17/movies/film-where-films-made-in-english-can-seem-a-cultural-betrayal.html (accessed July 25, 2010).

Wilkerson, Martha. "Explaining the Presence of Men Coaches in Women's Sports: The Uncertainty Hypothesis." *Journal of Sport and Social Issues* 20, no. 4 (1996): 411–26.

Wilkie, Janet Riblett. "The Decline in Labor Force Participation and Income, and the Changing Structure of Family Economic Support." *Journal of Marriage and the Family* 53 (February 1991) 111–122.

Williams, E.A. "Bakhtin and *Borat*: The Rogue, the Clown, and the Fool in Carnival Film." *Philament* 20 (2015): 105–128.

Williams, Linda. "Melancholy Melodrama: Almodóvarian Grief and Lost Homosexual Attachments." In *Melodrama! The Mode of Excess from Early America to Hollywood*, edited by Frank Kelleter, Barbara Krah, and Ruth Mayer, 353–371. Heidelberg: Universitätsverlag, 2007.

———. "Melodrama Revised." In *Refiguring American Film Genres*, edited by Nick Browne, 42–88. Berkeley: University of California Press, 1998.

Wilson, Alexander. *The Culture of Nature: North American Landscapes from Disney to the Exxon Valdez*. Cambridge, MA: Blackwell, 1992.

Wise, Mike. "NBC's Ebersol Puts His Games Face On, Comes Up a Winner." *The Washington Post*, August 28, 2004.

Wiseman, Matthew S. "Origins of the Cold War—The Canadian Perspective." February 25, 2013. http://www.mattwiseman.ca/origins-of-the-cold-war-the-canadian-perspective/ (accessed February 28, 2014).

Worster, Donald. "Two Faces West: The Development Myth in Canada and the United States." In *One West, Two Myths: A Comparative Reader*, edited by Carol L. Higham and Robert Thacker, 23–45. Calgary: University of Calgary Press, 2004.

Wulff, Hans. J. "Suspense and the Influence of Cataphora on Viewers' Expectations." In *Suspense: Conceptualizations, Theoretical Analyses, and Empirical Explorations*, edited by Peter Vorderer, Hans J. Wulff, and Mike Friedrichsen, 1–18. Mahwah, NJ: Lawrence Erlbaum Associates, 1996.

Yaffe, Samantha. "Production Still Booming." *Playback*, March 5, 2001. http://www.playbackonline.ca/articles/magazine/20010305/Productions.html?word=2001&word=Production&word=booming.

Young, M. Crawford. "The National and Colonial Question and Marxism: A View from the South." In *Thinking Theoretically About Soviet Nationalities*, edited by Alexander J. Motyl, 67–97. New York: Columbia University Press, 1992.

Young, Scott, and George Robertson. *Face-Off, a Novel.* Toronto, Ontario: Macmillan of Canada, 1971.

Zillmann, Dolf. "Mechanism of Emotional Involvement with Drama." *Poetics* 23 (1994): 33–51.

_____. "The Psychology of Suspense in Dramatic Exposition." In *Suspense: Conceptualizations, Theoretical Analyses, and Empirical Explorations,* edited by Peter Vorderer, Hans J. Wulff, and Mike Friedrichsen, 199–231. Mahwah, New Jersey: Lawrence Erlbaum Associates, 1996.

_____. "The Psychology of the Appeal of Portrayals of Violence." In *Why We Watch: The Attractions of Violent Entertainment,* edited by J.H. Goldstein, 179–211. New York: Oxford University Press, 1998.

Index

Aaron, Michele 255, 256
Abel, Allen 280n9; see also Going South
Academy of Motion Picture Arts and Sciences 6
action/sports (male genres) 4, 6, 9, 15, 16, 17, 19, 21, 22, 29, 39, 40, 47, 51, 88, 91, 93, 124, 154, 159, 202, 220, 235, 239, 243, 247, 250, 255, 272n87, 302n8, 304n15; see also biopic (sports); buddy-cop (genre); combat/war (genre); road movie
Adams, Jack: in Net Worth 83, 84, 154
Adams, Mary Louise 220, 273n111
Airborne 114
Aitken, Stuart: and Christopher Lee Lukinbeal 98, 282n58; Leo Zonn 256
Alaska 91, 94, 96
Allain, Kristi 272n88, 280n56
Allen, Holly 271n61
Altman, Rick 6, 269n25
American Broadcasting Corporation (ABC) 168, 173, 175, 226, 252, 282n55, 284n18, 291n6, 292n10, 294n45, 294n47
American Dad: "The Return of the Bling" 292n9
American Dream 8, 12, 16, 54; see also social mobility
American Hockey League (AHL) 96, 298n15
American identity 5, 8, 10, 11, 12, 13, 16, 19, 27, 29, 30, 31, 32, 38, 39, 42, 45, 47, 53, 72, 81, 90, 91, 94, 95, 96, 97, 116, 120, 128, 132, 133, 141, 147, 161, 178, 232, 247, 252, 262, 263
Americanization of Canada 18, 82; Canada as U.S. branch plant 27–28, 29, 30, 79, 113, 282n34; see also Innis, Harold E.; Innisian critique
Americanization of hockey 27–

28, 38, 82, 108–109, 289n71; see also Canadian crisis of identity; NHL Sun Belt migration
Anaheim Ducks 276n34, 285n40; see also Disney/The Mighty Ducks of Anaheim
Anglo-French divide/duality/rivalry 11, 29, 130, 131, 133, 135, 138, 148, 163, 160, 162, 165, 166, 201, 261
Anglophone 29, 130, 131, 133, 142, 158, 162, 165, 193, 201, 207, 245, 285n54, 289n71; Anglophone boss/manager in Quebec film 153, 157, 157, 158, 290n94, 304n1
archival footage 251–254
Arledge, Roone 291n6
Armstrong, George Edward "Chief": in Face Off 78–79
Atwood, Margaret 18, 273n98
Aubut, Marcel: in Bon Cop, Bad Cop 161
Auge, Lester: in Miracle on Ice 170

Babington, Bruce 7, 8, 56, 71, 240, 251, 299n30
Baker, Aaron 51, 53, 229, 236, 263
Baker, Brian 53, 278n20
Baker, Hobey 75, 272n71
Bakhtin, Mikhail 277n1; Bakhtinian archetypes 277n2, 298n13
Baldwin, Howard 86
Baldwin, Karen Elise 86
Baruchel, Jay 67, 68, 72, 279n44, 279n49, 279n50, 279n51, 291n123
baseball 1, 8, 9, 13, 14, 170, 227, 262, 277n64, 281n25, 301n28
Beardsley, Doug 84, 158, 275n12, 296n65
Beaty, Bart 6, 38, 47, 265n15, 269n15, 276n44
beaver 11, 161
Béliveau, Jean 261; in Here's Hockey 23; in Il était une fois les

Boys 152; in The Mystery of the Million Dollar Hockey Puck 133, 134
Bell Centre 128, 287n24
Bell-Metereau, Rebecca 171
Benshoff, Harry, and Sean Griffin 3
Berenson, Red 296n63
Berland, Jody 271n46
Bernie, Louis, and Mac (as Jack, the Chimp) 285n57
Berry, Robert, and William Gould 85
Berton, Pierre 119
Bettman, Gary 82, 89, 106, 107, 108, 280n12, 282n38, 284n20, 297n88; in Bon Cop, Bad Cop 160, 161, 166
Binamé, Charles 153
biopic (sports) 8, 35, 74, 157, 158, 167, 169, 184, 197, 241, 251, 252, 253, 254, 304n11
Blades and Brass 24, 274n128
Blake, Hector "Toe": in Slap Shot 3: The Junior League 124, 255
Blake, Jason 15, 190, 193, 197, 235, 261, 303n19
Bobines d'Or 140
Bobrov, Vsevolod: in Canada Russia '72 178, 183, 184
Bollywood 202, 299n26
Bon Cop, Bad Cop 134, 159–166, 259, 261, 290n116, 291n126; Anglo-French divide 160, 161, 162, 166, 290n118; carnivalesque humor 164; English-and French-Canadian masculinities 163, 164; plunder of hockey by American interests 161, 164; see also Americanization of hockey
Bordwell, David 269n19
Bossy, Mike: in Les Boys IV 140
Boston: and hockey 14, 105, 126, 168, 170, 262; see also Dowd, Nancy
Boston Bruins 51, 56, 67, 82, 83,

105, 128, 155, 191, 261, 262, 304n9; "Big Bad Bruins" 28, 56, 178
Boston Garden 191, 192
Bouchard, Émile "Butch": in *Maurice Richard/The Rocket* 156
Bourque, Ray: in *Les Boys IV* 140; in *Sticks and Stones* 128
The Boy Who Drank Too Much 105–106, 149, 250
Les Boys tetralogy 20, 139, 140–147; Anglo-French divide 146, 289n71; carnivalesque/*Slap Shot* intertextuality 140, 141, 142, 143, 145, 146, 147, 299n78; commercial success 139–140, 288n47; father-son relationship 141; hockey as social leveler 142; Jean-Charles 140, 141, 142, 143, 299n238; physicality 141, 142, 145; Quebec-France relationship 144; Quebec myths 143, 144, 145, 146, 147, 289n70; 289n80; secession 145, 146; *see also* Francophone Dream in sport; Quebec cinema/industry
Branch, John 25, 279n37, 279n45, 279n48
Brault, Michel 132; *see also* Montréal vu par... La Dernière Partie
breadwinning 5, 14, 16, 41, 74, 75, 97, 98, 126, 141, 149, 169, 185, 251, 279n51
Breakaway/The Speedy Singhs 23, 203–207, 6, 255, 256, 259, 260, 298n21; bully hockey and race 203, 204, 205, 206, 299n25; father-son relationship 124, 149, 203, 213; *Youngblood* 204–205, 242, 298n20; *see also* Bollywood
Breakfast with Scot 23, 211–215; father-son relationship 213, 215; *see also* physicality and the gay player
Britain: and Canada 11, 16, 32, 190, 191, 193, 275n28, 280n10, 304n1; and French-Canada 144, 162, 163; *see also* Elizabeth II, Queen
British Columbia 35, 36, 38, 119, 120, 122; and British Columbia film industry 116, 119, 120, 122, 285n41
Brode, Douglas 228
Brodeur, Martin: in *Les Boys IV* 140
Brooks, Herb 225, 282n9, 292n19, 292n20, 293n22, 295n50, 303n24; approach to hockey 45, 176, 293n28, 293n33, 294n40, 294n43, 295n53; in *Miracle* 170, 171,

172, 173, 174, 175, 176, 255, 292n18, 295n51; in *Miracle on Ice* 168, 171, 172, 173, 175, 176
Brown, Noel 107, 109, 128, 274n119, 283n3, 283n5, 284n35, 285n35, 302n2
Brunet, Benoît: in *Les Boys IV* 140
Bruzzi, Stella 4, 87, 92, 213, 260, 283n7, 293n24
buddy-cop, *policiers* (police dramas) 139, 162, 163, 165, 270n32
bully 22, 27–28, 32, 33, 34, 35, 38, 39, 40, 42, 43, 44, 46, 47, 96, 111, 263; enforcer 25, 38, 39; *see also* Canadian cultural debate about hockey; Fothergill, Robert
bully-clown 22, 48, 49, 51, 54, 56, 57, 58, 59, 60, 61, 62, 63, 65, 66, 67, 69, 73, 76, 123, 206, 211, 263, 279n36; *see also* carnivalesque; Fothergill, Robert
Buma, Michael 5, 15, 19, 93, 114, 142, 185, 218, 270n34, 273n105, 276n40, 286n63, 286n66, 297n73, 299n35
Bush, George W. 161, 171, 298n18
Bush, Walter: in *Miracle* 172

Calgary Flames 82, 218
Campbell, Clarence: in *Maurice Richard/The Rocket* 157; in *Net Worth* 83; Summit Series 295n56
Canada Amateur Hockey Association (CAHA) 14, 177
Canada Russia '72 22, 145, 177–185, 191, 192, 256, 259, 262, 295n54, 304n11; *see also* Summit Series, Summit Series documentaries
Canadian Association of Film Distributors and Exporters (CAFDE) 119, 285n41, 285n44
Canadian Broadcasting Corporation (CBC) 22, 26, 28, 32, 34, 35, 36, 38, 280n10, 303n28; hockey guidelines 62–63; *see also* Going South; Hockey Night in Canada
Canadian canonical film 9, 18–19, 20, 21, 26, 27, 38, 46, 47, 49, 118, 123, 147, 151, 157, 164, 180, 181, 184, 185, 202, 207, 210, 218, 220, 258, 259, 262, 271n46, 272n96, 273n101, 275n16, 275n17, 299n30; *see also* Canadian Cost Allowance; Innisian critique; loser hero; social realism
Canadian Cost Allowance (CCA) 29, 30, 32, 272n96, 275n15
Canadian crisis of identity 82,

161, 281n13, 281n17; *see also* Americanization of hockey
Canadian cultural debate about hockey 16, 18, 26–27, 28, 76, 77, 180, 205, 210, 259, 274n116
Canadian Film Development Corporation (CFDC) 135, 139, 275n15, 275n16
Canadian identity 5, 9, 10, 11, 18, 19, 27, 28, 29, 32, 38, 47, 77, 120, 121, 128–129, 132, 181, 182, 197, 202, 247, 304n1; *see also* Prairies
Canadian Television Network (CTV) 126, 127, 284n32
Canuel, Érik 140, 159, 290n119
capitalism 12, 53, 54, 78, 90, 144, 161, 181, 271n64, 280n3
Carlson, Jeff, Steve Carlson and Dave Hanson *see* Hanson Brothers
the carnivalesque 48, 51, 54, 56, 59, 61, 63, 66, 73, 102, 140, 141, 142, 143, 146, 147, 148, 164, 201, 202, 219, 239, 258, 259, 264, 289n78, 298n8, 298n13; *see also* Bakhtin, Mikhail
Carrier, Roch 137, 138, 141; *see also The Sweater*
Carter, Jimmy: Crisis of Confidence speech 292n17; in *Miracle* 170, 252
Cartier, Jacques 130
Cashman, Wayne 181; in *Canada Russia '72* 179
catharsis 54, 239, 246, 257, 303n19
center-margins 29, 38, 276n44
Cermak, Iri 289n69, 284n32, 294n41, 296n64, 296n66, 296n70
Le Chandail see *The Sweater*
Chandler, Daniel 269n19
Charette, Michel 148; *see also Les Boys* tetralogy
chase (genre) 134
Chelios, Chris: in *Slap Shot 2: Breaking the Ice* 100
Chernishev, Arkadii: in *Canada Russia '72* 182, 184
Cherry, Don 73, 74, 75, 76, 160, 163, 164, 190, 191, 192, 193, 194, 197, 215, 272n88, 280n52, 280n54, 280n56, 280n57, 281n13, 297n87, 297n88, 304n11; in *Breakfast with Scot* 215; in *Il était une fois les Boys* 233; in *Waking Up Wally*, 196; *see also* Keep Your Head Up, Kid; Wrath of Grapes
Chicago Blackhawks 83, 84, 86, 87, 253, 281, 292n9
Chicks w/Sticks 23, 228–230, 260, 301n24

Chiefs, the Charlestown *see* Hanson Brothers; *Slap Shot*; *Slap Shot 3: The Junior League*
the Church *see* Roman Catholicism
Ciardi, Mark 247, 278n35
cinematography 23, 24, 31, 51, 60, 100, 124, 125, 129, 155, 132, 183, 188, 195, 218, 235, 240, 241, 242, 245, 246, 247, 248, 250, 254, 256
Clapper, Aubrey Victor "Dit": in *Slap Shot 3: The Junior League* 124, 255
Clark, Wendell: in *Wrath of Grapes* 192
Clarke, Bobby 85, 275n12, 278n16; in *Canada Russia '72* 179, 181, 182
Clarke, Chris 121
class (culture/sport) 13, 14, 47, 29, 110, 142, 150, 153; differences 14, 26, 27, 47, 49, 56, 105–106, 142, 158, 180, 259, 272n70; middle-class 13, 40, 48, 53, 54, 104, 105–106, 169, 272n70, 283n3, 297n76; upper-class 13, 48, 49, 51, 52, 58, 169, 180, 304n1, 304n14; working-class 13, 14, 25, 39, 45, 47, 57, 72, 75, 87, 102, 104, 135, 142, 143, 157, 169, 180, 204, 205, 210, 211, 249, 251, 268n2, 272n70, 279n51, 290n94, 292n14, 292n16, 304n1; *see also* gamesmanship; sportsmanship
coaches 4, 22, 45, 47, 52, 71, 75, 78, 125, 126, 148, 149, 167, 172, 183, 184, 185, 186, 277n54, 292n19, 293n37, 294n41, 296n67, 302n40, 304n11; *see also* Brooks, Herb; Cherry, Don; Gretzky, Walter; Murray, Athol
Coach's Corner 190, 197; in *Bon Cop, Bad Cop* 160; in *Wrath of Grapes* 192, 193, 196
Coakley, Jay 239, 246
Cohen, Leonard: in *Canada Russia '72* 180, 184, 256
Cold War 168, 173, 174, 175, 176, 177, 181, 182, 183, 185, 252, 253, 263, 281n25, 285n36, 291n6, 292n11, 292n12, 295n52, 296n66, 303n26; post–Cold War 113, 174, 176, 253, 295n52; *see also* Arledge, Roone; Soviet Union
colonialism/colonization 11, 12, 18, 20, 27, 29, 33, 79, 91, 130, 144, 162, 163, 209, 280n10, 291n31
Colorado Avalanche 82, 164, 181, 280n12, 289n71

Columbia Broadcasting Corporation (CBS) 40, 105
combat/war (genre) 9, 168, 171, 172, 198, 270n32
comedy (genre) 32, 48, 50, 51, 56, 58, 62, 139, 140, 141, 146, 147, 159, 189, 190, 227, 237, 270, 277n2, 278n6, 278n32, 292n9, 298n10; *see also* the carnivalesque; satire
commercialism (in hockey) 24, 38, 79, 116, 160, 161, 162, 209, 259, 262; *see also* Americanization of Canada; Americanization of hockey
communism 101, 145, 176, 181, 189, 193, 281n25, 291n6, 292n11, 296n63
Connell, R.W., and James W. Messerschmidt 268n2
conquest 10, 25, 174, 292n11; *see also* the Conquest/*la Conquête*
The Conquest/*la Conquête* 130, 144, 145, 163, 166
Consol Energy Center 292n40
consumer culture/consumerist 4, 18, 20, 53, 89, 97, 103, 106, 107, 108, 111, 112, 144, 161, 167, 173, 184, 231, 252, 256
Co-operative Commonwealth Federation Party (CCF) 189, 297n81
corruption in sports 7, 14, 49, 94, 100, 115, 116, 188, 232, 233, 259; and authority 171, 189
counterculture 77, 78, 277n52, 280n3
Cournoyer, Yvan: in *Canada Russia '72* 180, 184
Craig, Jim 177, 293n21, 293n22; in *Miracle* 170; in *Miracle on Ice* 168, 170, 171, 176
crisis *see* Canadian crisis of identity; Carter, Jimmy
Crosson, Séan 7, 20, 269n19, 269n25, 270n28, 274n117, 304n2
Cruise, David, and Alison Griffiths 83
cultural nationalism 29, 38, 79, 146, 180, 202, 259, 273n103, 278n36, 280n3
Cummins, Glenn 207, 243, 302n16, 303n17
Custen, George 167
The Cutting Edge 117
Czechoslovakia, Czech Olympic hockey team 192, 224, 225, 294n41

Dancyger, Ken, and Jeff Rush 7, 9, 21, 255, 257
The Deadliest Season 21, 22, 40–43, 51, 77, 80, 246, 259, 261

decline-and-fall storylines 18, 19, 21, 29, 31, 33, 34, 35, 85, 95, 99, 237, 251; *see also* loser hero
Den Brother 22, 113, 115–116, 259
destiny: and expansion 120, 161, 168, 174, 292n11, 295n52, 304n1; national 12, 159, 190, 271n57; storylines 16, 111, 164, 172, 175, 180
Detroit Red Wings 3, 82, 83, 84, 132, 154, 155, 218, 2621, 281n21
development myths 10
didacticism and sport 26, 28; and sports/family fare 9, 48, 76, 114, 129, 187, 228, 233, 234, 241, 256, 259, 286n62
Diduck, Ryan 20, 273n112
The Dilemma 292n9
The Disney Company 1, 6, 113, 116, 119, 282n55, 284n19, 285n36, 285n45; children's brand 109, 283n12, 284n34, 284n35, 301n20; Disney, Walt 172, 262n55; and hockey films 22, 72, 90, 116, 125, 216; and NHL/The Mighty Ducks of Anaheim 22, 81, 88, 90, 96, 106, 107–109, 280n12, 280n30, 284n32, 285n40, 301n22; *see also* Donald Duck; Eisner, Michael
Dizikes, John 52
Do You Believe in Miracles? *see* Home Box Office (HBO)
Dokoupil, Tony, and Rick Marin 279n51; and Andrew Romano 282n64, 300n2
Donald Duck 107, 109, 112
Dowd, Nancy 49, 51, 52, 54, 278n7
dreams/dreaming 21, 30, 45, 152–153, 158, 222, 225, 257, 282n55, 292n18, 292n19; *see also* American Dream; Francophone Dream in sport
Dryden, Ken: in *Canada Russia '72* 179
The Duke of West Point 23, 124
Duplessis (Maurice) era 135, 156, 290n91, 290n120
Dupuis, Roy 157, 290n95

Eagleson, Alan 295n56; in *Canada Russia '72* 178, 184
Eastern Canada Amateur Hockey Association 14
Eaton's Department Store 137
Ebersol, Dick 291n6
Edensor, Tim 19
editing 23, 24, 36, 38, 71, 72, 95, 128, 165, 176, 188, 195, 240, 241, 242, 243, 244, 245, 246, 247, 52, 254, 255, 256
Edmonton Oilers 34, 82, 106, 161, 196, 276

Eisner, Michael 81, 106, 107, 108, 284n33
Elcombe, Tim 295n62
Elias, Norbert, and Eric Dunning 25–26
elite sport/athletes 4, 8, 27, 37, 42, 77, 78, 79, 80, 85, 89, 90, 102, 106, 107, 115, 177, 183, 185, 203, 207, 220, 222, 263, 276n34, 281n12, 283n7, 301n18, 304n11; elite (governing) 11, 12, 13, 14, 25, 26, 27, 48, 57, 76, 130, 133, 135, 144, 157, 162, 164, 278n36, 280n8, 290n120, 282n12, 292n14, 304n1
Elizabeth II, Queen 71, 280n10
Ellerman, Evelyn 297n74, 297n75, 304n14
Ellis, Mark 247
Elmwood, Victoria 276n50
enforcer *see* bully
England *see* Britain
Entertainment and Sports Programming Network (ESPN) 280n12, 299n40, 300n4
environmental determinism 10, 270n40
Eruzione, Mike 292n19, 293n21; in *Miracle* 171, 173; in *Miracle on Ice* 170, 171, 176
Esposito, Phil 181, 296n63; in *Canada Russia '72* 179, 180, 183, 184
ethnicity 7, 15, 20, 22, 57, 110, 130, 143, 144, 162, 199–207, 260, 263, 270n32, 273n111, 286n14, 297n6, 298n14, 299n25, 299n26; *see also* minorities; multiculturalism
Everett, Wendy 98, 282n59
exemplar *see* hockey/sports exemplar
expectations/audience *see* grammar of film

Face Off (film) 19, 22, 29, 77–81, 141, 240, 250, 252, 259, 280n8, 303n41
Face Off (novel) 78, 280n8
family: dysfunctional/breakdown 46, 98, 104, 118, 127, 128, 149; and the sports hero 7, 21, 17, 44, 255, 242; team as 83, 136, 141, 150, 162, 171, 228, 260; *see also* orphan
family film 2, 9, 22, 23, 61, 67, 72, 104, 105, 106, 107, 108, 109, 114, 116, 117, 118, 119, 121, 122, 123, 125, 126, 128, 129, 142, 149, 150, 151, 152, 171, 233, 235, 237, 239, 255, 259, 260, 262, 263, 264, 283n3, 283n5, 283n34, 283n35; corporate entertainment/sanitized

hockey 72, 77, 88, 99, 100, 101, 102, 103, 111, 112, 125, 126, 127, 129, 205, 209, 217, 227, 248
fan/s 19, 25, 51, 59, 184, 192, 276n40, 278n16, 294n43, 298n17; marketing/business 27, 38, 67, 85, 86, 90, 98, 101, 107, 108, 166, 167, 192, 230, 256, 257, 274n116, 283n65, 283n67, 302n41; traditional constituencies 3, 31, 33, 38, 41, 47, 64, 72, 77, 84, 97, 99, 109, 132, 137, 206, 244, 283n67, 286n60, 291n123
father/family man 5, 13, 17, 128, 148, 260, 277n64; father-daughter relationship 215, 216, 222, 223, 235, 260; father-son relationship 5, 33, 36, 38, 40, 46, 54, 73, 75, 80, 87, 89, 92, 104, 105, 106, 111, 124, 126, 128, 129, 149, 141, 150, 170, 176, 190, 195, 197, 203, 204, 217, 219, 233, 234, 251, 260, 283n7; surrogate father 61, 105, 112, 125, 186, 210, 212, 213, 214, 218, 260, 283n7; *see also Waking Up Wally*
Felske, Lorry, and Beverly Rasporich 79
Ferguson, John: in *Canada Russia '72* 178, 180, 181, 183, 184
fighting *see* violence
Finland/Finnish hockey 32, 33, 34, 35, 176, 276n35
Finley, Margot 117
First Nations 11, 18, 79, 91, 92, 95, 131, 282n46
Fiske, John 14, 26, 48, 56, 164, 277n1
Flannery, Tim 294n44
Fleras, Augie, and Shane Michael Dixon 304n14
Florida Panthers 38, 81, 85, 280n12
football 1, 9, 13, 24, 39, 55, 170, 262, 278n16, 281n15, 304n14
Forum *see* Montreal Forum
Fothergill, Robert 29, 34, 48, 49, 297n5
Fowler, Roger 168
Fox Networks 82, 161, 201, 280n12, 281n15; FoxTrax puck 82, 99; 20th Century Fox 60, 247
Francaviglia, Richard 172, 282n55
France: and Quebec 130, 134, 140, 144, 163, 288n62
Francophone Dream in sport 20, 143, 153, 234
Frappier, Roger 147
Freda, Isabelle 171
French-Canadian/Québécois

identity 5, 22, 29, 130, 131, 132, 134, 135, 136, 137, 138, 142, 144, 145, 147, 162, 164, 166, 261
Front de Libération du Quebec (FLQ) 133
frontier 25, 27, 39, 42, 47, 48, 53, 65, 80, 90, 91, 93, 94, 95, 96, 120, 121, 172, 193; cultural archetypes 9–10, 15, 16, 198, 246, 258, 260, 263, 270n35; The North/Canada 10, 11, 16, 18, 121, 190, 254, 275n28; The North/French-Canada/ 10, 11, 130, 162, 166, 270n43, 304n1; The West/U.S. 12–13, 16, 172, 270n39, 271n56, 271n57, 276n50; 278n25, 282n44, 282n55, 292n11, 294n44, 295n52, 304n1; "Wild West" vs. "Mild West" 31–32, 180, 278n28, 278n29; *see also* North America; sports/hockey exemplar
Frye, Northrop 18, 273n98
Fuller, Linda 284n18
funding (Canada film) 62–63, 136, 139, 287n41, 278n36, 288n44, 288n47; *see also* Canadian Cost Allowance; Canadian Film Development Corporation; National Film Board of Canada; Société de développement des enterprises culturelles; Telefilm Canada
Fürsich, Elfriede 8, 22, 270n29, 274n119

Gagné, Simon: in *Les Boys IV* 140
Gallivan, Danny: in *The Mystery of the Million Dollar Hockey Puck* 133, 134, 136
The Game That Kills 23
gamesman/gamesmanship 52, 53, 54, 111, 116, 129, 131, 142, 258, 278n16
Gasher, Mike 120, 285n41, 285n45
Gay Blades 23
Gee, Sara 304n15
Gehring, Wes 48, 49, 57, 277n2
Genie Awards 153, 290n116, 297n74
genre(s) 6–9, 16, 18, 19, 20, 29, 240, 262, 263, 269n19, 270n30, 270n31; hybridity 9, 270n32, 274n18; *see also* melodramatic mode
Gerson, Geoffrey 302n40
Gidén, Carl, Houda, Patrick, and Jean-Patrice Martel 270n35
Gillmor, Don 277n60, 278n27
Girard, Rémy 140, 148, 157; *see also Il était une fois les Boys*; *Les*

Boys tetralogy; Maurice Richard/*The Rocket*
globalization/transnational markets (and sport) 34, 38, 81, 97, 98, 102–103, 113, 121, 125, 139, 147, 167, 175, 197, 207, 262, 276n48, 294n44, 298n14; *see also* The Disney Company
Go Figure 23, 226–228, 230, 236, 250, 260, 301n17, 304n11
Going South 38, 81, 89, 280n9
Goldberg, Evan 67
Golden Reel Awards 140
golf 55, 56, 57, 122, 164, 275n31
goon *see* bully
Goon 21, 22, 67–73, 244–246, 247, 248, 249, 255, 259, 263, 279n44, 279n50, 291n123, 304n11
Gorman, Tommy: in *Maurice Richard/The Rocket* 153
Goudreau, Richard 139
Gouge, Catherine 12, 278n25
grammar (of hockey in film) 239–240, 247, 254, 257, 302n7; audience expectations 8–9, 239, 240, 257
La Grande Noirceur see Duplessis (Maurice) era
Les Grands Duels du Sport: Hockey sûr glace: Canada–URSS 181; *see also* Summit Series documentaries
Gray, Gordon 247
Greene, Eric 120, 270n30
Gretzky, Walter 194, 195, 197; *see also Waking Up Wally*
Gretzky, Wayne 64, 85, 102, 106, 107, 112, 193, 230, 280n57, 283n65, 284n31; in *Bon Cop, Bad Cop* 160, 161; in *Chicks with Sticks* 229, 230; in *D2: The Mighty Ducks* 112; in *MVP: Most Valuable Primate* 121; 1988 Canada–U.S. Free Trade Agreement 164, 197, 297n90; in *Waking Up Wally* 194, 195, 197
Grey, Zane 275n23
Groen, Rick 279n36
Gross, Paul 276n43, 276n47
Gross Misconduct 19, 35–39, 75, 84, 253, 254, 259, 276n43, 276n47, 303n41
Grown Up Movie Star 23, 215–217, 259, 260
Gruneau, Richard, and David Whitson 16, 19, 83, 102, 147, 221, 222, 262, 276n49, 301n11, 301n12
Guber, Peter 6, 167
Guérin, Luc 148; *see also Il était une fois les Boys*; *Les Boys* tetralogy

Hanson Brothers 263–264, 278n6, 278n27, 286n60, 304n12; in *Chicks with Sticks* 229; in *les Boys* tetralogy/intertextual 141; National Lampoon's *Pucked*/intertextuality 231; other characters 60, 61, 66, 69, 111, 201; in *Slap Shot* 49, 50, 51, 52, 53, 54, 246; in *Slap Shot 2: Breaking the Ice* 99, 100, 101, 102; in *Slap Shot 3: The Junior League* 122, 123, 124, 125, 126, 236, 255
Happy Gilmore 22, 54–58, 59, 61, 258, 278n31
Harcourt, Peter 32, 303n28
Hardy, Stephen 14, 172, 304n10
Harper, Stephen 296n65, 299n25
Harrer, Tim: in *Miracle* 171
Harrison, Dick 31, 275n23
Harrison, Richard 54, 295n56
Harvey, Jean 131, 132, 158
Hays, Matthew 165
H-E-Double Hockey Sticks 113–115, 123, 259
Helstein, Michele 268n2
Henderson, Paul 190, 296n66; in *Canada Russia '72* 179, 180, 181, 184
Here's Hockey 24, 274n127
hero/heroism (sport film) 4, 17–18, 76, 111, 144, 147, 163, 167, 197, 199, 202, 239, 246, 254, 255, 256, 258, 263, 264, 273n105, 304n15; *see also* family and the sports hero; nostalgia
heteronormative 5, 141, 142, 211, 218, 261
heterosexuality 4, 117, 142, 143, 199, 211, 217, 218, 219, 258, 260, 268n2, 304n15
Hockey: A People's History 272n87
The Hockey Champ 109, 284n23
Hockey Homicide 109, 284n24
hockey in media/film (study of) 1–2, 6–9, 17–20, 23, 24, 261, 262
Hockey Match on the Ice 23, 274n121
Hockey Night 23, 221–224, 229, 230, 235, 249, 260, 261
Hockey Night in Canada 22, 36, 82, 134, 192, 197, 200, 253, 262
hockey player (in popular culture/film/media) 3–6, 9, 18, 19, 20, 22, 23, 25, 27, 29, 37, 65, 66, 67, 70, 75, 77, 81, 94, 100, 114, 117, 118, 144, 201, 207, 209, 211, 213, 215, 217, 218, 224, 225, 227, 230, 240, 246, 248, 249, 253, 258, 259, 260, 272n88, 278n35, 280n56, 298n35, 304n15
hockey/sports (development)

programs 79, 104, 112, 187, 221, 259, 281n13, 282n57, 284n32, 297n77, 302n40
hockey/sports film (characteristics) 6, 7, 19, 167, 181, 190, 199, 235, 250, 257, 258, 270n28, 274n18, 304n2; *see also* didacticism; intertextuality; melodramatic mode
hockey/sports literature 5, 15–16, 32, 39, 78, 93, 142, 185, 190, 207, 256, 270n34, 272n80, 273n105, 275n3, 276n40, 277n64, 280n8, 286n63, 286n66, 287n19, 299n35, 304n4
Holiday in Handcuffs 237
Hollands, Robert 15, 78, 79, 272n80, 280n8, 287n19
Hollywood film: 1970s 2, 42, 54, 79, 80, 92, 104, 106, 169, 170, 171, 264, 278n24, 277n52; 1980s 2, 43, 104, 105, 169, 264; 1990s 239, 256; *see also* family film; "New Manhood"
Holman, Andrew 270n34, 272n77, 288n67, 295n60, 296n67
Home Box Office (HBO), *Do You Believe in Miracles?* (documentary) 292n17, 301n19; *Real Sports with Bryant Gumbel* 279n47
homosexuality 22, 23, 67, 99, 102, 148, 199, 207, 209, 211, 212, 213, 214, 215, 216, 217, 218, 219, 260, 268n2, 269n15, 288n54, 297n88, 299n35, 299n40, 300n40, 300n42; *see also Les Boys* tetralogy, Jean-Charles; physicality and the gay player
Hopkins, Jeff 239
Horne, Gerald 31
Hot Ice: The Anatomy of Hockey, Canada's National Game 23
Houle, Michel 134, 135, 136, 150, 156, 287n27
The Hounds of Notre Dame 22, 186–190, 259, 260, 261, 297n74, 297n75; *see also* Murray, Athol; muscular Christianity
Howe, Gordie: in *Net Worth* 64; in *Slap Shot* 50; in *Slap Shot 3: The Junior League* 124, 255
Huard, Patrick 159, 165, 166, 291n130
Hughes-Fuller, Patricia 79, 273n105
Huizenga, Wayne 81, 85, 89
Hunt, Patricia 275n32

Ice Angel 21, 23, 224–226, 228, 236, 249, 260, 263, 301n19, 304n11

Ice Castles 22, 39, 47, 104, 261
identity (male/social/sport) 4, 5, 6, 7, 8, 9, 10, 12, 15, 21, 23, 27, 29, 30, 38, 61, 78, 80, 81, 93, 98, 113, 131, 145, 147, 167, 180, 199, 202, 207, 209, 212, 213, 215, 217, 218, 219, 227, 229, 264; *see also* national identity; regional identity
ideology: of sport 4–5, 8, 14, 15–16, 17, 18, 20, 25–27, 47, 198, 261, 284n31; in sports media 8, 9, 16, 17, 23, 220, 239–240, 241, 243, 254, 256, 257, 262, 302n8; *see also* American dream; social mobility
Idol of the Crowds 23, 24, 274n131
Il était une fois les Boys 148–153; *see also* dreaming; Francophone Dream in Sport
indigenous peoples *see* First Nations
individualism (in sport/media narratives) 4, 7, 12, 15, 16, 17, 78, 114, 115, 116, 171, 228, 125, 249, 258, 260, 271n56, 284n35
Ingram, David 282n46
Innis, Harold E. 11, 12
Innisian critique 18, 19, 27, 30, 161, 181, 273n113, 280n10; Canadian cultural industries, 271n46
International Ice Hockey Federation (IIHF) 177, 295n58, 303n26
intertextuality (sports/hockey film) 72, 118, 122, 140, 143, 148, 152, 166, 205, 225, 231, 242, 263, 298n8; *see also Les Boys* tetralogy, *Slap Shot*; Miracle on Ice allusions
Irvin, Dick: in *Maurice Richard/The Rocket* 153, 159
Is Commercialism Changing Canadian Sport? 23–24

Jack Frost 283n7
Jackson, Joshua 110, 117, 118
Jackson, Steven 164
Jagr, Jaromir: in *Sticks and Stones* 126
James, Graham: in *The Sheldon Kennedy Story* 217, 218
Un Jeu si simple 132, 286n15
Johnson, Dwayne "The Rock" 58, 59, 60, 62; *see also* Tooth Fairy
Johnson, Mark 293n37
Jones, Glen 6
junior hockey 33, 44, 45, 65, 112, 119, 121, 122, 153, 192, 196, 205, 217, 263, 277n60, 303n24, 304n11
Just Friends 22, 61–62

Kariya, Paul: in *D3: The Mighty Ducks* 113
Kashmere, Brett 181, 103n290, 296n65
Katerberg, William 11, 120, 271n47, 275n28
Katz, Sidney 157–158, 289n83
Kaye, Janice 6, 29, 160, 189, 209, 211, 269n15, 272n96, 275n16, 275n17, 275n29
Keaton, Michael 105, 283n7; *see also Jack Frost*; *Touch and Go*
Keep Your Head Up, Kid: The Don Cherry Story and *Wrath of Grapes* 21, 22, 73–76, 190–193, 210, 251, 259, 261, 280n52; *see also* Cherry, Don
Keeso, Jared 74; *see also Keep Your Head Up, Kid*; *Wrath of Grapes*
Kelly, Robert "Battleship": in *Wrath of Grapes* 191
Kennan, George 292n12
Kennedy, Brian 256, 290n102, 296n66, 296n67, 303n40
Kennedy, Kathleen 6
Kennedy, Sheldon: in *The Sheldon Kennedy Story* 217–218
Kharlamov, Valeri 275n12; in *Canada Russia '72* 179, 181, 182, 183
Khouri, Malek, and Darrell Varga 275n24
Kibby, Marjorie 17, 273n111, 304n15
Kidd, Bruce, and John Macfarlane 275n24, 280n8
Kimmel, Michael 102
King, Geoff 277n52
King, Richard C., and David Leonard 199, 273n111, 297n2
King of Hockey 23, 24, 274n123
Knelman, Martin 275n15
Knight, Bill 108, 281n13
Kollin, Susan 91, 94
Kronjuvelerna 219
Krutov, Vladimir 174; in *Miracle* 294n47
Kubyshkin, Alexander 297n67
Kurri, Jari 276n35

Laberge, Suzanne, and Mathieu Albert 142
labor (sport/athlete as) 25, 40, 47, 53, 74, 75, 81, 84, 85, 88, 155, 244, 259, 260, 276n34, 281n34, 295n57, 304n14
lacrosse 11, 13
Lafleur, Guy 261; in *Les Boys IV* 140
Lafortune, Roc 142, 148; *see also Il était une fois les Boys*; *Les Boys* tetralogy
Lance et compte—Le Moment de vérité 218, 219

Landau, Misia 252, 272n91
The Last Season (film) 19, 22, 26, 28, 32–35, 37, 46, 77, 259, 261, 303n41
The Last Season (novel) 275n33, 276n40
Laycoe, Hal: in *Maurice Richard/The Rocket* 156, 157
Leach, Jim 18
A League of Their Own (baseball) 301n28
"A League of Their Own" (hockey) 301n8
Lebeau, Pierre 140, 148, 150; *see also Il était une fois les Boys*; *Les Boys* tetralogy
Légaré, André 10
Lembeck, Michael 247
Lemieux, Mario 89, 102, 193, 282n38, 283n65; in *Wrath of Grapes* 193
Leonsis, Ted 81
Lesage, Jean 153, 156
Lidström, Nick: in *Sticks and Stones* 129
Limerick, Patricia Nelson 270n39, 292n11
Lindros, Eric: in *Bon Cop, Bad Cop* 160, 164; "Lindros Affair" 164
Lindsay, Ted 84, 158, 281n20, 281n21, 281n22, 281n28; in *Net Worth* 82–85, 154, 155, 158
literature 10, 18, 31, 35, 39, 94, 138, 271n56, 275n32, 297n76, 376n50; *see also* sports literature
Loco Locass 159
Loiselle, André 6, 20, 136, 139, 141, 143, 146, 157, 158, 269n15, 289n70, 289n78, 290n94, 299n78; and Gina Freitag 147
Lorenz, Stacey, and Osborne, Geraint 14, 272n70
Los Angeles Kings 59, 61, 85, 89, 100, 106, 107, 112, 121, 160, 161, 164, 192, 195, 197, 199, 201, 247
loser hero 18, 19, 20, 21, 27, 29, 32, 35, 140, 180, 273n98, 275n16, 275n17; *see also* Frye, Northrup
The Love Guru 21, 23, 199–203, 207, 230, 249, 260, 298n8, 298n10, 298n13, 298n16, 298n17; *see also* Myers, Mike
Love Story 22, 39–40, 47, 104
Lovers in a Dangerous Time 46
Lowe, Rob 205, 298n20; *see also Breakaway/The Speedy Singhs*; *Youngblood*
Luzhniki Palace of Sports/hockey arena 184
Lyden, John 88

MacGregor, Roy 32

Index

Mackenzie, Scott 131, 287*n*31, 290*n*120
Mackey, Eva 128, 199, 207, 209, 273*n*100, 276*n*46, 280*n*10, 281*n*17
Maclean, Ron: in *Waking Up Wally* 197
MacNeill, Margaret 253, 281*n*16
MacRury, Malcom 180
MacSkimming, Roy 295*n*56, 295*n*62, 296*n*67
Madison Square Garden 173, 174
Maguire, Joseph 5, 33, 34, 35, 276*n*34
Mahovlich, Frank: in *Canada Russia '72* 181, 183
Makarov, Sergei 174
Malden, Karl 171, 292*n*19; *see also Miracle on Ice*
Malone, Joe: in *Maurice Richard/The Rocket* 155, 157
Mandel, Eli 31
Markle, Peter 45
Marsh, Margaret 297*n*77
Marshall, Bill 143, 144, 162, 269*n*15, 290*n*120
Martin, Brian 270*n*43
masculinity characteristics/functions 3–5, 8, 9, 10, 11, 13, 14, 15, 16, 17, 18, 19, 20, 40, 77, 79, 80, 92, 93, 97, 98, 102, 104, 111, 112, 117, 125, 128, 129, 130–131, 142, 143, 145, 147, 164, 166, 167, 180, 186, 190, 197, 199, 218, 258, 259, 260, 268*n*2; crisis of 13, 87, 93, 263–264, 282*n*64, 304*n*14; *see also* bully; bully-clown; "New Manhood"
Mason, Daniel 82, 281*n*12, 281*n*15; and Gregory Duquette 272*n*73
Maurice Richard/The Rocket 22, 153–159, 176, 185, 240, 258, 259, 261, 269*n*15, 289*n*82, 290*n*94; *see also* Dupuis, Roy
McCartney, Andra 273*n*98
McClanahan, Rob: in *Miracle* 170, 250; in *Miracle on Ice* 169–170
McDermott, John: in *Score: A Hockey Musical* 67
McGowan, Michael 65
McGrath, Alister 297*n*76, 197*n*77
McGrath, Charles 94, 280*n*43
McKay, Jim, Toby Miller, Geoffrey Lawrence and David Rowe 271*n*64
McMurtry, William: and *Investigation and Inquiry into Violence in Amateur Hockey* Report 42, 277*n*54
McNall, Bruce 106, 107
McSorley, Marty: in *Wrath of Grapes* 192

media conglomeratization 4, 67, 81, 90, 96, 116, 117, 161, 167, 198, 262
media content/programming 3, 22, 220, 262, 269*n*14, 277*n*53; Canada 29, 194, 217, 278*n*36, 285*n*54; Quebec 139, 158; *see also* North America/film markets
media/sport consumption 4, 18, 20, 22, 158, 194, 198, 231, 246, 252, 256, 274*n*119, 278*n*36, 284*n*35, 285*n*41, 285*n*54
Mellanby, Ralph: in *Wrath of Grapes* 192, 193
Mellen, Joan 42
Melnyk, George 138, 139, 275*n*15, 286*n*1, 287*n*21
melodramatic mode 9, 17, 18, 19, 20, 47, 96, 103, 111, 143, 153, 154, 155, 156, 157, 159, 76, 179, 182, 184, 202, 205, 242, 243, 255, 258, 269*n*19, 272*n*90, 294*n*41
Melrose, Barry: in *Slap Shot 2: Breaking the Ice* 100
Messier, Marc 48, 141, 148, 149; in *Slap Shot 3: The Junior League* 125, 126; *see also Il était une fois les Boys*; *Les Boys* tetralogy
Messner, Michael 4, 199, 253, 288*n*54, 300*n*1; and Donald Sabo 218
Meyrowitz, Joshua 240, 254, 302*n*7, 303*n*42
Michaels, Al : in *Miracle* 294*n*47; in *Miracle on Ice* 175, 176
The Mighty Ducks, D2: The Mighty Ducks, D3: The Mighty Ducks 1, 21, 22, 72, 106, 108, 110–115, 117, 118, 119, 123, 125, 128, 236, 249, 251, 256, 258, 259, 260, 261, 263, 284*n*17, 284*n*18, 292*n*22
Mikhailov, Boris: in *Canada Russia '72* 183; in *Miracle* 174
Millbury, Mike: in *Wrath of Grapes* 192
Miller, Mary Jane 34, 223
mimicry 189, 243
Minnesota North Stars 173
minorities (cultural) 4, 22, 23, 81, 131, 155, 199, 202, 205, 206, 207, 261, 263, 268*n*2, 273*n*111, 300*n*4
Miracle on Ice (event) 167, 168, 291*n*7, 291*n*6, 292*n*8, 292*n*11, 293*n*31, 293*n*32, 293*n*27, 295*n*50, 298*n*48, 303*n*24
Miracle on Ice and *Miracle* (films) 1, 6, 21, 22, 167, 168–177, 285*n*36, 292*n*10, 292*n*14, 292*n*16, 293*n*24, 294*n*41, 294*n*43, 294*n*44, 294*n*45, 294*n*47; *see also* HBO/*Do You Believe in Miracles?*
"Miracle on Ice" allusions (in hockey movies) 72, 113, 123, 152, 289*n*81, 292*n*9
Monk, Katherine 27, 133, 301*n*29
Montreal 14, 88, 126, 128, 132, 139, 140, 144, 145, 147, 153, 158, 159, 160, 177, 261, 262, 286*n*7, 286*n*16, 288*n*44, 291*n*123, 295*n*59
Montreal Canadiens 23, 85, 132, 133, 134, 135, 136, 137, 148, 152, 153, 155, 156, 159, 160, 161, 166, 178, 261, 262, 286*n*14, 304*n*9; Anglo-French rivalry 131, 138, 161
Montreal Forum 132, 133, 134, 136, 137, 152, 156, 157, 287*n*24
Montréal vu par—"La Dernière Partie" 132, 286*n*16; *see also* Brault, Michel
Montreal Wanderers 14
Morris, Peter 189
Motley, Clay 53
multiculturalism 3, 9, 92, 109, 111, 129, 150, 151, 194, 202, 205, 206, 207, 289*n*17, 298*n*25
Murray, Athol 186, 187, 188, 189, 190, 193, 297*n*78, 297*n*82; *see also The Hounds of Notre Dame*
Murray, Catherine 278*n*36
muscular Christianity 186, 187, 193, 271*n*64, 297*n*76, 297*n*77
MVP: *Most Valuable Primate* 22, 119–122, 123, 236, 256, 258, 285*n*45, 285*n*57
Myers, Mike 202, 203, 298*n*10, 298*n*13, 298*n*17, 298*n*18, 298*n*26; *see also The Love Guru*
Myshkin, Vladimir: in *Miracle on Ice* 175
Mystery, Alaska 1, 22, 90–96, 99, 149, 206, 255, 260, 261, 262, 282*n*55, 303*n*41
The Mystery of the Million Dollar Hockey Puck 22, 132–137, 150, 240

National Broadcasting Company (NBC) 220, 232, 294*n*41, 304*n*12; *see also* Arledge Roone
National Film Board of Canada (NFB) 23, 137, 158, 274*n*126, 290*n*103, 303*n*28
National Hockey League (NHL): business aspects 18, 19, 22, 81, 82, 83, 85, 86, 89, 90, 96, 99, 102, 155, 161, 202, 222, 240, 246, 278*n*31, 280*n*8, 280*n*12, 281*n*15, 282*n*38, 283*n*67, 283*n*11, 284*n*30, 295*n*56, 298*n*11; cultural dream/social mobility 30, 31, 33, 74, 83, 99,

170, 203, 260, 296n66; expansion/migration, Sun Belt 27, 38, 79, 81, 121, 161, 162, 164; and identity 3, 30, 34, 56, 80, 81, 136, 140, 144, 161, 164, 181, 184, 193, 202, 213, 216, 230, 254, 261, 262, 281n13, 296n66; lockout (partial) 1994–1995, 82, 86, 90; lockout (total) 90, 102; systemic pressures 28, 34, 79, 80, 81, 84, 87, 94, 95, 170, 173, 191, 252, 279n47, 279n48; *see also* Disney; *Going South*; Original Six

National Hockey League Players Association (NHLPA) 83, 75, 83, 85, 86, 177, 178, 281n20, 281n22, 281n25, 281n28, 300n14

national identity/nationalism 3, 5, 7, 8, 9, 12, 19, 96, 112, 122, 130, 131, 162, 185, 197, 260, 261, 262, 280n1; *see also* cultural nationalism

National Lampoon's *Pucked* 23, 221, 230–232, 234, 260

Native Americans *see* First Nations

Neale, Stephen 4, 269n19

Neely, Cam: in *Sticks and Stones* 128

Nesterenko, Eric: in *Youngblood* 44, 46

Net Worth (film) 19, 22, 82–85, 88, 154, 155, 161, 281n20, 281n22, 281n24, 281n25, 281n28

Net Worth: Exploding the Myths of Pro Hockey (book) 83

New Brunswick 126, 162, 286n61, 295n54

New Man/New Manhood 87, 112, 261, 284n27

New York Islanders 106, 221, 126, 128

New York Rangers 7, 83, 85, 90, 92, 93, 94, 95, 96, 121, 255

Newman, Paul: in *Les Boys IV* 146; in *Slap Shot 3: The Junior League* 286n58; *see also Slap Shot*

NHL *see* NationalHockey League

No Sleep 'til Madison 22, 97–99, 102, 259, 282n57

Nordicity/North *see* frontier; scripts of nationhood

Norris, James 281n20; in *Net Worth* 84

North America 4, 10, 130; game footprint/leagues 3, 22, 29, 29, 85, 88, 90, 98, 99, 136, 201; TV/film market(s) 117, 118–119, 121, 122, 126, 136, 139, 165, 247, 264; *see also* hockey/sports exemplar; scripts of nationhood

nostalgia 13, 54, 92, 97, 98, 99, 111, 128, 129, 151, 158, 167, 251, 252, 304n15; *see also* hero/heroism

novels *see* sportsliterature

O'Callahan, Jack: in *Miracle* 170, 250

O'Connor, Gavin 170–171, 253, 292n18

Octagon/Street and Smith's *SportsBusiness* publications 269n18, 298n16; World Congress of Sports 6, 269n18

Of Sport and Men 290n103

Olson, Scott Robert 269n14

Olympic Games 13, 45, 72, 112, 140, 145, 170, 271n64, 280n1, 302n41; 1972 Sapporo Winter Games 45, 169; 1980 Lake Placid Winter Games 1, 45, 72, 113, 168, 169, 173, 176, 252, 292n14, 293n31, 294n41, 294n45, 294n46; 1988 Calgary Winter Games 161, 164, 184, 276n35; 1992 Albertville Winter Games 294n41; 1994 Lillehammer Winter Games 276n35, 284n32, 294n41, 294n44; 1998 Nagano Winter Games 225, 226, 263, 276n35; 2002 Salt Lake Winter Games 228, 284n31, 291n7; 2006 Torino Winter Games 276n35; 2010 Vancouver Winter Games 161, 220; 2014 Sochi Winter Games 276n35; *see also* "Miracle on Ice"

Oriard, Michael 13, 52, 271n57, 272n84, 277n64, 278n16

Original Six (NHL teams) 56, 83, 199, 261, 262

origins 10, 16, 17, 18, 80, 120–121, 131, 134, 144, 159, 172, 176, 270n35, 271n57, 272n91, 291n7, 295n52; *see also* environmental determinism

orphan/orphaning 121, 122, 123, 124, 125, 132, 133, 134, 135, 136, 138, 150, 212, 255

Orr, Bobby 64, 190, 275n12; in *Gross Misconduct* 38; in *Hockey Night* 222; in *Slap Shot* 50; in *Waking Up Wally* 196; in *Wrath of Grapes* 191

Oscars 6

Ottawa Silver Seven 14

Our Game (Electronic Arts) 3–5, 268n1

Owen, George 75

Paperback Hero 19, 21, 22, 29–32; *see also* Prairies

Paquin, Laurent 148; *see also Il était une fois les Boys*

Paramount Pictures 40, 202, 249

Parisé, Jean-Paul (J-P): in *Canada Russia '72* 184

Parpart, Lee 27, 161, 181, 274n118

Pearson, Demetrius W., Russell L. Curtis, C. Allen Haney, and James J. Zhang 1, 277n52

Les Pee Wee 3D: l'hiver qui a changé ma vie 23, 149, 232–235, 236, 256, 258, 259, 260, 261, 263, 304n11

Pelletier, Émilie 162

Perfectly Normal 23, 207–211, 218, 248, 249, 260, 299n30

petit pays see "small nation"

Phan, Peter 69

Philadelphia Flyers 26, 160, 181, 232; Broad Street Bullies 28, 32, 33, 72, 263, 276n49

Phoenix Coyotes 82, 102, 281n12

physicality and the gay player 211, 212, 213, 214, 215, 216, 218, 219

physicality vs. skill *see* skill vs. physicality

picaresque 150, 189, 190, 259, 277n2

Pittsburgh Penguins 37, 86, 87, 88, 89, 90, 102, 282n40, 293n28, 293n37; *see also* Lemieux, Mario

Plains of Abraham (Battle of the) 130, 146, 163

Players Association *see* National Hockey League Players Association (NHLPA)

Pocklington, Peter 106; in *Bon Cop, Bad Cop* 161

Podruchny, Carolyn 131, 286n7, 286n8

police 30, 32, 50, 51, 72, 79, 126, 133, 148, 159, 160, 164, 184, 231; Royal Canadian Mounted Police (RCMP) 32, 275n28, 275n32, 281n25, 304n1; *see also* buddy-cop (genre)

pond hockey/game 62, 90, 92, 94, 95, 96, 101, 109, 110, 118, 121, 141, 187, 206, 251, 256, 257, 263, 282n43, 283n7; *see also* shinny

Ponton, Yvan 140, 148; *Le Moment de vérité* 218; *see also Il était une fois les Boys; Les Boys* tetralogy, Jean-Charles

Populism 53

populism (and sport/hockey) 5, 12, 16, 26, 48, 53, 57, 58, 61, 63, 66, 67, 72, 76, 77, 92, 102, 125, 132, 133, 134, 135, 137, 138, 141, 142, 143, 159, 161, 162, 164, 166, 169, 190, 192, 202, 229, 241, 258, 259, 262, 263, 280n57, 284n35, 289n71

Poulton, Emma, and Martin Roderick 6, 299n22
Powers, John 175
Prairies 30, 31, 32, 187, 275n24, 275n32; see also Mandel, Eli
Prix Jutra 289n82
Proteau, Adam 278n7

Quebec: and the Church 11, 130, 131, 133, 135, 136, 137, 138, 141, 150–151, 156, 159, 163, 164, 166, 290n91, 304n1; family 149, 163, 165, 166; identity 130, 131, 136, 137, 139, 142, 146, 147, 151, 159, 160, 164, 259, 289n70, 280n80, 291n131; French-Canadians/North America 130, 136, 139, 144, 149, 259; hockey as Francophone 131, 132, 133, 134, 137, 139, 143, 144, 147, 149, 153, 157, 161, 165, 166, 219, 249, 261, 286n14, 287n24, 288n62, 288n67; key historical/political events 130, 131, 135–136, 145, 158, 159, 162, 163, 166, 193, 281n17, 289n83, 290n91, 290n120; social mobility 136, 144, 151; see also frontier; Quiet Revolution; "small nation"
Quebec cinema/industry 134, 135, 136, 138–139, 147, 259, 268n4, 269n15, 285n41, 286n1, 287n27, 288n44, 288n47, 289n82, 290n95, 291n126, 298n8
Quebec City 133, 233, 234, 280n12
Quebec Colisée 34
Quebec Nordiques 85, 160, 261; relocation see Colorado Avalanche
Quiet Revolution (Révolution tranquille) 131, 135, 136, 153, 156, 158, 166, 286n1, 290n120

race see ethnicity
Ragulin, Alexander: in Canada Russia '72 179
Raising Helen 200
Ramsay, Christine 276n44
Ransom, Amy 5, 6, 132, 141, 143, 147, 158, 164, 219, 261, 262, 269n15, 269n19, 286n14, 287n24, 288n67, 290n87, 300n42
Ratelle, Jean: in The Boy Who Drank Too Much 105
realism see versimilitude
regional identity (and hockey/sport) 3, 5, 7, 9, 30, 31, 34, 38, 77, 96, 97, 99, 108, 122, 126, 168, 170, 202, 260, 261, 262

Report of the National Commission on the Causes and Prevention of Violence 41
The Return of the Bling see American Dad
Révolution tranquille see Quiet Revolution
Rhéaume, Manon 234, 302n35
The Rhino Brothers 46, 237, 261
Richard, Maurice 83, 137, 138, 153, 158, 159, 166, 190, 261, 290n103; "Richard Riot" 153, 158, 289n83; see also Maurice Richard/The Rocket; The Sweater
Riess, Steven 284n17
ritual (sport as) 3, 5, 28, 58, 67, 77, 98, 131, 132, 134, 138, 169, 196, 201, 246, 255, 270n28
road movie 98–99, 282n59
Roberts, Katharine Ann 291n131
Robidoux, Michael 11, 219, 285n38
Robins, Kevin 298n14, 299n26; and David Morley 171
Robitaille, Luc 87, 115
Rochester Americans 74
The Rocket: The Legend of Maurice Richard see Maurice Richard/The Rocket
Rocky (films) 282n64
rollerblade (game) 225, 226, 255
Roman Catholicism 11, 130, 131, 133, 135, 136, 137, 150, 151, 156, 159, 163, 164, 166, 189, 290n91, 297n77, 304n1
Ronnie and Julie 22, 117–119, 256, 258, 285n43, 304n11
Roosevelt, Theodore 13, 16, 271n57, 297n77
Rowe, David 239, 269n25, 271n64
Russian/s 45, 112, 118, 145, 173, 174, 175, 178, 181, 183, 184, 185, 192, 209, 221, 225, 226, 234, 263, 284n32, 291n6, 293n37, 294n41, 294n44, 295n50, 304n11; see also Soviet/s

Sabo, Donald, and Sue Jansen Curry 217, 299n33
Saïa, Louis 139, 142, 147
Salutin, Rick 159
Sanders, Eric Henry 269n19
Sanderson, Derek 28
Sandler, Adam 54, 58, 278n32; see also Happy Gilmore
Santa Baby 237
satire 40, 48, 54, 132, 140, 141, 142, 147, 148, 151, 190, 201, 202, 219, 231, 269n15; see also the carnivalesque
Savard, Serge 296n63; in Canada Russia '72 182
Scheurer, Timothy 256

Score: A Hockey Musical 22, 63–67, 275n40
Scott, Seann William 279n50; see also Goon
scripts of nationhood 10–13, 20, 25, 26, 30, 167, 270n37, 270n40; see also origins
Seagram Company, Ltd. 88, 90
Sedgwick, Eve K. 142, 278n20
Seibert, Earl: in Maurice Richard/The Rocket 154
Seiler, Robert 272n88
Selänne, Teemu 276n35
September 1972 181, 296n68; see also Summit Series documentaries
La Série du siècle see Summit Series
Shadrin, Vladimir: in Canada Russia '72 183
The Sheldon Kennedy Story 23, 217–218, 303n41
shinny 63, 65, 67, 196, 216, 235
Shore, Eddie: in Keep Your Head Up, Kid 74, 75
sibling bonding/rivalry 5, 45–46, 196, 301n28
Silk, Michael, Jamie Schultz and Brian Bracey 171, 269n15, 293n24
Sinden, Harry 296n66; in Canada Russia '72 178, 180, 184; in Wrath of Grapes
skill vs. physicality (hockey) 3, 18, 24, 26, 43, 45, 56, 77, 84, 109, 118, 123, 158, 180, 205, 210, 243, 276n49, 229, 246, 248, 250, 259, 299n22
Slap Shot 7, 8, 9, 22, 40, 47, 49–54, 61, 77, 104, 108, 123, 140, 141, 143, 146, 201, 229, 231, 232, 246, 249, 258, 259, 263, 264; see also Dowd, Nancy; Hanson Brothers
Slap Shot 2: Breaking the Ice 22, 67, 99–102, 123, 124, 210, 231, 236, 259, 261, 263, 282n64, 303n41, 304n11
Slap Shot 3: The Junior League 22, 122–126, 236, 242, 249, 255, 256, 258, 261, 263, 264, 286n58
Slotkin, Richard 12, 42, 270n31, 270n35, 277n52, 304n1
"small nation" (petit pays) 130, 132, 145, 147, 157, 163, 166
Smith, Anthony D. 270n37
Social Darwinism 13, 111, 113, 116, 260, 271n64
social mobility (sport and) 31, 42, 43, 45, 53, 54, 58, 96, 205, 241, 258, 304n1
social realism 18, 19, 151, 157, 180, 190

Index

Société de développement des entreprises culturelles (SODEC) *see* Quebec cinema/industry
Sontag, Susan 241
Soul of a Nation, Hockey: A People's History 296n68; *see also* Summit Series documentaries
sound (soundtrack/sound effects/music) 21, 23, 24, 36, 57, 65, 66, 67, 70, 71, 72, 73, 74, 91, 95, 112, 118, 124, 138, 170, 172, 183, 195, 206, 209, 210, 212, 217, 218, 235, 240, 241, 242, 243, 245, 246, 248, 250, 255, 256
Soviet rivalries, methods/influence 167, 168, 173, 174, 176, 177, 179, 183, 185, 263, 288n67, 289n68, 292n8, 292n14, 293n37, 294n47, 296n66, 296n67; *see also* Tarasov, Anatoli
Soviet Union 173, 174, 175, 176, 181, 183, 184, 252, 284n32, 291n6, 292n11, 292n12, 294n41, 295n50, 295n52, 295n59
Soviets in hockey repertoire 112, 113, 118, 123, 142, 145, 173, 174, 221, 225, 284n32, 286n62, 288n67, 304n11; in *Canada Russia '72* 178, 179, 182, 183–184; in *Miracle* 174, 175, 176; in *Miracle on Ice* 173–174
spectacle 23, 96, 97, 98, 106, 108, 109, 126, 134, 156, 239, 240, 241, 243, 245, 250, 254, 255, 256, 257, 277n1
Spencer, Brian "Spinner" 35, 36; *see also Gross Misconduct*
sponsor/corporate partnerships 22, 41, 55, 57, 90, 91, 97, 97, 99, 100, 101, 102, 110, 111, 122, 125, 126, 167, 173, 202, 203, 220, 221, 222, 228, 235, 260, 262, 264, 278n32, 281n15, 284n18
sports (values): competition 13, 15, 16, 17, 24, 25, 26, 52, 77, 116, 237, 241, 284n35, 304n14; *see also* gamesmanship; skill vs. physicality; sportsmanship
sports/hockey exemplar 3–5, 15, 16, 17, 25, 57, 78, 80, 85, 89, 102, 124, 126, 140, 144, 155, 167, 185, 193, 196, 201, 207, 220, 222, 241, 246, 248, 251, 258, 259, 260, 297n76
Sports Illustrated 90, 92, 94, 278n6, 290n104, 292n10, 296n65, 302n11
sportsmanship 13–14, 16, 26, 43, 50, 52, 54, 76, 101, 125, 128, 141, 142, 182, 190, 223, 235, 241, 251
Springfield Indians 74

Stanley Cup 28, 32, 33, 86, 89, 114, 134, 138, 153, 178, 192, 196, 197, 199, 230, 267n24, 281n21, 284n18, 295n62, 299n26
Stark, Tobias 295n58
Stebbins, Robert A. 37–38
Stevens Julie 301n31; and Carly Adams 230
Sticks and Stones 22, 126–129, 233, 235, 259, 261, 263, 286n61, 286n62, 304n11
Strate, Lance 255
Sudden Death 22, 86–90, 161, 162, 240, 258
Sullivan, Rebecca 156, 290n91
Summit on Ice 296n63, 296n68; *see also* Summit Series documentaries
Summit Series 22, 127, 140, 142, 145, 167, 288n67, 295n56, 295n59, 295n62, 296n66, 296n67
Summit Series documentaries 181, 184, 185, 296n63, 296n68
The Sweater (animation) 137–8, 287n32
Swift, E.M. 171, 292n10, 292n19, 303n22

Tarasov, Anatoli 45, 145, 289n68, 293n37, 296n66; in *Canada Russia '72* 182, 183, 184
Tchofen, Monique 276n48
Telecommunications Act (1996) 280n11
Telefilm Canada 203, 272n96, 278n38, 279n36, 288n44, 288n47
television 1, 3, 5, 20, 22, 29, 47, 82, 179, 277n53, 279n47, 280n12, 282n55, 300n4, 304n14
Telotte, J.P. 284n19
textual analysis 21, 22, 270n29, 274n119; media studies approach to hockey in film 1, 22, 302n8
13 Going on 30 7–8
Thornton, Joe: in *Sticks and Stones* 128
Tikhonov, Viktor 118, 175, 294n41, 304n11; in *Miracle* 174–175
Tikkanen, Esa 276n35
Tollin, Mike 6
Tooth Fairy 21, 22, 58–61, 62, 72, 115, 246, 247, 250, 261, 278n35
Toronto 14, 38, 140, 159, 160, 161, 162, 177, 179, 195, 199, 202, 205, 233, 261, 289n71; and film industry 121, 139, 276n44, 285n41, 288n44
Toronto International Film Festival (TIFF) 140

Toronto Maple Leafs 36, 37, 38, 78, 79, 80, 81, 83, 84, 132, 137, 138, 152, 159, 199, 200, 201, 202, 203, 206, 211, 212, 213, 218, 252, 261, 262, 298n12, 298n15, 298n17, 300n40, 304n9; Maple Leaf Gardens 192
Toronto Marlies 298n15
Torres, Cesar, and Mark Dyreson 176
Touch and Go 105, 213, 260, 261, 283n7, 291n123
Tranquilla, Ronald 31, 32
Tremblay, Michel 138, 289n78
Tretiak, Vladislav: in *Canada Russia '72*, 183; in *Miracle* 174; in *Miracle on Ice* 175
tricksterism/gimmickry 53, 56, 100, 111, 112, 113, 114, 116, 118, 119, 121, 122, 124, 125, 129, 142, 150, 232, 249, 258
Truckey, Don 228
Trudeau, Pierre Elliott 133, 177, 295n59
truncated quests *see* decline-and-fall storylines
Tudor, Deborah 220, 224, 229, 237
Turner, Frederick Jackson 12, 13, 16, 42, 53, 54, 91, 94, 161, 232, 271n49, 271n57, 278n25, 282n44, 282n55
Two Solitudes 162, 166, 269n15; *see also* Anglo-French divide/duality/rivalry

underdog 16, 23, 25, 54, 58, 89, 96, 110, 112, 113, 124, 142, 143, 145, 152, 158, 180, 242, 243, 263
Union Nationale 156; *see also* Duplessis (Maurice) era
Universal Studios 24, 86, 88, 90, 100
upmarketization (of hockey/sport) 85, 89, 97, 103, 106, 108, 111, 112, 116, 159, 161, 259, 281n12, 280n12, 282n15, 283n67
Urquhart, Peter 20, 273n103, 273n113, 273n114, 275n119
USSR *see* Soviet Union
utopian (narratives) 7, 12, 18, 63, 90, 143, 269n15; *see also* destiny storylines

Vancouver, British Columbia 116, 119, 117, 179, 181; British Columbia, 36, 38
Vancouver Olympics *see* Olympic Games/Vancouver Winter Games
Van Damme, Jean-Claude 86, 87, 88; *see also Sudden Death*

verisimilitude (realist aesthetic) 17, 22, 23, 67, 109, 240, 258, 302n11

Véronneau, Pierre 20, 22, 150, 274n120, 289n80

violence: as commodity/spectacle 4, 8, 14, 15, 18, 25, 27, 38, 41, 42, 43, 54, 61, 231, 259; as excess/corruption 14, 18, 27, 30, 31, 32, 33, 34, 38, 39, 40, 51, 88, 109, 155, 157; as frontier expression 25, 27, 28, 32, 36, 37, 42, 46, 47, 51, 53, 54, 57, 72, 87, 89, 103, 126, 201, 247, 258; as policing 25, 28, 37, 65, 68, 73, 75, 212, 244, 246, 253, 279n48; as resistance 20, 25, 26, 39, 48, 53, 58, 76, 102, 130, 143, 166, 217, 229, 258, 259; as social problem 19, 28, 41, 42, 45, 253; as strategy to garner wins 27, 28, 32, 34, 42, 43, 52, 177, 259; as working-class 13, 25, 26, 45, 46, 47, 49, 51, 52, 54, 57, 70, 71, 72, 75, 87, 102, 104, 106, 142, 157, 204, 211, 247, 248, 251, 279n51; see also McMurtry, William; physicality and the gay player

Virmani, Vinay 205, 206

Vlahos, Michael 292n11

Waking Up Wally: The Walter Gretzky Story 194–197; see also Gretzky, Walter

Walkerdine, Valerie 25, 39

Ward, Jeremy Michael 107, 269n15, 283n12, 284n27

warrior codes (and hockey) 4–5, 71, 128, 142, 117–118, 188, 198, 204, 206, 207, 232–233, 239, 260, 304n15; see also combat/war genre

Washington Capitals 106

Wayne, John 24, 274n131

Wead, George, and George Lellis 270n30

Wensik, John: in *Wrath of Grapes* 192

The Westering/West *see* frontier; scripts of nationhood

western (genre) 6, 9, 24, 29, 32, 39, 46, 53, 57, 87, 88, 89, 92, 95, 172, 201, 242, 269n19, 270n32, 271n56, 278n20

Whannel, Garry 6, 273n105, 299n22

White, Richard 174, 270n39

White, Robert 291n7

White Lightning 23

Whitson, David 278n36, 283n67; see also Gruneau, Richard, and David Whitson

Wilkerson, Martha 236

Williams, Brian: in *Wrath of Grapes* 191–192

Williams, E.A. 277n2, 298n13

Williams, Linda 17, 19, 20, 154, 243, 272n90

Williamson, Murray 45

Wind, Herbert Warren 158

Winnipeg Jets 81, 85, 89, 280n12; see also Going South

Winsor, Ralph 14

Winter Carnival 134, 136, 298n18

Winter Classic 304n12

women (and society) 3, 4, 13, 22–23, 29, 34, 77, 80, 92, 93, 127, 131, 194, 210, 268n2, 282n64, 286n16, 300n1, 300n2, 300n4, 300n5; athletes/hockey players 140, 219–221, 260, 261, 300n1, 300n9, 301n26, 301n31, 301n33, 302n40, 302n41, 303n24; leagues Canadian Women's Hockey League (CWHL) 220, 301n9; National Women's Hockey League (NWHL) 301n9; Olympics/Canadian women's Olympic team 140; U.S. women's Olympic team 263, 280n1

working-class (hockey as) *see* violence

World Hockey Association (WHA) 85, 177, 295n56, 295n56

Worster, Donald 10

Wrath of Grapes see Keep Your Head Up, Kid

Young, Scott, and George Robertson 78

Youngblood 1, 22, 43–47, 66, 72, 77, 105, 123, 149, 204, 205, 242, 246, 248, 250, 255, 258, 259, 260, 303n41

Zeidel, Larry "The Rock": in *Keep Your Head Up, Kid* 74

Zeisel, Laurel 24

www.ingramcontent.com/pod-product-compliance
Lightning Source LLC
Chambersburg PA
CBHW081537300426
44116CB00015B/2667